THE NEW TESTAMENT

AN INTRODUCTION TO THE STUDY OF THE NEW TESTAMENT

BY

A. H. McNEILE

SECOND EDITION REVISED BY

C. S. C. WILLIAMS

OXFORD
AT THE CLARENDON PRESS

Oxford University Press, Amen House, London E.C.4

GLASGOW   NEW YORK   TORONTO   MELBOURNE   WELLINGTON

BOMBAY   CALCUTTA   MADRAS   KARACHI   KUALA LUMPUR

CAPE TOWN   IBADAN   NAIROBI   ACCRA

FIRST EDITION 1927

REPRINTED 1950

SECOND EDITION 1953

REPRINTED LITHOGRAPHICALLY IN GREAT BRITAIN
AT THE UNIVERSITY PRESS, OXFORD
FROM CORRECTED SHEETS OF THE SECOND EDITION
1955, 1957, 1960

PREFACE TO THE SECOND EDITION

To one who has been brought up theologically from undergraduate days in 1927 upon McNeile's *Introduction*, the attempt to produce a revised edition of it after a quarter of a century has not been easy. Justification for a revision must be that research has not stood still during this period and that some of McNeile's landmarks have been removed. He himself might well have changed his views, had he lived, on three points, to mention no more: the evidence for the early death of St. John, the son of Zebedee; the chronological order of the chapters in 2 Corinthians; and the authorship of Ephesians. Here and elsewhere one cannot be quite so certain as he was in 1927; alternative solutions to various problems need to be mentioned, even if on many questions his verdict still stands good.

One criticism made of the first edition was that it included no references, except in passing, to the then new subject of Form-criticism and few in general to foreign and English books and periodicals dealing with the subject under discussion. A student whose appetite is whetted by an *Introduction to the New Testament* needs to be told where he can satisfy himself more fully. But to those who know McNeile's writings, both devotional and academic, he will remain, as he said of Dr. Salmon, a 'master and a giant'.

C. S. C. W.

MERTON COLLEGE, OXFORD
Epiphany, 1952

PREFACE TO THE FIRST EDITION

THE following sketch of the history and contents of the New Testament is necessarily a sketch only. Historical, literary, and textual criticism, and the question of the Canon, require increasing specialization, which makes a whole library necessary for a full treatment of the New Testament. But as the study advances there is need at intervals for a brief conspectus of the material in one volume, such will put the reader who is not an expert or a professed student in possession of the salient points. He wants to know in outline how the New Testament as a whole, and each book in it, reached its present form, when and where each acquired canonical authority, the chief problems which the study of them raises, historical, literary, and textual, and broadly what each is about and what it contains. It is the aim of the present volume to supply such a need.

I greatly regret that I was unable to make use of Provost (formerly Archbishop) Bernard's work on the Fourth Gospel in the International Critical Commentary, but I am glad to find that the views that I have expressed agree to a large extent with his.

It is venturesome to write an Introduction to the New Testament in Dublin, where Dr. Salmon's learning, enriched with brilliance and humour, has caused his name to be revered as that of a master and a giant. But a large proportion of this book is concerned with results reached since his day, which are so numerous that the attempt to record them may be forgiven.

A. H. McN.

TRINITY COLLEGE, DUBLIN
  Easter, 1927

CONTENTS

CONTENTS

ABBREVIATIONS

Ex.T., Expository Times.
J.B.L., Journal of Biblical Literature.
J.T.S., Journal of Theological Studies.

I

THE NEW TESTAMENT

THIS title, as applied to the collection of sacred Christian writings, is often used with no clear understanding of its meaning. A 'testament' is strictly a 'will', a last will and testament made by someone before his death and binding upon his survivors after it. But that does not explain the title. The Latin *testamentum* also has this meaning, apart from the Bible and writings connected with it. In non-biblical Greek the word διαθήκη (*diathēkē*), of which *testamentum* is the equivalent, means similarly a 'will'. But a will is only a particular instance of a binding arrangement or disposition; and in the Bible *diathēkē* bears that wider meaning in various applications. In the Greek Old Testament it is the rendering of the Hebrew בְּרִית (*bᵉrith*), which never means a 'will'. It is with the Hebrew meanings, therefore, that a study of the word must begin.

(*a*) Either God or man can lay a binding obligation upon himself. It is then an 'undertaking' or 'promise'. (*b*) It can be imposed upon another, in the form of an 'ordinance' or 'command'. (*c*) When an undertaking is mutually entered into by two parties, it is a 'covenant' or 'agreement' or 'pact'. The Israelite nation were deeply influenced by the thought that when they became Yahweh's people at Sinai He and they entered into such a covenant; they received from Him a body of commands, and He promised His blessing and protection in the event of their obedience (διαθήκη occurs in this sense of mutual agreement in Aristoph. *Birds*, 440, but normally in non-biblical Greek the word used for that is συνθήκη). Since διαθήκη was the LXX equivalent of *bᵉrith* in all these various senses, it was taken over by New Testament writers with the same elastic force. But they added to it two other meanings. (*d*) Both St. Paul (Gal. iii. 15) and the author of Hebrews (ix. 17) illustrate the dealings of God with His people by reference to the ordinary non-biblical meaning, a human 'will' or 'testament'. (*e*) Finally, we reach the sense from which was derived the use in our title, i.e. a 'dispensation', 'régime'. There were two eras in the world's history, in which there were two *diathēkai*, the one involving slavery, the other freedom (Gal. iv. 24–26). The conditions of the 'old *diathēkē*' were written on tablets of stone; and if the giving of them, says St. Paul, was accompanied by divine glory, how much more glorious must be the 'new *diathēkē*' (2 Cor. iii. 4–11). What we call the Old and the New Testaments are two collections of writings containing the divine message which belong respectively to the two dispensations. Melito, Bishop of Sardis (*c.* A.D. 170), speaks of 'the books of the old *diathēkē*' (*ap.* Eus. *H.E.* iv. 26); and at about the end of that century Clement of Alexandria and Tertullian employ the expressions παλαιὰ διαθήκη, *vetus testamentum*, and νέα διαθήκη, *novum testamentum*, as the actual titles of the two collections of books.

BOOKS

J. Behm, διαθήκη, *Theologisches Wörterbuch zum neuen Testament* (G. Kittel), ii. 106–37.
J. O. Cobham, article 'Covenant' in *A Theological Word Book of the Bible*, edited by A. Richardson, pp. 54–56.
J. Hastings's *Dict. of the Bible*, articles 'Covenant' and 'Testament'.
J. B. Lightfoot, *Galatians*, p. 141.
A. H. McNeile, *Exodus*, pp. 150–2.
J. H. Moulton and G. Milligan, *Vocabulary of the Greek Testament*, s.v. διαθήκη.
B. F. Westcott, *Hebrews*, pp. 298–302.

II

THE SYNOPTIC GOSPELS

§ I. EARLY STAGES

A LITTLE group of Jews in the capital of Judaism began one day to proclaim to all and sundry that a Young Man, who had just been executed as a revolutionary, had risen from the dead, and was the Messiah. This obviously invited derision, and worse, unless convincing proof were forthcoming. The repeated and confident witness of those who had seen Him alive after His death, and the ecstatic and moving inspiration with which they pressed their message, were enough at the outset to convince quite a number of persons. But in the conservative air of Judaism no message could gain wide acceptance without the only sort of proof that was felt to be worth anything—the proof from Scripture. If Jesus was the Messiah, Scripture must have foretold His death and resurrection. The early Christians found no difficulty in showing that it did. Very soon the apostolic preaching (κήρυγμα) (as opposed to teaching (διδαχή) which consisted mainly of ethical exhortation) began to follow a pattern, as Dr. C. H. Dodd[1] has shown from an examination of the Pauline epistles and the speeches in the book of Acts:·

Old Testament prophecies have been fulfilled and the promised Messianic age has dawned at the coming of Jesus,
Who was born of David's seed,
Who died for us according to the Scriptures to deliver us from the power of this present evil age,
Who was buried and rose again on the third day according to the Scriptures,
Who has been exalted at the right hand of God as God's Son, to be Lord of quick and dead,
Who will come again as Judge and as Saviour,
Therefore repent and be baptized, receiving the Holy Spirit.

Christian preaching inevitably took the form of *apologia*, 'proving that this is the Messiah' (Acts ix. 22). When St. Paul

[1] *The Apostolic Preaching and its Developments*, 1936.

had given this message at Beroea, his hearers each day looked up in the Scriptures the passages adduced in order to verify and understand them (Acts xvii. 11).

It was from this invariable need of *apologia* that Christian literature must have taken its rise, in the writing down of Old Testament passages, perhaps together with the events in which they found fulfilment. This practice began at an early date; and the writings would be in the native Aramaic of Palestinian Jews. J. R. Harris and V. Burch[1] have shown that *testimonia* or Old Testament proofs of an anti-Judaic character were drawn up in lists and known not only to Barnabas, Justin, Irenaeus, Cyprian, and other Fathers but also to the Evangelists themselves. Recently a papyrus[2] has been discovered which contains such *testimonia*.

While proofs were needed to convince opponents, believers in Jesus as Messiah would seek for more information about Him, not perhaps at the very beginning, when His advent was expected any day in the immediate future, but increasingly as time elapsed. What manner of man was this? How did He spend His time? Above all, what did He teach? Thus round the reminiscences of the events for which Old Testament predictions could be adduced other reminiscences would grow, all glowing with the character and spirit of Him who was believed to be the foreordained Son of God.

Behind our Gospels, then, lay these two *strata*—written *testimonia*, or Old Testament proofs, and oral reminiscences; the latter, however, in many cases would before long be written down, also in Aramaic, and treasured as fresh material by mission preachers, teachers, and exorcists. (For the study of the Gospel tradition during its oral stage, see on Form-criticism below, Ch. III.) The *testimonia*, according to many, are referred to in the statement of Papias, Bishop of Hierapolis, in the first half of the second century, for which he claims the authority of an 'Elder', i.e. probably a Christian of an earlier date, who lived very near to the events which he relates: Ματθαῖος μὲν οὖν Ἑβραΐδι διαλέκτῳ τὰ λόγια συνεγράψατο· ἡρμή-

---

[1] *Testimonies*, ii, 1920.
[2] Papyrus of the 4th cent., *Catalogue of the Greek and Latin papyri in the John Rylands Library*, iii, by C. H. Roberts, pp. 10–13.

νεῦσε δ' αὐτὰ ὡς ἦν δυνατὸς ἕκαστος. 'Matthew compiled the logia¹ in the Hebrew [i.e. Aramaic] language, and each person interpreted them as he was able' (ap. Eus. H.E. iii. 39). The First Gospel is not a translation from the Aramaic; so that if the evidence of Papias is to have any weight, the work of the apostle, whatever it was, must have been earlier. But since much of it may have been incorporated in the First Gospel, his name became attached to it in tradition. The occurrence in the First Gospel of expressions such as 'that it might be fulfilled' (ii. 15, 17, 23; iv. 14; viii. 17; xii. 17; xiii. 35; xxi. 4) is thought to favour the idea that the apostle made the earliest, or the most popular, collection of proof texts from the Old Testament, and that each reader 'interpreted', i.e. thought out for himself, to the best of his ability the fulfilments of them; or that to his collection of texts he himself added short accounts of the events in which they were fulfilled, and each reader 'translated' them from Aramaic into his own tongue. But the passages in Matthew which speak of the fulfilment of the Old Testament are not, after all, numerous or important enough to have caused the compiler's name to be attached to it.

A better explanation is that the apostle compiled in Aramaic² a collection of Gospel material of which the discourses and

¹ Papias himself wrote a work in five books entitled (according to Eus., loc. cit.) 'Expositions of Oracles of the Lord', λογίων κυριακῶν ἐξηγήσεως (sic; probably -γήσεις or -γησις). Dr. Lawlor ('Eusebius on Papias', in Hermathena, vol. xx) argues that logia does not mean simply 'Sayings'. He suggests that the expression λόγια κυριακά is borrowed from Papias by Irenaeus, who seems to use it in the sense of 'matters relating to the Lord', from which heretics drew false inferences. He also has the expression τὰ λόγια τοῦ κυρίου, which appears to mean specifically 'the Gospels'. If so, the work of Papias was, in fact, an exposition of some of the contents of the Gospel. Similarly H. J. Lawlor and J. E. L. Oulton, Eusebius, Ecclesiastical History, ii. 112, said that the 'Dominical Oracles' are apparently authoritative writings relating to the Lord Jesus Christ, giving an account of His deeds as well as His sayings, i.e. Gospels, though not necessarily our canonical Gospels. But when Papias quotes the Elder as saying simply that Matthew compiled the λόγια, he cannot mean 'the Gospels'; and the article forbids either 'a Gospel' or 'some of the contents of the Gospel'. Bp. Westcott thought that the word must be given 'its necessary notion of scriptural authority'; but its notion of sacred authority is all that is necessary. Streeter explains it as 'the (original) discourses'. They were sacred and authoritative, they were divine oracles, because they were Christ's.

² Dalman, The Words of Jesus (trans. Kay, 1902, pp. 57-71), is sceptical about any written Semitic original. On this see Stanton, The Gospels as Historical Documents, ii. 63 f.

sayings of Jesus formed the larger part, with perhaps short narratives describing the occasions on which they were uttered; and various persons translated it according to their ability. An even better suggestion has been made by Dr. T. W. Manson,[1] according to whom the statement of Papias cannot be made to fit the Gospel of Matthew but does, 'when taken in its simple and natural meaning, fit a document such as Q [the other source besides Mark common to Matthew and Luke] like a glove'. (For Q see below, pp. 79–84).

Other apostles, disciples, and eye-witnesses of the Lord's ministry would constantly relate reminiscences of His sayings and doings. What the Elder says about St. Peter (Eus., ibid.) must have been true of them all, that they related them πρὸς τὰς χρείας, as the needs, moral or apologetic, of their audiences on each occasion required, and not as making a σύνταξις, a formal or logical arrangement. Early tradition, starting with this passage of Papias, has it that Mark followed Peter as his interpreter. And he collected, as fully and accurately as he could, and wrote down in Greek, as much as he could remember of these scattered and occasional teachings of the apostle. The passage is full of ambiguities, and each reader must 'interpret it as he is able':

Καὶ τοῦθ' ὁ πρεσβύτερος ἔλεγε. Μάρκος μὲν ἑρμηνευτὴς Πέτρου γενόμενος ὅσα ἐμνημόνευσεν ἀκριβῶς ἔγραψεν, οὐ μέντοι τάξει, τὰ ὑπὸ Χριστοῦ ἢ λεχθέντα ἢ πραχθέντα. οὔτε γὰρ ἤκουσε τοῦ Κυρίου οὔτε παρηκολούθησεν αὐτῷ· ὕστερον δέ, ὡς ἔφην, Πέτρῳ, ὃς πρὸς τὰς χρείας ἐποιεῖτο τὰς διδασκαλίας, ἀλλ' οὐχ ὥσπερ σύνταξιν τῶν Κυριακῶν ποιούμενος λόγων· ὥστε οὐδὲν ἥμαρτε Μάρκος, οὕτως ἔνια γράψας ὡς ἀπεμνημόνευσεν. ἑνὸς γὰρ ἐποιήσατο πρόνοιαν, τοῦ μηδὲν ὧν ἤκουσε παραλιπεῖν ἢ ψεύσασθαί τι ἐν αὐτοῖς.

This also the Elder used to say: Mark, having been Peter's interpreter,[2] wrote down accurately—not, however, in order—all that he remembered of the things either said or done by Christ. For he was neither a hearer nor a follower of the Lord, but a follower, as I have said, of Peter at a later time; and Peter delivered his instructions to meet the needs [of the moment], but

---

[1] *The Sayings of Jesus*, 1949, p. 18; cf. K. Lake, *An Introduction to the New Testament*, p. 26. Contrast G. D. Kilpatrick, *Origins of the Gospel according to St. Matthew*, 1946, pp. 3–7.
[2] 'Private secretary or *aide-de-camp*', T. W. Manson, *The Teaching of Jesus*, p. 23, n. 1.

with no attempt to give the Lord's words in any systematic arrangement. So that Mark was not wrong in thus writing down some things as he recollected them, for the one thing that he was careful of was to omit nothing of what he had heard or to make any false statement.[1]

Thus behind our Gospels two lines of tradition are traceable —an Aramaic collection (St. Matthew's?) of the Lord's sayings, and St. Peter's Aramaic instructions. Other lines which cannot be traced are the Aramaic instructions given by the apostles and others, which doubtless left a precipitate in the sources used by the evangelists. (See on Form-criticism below.) The first stages of the written sources, the development in Greek of 'St. Matthew's collection', known as Q, St. Mark's Greek reproduction of St. Peter's teaching, and others, will be studied later; and the way in which the authors of the First and Third Gospels seem to have used them to build up their writings. These two, together with St. Mark's, are called 'synoptic' because the three give in general the same view of our Lord's life, and follow broadly the same narrative framework, with a similarity in language, vocabulary, and the selection of material, which marks a kinship in which they stand apart from the Fourth Gospel.

But all four evangelists aimed at setting forth the 'Gospel', the good tidings of Jesus Christ. So that some time after the separate Gospels had become known and reverenced everywhere, there were prefixed to them in the earliest manuscripts that we possess (dating from the fourth century) the titles κατὰ Μαθθαῖον, κατὰ Μάρκον and so on—the one Gospel 'according to Matthew', &c.

Streeter, however, suggests that following the Jewish custom of referring to books by one of the opening words, Christians

---

[1] Dr. A. M. Farrer (*A Study in St. Mark*, 1951), who finds that Mark conforms to a pattern (pp. 30 ff., 187–202), rejects Papias's evidence as being 'too clever by half'; he thinks that the Papian tradition arose to account for the tradition that there were two Gospels, Matt. and Mk., in two languages. He thinks, too, that this tradition of Papias would explain the discrepancies between the two Gospels (pp. 11–21). 'Papias is simply describing the standing of the two Gospels in the Greek Church at an imaginary time before St. Matthew had been translated (*sc.* from the Aramaic)' (p. 18). But Papias's evidence conflicts with Dr. Farrer's hypothesis that an 'over-all' pattern of Mark exists owing to the influence of the Holy Spirit.

would refer to Mark by 'Gospel' from Mk. i. 1. Later the titles 'according to . . .' had to be added to differentiate between the 'Gospels'. (*The Four Gospels*, pp. 497 f.)

§ 2. CHARACTERISTICS AND MOTIVES

But historians are not mere chroniclers of bare events. To the true historian the past is not the 'dead past' which can be left to bury its dead; it is alive, with a meaning for the present. And an ancient historian generally allowed his conceptions of its meaning to set their mark upon his narrative more strongly than is permitted by the modern feeling of the importance of accuracy. He always wrote with presuppositions and a purpose, political, moral, religious, and so on. And the writers of the Gospels show that they were not exceptions; each of them emphasizes particular aspects of the message which he felt to be important.

(*a*) MATTHEW. Although the First Gospel was composed from existing material, the evangelist used it in such a way as to serve a definite purpose. By selection, arrangement, and comment, and by numerous alterations of wording, he made clear the meaning that he found in the events and in the utterances of Jesus. His aim was to show that Christianity was the true consummation of Judaism. It was an *apologia pro vita sua* of the Christian Church, offered to the Jews. 'Jesus the true messiah, born and trained under the Jewish law, and yet Lord of a Church whose inward faith, organization, procedure, and world-wide scope transcended the legal limitations of Judaism —this is the dominant conception of Matthew's Gospel from beginning to end.' 'He wishes to show that, in spite of the contemporary rupture between Judaism and Christianity, there has been a divine continuity realized in the origin and issues of faith in Jesus as the Christ.' 'The three sacred possessions of Judaism'—the chosen People, the Temple, and the Law— 'have thus passed into higher uses, as a result of the life of Jesus the Christian messiah. It is Matthew's aim to justify this transition by showing from the life of Jesus how it was not the claim of a heretical sect who misread the Bible by the light of their own presumptuousness, but the realization of a divine purpose and the verification of divine prophecies in the sphere of history.'[1] The same thought, that Christians are the true Israel, is expressed in other ways elsewhere in the New Testament, in the Lucan writings, Hebrews, 1 Peter, and the Apocalypse. It is not a leading thought of St. Paul; he was too much occupied with the 'contemporary rupture'. But when his victory for the Gentiles was won, the continuity was recognized to be an essential factor in the Church's life, which it was important to claim and prove. But the First Evangelist does it by a method peculiar to himself. He was both a thorough Jew, acquainted with Rabbinic thought, and not averse to the use of Midrash, and at the same time a Christian Churchman; and he fuses sources written from different points of view in such a way that the two aspects sometimes appear side by side, so that they can be studied separately.

(1) As a Jew he is interested in everything which can be interpreted with a particularistic force, showing the importance and permanence of Jewish ideas and customs: e.g. v. 18, 19; vii. 6; viii. 7,[2] 11; x. 5b, 6; xiii. 52; xv. 24; xix. 28; xxiii. 2, together with the many eschatological utterances attributed to Jesus. And he reveals his Rabbinic habit of mind by the devices which he adopts in the arrangement of his material. For convenience to the memory in Church instruction he groups incidents and sayings in twos, threes, fives, and sevens,[3] and the Genealogy in fourteens, thus offering what appears to be a sort of acrostic on the name David, of which the numerical value of the Hebrew letters is fourteen.[4] That which made it possible for him to be a scribe, bringing forth from his treasure things new and old, was the fact that Jesus who wields universal sovereignty was at the same time the Messiah of Hebrew ancestry. This is taught in the Genealogy traced through the royal line, and in the worship offered by the Magians to Him that was born King of the Jews. The royal authority of the King is seen in the repeated 'But I say unto you' in the Sermon on the Mount, expressing His independence in interpreting

[1] J. Moffatt, *Introd. to the Literature of the N.T.*, p. 244.
[2] If, as is probable, the words are to be understood as a question.
[3] See W. C. Allen, *St. Matthew*, p. lxv.
[4] G. H. Box, *Interpreter*, Jan. 1906.

the Jewish law in its true inwardness. The same independence is shown in His repudiation of some of the enactments in the 'tradition of the elders'. And if He was superior to the law and the tradition, He was superior to the law and the prophets, a truth conveyed in the vision of the Transfiguration. Again, He was superior to the claims of Caesar the earthly monarch, as He asserted in the statement that 'the children are free' of the duty of paying the stater or didrachm, which He paid only to avoid giving offence. Eight times His royal descent is recognized when He is addressed as 'Son of David', and the same title is given to Joseph (i. 20). The entry into Jerusalem was a manifestation of loyalty to One who was popularly supposed to be about to restore the Jewish monarchy; and He accepted it as symbolic of something greater and more spiritual. When Pilate asked Him, 'Art thou the king of the Jews?' He again accepted the title, but as expressing something which the procurator was quite unable to understand. And there was a deep irony in the mockery by the soldiers, and in the *titulus* on the Cross.

The evangelist saw in Him also the more spiritual hopes of the Jewish apocalyptic. St. Peter's confession of His Messiahship forms an important turning-point in His history. Jesus then began to speak of Himself as 'the Son of Man', and openly to predict His future Messianic glory, His Advent and Judgement. Finally, He claimed to have been given all authority in heaven and on earth. Add to these the references to the fulfilment in Him of Old Testament predictions, and it will be seen that the author's heart, like the Psalmist's, overflowed with a goodly matter: he spoke of the things that he had made touching the King.

(2) But with the King is bound up the Kingdom. If Christ was the fulfilment of Israelite hopes, the Christian Church was the fulfilment of Israel. The national privileges of the Jews had passed into the possession of the few who were the true Israelites: see iii. 12; viii. 11 f.; xiii. 11–17, 36–43, 47–50; xix. 27–30; xxi. 28–31, 33–43; xxii. 8–10, 14; and all the teaching on those who were fitted to enter or possess the Kingdom. They were the sacred *ecclesia* as it ought to be. The evangelist writes as a 'Churchman', and shows a strong ecclesiastical interest.

Christ's followers were His *ecclesia* which He would build upon the rock, the sure foundation of His Messiahship which St. Peter had confessed (xvi. 18). To St. Peter (*v.* 18) and to the members of the Church as a body (xviii. 18) was given the authority to bind and loose, i.e. to declare things forbidden and permitted; and the latter passage immediately follows an injunction (*v.* 17) to report an offending and contumacious brother to the *ecclesia*; and, if he disregarded the *ecclesia*, to treat him as outside the pale of society. They were to possess, therefore, the powers, such as were exercised in the Jewish Church, of legislature and excommunication. To St. Peter would be given administrative power, 'the keys of the Kingdom of Heaven' (xvi. 19), and all the Twelve should sit on thrones judging the twelve tribes of Israel (xix. 28). Membership in this community was to be acquired by Baptism (xxviii. 19). Wherever two or three members met for prayer, Christ would be in their midst (xviii. 20). And, as in the Jewish Church, there would be prophets (x. 41; xxiii. 34), wise men (xxiii. 34), and scribes (xiii. 52; xxiii. 34).

The working out of this conception that Christ and His *ecclesia* are the fulfilment of the Jewish Messianic hopes and of the Jewish sacred people explains the presence in the Gospel of a strong anti-Pharisaic polemic (see Allen, pp. lxxvi ff.), since it was the Pharisees who prevented the Jewish *ecclesia* from being what it might be. At the same time the evangelist was glad to include passages which pointed to the drawing in of the Gentiles into the embrace of this Church which has reached that for which the Jewish Church was destined. This is not the universalism of St. Paul or St. Luke, but of the highest minds in Israel of old. Magians from the East (ii. 1–12), 'Galilee of the Gentiles' (iv. 14–16), a centurion's servant (viii. 5–13; see especially *vv.* 11 f.), a Canaanite woman (xv. 22–28), 'all the world' (xxvi. 13), could share in the blessings available through the coming of the King. 'In His name shall the Gentiles trust' (xii. 21). 'This Gospel shall be preached in all the world for a witness unto all the Gentiles' (xxiv. 14). 'Go, therefore, and make disciples of all the Gentiles' (xxviii. 19).

Lastly, for life in the new *ecclesia* the Jewish law and tradition are transcended by the law as interpreted by the Messiah

(v. 21–48; vi. 1–18; ix. 10–13; xii. 1–8, 9–14; xv. 1–20; xvi.
11 f.; xvii. 1–5; xxii. 23–33, 34–40; xxiii. 1–28; xxv. 31–46).

The keynote of the Gospel is 'I am not come to destroy but
to fulfil'. That principle conserved all that was good in Judaism
by finding it in Christianity. Particularism and universalism
thus stand side by side as in post-exilic Judaism. And it is unnecessary to think of either as introduced by interpolation or
editing; the author, as has been said, used sources written from
the two points of view, and his own bent of mind was such that
he would not neglect either of them, but amalgamated them.

(3) The First Gospel is a 'revised Gospel lectionary', as Dr.
G. D. Kilpatrick has shown.[1] It was composed for liturgical
use, which had already modified a large part of the material
used by the First Evangelist. To this extent he reflects the
situation in the life of the Church of his day.

(b) MARK. The Second Gospel is less complex in its character and purpose. 'Messiah' did not connote for the writer the
royalty of the Son of David but the power of the Son of God.
All that was contained in his reminiscences of apostolic teaching impressed him deeply with this great fact. His Gospel is not
an *apologia* to Jews but an *apologia* to the world of the truth of
Christianity. He therefore makes small use of proof-texts, and
few suggestions that Christianity is the real and 'fulfilled'
Judaism. His sole 'proofs' are the actual words and deeds of
the Master and the effects which they produced. He uses Old
Testament references subtly and allusively to show that Jesus
is the Messiah; e.g. the use of $\mu o\gamma\iota\lambda\acute{a}\lambda o\varsigma$ in vii. 32 indicates that
Isa. xxxv. 4–6 is now fulfilled;[2] in ix. 2–8 he alludes to Exod.
xxiv. 13 ff.; in xi. 1–10 to Zech. ix. 9; in xii. 1–12 to Isa.
v. 2 ff.; it is probable that Jesus—not the 'community behind
Mark' nor an eyewitness like St. Peter nor Mark himself—was
the first to perceive the relevance of some at least of these
allusive references to the LXX, *pace* the Form-critics. He offers
his portrait of the Christ to speak for itself. The power is seen
first and foremost in His preaching. 'After John was delivered
up Jesus came into Galilee preaching the good tidings of the

---

[1] *The Origins of the Gospel according to St. Matthew* (1946).
[2] Sir E. C. Hoskyns and N. Davey, *The Riddle of the New Testament*, pp. 167–8
and the former in *Mysterium Christi*, p. 73.

Kingdom of God' (i. 14). The first effect was the immediate attachment to Him of the two pairs of brothers, Simon and Andrew, James and John (*vv.* 16–20). On the Sabbath He entered into the synagogue and taught, 'and they were astonished at His teaching, for He used to teach as one having authority and not as the scribes' (*v.* 22). At Capharnaum 'they were all amazed, so that they questioned among themselves saying, What is this? A new teaching!' (*v.* 27). After praying in a deserted place He said, 'Let us go elsewhere into the adjoining villages that I may preach there also, for therefore came I forth. And He was preaching in their synagogues throughout the whole of Galilee'. (*vv.* 38 f.). In Capharnaum, again, a crowd came to the house, 'and He spake to them the word' (ii. 2). And by the sea 'the whole multitude came to Him and He taught them (*v.* 13). The number of his followers increased (*vv.* 13–15). 'And again He began to teach by the sea, and a very great multitude was gathered unto Him' (iv. 1). Later He returned to His own country and preached in the synagogue, and 'the majority were astonished', though they stumbled at the possession of such power by a local carpenter (vi. 1–5). 'And He went round the villages in circuit preaching' (*v.* 7), and was besieged by crowds (*vv.* 31–33). At the Transfiguration the Voice said, 'This is My Son, the Beloved [i.e. unique]; hear Him' (ix. 7). When He moved into Peraea 'multitudes came together again unto Him, and as He was wont He taught them again' (x. 1). And in Jerusalem the authorities hesitated to arrest Him 'for all the multitudes were astonished at His teaching' (xi. 18). Though the evangelist records very few of His words, he emphasizes by this reiteration the effect which they produced.

But His preaching called forth the recognition of evil spirits, and His power showed itself in their exorcism, to the amazement of those who witnessed it (i. 23–27, 39; iii. 11, 22; v. 2–16; vii. 25–30; ix. 14–27). He gave His disciples the same power (iii. 15); and one man, though he was not of their number, was found exorcizing spirits in His name (ix. 38). But this at once led people with all kinds of diseases to come to Him for healing, and He showed His power, and astonished those who saw it, by performing the cures (i. 29–34, 40–45; ii. 3–12;

iii. 1–5, 8–10; v. 21–42; vii. 32–35; viii. 22–26; x. 46–52). This growing popularity as a healer troubled Him. He was 'angry'[1] (with righteous indignation against the forces of evil seen in human suffering) when the leper came for healing (i. 41), and sternly charged him to tell no one about it. When unclean spirits recognized Him, 'He rebuked them much that they should not make Him manifest' (iii. 12). And when He healed the daughter of Jairus, 'He enjoined them much that no one should know this' (v. 43) : see also vii. 36; viii. 26. Finally, His power is shown in miracles other than healing—the stilling of the sea (vi. 47–51), the feeding of the five thousand (vi. 35–44) and the four thousand (viii. 1–9), and the withering of the fig-tree (xi. 13 f., 20).

All this is the power of the Messiah, the Son of God. That Sonship is repeatedly emphasized (i. 11; iii. 11; v. 7; xiii. 32; xv. 39); He is called 'the Holy One of God' (i. 24); and in the power of the 'Holy Spirit' He cast out demons (iii. 29).

(c) LUKE. The leading note of the First Gospel is royalty, and of the Second power, that of the Third is love. The writers of the two former appear to have had apologetic needs in mind; and the same must be said of St. Luke. In writing to offer to the Gentile Theophilus a true presentation of Christian facts, he depicts the Messiah as the Saviour of all men and the Satisfier of all human needs, the anointed Prophet who brings good tidings to the poor, the blind, and the bruised (iv. 18 f.). But there is no argument or display of any apologetic intention. While he writes with a purpose, he is himself absorbed in the beauty of the fairest human life. This is the first and abiding impression felt by the reader; and some of the narratives, notably those of the Nativity, are among the gems of literature. The other evangelists sometimes tell the same stories, but the aesthetic effect is not quite the same. St. Matthew impresses us by what Moffatt calls the 'massive unity' of his Gospel; St. Mark by the steady force and directness of plain, even uncouth, language; St. Luke by the artistry of grace.

---

[1] ὀργισθείς, so D a ff[2]. The v.l. σπλαγχνισθείς has the mass of support; but it would be so natural for that to be substituted that the harder word is probably right; cf. C. S. C. Williams, *Alterations to the text of the Synoptic Gospels and Acts*, pp. 23 f.

St. Luke emphasizes the universality of salvation, and of the satisfaction of human needs. The very word 'salvation', which does not occur in the first two Gospels, is found thirteen times in Luke and Acts. In the account of the Baptist in Matthew and Mark Is. xl. 3 ff. is quoted as far as the words 'make His paths straight'; but in Lk. iii. 4 ff. it is continued to the words 'and all flesh shall see the salvation of God'. The full meaning, moreover, is given to 'all flesh'; it includes not only Jews, but Samaritans whom the Jews despised as being more than half Gentiles (ix. 51–56; x. 30–37; xvii. 11–19), and Gentiles (ii. 32; iv. 25 ff.; vii. 2–10; xiii. 29; xxiv. 47); and the mission of the Seventy is generally understood as a mission to Gentiles (x. 1 ff.: compare v. 7 with 1 Cor. xi. 25–27). But within the Jewish nation there were those whom the upper classes treated as beyond the pale of respectable society. The religious leaders, learned in the Law, thought of the populace, the *'am hā'āreṣ*, with pious scorn.[1] But to the Lord, who was one of them, the poor were very dear (iv. 18; vi. 20 f.; vii. 22; xiv. 13, 21; xvi. 19 ff.); and not only the poor, but the disreputable—customs officers and sinners (v. 27–32; vii. 37–50; xv. 1 ff., 11–32; xviii. 9–14; xix. 2–10; xxiii. 43). At the same time He did not avoid the rich and respectable (vii. 36; xi. 37; xiv. 1; and see xxiii. 50–53). Again, women were little accounted of in Jewish life; 'but all through this Gospel they are allowed a prominent place, and many types of womanhood are placed before us: Elizabeth, the Virgin Mary, the prophetess Anna, the widow at Nain, the nameless sinner in the house of Simon, Mary Magdalene, Joanna, Susanna, the woman with the issue, Martha and Mary, the widow with the two mites, the 'daughters of Jerusalem', and the women at the tomb' (Plummer, *St. Luke*, xlii f.; he quotes Dante who speaks of the evangelist as *scriba mansuetudinis Christi*).[2]

Not all, but a large number, of these incidents and passages are peculiar to the Third Gospel. The same purpose is seen in the Genealogy (iii. 23–38), in which the human descent of Jesus is traced to 'Adam the son of God', whereas in Matthew the royal descent is traced to Abraham the father of the Jewish

---

[1] See Jackson and Lake, *The Beginnings of Christianity*, i. i, App. E.
[2] *De Monarchia*, i. 18.

race. Notice also the favourable description of a Gentile given only in Luke (vii. 5); the omission of the incident of the Canaanite woman who obtained a blessing with great difficulty, and as a dog ate of the children's crumbs (Matt. xv. 21–28; Mk. vii. 24–30); the indication that the family of Jesus was poor (ii. 24); and the special references to the poor (i. 53; ii. 8), and to customs officers (iii. 12); and the woes pronounced against the rich (vi. 25).

The aspects of Christianity revealed in the Gospel are those of a personal and spiritual religion resulting from the experience of God's love and forgiveness. As compared with the first two Gospels there is a frequent use in Luke and Acts of such words as 'repentance', 'grace', 'mercy', 'merciful', 'forgiveness of sins'. The expression 'Holy Spirit', which occurs nine times in Matthew, Mark, is found twelve times in Luke and forty-one times in Acts. And the attitude of God to man which is thus indicated is met on man's side by prayer and praise. The prominence of these is shown in detail by Plummer, pp. xlv f. These instances are far from exhausting the characteristic features of the Third Gospel; but they serve to show their general colour, and to place in a bright light the warm and human character of the evangelist, to whom these aspects of the Lord's Person and work made a special appeal.

A recognition of these characteristics of the Synoptic Gospels is essential to their study. They were understood and made use of at an early date. Matthew, the Jewish Gospel, was preferred by Jewish Christians, orthodox and unorthodox, if the modern expression is allowable, and was the basis of apocryphal Gospels such as the *Gospel of the Nazarenes*.[1] Conversely, Luke, the non-Jewish Gospel, was congenial to Marcion, who issued it in a mutilated recension. And even Mark is said to have been a favourite with a certain class. Irenaeus (*Haer.* iii. xi. 7) speaks of 'those who separate Jesus from Christ, and say that Christ remained always impassible, but that Jesus suffered, preferring that Gospel which is according to Mark'. Whether the state-

---

[1] There was considerable confusion in Patristic writers between this, and the *Gospel of* [or *according to*] *the Hebrews* (written in Greek), the closely allied *Gospel of the Ebionites*, and the *Gospel of the Twelve* [*Apostles*]. See Moffatt in Hastings's *D.A.C.* i. 489–94, and Schmidtke, *Texte u. Untersuch.* (Harnack and Gebhardt), xxxvii.

ment is trustworthy or not, it shows that the picture of divine power which St. Mark draws could be interpreted in a docetic sense, the Son of God being thought of as separable from the human Jesus.

§ 3. ARRANGEMENT

I. MATTHEW. As was usual in ancient times the evangelist incorporated existing documents and traditions. To determine what these were is part of the Synoptic problem (Ch. IV). Here we must note his arrangement of the material. As the following table shows, he closely followed the general outline and framework of St. Mark, with only the few departures from his order which are italicized:

Mark		*Matthew*
i. 1–8[1]	John the Baptist and his message	iii. 1–6, 11, 12
9–11	The baptism of Jesus	13–17
12, 13	The temptations	iv. 1–11
14, 15	Jesus moves to Galilee; His message	12, 17
16–20	Call of the first disciples	18–22
39	Preaching in Galilee	23–25
22	He taught with authority	vii. 28, 29
40–45	Healing of a leper	viii. 1–4
29–34	Healing of Simon's mother-in-law, and others	14–17
iv. 35–41	Proposal to cross the lake: the storm	18, 23–27
v. 1–20	The Gerasene demoniac	28–34
ii. 1–12	Healing of a paralytic at Capharnaum	ix. 1–8
13–17	Call of Levi (Matthew), and reply to the complaint that He ate with publicans	9–13
18–22	Question about fasting	14–17
v. 21–43	Daughter of Jairus, and woman with issue	18–26
iii. 13–19	Mission of the Twelve, and their names	x. 1–4
vi. 7–11	Charge to the Twelve	9–11, 14
ii. 23–28	Plucking ears on Sabbath	xii. 1–8
iii. 1–6	Man with withered hand	9–14
7–12	Crowds and healings	xii. 15, 16
iii. 22–30	Beelzebub	22–32

[1] Dr. R. H. Lightfoot holds that Mark's Prologue consists of i. 1–13 not 1–8 and that it corresponds to the Prologue in the Fourth Gospel (*The Gospel Message of St. Mark*, 1950, pp. 15–19).

¹ The best manuscripts of the Alexandrian, African, Syriac, Armenian, and Georgian 'families' omit v. 26.

Mark		*Matthew*
xiii. 1–32	Eschatological discourse	xxiv. 1–36
xiv. 1–	Passion and Resurrection	xxvi. 1–
xvi. 8		xxviii. 10

The following passages of Mark are absent from Matthew:
i. 1 Heading. i. 21, 23–28[1] Unclean spirit at Capharnaum; 32–
34 Many sick brought at eventide; 35–38[1] The disciples seek
Jesus; 'therefore came I forth'. ii. 27 'The Sabbath was made
for man'. iii. 20, 21 'He is beside himself'. iv. 21–24[1] Miscellaneous sayings; 26–29 Parable of Seed growing secretly. vi. 12,
13 The Apostles' work; 30 Their return from their tour. vii.
3, 4 The Jews' tradition of washings; 32–37 Ephphatha. viii.
22–26 Blind man healed gradually. ix. 38–41[1] The exorcizer;
49, 50 Miscellaneous sayings. xii. 40[1] 'Who desire widows'
houses'; 41–44[1] The widow with two mites. xiii. 33–37[2] Sayings and a parable on watching. But to some of these—parts of
iv. 21–24 and xiii. 33–37—Matthew has equivalents elsewhere;
and when Mark tells of the dumb man to whom our Lord said
Ephphatha, Matthew, in the same Marcan context, has a
general account of healings and mentions similarly the wonder
of the multitude (xv. 29–31). The omissions are extraordinarily
few, and more or less probable reasons can be given for them
in nearly every case. The return of the Apostles Matthew has
altered into a statement about John's disciples (xiv. 12). The
incidents in Mk. iii. 20, 21 and ix. 38–40 he probably avoided
because he did not like them, and perhaps thought that the use
of material means in vii. 32–37 detracted from the dignity of
the cure. The story of the Two Mites he omitted probably to
bring the statement 'Jesus having gone out of the temple went
His way' (Matt. xxiv. 1) into conjunction with the saying
'Behold your house is left unto you, &c.' (xxiii. 38 f.). In the
story of the Passion two incidents, the young man's flight from
the garden (Mk. xiv. 51), and Pilate's inquiry as to the death
of Jesus (xv. 44 f.), were omitted for no traceable reason;
possibly they were later additions in Mark, but there is no
textual evidence against either passage.

[1] Given in Lk.
[2] Similar material in Matt. xxiv. 42; xxv. 13–15; cf. also Lk. xii. 38–40;
xix. 12.

The departures from the Marcan order at the beginning of the Ministry are noteworthy. The Marcan order is:

1. i. 21–38. First Capharnaum visit and proposal to preach throughout Galilee.
2. i. 39–45. Preaching in Galilee and the healing of the leper.
3. ii. 1–iv. 34. Second Capharnaum visit.
4. iv. 35–v. 20. Crossing of the lake and healing of the demoniac.
5. v. 21–43. Third Capharnaum visit; daughter of Jairus; woman with issue.

In Matthew our Lord's preaching in Galilee is made the first and all-important event in the Ministry, though the settling at Capharnaum and the calling of the first disciples are related in anticipatory notes (iv. 12–22). The words of Mk. i. 22 were taken from their context to form a useful comment at the end of the Sermon on the Mount (chs. v–vii), and consequently their context was omitted, i.e. the arrival at Capharnaum and the events in the synagogue (Mk. i. 21, 23–28), and the subsequent proposal to preach throughout Galilee (vv. 35–38). Thus Mark's No. 1 melts away, except the healing of Simon's mother-in-law and others, which Matthew inserts later. No. 2 is expanded into the Sermon on the Mount, followed by the healing of the leper. Then comes in Matthew the *first* Capharnaum visit, where are placed the healing of the centurion's servant (absent from Mark) and others. All the events of No. 3 are held over till No. 4 has been related, and are finally combined with the stories of Jairus's daughter and the woman with the issue in Matthew's *second* Capharnaum visit. The mission of the Twelve, with the parenthetical mention of their names, is placed at a point which the compiler found convenient for the discourse collected from various quarters into ch. x. The only other departure from the Marcan order is the placing of the cleansing of the Temple immediately on the arrival at Jerusalem, so that the cursing and the withering of the fig-tree are brought together.

But while adhering thus closely to the Marcan framework, the First Evangelist has enriched his Gospel with numerous parables and sayings of our Lord, the latter of which he has for the most part collected into five extended discourses (chs. v–vii, x, xiii, xviii, xxiii–xxv) each concluded with the formula,

'And it came to pass when Jesus had finished these words', or the like. In so far as these parables and sayings are found closely similar in Luke, they may, with some confidence, be explained as derived from Q, but it must remain doubtful which of the others were derived from Q and which from other sources. Matthew contains also a few narratives which are found in Luke but not in Mark: the three Temptations (iv. 2–10), the centurion (viii. 5–13), the two [Lk. three] aspirants (viii. 19–22), the Baptist's question and the reply (xi. 2–6); and several which are peculiar to the Gospel, some of which may be Midrashic comments on Christian traditions: two blind men (ix. 27–31), a deaf demoniac (ix. 32–34), healing on the mountain (xv. 29–31), the didrachm (xvii. 24–27), the remorse of Judas, and the potter's field (xxvii. 3–10), Pilate's hand-washing (xxvii. 24, 25), earthquake at the Crucifixion (xxvii. 51b–53), sealing of the tomb (xxvii. 62–66), earthquake, and rolling away the stone by an angel (xxviii. 2–4), payment of the soldiers (xxviii. 11–15).

2. MARK. Papias, in giving the statement of 'the presbyter' that St. Mark wrote down accurately what he remembered of St. Peter's preaching of the words and deeds of Christ, adds 'not however in order', which may be a parenthesis of his own, not the words of the presbyter. Very likely it implies a contrast with the Fourth Gospel. It strikes as disparaging a note about the order of events in Mark as a modern Form-critic would do.

But from St. Peter's teaching, and possibly from that of St. Paul and St. Barnabas and others, three main chronological divisions of the Ministry stood out in his memory, and he prefixes to them a brief survey of incidents preparatory to it, viz. the Ministry of the Baptist (i. 1–8), his Baptism of Jesus (vv. 9–11), and the Temptation (vv. 12, 13).

i. The *Galilean Ministry* (i. 14–ix. 50) carried on in two districts: (*a*) Eastern Galilee, with Capharnaum as its centre (i. 14–vii. 23), including one crossing to Gerasa (v. 1), and one to Bethsaida (vi. 45). (*b*) North and east of Galilee, the Tyrian district, Decapolis, Dalmanutha,[1] Bethsaida, Caesarea Philippi

---

[1] This place-name has not been identified. The variant Magedan (P⁴⁵) may be original; 'Dalmanutha' appears to be ܕ݁ܐܝܬ݂ ܠܩܘܒ݂ܠ 'quod est iuxta partes';

(vii. 24–ix. 29), after which Jesus passed through Galilee and returned to Capharnaum before moving southwards (ix. 30–50). There is a strong but unwarranted tendency among Form-critics to suspect notes of place and notes of time (mentioned below) in this Gospel, as though it were a mere religious drama to which an editor has attached geographical and temporal links at random. ii. The *Judaean Ministry* (x. 1–xiii. 37). (*a*) He travelled on the eastern side of the Jordan (x. 1–45), i.e. through Peraea; then (*b*) across the river to Jericho (x. 46–52), whence to Bethphage, Bethany, and the Mount of Olives (xi. 1), from which He made the triumphal entry into Jerusalem (xi. 1–10). (*c*) Arrived at Jerusalem He went out to Bethany each night, and on successive days He cleansed the Temple, engaged in controversies with the authorities, and delivered the eschatological discourse (xi. 11–xiii. 37). iii. The *Passion* and *Resurrection* (xiv–xvi. 8).

The compiler of Matthew, as we have seen, follows this outline substantially. But in the traditions incorporated in Luke there appear to be indications of work in Judaea before the closing visit to Jerusalem (see p. 24). If this is accurate, we must suppose that St. Peter and other sources, being interested mainly in Galilee, were silent about earlier visits to the south, or mentioned them only incidentally, so that St. Mark did not recall them as important. It is noticeable that in the last of his three divisions St. Mark gives careful notes of time, assigning events to each day in the week (xi. 11; xi. 12; xi. 19, 20; xiv. 12; xv. 1; xvi. 1; xvi. 2). But in the first two divisions there is only one definite note of time: the Transfiguration took place 'after six days' (ix. 2), for which Lk. ix. 28 has more vaguely 'about eight days'. Elsewhere St. Mark contents himself with such expressions as 'in those days' (i. 9; viii. 1); 'and after John was delivered up' (i. 14); 'on the Sabbath' (i. 21; ii. 23); 'after an interval of some days' (ii. 1), 'again' [*sc.* on the Sabbath] (iii. 1). There is therefore plenty of room for visits to Judaea; and such are clearly related in the Fourth Gospel. It is thus impossible to think that St. Mark had any accurate knowledge of the sequence of individual events. But the broad

cf. Dalman, *Ex. T.* ix, 1897, p. 45; P. R. B. Brown, *Theology*, 1935, p. 350, F. C. Burkitt, *J.T.S.* xvii, 1915–16, p. 16.

divisions are historically important. In eastern Galilee the Lord's ministry began with a large measure of success; disciples joined Him, the fame of His miracles of healing spread rapidly, and crowds followed Him, though St. Mark places some collisions with the authorities at an early date. The collisions culminated in a deliberate gathering of Pharisees and scribes against Him, and His repudiation of Jewish traditions of ceremonial pollution (vii. 1–23). This sufficiently explains His retirement to the north. At the only meeting with the Pharisees recorded during His movements in the north they are described as 'tempting Him' (viii. 11); He warned His disciples against their 'leaven' (v. 15), and then began to predict to them His Passion (v. 31), and to speak of their 'losing their life for His sake' (v. 35). It was a deepening presentiment of evil. And as He moved on the east of the Jordan 'tempting' by the Pharisees began again (x. 2), and the shadow of the Passion darkened upon Him (x. 32–34, 38 f., 45). This course of events has the ring of truth,[1] and the stages of the ministry are represented as an apostle might relate it in his teaching of Christians.

3. LUKE. There is no sign that the Third Evangelist was able to follow any more exact sequence than St. Mark. The words in the prologue, 'to write *in order* unto thee, most excellent Theophilus', cannot be adduced to support the accuracy of his chronological order. Καθεξῆς can mean 'one by one', 'successively' (so Syr.[sin] Sah); cf. Acts xi. 4; xviii. 23. Burkitt writes,[2] 'it certainly does imply, in a general way, chronological order. But it does not necessarily imply a claim of superior chronological order to other "Gospels" or even to Mark. Rather it is a claim to present a chronological order, as contrasted with a systematic or doctrinal one.' Cadbury, however (op. cit., p. 505), will not admit as much as that. He thinks it is a merely formal and literary word. St. Luke purposes to relate the events in a consecutive narrative. It might even mean 'as follows', 'hereinafter'; cf. Lk. viii. 1 ('soon afterwards'); Acts. iii. 24 ('followed after').

After the Infancy narratives he starts off, in iii. 1–iv. 30,

---

[1] Cf. F. C. Burkitt, *Jesus Christ, an historical outline*, 1932, pp. 65–71.
[2] *The Beginnings of Christianity*, ii. 485.

with a block of non-Marcan material. The order of the opening events, the Baptist's work, the Baptism, Temptation, and
return to Galilee, would necessarily be the same as in Mark.
But except for a sentence or two he seems to prefer his other
sources. With the removal to Capharnaum (iv. 31) he turns to
Mark, and until vi. 19 follows Mk. i. 21–iii. 19 fairly closely.
vi. 20–viii. 3 is his second non-Marcan block, the so-called
'Lesser Insertion', which completes the non-Marcan account
of the Galilean ministry. But the next group of incidents in
viii. 4–ix. 50, which are taken from Mk. iv. 1–ix. 40, are still in
Galilee. (Spitta, indeed, on the basis of the reading 'Ἰουδαίας
in iv. 44, suggests that the whole of Lk. v. 12–vi. 49 (v. 1–11 is
out of its true context) relates a ministry in *Judaea*.[1] (See A. H.
McNeile's *St. Matthew*, pp. 48 f.) St. Luke does not, however,
use the whole of this piece of Mark. Whether intentionally or
not, he omits vi. 45–viii. 26, which is sometimes called the
'Great Omission'. For Streeter's suggestion that his copy of
Mark may have been mutilated see below, p. 77. The next
non-Marcan block, ix. 51–xviii. 14, containing more than
30 per cent. of the Third Gospel, is often called the 'Great
Insertion'. It has also been named the 'Peraean section', because in Mk. x. 1–45 our Lord travels towards Jericho, on the
way to Jerusalem, through Peraea, i.e. on the other side of the
Jordan; but there is not a hint of this in Luke. His collection of
narratives pictures Him simply as moving from village to village towards Jerusalem (see ix. 51 f., 56 f.; x. 38; xiv. 25; xvii.
11), till He reached Jericho. From the first and the last of these
references we should gather that the route was not across the
Jordan but through Samaria. Another name, 'the travel document', is—as Streeter says—'from the critical standpoint, an
even more dangerously misleading title, as it implies that this
section once existed as a separate document'. Besides, closer
examination shows that the author riveted the theory of a
journey upon his material in this section. Streeter adds: 'The
only safe name by which one can call it is the "Central Section"—a title which states a fact but begs no questions.' It is
probable that St. Luke has here made no use at all of Mark.
The passage about Beelzebub and the parable of the Mustard

---

[1] Cf. H. Bryant Salmon, *Church Quarterly Review*, xcix, 1924, pp. 59–68.

Seed are from Q. In a few isolated sayings he may have been influenced by Mark; but in every case it is possible to suppose that his other sources overlapped Mark at these points, and that he preferred the former. After using, in xviii. 35–43, the Marcan story of the blind man at Jericho, he has a short non-Marcan block, xix. 1–28. And then from the entry into Jerusalem and onwards he amalgamates Marcan material with much from his other sources. He bases the eschatological discourse in ch. xxi on Mark's 'little Apocalypse', but adds three verses at the end. From xxii. 14 to the end it is scarcely possible to distinguish what is Marcan from the rest. It has been much debated whether in this section St. Luke used his non-Marcan material as his primary source and the Marcan as his secondary or the reverse. B. H. Streeter[1] and V. Taylor[2] support the former view, J. M. Creed[3] and M. Goguel[4] the latter. Mark seems to have supplied the greater part of the accounts of Peter's denial, Simon of Cyrene, the Crucifixion, and the Entombment. But the appearances after the Resurrection, which are confined to Jerusalem and its neighbourhood, are entirely independent of Mark.

§ 4. DATE

For the dates of the first three Gospels we are dependent largely upon evidence within the New Testament itself. The patristic traditions, which afford little help, are as follows:

Patristic Tradition

MARK. Divergent theories were held as to the date of the Second Gospel, some placing it in Nero's reign, and some in that of Claudius. Late, but not early, traditions date it within St. Peter's lifetime. (1) According to Irenaeus, III. i. 1 (Eus. *H.E.* v. 8), 'And after their exodus [i.e. the death of Peter and Paul] Mark, the disciple and interpreter of Peter, having committed to writing the things that Peter used to preach delivered them to us'. The interpretation, indeed, is disputed.

---

[1] *The Hibbert Journal*, Oct. 1921, and *The Four Gospels*, pp. 199–222.
[2] *Behind the Third Gospel: a study of the Proto-Luke hypothesis.*
[3] *The Gospel according to St. Luke*, pp. lviii, lxiv, 86, 140, 253, 262, 274.
[4] *Harvard Theol. Rev.* xxvi, 1933, pp. 1–55.

Some explain 'having committed to writing' (ἐγγράφως) as referring to a time before St. Peter's death, while only 'delivered them to us' belong to the time after 'their exodus'. But this is strained and unnatural. Others, very improbably, understand 'exodus' to mean 'departure' not 'death'.[1] If the words are taken in their plainest meaning, Irenaeus dates the Second Gospel c. 64–67. (2) In the English edition of Huck's *Synopsis* the evidence of the Anti-Marcionite Prologues is given after Papias's evidence. Thus they are put before the evidence of St. Irenaeus as though they were prior to and independent of his works; if so, they may be dated about 160–80. Dom de Bruyne[2] pointed to their homogeneity and Anti-Marcionite tendency. His arguments convinced A. von Harnack[3] and F. L. Cross.[4] However, M. J. Lagrange[5] concluded after a careful study of the evidence that the Prologue-writer knew Irenaeus's *Adversus Haereses*. The Prologues, which are found in thirty-eight Latin biblical manuscripts, were written originally in Greek, to judge from internal evidence, but only the Lucan Prologue is extant in Greek, the other two being in Latin. The Prologue to Matthew and the opening of the Prologue to Mark are lost, the fragment of the latter being as follows:[6] '. . . Marcus adseruit, qui colobodactylus est nominatus, ideo quod ad ceteram corporis proceritatem digitos minores habuisset. iste interpres fuit Petri, post excessionem ipsius Petri descripsit idem hoc in partibus Italiae evangelium.' *Colobodactylus* was an epithet applied to Mark especially at Rome before Latin became the ordinary tongue of Christians there. Streeter[7] quotes this epithet as applied to St. Mark by Hippolytus and he cites the explanation given by Wordsworth and White[8] who took it to describe a man who cut off his thumb to escape military service, a 'shirker'. If the word

[1] Cf. Lk. ix. 31; 2 Pet. i. 15.   [2] *Revue Bénédictine*, 1928, pp. 193 ff.
[3] *Sitzungsberichte der Preussischen Akademie, Phil.-hist. Kl.*, 1928, pp. 322 ff.
[4] Cf. Dr. Cross's letter to the London *Times*, 13 February 1936.
[5] *Revue Biblique*, xxxviii, 1929; pp. 115–21; cf. his *Introduction à l'étude du Nouveau Testament: deuxième partie: critique textuelle, II. La Critique rationelle*, p. 265; cf. B. W. Bacon, *J.T.S.* xxiii. 134 ff.
[6] Huck-Lietzmann, *A Synopsis of the First Three Gospels*, English edition by F. L. Cross, pp. vii–viii.
[7] *The Four Gospels*, pp. 336–7.
[8] J. Wordsworth and H. J. White, *Nouum Testamentum Latine*, p. 171.

described a 'shirker' in general, it may have carried a reference to the story in Acts xv. 38, according to which John Mark deserted Paul and Barnabas on the first missionary journey and went home. Streeter somewhat too ingeniously suggests that the epithet had a double meaning, 'the author was a shirker, his gospel a torso', for the original ending of Mark if it ever existed after xvi. 8 is lost. Others would connect the word κολόβον, an undervest with short sleeves, with the story peculiar to Mark of the young man who fled 'naked', wearing only his inner garment, xiv. 52; others would say that the epithet was conferred on St. Mark because of the brevity of his Gospel compared with St. Matthew's; even St. Augustine[1] was to describe Mark wrongly as a successor of Matthew and a lackey and abridger of him. Another suggestion is that the epithet was due to the legend that Mark, cousin to the Levite Barnabas,[2] mutilated his thumb to escape Levitical service in the Temple; in an age when Christians loved to gossip about the apostles and their followers, as the Western text of Acts and the Apocryphal Gospels show, this legend arose to which Hippolytus[3] refers. The Prologue-writer, however, appears to have interpreted the epithet to mean that Mark had rather short fingers in relation to his general bodily stature and not that he was mutilated.[4] The last sentence in the Prologue, containing *interpres Petri* and *excessio*, resembles closely the evidence of Papias and of Irenaeus and is probably dependent upon them.

(3) In Alexandria the wish was felt for an apostolic guarantee for St. Mark's work. Clement of Alexandria places it at a date after St. Peter had worked and taught at Rome, but before his death. Eusebius cites his testimony in two somewhat different forms. In *H.E.* ii. 15 he relates, on the authority of Clement in the sixth book of his *Hypotyposes*, that the hearers of Peter at Rome earnestly entreated 'Mark, whose Gospel is extant, who was a follower of Peter', to preserve in writing the oral teaching which they had received;[5] and that Peter 'was pleased with the

---

[1] 'tanquam pedisequus et breviator eius videtur', *De cons. ev.* ii.
[2] Acts iv. 36. [3] *Philosophoumena*, vii. 30.
[4] Cf. H. B. Swete, *The Gospel according to St. Mark*, pp. xxi f.
[5] H. B. Swete remarks that 'this feature in the story bears a suspicious resemblance to the account which the Muratorian fragment gives, and Clement repeats, in reference to the Gospel of St. John' (*St. Mark*, p. xx).

zeal of the men, and authorized the writings to be read by the Churches'. In *H.E.* vi. 14 Clement is reported to have said in the same work that 'when Peter knew it he used no persuasion either to hinder him from it or to urge him to do it'. And Origen said (*ap.* Eus. *H.E.* vi. 25) that Mark made his Gospel 'as Peter instructed (ὑφηγήσατο) him', which seems to imply his personal supervision. Jerome (*De vir. ill.* 8) says much the same as Clement in the former of the two passages of Eus., appealing to Papias as well as to Clement; yet he states (*ad Hedib.* 11) that the Second Gospel was produced 'Petro narrante et illo scribente'. (4) Eusebius himself, on the other hand (*H.E.* ii. 14, 17), brings the Apostle to Rome to oppose Simon Magus in the reign of Claudius (A.D. 41–54). Hence it is stated by Theophylact, and in the subscriptions of some late manuscripts,[1] that the Gospel was written ten or twelve years after the Ascension.

MATTHEW. The persistent belief that St. Matthew the Apostle wrote his Gospel for 'Hebrews', i.e. residents in Palestine, carried with it an early date. Iren. III. i. 1 (Eus. *H.E.* v. 8): 'Matthew also put forth a Gospel writing among the Hebrews in their own language [i.e. Aramaic], while Peter and Paul in Rome were preaching the Gospel and founding the Church.' Clement Alex. (Eus. *H.E.* vi. 14): 'The Gospels which contain the genealogies were written first.' Origen, *in Evang. Joh.*, tom. vi. 32: 'Matthew who, according to tradition, before the others published the Gospel for the Hebrews.' Eus. *H.E.* iii. 24: 'Matthew, having first preached to the Hebrews, when he was about to go to others, compensated for the loss of his presence those whom he was obliged to leave by delivering to them in writing his Gospel in their native language.' And Jerome follows the same tradition stating repeatedly that Matthew wrote first, and in Judaea.

LUKE. The facts as to the origin of the Third Gospel appear to have been no better known. Irenaeus (loc. cit.) writes: 'And [*sc.* also after the death of Peter and Paul] Luke, the follower of Paul, recorded in a book the Gospel preached by Paul.' Eusebius even implies (*H.E.* iii. 4) that his Gospel was written within St. Paul's lifetime, recording a tradition

---

[1] 13, 124, 346, 543, 160, 161, 293, 209².

($\phi\alpha\sigma\acute{\iota}$) that St. Paul referred to St. Luke's writing whenever he said 'according to my Gospel' (cf. Rom. ii. 16). The tradition is, of course, worthless; but it shows how unintelligently conclusions could be formed, after two or three centuries, as to the dates of New Testament writings.

Reference here may be made to two other pieces of evidence.

(1) The Anti-Marcionite Prologue to Luke (see above, p. 26) may contain valuable information. It runs:

Luke is a Syrian of Antioch, a doctor by profession. Having been a disciple of the Apostles and later having accompanied Paul until his [Paul's] martyrdom, he served the Lord without distraction,[1] unmarried, childless, and he fell asleep at the age of eighty-four in Boeotia, full of Holy Spirit. This man, when Gospels already existed—that according to Matthew written down in Judaea and that according to Mark in Italy—impelled by Holy Spirit composed the entire Gospel in Achaia, showing through his preface this very fact that before him other [Gospels] had been written, and also that it was necessary to produce an accurate account of the dispensation for the faithful ex-Gentiles so that they should neither be distracted by Jewish myths nor be led astray by heretical and empty imaginings and miss the truth. Therefore we have transmitted to us at once at the beginning as being most necessary [the record of] the birth of John, who is the beginning of the Gospel, having been forerunner of the Lord and a participator in the preparation of the Gospel [Latin: of the people], in the baptismal instruction [Latin: in the introduction of baptism] and in the fellowship of the Spirit [Latin: in the fellowship of suffering]. A prophet[2] among the Twelve mentions this dispensation. And indeed afterwards the same Luke wrote the Acts of the Apostles while, later, John the Apostle, one of the Twelve, wrote the Apocalypse in the isle of Patmos and, after that, the Gospel.

That Luke wrote in Achaea and that he lived to be eighty-four and died unmarried and childless cannot be inferred from the evidence of the New Testament itself nor taken as Anti-Marcionite polemic. It may be accepted that Luke wrote later than Mark but it is more doubtful whether he wrote later than the First Evangelist.

---

[1] $\dot{\alpha}\pi\epsilon\rho\iota\sigma\pi\dot{\alpha}\sigma\tau\omega s$, cf. P[46], Heb. xii. 2, $\epsilon\dot{\upsilon}\pi\epsilon\rho\acute{\iota}\sigma\pi\alpha\sigma\tau o\nu$, and 1 Cor. vii. 35.

[2] Malachi.

(2) The Muratorian Canon was published by Muratori from the eighth-century MS. Bibl. Ambros. Cod. 101 at Milan. Four small fragments of the same Canon were discovered in manuscripts of the eleventh and twelfth centuries at Monte Cassino. The bad Latin is no doubt a translation from the original Greek, the author of which may well have been Hippolytus.[1] The Canon contains the following: 'The third book of the Gospel (according to Luke), Luke, that physician whom after the ascension of Christ Paul had taken with him as one zealous for the law,[2] composed in his own name on the basis of report. However, he did not himself see the Lord in the flesh and therefore as he could "trace the course of events" he set them down. So also he began his story with the birth of John.' There is nothing here, however, which could not have been inferred from an intelligent reading of the New Testament.

All the Patristic evidence is set out fully by H. J. Cadbury in F. Jackson and K. Lake, *The Beginnings of Christianity*, ii, 1922, pp. 209 ff. Cadbury (ibid., pp. 243 f.) gives the Monarchian Prologue, as it has been called, with which the Anti-Marcionite Prologue quoted above should be compared.

Internal Evidence

MARK. Irenaeus was doubtless right in saying that St. Mark wrote his Gospel after St. Peter's death. It was then that a record of the Apostle's preaching would be needed. Apart from that fact, which presupposes a date after 64, and the sure conclusion which has been reached by synoptic study that Matthew and Luke were later than Mark, the only indication of date is supplied by the apocalyptic discourse in Mk. xiii. There is a fairly general, though not quite universal, consensus of opinion that the discourse, in its original form, was at one time in circulation as an independent pamphlet. It contains, no doubt, some sayings of our Lord; but in the form known to St. Mark it appears to have been the work of a Jewish Chris-

---

[1] Lagrange, *Revue Biblique*, xlii, 1933, pp. 161 ff.; B. Altaner, *Précis de Patrologie*, pp. 121 f.

[2] *iuris studiosum*; or *itineris socium*, a companion of his journey, or *litteris studiosum*, with a zeal for letters, or *quasi adiutorem*, in the role of assistant. The text is uncertain. Cf. M. Goguel, *Introduction au Nouveau Testament*, iii, 1922, p. 371.

tian who understood the Apocalypse of *Daniel* (as many have done ever since) as applying to the events immediately beyond his own horizon. 'The Abomination (*neuter*) of Desolation standing where *he* ought not' refers to the personal figure of Anti-Christ, which was a well-known feature of Jewish apocalyptic expectation. The writer, as always in eschatological thought, is sure that the dire catastrophe will occur soon. Not, indeed, actually at once, because deceivers, wars, earthquakes, famines, were to be only the 'beginning of travail pains'. This, in itself, had nothing to do with the fall of Jerusalem. But Mark incorporated the document because he, in turn, could apply the predictions to his own day and see their fulfilment immediately beyond his horizon. The end of this world-order is seen against the foreground of Jerusalem's fall and the distance between the two future events is foreshortened. There is no real connexion between *vv.* 1, 2 and the discourse which follows; but the fact that he could connect them shows that, for him, the destruction of the Temple was one of the imminent horrors of 'that tribulation'. If, however, he had been writing after it occurred, *v.* 2 would probably have contained a more explicit description of the fall of the city. At whatever earlier date, then, the Little Apocalypse may have been current, the use which St. Mark makes of it points to a date shortly before A.D. 70 for the writing of the Gospel. With this agrees the view of A. E. J. Rawlinson[1] that one object of the Gospel was to encourage Christians at Rome in the Neronian persecution.

This is against the view of Allen[2] who contends for an early date for all three Synoptic Gospels, and thinks that St. Mark wrote early in the time that St. Peter was absent from Jerusalem (A.D. 44–49) before returning for the Council, to compensate for the loss of his personal presence. And that being in Jerusalem it was naturally in Aramaic; but when St. Mark, soon afterwards, went with Barnabas to Antioch (44–47) the need was felt for its translation into Greek. Similarly C. C. Torrey,[3] who thinks that all four Gospels were based on written Aramaic sources, maintains that there is no reference in the Gospels or Acts to the Fall of Jerusalem. 'The supposed

---

[1] *St. Mark*, pp. xvi ff.   [2] *Dict. of the Apostolic Church*, i. 474.
[3] *The Four Gospels*, pp. 256 ff.

references . . . are merely repeated from the Old Testament prophecies . . . Zech. xiv. 2 . . . Dan. ix. 26 . . . Zech. xiii. 8.' He holds that when Caligula[1] threatened to set up his own image in the Temple in A.D. 40, Mark expected the fulfilment of Dan. ix. 27 and xii. 11. Caligula fortunately died on 24 Jan. A.D. 41 at the hand of an assassin. The Aramaic background of the Second Gospel is clear; but there is not enough evidence to prove that it was a translation (see pp. 42 ff.). He thinks, rightly, that there is nothing in the eschatological discourse which our Lord, with prophetic insight, could not have said. But, as we have seen, it is St. Mark's use of it which points to a later date for the Gospel. On the other hand M. Goguel[2] is among those who date Mark after A.D. 70 despite the allusiveness of xiii. 14. He urges that the saying in xiv. 57 about the destruction and rebuilding of the Temple in three days, which 'may not be authentic', is disavowed by the evangelist, i.e. after A.D. 70; it was false witnesses who reported it. But xiv. 58 was no doubt an authentic saying of Christ; cf. Acts vi. 14, Jn. ii. 19. When Goguel adds that he wonders whether the Parable of the Husbandmen would have ended before A.D. 70 so explicitly as xii. 9 does, he forgets that that Parable shows no sign of being retouched by Christians.[3]

It is scarcely necessary, in the face of all the work that has been done upon the Gospels, to discuss the arguments which used to be offered for bringing this Gospel down to the second century.

MATTHEW. If the arguments for dating Mark shortly before A.D. 70 are sound, all attempts to date either Matthew or Luke earlier than that must fail, since the writer of each of them used Mark virtually in its present form. Such attempts have been made, but none of the arguments adduced can outweigh that fact. The dates given by various scholars can be seen in

---

[1] Josephus, *Ant.* xviii. 5. 3.

[2] *Introduction au Nouveau Testament*, i, 1923, pp. 373 f.

[3] F. C. Burkitt, *Transactions of the Third International Congress for the History of Religion*, ii. 321–8; cf. C. H. Dodd, *History and Gospel*, p. 101, citing Matt. xxiii. 36 and Lk. xi. 49–51, Matt. xxiii. 37–39 and Lk. xiii. 34–35, Lk. xix. 41–44, Jn. ix. 39. 'The purpose of them all is the same; the rejection of Jesus by the Jews is a sign of divine judgement. . . .' Note that there is no reference in the Parable to the Resurrection of Christ.

Moffatt, *Introd. Lit. N.T.*, p. 213. The evidence for an exact
date is scanty. But such expressions as 'till now' ἕως ἄρτι
(xi. 12), 'till today' ἕως τῆς σήμερον (xxvii. 8), μέχρι τῆς
σήμερον ἡμέρας (xxviii. 15), suggest generally that some time
had elapsed since the days of Jesus. The destruction of Jerusalem seems to be referred to in xxii. 7 : 'he sent forth his armies
and destroyed those murderers and burnt up their city.' And
a comparatively late date is required by the following considerations : Mark, written at a place distant from Palestine,
probably Rome, had had time to reach Palestine or Syria with
an established value which the writer of Matthew could appre-
ciate. There are allusions to Church government (xvi. 19,
xviii. 18) and to excommunication (xviii. 17). The apostles are
so highly reverenced that the writer often softens or omits statements derogatory to them (see A. H. McNeile's *St. Matthew*, on
viii. 26). False Christian prophets had appeared (vii. 15, 22) ;
cf. *Didache*, xi–xiii. There had been time for apocryphal or
legendary details to become current, which the evangelist
adopts (e.g. xxvii. 52 f., xxviii. 2 ff.). And though, with other
writers of his day, he had not given up the expectation of the
imminence of the Advent, and freely recorded utterances of our
Lord to that effect, he could yet look forward to a period
during which the evangelization of 'all nations' would be
carried on (xxviii. 19 f.).

On the other hand, there are considerations which forbid a
late date. The Gospel was the first favourite in the early Church
although it lacked the prestige of the two chief centres of
Christendom, Rome and Ephesus ; and the prestige also of the
two chief apostolic names, Peter and Paul. And the strongly
Judaic elements in it would have discredited it if it had appeared in the second century. All of which imply its early,
widely known, and apostolic credit.[1]

External evidence is of no help earlier than Ignatius (A.D.
110–15). Echoes in James and Clement of Rome may be
accounted for by the probability that collections of the Lord's
sayings had been made before the evangelist's date, and were
still in use. But Ignatius certainly seems to refer to our Gospel
when he speaks of Christ (*Smyrn.* i) as baptized by John 'that

---

[1] See C. H. Turner, *J.T.S.* x, 1908–9, p. 172.

all righteousness might be fulfilled by Him' (cf. Matt. iii. 15). There is no reason to depart from the conclusion (McNeile's *St. Matthew*, p. xxviii) that 'these facts, which are in keeping with the impression produced by the Gospel as a whole, forbid a date earlier than *c.* A.D. 80, but do not require one later than 100'. A date about 80–85 is a probable one. 'I am not convinced that any of the reasons brought forward [by Dr. Kilpatrick] requires a date as late as A.D. 90', writes Dr. T. W. Manson.[1]

LUKE. Such evidence as we have is best satisfied by placing the Third Gospel in the same period, *c.* 80–85. Dr. T. W. Manson would date the writing of Luke–Acts *c.* 70. An argument for an earlier date has been drawn from the conclusion of the Acts. Since the narrative leaves St. Paul in imprisonment at Rome, without going on to record his death, some have thought that St. Luke wrote at that point of time, i.e. before 64; and that the Gospel must be earlier still. But it is possible that Acts was written after a compilation of Q and L material and before the third Gospel as we have it.[2]

The study of the synoptic problem will show that it is very doubtful if there is any dependence of Matthew on Luke, or vice versa; and their independence can most easily be explained if they wrote at about the same time.

A comparison of St. Luke's treatment of the eschatological discourse with St. Mark's (see Lk. xxi. 20–24) makes it probable that while St. Mark expected the destruction of the Temple in the future, St. Luke looked back to the siege and sack of the city in the past.[3]

It is possible that the Fourth Evangelist knew Luke.[4] Streeter[5] concludes as follows: 'The interest shown by John in identifying and connecting persons and places, or in elaborating incidents, mentioned in Luke is more likely if they occurred

---

[1] *J.T.S.* xlviii, 1947, p. 218.

[2] C. S. C. Williams, *J.T.S.* xlix, 1948, p. 204. The end of Acts and its bearing on the date of Luke–Acts have been discussed by M. Goguel, *Introduction au Nouveau Testament*, iii. 326–41, and by K. Lake and H. J. Cadbury, *Beginnings of Christianity*, iv. 349 f. and by Cadbury, v. 326–38.

[3] Dr. C. H. Dodd denies this. Luke quotes the LXX and does not refer to horrors of the siege. (*The Journal of Roman Studies*, xxxvii, 1937, pp. 47–54.)

[4] See Windisch, *Johannes und die Synoptiker*, pp. 48–50.

[5] *The Four Gospels*, pp. 401–8.

in some document regarded by his readers as a standard account of the life of Christ rather than in a mere floating tradition.' And after a further examination of the question whether the source known to him was our Luke or the earlier Proto-Luke which was incorporated in it, he says 'Neither singly nor together do these points amount to demonstrative proof that what John knew was, not Proto-Luke, but our Gospel of Luke; yet, to my mind, they make the balance of probability incline still very decidedly in that direction.'

The question whether St. Luke had read Josephus's *Antiquities*, which was written *c.* A.D. 93, has been disputed by competent scholars.[1] Coincidences of language prove nothing. Two historians, writing Hellenistic Greek in the same quarter, or third, of the first century, would naturally show similarities of vocabulary. But the two chief considerations offered as proof that St. Luke had read it—and not only read, but in each case misread—are as follows:

(*a*) Josephus[2] gives an account of the abortive insurrection of Theudas in the procuratorship of Fadus, i.e. A.D. 44–46. He attracted a large following, but a Roman squadron of cavalry cut them in pieces, and Theudas was captured and beheaded. He then relates that Alexander, the next procurator of Judaea (46–48), executed some of the sons of Judas the Galilean. This person had incited the Jews not to pay taxes, forty years before in the time of Quirinus. Here we have Theudas followed by the *sons* of Judas. But in the speech of Gamaliel (Acts v. 34 ff.) we hear of an insurrectionary Theudas followed by an insurrectionary *Judas*. And, as Burkitt says:[3] 'Here, if anywhere in the Acts, the details of the speech must be due to the author, for all the Christians had been put outside.' If St. Luke had read the *Antiquities* his remembrance of the passage is faulty, since he writes 'Judas' instead of 'the sons of Judas'. But further, if his Theudas is the same as the Theudas of Josephus he has committed a startling anachronism, because Gamaliel was speaking not less than twelve years *before* that insurrection took

[1] F. J. F. Jackson and K. Lake, *Beginnings of Christianity*, ii, 1922, pp. 355–8; E. Meyer, *Ursprung und Anfänge des Christentums*, i, 1921, pp. 47 ff., ii. 404 f., iii. 11; F. C. Burkitt, *Gospel History and its Transmission*, (3rd ed. 1911), pp. 105 ff.

[2] *Antiq.* xx. 5.

[3] *The Gospel History and its Transmission*, 1911, p. 107.

place. If he had not read it, we must suppose that he possessed some source of information from which he derived the names Theudas (an abbreviation of Theodorus and of other names) and Judas as rebels, and their stories in this chronological order.

(b) Lysanias was tetrarch of Abila, and according to Strabo (XVI. ii. 10) had been executed by Mark Antony in 36 B.C., but the district continued to be called by his name. Josephus[1] speaks of Ἀβίλαν τὴν Λυσανίου 'Abila of Lysanias', and (B.J. II. xi. 5) of βασιλείαν τὴν Λυσανίου καλουμένην, 'the so-called kingdom of Lysanias'. And he says of Abila[2] Λυσανίου δ' αὕτη ἐγεγόνει τετραρχία, 'now this had been the tetrarchy of Lysanias'. But in Lk. iii. 1, 2 the beginning of the Baptist's ministry is dated 'in the fifteenth year of Tiberius Caesar', and, together with four other synchronisms, 'Lysanias being tetrarch of Abilene'. Unless there was a second Lysanias, tetrarch of Abila, of which there is possibly evidence,[3] St. Luke makes him tetrarch sixty-five years after his death. If, then, he did not get his information about an unknown man from an unknown source, he had learnt that the Abilene district was known as the tetrarchy of Lysanias, and erroneously concluded that Lysanias was alive at the time; and it is claimed that he learnt it from the *Antiquities*. Torrey[4] thinks that both St. Luke and Josephus are dependent upon earlier sources. M. Goguel agrees,[5] suggesting that Luke and Josephus used a history of Herod which went up to A.D. 79 and quoting G. Hölscher.[6] Streeter[7] suggests that St. Luke had—not read the *Antiquities* but—heard Josephus lecture previously in Rome, and had made some slips when he took down hurried notes. The theory of indebtedness cannot be considered proved. But if it is accepted, he wrote later than 93. Such a date is not impossible for a companion of St. Paul; but since he was, presumably, a physician before he joined the Apostle on his travels, he can hardly have been born much later than A.D. 20, and was there-

---

[1] *Antiq.* XIX. v. 1.   [2] Ibid. xx. vii. 1.
[3] Cronin, *J.T.S.* xviii. 147–51.
[4] *The Composition and Date of Acts*, 1916, pp. 69 ff.
[5] *Introduction au Nouveau Testament*, iii. 117 ff.
[6] *Die Quellen des Josephus für die Zeit vom Exil bis zum jüdischen Kriege*, 1904.
[7] *The Four Gospels*, pp. 557 f.

fore some seventy-five years of age when he wrote both the
Gospel and the Acts, which is a somewhat advanced age for
the execution of such a work, though not impossible; cf. the
Anti-Marcionite Prologue (p. 29). If the Acts was written
about 90, and the Gospel 80–85, all the evidence (apart from
Josephus) is satisfied; however, dependence on Josephus is
unlikely. As Dr. T. W. Manson[1] urges, Luke's ignorance of a
collection of Pauline epistles is a stronger argument against a
late date in the first century than any problematical acquaintance with the *Antiquities* can be for it.

§ 5. PLACE OF WRITING

MARK. (1) In 2 Tim. iv. 11 (a passage from St. Paul's own
hand) directions are given for St. Mark to be brought to
Rome. (2) Very soon afterwards 1 Pet. v. 13 implies that he is
there. Even if the Epistle was not the work of St. Peter, it must
have been written early enough for Polycarp to know it; i.e.
the presence of St. Mark with the Apostle at Rome must have
been accepted as a fact by, say, 110. Merrill[2] contends, as
many writers in the past have contended, that 'Babylon' (in
1 Pet., loc. cit.) means the Mesopotamian city, and that St.
Peter never visited the capital. But this criticism has com-
mended itself to few. See Streeter's note, op. cit., p. 489. If
he was not in Rome, something is required—supposing the
Epistle not to be authentic—to account for the belief that he
was. That belief is perhaps implied by Ignatius in his letter to
Rome (iv. 3): 'I do not enjoin you like Peter and Paul'; and
even more clearly by Clement of Rome, who, in his letter to
Corinth (v. vi) speaks of the deaths of Peter and Paul in close
connexion with the Neronian persecution. But, as Streeter
argues, if a mistaken inference was drawn from Clement's
words, the acceptance of that inference would be rendered
easier if there was a prior belief that a Gospel, representing
St. Peter's reminiscences, had emanated from Rome. 'Thus
the hypothesis that Mark was written in Rome is a legitimate
inference from the tradition that Peter and Mark were together

---

[1] *Bulletin of the John Rylands Library*, xxviii, 1944, p. 398.
[2] *Essays on Early Church History*, pp. 311 f.

in Rome, if that is historical; or, if that tradition is not historical, then it helps to explain its origin.' (3) Irenaeus (quoted on p. 25) adds to the statement of Papias the significant fact that St. Mark wrote after the death of St. Peter and St. Paul, who had been (as he says in the previous context) 'preaching and founding the Church in Rome'. This would have little point unless he thought that he wrote at Rome, carrying on their work. (4) Clement Alex. evidently understood it so, for he explicitly places St. Mark's work at Rome in the lifetime of St. Peter (see p. 27). (5) The Second Gospel was the least popular of the four; and without the backing of some strong authority such as that of the Roman Church, might not have been included in the Canon at all.

Two points of internal evidence are sometimes adduced which cannot be allowed much weight: (a) The writer uses Latinisms.[1] But this might be done anywhere in the Roman Empire. In Egypt, for example, the papyri show how easily Latin could penetrate the popular Greek. Even the First Evangelist could adopt *quadrans* (v. 26) from a Jewish-Christian source, and *praetorium* (xxvii. 27) from Mark. (b) He mentions Rufus as a son of Simon the Cyrenaean (xv. 21); and St. Paul sends greeting to a Rufus in Rom. xvi. 13. They were not necessarily the same person; the name was common. But even if they were, it is very probable that Rom. xvi was written not to Rome but to Ephesus, perhaps added to a copy of Rom. i–xv sent to Rome (see pp. 154 ff.).

Tradition afterwards placed St. Mark at Alexandria. But the Gospel cannot have been written there (as stated in the subscriptions of the MSS. Y and 473), because, as Turner[2] says, 'Alexandrine Christianity, during more than a century and a half after Christ, stood almost completely aloof from the main current of Church life'. The motive, no doubt, for the tradition was to suggest that Alexandria ought to stand to Rome as St. Mark had stood to St. Peter, as subordinate.

MATTHEW. One of the chief merits of Streeter's work on the Four Gospels is its insistence on the fact that each of them must have had its original home in one of the great apostolic

---

[1] See Thumb, *Dict. of the Apost. Church*, i. 555.
[2] *J.T.S.* x, 1916–17, p. 169.

Churches, to which appeal was made against the Gnostic claim to a secret tradition. The First Gospel is anonymous; and therefore its author must have been known, and it must have been read and honoured, in one of the great Churches, or it would not have become the favourite Gospel; it would not, indeed, have enjoyed any circulation at all.

The tradition, traceable to Irenaeus, who in turn was dependent upon the words of Papias, that the First Gospel was written for 'Hebrews', though its Aramaic origin cannot be maintained, points at least to the East as the place of its origin. And there is evidence that it was largely used by Jewish Christians. This makes Rome, Ephesus, or Alexandria impossible. There are left Caesarea or some Church in Palestine, and Antioch. With regard to the first, Streeter's reasoning (op. cit., pp. 502 f.) that 'the official Gospel of a Church which was the port of entry of Samaria was not very likely to have contained the command, "Enter not into any city of the Samaritans" ' is not very convincing. And against any Church in Palestine he argues that the 'haggadic' use of Mark in Matthew shows that Mark must have been known in the Church where the latter was written 'long enough to have become an established authority—a document which teachers and preachers expounded by methods familiar in the exposition of Scripture'. But he does not make it clear why this would be impossible anywhere in Palestine. The writer, however, seems to have lived at some place where the Christians were not in close touch with Jerusalem. He apparently had no knowledge, or at least made no independent use, of the Hebrew Old Testament, and employs no distinctively Jerusalemite traditions. Antioch, therefore, is the place which seems to satisfy the conditions best. Streeter refers to Burkitt who points out that the use of the verb ἐπιφώσκειν, Matt. xxviii. 1, implies the Gentile mode of reckoning time and suggests Antioch. And if that was the place of writing, the use of the Gospel by Ignatius, Bishop of Antioch, is explained (see pp. 33 f.). Dr. G. D. Kilpatrick, however, thinks that Matthew was composed in some prosperous city in Syria, perhaps in one of the Phoenician sea-ports.[1]

LUKE. There was a tradition that St. Luke was a native of

---

[1] *The Origins of the Gospel according to St. Matthew*, 1946, pp. 133 f.

Antioch,[1] as the 'Anti-Marcionite' Prologue says, which is in keeping with the large part which Antioch plays in the narrative of the Acts.[2] But it does not follow that he wrote his Gospel there. Streeter (op. cit., p. 533) points out that 'no Church writer and no MS. "subscription" says that Luke wrote at Antioch'. And he adds, 'the fact that the connexion of Peter with Antioch—the proudest boast of that Church—is completely ignored is fatal to the theory of some modern scholars that the book was written in and for that Church'. It may also be said that if Matthew was written at Antioch Luke was not. The tone and language and general atmosphere are too different. A large part of his sources was no doubt collected in Palestine; he had access, in particular, to Jerusalemite and Caesarean traditions. But he wrote for the Gentile Theophilus and other readers who were unacquainted with Palestine, since topographical explanations are given of Nazareth (i. 26), Bethlehem (ii. 4), Capharnaum (iv. 31), the country of the Gerasenes (viii. 26), Arimathaea (xxiii. 51), Emmaus (xxiv. 13).

Moreover, the same Prologue places the writing of the Gospel in Achaea; and that is assumed by Gregory Naz. (*Orat.* xxxiii. 11), and the tradition is reflected by Jerome (*Praef. in Matt.*). But the latter also places the writing of the Acts in Rome, a conclusion which can be safely drawn from the contents of the book. The Gospel and the Acts were not necessarily written in the same place; there was probably some interval between the two, during which St. Luke could have moved from Achaea to Rome. There was, further, a tradition that he was buried at Thebes in Boeotia; this had been well accepted by the time of Constantine, who removed what he believed to be his bones to Constantinople. None of the evidence is decisive, but if we are to indulge in conjecture, that of Streeter is as likely as any:

The name Theophilus in the Lucan Prefaces looks like a pru-

---

[1] Found in the 'Monarchian Prologue' to the Gospel, and in Eus. *H.E.* iii. 4, the tradition being carried on by Jerome (*Praef. in Matt., De vir. ill.* 7). If Eus. was independent of the Prologues, as Harnack thinks, they go back to a very early common source. Possibly, but not necessarily, the tradition is an inference from the reading of D at Acts xi. 27: 'and when *we* were gathered together, one of them named Agabus, &c.' If so, the evidence for the reading is greatly strengthened.

[2] See Harnack, *Luke the Physician*, pp. 20–24.

dential pseudonym for some Roman of position—κράτιστε might be translated 'your Excellence'; and if Luke had a special connexion with some personage who, after a provincial governorship (perhaps of Achaea, resident at Corinth), subsequently returned to Rome, all the conditions would be satisfied. But in that case a copy of the Gospel would have been brought to Rome by Luke himself so soon after it was written, that from the point of view of its circulation in the Church at large, it may practically be reckoned as a second Roman Gospel [op. cit., pp. 534 f.].

It is possible that a collection of Q and L material was addressed to Theophilus as the 'first account' (Acts i. 1) and that Acts formed the second work addressed to Theophilus after a copy of Mark had come into Luke's hands (for Acts echoes passages of Mark not used in the Third Gospel) and that finally perhaps at Rome or perhaps still in Achaia, if one may credit the phrase found in the Anti-Marcionite Prologue ἐν τοῖς περὶ τὴν Ἀχαίαν τὸ πᾶν τοῦτο συνεγράψατο εὐαγγέλιον, Luke composed the 'whole Gospel' using Mark as his chronological framework, as the Q and L material was not provided with one.

§ 6. ORIGINAL LANGUAGE

The opinion, long universally held, that all the three synoptic Gospels were originally written in Greek has been controverted in modern times, partly in consequence of an ancient tradition about Matthew, and partly from internal evidence. The question of the language of the Gospels as they stand must be carefully distinguished from that of their sources. It is probable (see p. 88) that Lk. i, ii are a translation, or at least based upon a translation, from a Hebrew document; and perhaps the same must be said of Matt. i, ii. Also that someone, perhaps St. Matthew the Apostle, made an Aramaic collection of *logia*, which was expanded into different Greek recensions, from two of which a portion of Matthew and Luke was derived. And any oral tradition of our Lord's words and deeds handed down by His Palestinian contemporaries ultimately goes back to Aramaic, which was the vernacular of Palestine. But Matthew and Luke embody much of Mark in its Greek dress, not an Aramaic one; almost certainly therefore they were both written in Greek originally, even if they included translations of some Aramaic sayings.

MARK. There is no early tradition that the Second Gospel is a translation, but that is maintained by some modern scholars. The treatment of the subject by Blass[1] is not, indeed, convincing. He thinks that the first part of the Acts was based on an Aramaic writing by St. Mark which formed a continuation of his Gospel, and therefore that the Aramaisms to be found there were St. Mark's Aramaisms. Hence 'if Mark's second part was written in Aramaic, then his first part, that is the Gospel, must have been originally written in the same language'. As evidence that the Gospel was written in Aramaic he notes textual variations which suggest 'the idea that there existed a plurality of versions [or rather redactions] of a common Aramaic original, and that St. Luke "used another Mark"'. 'Before writing his own Gospel he made a Greek redaction of that of Mark.' 'Another translation of Mark, or other translations, were made by other persons, and one version among these was that which eventually predominated, but the others have at least left their traces.' But in no single case of variant readings does Blass try to show that one of the readings reveals an Aramaic original. Variants can be accounted for in many other ways, and his conjectures cannot be said to have created the least probability of an original Aramaic Mark.

But a stronger case is made by linguistic arguments. Wellhausen[2] points to the general Semitic colouring of style and syntax, a few only of his numerous instances being specifically Aramaic. (He shows also that when Matthew and Luke differ, especially in words of our Lord, the difference can occasionally be explained by reference to the Aramaic which He spoke.) Allen[3] cites the frequent use of certain particles; $\kappa\alpha\acute{\iota}$ = וְ, $\epsilon\mathring{v}\theta\acute{v}s$ = מִיָּד, $\pi\acute{\alpha}\lambda\iota\nu$ = תּוּב, $\ddot{o}\tau\iota$ recit. = דְּ. In syntax he refers to instances of asyndeton, to the frequent historic present corresponding to the Aramaic participle, and to the use of the participle with the verb 'to be' as a periphrasis for a verb in a past sense. And he adduces some expressions which seem to reflect

---

[1] *Philology of the Gospels*, ch. xi.
[2] *Einleitung in die drei ersten Evangelien*, pp. 14–42.
[3] *Expositor*, June 1900, and *St. Mark*, pp. 48–50.

Aramaic idioms. The phenomena certainly point to Aramaic, but the question is whether they imply actual translation or only the work of a bilingual writer whose Greek was influenced by the fact that he habitually thought in Aramaic. Allen and Wellhausen decide in favour of the former. And the theory was supported by Torrey,[1] who believed in the Aramaic origin of all the four Gospels (as well as of Acts i–xv). On the other hand, Allen's results are tested by Burney,[2] who shows that the Aramaic colouring of Mark is not nearly as striking as that of John, and says rightly (p. 19), 'What is needed to substantiate the theory of an Aramaic original for Mark is some cogent evidence of mistranslation; and this has not yet been advanced'. However, Torrey produced his *Four Gospels* in 1933, which like his *Our Translated Gospels* aimed at corroborating his theory and presenting evidence of such mistranslations. This evidence has been sifted and discussed by other Aramaic scholars, who have not been convinced by it in detail, such as J. T. Hudson,[3] W. F. Howard,[4] G. A. Barton,[5] Matthew Black,[6] and E. Littmann.[7] As Howard says, 'Mark's Greek is always Greek, yet translation Greek: not that he translates an Aramaic writing but because he reproduces an Aramaic κατήχησις' (op. cit., p. 481). This is also the conclusion reached by M. Goguel.[8]

MATTHEW. That St. Matthew wrote for Hebrews in 'Hebrew' (i.e. Aramaic)[9] was a tradition which can be traced to Irenaeus. See the passage quoted on p. 28, where the testimonies of Origen, Eusebius, and Jerome to the same effect are given. To these may be added those of Cyril Jerus., *Catech*. xiv, 'Matthew who wrote the Gospel in the Hebrew tongue', and Epiphanius, *Haer*. ii. i. 51, 'And this Matthew writes the Gospel in Hebrew [ἑβραϊκοῖς γράμμασι], and preaches, and begins not from the beginning but gives the genealogy from Abraham'.

Two causes seem to have created this tradition—firstly the

---

[1] *Harvard Theol. Rev.*, Oct. 1923.
[2] *The Aramaic Origin of the Fourth Gospel.*
[3] 'The Aramaic Basis of St. Mark', *Ex. T.*, May 1942, pp. 264 ff.
[4] Moulton's *Grammar of New Testament Greek*, ii, Appendix.
[5] *J.T.S.* xxxvi, 1935, pp. 357 ff.
[6] *An Aramaic Approach to the Gospels and Acts*, 1946.
[7] *Zeitschr. f. d. neutest. Wiss.* 34, 1935, pp. 20–34.
[8] *Introduction au Nouveau Testament*, i. 1923, pp. 352–6.
[9] Cf. Dalman's *Grammatik*, 2nd ed., § 1.

words of Papias, 'Matthew composed the *logia* in the Hebrew language' (see p. 4), and secondly the existence of apocryphal Gospels, current in Jewish-Christian circles, which were closely related to Matthew (see p. 16 n.). In particular the *Gospel of the Nazarenes* was written in Aramaic, and used by a Jewish-Christian sect in Beroea in Coele Syria. It was clearly based on our Gospel, but by Jerome and others it was identified with it. Zahn,[1] though he recognizes this, accepts the tradition, and believes that the First Gospel was originally written in Aramaic. But he makes no attempt to support his theory linguistically, and in fact it cannot be done. An ancient translation from a document in another language always betrays itself in vocabulary and syntax. Some of our Lord's words in Matthew and Luke, as has been said above, show traces of their Aramaic origin, but both Gospels as wholes are entirely free from Aramaisms. The tradition reflected in Irenaeus and the others cannot compete with the fact that, apart from Old Testament quotations, Matthew is quite innocent of 'translation Greek'. Nor can it compete with the fact that the writer transparently uses the Greek Mark.

LUKE. St. Luke, a Hellenist, some even think a Gentile, cannot, probably, himself have written in a Semitic language, even if he could read it. The probability of a Hebrew source for chs. i, ii is discussed on p. 88, and of Aramaic sources for some, or the whole, of Acts i–xv on pp. 101–3. It is improbable that he translated them, but he incorporated translations, which he touched up, as usual, with his own distinctive style and vocabulary. The remainder of the Gospel shows no sign of a Semitic origin, with two exceptions. In some of our Lord's utterances from Q His original Aramaic can be detected behind the Greek; and the LXX, itself a translation, was employed for Old Testament quotations, and deeply colours the whole work, giving it an archaic, Semitic tinge, which St. Luke no doubt thought more suitable than the artificial, rhetorical Greek of the period (which is found only in i. 1–4) for the narration of the Lord's words and deeds, which were as sacred as the Old Testament, and required a biblical style.

[1] *Introd. to the N.T.* (trans. Trout), vol. ii, § 54.

INTRODUCTIONS TO THE NEW TESTAMENT

F. B. Clogg (1937), P. Feine (9th ed., 1950), M. Goguel (1922–6), E. J. Goodspeed (1937), R. Heard (1950), K. Lake (1938), J. Moffatt (3rd ed., 1918), J. Wellhausen (2nd ed., 1911).

BOOKS

F. C. Burkitt, *The Gospel History and its Transmission*, 3rd ed., 1911.
A. von Harnack, *Luke the Physician*, 1907.
Sir E. C. Hoskyns and N. Davey, *The Riddle of the New Testament*, 1931.
T. W. Manson, *The Sayings of Jesus*, 1949.
V. H. Stanton, *The Gospels as Historical Documents*, 1903–20.
B. H. Streeter, *The Four Gospels*, 1924.
V. Taylor, *Behind the Third Gospel*, 1926.

COMMENTARIES

Matthew: W. C. Allen (1907), G. H. Box (1922), F. W. Green (1936), A. H. McNeile (1915), P. A. Micklem (1917), A. Plummer (1909), B. T. D. Smith (1927).

Mark: W. C. Allen (1915), A. W. F. Blunt (1929), B. H. Branscomb (1937), E. Klostermann (3rd ed., 1936), M. J. Lagrange (1947), E. Lohmeyer (1937), A. E. J. Rawlinson (1925), H. B. Swete (1902), V. Taylor (1952), J. Wellhausen (1909).

Luke: W. F. Adeney (2nd ed., 1922), H. Balmforth (1930), J. M. Creed (1930), B. S. Easton (1926), W. Manson (1930), A. Plummer (1896), L. Ragg (1922), J. Wellhausen (1904).

Synoptic Gospels: A. Loisy (1907–8), C. G. Montefiore (1927).

III

FORM-CRITICISM

ST. MARK's Gospel was not written till some thirty or forty years after the Lord's Resurrection. During that period, c. A.D. 33 to 65–70, many apostles and other eyewitnesses were alive and the hope of the Parousia was intense. When death began to remove the apostles and their contemporaries and when the hope of the Second Coming was deferred until the hearts of many grew sick, as the denunciations in Jude and 2 Peter indicate, the necessity for written accounts of Jesus' sayings and deeds was seen to be urgent. The liturgical needs of the community also could be satisfied only by written Gospels. During this 'tunnel period' of one generation, some sayings of Jesus were written down, such as Q, but the tradition of the Good News was mainly oral.

Can we think of Mark as the product of this period of life and thought in the early Church? Can we conceive it as the end of the process of oral tradition rather than as the beginning of a literary movement which produced the Four and the Apocryphal Gospels? Can we go behind the literary sources of the synoptic critic to study the pre-literary forms of the Gospel tradition, to classify them and to set them in the context of the life of the Church? An affirmative answer to these questions was given by a school of Form-critics ('Form-historians' would be a more literal translation) who appeared in Germany after the war of 1914–18, many of whom worked at first independently one of another. They included the following authors whose works are noted: K. L. Schmidt, *Der Rahmen der Geschichte Jesu* (1919); R. Bultmann, *Die Geschichte der synoptischen Tradition* (2nd ed., 1931); M. Dibelius, *Die Formgeschichte des Evangeliums* (1919), translated by B. L. Woolf, *From Tradition to Gospel* (1934). Bultmann published a summary of his views in the *Journal of Religion*, vi, 1926, pp. 337 ff. Valuable introductions and criticisms of the new method are to be found in B. S. Easton's *The Gospel before the Gospels* (1928) and *Christ in the Gospels* (1930); W. K. L. Clarke's *New Testament Problems* (1929), pp. 18–30; M. Goguel's article in the *Revue de l'histoire des religions*, xciv, 1926, pp. 114–60; V. Taylor's *The Formation of the Gospel Tradition* (1933); W. Manson's *Jesus the Messiah* (1943), pp. 20–32; F. C. Grant's *Form Criticism* (1934); E. B. Redlich's *Form Criticism, its value and limitations* (1939); E. Scott's *The Validity of the Gospel Record* (1938); L. J. McGinley's *Form-criticism of the Synoptic Healing Narratives* (1944). The theory did not go without its critics in Germany, notably E. Fascher in his *Die formgeschichtliche Methode* (1924), but a sympathetic approach to Form-criticism was made in England by R. H. Lightfoot, *History and Interpretation in the Gospels* (1934); the same writer championed the Form-critics in reply to F. J. Badcock's attack, *Expository Times*, liii, 1941, pp. 16 ff. by an article (ibid., pp. 51 ff.) which he reprinted with certain admissions as ch. viii of his *The Gospel Message of St. Mark* (1950).

On the Form-critics' view the tradition of the Good News did not rest during the 'tunnel period' with an isolated individual like St. Peter but was the work of the Church composed of communities scattered about the Mediterranean world and enjoying a common life of Christian worship, missionary enterprise, and polemical activity. The stories about Jesus were told and retold many times, before they reached St. Mark or other evangelists, by missionary preachers, teachers, exorcists, and miracle-workers, all of whom left a mark on the mould of the tradition. For Dibelius 'in the beginning was the sermon'. The needs of the community determined the choice of the material eventually written down and its form. The folk-lore of any primitive community has certain marked traits so that the separate stories embodied in folk-lore tradition can be classified and 'rules' can be formulated about them. The originally separate stories found in the Gospels respond to similar treatment. So the Form-critics tried to fix attention on the primary elements of the synoptic Gospels, the units of speeches and narrative, and to apply to them the 'laws' of Form-criticism, seeing those units in their 'situation in life', the *Sitz im Leben* not of Jesus but of the community.

In their approach to the study of the small sections of Mark

the Form-critics were largely indebted to Gunkel's[1] treatment
of the stories in Genesis. Many stories there may have been
the products of popular tradition orally transmitted from one
generation to another, perhaps around the well or the city gate
or the camp fireside or the family hearth. A rule about such
traditions appears to be that a cycle of legends is less primitive
than the separate story, which serves as the basic unit. Each
unit has its particular colouring so that if two stories are combined the colours are blurred. In a primitive unit the actors
are few and the action is short, vivid, and direct. The unit is
apt to end with an oral generalization or to include a striking
saying which would be easily remembered and for which the
framework of the story may serve simply as the scaffolding. It
was not difficult for Schmidt to show that the stories in Mark
up to but not including the Passion narrative, which was
welded into a unity in the crucible of missionary preaching
according to most Form-critics except Bultmann, fall into
separate sections, as a glance at a Greek Synopsis would show.
Each section has usually a short, rather vague introduction
such as καί, καὶ εὐθύς; Matthew and Luke allowed themselves
great freedom in altering Mark's notes of time and place connecting stories together. On the Form-critics' view the outline
of events and the connecting links are not so old or so reliable
as the stories themselves. The episodes did not have any strict
chronological connexion originally, the links between them
being due to the Evangelist, whose setting of them was due to
the community's soteriological motives in presenting the Gospel. Where they occur in Mark the connecting links of time or
place were liable to textual corruption and Matthew and Luke
present often a different order of events from Mark's. Often one
word or saying of Jesus suggested another similar one and so
the evangelist placed them side by side. He was responsible for
threading on to strings the pearls which had long been polished
—or marred?—by passing through the hands not of an eyewitness of the ministry of Jesus but of many to whom the
interests of the community of Christians were paramount.

The immediate effect of Form-critical thought was to undermine the value of the chronology of Mark and to make

[1] *Handkommentar zum A.T.*, 1910, and *Das Märchen im A.T.*, 1917.

students refuse to treat it any more than John as in any sense a biography. The source-critics had hoped to recover the 'plain biography' of the 'Jesus of History'; today it is generally admitted that it is impossible to write a 'life of Christ' for 'Strictly speaking, no framework, no outline is present in Mark'.[1]

The two best-known classifications of Gospel material are those of Dibelius: (a) Paradigms, which correspond roughly to Bultmann's Apophthegmata or V. Taylor's Pronouncement-stories, and (b) Novellen or Miracle-tales. (a) A paradigm is a small section based on the apostolic kerygma and including a striking saying of Jesus. Later the evangelist grouped together such paradigms to form part of his Gospel. However, Dibelius maintains that only eight 'pure' paradigms are discernible in Mark, ii. 1–12, 18–22, 23–28, iii. 1–6, 31–35, x. 13–16, xii. 13–17, and xiv. 3–9 while there are eight others also, less 'pure', i. 23–28, ii. 13–17, vi. 1–6, x. 17–22, 35–45, 46–52, xi. 15–18, xii. 18–27. The heart of each paradigm was a saying of Jesus, 'which will usually imply a principle of universal application, and in it is to be found the purpose of the story, the framework being needed to give the occasion when the utterance was spoken, and the motive which called it forth'.[2] A paradigm is rounded off with a formula; the unit is concise; biographical details are almost entirely absent, the story being told for the sake of the saying that it enshrines. (b) 'Novelle' was Dibelius's name for a miracle-story. He discerns nine in the first nine chapters of Mark; i. 40–45, iv. 35–41, v. 1–20, 21–43, vi. 35–44, 45–52, vii. 32–37, viii. 22–26, ix. 14–29. Unlike the paradigms the Novellen are full of details, often apparently otiose. For example, Matthew and Luke omit many of Mark's superfluous details in the story of the Gerasene demoniac, Mk. v. 1–20. Jesus the Wonder-worker replaces Jesus the Teacher, say the Form-critics. The Gospel Novellen are told in the same way as the pagan miracle-tales. According to Bultmann all the limelight is shed on Jesus; the private sentiments of the victim before and after his cure are not revealed; he exhibits a 'Wunderglaube' towards Jesus. The Novellen conclude with

---

[1] Schmidt, op. cit., p. 90. Cf. T. W. Manson, 'Is it possible to write a life of Christ?', *Ex. T.* liii, 1941, pp. 248–51.

[2] R. H. Lightfoot, *History and Interpretation in the Gospels*, p. 46.

a note of fear, awe, and amazement. The origin of some *Novellen* may lie in paradigms which have been reshaped, e.g. Lk. xiii. 10–17, while that of others may lie in a desire to employ extraneous motifs or to remodel pagan stories. Bultmann[1] writes:

Since we know a great many miracle-stories, we can make a careful comparative study of the miracle-stories found in the Gospels. We then discover that the Gospel stories have exactly the same style as the Hellenistic miracle-stories. Accounts of miraculous healing run as follows: first, the condition of the sick person is depicted in such a fashion as to enhance the magnitude of the miracle. In this connection it is frequently said that the sickness had lasted a long time. Occasionally it is stated that many physicians had attempted in vain to cure the sick person. Sometimes the terrible and dangerous character of the sickness is emphasised. All these traits are found in the Synoptic narratives just as they also appear in the stories which are told concerning the pagan miracle-worker Apollonius of Tyana. After the introductory description of the illness comes the account of the healing itself. The Hellenistic miracle-stories often tell of unusual manipulations by the miracle-worker; the Gospel accounts, however, seldom mention this trait (Mk. vii. 33, viii. 23). The Gospels, however, do retain other typical items. They narrate that the Saviour came near to the sick person—perhaps close to his bed— that he laid his hands upon the patient and took him by the hand and then uttered a wonder-working word. Following a custom also characteristic of pagan miracle-stories, the narratives of healing in the Gospels occasionally reproduce this wonder-working word in a foreign tongue, as for example 'Talitha cumi' (Mk. v. 41) and 'Ephphatha' (Mk. vii. 34). Another typical trait appears when it is sometimes said that no one was permitted to see the actual working of the miracle (Mk. vii. 33 and viii. 23). The close of the miracle-story depicts the consequence of the miracle, frequently describing the astonishment or the terror or the approval of those who witnessed the miraculous event. In other cases the close of the narrative shows the one who is healed demonstrating by some appropriate action that he is entirely cured.

Bultmann's treatment of the sayings of Jesus may be considered next. His classification of them is as follows:

[1] *Journal of Religion*, vi, 1926, pp. 347 ff.

(*a*) Logia or Wisdom sayings like those of the Old Testament. Many Jewish proverbial sayings were attributed to Jesus.

(*b*) Prophetic and Apocalyptic sayings whose burden was, 'The Kingdom is coming', 'Repent'. Whereas 'some prophetic utterances which we read in the Synoptic Gospels may have originated in the Christian community', these being predominantly in the style of Jewish apocalypse, yet 'one can detect here with some probability genuine words of Jesus, for there can be no doubt that Jesus appeared as prophet and announcer of the Kingdom of God'.[1]

(*c*) Law-words and Community rules. Here, too, Bultmann is cautious. He accepts some precepts like those about purification and divorce, almsgiving, prayer and fasting, and especially the great antitheses in Matt. v ('It was said by them of old time . . . . But I say unto you . . .'). But he warns us that we find associated with these utterances others which can be regarded only as regulations for the community, disciplinary rules and regulations for missionary activity. 'These last can have originated only in the Christian community itself.'

(*d*) Sayings in the first person singular. Bultmann considers only a few of these to be authentic. Indeed, a study of the wording of the Isis aretalogy published by W. L. Knox[2] and reflection upon the presence in the Fourth Gospel of only a few parables but of many sayings in the first person singular attributed to Jesus may lead to agreement with Bultmann that not all such sayings in the Gospels are genuine.

(*e*) Parables and parabolic sayings. Although Bultmann doubts whether more than about forty sayings of Jesus go back to Him, he is willing to accept the authenticity of some in this category, chiefly those of an ethical and eschatological character.

This is not the place to describe in detail other classifications of Gospel material by Form-critics, such as 'Mythus' (' "Myth" means those deeds or words which are reported as from a divinity rather than from a teacher'[3]), or 'Paränese' (to

---

[1] Ibid., p. 358.
[2] *J.T.S.* xxxviii, 1937, pp. 230 ff.
[3] H. J. Cadbury, *Harvard Theol. Rev.*, xvi, 1923, p. 83.

Dibelius the Gospel in its original sense was not kerygmatic but paraenetic, as though it were good advice, not good news!).

Bultmann believed that we can neither write a 'life of Jesus' nor present an accurate picture of His personality. 'Even in regard to the question of His Messianic consciousness, we seem compelled to admit ignorance.' This seems a needlessly sceptical conclusion on a par with the closing paragraph of R. H. Lightfoot's *History and Interpretation in the Gospels*, p. 225, 'It seems, then, that the form of the earthly no less than of the heavenly Christ is for the most part hidden from us. For all the inestimable value of the gospels, they yield us little more than a whisper of his voice; we trace in them but the outskirts of his ways.' The same writer, however, in a footnote[1] to a revised article originally championing Form-critical methods against F. J. Badcock's[2] attack on them has tried to explain away the obvious meaning of the above quotation on the ground that he was (mis)quoting Job xxvi. 14. He admits now that 'it will be readily seen how liable the [Form-critics'] method is to exaggeration and abuse' but he does not criticize it.

The following criticisms of the method are a selection from many that can be made:

(1) The uncertainty of exact classification. Form-critics are often arbitrary in their selection of 'Forms' to which a particular section of the Gospel is attributed. As M. Goguel[3] has said, 'It does not appear in the name of what principle it can be maintained that such a section as could be used for preaching is not to be used at the same time for instruction, for controversy, for mission-work, and perhaps also quite simply to satisfy pious imagination and curiosity'. To illustrate Goguel's point L. J. McGinley's[4] words may be quoted, 'Neither Bultmann nor Dibelius will admit as Sitz im Leben for any of the categories of Gospel-form what Köhler terms "das biographische Interesse". Interest in the person of Jesus, a desire to know the life of Jesus—these are assigned no part in that life of the primitive Christians who formed the Gospel!'

---

[1] *The Gospel Message of St. Mark*, 1950, p. 103; cf. *Ex. T.*, Nov. 1941.
[2] Ibid., Oct. 1941, pp. 16 ff.
[3] *Revue de l'histoire des religions*, xciv, 1926, pp. 114–60.
[4] Op. cit., p. 21.

(2) The Community-myth. Form-critics have kept in mind the 'setting in the life' of the Church but not of Jesus. After 1918 German Protestantism rediscovered the importance of the 'community'. Acts, however, and the Pauline epistles do not reflect or narrate more than a small fraction of the history of the early Church. Can one argue from the little known to the less? Just as political theories assumed in different ages within society to be valid have reacted on the various Christian doctrines of the Atonement, so, it may be suggested, one of the reasons for the rise of the Form-critical school was that it came into being when politically eminent personalities were at a discount in Germany and when 'the community' became endowed with that mystic quality which befogged the minds of many Germans who paved the way for the emergence of the totalitarian state, in which the individual was nothing, and the community was everything. But communities do not create sayings of the kind found in the Gospels. 'It is quite impossible', writes W. Manson,[1] 'with Form-criticism to rule out the influence over the community of commanding personalities, apostles and others who had a share in its life'—to say nothing of the influence of Jesus Himself. So, too, McGinley[2] writes, 'The theory of the collective origin of the synoptic tradition would suppose that there arose almost spontaneously an intense faith in the divinity of a crucified Jew, a complete and sublime system of dogma and morals, an organized cult life—all without the dominant personal influence of Jesus or even Paul. . . . Such a supposition contradicts everything we know of the primitive communities.' Form-critics write as though the original eye-witnesses were all caught up to heaven at the Ascension and the Christian Church were put to live on a desert island. Dr. Lightfoot[3] writes as if St. Mark never put the natural question to St. Peter, 'Did *you* see the Risen Lord?'[4] but derived from obscure members of the community a sense of numinous awe producing a 'dramatic aposeiopesis'[5] after Mark xvi. 8 'unique

---

[1] *Jesus the Messiah*, p. 27.
[2] Op. cit., p. 7.
[3] *The Gospel Message of St. Mark*, pp. 80 ff.
[4] Lk. xxiv. 34, 1 Cor. xv. 5.
[5] W. L. Knox, *Harvard Theol. Rev.* xxxv, 1942, pp. 13–23.

in ancient literature of the narrative type.' But the Good News produced the community, not vice versa.

(3) The folk-lore analogy is dubious. As W. Manson says, 'It is an exceedingly dubious analogy which is chosen when the rise and development of the early Christian tradition is explained in terms of processes which have worked in the folk-literature of primitive peoples or in early Hebrew saga.' The period which divides Jesus' Resurrection from the date of Mark's composition is little more than one generation. Dibelius sought for an analogy and found it in the *Apophthegmata Patrum*, though the tradition about the desert Fathers took not thirty or forty years to form but about one hundred. It is not unusual for men even of slight intellectual ability to recall and relate clearly important events occurring thirty-five years previously.

(4) Form-critics neglect the tradition of Jesus' actual words. They make insufficient allowance for the existence of an authentic tradition of Christ's *ipsissima verba*, carefully preserved, as 1 Cor. vii. 10, 12, 25, xv. 3–11 reveal. It was a Jewish custom to memorize a Rabbi's teaching.[1] If there is any truth in C. F. Burney's[2] theory, much of our Lord's teaching goes back readily into Aramaic poetical form, easily memorized.

(5) Form-critics have invariably overstepped the limits of their method in passing judgement consciously or not upon the contents of the units of the Gospels. Theirs is a literary, not historical, instrument, as Fascher observed. If, for example, one sets out to tell a story in a popular way about a wonderful cure, one would inevitably adopt a form like that of the Gospel-miracles, though embellished with more 'scientific' terms. Parallels can be found in the advertisement columns of popular newspapers proclaiming the benefits of a panacea. The fact that letters from previous victims or patients now cured 'miraculously' have much the same form as Bultmann discerns in pagan and Christian miracle-stories can prove nothing for or against the historicity of the cures themselves. The Form-critic

---

[1] A good pupil was like 'a plastered cistern that loses not a drop' (*Mishna, Aboth*, ii. 8).

[2] *The Poetry of our Lord* (1925); cf. V. Taylor, *The Formation of the Gospel Tradition*, pp. 88–100 and E. G. Selwyn, *The First Epistle of St. Peter* (1946), pp. 396 ff., 442–58, 462–4.

has usually built upon preconceived hypotheses, for instance, that Jesus was primarily a preacher of ethics and eschatology, whom His followers made into a cult-hero, a wonder-worker, and a divine being. 'Whenever Bultmann denies the historic worth of a passage because of the supernatural content, he has ceased to be a Form-critic or even an historian evaluating sources. He is in the realm of philosophy and his criticisms have no value in the study of the Gospel text.'[1] Similarly the Form-critical assumption may be challenged that Christ's word or example was constantly quoted by early Christians as the 'authority by which conduct was to be regulated and controversies determined'. As Badcock[2] says, the whole of the rest of the New Testament outside the Gospels would seem to show that knowledge of them was not in mind. Furthermore, it may be noticed that when Form-critical preconceptions clash with the 'assured results' of Synoptic criticism, the latter are neglected.

(6) If there were any truth in the main contention of the Form-critics, the burning problems of the early Church would be reflected in the Gospels or the common practices of the Church would be recorded as having been discussed and determined by Jesus. As Easton[3] has shown, this is not what we find. The Gospels are remarkably free from references to such questions as the terms on which to include Gentile converts within the community or to such practices as that of Christians speaking with tongues under the inspiration of the Holy Spirit; cf. Acts ii, 1 Cor. xii, xiv. The references to the Holy Spirit attributed to Jesus in the Synoptic Gospels are remarkably few. The treatment of Christ's words during the oral period of transmission was conservative.

(7) The underestimate of the Marcan outline. The Form-critics inherited a German theory of the worthlessness of Mark as history. Wrede[4] thought that Mark's historicity was illusory; that the evangelist himself was responsible for the context and setting of sayings and narratives; that the separate incidents

---

[1] McGinley, op. cit., p. 71. [2] Op. cit., p. 18.
[3] *The Gospel before the Gospels* (1928).
[4] *Das Messiasgeheimnis* (1901); contrast A. E. J. Rawlinson, *St. Mark*, pp. 258–62.

which Mark connected were in the main historical; but that
Jesus was not believed to be Messiah until after the Resurrection; and that Mark's theory that Jesus was recognized as
Messiah at Caesarea Philippi[1] had no foundation in fact; and
that Mark riveted his theory of the Messianic consciousness of
Jesus upon his material. This theory was held to account for
the injunctions to silence given by Jesus after His miraculous
healings, Mk. v. 19 being exceptional. This view has had profound influence upon German critics,[2] such as Wellhausen.[3]
Not only does the theory overlook the cumulative evidence
that Jesus knew Himself to be in His own sense of the term
Messiah, but it also begs the question why the vision of the
Risen Lord or the belief that He was risen should have led the
disciples to the remarkable conclusion that He was the Messiah, unless He had already prepared them for such a faith
during His ministry. The theory also fails to recognize an outline of the Galilean ministry in Mark, forming a framework
into which the separate pictures of Jesus and His disciples were
set. But, as C. H. Dodd[4] has shown, this outline can be found in
Mk. i. 14–15, 21–22, 39; ii. 13; iii. 7b–19; vi. 7, 12–13, 30. Put
together, these passages form a structure. Dodd[5] has proved
that a summary outline of Christ's life is almost certain to have
formed part of the Church's early kerygma; cf. Acts x. 37–41;
xiii. 23–31. If the tradition of the contents of 'units' could be
handed on, so could the main outline of Jesus' ministry with
some regard to its topographical and chronological setting.[6]
To split up the Gospel records into minute parts and to treat
them as *Kleinliteratur* and then to assume on the basis of the
transmission of anecdotes that the topographical and chronological links in Mark are all equally worthless is to argue in a
circle. A careful examination of the topography of Mark, made
by C. C. McCown,[7] has shown the value of some but not all

---

[1] W. Manson, *Jesus the Messiah*, 1943; cf. A. E. J. Rawlinson, *The New Testament Doctrine of the Christ*, pp. 27–52.

[2] Cf. H. Ebeling, 'Das Messiasgeheimnis', *Beihefte zur Zeitschrift f. d. neutest. Wissenschaft*, xix, 1939; cf. W. H. Cadman, *The Last Journey of Jesus*, 1923, ch. iv.

[3] *St. Mark*, 2nd ed., 1903.   [4] *Ex. T.* xliii, 1931, 396–400.

[5] *The Apostolic Preaching and its Developments*.

[6] Cf. B. Redlich, *Form-criticism*, p. 71.

[7] *Journal of Biblical Literature*, li, 1932, pp. 109 ff. and lx, 1941, pp. 1–25.

such links; in Mk. i. 1–vi. 29 Schmidt may be right and the links be worth very little; in vi. 30–ix. 1 the journey related may be the construction of the evangelist; in ix. 2–xi. 11 we have a consistent story of Jesus' movements which is 'entirely reasonable'; in xi. 12–xvi. 8 we find nothing inconsistent, Mark being far more trustworthy here than Luke. McCown concludes, 'Fiction, fact and truth—all three are to be found in the geographical data in the Gospels, not fiction alone as Schmidt seems to suggest and as other Formgeschichtler walking in goose-step after him boldly declare. There is much of fiction especially in Luke, but in Mark much of fact.'[1] Dodd thinks that St. Mark had at his disposal three kinds of material, '(a) isolated material without any connection; (b) more complex material including Pericopae strung on an itinerary or connected by unity of theme; (c) the outline to the ministry designed to introduce the Passion story'. He points out that if this was so, St. Mark was likely to have been embarrassed by two facts; first, that his outline was far too meagre to provide a setting for all the detailed narratives at his disposal; secondly, that some materials came to him already grouped in ways which cut across a truly chronological order. (See on Mark's sources, pp. 67 ff.) 'St. Mark's natural inclination', he says, 'would be to compromise between a topological and a chronological order. When the outline gave a clue to the setting of a narrative, he used it; when he took over more complex material already arranged, he allowed its order to stand, relating perhaps only its opening to what seemed the most suitable point in the outline, e.g. ii. 1–12. Otherwise he was guided by topical considerations or by what he felt to be chronological requirements.' On the whole, as Dodd says, there is good reason to believe that in broad lines the Marcan order does represent a genuine succession of events within which movement and development can be found. With this verdict F. C. Burkitt would have agreed (*Jesus Christ: an historical outline*, 1932). Or as H. L. Goudge[2] wrote:

Form-criticism has little to teach us if we are familiar with the Old Testament. That the purpose of the Gospels is a practical

---

[1] Op. cit., p. 24.
[2] *The Church of England and Reunion* (1938), p. 204.

and devotional purpose, not primarily an historical one; that different forms of narrative are employed, which we may distinguish if we can do so; that strict chronological arrangement is absent; and that the narrative of the divine redemption has a place which is all its own—to say this is simply to say that the New Torah resembles the Old. Again, to say that the basis of the Synoptic Gospels lies in oral tradition is to say what is equally true of the Old Torah, and should never have been denied: Form-criticism is a return to Westcott. But unhappily our chief Form-critics seem to have little idea of the Church or of the Ministry: and so they confuse the guarded tradition of the Church with the floating tradition of primitive peoples. To guard the tradition was one of the first duties of the Christian Ministry, as it had been of the Jewish. The Lord by His teaching and training took care that they should be able to perform it. . . . St. Mark and St. Luke were in the closest association with the Apostles; and it is absurd to treat their narratives as if they had just been disinterred from the sands of Egypt and as if we knew nothing of their origin but what we can gather by our critical acumen.

It may not be going too far to apply to Form-critical views *mutatis mutandis* what John Drinkwater[1] wrote about our ballads:

We need have nothing to do with the fantastic notion that they [the ballads] were by some unexplained process communal productions. A poem must be written by a poet and that is all there is about it. These poems, surviving as they did from generation to generation by oral tradition alone, doubtless underwent many modifications in the process, but that has nothing to do with the question, which with rational people cannot be a question at all.

No Gospel section passed through such a long period of oral tradition as did any genuine ballad. B. H. Streeter,[2] a far from conservative critic, who did not discuss Form-criticism in his *Four Gospels* gave the following verdict on Form-critics' work: 'These endeavours are often suggestive; but in the opinion of the writer, they are always precarious and sometimes perverse.'

[1] *English Poetry*, p. 78.
[2] *Cambridge Ancient History*, xl, 1936, p. 260, n. 1; cf. C. J. Cadoux, *Bulletin of the John Rylands Library*, xxxix, 1945–6, pp. 269–85.

IV

THE SYNOPTIC PROBLEM

§ 1. THE PROBLEM

THE first three Gospels, as has been said, are called 'synoptic' because they give in general the same view of our Lord's life, and follow broadly the same narrative framework with a similarity in the selection of material and in language and vocabulary. In these respects they differ widely from the Fourth Gospel. And the problem, the study of which may be said to have begun with Gieseler and Schleiermacher early in the eighteenth century, is to determine their literary origin and the way in which each of them has come to be what it is.

When Westcott wrote his *Introduction to the Study of the Gospels* in 1860 he added his weight to the theory of 'an original oral Gospel, definite in general outline and even in language, which was committed to writing in the lapse of time in various special shapes, according to the typical forms which it assumed in the preaching of different Apostles' (pp. 174 f.). The definiteness of outline and language, he thought, was due to the fact that the Apostles 'remained together at Jerusalem in close communion long enough to shape a common narrative, and to fix it with the requisite consistency'. He was followed, among others, by Salmon: 'an oral Gospel which gave a continuous history o His [Christ's] life from His baptism by John to His crucifixion' (*The Human Element in the Gospels*, 1907, pp. 27 f.).[1] Other writers, e.g. A. Wright (*Synopsis of the Gospels in Greek*, 1896, 1903) and Plummer (*St. Luke*, 1896), continued to hold the oral hypothesis, but in modified forms under the pressure of the growing study of the problem. Today, though some effect of oral tradition on the formation of the Gospels is, and must be, recognized by everyone, the idea of a primary stereotyped *corpus* of preaching has been abandoned, chiefly for the

---

[1] But in his *Introduction to the N.T.*, 1885, 5th ed. 1891, he had declined to admit that the common source of the Gospels was purely oral (pp. 123 f.).

following reasons: (*a*) The preservation of the common outline both in order and language, in widely different places, before any sacredness of inspiration attached to it, must have been so difficult as to amount to an impossibility. (*b*) If the common outline included the teaching of Jesus as we have it in Matthew and Luke why is it almost wholly omitted from Mark? And why did the writers of the two former feel free to incorporate it so differently—St. Luke in three main portions of his Gospel, St. Matthew in extended discourses, each with its own aim and character? (*c*) It is very improbable that these two writers, in reproducing large quantities of non-Marcan material, would be able so consistently to revert to the original order of sections if their source was only the common oral outlines. And generally speaking it is difficult to imagine how, with all their purposive adaptations and additions, they adhered so steadily to the wording, often in minute and unimportant details, of the oral Gospel.

The theory on which there has been, for some time, an almost universal agreement, though with a multitude of differences in its detailed application, is known as the 'two document theory': (1) The writers of Matthew and Luke each used in a written form the Second Gospel virtually identical with ours. (2) To their reproductions of the Marcan material each makes large additions, consisting chiefly of sayings and discourses of our Lord, drawn from a common source Q, which has been noticed above (p. 7). (3) To this they further added material peculiar to each, drawn probably from a variety of written sources and from local oral tradition. The two documents which give the name to the theory are thus Mark and Q. But the name is inadequate, since it does not take account of the use of the large amount of special material found in both Matthew and Luke. And the 'four-document theory' urged by Streeter, whether or not his scheme is accepted in all its details, comes much nearer to representing the facts.

He gave foretastes of his theory in the *Hibbert Journal*, October, 1921; and he elaborated it in his important work *The Four Gospels*, 1924, to which references have already been made.[1]

---

[1] Further elaborated by Vincent Taylor, *Behind the Third Gospel*, 1926; contrast M. Dibelius, *Theologische Literaturzeitung*, 1927, pp. 146–7.

It is briefly as follows: The four documents are Mark, Q, M, and L. (1) Mark was the earliest of our written Gospels, and was used by the authors of Matthew and Luke; the former based his work on Mark, following it closely, and inserting Q and M into it by fusion; the latter had written the groundwork of his Gospel, 'Proto-Luke', consisting of a combination of L and Q, years before he came across Mark; and he inserted the Marcan material into LQ at intervals in blocks. (2) Q was a Greek document containing the collection which, according to Papias, St. Matthew had made in Aramaic of our Lord's sayings. This seems to have contained also narrative settings; and it was an important element in the formation of both Matthew and Luke. (3) M stands for a large residue of matter peculiar to Matthew, most of it having a more or less distinct Judaistic colouring. (4) L stands for a considerable quantity of material peculiar to St. Luke's work. He collected as much as he could in Palestine and in Caesarea; and when he became acquainted with Q, probably in Antioch, he wedged it into L, for the most part in blocks. The contents of L, according to Streeter, are given below (pp. 87 ff.). It will be seen that they form, in some sort, a Gospel in themselves.

Streeter claims, with justice, that his theory, while detracting in no way from the value of Mark and Q, raises M and L to a higher importance, enhancing their authority, generally speaking, for a knowledge of our Lord's life and teaching.

However, it may be questioned whether Proto-Luke is a real Gospel with a beginning, a middle, and an end. M. Goguel[1] takes Lk. iii. 1–6 to be an elaboration of Mark's narrative with the addition of a chronological note, and in iii. 1–viii. 4 he finds only twenty-five verses peculiar to Luke without any evidence of their unity of origin. Again, in the long central section, ix. 51–xviii. 14 he thinks that two passages have a tradition akin to Mark's, xiii. 10–17 and xiv. 1–6, and that only six passages, lacking unity between them, are peculiar to Luke, the rest coming from Q. Similarly J. M. Creed wrote, 'The subtraction of Marcan material leaves an amorphous collection of narrative and discourse the greater part of which is thrown without intelligible reason into the unsuitable form of a "travel-document".

[1] *Harvard Theol. Rev.* xxvi, 1933, pp. 1–55, especially pp. 9 and 17.

Moreover, signs of the use of Mark are clear both in the account of John's mission (iii. 3 and also probably iii. 16) and above all in the Passion narratives. . . .'[1] Goguel argues that Luke's Passion narrative was based on Mark's and combined with 'fragmentary traditions of no great importance';[2] similarly Creed says, with reference to Lk. xxii. 7–38, 'Luke has himself freely rewritten, rearranged, and enlarged Mark. He may sometimes preserve independent traditions, but the continuous thread of the narrative appears to be based upon Mark.'[3] However, while Goguel[4] charges Streeter with having exaggerated the force of his arguments for a Proto-Luke because he has studied the question in too general a fashion, taking the non-Marcan sections of Luke's narratives each as a whole, without looking closely enough at their internal structure and analysing their constituent elements, and also with confining himself too much to the relation between Mark and Luke, without taking into consideration the complex problems that arise if Matthew is included in the comparison, Creed[5] on the other hand, allows that his criticisms are not inconsistent with the hypothesis that Q and some of Luke's peculiar material may have been already combined, and may have lain before Luke as a single document. If there was a Proto-Luke, it was an early draft[6] of Gospel material mainly from L and Q, combined before Luke discovered Mark. It may well be that it did not contain a Passion narrative.

§ 2. THE MARCAN SOURCE

The earliest tradition that we possess with regard to Mark is in the passage given above (p. 6), which is quoted as a statement of the 'Presbyter' by Papias, Bishop of Hierapolis c. A.D. 140, and preserved by Eusebius (*H.E.* iii. 39). If Papias reproduces the statement, or the substance of it, correctly, and if his words are given accurately by Eus., it is a passage of great historical value. The word ἑρμηνευτής, accepted by Irenaeus III. i. 1

---

[1] *The Gospel according to St. Luke*, p. lviii, n. 1.
[2] Op. cit., pp. 26 f.   [3] Op. cit., p. 262.
[4] Op. cit., p. 39.   [5] Op. cit., p. lviii.
[6] It is possible that such an early draft of Luke survived and was used by the author of the *Gospel according to the Hebrews*; cf. P. Parker, *J.B.L.* lix, 1940, pp. 471–8.

(= Eus. *H.E.* v. 8), xi. 6, who is followed by Tertullian (*c.*
Marc. iv. 5), does not, as most writers agree, bear the meaning
usually attached to the word 'interpreter' in modern times. It
does not imply that while St. Peter was preaching in Aramaic
St. Mark gave to his audience a Greek translation of his words
sentence by sentence. Still less can it mean that St. Mark at
Rome translated into Latin St. Peter's Greek preaching.[1]
Papias means that St. Peter preached in Aramaic, and that
St. Mark at a later time—after the Apostle's death in fact—
set down in Greek for other circles of Christians all that he
remembered. This is perhaps the meaning of the opening
words of the mutilated Muratorian fragment (see p. 30):
'quibus tamen interfuit et ita posuit'; '[Peter's instructions] at
which,[2] nevertheless, he was present, and thus [i.e. in the
Gospel which we possess] committed to writing.' It may be
taken as very probable, despite the Form-critics, that in the
Second Gospel, practically as we have it, St. Mark wrote down
in Greek what he remembered of St. Peter's Aramaic discourses about Christ, together with the reminiscences of other
eyewitnesses.

The reason for the theory that this writing was used by the
authors of Matthew and Luke is that it accounts better than
any other for the following phenomena:[3] (*a*) While Matthew
and Luke are quite independent in their Infancy narratives,
they begin to agree with one another and with Mark at the
point where the latter begins—the ministry of the Baptist. (*b*)
Both Matthew and Luke contain nearly the whole of Mark's
subject-matter, and with a few exceptions Matthew follows
Mark's arrangement of the material (see pp. 17 ff.), though
both Matthew and Luke insert large quantities of other matter,
some of it peculiar to each, and some of it common to both but
differently placed and handled. (*c*) Each of them sometimes

---

[1] See J. B. Lightfoot, *Clement of Rome*, ii. 494, and West, *Interpreter*, July 1924,
pp. 295–9. Christianity had been brought to Rome by Greek-speaking people,
and the Church there was, for some time, largely composed of slaves and others
of the humblest classes, who were not Roman but Greek in origin or speech.
So that for more than a century after St. Peter's preaching at Rome no Latin
translation of his Greek was needed.

[2] Or perhaps [*ali*]*quibus*, 'at some of them'.

[3] See Stanton, *The Gospels as Historical Documents*, ii, 1909, p. 34.

omits Marcan material, but they very seldom agree in what they omit. (*d*) Each of them sometimes departs from the Marcan sequence of narrative, but they very seldom agree in doing so; when one departs from, the other retains, the Marcan sequence. (*e*) To a very great extent, as the study of a Greek synopsis will show, they are both in striking agreement with Mark in details of narrative and phraseology. Sometimes one or other—more often Matthew than Luke—agrees with Mark while the other diverges. And the cases in which the two agree in details of this kind while differing from Mark are extraordinarily few. The same facts are given more statistically by Streeter (pp. 159–68).

Other less successful theories have been advanced. Some writers have postulated a document which held the same relation to our Gospels as was held by the fixed catechetical tradition of the oral hypothesis. It was an *Ur-Evangelium*, a primitive written Gospel, some say in Hebrew, some in Aramaic, on which our Gospels were based. It is thought that Mark is practically a translation of parts of it, or that the Second Evangelist used it as did the first and the third. But in either case it is difficult to imagine why he should have omitted the large amount of narratives and discourses preserved in Matthew and Luke. Zahn held that the primitive Gospel was an Aramaic Matthew; that this was used by the writer of Mark; and that our present Matthew was formed by translation from the Aramaic *plus* the use of Mark. Other theories continue to be suggested: e.g. by W. Lockton (*Church Quart. Rev.*, July 1922), that Mark was formed out of Luke, the earliest Gospel, and Matthew out of both Luke and Mark; and conversely by H. G. Jameson[1] that Mark was formed out of Matthew, the earliest Gospel, and Luke out of Matthew and Mark.[2] Roman Catholic scholars must conclude according to the findings of the Pontifical Biblical Commission in 1912 on the Synoptic problem; their usual conclusion is that Matthew wrote his Gospel first in Aramaic, which Mark used; then the Greek translation of Matthew was made, partly based on Mark and substantially in conformity with the Aramaic original; then Luke wrote,

---

[1] *The Origin of the Syn. Gospels*, Oxford, 1922.
[2] See a review by Burkitt, *J.T.S.* xxiv, 1922–3, pp. 441 ff.

following Mark and to some extent Matthew or an edition of Matthew's 'Sayings of the Lord'. However, John Chapman, O.S.B., believed that the Greek Matthew was used by Mark.[1] But the theory that Mark and Q were two of the chief sources of Matthew and Luke is accepted by the mass of N.T. scholars as covering the facts more nearly than any other.

UR-MARCUS. Whether Mark as it stands was the original form of the work is another matter, on which scholars of the first rank have disagreed. Some think that St. Mark's work, in which he committed to writing his reminiscences of St. Peter's teaching, was edited by a compiler, who brought it to its present form by rearrangements and additions. The evidence adduced is mainly of three kinds: (a) Want of cohesion in the structure and order of the material. (b) Agreements of Matthew and Luke against Mark when they are employing Marcan material. (c) The presence in Mark of 'Paulinisms'[2] or other features thought to be secondary on subjective grounds.

(a) It is true that some dislocations and rearrangements may be due to the evangelist having incorporated fragments from earlier writings; but that is very different from the Ur-Marcus theory. And some may be the work of an editorial hand later than Matthew and Luke. Both these possibilities will be considered below. But the want of cohesion which is occasionally noticeable has been greatly exaggerated by some writers. When it occurs it may be largely explained by the fact that St. Mark, as Papias says, did not write τάξει; he was not careful to observe a literary or artistic order and smoothness in order to present his ideas systematically. He recorded some things parenthetically, as they occurred to him. This will account, for example, for the rapid sketch of the events in his prologue (i. 1–14) up to the time when Simon comes on the scene. No other literary explanation is needed, as, for example, that the editor is rapidly outlining familiar events to the point where his source, Ur-Marcus, begins; or that St. Mark is abridging Q; or that he is using Matthew or Luke or both. It will account also for the

---

[1] *Matthew, Mark, Luke. A study in the order and interrelation of the Synoptic Gospels*, 1937.

[2] Strenuously denied in the interesting study by M. Werner, *Der Einfluss paulinischer Theologie im Markusevangelium*, 1923.

position of the visit to Nazareth (vi. 1–6a), which Moffatt describes as an 'erratic boulder', for the following commission to the Twelve (vi. 6b–18), and some other loosely attached sections and chronological displacements.

(b) The agreements of Matthew and Luke against Mark do not amount to very much. See Burkitt[1] who examines twenty instances collected by Sir J. Hawkins.[2] 'Some of them', as he says, 'are concerned with very small points indeed, while in others the agreement between Matthew and Luke is best explained as due to special and fairly obvious causes.' In most cases they have independently polished Mark's more primitive style, so that, as Streeter says,[3] 'If the coincident agreements of Matthew and Luke can only be explained on the theory that they used a different edition of Mark to the one we have, then it is the earlier of the two editions, the Ur-Marcus in fact, that has survived.'

The most striking instance is in Matt. xxvi. 67 f. = Lk. xxii. 63 ff., which have the words 'saying' and 'who is he that struck thee?' which are absent from Mark.[4] They are more suitable, as Burkitt suggests, in Luke than in Matthew, and their insertion in the latter may be merely an early harmonization. And this is probably the explanation of agreements in some other cases. C. H. Turner[5] suggests further that the author of Matthew may have used a more corrupt text of Mark than our present one, and that some of its corruptions were in the text used by St. Luke.

The theory was revived by T. F. Glasson in the form that Matthew and Luke may have used a 'Western' text of Mark (Ex. T. lv, 1944, pp. 180 ff.), contrast C. S. C. Williams (ibid. lvi, 1944, pp. 41 ff. and lviii, p. 251).

Streeter[6] bids us 'renounce once for all the chase of the phantom Ur-Marcus, and the study of the minor agreements becomes the highway to the recovery of the purest text of the Gospels'.

(c) Some writers have gone to great lengths in this direction,

---

[1] Gospel History and its Transmission, pp. 42–58.
[2] Horae Synopticae, pp. 174 f.; cf. B. H. Streeter, The Four Gospels, pp. 293–331.
[3] Ibid., p. 305.   [4] Cf. ibid., pp. 325 ff.
[5] A New Commentary on Holy Scripture, C. Gore, H. L. Goudge, and A. Guillaume, pt. iii, p. 112.   [6] Op. cit., p. 331.

maintaining not only that an original Mark has been edited, but that there has been a combining and editing of more than one source, each source and each process of editing or redacting removing the Gospel farther from the simple, primitive picture of Jesus as a Rabbi desiderated by some modern liberal theologians. Moffatt,[1] who himself holds the *Ur-Marcus* theory, gives some examples of this ultra-analysis, which he rightly condemns. And see N. P. Williams's[2] study of Wendling's theory in which he illustrates the subjective character of this kind of criticism.

Burkitt[3] closes his examination of the *Ur-Marcus* theory by pointing out that the Gospel 'deals mainly with a cycle of events foreign to the life and interests of the growing Christian communities'. The evangelist desires, indeed, to produce the impression that Jesus Christ was the Son of God, but he does so by recording biographical details of the Ministry. What interested the early Church was, on the one hand, the series of main events, foretold, as was believed, in the Old Testament— the Nativity, Death, and Resurrection, on which Christianity depended, and which therefore became the basis of the Creeds; and on the other, the Ethics of Christianity, the foundation of which was the teaching of Jesus. And it is not easy to see what should have led a sucession of revisers and redactors to take the trouble to revise or redact a narrative which did not supply as much material for the former as either Matthew or Luke, and hardly any for the latter.

USE OF EARLIER SOURCES. If we did not have Mark it would be difficult to reconstruct it from Matthew and Luke. Similarly it is almost impossible to reconstruct with any certainty the sources used by St. Mark. Neither A. T. Cadoux[4] nor J. M. C. Crum[5] has succeeded in putting forward more than interesting hypotheses; the former suggested that St. Mark edited in a conservative way three narratives, the first connected with St. Peter's work in Palestine and dated *c.* A.D. 40, the second with St. Paul's work among the Gentiles and

---

[1] *Introd. Lit. N.T.*, pp. 227 f.
[2] *Oxford Studies in the Synoptic Problem* (W. Sanday and others, 1911), ch. xiii.
[3] Op. cit., p. 61.   [4] *The Sources of the Second Gospel* (1935).
[5] *St. Mark's Gospel* (1936).

dated *c.* A.D. 50, and the third, a pro-Jewish record, with workers among the Dispersion during the war of A.D. 66–70; the latter argued that Mark becomes two Marks, the one a simple, straightforward story of our Lord, 'such a story as might have been told by a man who had been very near to the original company of those who had been with Jesus of Nazareth'. 'The other was what was left when this story has been separated out from our Gospel';[1] its writer amplified, interrupted, and worked over the first writing. This second writer, whose date is about A.D. 65, used the language of the Septuagint, a document closely akin to Q, and a later Christian language and Christology. M. Goguel[2] considers that St. Mark used the 'Logia' (Q), Peter's reminiscences, and a Passion narrative with some other less important sources.

However, it is highly probable that St. Mark had access to a summary outline of Christ's life, found now in i. 14 f., 21 f., 39; ii. 13; iii. 7b–19; vi. 7, 12 f., and 30, and that this outline formed one of his sources written or oral (see pp. 56 f.). No doubt also St. Peter was one of his main sources. C. H. Turner[3] showed that Mark reflects an eyewitness account of many scenes; the third person plural passes frequently on to a third person singular, e.g. '*They* come to Jairus's house and *he* sees the tumult', v. 38; cf. i. 21; x. 32; xi. 12, 27; xiv. 32. The third person plural may be put back into the first person plural of the narrator, St. Peter, e.g. '*We* came into our house with James and John and *my* wife's mother was sick with a fever and so[4] *we* tell Him about her.' It is possible to take these first-person-plural passages, to study the contexts in which they are embedded and to draw up a tentative list of 'Petrine sections' which helped to make a Petrine source, oral probably rather than written. The following is Dr. T. W. Manson's[5] list: i. 16–39; ii. 1–14; iii. 13–19; iv. 35–v. 43; vi. 7–13, 30–56; viii. 14–ix. 48; x. 32–52; xi. 1–33; xiii. 3–4, 32–37; xiv. 17–50, 53–54, 66–72.

Again, a Conflict-source made up of Conflict-stories (*Streit-*

[1] Op. cit., pp. 1 f.
[2] *Introduction au Nouveau Testament*, 1, 1923, pp. 328–46.
[3] *A New Commentary on Holy Scripture*, pt. iii, pp. 42–124.
[4] καὶ εὐθέως may be the Semitic *waw consecutive*.
[5] *Bulletin of the John Rylands Library*, xxviii, 1944, p. 133.

gespräche) may underlie ii. 15–iii. 6 and xii. 13–27, as B. S. Easton[1] has suggested. iii. 6 ends with the statement that the Pharisees and Herodians plotted to kill Jesus while xii. 13 begins by saying that the Pharisees and Herodians sent men to snare Jesus in speech. Apart from Matt. xxii. 16, the parallel to Mk. xii. 13, these two passages, iii. 6 and xii. 13, are the only two in the New Testament where the word 'Herodian' occurs. This word in not unnatural in Mark's account of the Galilean ministry but is difficult to explain when applied to anyone during the ministry in Jerusalem outside Herod's domain. St. Mark seems to have split this source into two, putting the second part late in the ministry because Jesus on St. Mark's view reached Jerusalem only at the end of His ministry and because he thought that the incident of the tribute-money to Caesar, paid only in Judaea, must have taken place outside Galilee and therefore late in the ministry.[2]

Again, iv. 1–34 may well have been taken from a collection of Parables and sayings on the Parabolic Method. It includes iv. 1–9, the Parable of the Sower; 10–12, the reason for parables; 13–20, the interpretation of the Parable of the Sower (most scholars, except W. O. E. Oesterley,[3] take this interpretation to be the work not of Jesus but of a member of the Church who pressed the details of the parable to give them an allegorical meaning which cuts across that of the parable itself); 21–25, sayings on the right use of parables, the connexion with the preceding section being purely verbal probably, the word μυστήριον in 11 being echoed by κρυπτόν in 22; 26–29, the seed growing of itself; 30–32, the Parable of the Mustard Seed; 33 f., a summary to indicate that for the time being the use of a parabolic source is complete, verse 33 conflicting with verse 11, the former giving St. Mark's view that Jesus spoke to the simple in parables to make His meaning clear, the latter representing Mark's source according to which Jesus was intentionally difficult to understand when He spoke His parables.

Again, iv. 35–v. 43, already mentioned as a 'Petrine' section, may have formed a connected cycle of miracle-stories when

[1] *Studies in Early Christianity*, ed. S. J. Case, pp. 85 ff.
[2] Cf. T. W. Manson, op. cit.
[3] *The Gospel Parables in the Light of their Jewish Background*, 1936.

St. Mark used it. The two miracles in iv. 35–41 and v. 1–20 correspond closely one with the other, the storm on the sea to the tumult in the man's heart; in both, Jesus' word brings peace. As Hoskyns and Davey[1] say, both miracles reproduce the 'sequence and movement' of passages in the Psalms, e.g. Ps. xviii. 16 f., lxv. 5–7, lxix, lxxxix. 9, xciii. 3, and in the *Testament of Naphthali*, vi. Frequently in Mark the Old Testament and kindred literature are quoted with subtle allusiveness to indicate that Jesus fulfilled in Himself the highest hopes for a Saviour and Deliverer. The two miracles in v. 21–43, the healing of Jairus's daughter and that of the woman with an issue of blood, are dovetailed, the latter into the former. Perhaps St. Mark dovetailed the two incidents, perhaps he found them so arranged in his source: the number twelve in verses 25 and 42 may have served as a mnemonic link from the earliest times.

There can be no reasonable doubt that Jesus worked miracles according to the earliest evidence available as even the radical and sceptical Guignebert[2] admits.

vi. 17–29, the story of John Baptist's death probably came from a special source. Rawlinson[3] hints that it was due to 'bazaar gossip'. Bussmann[4] argued that this section was part of an independent tradition of Galilean origin, inserted into Mark at a late date; but there is no evidence textually for late insertion; the story was used in Matthew and in another context in Luke. Joseph Thomas[5] comments on the fullness of detail here, contrasting Mark's brief references elsewhere to the Baptist and suggesting that the participial form, ὁ βαπτίζων, in place of ὁ βαπτιστής points to an Aramaic source; he advances the theory that this story was preserved by the Baptist's disciples, as the last verse may indicate.

The events of viii. 1–26 are a duplicate of those related in vi. 31–vii. 37, as the following table shows. It will be seen that Matthew has parallels to all except the two miracles of healing with the use of saliva. But in xv. 29–31 there is a general mention of healings which stands over against

[1] *The Riddle of the New Testament*, pp. 93 ff.
[2] *Jesus*, trans. S. H. Hooke, 1935, pp. 185–204.
[3] *The Gospel according to St. Mark*, p. 82.
[4] *Synoptische Studien*, 1925.
[5] *Le mouvement baptiste en Palestine et en Syrie*, 1935, pp. 110 ff.

Mk. vii. 32–37. Luke omits the whole of both series, except the sayings in viii. 12 (= Lk. xi. 29) and viii. 15 (= Lk. xii. 1). The correspondence in the order of the narratives points to a certain fixation of order in the oral tradition, such as used to be claimed for the whole Gospel narrative to an undue extent by the upholders of the oral hypothesis. It has been noted above that vi. 30–56 was a 'Petrine section'. Part at least of the first cycle of stories may well have come from St. Peter, the second from another disciple. St. Mark no doubt included both cycles intentionally 'that nothing be lost'.

	Mk.	Matt.		Mk.	Matt.
(i)	vi. 31–44	xiv. 13–21	Miraculous feeding of a multitude somewhere on the east of the lake.	viii. 1–9	xv. 32–38
(ii)	45–52	22–33	Crossing the lake.	10a	39a
(iii)	53–56	34–36	Arrival at the west of the lake.	10b	39b
(iv)	vii. 1–23	xv. 1–20	Conflict with the authorities.	11, 12	xvi. 1–4a
(v)	24–31	21–28	Avoidance of the dominion of Antipas.	13–21	4b–12
(vi)	32–37	vacat	Healing on the east of the lake.	22–26	vacat

It is not enough with Dibelius[1] to treat x. 1–12 as a pre-Marcan unity. The whole section viii. 27–x. 52, which forms the central part of Mark, opens with the Petrine confession at Caesarea Philippi and the first prediction of suffering which strike the keynotes of the entire block. As Dr. T. W. Manson[2] has shown, after the Petrine confession certain words addressed to the disciples appear for the first time both in Mark *and in other synoptic strata too*. These words appear in and after the central section of Mark as part of the teaching of Jesus; even allowing for Mk. xiii being based on 'an Apocalyptic fly-sheet' they show the width of the circle of new ideas introduced after St. Peter's confession. It appears that Guignebert[3] makes insufficient allowance for these linguistic data when he takes the Confession of Peter, the Transfiguration, the apocalyptic utterances in which Jesus claims to be Son of Man, and the manifestations from heaven at the time of Jesus' baptism to

[1] *Formgeschichte des Evangeliums*, 2nd ed., p. 223.

[2] *The Teaching of Jesus*, 1931, pp. 320–3. St. Mark's words in this category include ἀνίστημι of the Son of Man, xiv. 58; (ἀπ)αρνέομαι, xiv. 68, 70, viii. 34, xiv. 30 f., 72; διάκονος, ix. 35, x. 43; δόξα of the glory of God or of the Son of Man, viii. 38, x. 37, xiii. 26; ἔσχατος as opposed to πρῶτος, ix. 35, x. 31, xii. 6, 22; ζωή in the sense of eternal life or as equivalent to the 'Kingdom of God', ix. 43, 45, x. 17, 30; καλόν ἐστιν, ix. 5, 42, 43, 45, 47, 50, xiv. 6, 21; κερδαίνω, viii. 36; πάσχω of the Son of Man, viii. 31, ix. 12; τέλος of the Final Consummation, xiii. 7, 13; ὥρα, crisis, xiii. 11, 32, xiv. 35, 41.

[3] *Jesus*, p. 291.

represent most probably not stages, in inverse order, in the Messianic consciousness of Jesus but stages in their order of development in the progress of primitive Christology. So, too, R. H. Lightfoot,[1] who admits that Jesus was conscious of being Messiah but who minimizes the significance of Peter's Confession, overlooks the linguistic data. For much of the central section has been attributed to a Petrine source, viii. 14–ix. 48 and x. 32–52. St. Mark's source, probably St. Peter, was fully aware of the change of tone and style in Jesus' words after the event at Caesarea Philippi for the event was the turning-point in Jesus' ministry. St. Mark had good grounds for placing this material precisely where he does. This argument strengthens the impression that St. Mark's outline is historically trustworthy. The account of St. Peter's confession is the watershed of Mark because the event there was the turning-point in Jesus' public career.

In an article on 'Mark and Divorce' F. C. Burkitt[2] came by another route to the conclusion that when he wrote Mk. viii. 15–x, Mark was 'in touch with the facts of history'.

In xiii, the 'little Apocalypse', we have the only long, connected discourse of Jesus in Mark, though the sayings contained in it are not entirely consistent. The tone of this chapter is so Jewish-Apocalyptic that many have supposed it to be based on a Jewish or Jewish-Christian Apocalyptic fly-sheet. Source-criticism of ch. xiii, which is not so popular now as in the past, has been able to suggest the following divisions:[3] (a) The Signs preceding the Parousia, 5–8, 24–27; (b) Logia on persecution, 9–13; (c) The Abomination of Desolation, 14–23; cf. 2 Thess. ii, Dan. xi. 31, xii. 11; (d) Logia on the need for watchfulness, 28–37. It is probable that (a) and (c) existed as a separate unit before St. Mark wrote, adapting it to encourage Christians during the Neronian persecution. He incorporated some authentic sayings of Jesus, e.g. xiii. 32, but it is doubtful how far Jesus gave His disciples details of the steps or stages leading to the Fall of Jerusalem or to the end of this

---

[1] *The Gospel message of St. Mark*, 1950, p. 34.
[2] *J.T.S.* v, 1904, pp. 628–30.
[3] Cf. Dr. V. Taylor, *Ex. T.* lx, 1949, pp. 94–98 and *The Gospel according to St. Mark*, 1952, pp. 499 and 636–44.

world-order. It seems that St. Mark has thrown on to his canvas a background of the End of theWorld and in the foreground he has painted a picture of the 'signs' of the Fall of Jerusalem. St. Mark or the 'community behind St. Mark' may have been responsible for the foreshortening which results in the one event appearing imposed on the other.

In xiv it is possible that St. Mark incorporated two sources, (a) 1-2 and 10-11, (b) 12-16. (a) would agree with the Johannine dating of the Last Supper in relation to the death of Jesus, taking it not to be the Passover meal but an anticipatory one, perhaps of a Kiddush or sanctification type, whereas according to (b) the Last Supper was a Passover meal, the view adopted by Matthew and Luke.[1]

In xv Mark records the Barabbas episode and the Mockery. It is impossible to dismiss the former (6-15) simply as an attempt to excuse the Romans and throw the blame upon the Jews, which Klostermann[2] does, or to argue that the release by the Romans of a criminal is most unlikely, which Guignebert[3] does. For parallels to such an amnesty have been found in Livy, v. 13, and on a papyrus dated A.D. 85.[4] Mark's source may have been influenced by the 'Carabas episode' at Alexandria related by Philo (contra Flaccum, ii) according to whom the populace of Alexandria in the time of Caligula, stirred by anti-Semitic feelings, insulted Agrippa upon his visit there by dressing up an idiot, Carabas (which meant 'cabbage'), as a mock king and by hailing him as 'Marin', a title based on the Semitic word for 'our lord'. Even so, Mark's source is not to be identified with Philo, as the mime of a 'temporary king' was widespread. Dio Chrysostom[5] (fl. A.D. 100) speaks of an annual King of the Sacaea, a Zoganes, chosen from the condemned

---

[1] In support of the historicity of (a) and the Johannine dating cf. H. Lietzmann, Messe und Herrenmahl, 1926, W. O. E. Oesterley, The Jewish Background of the Christian Liturgy, 1925, P. Gavin, The Jewish Antecedents of the Christian Sacraments, 1928, and A. E. J. Rawlinson, The Gospel according to St. Mark, 2nd ed., 1927, pp. 262-5. In support of the historicity of (b) cf. G. Dalman, Jesus-Jeschua, 1922, and J. Jeremias, J.T.S. l, 1949, pp. 1-10.

[2] Das Markusevangelium, 1936, p. 159.   [3] Jesus, pp. 468 ff.

[4] A. Deissmann, Light from the Ancient East, p. 269; cf. C. B. Chavel, 'The Releasing of a Prisoner on the Eve of the Passover in ancient Jerusalem', J.B.L. lx, 1941, pp. 273-8.

[5] De Regno, iv. 66.

criminals and treated for five days like a king before being scourged and hanged; this barbarous mime acted on 25 March is probably to be connected with an ancient fertility cult resembling that of the New Year ritual in Babylon or Egypt.[1] The horseplay inflicted on Jesus may have been due to the soldiers' knowledge of the mime and of His claim, according to His *titulus*, to be King of the Jews. It is probable that Barabbas's name was originally Jesus Barabbas, according to Matthew.[2] It may even have been simply Joshua (Greek 'Jesus') and Philo's story may have led to the Semitic form Barabbas being introduced as the second Jewish name, which has alone survived in Mark.

The Form-critics, except Bultmann, assume that the Passion narrative is a unity forged in the crucible of oral transmission by preachers, teachers, and apologists of the primitive community. Goguel's[3] argument carries conviction that St. Peter's reminiscences formed the bases of an elaboration of Mark's Passion narrative. At the same time it is uncertain how far Mark or his source was indebted to Old Testament testimonies in ch. xv. It is possible that citations from Ps. xxii were treated as a source directly or indirectly, Ps. xxii. 1 (LXX, xxi. 2) having been in Jesus' mind on the Cross, Mk. xv. 34; cf. Ps. xxii. 18 with Mk. xv. 24 (Jn. xix. 24); Ps. xxii. 7 with Mk. xv. 29 f., cf. Ps. lxxix. 12, lxxxix. 50 f. Cf., too, Prov. xxxi. 6 and Ps. lxix. 21 with Mk. xv. 23 and Matt. xxvii. 34; Joel iii. 16 with Mk. xv. 33 f., cf. Amos viii. 9, Jer. xv. 9; Is. liii. 12 with Mk. xv. 27, Lk. xxii. 37. It seems to Guignebert[4] on this evidence that Mark's Passion narrative was very largely created to fit the Old Testament prophecies. The more probable view is that St. Mark's source, who may well have been St. Peter, knew the facts and sought confirmation of them by 'searching the Scriptures (to see) if these things were so'. The question whether Q was another of Mark's sources is discussed below.

EDITORIAL ADDITIONS. It is possible, further, that his

---

[1] Cf. *The Labyrinth*, ed. S. H. Hooke, 1935.
[2] C. S. C. Williams, *Alterations to the text of the Synoptic Gospels and Acts*, pp. 31–33.
[3] *Introduction au Nouveau Testament*, i. 343.
[4] *Jesus*, p. 489.

work was 'touched up' at a later time than Matthew and Luke, so that passages and expressions in our present Mark are wanting in both. Among writers who adopt this view are Sanday[1] and Stanton.[2] This kind of agreement against Mark is not, indeed, in every case a criterion. In some points the writers of Matthew and Luke may have corrected Mark independently. And it would be rash to claim that we possess the true text of either Matthew or Luke; if we could arrive at it, some of their agreements would probably disappear.[3] It would be rash also to state with confidence what material either of them must have wished to omit or include. But, in fact, their agreements are probably the only criterion we have. They will be found collected in Abbott, *Corrections of Mark*, 1901.

A considerable fraction—about a quarter—of Mark is found in Matthew but absent from Luke. And some have held that this was added to Mark later than Luke. This is strongly maintained by Stanton,[4] though he admits that 'it is not, perhaps, absolutely necessary'. Some passages, he thinks, St. Luke found in Mark, but had reasons for omitting. But those for which he sees no reasons, which he enumerates on p. 167 n., he assigns to a later writer who might be called Deutero-Mark. They amount to between one-fifth and one-sixth of the Gospel. But the view has not found general acceptance. It is open to many of the arguments fatal to the *Ur-Marcus* theory. Hawkins[5] finds reasons for all the omissions, most of which are fairly adequate. But we cannot expect to know all St. Luke's reasons, while many of his omissions were probably due to the fact that it was necessary to keep his work within the limits of a portable papyrus roll, and he needed the room for much other material, more suitable to his purpose, which he had collected. He may also have preferred his non-Marcan source. Further, the question of style cannot be quite disregarded. If the portions of Mark due to an amplificator amounted to one-sixth of the Gospel, it is probable that differences would be discernible to an extent sufficient to betray his hand. Stanton suggests a

---

[1] *Oxford Studies in the Synoptic Problem*, pp. 21–24.
[2] *The Gospels as Historical Documents*, ii. 142–5.
[3] See Turner, *J.T.S.*, Jan. 1909, pp. 175 ff.; Streeter, *Four Gospels*, pp. 293–331.
[4] Op. cit., pp. 152–70.
[5] *Oxford Studies*, pp. 60–74.

few (pp. 204 ff.), but they are neither striking nor numerous enough to prove the theory. A natural inference from his view is that Luke was prior to Matthew; and on p. 152 he says that there are good grounds for thinking that this may have been so; but on p. 368 he writes, 'there do not appear to me to be sufficient reasons for giving precedence to either of them. Luke used the original unamplified work of Mark, and the author of St. Matthew the amplified one, but this may have been due to special circumstances'.

MUTILATIONS. It has been held by Spitta and others that Mark has been mutilated at the beginning, as at the end. The opening verses present, indeed, curious difficulties. After the heading (whether it is the first clause of the evangelist or a mere title by him or an editor) the Gospel opens with the words 'As it is written in Esaias the prophet', but this introduces a quotation not from Isaiah but from Mal. iii. 1. In *v.* 3 follow words from Is. xli. 3, and in *v.* 4 the narrative begins, the order being reversed in Luke. The theory of mutilation fails to account for these difficulties; they must be the result of editorial manipulation. It is just possible to make the words ἐγένετο ᾿Ιωάννης the apodosis of καθὼς γέγραπται, κτλ., 'according to the words in Esaias . . . John came'. But it is so artificial that only an editor who prefixed a quotation, and not the evangelist, can be credited with such a construction. The quotation from Malachi was probably interpolated from a list of *testimonia*; it is an independent version of the Hebrew, while that from Isaiah is from the LXX. Omitting the interpolation Rawlinson (*St. Mark*, pp. 5 f.), following Turner,[1] makes *v.* 4 the apodosis to *v.* 1: 'The starting-point of the Good News about Jesus Christ (in accordance with the scriptural words of the Prophet Isaiah . . .) was John, who baptized, &c.' An awkward parenthesis of this kind finds parallels in St. Mark's work, but a difficulty in this explanation is that the word 'Gospel' has a different meaning in *v.* 14, viz. the 'good tidings of God' which Jesus proclaimed, that 'the time is fulfilled and the Kingdom of God is at hand'. In *v.* 15, 'believe in the Gospel', the meaning is the same as in *v.* 1, as also the use of the word in viii. 35, x. 29.

---

[1] *J.T.S.* xxvi, 1925, p. 146. See the whole series of interesting articles on Marcan usage, xxvi–xxix.

A mutilation in the middle of Mark has been suggested as an explanation of St. Luke's 'great omission' of Mk. vi. 45–viii. 26. Streeter[1] thinks that, by an accident to the roll, the copy of Mark used by St. Luke—not by the author of Matthew—may have included merely the beginning of the 'great omission', as far as the words αὐτὸς μόνος, 'He alone', in vi. 47, and then went straight on to ἐπηρώτα τοὺς μαθητάς, 'He asked His disciples', viii. 27. St. Luke did his best with the wording at each end of the gap, and in ix. 18 writes, immediately after the Feeding of the Five Thousand, 'And it came to pass, as He was praying alone, the disciples met Him: and He asked them saying, Who do the multitudes say that I am?' And he inserts the place-name Bethsaida into the opening sentence of the story of the Feeding, though in other respects he closely follows the Marcan version of the story. Streeter offers this only as a tentative suggestion; and it must be admitted that it is not very attractive. But something, at present undetermined, is needed to explain St. Luke's omission of the section. It may be that Mark was not his primary source here and so to think in terms of an 'omission' is wrong.

That Mark is mutilated at the end is one of the most certain results of textual criticism. Most of the best manuscripts and versions, whether they contain additional material or not, indicate that the text stops short at ἐφοβοῦντο γάρ, 'for they feared' (xvi. 8), which is an impossible ending to a Gospel. Whether it has lost only the last sheet, as is commonly supposed, is uncertain. Burkitt[2] thinks it 'a more reasonable conjecture that Mark may have lost about a third of its original contents, and that the work once dealt with the period covered by Acts i–xii, including, for instance, the story of Rhoda, Mark's mother's maid'. Persecution might perhaps account for it, but that so much should have been lost by a mere accident to a roll is not likely. The conjecture is connected with the question of St. Luke's sources for those chapters. But why did St. Mark continue his Gospel so far? And if he did, why did he stop there?

As early as Tatian (170) and Irenaeus (185) there was

---

[1] Op. cit., pp. 176 ff.
[2] *Christian Beginnings*, p. 83.

current at Rome a passage known as the Longer Conclusion, which is found in several manuscripts (including D) either as an appendix or as a part of the text. It was printed in the Textus Receptus, and hence stands in our A.V. and R.V. as *vv.* 9–20. A few manuscripts and versions (but no patristic writers) give also a Shorter Conclusion, all, except the African *k*, before the longer one. And the Freer MS. W adds a further passage to the longer one after *v.* 14. The evidence for the view that neither conclusion was in the original text of Mark is discussed by Hort,[1] and additional evidence discovered since that date (1882), especially the absence of any conclusion in the Syr. sin, and the fact that in the Old Georgian and more ancient Armenian codices the Gospel ended at ἐφοβοῦντο γάρ, only strengthens his results.[2] R. H. Lightfoot[3] maintains that St. Mark intended to conclude his Gospel with ἐφοβοῦντο γάρ though no book can be cited with a comparable ending. To him the 'fear' denotes a numinous awe. He strains the sense of xiv. 28 and xvi. 7 to mean that Christ would be at work in and through His disciples in Galilee, and not that He would appear to St. Peter and others there. His arguments, which would involve the omission from the original Mark of all reference to a Resurrection appearance, though the Resurrection was one of the main elements in the Apostolic kerygma, have been refuted by W. L. Knox.[4]

This is not the place to discuss what the lost end of Mark may have contained. Streeter argues that it was lost before Matthew and Luke were written, and conjectures that it contained 'an Appearance to Mary Magdalene, followed by one to Peter and others when fishing on the Lake of Galilee, and that John derived his version of these incidents from the lost conclusion of Mark'.[5]

---

[1] *Introd. N.T. in Greek*, App., pp. 28–51.

[2] The evidence is fully set out in S. C. E. Legg's *Nouum Testamentum Graece secundum Marcum*, 1935, on Mk. xvi. 9–20; cf. C. S. C. Williams, *Alterations to the Text of the Synoptic Gospels and Acts*, pp. 40–45.

[3] *Doctrine and Locality in the Gospels*, chs. i and ii, and *The Gospel Message of St. Mark*, pp. 80–97.

[4] *Harvard Theol. Rev.* xxxv, 1942, pp. 13–23.

[5] Op. cit., pp. 343 f., 351–60.

§ 3. THE SOURCE KNOWN AS Q

The First Gospel is anonymous, but St. Matthew's name became attached to it in the Church where he worked. This was probably because it incorporated St. Matthew's writing, a collection of the *logia*, as Papias calls them—the sayings and discourses (or the substance of discourses) of our Lord (see p. 5 n.).[1] His work cannot have amounted to a γραφὴ εὐαγγελίου such as Irenaeus describes it. And that it was the only form in which sayings of our Lord found circulation is, of course, impossible; many of them must have been recorded by St. Peter and the other Apostles in their preaching and instruction. When it was issued 'each one', says Papias, 'interpreted it as he was able'. The word ἡρμήνευσε (like the word ἑρμηνευτής which Papias uses of St. Mark) must be given its strict meaning 'translated'. Salmon,[2] Stanton,[3] and others have understood it to mean 'gave extempore interpretations in his own language' to congregations in Church, similar to those of the Targumists who interpreted the Hebrew Scriptures in the synagogues in their vernacular Aramaic. But there is nothing to show that Papias was referring to Church services; he seems rather to have been dealing with the development of Christian writings. We are led to think of written documents in which St. Matthew's Aramaic collection was done into Greek. These would soon be enlarged and altered, becoming what we might call different recensions. Whether or not the authors of Matthew and Luke used two of these, they certainly used two different translations, which is occasionally discernible where their variations can be explained by slight differences in Aramaic words, or by Aramaic words which bear two distinct meanings.

Streeter, though he believes in the existence of Q, does not believe in the recensions. He suggests (rather speculatively) that the words of the Elder quoted by Papias may have been a protest by the Church of Ephesus against the newly introduced

[1] Dr. G. D. Kilpatrick (*J.T.S.* xlii, 1941, pp. 182–4) accounts for the disappearance of Q by suggesting that it was anonymous, rather amorphous and without a Passion narrative, and that the bulk of Q was taken over in Matt. and Lk.

[2] *The Human Element in the Gospels*, 1907, pp. 27 f.

[3] *The Gospels as Historical Documents*, i. 55–57.

Gospel of St. Matthew; and 'his language is a slightly contemptuous exaggeration intended to assert that the particular
Greek version (i.e. our Gospel of Matthew), to the authority
of which the critics of the Fourth Gospel were appealing, was
an anonymous version having no claim to direct apostolic
authority'. If the Elder were himself the author of the Fourth
Gospel, as Streeter thinks, 'it would only be the more necessary
to point out that Gospels like Matthew and Mark, which were
at times in conflict with it, were no more directly apostolic than
itself' (op. cit., p. 21). On the other hand, it has been thought
that the material used in Matthew and Luke respectively was
so largely dissimilar that while their common matter goes back
ultimately to St. Matthew's collection, they cannot be said to
have used, even in different recensions, a source which had
sufficient unity to be designated by one symbol Q. Stanton[1]
supposes that *fragmentary* translations of St. Matthew's collection were extant, and that the First Evangelist has occasionally
used one or more of these which were fuller than the version
used by St. Luke. A few writers, Burton[2] and Allen,[3] for example, hold that St. Luke did not use Q at all, but obtained the
material which he has in common with Matthew from a
variety of sources, one of which, Allen thinks, was possibly
Matthew itself (see below).

The question naturally arises whether the author of Matthew
or Luke shows the greater fidelity to their common source in
respect of wording and order. As to wording, many think that
the former adheres to it more closely than the latter, and that
St. Luke must have treated it, as he treated Mark, with the
freedom of an artist. A recent suggestion is that of Burney[4]
who claims that the Semitic parallelism of our Lord's sayings
is preserved more faithfully in Matthew than in Luke. On the
other hand, the custom of the former was to conflate the
language of his sources when they overlapped (see Streeter,
pp. 244–54), and hence he would probably reproduce the
language of any of them less exactly than St. Luke. This is the
case in some of the not very frequent passages where Q and

---

[1] Op. cit. ii. 78–102.
[2] *Introduction to the Gospels*, Chicago, 1904.   [3] *St. Matthew.*
[4] *The Poetry of our Lord*, 1925, pp. 87 f.

Mark overlapped, and therefore it is no doubt the case where Q overlapped his other source. But both causes must have operated, so that we cannot be sure, except when they are identical, that either of them preserves a verbatim report of Q.

As regards order also opposite opinions are held. In Matthew the sayings are mostly grouped into five discourses (v–vii. 27; x; xiii. 1–52; xviii; xxiii–xxv), each followed by the formula 'And it came to pass that when Jesus had finished these words', or the like. Lk. vii. 1 (parallel to Matt. vii. 28) has somewhat similarly: 'When He had completed all these sayings in the ears of the people.' This suggests that a formula of this kind stood in Q at the end of a discourse, which is supported by the fact that the common LXX expression καὶ ἐγένετο, which is used in Matthew in each case, is not found elsewhere in that Gospel. And since Papias arranged his 'Exposition of *logia* of the Lord' in five books, it is possible that the original Aramaic collection was similarly arranged (Nestle[1]), a not uncommon Jewish device; e.g. there are five books of the Law, and of the Psalms, and five divisions of the Rabbinic *Megilloth* and the *Pirqe Aboth* in their original form. If so, the grouping in Matthew might appear to follow the grouping in Q more closely than that in Luke, where the sayings are placed in very different positions, sometimes for artistic and literary purposes, and rearranged to admit passages from other sources. But it was not necessarily in Q that the sayings were grouped into five discourses. The author of Matthew probably did it himself and inserted the formula (derived from Q) at the end of each.

The opposite view is maintained by Stanton, who argues that in combining the Marcan with other material, in particular that drawn from Q, 'Luke decided on the easiest, though not the most artistic, plan of inserting the greater part of this material in two masses at two different points of the Marcan outline (vi. 20–viii. 3 and ix. 51–xviii. 14), so as to keep it as free as possible from his Marcan material. In the First Gospel, on the other hand, the Marcan and the non-Marcan are used *pari passu*, sayings from both being brought together when they referred to, or might naturally be taken to refer to, the same

---

[1] *Zeitschr. f. d. neutest. Wiss.*, 1900, pp. 252 ff.

occasion.' The same view was held by Streeter;[1] and in his work *The Four Gospels* he says, 'If we consider (1) Matthew's proved habit of piling up discourses from Mark, Q and M; (2) the fact that sayings like "Blessed are your eyes", Mt. xiii. 16–17, concerning offences, Mt. xviii. 7—being imbedded in extracts from Mark—cannot possibly be in their original context as they occur in Matthew, the presumption is plainly in favour of the view that *Luke's order is the more original*' (p. 275).

No less than sixteen reconstructions of the contents of Q are given by Moffatt,[2] besides a suggested outline of his own. And Streeter, on the basis of his four-document theory, gives another. His whole argument should be read (pp. 283–92).

Dr. T. W. Manson[3] has taken the reconstructions of Harnack, Streeter, and Bussmann, finding a large measure of agreement between them. Matter common to all three includes Lk. iii. 7–9; iv. 1–13; vi. 20–23, 27–33, 35–44, 46–49; vii. 1–10, 18–20, 22–35; ix. 57–60; x. 2–16, 21–24; xi. 9–13, 29–35, 39, 41, 42, 44, 46–52; xii. 2–10, 22–31, 33, 34, 39, 40, 42–46, 51, 53, 58, 59; xiii. 18–21, 24, 28, 29, 34, 35; xiv. 26, 27, 34, 35; xvi. 13, 16–18; xvii. 1, 3, 4, 6, 23, 24, 26, 27, 33–35, 37. On the basis of this irreducible minimum Dr. Manson has suggested further material that belonged to Q. He comments on the large amount of religious and moral teaching and the small amount of narrative that it contained. Despite F. C. Burkitt,[4] Q seems to have had no Passion narrative. It contained little polemical matter. In a valuable additional note[5] Dr. Manson discusses and rejects the arguments of W. Bussmann[6] that Q can be split into two sources, the older one ('R') having been in Aramaic and the other ('T') in Greek.

RELATION OF MATTHEW AND LUKE. There are differences of opinion as to whether either writer made use of the other's work. That the author of Matthew used Luke has had little serious support since Schulze.[7] But the converse, that St. Luke used Matthew, has been frequently maintained.[8] No

---

[1] *Oxford Studies in the Synoptic Problem*, p. 147.
[2] *Introd. Lit. N.T.*, pp. 197–202.   [3] *The Sayings of Jesus*, 1950, pp. 15 f.
[4] *Earliest sources for the Life of Jesus*, 1922, pp. 103–6.
[5] Op. cit., p. 20.   [6] *Synoptische Studien*, ii.
[7] *Evangelientafel*, ed. 2, 1886.
[8] For careful statements of this view see E. Simons, *Hat der dritte Evangelist den*

conclusive evidence, however, has been adduced; and the chief reason for thinking that the theory is improbable is that it is wholly unnecessary. When the two evangelists agree against Mark, a variety of causes may have operated: (1) they could not help agreeing in some improvements of St. Mark's Aramaic style and somewhat primitive Greek. (2) Streeter (pp. 298–305) discusses several which he calls 'deceptive agreements'. (3) Others, not very numerous, are the result of the overlapping of Q and Mark. (4) There is little doubt that textual corruption will account for some of the instances: e.g. a word or line which once stood in Mark, and was accidentally omitted in the copy from which all our manuscripts are derived, was preserved in Matthew and Luke; or assimilation of parallel passages has taken place, a very common form of corruption, commoner, perhaps, than has often been supposed. (5) To these may be added the possibility, mentioned above and maintained by Stanton and others, of editorial additions in Mark later than Matthew and Luke. Further, if Luke used Matthew (or vice versa) why did he differ so markedly from him, especially in his placing of the Q sayings?

RELATION OF MARK AND Q. The remaining problem, whether St. Mark knew and made use of Q, is closely connected with the foregoing. Opinions, once more, are divided. If St. Mark wrote shortly before 70, and Greek documents were growing up based on St. Matthew's Aramaic collection of *logia*, he might quite possibly have met with some form of Q at Rome (Q^R as Rawlinson[1] called it). But if he made any use of it, why did he use it so little? It is easier to suppose that, Q being current among his readers, he refrained from repeating its contents as unnecessary. That he lays emphasis on the authoritative power of our Lord's teaching (see p. 12), and yet records so little of it, is best explained if he knew that his readers were already in possession of a collection of sayings, and needed only a narrative to supplement them. Burkitt[2] gives a list of thirty or thirty-one isolated sayings in Mark

---

kanonischen Matthäus benützt? 1880. E. Y. Hincks, *Journal of Bibl. Lit.*, x, 1891, pp. 92–156. E. W. Lummis, *How Luke was written*, 1915.

[1] *The Gospel according to St. Mark*, p. xl.
[2] *Gospel History*, pp. 148–66.

which occur in more or less similar forms in *two* passages, either in Matthew–Luke or in one or other of them, one of which passages in each case appears to be derived from Mark and the other from Q. These are often called 'doublets', and are thought by some to imply literary dependence of St. Mark on Q. But, as in the case of the dependence of St. Luke on Matthew, the chief objection to the theory is that it is unnecessary. St. Mark may have recalled from St. Peter's preaching, or learnt by oral tradition, some sayings contained in Q. This would meet the cases in which Burney (loc. cit.) thinks that St. Mark has glossed Q, while the Semitic parallelism is better preserved in Matthew–Luke. As Moffatt says,[1] 'The theory assumes that Q had a monopoly of such sayings. But the tradition of the Churches was far too widespread to permit any such restriction of *logia*. Sayings of Jesus, such as come into question here, must have been circulating in many directions; and it is contrary to all probabilities that they were drawn into the single channel or canal of Q, so that any other writer had to derive them from this source.' Finally, an editor of Mark may have inserted a few sayings under the influence of Matthew–Luke. The theory of St. Mark's dependence on Q is due to a too hard and fast conception of the literary growth of the Gospels, and is improbable or at least not proved. For a detailed study of passages see Streeter, pp. 186–91.

§ 4. OTHER SOURCES OF MATTHEW AND LUKE

MATTHEW. That the evangelist drew from sources other than Mark and Q is obvious. The following comprise most of the material:[2]

(*a*) The narratives of the Nativity and Infancy, including the Genealogy, embody traditions wholly distinct from those in Luke and absent from Mark.[3] It is noticeable that Joseph plays a prominent part in them. And Stanton suggests that the narratives were current among his kindred and descendants, some of whom were highly honoured in the Palestinian Church.

[1] Op. cit., p. 205.

[2] Cf. Goguel, *Introduction au Nouveau Testament*, I, 1923, pp. 420–34.

[3] Spitta, *Urchristentum*, iii. 2, pp. 122–38, conjectures that the evangelist found them in Mk. before that Gospel was mutilated, as he thinks, at the beginning. But see above, p. 76.

But if so, the Jewish Christians did not shrink from shaping these and other narratives for apologetic purposes into *mid-rashim* on the stories of Moses and Israel (see A. H. McNeile's *St. Matthew*, p. 23). These may have been current orally, but the evangelist probably knew them in a written form, perhaps a Greek translation of a Hebrew document. The play in i. 21 on Jesus (ישוע) and 'shall save' (יושיע) is Hebrew, and impossible in Aramaic.

If the Genealogy is not his own composition it may have come from a written source, or it may possibly have been added later as a prelude to the Gospel. The heading (i. 1), at least, cannot be the work of the same writers as *v.* 18, since γένεσις is used with different meanings.

(*b*) References to the Old Testament are frequent, as is natural in a Jewish-Christian apologetic work. Normally the quotations and verbal allusions are clearly dependent on the LXX. But one class of quotations differs from the rest, i.e. the passages in which attention is drawn to the fulfilment of the Old Testament by a formula 'that it might be fulfilled which was spoken through . . .' or similar words. These are i. 23 (Is. vii. 14); ii. 6 (Mic. v. 2); ii. 15 (Hos. xi. 1); ii. 18 (Jer. xxxi. 15); ii. 23 ('through the prophets'); iii. 3 (Is. xl. 3); iv. 15 f. (Is. ix. 1 [Heb. viii. 23 f.]); viii. 17 (Is. liii. 4); xii. 18–21 (Is. xlii. 1–4); xiii. 35 ('through the prophet'; Ps. lxxviii. 2); xxi. 5 (Zech. ix. 9, with reminiscence of Is. lxii. 11); xxvii. 9 ('through Jeremias the prophet'; Zech. xi. 12 f.). And with the exception of iii. 3, which occurs in Mk. i. 3; Lk. iii. 4 (see p. 76), all are peculiar to Matthew. These quotations differ from the others in the First Gospel in adhering less closely to the LXX. They appear to be independent translations, though in some cases perhaps influenced by the LXX. Not only so, but some of them (i. 23; ii. 6, 15; iv. 15 f.; xii. 18 ff.; xiii. 35) differ from our Hebrew text as well as from the LXX, and in i. 23 the impersonal καλέσουσιν, 'people shall call His name', i.e. His name shall be called, is an Aramaic feature. It is possible, therefore, that the source for these quotations was a translation of an Aramaic collection of *testimonia*.[1]

[1] This source must have been one of the causes which led to the complex narrative in xxvii. 3–10.

(*c*) In his record of our Lord's discourses and sayings, Matthew has passages of three different kinds: (i) some which are so similar to those in Luke that they may safely be assigned to Q; (ii) some which are disconcertingly similar, but at the same time dissimilar to those in Luke; (iii) some which are peculiar to his Gospel. If the third are assigned to his source M, the second can be explained as due to collation of Q and M, while St. Luke remained truer to Q.

For the Sermon on the Mount the First Evangelist seems to have had two distinct sermons, one practically identical with the Sermon on the Plain in Luke (followed by the story of the centurion's servant), and the other—more than two-thirds of the whole—a more or less connected discourse, anti-Pharisaic in character, and dealing with Jewish controversy. Where they overlapped he conflated them. And to this conflated sermon he added certain passages parallel to Luke, i.e. taken from Q, which in Luke stand in other contexts. And the strongly anti-Pharisaic discourse in ch. xiii appears to be similarly a conflation.

In many of his parables also the use of M is probably to be seen. Two are derived from Mark (the Sower and the Wicked Husbandmen); two from Q (the Mustard Seed and the Leaven); and there are eleven others—or rather twelve, since xxii. 11–14 is really a parable distinct from the foregoing. Three of these overlap three of the nineteen in Luke, the Lost Sheep, the Marriage Feast (= the Great Supper), and the Talents (= the Pounds). But while these are parallel they are so dissimilar that they are probably to be assigned, with Streeter, to M and L respectively. And the remainder of the parables in Matthew can be assigned to M. All of them bear upon the Kingdom of Heaven, or the duty of being fit and ready for it: the Tares, Hidden Treasure, Pearl, Net, the Debtor who owed a thousand talents, the Vineyard Labourers, the Two Sons, and the Sheep and the Goats (which is not strictly a parable, but an apocalyptic prediction containing the simile of the sheep and the goats). Most of the parables in Luke are rather vehicles of moral teaching drawn from the daily life of men. But St. Luke applies the word 'parable' also to illustrations and similes which are not in the form of narratives. Sometimes an extended illustration or simile verged upon narrative, e.g. Lk. xii. 35–40; xv. 3–10. Neither Q nor the Marcan tradition appears to have been very rich in fully formed parables, though they were not without them; they preserved rather the authoritative *dicta* of the Master, with many of His illustrative comments, similes, and figurative expressions. But these were probably current in large numbers, in many degrees of elaboration in the direction of narrative; and the compiler of M collected those, for the most part, of a Jewish-Christian character, and the compiler of L (very likely St. Luke himself) those of a different kind. St. Mark evidently knew more than he recorded; see iv. 10–13 following a single parable. With regard to the sayings of Jesus and His parabolic teaching, Stanton refers to Weizsäcker's suggestive comparison between the Jewish *halacha* and *haggada*, the former of which was handed down with greater care and fidelity than the latter.

Jewish Christians delighted to emphasize the importance of St. Peter. And this appears in several narratives in which he plays a prominent part, which may be assigned to M: e.g. xiv. 28–32; xvi. 17 f., 19.

It is practically agreed that Q did not extend to the Passion. When St. Matthew made his collection of *logia* Christians did not need a reminder of the great events which they knew, but a record of the sayings during the Ministry which they did not know. And there are no passages in which Matthew and Luke agree against Mark which would suggest it. Mark is here followed very fully in Matthew, but there is some material peculiar to the First Gospel which must have been derived from the source or sources collected in M, which, as elsewhere, the evangelist inserted by fusion into the Marcan framework: xxvi. 50, 52–54; xxvii. 3–10, 19, 24 f., 36, 43, 51 b–53, 62–66; xxviii. 2–4, 11–20.

LUKE. It is generally easier to distinguish the material which St. Luke introduced from L, because, as has been said, his practice was to insert his Q and Marcan material in blocks with very little fusion. Streeter gives tentatively the contents of Q (p. 291) and of Proto-Luke (p. 222); hence those which he would assign to L are as follows: iii. 1, 15, 18–20, 23–28; v. 1–11; vi. 14–16; vii. 11–17, 36–50; viii. 1–3; x. 1, 25–42; xi. 1–8,

53 f.; xii. 13–21; xiii. 1–17; xiv. 1–10, 12–25, 28–33; xv. 1–32; xvi. 14 f., 19–31; xvii. 7–19; xviii. 1–14; xix. 1–10, 37–44; xxi. 18, 34–36; xxii. 14 to the end, apart from a few passages from Mark (xxii. 18, 22, 42, 46 f., 52–62, 71; xxiii. 3, 22, 25 f., 33, 34b, 38, 44–46, 52 f.; xxiv. 6), and some verses which 'may be derived from Mark, or represent Proto-Luke partially assimilated to the Marcan parallel' (xxii. 69; xxiii. 35, 49, 51; xxiv. 1–3, 9 f.).

The Infancy narratives (chs. i, ii) have every appearance of being derived from a special source. They are wholly independent of the Infancy narratives in Matthew. Style and language are our only guides as to sources. In the Prologue (i. 1–4) he lays himself out to write the studied, literary Greek of the period, polished and rhetorical. But at *v.* 5 there is a sudden, steep drop into Hebraic Greek. Harnack and others have supposed that he shows his literary genius by the conscious art with which he adapted the style and language of the section to its subject-matter, making his own the archaic religious style and language of the LXX. But apart from the fact that the Greek of the LXX, even of those books of which the original language was Hebrew, is far from uniform, the archaic religious style and language are those of translation-Greek. And it is impossible to see any reason why he should wish to imitate translation-Greek more closely in his first two chapters than in the rest of his Gospel which is redolent of the LXX—so closely, in fact, that they have the appearance of being a literal translation of a Semitic original. The theory, widely accepted at the present time, is much more probable, that they are a translation from a Hebrew document. Whether St. Luke translated them himself, or used a Greek translation which he touched up, according to his usual custom, with his own style and vocabulary, cannot be definitely decided, since we have no means of knowing whether he was acquainted with Hebrew. But since he shows no clear signs of it elsewhere, and his Old Testament quotations are invariably from the LXX, the latter is the more likely. That the original document was Hebrew, not Aramaic, may be regarded as certain, since distinctive Aramaisms, such as are seen in Mark and John and to a slight degree in Q, are absent, while Hebraisms abound as may be seen in any good commentary. If the original was Aramaic we should have to suppose that the translator was skilful enough to avoid Aramaisms while rendering Aramaic into Greek of the style of the LXX, which is very improbable.[1] Some portions of the chapters are poetical—the canticles, *Magnificat, Benedictus,*[2] and *Nunc Dimittis*, and the words of angels in i. 14–17, 32 f., 35; ii. 14. And the ease with which they can be rendered into rhythmical Hebrew is shown by Aytoun.[3] It is their Hebraic language, however, not the rhythm which points to Hebrew, since Aramaic could be no less rhythmical.[4] It is possible that these poetical passages were current separately, and incorporated by the Hebrew narrator, as may have been the case with the angel's words in Matt. i. 21. But it is more probable that the Infancy narratives in both the Gospels were written in Hebrew, and that the rhythmical passages were composed by the narrators themselves.

A further possibility is that the chapters were added to the Gospel at a later date. The word ἄνωθεν 'from the first' (i. 3) seems to mean from the beginning of the common apostolic tradition; and this was certainly the ministry of the Baptist (see Acts i. 21 f.), which was the earliest point at which eye-witnesses (Lk. i. 2) could communicate the facts. And the sixfold synchronism in iii. 1 looks like an elaborate opening to the Gospel. But neither of these is conclusive. St. Luke's main purpose, no doubt, was to give to Theophilus and to the Church of his day an account of the apostolic tradition, beginning with iii. 1. But there was nothing to prevent him from prefixing a prelude to his masterpiece, describing the birth and childhood of Him of whose public Ministry the common tradition treated.

---

[1] The vernacular of Palestine was Aramaic, and the mass of the people could not understand Hebrew; hence the need of Aramaic targums, or interpretations, given in the synagogues side by side with the reading of the Hebrew scriptures. But certain religious circles, such as those which produced some of the apocalypses, and those to which such men as Zacharias the priest, and Simon, who was 'righteous and devout', belonged, seem to have continued to cultivate the sacred language. Our Lord Himself could read *Isaiah* in the original (Lk. iv. 18 f.).

[2] A comparison of the Greek of the *Magnificat* and *Benedictus* with that of the LXX is given by J. M. Creed, *The Gospel according to St. Luke*, 1930, pp. 303–7.

[3] *J.T.S.* xviii, 1916/17, 274 f.

[4] See Burney, *The Poetry of Our Lord* (Oxford, 1926).

The Genealogy, which seems clearly intended to be a list of actual descent, and is thus distinct from that in Matthew which traces the royal succession, is perhaps not in its original form. From Terah (Θάρα) to Adam is 20 generations; from David to Abraham is only 14; and from Heli the father of Joseph to Nathan is 40, of which 20 are before the Exile and 20 after it. Moreover, St. Luke appears to have manipulated the list in two ways: (1) The value which it would have for the family of Jesus lay in the descent from David, and through him from Abraham the father of the race. The twenty names to Adam, with the addition τοῦ Θεοῦ, were probably from St. Luke's own pen as an expression of his universalism. This is supported by the fact that these names appear to have been drawn from the LXX, while corruptions in several of the others point to the Hebrew Bible.[1] (2) He seems to have inverted the order of the whole list, the original form having been simply a catalogue of names beginning with Abraham. Zerubbabel is called the 'son of Rhesa', a name which is not found in Matthew or 1 Chronicles. It is a probable suggestion, therefore, that the list was originally the work of an Aramaic writer (as would be natural) who wrote Salathiel, Zerubbabel the prince (rêshā), Johanan, &c.; and in the Greek form employed by St. Luke rêshā had become a proper name. This rightly makes the forty names reach to Joseph, not to his father Heli.[2]

The distinguishing of the several fragments of tradition, oral or written, collected in L must be largely tentative; but the search for the 'sources of sources' is still going on. Bacon, for example, finds a special source used for our Lord's teaching on Wisdom, and for the sections connected with it.[3] Details connected with the Herod family (xiii. 31 f.; xxiii. 8–12; and cf. i. 5; iii. 1, 19; ix. 7–9) may have been derived through Joanna the wife of Herod's steward (viii. 3), or Manaen the σύντροφος of Herod the tetrarch, who was among the prophets and teachers in the Church at Antioch (Acts xiii. 1). Some have seen an element of Ebionism in sayings and parables which

---

[1] See an elaborate study of the names by Kuhn in *Zeitschr. f. d. neutest. Wiss.*, xxii, 1923, pp. 206 ff.

[2] See Hastings's *Dict. of the Bible*, ii. 140.

[3] *Dict. of Christ and the Gospels*, ii. 825.

teach the religious value of poverty and the duty of alms-giving, and in warnings against covetousness. But on this see. Stanton.[1]

[1] Op. cit. infra, pp. 233-7.

BOOKS

F. C. Burkitt, *The Gospel History and its Transmission*, 3rd ed., 1911.

W. Bussmann, *Synoptische Studien*, 1925.

A. von Harnack, *The Sayings of Jesus*, tr. J. R. Wilkinson, 1908.

Sir J. C. Hawkins, *Horae Synopticae*, 2nd ed., 1909.

F. J. A. Hort, *The N.T. in Greek, Introd., Appendix*, 1896, pp. 28-51.

A. Huck, *Synopse der drei ersten Evangelien*, Eng. ed. by F. L. Cross, 1936.

G. D. Kilpatrick, *Origins of the Gospel according to St. Matthew*, 1946.

J. Moffatt, *Introduction to the Literature of the N.T.*, 3rd ed., 1918.

A. Richardson, *The Gospels in the Making*, 1938.

W. Sanday, ed., *Oxford Studies in the Synoptic Problem*, 1911.

V. H. Stanton, *The Gospels as Historical Documents*, vol. ii, 1909.

B. H. Streeter, *The Four Gospels*, 1924.

V

THE ACTS

THE historical and literary problems of the book of the Acts are as great as any in the New Testament. There is practically universal agreement that it was written by the author of the Third Gospel,[1] but the agreement is not at all universal as to who the author was. And the question of authorship is bound up with nearly every other problem that meets us in the two books. The traditional view, unquestioned till the close of the eighteenth century, but seriously questioned in the nineteenth, was that St. Luke, the companion of St. Paul mentioned in Col. iv. 14; Philem. 24; 2 Tim. iv. 11, was the author, and that he wrote it in Rome at the point of time at which the narrative ceases, when St. Paul had been a prisoner for two years and was still preaching unhindered to all who came to him.

§ 1. THE PURPOSE OF THE ACTS

This was the first question to which historical criticism of the book turned its attention. It was noticed that the contents did not really answer to the title 'The Acts of the Apostles'. Chapters i–xii contain a few early scenes in the Church's life, in which, apart from St. Paul's conversion, attention is directed chiefly to St. Peter; and chapters xiii–xxviii contain accounts, some in full detail, others slight and rapid sketches, of some of St. Paul's movements. The variety of suggestions made as to the purpose and nature of the book may be seen in McGiffert's useful survey of 'Historical criticism of Acts in Germany' in *The Beginnings of Christianity*, ii. 363 ff. The theory of the Tübingen school of F. C. Baur and his followers that the early Church was rent asunder by Pauline and Judaizing factions, and that both the Third Gospel and the Acts were attempts to reconcile them, has now been generally abandoned, at least in

[1] Contrast A. C. Clark, *The Acts of the Apostles*, 1933, pp. 393 ff. His linguistic arguments have been convincingly refuted by W. L. Knox, *The Acts of the Apostles*, 1948, pp. 1–15, 100–9.

its earlier and more uncompromising form. Under the influence of it Bruno Bauer held that Acts was a quite unhistorical description, in the form of narrative, of the condition of peace and harmony between the two factions which developed Judaism had evolved. And Overbeck's view was a variation of this— that the Church never accepted pure Paulinism; it was influenced from the first by Judaism; and Acts represents not Paulinism but a *rationale* of the conceptions about the Apostle which were formed by Christian Judaism. It was not an eirenicon, but the work of one who knew of no condition of things except the developed Christian Judaism of his day. Speaking generally, the view which was widely held fifty years ago was that the author reproduced the idealized picture formed by the Christians of his time of the origin and early years of the Catholic Church. But the work done since J. B. Lightfoot, especially by English-speaking scholars, has made it increasingly clear that the author intended to write history, and that an injustice is done to him if his own words about himself are not taken in their prima facie meaning. There is little doubt that the preface prefixed to his Gospel was intended to cover both Gospel and Acts, and that Acts i opens with a secondary preface introducing his second volume.

It is necessary once more to remind the reader that it was the custom in antiquity, on account of the purely physical conditions of writing, to divide works into volumes, to prefix to the first a preface for the whole, and to add secondary prefaces to the beginning of each later one. The impression made on the English reader by Acts i. 1, that the author is making a new start or at least preparing a kind of sequel to his gospel, would not occur to an early reader. The book of Acts is no afterthought. The word 'treatise' implies a more complete work than does λόγος. The reference to the preceding book, and the renewed address to the patron, are typical of these secondary prefaces in Greek and Latin literature, and are intended to recall the original preface to the reader. Luke i. 1–4 therefore is not merely of indirect value to the student of Acts as an introduction to another work written by the same author and addressed to the same patron. It is the real preface to Acts as well as to the Gospel, written by the author when he contemplated not merely one but both volumes.[1]

[1] Cadbury, in *Beginnings of Christianity*, ii, 1922, 491 f. In the opening of the

In *v.* 4 he states that he is writing that Theophilus may know the certainty concerning the things of which he has been informed. Claiming accurate acquaintance with the facts by careful research and inquiry, he can give him information that he can safely accept as trustworthy. What is not so certain is the purpose that he had in view in giving him this information. Cadbury's notes on the passage show that there are hardly any words in it whose exact significance is beyond dispute. There is no good reason for thinking that Θεόφιλος is an adjective, symbolical of 'the Christian reader', 'the God-lover' in general. But we cannot be sure whether the person addressed was a high official, in which case κράτιστε is a recognized title of respect and Theophilus perhaps a prudential pseudonym, or simply a friend or acquaintance of St. Luke to whom he wished to be polite. Perhaps the formality of the address is merely a literary convention. The word κατηχήθης does not necessarily imply that he was a Christian who had received catechetical instruction; it can have the same force as in Acts xviii. 25, where it is used of receiving information which was accurate but incomplete, and in xxi. 21, 24 where the information is inaccurate. If Theophilus was a Roman official, St. Luke appears as the first Christian apologist, and his work in two parts had an object similar to that of the *Epistle to Diognetus*. It was to show him, and all others whom it might concern, what Christianity really was, its origin and character, and the nature of and reasons for its expansion from its Jewish nucleus till it embraced Gentiles as far as the capital of the empire. Its origin and character are shown in the first volume by an account of Him from whom it sprang; its development in the second, together with indications of the friendly, or at least neutral, attitude towards it which had been taken by one Roman official after another. But if Theophilus was an official he cannot have been a pagan. At least he must have been very favourably disposed towards Christianity to have been influenced by the detailed accounts of our Lord's words and deeds in the Gospel, or,

Acts a résumé is given of the contents of the πρῶτος λόγος, which might naturally have been followed, as commonly in such cases, by a statement of how much the δεύτερος λόγος was intended to embrace. And it is a likely conjecture that such a statement (in which the μέν of *v.* 1 found its answering δέ) has been lost after ἀνελήφθη. See Norden, *Agnostos Theos*, pp. 311 ff.

indeed, to have read them at all. The characteristics of the Gospel noted on pp. 14 ff. go far beyond anything required for merely apologetic purposes. And only one who had breathed, to some extent, the Christian atmosphere could have appreciated the thought which runs through the whole of the Acts, that what Christ had said and done on earth He was continuing to say and do through His Spirit in the Church (see ii. 4, 33; v. 9, 32; vii. 55; viii. 15 f., 39; x. 44 f.; xi. 12, 28; xiii. 2; xv. 28; xvi. 6 f.; xix. 2–6; xx. 28; xxi. 11). It is easier to suppose that Theophilus was a Christian or inclined to the Christian faith; perhaps an official, but at any rate someone in a good social position at Rome. And we know that in the reign of Domitian Christianity may have begun to penetrate to the Roman aristocracy.[1] In addressing him St. Luke no doubt wrote for a wider public, as was commonly the case with Greek writers who addressed their work to individuals. And the *apologia* in the Acts would be useful in the circumstances of the time. Theophilus and many others had heard Jewish-Christian doctrine and also specifically Pauline doctrine. Did this mean that the Jewish apostles and St. Paul had been at variance? The tension that existed between pro-Jews and pro-Gentiles in the Church could still be felt, although the leaders on both sides had done their best to allay it. They knew that the Church of that day embraced Gentiles throughout the empire, and that it had not always done so. Was this universalism a new Pauline departure, or could its roots be traced back into the régime of the first Apostles? And if so, farther still into the action and teaching of Jesus? Rome had begun to persecute Christians, but everyone knew that she had not always done so; before the latter part of Nero's reign the Romans had not distinguished them from Jews, whose religion was officially recognized. On all these and many other points St. Luke felt himself able to provide reliable information, which would show how the Church of his day stood in relation to the Church at the beginning, and he therefore wrote an account of 'the *origines* of the Christian "way"' (Burkitt). He had no wish to write biographical notices of the first Apostles or of St. Paul;

---

[1] See Lightfoot, *Clement*, i. 29 ff.; Streeter, op. cit., pp. 535–9. Cf. R. L. P. Milburn, *Church Quarterly Review*, cxxxix, 1945, pp. 154–64.

and to relate the death of the latter or of St. Peter was foreign to his purpose. That purpose led him to bring the narrative down to the point when Christianity had grown from its embryonic Jewish form till it embraced Rome itself in its catholic embrace; so he concluded with the triumphant account of the greatest of missionaries preaching in the heart of the empire 'unhindered'. 'I believe that the Gospel and the Acts form the two halves of a simple and connected scheme, and that in order to understand it we have only to attach to the two books some such labels as these: Λόγος α', 'How Jesus the Christ preached the Good News to the Jews, and how after His Death and Resurrection He commissioned His apostles to preach it to the Gentiles'; Λόγος β', 'How they brought the Good News from Jerusalem to Rome'. 'With the two years' unhindered proclamation of the Kingdom in the capital of the world, the evolution of the Jewish-Christian sect into the Universal Church was symbolically accomplished' (Turner[1]). 'In a word, the title of the Acts might well have been "The Road to Rome"' (Streeter[2]). A third volume[3] of up-to-date history, such as some writers think that he contemplated, could add little to the practical, instructive value of what he had written; and in itself is very unlikely if, as is highly probable, no release of St. Paul and travelling and preaching and second imprisonment intervened before his death (see pp. 196 f.). To suppose that St. Luke wrote with one chief purpose or *tendency* is to misunderstand his work. It is an attempt to describe, in its essentials, his conceptions of Christianity as it was, in order that Theophilus, and others, may rightly understand it as it is, i.e. Judaism in its true form, the Judaism of the true Messiah such as God intended it to be; to show that Christianity as it is results from the continuation in the Church by means of the Holy Spirit of what Jesus 'began both to do and to teach' when He was on earth. How much of the history is accurate according to modern standards must be decided point by point. The

---

[1] *The Study of the New Testament 1883 and 1920*, p. 30. An inaugural lecture, Oxford.

[2] *The Four Gospels*, p. 532.

[3] πρῶτον (i. 1) should more strictly have been πρότερον, but that is a word which St. Luke never uses. Cf. vii. 12, where πρῶτον (adv.) means 'the first time' followed by καὶ ἐν τῷ δευτέρῳ.

trustworthiness of many of its details has been abundantly vindicated in recent years.[1] But the writer's object was not to draw up a chronicle of events; he wrote aetiological history, in the sense of a selection of narratives such as seemed to him to account for and substantiate the Christianity of his own date. 'His theme was the advance of Christianity from Jerusalem to Rome as the result of the work of his hero Paul, and the form which imposed itself on him was that of a travel story' (W. L. Knox, op. cit., p. 55).

§ 2. THE ARRANGEMENT

If the Acts sketches the expansion of Christianity from Jew to Gentile and from Jerusalem to Rome, it is natural to expect a writer as careful and artistic as St. Luke to give some indication of a methodical treatment of his material. And he does not disappoint us. He cuts the history into 'panels',[2] each concluding with a remark which looks back over the events just related and sums up the success attained. Turner finds six such panels, with the following result: (i) *First Period*, i. 1. The Church in Jerusalem and the preaching of St. Peter: summary in vi. 7 'And the word of God was increasing, and the number of disciples in Jerusalem was being greatly multiplied, and a large number of the priests were becoming obedient to the faith'. (ii) *Second Period*, vi. 8. Extension of the Church through Palestine; the preaching of St. Stephen; troubles with the Jews: summary in ix. 31 'The Church, then, throughout all Galilee and Judaea and Samaria was having peace, being built up, and walking in the fear of the Lord and in the consolation of the Holy Spirit was being multiplied'. (iii) *Third Period*, ix. 32. Extension of the Church to Antioch; St. Peter's conversion of Cornelius; further troubles with the Jews: summary in xii. 24 'And the word of the Lord was increasing and being multiplied'. (iv) *Fourth Period*, xii. 25. Extension of the Church to Asia Minor; preaching of St. Paul in 'Galatia';

---

[1] Especially by Sir William Ramsay in *Saint Paul, the traveller and Roman citizen* (1895) and *The bearing of recent discovery on the trustworthiness of the New Testament* (1915).

[2] This descriptive word is used by Professor C. H. Turner in his valuable article 'Chronology of the New Testament' in Hastings's *D.B.* i. 421.

troubles with the Jewish Christians: summary in xvi. 5 'The Churches, then, were being confirmed in the faith, and were abounding more in number daily'. (v) *Fifth Period*, xvi. 6. Extension of the Church to Europe; St. Paul's missionary work in the great centres, such as Corinth and Ephesus: summary in xix. 20 'So forcibly was the word of the Lord increasing and prevailing'. (vi) *Sixth Period*, xix. 21. Extension of the Church to Rome; St. Paul's captivities: summarized in xxviii. 31 'proclaiming the Kingdom of God and teaching the things concerning the Lord Jesus Christ with all boldness unhindered'. Of these six sections the protagonist in the first three is St. Peter, in the last three St. Paul; and the two halves into which the book thus naturally falls make almost equal divisions at the middle of the whole period covered.

That the 'panels' comprise chronological periods is accepted and elaborated by C. J. Cadoux[1] and Bacon.[2] The former notes an earlier summary statement in ii. 47b ('and the Lord was adding those that were being saved daily together[3]'), from which the chronological series starts.[4] And by identifying the visit of St. Paul to Jerusalem of Gal. ii with that of Acts xi (see pp. 118 ff.), and making use of the Gallio inscription found at Delphi (see p. 124), which was published seven years later than Turner's article, he dates the summaries as follows: (1) ii. 47b, immediately after Pentecost A.D. 29; (2) vi. 7, in the middle or early part of 34; (3) ix. 31, between 36 and the early months of 41; (4) xii. 24, after Nisan 1st, 44, and before the beginning of 47; (5) xvi. 5, a few weeks before the Passover of 49; (6) xix. 20, between Jan. 53 and March or April 55; (7) xxviii. 31, in the early part of 59. He further makes the ingenious (perhaps

---

[1] *J.T.S.* xix, 1918, pp. 333 ff.

[2] *Harvard Theol. Rev.*, April 1921, pp. 137–66.

[3] Ἐπὶ τὸ αὐτό. This difficult expression led to the reading of E P, τῇ ἐκκλησίᾳ followed by ἐπὶ τὸ αὐτὸ δὲ Πέτρος κτλ., adopted in the Tyndale, Cranmer, Geneva, and Authorized Versions. See Burkitt, *J.T.S.* xx, 1918–19, pp. 321–4. Cf. F. J. Foakes Jackson, *Harvard Theol. Rev.* x, 1917, reviewing C. C. Torrey's *The Composition and Date of Acts* (1916). Luke's ignorance of Palestinian Aramaic probably made him take לחדא 'greatly' as if it were יחדו and so he translated it ἐπὶ τὸ αὐτό.

[4] Jackson and Lake (*Beginnings of Christianity*, ii. 177) further suggest xi. 21, but that is not so clearly a summary of a period intended to articulate the history.

over-ingenious) suggestion that St. Luke splits the history into six periods of five years each, beginning with the Pentecosts of 29, 34, 39, 44, 49, 54, thus covering a total period of thirty years, which was about the length of time covered by his Gospel.

Bacon agrees with the quinquennial arrangement, and strives to substantiate it with some drastic criticism of St. Luke's accuracy, both in facts and in the order of events.

These periods correspond to some extent with stages in the geographical progress of Christianity, as Turner points out.[1] The geographical steps, however, are not strictly distinct. The extension through Palestine (2nd period) is partly parallel to the extension to Antioch (3rd period); and xvi. 5 occurs in the middle of a journey in which St. Paul *revisits* places already evangelized. Moreover, there were Christians in Damascus (ix. 10 ff.), Ephesus (xviii. 19 f., xix. 1 f.), Troas (xx. 7–12), Puteoli (xxviii. 13 f.), Rome (? xviii. 2 f., xxviii. 14 f.) before St. Paul is recorded to have preached in those towns. Goguel,[2] however, questions the views of Turner, Cadoux, Moffatt, and Bacon on the grounds that the development of the narrative of Acts is not at all 'rectilinear' and that an author intending to divide his account into equal chronological periods would have left more precise indications of his intention than the author of Acts does.

This is not the place to discuss the chronology of the Acts; but it seems possible that St. Luke arranges and divides his narrative according to a deliberate plan, which heightens the impression of a steady and regular forward movement, even if he goes back sometimes to pick up the threads of his story.

§ 3. THE SOURCES

That St. Luke gained from others information about events in the first years of the Church is evident; and if the Preface (Lk. i. 1–4) was intended to cover the Acts, as has been said, as well as the Gospel, he states that he did. And if he used written sources for the Gospel, it is natural that he should do

---

[1] So Moffatt, *Introd. Lit. N.T.*, pp. 284 f.
[2] *Introduction au Nouveau Testament*, iii, 1922, p. 154, n. 1, pp. 148–53 providing his grounds for his first point.

so for its sequel, though it cannot be demonstrated in the latter case in the same way as in the former because we possess no documents analogous to Mark, with Matthew for comparison.

All narratives, of course, are ultimately traceable to the places where the actors lived and moved. In the infancy of the Church these were principally Jerusalem, Caesarea, and Antioch. It does not necessarily follow that *written* accounts emanated from each of these centres. Harnack[1] finds a Jerusalem source, A, in iii. 1–v. 16, and parallel to it a series of (less trustworthy) Jerusalem narratives, B, in ch. i (possibly), ii. 1–47; v. 17–24. He ascribes viii. 5–10; ix. 31–xi. 18; xii. 1–23 to a Jerusalem-Caesarean source or group of traditions, which is perhaps to be identified with A; vi. 1–viii. 4; xi. 19–30; xii. 25–xv. 35 to a Jerusalem-Antiochene source based on the authority of Silas; and ix. 1–30 to a Pauline source. The remainder of chs. i–xv, and the whole of xvi–xxviii are the work of St. Luke.

The history of the source-criticism of Acts has been summarized by Goguel, op. cit., pp. 51–57. To his bibliography on the subject must be added W. L. Knox, *The Acts of the Apostles*, pp. 19–21, 23–25, where Harnack's theory meets with searching criticism. Knox writes:

I would suggest that apart from the speeches, representing a more or less fixed pattern of preaching, which may have been reduced to writing, we have in these chapters (i–xii) no written sources with the possible exception of chapters i–v inclusive, but excluding most of the speeches. This source may have duplicated the trials before the Sanhedrin and included a miraculous escape from prison of dubious historical value; but it reached Luke with the doublets already in it. It remains possible that the whole section represents what Luke collected by way of oral tradition for himself [p. 39].

Schutz,[2] proceeding upon Harnack's lines, finds two sources emanating from Jerusalem and from some Hellenistic quarter, perhaps Antioch. The former upholds the Jerusalem ('Ιερου- σαλήμ) tradition of the *twelve* apostles, with their claim to supreme ecclesiastical authority and to the sole prerogative of

---

[1] *The Acts of the Apostles* (trans. Wilkinson), 1909, pp. 175–202.
[2] *Apostel und Jünger*, 1921.

dispensing the gift of the Spirit. The latter represents the position of the followers of the Lord outside Jerusalem ('Ιεροσό-λυμα), in Galilee, the Gentile Decapolis, and Syria; and the apostles are not twelve, but a larger, undefined body of missionaries, as St. Paul understood them, for whom 'disciples' is the description chiefly used; Christianity does not 'emerge peacefully from the bosom of Judaism', but with conflict between the equally original Judaic and Gentile elements. In accordance with this theory the sources are distinguished as follows: A and M (for *Apostoloi* and *Mathētai*) are the 'Apostle' source and the 'Disciple' source. A: chs. i–v; vii. 2–47; viii. 1 (the words 'except the apostles'); viii. 14–25 (Peter and John in supreme authority in Samaria); ix. 27 f. (St. Paul with the Jerusalem apostles); ix. 31–xi. 18, 19b (St. Peter and the Gentiles); xv. 1–33 (34) (the decision of the apostles concerning Gentile converts); xvi. 3b, 4 (St. Paul circumcises Timothy. The apostolic decrees); xix. 2–7 (the baptism of John's disciples); xxi. 20–27a (St. Paul's Nazirite vow). M comprises all the rest of the book.

Briggs[1] and Blass[2] are content with a single Jerusalem source due to John Mark; and they suggest that he wrote it as a continuation to his Gospel, which they think ended at xvi. 8, and that St. Luke made the same use of it as he had made of the Second Gospel.

New ground was broken by Torrey,[3] who maintained that i. 2–xv. 35 is St. Luke's translation of a single Aramaic document emanating from Jerusalem, whose 'chief interest was in the *universal mission* of Christianity', and which was intended to show 'how Antioch became the first great Gentile centre of Christianity'. It was written in A.D. 49 or early in 50, for its author did not know (see xv. 32 f.) that Silas had started on a new missionary journey in company with St. Paul. It came into St. Luke's hands after his arrival in Rome in 62. Two years later he added to it the second half of the work, thus forming

---

[1] *New Light on the Life of Jesus*, pp. 135 f.
[2] *Acta Apostolorum*, 1895, pp. iv f.; *Philology of the Gospels*, 1898, pp. 141 f.
[3] *The Composition and Date of Acts* (Harvard Theological Studies, 1916). Contrast de Zwaan, *Beginnings of Christianity* ii. 50 ff., C. H. Dodd, *The Apostolic Preaching*, p. 35, n. 1, and W. L. Knox, op. cit., p. 20 f. Torrey has not proved his case for more than the speeches and chapters i–v. 16.

our present book, as a sequel to his Gospel which was already written before 61 and probably in 60. The linguistic argument has been criticized by Burkitt[1] and others, but Torrey has at any rate made clear the strong Aramaic colouring of the narratives. It is quite possible that they rest on Aramaic documents; but what he has not satisfactorily proved is that they rest on a single document. All written sources that had their home in Jerusalem would naturally be in Aramaic; and if written sources were used, translators might sometimes misunderstand their idiom.

Jackson and Lake[2] hold a theory of sources on lines similar to Harnack's, together with the recognition that some of them were in Aramaic; but they are inclined, with Ramsay and others, to connect the local traditions more closely with individual persons—Peter, Philip, John Mark. And they make the suggestions: (1) that the John who accompanies St. Peter in the early scenes was, in the original form of the tradition, not the son of Zebedee but John Mark, who afterwards associated with St. Peter; (2) that Harnack's source B is a continuation of the Jerusalem source used by St. Luke in his Passion and Resurrection narratives; (3) that the story of Stephen contains a duplicate account of the accusation brought against him: (a) vi. 9–11, and (b) 12–14, and of his death: (a) vii. 54–58a, and (b) 58b–60. They admit, however, that the doublets may have been accidental.

The theory of a written Aramaic source as propounded by Torrey is strongly opposed by Goodspeed.[3] He thinks that in the earliest days the expectation of the immediate coming of the End would prevent Jewish Christians from writing histories. And the writing of history by using detached stories from different sources required an 'insight and restraint and historical scent' which were distinctively Greek. There was a 'general Aramaic indisposition to literary composition at the time in question'. Moreover, the purpose of the Acts was to trace the emergence of Greek out of Jewish Christianity; and 'that there should have been a Palestinian Christian Aramaic

---

[1] *J.T.S.* xx, 1918–19, pp. 320–9.
[2] *The Beginnings of Christianity*, ii, 1922, pp. 145 ff.
[3] 'The Origin of Acts' in *Journ. Bibl. Lit.* xxxix, 1920, pp. 83–101.

reading public about A.D. 50, interested to read how the Gospel was already feeling its way past them into the Greek world, seems very near the height of improbability'. 'What Palestinian circle of Aramaic readers reacted to this up-to-date pro-Gentile historical sketch, and scattered copies of it as far as Rome?' But while this has some weight against Torrey's single document which came into St. Luke's hands at Rome, it has little against the theory of shorter Aramaic narratives. They contained accounts of events startling enough for even Jewish Christians to record; and it was St. Luke who arranged them and worked up the pro-Gentile historical sketch.

It is unnecessary to enlarge upon more complicated theories of sources traceable through the whole book with additions by one or more redactors. Some of them may be seen in Moffatt's *Intr. Lit. N.T.*, pp. 286–9 and Goguel, op. cit., pp. 51–72.

§ 4. THE AUTHORSHIP AND HISTORICAL VALUE

These two questions are so closely bound together that they cannot easily be treated apart. Hitherto the author has, for convenience, been called St. Luke. But if he was St. Luke it cannot be assumed, without testing of the evidence, either that he was a companion of St. Paul during any of the apostle's movements that he relates,[1] or that his narratives, even in the latter half of the book, must be in all respects accurate. It might be expected from a companion of St. Paul, who wrote his history after the apostle reached Rome, that he would show an intimate knowledge of his epistles, and therefore both of his doctrine and of those events of his life which the apostle himself records. But none of these is the case. Some of the most difficult problems in the New Testament are occasioned by the divergences between his narratives and St. Paul's accounts of events. And it is doubtful if he gives any sign of having read one of his epistles. Here and there he uses Pauline language: 'In this Man every one that believeth is justified from all the things from which ye could not be justified in [the system of] the law of Moses' (xiii. 39); 'faith in Me' (xxvi. 18); 'the

---

[1] We know that he was with St. Paul when Col. iv. 14, Philem. 24, and probably 2 Tim. iv. 11 were written; but that is the only direct evidence that we possess. His name occurs nowhere else in the New Testament.

Gospel of the grace of God' (xx. 24); 'the word of His grace' (v. 32); the reference to redemption by Christ's death (v. 28), and to the day when He would judge the world (xvii. 31). If he received accurate reports of St. Paul's speeches, in which these occurred, he needed no knowledge of his epistles. But anyone who had heard St. Paul's doctrine preached or discussed by others could rightly attribute such phrases to him. The Acts contains very little trace of distinctively Pauline thought. On the other hand there are marked differences which show that the writer's thoughts moved on a plane nearer to that of the primitive Church than St. Paul's. This would be natural if the writer was using a pattern of the Apostolic kerygma as his model, inserting remarks appropriate in the mouth of the speaker.

The speeches which he records stand in two different categories. The *Petrine speeches* (i. 16–22, ii. 14–40, iii. 12–26, iv. 9–12, x. 34–43, xi. 5–17) were derived from sources (see § 3); and we have no means of knowing what opportunities were open to the writers of the sources of obtaining trustworthy accounts of what St. Peter said. It is clear that we possess only their substance, since six speeches comprise only seventy-six verses; but it is very likely that their substance is adequately represented. It is noticeable that they reflect an early stage of Christian thought, such as might be expected in St. Peter's earliest preaching, which provides an early instance of the Apostolic kerygma. On the other hand the *Pauline speeches* (xiii. 16–41; xiv. 15–17; xvii. 22–31; xx. 18–35; xxii. 1–21; xxiv. 10–21; xxvi. 2–23), which cannot with anything like the same probability be traced to written sources, can hardly be said to contain what might be expected from the apostle. 'We cannot imagine St. Paul preaching a mission sermon to Jews or pagans without the fire of appeal to the Cross or of warning of the Judgement to come. The latter appears once (xvii. 31; cf. xxiv. 25), but the former never.' And though there are echoes of Pauline phrases, there are ideas about Christ's Resurrection (xvii. 31, xxvi. 23) and that of other men (xxiv. 15; xiii. 32; xxvi. 6–8), and a few expressions, which are not found in his epistles.[1]

[1] See A. H. McNeile's *New Testament Teaching in the Light of St. Paul's*, 1923, pp. 118–35.

The speech at Miletus (xx. 18–35), the only one addressed to Christians, is probably the nearest in substance to St. Paul's words. The writer of the 'we'-sections (see below) seems to have been present; and in any case the elders to whom it was spoken could hand down much of what was said. But for the most part we must probably be content with the conclusion that St. Luke, who wrote several years after the apostle's death, and who probably was not present at any of the speeches that he records except that at Miletus and the speech, begun in Aramaic, to the crowd in Jerusalem (xxii. 1–21), followed a common custom of ancient historians in writing the Pauline speeches himself. He gives them in the form of brief summaries, seven speeches occupying 111 verses. In those of them that he heard his own distant reminiscences would play a part, and in some, probably, reports from other. A confused report may have been the cause of the obscurities in the self-defence before the Sanhedrin (xxiii. 1–8), and of the duplication which is noticeable in that before Felix (xxiv. 10–21).[1]

THE 'WE'-SECTIONS. This title is usually given to the following passages: xvi. 9–18 (from Troas to Philippi on the second tour), xx. 4–16 (from Philippi to Miletus on the third tour), xxi. 1–18 (from Miletus to Jerusalem), xxvii. 1–xxviii. 16 (from Caesarea to Rome). These are generally held to be the most trustworthy portions of the book from an historical point of view. The author, whether St. Luke or not, is thought to have incorporated material from a travel narrative or diary written by an eyewitness who used the first person plural.[2]

The remaining narratives in chs. xvi–xxviii, with which the 'we'-sections are combined, are composed of a variety of

[1] See below, p. 117. The Pauline speeches are discussed by P. Gardner, Professor of Classical Archaeology, Oxford, in *Cambridge Biblical Essays* (1909), pp. 381–419; also by W. L. Knox, op. cit., pp. 70–78; cf. p. 84 on the Petrine speeches, pp. 23 f. on St. Stephen's. E. Norden (*Agnostos Theos*, 1913) tried to prove that the speech at Athens (xvii. 23–31) was consciously modelled on a speech περὶ θυσιῶν of Apollonius of Tyana at Athens, preserved in his *Life* (vi. 3) by Philostratus. This was severely handled by Burkitt, *J.T.S.* xv, 1914, pp. 455–64. And see Harnack, *Texte u. Untersuchungen*, xxxix. 1–46.

[2] In xi. 27 also, after the word 'Antioch', D has 'And there was great exultation. And when *we* were gathered together one of them named Agabus signified saying, &c.' This is not part of a travel-narrative. The passage may not be genuine, but it is interesting as reflecting the tradition that St. Luke was a native of Antioch (see p. 40).

material as to the historical value of which very different opinions are held. And opinions differ even more widely in respect of chs. i–xv. Jackson and Lake[1] speak of four possibilities which have received considerable assent: (1) The traditional view is that the diarist is identical with the compiler of Acts and uses the first person to show that he was present during these parts of the events narrated. (2) The diarist is not the compiler of Acts, but added to his own diary the intervening sections of narrative, thus producing a connected whole, which was later taken over by the compiler of Acts and formed the main source of Acts xvi–xxviii. (3) The diarist wrote nothing except the 'we'-sections; another writer added the intervening parts in Acts xvi–xxviii, and the final editor added this composite work to Acts i–xv. (4) The diarist wrote nothing except the 'we'-sections, and the compiler added the intervening sections as well as Acts i–xv from other information. They are sceptical as to the diarist being St. Luke. And the Third Gospel and Acts being anonymous, Cadbury[2] discounts the whole of the early and undisputed attribution of both volumes to St. Luke on the ground that it arose solely by inference from their contents. Many will feel this to be unduly cautious. 'The wide area over which our evidence extends seems to imply that the ascription to St. Luke is a genuine tradition, and not a mere critical deduction.'[3] But as regards the diary, if the writer of it was a companion of St. Paul, the name Luke is as good as any other.[4] A companion who wrote a diary or travel-notes probably gives the nearest approach to historical accuracy to be found in the New Testament. The important thing is to decide the relation of the 'we'-sections to the rest of the book.

It has been clearly shown, by Hawkins[5] and Harnack[6] among others, that the style and vocabulary of these sections and of the rest of the book are closely similar. But this is not in itself a proof that the whole book was a homogeneous work

---

[1] *Beginnings of Christianity*, ii, 1922, 158 f.   [2] Ibid., pp. 250 ff.
[3] Bp. Headlam in Hastings's *D.B.* i. 27a.
[4] Epaphroditus, for example (Blaisdell, *Harvard Theol. Rev.* xiii, 1920, pp. 136–58); cf. Goguel, op. cit., pp. 158 f. for this and other suggestions.
[5] *Horae Synopticae*, ed. 2, pp. 182 f.
[6] *Luke the Physician* (trans. Williamson, 1907), ch. ii.

rather than a compilation. The author, whoever he was, was quite capable of revising his sources, so that his style and vocabulary predominate throughout. This is seen by the way in which he incorporated in his Gospel the material drawn from Mark, Q, and elsewhere. But, as Harnack points out, his revision or rewriting of his Marcan material was not carried out to the extent of obliterating all signs of its Marcan origin. His parallels to Mark are not, in fact, so distinctively 'Lucan' in style and vocabulary as the 'we'-sections. If this is accepted it tells against the view that the compiler of Luke–Acts incorporated and revised sections from another person's diary. See V. H. Stanton[1] in opposition to Cadbury[2] and others who tend to discard the evidence of style and vocabulary as of no weight at all.

The second of the alternatives mentioned above has little to commend it. It sharply divides the Acts into two portions, denying chs. i–xv to St. Luke, but assigning to him the bulk of the remainder. But if he wrote the latter, there is no sufficient reason for denying to him the former. Chapters i–xv contain narratives of events at which it is practically certain he was not present, and he was therefore dependent—as in his Gospel—upon sources. Any difficulties which may be found in those chapters were difficulties in his sources, which even a companion of St. Paul was not in a position to avoid; he could only make use of them as he made use of Mark and Q.

The third alternative is in no way preferable to the second. There is nothing which clearly suggests the hand of a third person. The decision must lie between the first and the last—the Lucan authorship of Luke–Acts as a whole or the Lucan authorship of the diary alone (or possibly the diary *plus* some of the narratives which immediately border on it). The former is the conclusion reached in the course of this chapter. And if it is accepted, the only remaining question with regard to the 'we'-sections is whether they were, after all, parts of a diary or not.

(1) If they were, two things require to be noted: (*a*) We obviously do not possess the whole diary, and therefore the writer of it may have been in St. Paul's company over a longer

---

[1] *J.T.S.* xxiv, 1923, pp. 374–81. [2] *Beginnings of Christianity*, ii. 161–6.

period than the extracts cover. If, for example, the introduction of the first person in xvi. 10 is felt to be abrupt, it is because the diary must originally have related how St. Luke came to be with St. Paul at Troas. In xx. 5 it is generally assumed that the first person reappears at Philippi because it ceased at Philippi, and that St. Luke had stayed on there in the intervening time.[1] But this is quite uncertain, and, if he belonged to Antioch, improbable. In any case the diary must have contained some statement to the effect that he and St. Paul met again, wherever it was (? Corinth), before the remark 'And these went before and awaited us at Troas'.[2] He must also have been with the apostle in Jerusalem, taking part in many of the events which follow xxi. 17, and in Caesarea in the period preceding xxvii. 1. (b) The exact extent of the extracts is uncertain. Did they include the story of Eutychus, for example (xx. 9–12), or anything of the events at Miletus (xx. 17–38) or Jerusalem or Caesarea (xxi. 18–xxvi. 32)? The writer of the 'we'-passages would appear to have been present on these occasions; and where he had no reason to mention St. Paul's companions, and himself among them, it does not follow that the narratives did not form part of the diary. Still, a diary would not be likely to contain extended narratives; it would rather be a journal, daily notes of the writer's movements with St. Paul.

(2) If they were not, we must conclude that the introduction of the first person did not feel as abrupt to St. Luke as it does to us. He uses the words 'I' and 'me' in Lk. i. 3, Acts i. 1; both parts of the work are addressed to Theophilus, and purport to contain information given to him personally. And thus 'we' might come in quite naturally, indicating somewhat loosely that he was present at several of the scenes that he describes.[3]

That he made extracts from his own diary seems to the present writer on the whole rather more probable. Several

---

[1] Ramsay even argues (*St. Paul the Traveller*, pp. 202 ff.) that he was a native of Philippi.

[2] D (not d) reads αὐτόν for ἡμᾶς—apparently an attempt to smooth the abruptness.

[3] So Stanton (op. cit.) following Harnack. Norden, *Agnostos Theos*, 1923, pp. 318–27, cites parallels, such as Cicero *to Atticus* (v. 20) and to Cato (*ad Fam.* xv. 4); cf. Goguel, op. cit., pp. 157 ff.

details, for example, especially the itinerary of xx. 13–15, are more likely to have been written on the spot than recorded from memory twenty years or more afterwards. But to those who accept the Lucan authorship of the whole book the question is not very important.

THE PHYSICIAN. One argument for the Lucan authorship of the Gospel and Acts must probably be allowed less weight than has usually been given to it—that of the medical language found in the two writings. St. Paul speaks of 'Luke the beloved physician' (Col. iv. 14). Erasmus thought that this description was for the purpose of distinguishing him from the evangelist, but he is generally identified with him. An elaborate attempt was made by Hobart[1] to show that the vocabulary of the Gospel and Acts is so rich in medical terms, and words found in medical writings, that only a physician is likely to have written it. Most English writers have accepted his main results without close examination. Some scholars,[2] however, recognize that Hobart, with his array of more than 400 words, tried to prove too much, and offer more modest lists; but they think that they are conclusive.

But the evidence is drastically sifted by Cadbury,[3] who points out the following facts: (1) Many of Hobart's words are so common that their appearance in Luke–Acts and in medical writings was inevitable. (2) More than 80 per cent. of his words (as Plummer says) are found in the LXX; 300 of them also in Josephus; 27 in the LXX but not in Josephus; and 67 in Josephus but not in the LXX. That is, 90 per cent. are covered by these writings. (3) More than 90 per cent. are covered by Plutarch and Lucian. (4) Several of the medical words cited, not only by Hobart, but by Zahn, Harnack, and Moffatt, are used by St. Luke in non-medical senses. (5) Sixteen medical words can be cited from Matthew and Mark which are not found in Luke–Acts. (6) St. Luke shows a higher degree of culture and education than the first two evangelists,

---

[1] *The Medical Language of St. Luke*, 1882.
[2] e.g. Plummer, *St. Luke*, pp. lxiv f.; Moffatt, *Introd. Lit. N.T.*, pp. 298 ff.; Zahn, *Introd. N.T.* iii. 146 ff., 160 ff.; Harnack, *Luke the Physician* (trans. Williamson), pp. 13–17 and Appendix I; Goguel, op. cit., pp. 142–6.
[3] 'The Style and Literary Method of Luke', *Harvard Theol. Stud.* vi, part i, 1919.

and naturally has command of a larger vocabulary, and so uses words found in the writings of medical men, who were also cultured and educated. Greek medical terms did not make up a technical vocabulary such as the medical profession employs today; they were genuinely Greek, and spoken Greek. Galen, who wrote later than St. Luke, claims for the sake of clearness to 'employ those terms which people in general (οἱ πολλοί) are accustomed to use'.[1] And in *Harvard Theological Review*, 1921, p. 106, Cadbury notes that Galen makes a similar claim for his predecessor Hippocrates (who wrote six centuries earlier): 'he appears to me to use the most usual and therefore plainly intelligible terms, such as rhetoricians are accustomed to call πολιτικά.'[2] Cadbury concludes his inquiry by an examination of Lucian on Hobart's lines, and produces results very similar to those which the latter claims for St. Luke. He tends, as said above, to reduce the significance of Lucan style and vocabulary to a minimum, believing that Luke–Acts was not written by 'the beloved physician'. But he has certainly reduced the strength of the case for the medical language.[3]

MIRACLES. Many think that the narratives in the Acts, especially in chs. i–xv, contain matter that is legendary and unhistorical, e.g. the story of Pentecost, the deliverance of the apostles from prison, and of St. Peter, and the raising of Dorcas from death. This is not the place to discuss the perennial problem of miracles.[4] Nor can all the accounts of miraculous

---

[1] Quoted in op. cit., p. 64, n. 91.

[2] i.e. used by the ordinary citizen, the plain man.

[3] Stanton (op. cit. ii. 262 f.) expresses the utmost that can be said for it: 'It seems to me probable that one who in former years had had some medical knowledge, but whose main interest in the miracles could no longer be in any sense a scientific one, and who was writing a narrative intended simply to set forth to general readers the facts as to that New Faith and its spread among men, to the progress of which he had come to be wholly devoted, might not improbably show signs of early training agreeing with what we notice in the "Lucan" writings.' It is worthy of remark that Jerome (*De vir. illustr.* 7) could speak of 'Luke a physician of Antioch *as his writings indicate*'.

[4] See A. Richardson, *Miracle-stories of the Gospels*, 1941, and *Christian Apologetics*, 1947, pp. 154–76. Given an outburst of religious enthusiasm in Palestine in the 1st century A.D., it would have been a miracle if no miracles had happened. It would also have been a miracle if some miracles were not exaggerated; but if on other grounds we see reasons to believe that the Incarnation represents an unique act of God in history, we may be inclined to suppose that miracles attended it. In any case, belief in miracles goes back to the earliest

happenings be treated as standing on the same level. Here it is necessary to point out that there is no justification whatever for thinking that if these accounts are legendary and unhistorical St. Luke could not have incorporated them, while another compiler could. Miracles were not an obstacle to faith, but the reverse. Records of miracles were the expression of a profound conviction of the truth that Christianity is itself miraculous; and when such records reached St. Luke, he did not criticize them; he delighted in them, and published them for his contemporaries as an important element in his *apologia* for the Christian Church, illustrations of its true inwardness and character and power.

PARALLELISMS. More or less striking parallelisms are pointed out between events in the two halves of the Acts. St. Peter and St. Paul 'both began their ministry with the healing of a lame man; both work miracles, the one with his shadow, the other with napkins. Demons flee in the name of St. Peter and in the name of St. Paul. St. Peter meets Simon Magus: St. Paul Elymas and the Ephesian magicians. Both raise the dead. Both receive divine honours. Both are supported by Pharisees in the council. St. Paul is stoned at Lystra, Stephen at Jerusalem. St. Paul is made to adopt the language of St. Peter, St. Peter of St. Paul, and so on' (Bp. Headlam[1]). If this is detrimental to the historical value of the narratives, as some have held, it is the second half of the book that suffers rather than the first, if the first half came to the author in the form of written sources. As Dr. Headlam says, 'Because the writer finds parallels between the lives of two men, it does not prove that his narrative is fictitious'. The idea that it does arose from the Tübingen conception of the book as a tract for the times mediating between the Judaic and the Pauline factions; many of St. Peter's deeds and words were similar to many of St. Paul's, and each was as good as the other.

COMPARISON OF ACTS AND EPISTLES. When due weight has been given to considerations of style and vocabulary, and of the author's plan and method, there still remains the larger

---

stages of the tradition and cannot be used as evidence that a particular story is 'late' or 'secondary'.

[1] Hastings's *D.B.* i. 31a.

and more pressing part of the problem. We have seen that a companion of St. Paul need not necessarily have known his epistles or reflected his distinctive theological ideas. But did he in his narrative relate or omit things about St. Paul which it is impossible to suppose that a companion of the apostle could have related or omitted? A comparison must be drawn between narratives in the Acts and statements in St. Paul's epistles, of which, for this purpose, Galatians is the most important.

(1) Is St. Luke likely to have omitted St. Paul's visit to Arabia (Gal. i. 17)? He certainly seems to leave no room for it in Acts ix. 19, 20. But it would have contributed nothing to his purpose. The spread of Christianity from Jews to Gentiles, which he wanted to trace, and of which St. Paul's conversion was one of the chief turning-points, was not notably advanced by his retirement for a few days to the regions outlying Damascus.[1]

(2) The accounts of the apostle's first visit to Jerusalem after his conversion are more difficult. St. Paul is emphasizing the fact that he received his Gospel without any authorization or instruction from men. On that account he did not go at once to Jerusalem to the original apostles, but to Arabia and back to Damascus. Not till three years later did he go to the capital (Gal. i. 18–24); and then it was for a purely private visit to make St. Peter's acquaintance. He spent fifteen days with him, and saw also St. James, the chief presbyter of the Church in Jerusalem; but did not come into contact with the Christians in the towns and villages in Judaea outside the city. 'I was unknown by face to the Churches of Judaea which are in Christ.' In the Acts (ix. 26–29) the author, writing long afterwards, with no desire whatever to press the fact of St. Paul's independence in his knowledge of the Christian Gospel, but only wishing to carry his account of the spread of Christianity a stage farther, describes Saul's reception by 'the apostles' in Jerusalem, owing to the good offices of Barnabas, and then his vigorous preaching, which included disputings with Hellenists. The two accounts differ widely; and their difference makes it

---

[1] This is probably the meaning of Arabia. See Ramsay, *St. Paul the Traveller*, p. 380. But the same, of course, is true if Arabia means the district in which Mt. Sinai stands (Lightfoot, *Galatians*, 10th ed., 1890, pp. 88 f.).

obvious that the author had not read Galatians. But though the epistle must be preferred to the Acts, it is possible that both writers may have heightened unconsciously the colour of their respective accounts under the pressure of their respective purposes. St. Paul no doubt met only St. Peter and St. James, as he says and asseverates; hence 'the apostles' must be taken as a generalization by one who did not know the exact facts. But the newly converted Saul was not one to keep silence for a fortnight, and very probably preached in the city. The words 'coming in and going out at Jerusalem' do not mean that he visited places outside the city, but that he moved about freely and fearlessly in and out of houses in the city.

(3) Having embarked upon his ministry, fired with the conviction that he was called to be an apostle to the Gentiles, it might be thought that St. Paul would confine his attention to them, or at least make them his first object. But according to the Acts his practice, of which the epistles give no hint, was to speak first to Jews when he arrived at a town for the first time. He turned to Gentiles when Jews proved hostile. It would be easy to exaggerate this into a fundamental disagreement between the apostle's picture of himself and the historian's conception of the whole purpose and method of his ministry. But in a strange town it would, in fact, be very difficult for him at once to secure a Gentile audience. A Jewish audience he could always get where there was a synagogue; and that gave him the opportunity of reaching any Gentiles who were attached, or attracted, to Judaism closely enough to be present. Having become known in the place (cf. Acts xiii. 44), he would frequently be rejected after a short time by the synagogue, but he would have gained a nucleus of Gentiles to whom he could go on preaching elsewhere. His deliberate turning from the one to the other may be pictured a little too sharply in xiii. 46, xviii. 6; cf. xxviii. 25–28; but the divergence between the Paul of the Acts and the Paul of the epistles is not wide enough, in this respect, to preclude the Lucan authorship. His freedom and charity, and desire to be all things to all men in order to win as many as possible, led him sometimes to speak and act in such a way that he was charged with inconsistency, as we know from his own pen. And St. Luke's accounts of his preaching

first to Jews only serve to illustrate that side of his behaviour which is expressed in the words, 'I became to the Jews as a Jew, that I might win Jews (1 Cor. ix. 20).

(4) According to Acts xvii. 15; xviii. 5, St. Paul on arriving at Athens sent back by the Beroeans, who had brought him thither, a message to Silas and Timotheus, who had been left. at Beroea, bidding them to 'come to him as soon as possible'. And after he had gone on to Corinth, they came. If the Acts stood alone, it would be natural to conclude that their arrival at Corinth was in obedience to the message received. But in 1 Thess. iii. 1–6 St. Paul states that in order to encourage the Thessalonians in their afflictions he sent Timotheus back to them *from Athens*: 'Since we could no longer forbear, we thought it good to be left in Athens alone, and sent Timotheus . . . to strengthen you.' There were, therefore, journeys of Timotheus (1) from Beroea to Athens, and (2) from Athens back to Thessalonica, which are omitted in Acts. His return to the apostle at Corinth coincides with the words (*v.* 6): 'But when Timotheus just now came to us from you . . . we were comforted'; and on that account 1 Thessalonians may be assumed to have been written at Corinth. Possibly a double journey of Silas has also been omitted. If the plural pronoun in '*we* could no longer forbear' includes him, he had come without Timotheus to the apostle at Athens, and had stayed with him there, in which case he must afterwards have been sent back to Thessalonica for some purpose and then with Timotheus rejoined St. Paul at Corinth. But since in *v.* 5 St. Paul uses the first person singular—'when *I* could no longer forbear'—the pronoun in *v.* 1 is probably an epistolary plural referring to the apostle alone. Conjectures have been made which exonerate St. Luke from ignorance of the movements of Timotheus.[1] But his ignorance would be no serious objection to the Lucan authorship of the Acts, since there is no evidence that the writer was with St. Paul at Athens or at Corinth. And if he was not ignorant, the omission can be accounted for by his wish to trace the rapid spread of Christianity, for which he confines himself mainly to the movements of St. Paul, and omits many details which do not serve his purpose.

[1] See Lake, *The Earlier Epistles of St. Paul*, p. 75, n. 2.

(5) St. Paul was at Ephesus for a considerable time in the course of his third missionary tour, and the writer was apparently not with him. This is enough to account for the fact that he gives a very rapid and sketchy record of the apostle's work there (xviii. 19–xix. 22), and says nothing of the violent opposition and danger which he encountered, and which he describes in 1 Cor. iv. 9–13; xv. 32; 2 Cor. i. 8; iv. 8–12. (For the story of the riot (Acts xix. 23–41) he must have been dependent upon a source other than St. Paul, since, according to his narrative, the apostle was not involved in it. His reason for relating it was no doubt the tolerant and pacific attitude taken by the civil official, which he takes every opportunity to emphasize.) The writer's absence will also explain his omission of a visit which St. Paul paid to Corinth from Ephesus in the same period. In 1 Cor. iv. 18 f., 21; xi. 34, St. Paul states his intention of paying the visit, and in 2 Cor. xii. 14; xiii. 1 f., he refers to it as having been paid (see p. 134). And even if St. Paul, at some time during their companionship, had informed him of all these facts, it was not to his purpose to recount the apostle's personal sufferings of body and mind, or his anxious dealings with the Corinthians.

(6) On the other hand the writer was with St. Paul when he went up to Jerusalem (Acts xxi. 15–17) and when he sailed from Caesarea to Rome (xxvi. 1–xxviii. 16), and therefore was presumably present at the events in Jerusalem which he describes (xxi. 17–xxiii. 30). We have no epistles at this point with which to check his narrative, but some difficulties have been raised. For St. Paul it was a matter of pressing importance that he should bring the contributions made by several Gentile Churches for the poor in Jerusalem. In Rom. xv. 25–28 he speaks of it as though it were his only object in going thither. This purpose is just mentioned in the Acts in a speech of St. Paul (xxiv. 17), but there is not a word to relate that it was handed over. This would be surprising if St. Luke's purpose had been simply biographical, and much more surprising if it had been to write an eirenicon to reconcile Pauline and Jewish factions. Nothing that he could relate about St. Paul could have been more germane to his purpose. But the importance for him of the events in Jerusalem lay simply in the fact that

they were the stage in the apostle's career which immediately led up to his journey to Rome.

(7) Difficulty has been felt in St. Paul's action in taking upon him a vow,[1] at the request of St. James, and paying the expenses of four men who were completing their vows (xxi. 23b–26). The details are somewhat obscure,[2] but to behave as a Jew to Jews, especially when the need was represented to him as pressing, was entirely in accordance with his principles of freedom and charity: and this was a good opportunity of illustrating them by an object lesson.

There is, indeed, some difficulty in the parenthetical remark of St. James (v. 25), 'But concerning the Gentiles which have become believers we sent[3] deciding that they should keep themselves from that which is sacrificed to idols and blood and [anything] strangled and fornication.' If St. Paul needed this information he cannot have been present at the Council of Jerusalem, nor have been sent to Antioch with the bearers of the letter from the Council, as is stated in ch. xv, nor have published the decrees in Asia Minor with Barnabas and Timotheus, as related in xvi. 4. It is not impossible, however, to understand 'we sent' as meaning 'we sent, as you know'; in that case St. James says in effect, 'It is not as though I were asking you to show Jewish sympathies in connexion with Gentiles; they, of course, know the decrees that we sent to them; it is only Jews that are at present in question.' Still the passage is certainly awkward, and v. 25 may be gloss. Goguel, however, finds 'absolutely decisive reasons for not finding a redactional element in this small section' (op. cit., pp. 297–300).

(8) Difficulties increase when we come to St. Paul's speeches at Jerusalem and Caesarea. In chs. xxii and xxvi he relates to two different audiences (to the former in Aramaic) his vision on the Damascus road, accounts which agree broadly with the narrative in ch. ix, but differ markedly in some details, showing that the three narratives must have been dependent upon

---

[1] Apparently a Nazirite vow, and for the period of a week (xxi. 27).

[2] See A. H. McNeile's *St. Paul: his Life, Letters, and Christian Doctrine*, pp. 96 ff.; *Beginnings of Christianity*, iv, 1933, p. 273.

[3] ἀπεστείλαμεν (Westc.–Hort) B Ψ D 1898 467 614 Syr.hl Arm. Cop.bo is widely attested. The reading ἐπεστείλαμεν (Tisch.) 'we enjoined' has some strong support; but it may have been due to harmonization with xv. 20.

different sources.[1] If St. Luke had written the Acts in St. Paul's company he could, of course, have gained more accurate information on many points. But since he probably wrote it several years after his death, he was dependent upon such reports as he had heard, and on their basis wrote up the speeches without making them agree with the account given in his source for ch. ix. There is no reason for thinking that such a procedure, while possible for a compiler other than St. Luke, was impossible for St. Luke himself.

The speech of St. Paul before the Sanhedrin (xxiii. 1–6) is confused and obscure. In *v.* 6 he says, 'Concerning the hope [i.e. possibly the Messianic hope or that of resurrection] and the resurrection of the dead I am being tried'; but neither of these was the cause of his arrest.[2] Though St. Luke cannot have been present at the trial, he might have learned from St. Paul an accurate account of what he said when he was with him afterwards at Caesarea. But he probably did not think of writing his book, or of collecting material for it, till long afterwards, when a correct version of the speech was no longer available.

The speech before Felix (xxiv. 10–21), at which St. Luke can hardly have been present, falls into two parts, *vv.* 10–16 and *vv.* 17–21, which seem to be duplicate accounts of the same speech. Four chief points appear in both: (*a*) St. Paul's reason for going to Jerusalem was a religious one, in harmony with, and not opposed to, the Jewish religion. (*b*) Denial of making a disturbance. (*c*) Challenge to the prosecutors. (*d*) Admission regarding a resurrection. As before, it was open to St. Luke, as to any other compiler, to compose the speech on the basis of reports.

(9) Difficulties reach their climax in the narrative of the Council of Jerusalem (Acts xv). We have three accounts in

---

[1] Contrast K. Lake: 'The three accounts of the vision in Acts are almost identical; they clearly represent a single tradition, and probably a single source. The phraseology in all three is generally similar, but manifests Luke's tendency slightly to vary his phrases when repeating the same story.' *Beginnings of Christianity*, v (1933), note xv, p. 189.

[2] McNeile's *St. Paul*, p. 101. Contrast K. Lake, op. cit., note xvii, p. 214, who says that St. Paul was a reformer seizing his chance to preach, and that to St. Paul the Resurrection was central while his claim to be about the only true Pharisee was justifiable.

chs. i–xv and Galatians of visits of St. Paul to Jerusalem later than the private visit (ix. 26–30; Gal. i. 18 f.) mentioned above: (i) The Christians of Antioch sent alms during a famine by the hands of Barnabas and Saul (xi. 30); and, after an intervening narrative about St. Peter, xii. 25 appears to conclude the statement that the visit was made: 'So Barnabas and Saul returned to Jerusalem fulfilling[1] (πληρώσαντες) their ministry.' (ii) A visit with Barnabas and Titus, in which St. Paul consulted with the leaders of the Church, James, Cephas, and John, and it was agreed that they should evangelize Jews, and he and Barnabas Gentiles (Gal. ii. 1–10). (iii) A visit with Barnabas for the Council (Acts xv).

St. Paul is describing his movements for the purpose of showing that he did not receive his Gospel from men because he had held no communication with the apostles before they had formally admitted his right to evangelize uncircumcised Gentiles. And yet he seems to have omitted the famine visit. If so, it must have been because it involved no communication with the apostles, and did not affect his argument. The alms were sent to the 'elders', and the apostles are not mentioned. This is the view of those who, with Lightfoot,[2] identify the visit of Gal. ii with the Council visit. There is much similarity between the two accounts, both being visits concerned with the question of the circumcision of the Gentiles. Lightfoot thinks that St. Paul describes a private consultation with the leaders, which probably preceded the public meeting.

Others feel the difficulty of St. Paul's omission of the famine visit so much that they identify it, and not the Council visit, with the visit of Gal. ii. So, for example, Sir W. Ramsay,[3] C. W. Emmet,[4] and (formerly) K. Lake.[5] According to this

---

[1] The aorist participle is so difficult that Westc.–Hort mark the clause as a primitive corruption, and suggest 'from (ἐξ) Jerusalem'. C. D. Chambers (*J.T.S.* xxiv, 1923, pp. 183–7) thinks that the aorist participle following a verb of motion can express the *purpose* of the motion: 'returned to J. *to fulfil* their ministry', and cites as parallels xxv. 13; 2 Mac. xi. 36; 4 Mac. iii. 13; Heb. ix. 12 (the last should certainly be excluded). As the textual evidence favours εἰς not ἐξ, it may be suggested that St. Luke inadvertently wrote 'Jerusalem' after it instead of 'Antioch'.

[2] *Galatians*, p. 530.   [3] *St. Paul the Traveller*, &c., pp. 55 ff.
[4] *Galatians*, pp. xvi ff. *Beginnings of Christianity*, ii. 277 ff.
[5] *The Earlier Epistles of St. Paul*, 1911, pp. 279 ff.

view St. Luke's object in his narrative was quite different from St. Paul's. The former was interested in the broad-mindedness and kindly spirit shown by Gentile Christians in the young Church at Antioch, in sending contributions to Jewish Christians, while the sole object of the latter was to record the official recognition of his work among Gentiles given by the Jewish Christian leaders. And when they asked him only to remember the poor, he could add with special point 'which was the very thing that I was keen to do' (Gal. ii. 10), as his conveyance of the Gentile alms clearly showed. It is true that the narratives in Gal. ii and Acts xi are entirely different; but there is no reason why St. Paul should not be supposed to have done two entirely different things at Jerusalem.

The difficulty attaches even more strongly to a third suggestion that all three narratives (Gal. ii; Acts xi, xv) are accounts of the same visit; and that the two latter, reaching St. Luke from two different sources, were not unnaturally understood by him to refer to two different occasions. This is the view to which Jackson and Lake[1] incline, and Windisch[2] thinks it possible.

Streeter (p. 557 n.), following Renan, cuts the knot with the suggestion that 'the delegates who brought the famine contribution from Antioch (Acts xi. 30) were Barnabas and another; Luke erroneously imagined that other to be Barnabas's (future) colleague, Paul'.

But a further difficulty is felt with regard to St. Paul's account and the decree of the Council. The decree, besides giving Gentile Christians freedom from circumcision, was fourfold, according to the ordinary reading (xv. 20, 29). In D and some Latin writers πνικτοῦ (-τῶν), 'things strangled', is omitted, producing the appearance of moral injunctions against idolatry, murder, and fornication. But this as 'a sort of moral catechism', as Windisch says, 'would be noticeably incomplete. What mention is made of theft, avarice, litigiousness, lying—prominent vices among the Gentiles—which are combated everywhere else?' And it may be added that 'abstain (ἀπέχεσθαι) from blood' is a strange equivalent for 'do no

---

[1] *Beginnings of Christianity*, ii. 322. Cf. Lake, ibid. v, note xvi, pp. 195 ff.
[2] Ibid. ii. 322.

murder'. He rightly adheres to the ordinary text, i.e. four rules bearing on Jewish ritual observance.[1] But he thinks it impossible that the story of the Council which laid down these rules was written by St. Luke, or is historical, because St. Paul makes no mention of the decrees in writing to the Galatian Gentiles about the Law, and shows in 1 Cor. viii–x that neither he nor the Corinthians knew anything about a decree on idol-foods. Of those who hold this view some think that the story is pure fiction, but this is improbable from the fact that the writer of Rev. ii. 24 ('I lay upon you no other burden'), who could hardly have quoted from the Acts, seems to have known the decrees. Others suggest that a Council was held after Galatians and 1 Corinthians were written, but antedated in the Acts. Or that it is related in its right place, but that St. Paul and Barnabas were not present at it. But do any of these conclusions necessarily follow? The letter containing the decree was sent only to the Gentiles in Antioch, and generally in the province of Syria and Cilicia (xv. 23), i.e. to those who were in immediate contact with the Jewish nation in its own country, and therefore with Jewish Christians with whom a *modus vivendi* was necessary.[2] No one can suppose that St. Paul liked the decrees, but—in respect of Gentiles in close contact with a large number of Jewish Christians—he submitted to them in the spirit of charity which he enjoins in 1 Cor. x. 19–33. Enlightened Christians knew that an idol was nothing at all (viii. 4, x. 20); but 'weak', i.e. scrupulous, Christians felt, as pagans did, that things offered to idols were offered to demons; and in that case they were pollution. Therefore, while all things were lawful for the enlightened Christian, all things were not expedient. But he was not under the least necessity, in writing to Corinth, of citing the decrees, of which the Corinthians had probably never heard, and which did not

---

[1] Cf. C. S. C. Williams, *Alterations to the Text of the Synoptic Gospels and Acts*, pp. 72–75. The Chester Beatty papyrus P^{45} omits the reference to 'fornication' but not to 'what is strangled'.

[2] This throws doubt on the statement in xvi. 4 that 'as they passed through the cities'—whether of south or of north Galatia—St. Paul with Barnabas 'delivered to them the decrees to keep'. The decrees were not laid down as binding on every Gentile who should thereafter become a Christian. It was a provision for a special need arising out of the Antioch mission. The verse is probably an erroneous addition and was not the work of St. Luke.

concern them. In Galatians there was even less reason for citing them, because he was writing from a wholly different point of view. Even if the decrees were published in Galatia on his second tour, the refraining in a spirit of charity from four things which were displeasing to Jewish Christians, in order to preserve the *modus vivendi*, was quite alien to his argument against the acquiring of 'righteousness' by obedience to Jewish ordinances.

These difficulties, which many have felt with regard to the decrees, would, indeed, disappear if Galatians was written before the Council (see p. 147) and reflects the beginning of the controversy with the Judaizers at Antioch after the first tour and before the apostle went to Jerusalem. This has the further advantage of placing St. Peter's action which occasioned St. Paul's rebuke (Gal. ii. 11–14) before and not after the Council, thus exonerating him from what St. Paul felt to be flagrant disloyalty to the agreement which he had taken a leading part in bringing about. And 'certain persons from James' (*v.* 12) are thus the same as 'certain persons who came down from Judaea' (Acts xv. 1). Turner[1] and Zahn[2] feel the difficulty of this disloyalty so much that, though they identify the visit of Gal. ii with the Council visit, they think that St. Paul, in giving his account of the rebuke, is referring to an incident of an earlier date.

But 'disloyalty' is hardly a fair word to use. St. Peter had been broad-minded enough to visit the Gentile Cornelius and baptize him when the Spirit was poured upon him; and he had been able to defend himself in Jerusalem when his action was disputed. Then he took the further strong step of going to Antioch and eating with Gentile Christians, until, in Streeter's words (p. 547):

Under pressure from 'certain who came from James', Peter at Antioch went back on his pro-Gentile liberalism. It was doubtless represented to him that if he continued thus openly to break the law he would ruin all possibility of converting 'the circumcision' to Christ. Peter has been much abused for giving way; but in all probability those who urged this judged the situation correctly. Peter was really face to face with the alternative of, either ceasing

---

[1] Hastings's *D.B*, i. 423 f.   [2] *Galatians*, pp. 110 f.

to eat and drink with Gentiles, or wrecking that mission to the circumcised which he felt to be his primary call (Gal. ii. 9). Is he to be blamed because he declined to take that risk? . . . The fact is that the relations of Jew and Gentile since the persecution of Antiochus Epiphanes and the Maccabean revolt had brought things to such a pass that to surrender the obligation of the Law meant the failure of the Jewish mission, while to retain it was to sacrifice the Gentile. It was one of those tragic situations that do sometimes occur when the best men for the best motives feel compelled to differ upon a vital issue.

Such are some of the problems which arise round the question of the historical value and the authorship of the Acts. They are many and complex. But a final consideration in favour of the Lucan authorship must not be lost sight of, namely, that if there are things which it is difficult to believe that a companion of St. Paul could have written, or omitted, it is even more difficult to think, in many cases, that they could have been written or omitted by a later compiler who would presumably be in possession of the epistles, and could keep all his statements in harmony with them. Though there is little certain evidence that anyone in the sub-Apostolic age quoted Acts (see below, p. 326), yet W. L. Knox[1] can argue:

We have to imagine a compiler who is interested enough in Paul to write his life, yet does not know his Epistles, since he has never read Galatians. Yet he is early enough for his works to be accepted by the author of 2 Tim., who again is early enough for Ignatius to be familiar with it and to treat it as Scripture, while Ignatius was martyred before A.D. 117. Yet again he is not early enough to have access to any authentic account of Paul's travels or Paul's theology.

That the Acts is a compilation is clear, at least in the earlier half; and it is unsafe to assume that a companion of St. Paul must always have avoided what was inaccurate in the sources from which he drew. But if St. Luke himself was the compiler at a later date in his life, several years after St. Paul's death, the great majority of the phenomena are sufficiently explained,

[1] *The Acts of the Apostles*, p. 41. He compares Ignatius, *Trall.* vii. 2 with 2 Tim. i. 3; *Philadelph.* ii. 2 with Jn. x. 12, Acts xx. 29, and 2 Tim. iii. 6; *Smyrn.* i. 1 with 2 Tim. iii. 15 and ix. 1 with 2 Tim. ii. 25 and x. 2 with 2 Tim. i. 16; *Polyc.* vi. 2 with 2 Tim. ii. 4. He takes 2 Tim. iii. 11 to point back to Acts iii. 50, xiv. 5 and 19.

room being left open for small additions and alterations. The correctness of a large number of his details in matters of archaeology, geography, and local politics has become increasingly evident in recent years, largely owing to the researches of Sir W. Ramsay. But correct details are only the outward framework of the record. The historical value of the book as a whole lies, not in the accuracy of the words or actions of the persons in the drama, or the exhaustiveness of its contents, but in the general picture which the author gives of the Christianity of the time, with its endowment of spiritual enthusiasm, the conditions under which it struggled, and its rapid advance from Jerusalem through a large part of the empire to Rome.

BOOKS

F. C. Burkitt, *Christian Beginnings*, 1924.

M. Goguel, *Introduction au Nouveau Testament*, iii, 1922.

A. von Harnack, *The Acts of the Apostles* (transl. Wilkinson, 1909).

F. J. A. Hort, *Judaistic Christianity*, 1894.

F. J. F. Jackson and K. Lake, *The Beginnings of Christianity*, vols. i–v, 1920–33.

H. Lietzmann, *The Beginnings of the Christian Church* (transl. B. L. Woolf, 1937).

A. H. McNeile, *St. Paul, his Life, Letters, and Christian Doctrine*, 1920.

J. Moffatt, *Introduction to the Literature of the New Testament*, 3rd ed., 1918.

Sir W. M. Ramsay, *The Church in the Roman Empire*, 1893, and *St. Paul the Traveller and Roman Citizen*, 1895.

B. H. Streeter, *The Four Gospels*, 1924, ch. xviii.

C. C. Torrey, *The Composition and Date of Acts*, 1916.

C. H. Turner, *The Chronology of the New Testament* (in Hastings's *D.B.*, vol. i).

J. Weiss, *History of Primitive Christianity*, vols. i and ii (transl. 1937).

COMMENTARIES

A. W. F. Blunt (1922), F. F. Bruce (1951), W. M. Furneaux (1912), H. J. Holtzmann (3rd ed., 1901), F. J. F. Jackson (1931), K. Lake and H. J. Cadbury (*Beginnings of Christianity*, iv, 1933), A. Loisy (1920), T. E. Page (1918), R. B. Rackham (10th ed., 1925), H. H. Wendt (9th ed., 1913).

VI

THE EPISTLES OF ST. PAUL

EVEN including Philemon, which deals with the private matters of an individual, all St. Paul's writings that have come down to us are addressed to Christian communities, and intended to be read aloud (1 Thess. v. 27; Col. iv. 16). Most of them are real 'letters', dealing with the particular circumstances and needs of particular Churches, but the Apostle made them the vehicle of a large amount of doctrinal and homiletic instruction. The evolution of didactic epistles, or epistolary homilies, and the adoption of them by Christians, is described by Moffatt,[1] and the ordinary form and method of ancient Greek letter-writing by G. Milligan.[2]

The exact dates of St. Paul's life are not yet determined. For those which are here given for the epistles an alternative of a year earlier throughout is possible. The chronological position of Galatians and Philippians is disputed, and also of certain portions, e.g. the two parts of 2 Corinthians (chs. i–ix and x–xiii), and within the former part vi. 14–vii. 1; also Rom. xvi, and Phil. iii. 2–iv. 1. But the following is the order in which they are usually studied:

	A.D.
1 and 2 Thessalonians	51
1 Corinthians	55 or 56
2 Corinthians	56
Galatians	56 (?49)
Romans	57
Colossians, Philemon, Ephesians	c. 61
Philippians	c. 62 (?54–56)

These dates are determined by working backwards and forwards, according to indications in the Acts and Epistles, from the midsummer of 52 or 51, at which time we learn from an inscription found at Delphi that Gallio (see Acts xviii. 12) entered upon office as proconsul of Achaia.[3]

[1] *Introd. Lit. N.T.*, pp. 44–50.   [2] *Thessalonians*, 1908, pp. 121–30.
[3] See Deissmann, *St. Paul*, Appendix I, and A. H. McNeile's *St. Paul*, pp.

A. FIRST GROUP OF EPISTLES

§ I. I THESSALONIANS

Throughout his life St. Paul cherished the warmest affection for his converts in Macedonia, which he first visited in the course of his second missionary tour. The spiritual guidance which had led him to Troas (Acts xvi. 6–8), and the vision which he had there of the man of Macedonia (v. 9), caused him to take the important step of enlarging his labours beyond the areas of Syria and Asia Minor. In the towns of Macedonia he found audiences more simple-minded, less sophisticated, than those in Asia Minor, who were beginning to fall under the influence of the rising tide of theosophical syncretism from the East and Egypt. His converts at Philippi and Thessalonica became attached to him in the closest friendship; and those in the latter town, as he says himself (1 Thess. i. 7 f.), became very widely known for their Christian devotion. He must have stayed with them for some time, because he settled down to his hand labour (cf. Acts xviii. 3, xx. 34) in order to maintain himself and not be burdensome to them as a guest (1 Thess. ii. 9; 2 Thess. iii. 8), and because during his stay his devoted converts at Philippi sent him supplies at least twice (Phil. iv. 16). But at last the Jews of the place, enraged at his success, incited the populace against him and Silas, who accompanied him. They fortunately were not able to lay hands on them, but Jason, in whose house they seem to have lodged, and some other Christians, were brought up before the politarchs, the local magistrates, on a charge of sedition against Caesar. Jason was bound over to keep the peace, and St. Paul and Silas (with their young companion Timothy, whom St. Luke does not mention) were hurried away by their friends (Acts xvii. 5–10). But his converts continued to suffer at the hands of the Jews (1 Thess. ii. 14 f.). After he had arrived, via Beroea and Athens, at Corinth, Silas and Timothy rejoined him (Acts xviii. 5; see p. 114), and Timothy, whom he had sent back to them from Athens, brought him a report of their spiritual and

---

xv–xviii, cf. W. L. Knox, *St. Paul and the Church of Jerusalem*, 1925, p. 278, n. 36. Knox gives reasons for thinking that Gallio's term of office ran from July A.D. 51 to July A.D. 52.

temporal position which relieved his mind of great anxiety and drew from him this letter.

Writing, as he always did, out of the fullness of his heart, he made no attempt at literary or artistic arrangement. But the letter falls naturally into two parts: *A*. Personal matter; *B*. Instruction.

In *A* he utters a thanksgiving for their zeal and endurance (i. 2–10), which was itself a proof of what his work for them had been, and gave him the opportunity of defending himself against false charges which had been made against his preaching and manner of life among them (ii. 1–12). He thanks God again for their endurance under Jewish persecution (ii. 13–16), and recalls his relations with them since his banishment, the mission of Timothy, and his report (ii. 17–iii. 10), concluding with a prayer (iii. 11–13).

In *B* he warns them against immorality, which was all too easy for newly converted Christians, especially Gentiles, surrounded by pagan life (iv. 1–8), and exhorts them to increase in mutual love, to keep quietly to themselves instead of mixing themselves up with the pagan society of the city, and to work with their hands, which would create a good impression among non-Christians and make them independent of charity (iv. 9–12). He had learnt from Timothy's report that because Christ's Advent, which they were momentarily expecting, had not yet occurred, and some of their number had died, they were in doubt and distress as to whether the dead would share in it. He assures them that they will, foretelling the Lord's descent from heaven, the rising of the Christian dead, and then the rapture of the risen and the living together 'in clouds to meet the Lord in the air; and so shall we ever be with the Lord' (iv. 13–18). He adds that sober watchfulness is needed because the Advent will be sudden (v. 1–11). And after some miscellaneous injunctions as to their manner of life as Christians (v. 12–22), a short conclusion brings the letter to an end.

Apart from some difficulties of language, which are discussed in commentaries, there is little that calls for special attention except the apostle's teaching on the Advent, for which reference should be made to R. H. Charles's work.[1] Its

---

[1] *Eschatology, Hebrew, Jewish and Christian*, 1913, pp. 437–75.

delay had begun to cause heartburnings, and St. Paul found himself constrained, as the years went on, to lay continually less stress on its immediate imminence and more on mystical union with Christ. And at the end of his life the thought of the Parousia, in the Jewish sense of a catastrophic event at a future moment of time, had practically faded from his mind.[1]

§ 2. 2 THESSALONIANS

This epistle, apart from the autographic conclusion (iii. 17 f.), falls into three parts, each concluding with a prayer (i. 11 f.; ii. 16 f.; iii. 16): *A*. A thanksgiving for the zeal and endurance of the readers (i. 3–5) leads to the thought of their recompense at the Advent of the Lord Jesus with His angels, when sinners will be destroyed (i. 6–10). *B*. The final End has not yet begun; the Advent must be preceded by the Lawless One, who is at present checked by a hindering power, but whom Jesus will destroy when He comes (ii. 1–12). This leads to a thanksgiving for the spiritual privileges of the readers, and an exhortation to hold fast the Christian tradition (ii. 13–15). *C*. A request for their prayers, and expressions of confidence (iii. 1–5). Injunctions to work quietly for their own living, and to avoid and admonish those Christians who do not (iii. 6–15).

PLACE OF WRITING. The opening salutation includes the names of Silvanus (= Silas) and Timothy. Since they had both rejoined St. Paul at Corinth (see above), and both are referred to as preaching with him there (2 Cor. i. 19), it is a natural conclusion that Corinth was the place where this epistle, as well as the preceding, was written. But the conclusion is uncertain. Silvanus at this point disappears from history altogether, and Timothy disappears for some time. St. Paul, after staying more than eighteen months at Corinth, returned to Syria via Ephesus, visited Jerusalem, spent some time at Antioch, passed through cities he had evangelized in Asia Minor ('the Galatic region and Phrygia'), and returned to Ephesus, where, after more than two years of the apostle's work, Timothy reappears in St. Luke's narrative (Acts xix. 22). Timothy, therefore, may have been left at Ephesus when

---

[1] But cf. Phil. i. 6, 10; ii. 16; iii. 20 f.; iv. 5, Col. i. 5, iii. 4.

St. Paul sailed thither from Corinth. But it is equally possible that he and Silvanus remained with the apostle throughout, in which case, so far as the inclusion of their names in the salutation is concerned, the epistle might have been written at any time in the four years or so between Timothy's arrival at Corinth and the mention of him at Ephesus. Moffatt cites iii. 2 as indicating Corinth: 'Pray, brethren, for us, . . . that we may be delivered from wicked and evil men'; but 'wicked and evil men' might point equally well to Ephesus.

RELATION TO I THESSALONIANS. The epistle is somewhat of an enigma. The difficulties which it raises are mainly three: 1. In a large part of it there is a marked similarity of language and subject-matter to those of the First Epistle.[1] This would be natural if St. Paul were writing soon afterwards to *another* Church. But why should he write two letters to the *same* Church in terms so similar, and at an interval of time so short, that one was an echo of the other? If, on the other hand, the interval was long—say three years or more—the similarity requires us to suppose that he re-read his copy of the first letter and imitated its language, which is very improbable. 2. But with the similarity there is a difference in tone which can be felt rather than described. The epistle is less frankly warm and affectionate than the first, more formal, more 'official and severe' (Milligan); and greater emphasis is laid on the apostle's teaching and example (ii. 15; iii. 6–14). If there was a considerable interval between the two writings, the news which the apostle received (cf. iii. 11) of the Thessalonians could well account for the change. But if they were written almost at the same time, the difficulty is greater. 3. While eschatology is a feature in both, St. Paul not only devotes a larger space to it in the second epistle (i. 7–10; ii. 1–12), but treats the subject very differently. In the First Epistle the Thessalonians, as said above, were troubled as to whether Christians who had died would share in Christ's Parousia. In the Second, the difficulty that has to be met is described in the words (ii. 1, 2), 'But I ask you, brethren, concerning the Parousia of our Lord Jesus Christ and our gathering together unto Him, that ye be not hastily shaken from your mind nor frightened either by spirit [i.e. a communi-

[1] See Milligan, *Thessalonians*, pp. lxxxi f.

cation delivered by one in a spiritual ecstasy] or by word or by
letter as purporting to be by us,[1] as that the day of the Lord is
[already] present'. The last word ἐνέστηκεν must not be rendered 'is imminent', cf. Kittel, *Theologisches Wörterbuch*, ii,
p. 540 (Oepke) ; of the imminence of the Parousia St. Paul was
himself deeply convinced at this period of his life. But the
readers had, from some cause, begun to think that the eschatological world-crisis had actually begun, perhaps because they
misunderstood the 'realized eschatology' according to which
the Kingdom had already come in some sense with Jesus' first
advent. And the apostle was obliged to repeat, perhaps in
different and clearer language, what he had taught them orally
when he was with them (ii. 5), and to beg them (*v*. 15) to
adhere to that teaching given by word of mouth (διὰ λόγου),
and also to what he had told them in his previous letter (δι'
ἐπιστολῆς ἡμῶν). It would not take long for some in Thessalonica, who had misunderstood his teaching, to rouse an un-
healthy nervous excitement in the community by fostering the
idea that the events of the final Drama had begun. And it is
perhaps natural that a touch of sharpness and frigidness should
enter into St. Paul's repetition of his teaching, of which a
mistaken—possibly with some a malicious—use had been
made.

'Paul may well have received a second messenger saying
that a number of Thessalonians believed that the day of the
Lord had already dawned and that those who were unwilling
to work had become more troublesome' (A. D. Nock[2]). 'A
sufficient explanation would be that the evils of which St. Paul
complains in 1 Thess. iv. 10 seemed so serious that after sending the first letter, he decided to follow it up with another more
severe in tone to make certain of suppressing them. But the
data for a full explanation are lacking' (W. L. Knox[3]).

Other explanations have been suggested. 1. J. C. West,[4] following Ewald and others, argues that the Second epistle preceded the First, and places the writing of it at Beroea. He says,

---

[1] It is very likely that the words 'as purporting to be by us' refer to all three
—ecstatic utterance, preaching, and a letter.

[2] *St. Paul* (1938), p. 160.

[3] *St. Paul and the Church of Jerusalem*, p. 281.

[4] *J.T.S.* xv, 1913, pp. 66–74.

'No misunderstanding on the part of the Thessalonians of anything in 1 Thessalonians can be discovered which will fit the
case'. But according to the above explanation, following St.
Paul's own words, what they had misunderstood was not his
first letter but his oral teaching given when he was with them.
West holds that the eschatological teaching in 1 Thessalonians
represents 'a wider and more Gentile outlook', while in 2 Thessalonians it is 'crude and Judaistic', and that the latter must
have preceded the former. But is it possible to suppose that
St. Paul's ideas developed so quickly in the brief interval
between leaving Beroea and arriving at Corinth? In any
case his oral teaching preceded any epistle, and it is that
which he expressly claims to be repeating. It is true that the
Jewish scenic descriptions of terror and retribution, and the
Jewish tradition, in a Christianized form, of the Man of
Lawlessness, the devilish counterpart to the Messiah, are to
be seen in the Second Epistle. But the need, as said above,
was different. In 1 Thessalonians his converts required comforting concerning the dead; in 2 Thessalonians his teaching
on the Parousia in general, which they had begun to mis-
represent, had to be reinforced. Two further considerations
favour the priority of 1 Thessalonians: firstly, the fact that
St. Paul's references in 1 Thess. ii. 17–iii. 6 to events which
had occurred since he left are more natural in the first
letter that he wrote after his departure than in a second;
secondly, the mention of 'the token in every epistle' (2 Thess.
iii. 17), to warn the readers against a letter, or letters, purporting to be by him, is rather more suitable in a second letter than
in a first.

2. Burkitt[1] thinks that both letters were drafted by Silvanus
(Silas), and that St. Paul approved them and added 1 Thess.
ii. 18 and 2 Thess. iii. 17 with his own hand.

3. Harnack suggests that the Gentile and the Jewish Christians at Thessalonica formed distinct groups, to which the two
epistles were written respectively. This is attractive, and would
explain some of the difficulties, and the Judaic language of the
Second Epistle. But it is a conjecture without evidence. The

[1] *Christian Beginnings*, pp. 128–32; cf. E. G. Selwyn, *The First Epistle of St.
Peter*, 1946, pp. 14–17.

salutation in each case is 'To the Church of the Thessalonians', with no hint of distinct groups; and the injunction in 1 Thess. v. 27 is to read the epistle to *all* the Christians.

4. Many writers have denied the genuineness of 2 Thessalonians. It is thought to be a later work by a Paulinist (possibly Silvanus), partly on account of the difficulties mentioned above —the similarities and differences—and partly on the ground of style and language. But this raises difficulties as great as those which it solves. The Thessalonians possessed, and no doubt knew almost by heart, the First Epistle. And we have to suppose that after St. Paul's death someone wrote an epistle addressed to the same Church, consisting partly of a cento of phrases from the First Epistle, and partly of some new and startling eschatology which he represented St. Paul as having taught by word of mouth in Thessalonica. And the boldness, or worse, of adding iii. 17 is greater than we can admit to be possible, even in an age when pseudonymity was a recognized literary artifice.

Some have gone so far as to reject the First Epistle on such grounds as the suspicious similarity of its language to that of 1, 2 Corinthians, the discrepancies between its historical notices and those in the Acts, the presence of words not used elsewhere by St. Paul, and the absence of distinctively Pauline ideas about the Law and the Cross. The reader is referred to the discussion on these points by Moffatt.[1] The similarity to 1, 2 Corinthians in language, in the apostle's attitude of self-defence, and in some of the difficulties felt by the readers is undoubted, and constitutes an argument for the genuineness of 1 Thessalonians. It leads W. Hadorn[2] to date it in the long stay at Ephesus in close conjunction with 1, 2 Corinthians. He thinks, however, that 2 Thessalonians preceded it, and can belong to the first stay at Corinth. But the general situation of the two epistles is too similar to make this interval and difference of place probable. This late date for the First Epistle, or both, is 'forbidden by the fact that in 1 Thessalonians the impressions of the first contact are still so fresh, much fresher than in 1 Corinthians or Philippians . . . and it is wholly improbable

---

[1] *Intr. Lit. N.T.*, pp. 70 ff.
[2] *Zeitschr. f. d. neutest. Wiss.*, xx, 1919, pp. 67–71.

that Paul should have sent no letter to the Thessalonians during his eighteen months in Corinth' (Windisch[1]).

5. It is suggested that the Second Epistle is composite. A pre-Christian or Jewish-Christian apocalypse has been incorporated by a Paulinist, or, conversely, an epistle has been built up round the Pauline fragment ii. 1–12, or a letter by St. Paul has been edited and partly rewritten. Moffatt (op. cit., p. 81) rightly says that 'little is really gained by postulating such a restricted activity on the part of the editor. For his purpose it would have been as simple and more effective to compose an entire epistle, and the section ii. 1–12 is so cardinal a feature of the canonical writing that the latter may be said to stand or fall with it.'

6. M. Goguel[2] adopts a theory suggested but discarded by Harnack that 2 Thessalonians was written to the Church at Beroea. Christians there seem to have been mainly converted Jews, 'more noble' than those in Thessalonica, who examined the Scriptures daily for Testimonies (Acts xvii. 11). Eschatological teaching to them needed a different emphasis. Though the Lord is at hand, certain Signs must first be seen, cf. Mk. xiii. The literary relationship between 1 Thessalonians and 2 Thessalonians would be explained if both letters were penned one after the other.

B. SECOND GROUP OF EPISTLES

§ 3. 1 CORINTHIANS

CIRCUMSTANCES. The First Epistle was written from Ephesus. This is shown in xvi. 8, 9. After saying that he would visit his readers when he had passed through Macedonia, and hoped to stay some time with them, the Apostle adds, 'But I am staying on at Ephesus till Pentecost, for a great and effectual door is open to me'. In keeping with this he sends salutations (*v.* 19) from 'the Churches of Asia', and from Aquila and Priscilla, who, according to Acts xviii. 18 f., had travelled with him to Ephesus. He had left them there, and had travelled to

---

[1] *Harvard Theol. Rev.* xv, 1922, pp. 173 f. The whole number is a very useful summary of German work on the New Testament, 1914–20.

[2] Op. cit., pp. 335–7.

Jerusalem and then to Antioch. After some time he retraversed the route which he had taken in his second tour, through Derbe, Lystra, Iconium, and Pisidian Antioch, and arrived at Ephesus.

The time of writing is doubtful, but his own words show that he wrote shortly before a Pentecost, say early in May; and he implies, in xvi. 1, 2, that the Corinthian collections for the poor of Jerusalem had not yet been begun. But in 2 Cor. viii. 10; ix. 2, he speaks of the Corinthians as having begun the collection 'last year' (ἀπὸ πέρυσι). The relation between the dates of the two epistles depends upon this phrase. 2 Corinthians was written from Macedonia after he had left Ephesus (see below), and after that he was three months at Corinth (Acts xx. 3) before leaving Philippi for Jerusalem 'after the days of Unleavened Bread' (v. 6). This would be at about the end of March, so that 2 Corinthians must have been written in the previous November or perhaps earlier. Now when St. Paul says 'last year' he may have reckoned the year either as a Roman from January or as a Jew from September–October. In the former case 'last year' for one writing in November would mean the previous December at latest. But in the latter it might mean any time up to the autumn New Year, just over a month before he wrote, though the context renders this improbable. If, however, he arrived in Macedonia and wrote 2 Corinthians in September, just before the autumn New Year, then 'a year ago' would mean that the collection was begun in the previous September at the latest. Thus if 2 Corinthians was written in September–November, 1 Corinthians was written in the spring either of the same, or of the previous, Roman year, i.e. five or six months before, or a year and five or six months before.[1]

After dealing with the first matter that required attention, party factions at Corinth, he states that he has already dispatched Timothy to Corinth, and announces his intention of visiting them himself (iv. 18 f., 21; xi. 34). Meanwhile he wanted to stay on at Ephesus till Pentecost, and was sending them this letter, which would evidently reach them before Timothy. He asks them to receive him well and not despise

---

[1] M. Goguel discusses the date more fully (op. cit. iv. 2, pp. 144–6) but he regards the two letters as composite (ibid., p. 86).

him, and to forward him in peace on his journey back to him with the brethren, who were probably the bearers of the letter (xvi. 10, 11). This seems to be the same mission of Timothy as that mentioned in Acts xix. 22, where it is said that Timothy and Erastus were sent to Macedonia. This would explain why the letter—sent straight across the sea—would reach Corinth first. But St. Paul does not mention Erastus, and Acts does not relate Timothy's arrival at Corinth. It is not certain, therefore, that he arrived there; something may have occurred to prevent him from doing what he was sent to do. St. Luke was not in possession of all the facts of this troubled period. We know only that Timothy was in Macedonia when 2 Corinthians was written, for he joins in the opening salutation. But whether from Timothy or from other sources St. Paul heard news that made him pay the visit to Corinth which he had intended, of which Acts says nothing. But the report was evidently so bad that he felt it imperative to go to them as soon as possible. So, on the hypothesis that 2 Corinthians is a unity as it stands now in our Canon, he made up his mind to visit them *twice*, once immediately, crossing direct by sea from Ephesus, and then again after going from them to Macedonia (2 Cor. i. 15, 16). The former of these was paid; but the visit was so painful that he could not bring himself to go a second time. There was thus a double change of plan: he did not stay in Ephesus till Pentecost, and he did not visit Corinth twice. For this he was accused of vacillation, against which he defends himself in 2 Cor. i. 17–ii. 1. His reason for refraining from the second visit is given in i. 23: 'But I call God as a witness upon my soul that to spare you I came no more[1] (οὐκέτι ἦλθον) to Corinth', and ii. 1: 'I determined this for myself that I would not come again to you with sorrow.' The painful visit, not recorded in the Acts, was the second that he had actually paid them; he went to them for the first time on his second tour (Acts xviii. 1–17), when he wrote to the Thessalonians. Hence he says, 'This is the third time I am ready to come to you' (2 Cor. xii. 14); 'This is the third time I am coming to you . . . I say

---

[1] 'I forbear to come' (R.V.), and 'I came not as yet' (A.V.) are incorrect renderings, which seem to have been occasioned by the desire to avoid the admission that St. Paul paid a visit to Corinth unrecorded by St. Luke.

beforehand as [I said] when I was present the second time'
(xiii. 1, 2). The visit was the more painful because it proved a
sad failure. St. Paul returned, as we have seen, to Ephesus
instead of going to Macedonia, and in the depths of depression
wrote a sorrowful letter (2 Cor. ii. 4), which he even feared
might have been too stern (vii. 8). It was taken by Titus. Then
St. Paul went up via Troas to Macedonia, and at last, to his
infinite relief, Titus came with the good news that the letter
had done its work and produced in them a repentant sorrow
(vii. 6–16). This made him write what we know as 2 Corinthians. The reason for the painful visit and this sorrowful letter
is not clear. It is perhaps something quite unknown to us; but
if it is one of the subjects with which 1 Corinthians deals, it may
be either the factions, or the crime of incest, or the litigation in
heathen courts. Possibly the last two were connected; some
have thought that it was the injured father who brought the
son before a heathen court.[1] Many have thought that part of
the sorrowful letter is preserved in 2 Cor. x–xiii. 10; others that
it is lost, and that 2 Corinthians is a unity (see below).

THE UNITY OF 1 CORINTHIANS. One exception, at least,
to its unity is widely recognized. 1 Corinthians is not the first
letter that the apostle wrote to the Church of Corinth. In
1 Cor. v. 9 he says, 'I wrote to you in my letter not to be mixed
up with fornicators'; and there is nothing in the opening
chapters of the epistle to which the words could refer. He
seems to have heard that some of them were behaving in an
unworthy manner with regard to the immorality with which
Corinth was saturated. But when he wrote to protest, they had
misunderstood him, and he was obliged to explain that he did
not mean that they must separate themselves entirely from all
fornicators, otherwise they would have to leave the world
altogether, but that they must keep clear of any *brother*, i.e.
Christian, who was guilty of the sin. It is very probable that a
fragment of this letter has been preserved in 2 Cor. vi. 14–
vii. 1, a passage which might have been so misunderstood, and
which breaks the close connexion of thought between vi. 13,
'be ye also enlarged' (i.e. enlarge your hearts towards me),
and vii. 2, 'make room for us' (*sc.* in your hearts).

[1] See J. H. Bernard, *Studia Sacra*, 1917, ch. ix.

Furthermore, J. Weiss[1] drew attention to 'different points of view or attitudes' in 1 Corinthians which led him to split this letter into three parts: '*A*. The rigorous demands concerning idolatry and fornication, the discussion about the unveiling of women and the common meals (x. 1–23, vi. 12–20, xi. 2–34, xvi. 7?, 8 f., 20 f.?). *B*. 1. The vigorous expositions on marriage, eating idol meat, Paul's renunciation, spiritual gifts, resurrection (vii, viii, ix, x. 24–xi. 1, xii–xv, xvi. 1–6 (7?), 16–19?). *B*. 2. The expositions on parties, the incestuous person, the law-suits before heathen magistrates (i. 1–9, i. 10–vi. 11, xvi. 10–14, 22–24). Similarly J. Héring[2] contrasts iv. 19 with xvi. 5 f., the references to arrival, and x. 1–22, the rigorist attitude to pagan sacrifice, with viii, x. 23–xi. 1, the liberal attitude to 'weak' or scrupulous brethren; and he notes that ix picks up abruptly the problem of the apostolate already discussed in i–iv. He splits the letter into two: *A*. i–viii, x. 23–xi. 1, xvi. 1–4, 10–14 and *B*. ix, x. 1–22, xi. 2–xv, and the rest of xvi (xiii 'étant d'ailleurs de toute manière un hors-d'œuvre'!). M. Goguel (see below on 2 Cor.) divides 1 Corinthians rather differently.

There is no textual evidence at all in favour of these partition views. The oldest papyrus of Paul's letters, the third-century Chester Beatty codex P[46] treats each of the two letters as a unity in the order familiar to us. However, it is possible that the first collector of St. Paul's Corinthian correspondence found his material on different pieces of papyrus and put together two letters as best he could and that all our textual evidence is derived from his arrangement. It is equally possible that St. Paul was great enough to be inconsistent at some points and that he did not have the thoroughness of the German or the lucidity of the French mind.

CONTENTS. Taken as it stands, 1 Corinthians is the most intensely practical of all St. Paul's letters. It was written to meet immediate needs of his converts, of which he heard from, apparently, three sources. 1. He was informed by 'them of Chloe' (i.e. probably Christian slaves of a Corinthian lady who had come with her, or had been sent by her, to Ephesus) that

---

[1] *The History of Primitive Christianity* (Eng. trans., 1937), i. 340 f.
[2] *La première épître de S. Paul aux Corinthiens*, 1948, p. 11.

the Corinthian Church was rent by party factions. He deals with this in i. 10–iv. 21. He learnt, probably from the same source, that a Christian in Corinth had committed incest with his stepmother (ch. v), that Christians were bringing lawsuits against Christians before heathen, Roman, courts (vi. 1–11), and that with an abuse of Christian 'liberty' some were yielding to the prevalent pagan vice of fornication (vi. 12–20). 2. But after dealing, with passionate eagerness, with these four matters which had reached him by report, he had to discuss some points apparently raised by the Corinthians themselves in a letter brought by Stephanas, Fortunatus, and Achaicus. He refers to each point in turn with the same formula :

'Now concerning what you wrote'		[with regard to marriage]	
			vii. 1–24
,,	,,	virgins'[1]	vii. 25–40
,,	,,	idol-foods'	viii. 1–xi. 1
,,	,,	Spirit-filled persons'	xii. 1–xiv. 40
,,	,,	the collection'	xvi. 1–11 (combined with some personal matters)
,,	,,	Apollos'	xvi. 12.

3. In addition to these the apostle treats of three other matters on which he learnt, probably from the bearers of their letter to him, that rebuke and counsel were needed: Irregularity, of which some women were guilty, with regard to dress at public worship (xi. 2–16); Unworthy behaviour on the part of some of the richer Christians in the eating of the food at the Eucharistic feasts (xi. 17–34); Denial by some Christians, probably Gentiles only, that there would be a Resurrection of the dead,

---

[1] In vii. 36–40 'daughter' has been added to the R.V. translation on the assumption that the problem was, should a father allow his unmarried daughter to marry before the Parousia? but the reference may be to the practice in pre-monastic days of men and women, dedicated to celibacy, living under the same roof, cf. Hermas, *Sim.* ix. 11; Eusebius, *H.E.* vii. 30. 12 and Canon 3 of the Council of Nicaea; cf. M. Maude, 'Who were the B'nai Q'yâmâ?', *J.T.S.* xxxvi, 1935, pp. 13–21. (Contrast Allo, *1 Corinthians*, Excursus, vii, and E. Alzas, *Revue de théologie et de philosophie*, xxxviii, 1950, pp. 226–32.) If so, the problem was, should a virgin dedicated to Christ marry a Christian man living perhaps under the same roof?

which St. Paul meets first by arguing from the Resurrection of Christ, as he had received it in tradition, and which he takes for granted (xv. 1–28), and on other grounds (vv. 29–34), and then by discussing the nature of the Resurrection body, granting, of course, the contention of his opponents that the material body could not inherit the divine kingdom (vv. 35–58). He concludes with some personal matters and salutations (xvi. 19–24). No other writing in the New Testament reveals more vividly the meaning of the words, 'that which cometh upon me daily, the care of all the Churches'.

§ 4. 2 CORINTHIANS

The above sketch of the *Circumstances* shows that this epistle was written at a moment of intense revulsion of feeling. St. Paul's temperament was such that he felt things more acutely than most people. His converts from paganism, who included 'not many wise, not many powerful, not many of noble family', but probably many slaves, and others who belonged, for the most part, to the humblest and uneducated classes, were in greater need than those of any other Church of being supported and controlled by the strong hand of authority. He had been racked with fear that they might defy his authority by refusing to listen to the pleadings and to follow the directions in his sorrowful letter. His relief was unbounded when he heard from Titus that they had accepted his letter in the right spirit, and had shown their penitence by dealing strongly— almost too strongly—with the offender. And he at once wrote this letter. It was not a moment for dealing with Christian doctrine or Church practice; the letter is simply a pouring out of the man himself. We learn from it more of his personal character and temperament than from all his other writings put together.

After the opening salutation (i. 1, 2) and thanksgiving (vv. 3–14), the latter of which, owing to the circumstances, is much more than an epistolary convention, the epistle falls into three main parts:

A. He dwells on (*a*) his relations with the Corinthians (i. 15– ii. 13), and (*b*) his apostolic authority (ii. 14–vii. 4). In the latter section he describes (i) his *office*: the nature of his work—

a sacrificial odour rising to God (*vv.* 14–16); the sincerity of his teaching (*v.* 17); his independence of human commendation, since his converts themselves are his living and visible commendation (iii. 1–3); the divine dignity of his ministry, as that of the New Covenant (*vv.* 4–18), and its high character in keeping with this (iv. 1–6). (ii) His *sufferings* (iv. 7–v. 10). (iii) His *life* (v. 11–vi. 10); its motive (v. 11–15), its nature (v. 16–vi. 2), and the earthly marks which show its nature, i.e. sufferings (vi. 3–5), character (*vv.* 6, 7), and a spiritual independence of circumstances (*vv.* 8–10). (iv) His *personal feelings* for the Corinthians (vi. 11–13 and vii. 2–4). (The intervening passage, vi. 14–vii. 1, as said above, is probably a fragment of an earlier letter.)

B. The Collection (viii, ix). He presses upon them the duty of almsgiving, and tries to spur them to liberality by pointing to the example of the Macedonians.

C. But the submission of the majority of the Corinthians did not mean that he had no opponents left. And to these he turns in the remainder of the letter (x–xiii). He reasserts his authority, and utters stern rebukes and warnings, sharpening the edge of them with touches of mordant irony.

THE SORROWFUL LETTER. Many have thought that this is not wholly lost, but is partly preserved in Section *C* (x. 1–xiii. 10), so that 2 Corinthians consisted originally of only Sections *A* and *B*, with the conclusion (xiii. 11–13). But A. H. McNeile was inclined to the opposite view, that the sorrowful letter is lost to us, and that the epistle as we have it[1] is a unity.

The principal arguments for the former view[2] are as follows, the corresponding arguments for the latter view being given where necessary.

1. In chs. i–ix the apostle's language expresses relief that the trouble is over, and he writes in a friendly tone of satisfaction; but chs. x–xiii are written in remonstrance, anger, satire, and self-defence. The difference, however, cannot be so sharply

---

[1] Apart from the fragment vi. 14–vii. 1.
[2] This view is best stated by J. H. Kennedy, *The Second and Third Epistles of St. Paul to the Corinthians*; cf. R. H. Strachan, *2 Corinthians*, pp. xiv–xxii; J. Weiss, op. cit., pp. 347–57.

defined. In the former part he shows that there was a minority in serious opposition to his authority and teaching. They charged him with fickleness (i. 17–22). They are evidently included in 'the many who insincerely made profit out of the word of God' (ii. 17); some still handled the word of God deceitfully, their own hearts being in obscurity; and they preached themselves, not Christ Jesus, as Lord (iv. 2–5). They gloried in appearance, not in heart (v. 12), and scoffed at St. Paul as being 'beside himself' (*v.* 13). These and other passages show that while he was pleased with the majority, the minority still gave great trouble; and the rebuke and satire of chs. x–xiii are not absent from chs. i–ix.

2. If chs. x–xiii were the sorrowful letter, written before the happier letter, chs. i–ix, an explanation is needed of the references to a coming visit in xii. 14–xiii. 3: 'this is the third time I am ready to come to you'; 'I fear lest when I come to you I shall not find you such as I wish'; 'lest when I come again God may humble me before you'; 'this is the third time I am coming to you'; 'as I said before when I was present with you the second time'; 'if I come again I will not spare'. The words are explained to mean, 'I *may be* obliged to come to you if this sorrowful letter and the exhortations of Titus prove unsuccessful'.[1] But if the epistle is a unity the words can be understood in their natural sense. St. Paul *was* about to come to Corinth from Macedonia.

3. It has been ingeniously suggested that three passages in chs. x–xiii point *forward* to the possibility of this visit, while three passages written later, in chs. i–ix, point *backward* to the fact that he had not been obliged to pay it.[2]

'Being in readiness to avenge all disobedience when your obedience shall be fulfilled.'—2 Cor. x. 6.	'For to this end also did I write that I might know the proof of you, whether ye are obedient in all things.'—2 Cor. ii. 9.
'If I come again I will not spare.'—2 Cor. xiii. 2.	'To spare you I came no more to Corinth.'—2 Cor. i. 23.

[1] Cf. R. H. Strachan, op. cit., pp. 62 ff.
[2] Cf. K. Lake, *An Introduction to the New Testament*, 1938, pp. 121–3.

'For this cause I write these things from a distance, that I may not when I come deal sharply.'—2 Cor. xiii. 10.

'And I wrote this same thing that when I came I might not have sorrow.'—2 Cor. ii. 3.

According to K. Lake, 'These three pairs of passages are very striking and lose nothing if read in their context. It seems impossible to deny that in each pair the same thing is referred to twice; in 2 Cor. x–xiii in the present or future tense and in 2 Cor. i–ix in the past.' However, according to McNeile, the two sets of passages do not necessarily refer to the same visit. Those in the second column look back to the fact that the apostle substituted the sorrowful letter for a visit from which he shrank. Those in the first look forward to the visit which he did in fact pay, according to Acts xx. 2, 3, when he went from Macedonia into Greece. His disciplinary measures upon the minority would be much easier to enforce, now that he had the support of the majority.

4. The following passage (xii. 17, 18) occurs, *ex hypothesi*, in the sorrowful letter that was taken by Titus: 'Did I take advantage of you by any one of them whom I have sent unto you [*sc.* in the past]? I asked Titus [to go], and I sent the brother with him. Did Titus take any advantage of you? Walked we not by the same spirit, in the same steps?' Since these words cannot refer to the conduct of Titus on the occasion on which he took the letter, the sentence 'I asked Titus, &c.' causes great difficulty. 'I asked' and 'I sent' are explained as epistolary aorists, i.e. 'I am asking Titus to go with this letter, and I am sending the brother with him'. But it is impossible to see any reason for St. Paul's insertion of this parenthetical remark about the sending of Titus. Lake's paraphrase,[1] 'Titus, who is now coming to you, has never made any profit', only serves to show how difficult the parenthesis is which needs to be so blurred. Whether παρεκάλεσα is to be rendered 'exhorted' (R.V.) or simply 'asked', 'desired' (A.V.), it must refer to the same time as the following clause; and the only natural explanation is that the apostle is referring to the conduct of Titus when he went, at his desire, with the sorrowful letter.[2]

[1] *The Earlier Epistles of St. Paul*, p. 166.
[2] See, however, R. H. Strachan, op. cit., pp. 34 f.

5. 'Are we beginning again to commend ourselves?' (iii. 1). 'We do not again commend ourselves to you' (v. 12). These are thought to be references to his energetic self-commendation in the sorrowful letter, i.e. chs. x–xiii. But the reference is really to some of his opponents who armed themselves with commendatory letters, whom he attacks in *both* parts of the epistle (iii. 1; x. 12, 18). iii. 2 explains his meaning: he ought to require no commendation other than the work that he had done among them; they were themselves his letter of recommendation.

For the theory that chs. x–xiii are the sorrowful letter it is unfortunate that the occasion which called it forth, the wrongdoing of an individual offender, and the attitude that St. Paul desired the Corinthians to take towards him (see ii. 5–10), are not so much as mentioned in the chapters. And the supporters of the theory are obliged to suppose that chs. x–xiii are only a fragment, the portion dealing with the offender having been lost or suppressed. But this, of course, is not impossible. The portion which was not lost or suppressed may have been added to the Pauline *corpus* when all the available fragments from his pen were collected. J. Weiss[1] accepts the view that chs. x–xiii originally preceded i–ix but he put together with x–xiii both ii. 14–vi. 13 and vii. 2 ff. and then the rest of i–ix. Goguel[2] splits 2 Corinthians into three parts (not counting vi. 14–vii. 1), x. 1–xiii. 10; i. 1–vi. 13 and vii. 2–viii. 24; ix. 1–15, leaving xiii. 11–13 as an indeterminable element. In a footnote he lists other divisions of this letter.

It is probable that all four theories will continue to find supporters; and it may be that final agreement will never be reached.

---

[1] Op. cit., pp. 347–57.

[2] Op. cit., pp. 72–86. Goguel's résumé of the classification of the elements in both letters is:

A. II, vi. 14–vii. 1. I, vi. 12–20, x. 1–22.

B. I, v. 1–vi. 11; vii. 1–viii. 13; x. 23–xiv. 40. xv. 1–58(?). xvi. 1–9, 12.

C. I, i. 10–iv. 21; ix. 1–27; xvi. 10 f.

D. II, x. 1–xiii. 10.

E. II, i. 1–vi. 13; vii. 2–viii. 24.

F. II, ix. 1–15.

B or *C.* I, xvi. 15–18.

Indeterminable elements: I. i. 1–9; xvi. 13–14, 19–24; II, xiii. 11–13.

§ 5. GALATIANS

DESTINATION. This has been the subject of much dispute. In the course of his first missionary tour St. Paul with Barnabas visited Pisidian Antioch, Iconium, Lystra, and Derbe (Acts xiii. 14, 51; xiv. 6, 20), which lay in the Roman province of Galatia. In this narrative, however, the name of the province is not mentioned. In the second tour he traversed, with Silas, the same route in the converse direction, revisiting Derbe and Lystra (xvi. 1). It is then added that as they passed through the cities they delivered to them the decrees of the Council, and that 'panel' of the history (see p. 97) is closed with the usual summary (v. 5). The next panel contains their arrival in Europe via Troas, the beginning of the journey thither being described in v. 6: 'And they passed through τὴν Φρυγίαν καὶ Γαλατικὴν χώραν having been forbidden by the Holy Spirit to speak the word in Asia.' The one article τήν, according to the most probable interpretation, makes Φρυγίαν to be an adjective as well as Γαλατικήν, both qualifying χώραν.[1] There is thus produced the compound term 'the Phrygian-and-Galatic regions', i.e. Galatic Phrygia.[2] This distinguishes it from the larger portion of Phrygia which lay in the province of Asia—Asian Phrygia—and also from Galatic Lycaonia through which St. Paul had just passed.[3] The question arises whether the Galatia to which St. Paul wrote was this southern portion of the Roman province, Galatic Phrygia and Galatic Lycaonia, as an increasing number of scholars now think, or whether it was the northern portion of it stretching up beyond Phrygia to Bithynia and Pontus, with Pessinus, Ancyra, and Tavium

[1] Moffatt (Intr. Lit. N.T., p. 93) adduces to the contrary διελθὼν τὴν Μακεδονίαν καὶ Ἀχαίαν (xix. 21), and κατὰ τὴν Κιλικίαν καὶ Παμφυλίαν (xxvii. 5). But the absence of χώραν prevents them from being true parallels. A nearer one is τῆς Ἰτουραίας καὶ Τραχωνίτιδος χώρας (Lk. iii. 1). How is it that Γαλ. χώραν without the article can be used as equivalent to a proper name in Acts xvi. 6 and yet needs the article in xviii. 23? On the other hand it must be admitted that there is no inscriptional evidence for 'Phrygia Galatica' as there is for 'Pontus Galaticus'; and if St. Luke had wanted to say the former, would he not have used the phrase ἡ Γαλατικὴ Φρυγία? Cf. K. Lake, Beginnings of Christianity, v, note xviii, pp. 234–9.

[2] Ramsay, St. Paul the Traveller, pp. 104, 210, and Hastings's D.B., art. 'Galatia'.

[3] See A. H. McNeile's St. Paul, p. 37.

among its principal towns, once the kingdom of the Galatae from which the Roman province took its name. Whether the name is more naturally used by St. Luke, and by St. Paul a Roman citizen, of the Roman province or in the popular sense of the northern district is hotly disputed by the supporters of the south and the north Galatian theories respectively. Ramsay and others, who hold the southern theory, caused unnecessary difficulty by interpreting *v.* 6 as a résumé of the movements concluded by *v.* 5. But St. Luke's 'panel' system, if that, despite Goguel, was his system, makes this very improbable; and the grammar of κωλυθέντες is extremely awkward, unless it can be taken to mean that they made the journey with the prohibition already laid upon them from the start. But this is obviously not what St. Luke means. Nor is there the least warrant for accepting the late[1] reading διελθόντες to the neglect of all the best manuscripts. St. Luke's quite intelligible narrative is in no way opposed to the southern theory. After visiting Derbe and Lystra in Galatic Lycaonia St. Paul and his party might have moved westward, straight into Asia. But receiving a divine intimation that they were not to do so, they moved north-west into Galatic Phrygia, where they no doubt revisited Iconium and Pisidian Antioch. Travelling on northwards they could not preach in Mysia, since that was in Asia, so they went κατὰ τὴν Μυσίαν, i.e. 'along the [eastern] length of Mysia', 'up as far as the northern border of Mysia', till, forbidden to enter Bithynia, they turned westward, avoiding Mysia all the time, and reached Troas.[2] As we do not know the exact point where they turned westward, we do not know whether any part of this route lay through the western edge of north Galatia or not. It is, of course, possible. And thus Moffatt, following P. W. Schmiedel[3] and others, feeling the great difficulty of Lightfoot's view that St. Paul carried his mission throughout all parts of north Galatia, places the converts to which St. Paul wrote in a few towns in the west of the district, such as Pessinus and Germa.

---

[1] Attested only by the late Alexandrian evidence Ψ and 104, and by the groups listed in Merk as 5ss, 920–1311, 383s.

[2] For an alternative route cf. Lake, op. cit., p. 236.

[3] *Encycl. Bibl.* 1606. 7. A very able modern defence of the north Galatian theory is given by M. Goguel, op. cit. iv. 2, pp. 147–66.

In xviii. 23 St. Luke again refers to Galatia. St. Paul, starting from Syrian Antioch is spoken of as 'passing successively through the Galatian region and Phrygia, strengthening all the disciples'; and 'having passed through the upper parts came to Ephesus' (xix. 1). That is to say he revisited his converts along a route from Antioch to Ephesus. This does not suggest a journey deliberately undertaken across country to the north Galatian towns and then south-west through Asian Phrygia to Ephesus. Moffatt's paraphrase, 'he went off on a tour through', suggests a more extended area than ἐξῆλθεν διερχόμενος καθεξῆς. St. Luke's geographical expression is less explicit than in xvi. 6. He was obliged to alter it, because St. Paul passed through not only districts in the province of Galatia but also parts of Asian Phrygia to reach Ephesus.

Apart from these geographical terms, there are other considerations which point to south Galatia. (a) Even if the Acts implies a journey along the western border of north Galatia, it contains no trace of any mission work there. St. Luke, of course, omits many of St. Paul's activities, but he does take the trouble to relate in some detail his work in the south of the province. And it would be surprising if the apostle wrote to converts in the north of whom the Acts relates nothing, and made not the slightest reference in his epistles[1] to his work and sufferings nearer home in the region of Antioch, Iconium, Lystra, and Derbe, which figure prominently in St. Luke's narrative. (b) In Gal. ii. 1, 9, 13 Barnabas is named as though known to the Galatians; and the Acts contains no suggestion as to how his name could have meant anything to Galatians in the north. He is named, indeed, in 1 Cor. ix. 6 also, and we have no evidence that he ever visited Corinth. But in Gal. ii. 13 the words 'even Barnabas was carried away with them in their dissimulation' imply that the readers knew him personally well enough to understand that it was surprising that he should be carried away. (c) In 1 Cor. xvi. 1–4 St. Paul speaks of directions which he gave to 'the Churches of Galatia' regarding the collection for the poor in Jerusalem. Each

[1] With the exception of 2 Tim. iii. 11, the Pauline authorship of which is doubtful.

Church was to appoint its own representatives to take it; and if St. Paul went himself, they could accompany him. He did go himself; and in Acts xx. 4 the names are given of representatives who accompanied him. Two[1] are south Galatians, Gaius and Timothy from Derbe and Lystra, and no north Galatians are mentioned. That they intended to go with him to Jerusalem seems obvious. For what other purpose would a Beroean, two Thessalonians, two south Galatians (or one at least), and two Asians gather to his side when he was just about to sail for Syria? Indeed it is not impossible that the knowledge that the party were carrying money was one of the reasons for the plot hatched by the Jews which caused the change of route. Schmiedel[2] objects that 'it would have been quite irrational to convey monies from south Galatia to Jerusalem by way of Macedonia, and run all the risks (2 Cor. xi. 26) of such a journey'. But they had had no such intention. If they crossed from Ephesus to Corinth to get a boat which would take them all the way to Syria by sea, that was at least as safe as any other route they could have taken. But when St. Paul was forced to go via Macedonia, they would not leave him in the lurch. St. Paul stated at this very time to the Romans (xv. 25) that his object in going to Jerusalem was to take the money, and in his speech before Felix he is reported to have said the same (Acts xxiv. 17).

The north Galatian theory in one form was upheld by Lightfoot,[3] and in another less improbable form is vigorously defended by Moffatt[4] and Goguel,[5] who give many names on either side and exercise much ingenuity in controverting south Galatian arguments. The final settlement of the problem is still in the future; but the trend of opinion in recent years has been setting towards south Galatia.

DATE AND PLACE OF WRITING. Numerous dates have been assigned, some of them possible only on the south Gala-

---

[1] Unless, as is almost certain, we should read 'Gaius the Do(u)berian' following D and g. A. C. Clark showed that the Δόβηρες existed in Greece and not in Asia (*The Acts of the Apostles*, pp. xlix f. and 374 ff.), cf. C. S. C. Williams, *Alterations to the Text of the Synoptic Gospels and Acts*, p. 70.

[2] *Encycl. Bibl.* 1612. [3] *Galatians*, pp. 18 ff.

[4] Op. cit., pp. 90–101. [5] Op. cit., pp. 147–66.

tian theory. Several writers date it after St. Paul's first tour,
before he went with Barnabas to Jerusalem for the Council as
related in Acts xv. 2, 3. This makes it the earliest of his epistles
that we possess. It has the advantage of explaining some of the
knotty difficulties (see p. 121) raised by a comparison of St.
Paul's account of a visit to Jerusalem (Gal. ii. 1–10) with the
accounts in the *Acts* of two visits, one to take help in the famine
(xi. 30) the other for the Council (xv. 1–29). That St. Paul does
not mention the Council or its decrees would be explained if
the epistle was written before it took place. Some think that
he wrote it from Antioch before he started, others *en route* for
Jerusalem; in the latter case 'all the brethren who are with me'
(Gal. i. 2) are his travelling companions. This date is not
necessarily forbidden by the words 'Ye know that on account
of infirmity of the flesh I evangelized you τὸ πρότερον' (iv. 13).
In classical Greek this would mean 'the former of two times',
and would imply that St. Paul had preached to the Galatians
twice before he wrote to them. 'This', says Moffatt, 'must be
maintained resolutely against all attempts, especially in the
interests of a theory, to make τὸ πρότερον = πάλαι or *jam-
pridem.*' But in the interests of accuracy it must be noted that in
Hellenistic Greek it could have that meaning, 'formerly',
'originally', 'in the past', and clearly has in Jn. vi. 62; ix. 8;
1 Tim. i. 13; it is like πρότερον without the article in 2 Cor. i.
15; Heb. iv. 6; and nowhere else in the New Testament does
it bear the classical meaning here claimed for it. If it does not
refer to two visits, it does not forbid the view that St. Paul is
referring to his work in south Galatia during his first tour, and
has, in fact, no bearing on the date.

If we date the epistle before the second tour we have to face
the fact that in the course of that tour St. Paul circumcized
Timothy. On the theory of a date after the tour it may have
been that action which led to the charges lying behind Gal. i.
10; v. 11. But to do it after writing Gal. v. 2 was a defiance of
logical consistency for practical purposes which cannot be
pronounced impossible for St. Paul.

The strict force of τὸ πρότερον is maintained by some upholders both of the south and of the north Galatian theories.
For the former, the two visits to Galatia are those of the first

tour (Acts xiii, xiv) and the beginning of the second (xvi. 1–6). But the places and dates assigned to it between the latter and the next visit (xviii. 23) are various. Macedonia, Athens, and Corinth have all been suggested, the last having the strong support of Zahn, Bacon, and J. Weiss. Volkmar and Renan bring it later still, to Antioch before the third tour.

But many supporters of both theories agree, independently of τὸ πρότερον, in choosing dates in the course of the third tour, mainly on the ground that the style and thoughts of the epistle stand in close affinity with those of 1, 2 Corinthians and Romans. Two alternatives have some probability: (a) during the stay at Ephesus (xix. 1, 8–10), or (b) during the journey thence via Macedonia to Corinth, or at Corinth itself (xx. 1–3). (a) Lightfoot[1] rightly argues that the period of the stay at Ephesus cannot be deduced from the expression in Gal. i. 6, 'I marvel that ye are οὕτως ταχέως changing from Him that called you, unto another Gospel', as though it could mean 'so soon after I left you'. They had received the true Gospel on his first visit some time before, and had now 'rashly', 'precipitately', abandoned it owing to Judaistic pressure. If Ephesus was the place,[2] it was probably written just before he left. In iv. 20 he says, 'I wish I could be present with you now.' Both north and south Galatia were accessible from Ephesus. We do not know enough of the events there to know whether he could have paid them a flying visit as he did to Corinth (p. 134), but he was either leaving the city immediately, or had already left it, for some urgent cause. (b) The epistle is placed at some moment between his resolve to go to Macedonia to get news of the Corinthians from Titus and the writing of Romans at Corinth. On the ground of language and thought, Lightfoot places it between 2 Corinthians and Romans, but the criterion must not be applied too rigidly; 1, 2 Corinthians are both written to meet particular pressing needs, and might both have stood between two epistles chiefly dealing with the Jewish controversy. If

---

[1] *Galatians*, p. 41.

[2] As stated in the Latin prologue to the Epistle. See Harnack (*Zeitschr. f. d. neutest. Wiss.*, 1925, pp. 204–18), who is the ablest defender of the widely accepted view that the prologues to the Pauline epistles which are preserved in some Vulgate MSS. are Marcionite in origin. Contrast M. J. Lagrange, *Revue biblique*, xxxv, 1926, pp. 161–73.

Romans was originally written in its present form, our epistle is perhaps most easily understood if it is placed at some moment between the writing of the sorrowful letter to Corinth and the meeting with Titus in Macedonia, i.e. immediately before (or, of course, it may have been immediately after) 2 Corinthians. But if the original Romans was a shorter, general epistle (see pp. 157 f.), then the argument from style is equally valid if that shorter form and Galatians were both written before the Council.

CAUSES OF WRITING. The Galatians, whether northern or southern, were mostly Gentiles. At the Council he had won his victory over the Judaizers who had tried to persuade the Gentile Christians in Antioch that their salvation was impossible unless they became members of the Jewish Church by circumcision. But opponents went farther afield. At some time shortly before he wrote the epistle he must have heard that they had visited Galatia and tried to pervert his converts. He wanted to go to them himself, but being unable to do that (iv. 20) he wrote in sorrow and indignation with an intense longing to keep them true to the principles of his universal Gospel. The Judaizers appear to have used two arguments: Firstly, they tried to undermine his influence and authority by telling the Galatians that St. Paul was an unauthorized upstart, whose position in the Church was greatly inferior to that of the original apostles who had lived with our Lord; and that his teaching of freedom from Jewish ordinances was his way of making his religion of salvation easier and more acceptable; he tried to 'please men' (i. 10). Secondly, they told them, as they had told the Christians at Antioch, that to become Christians they must first be joined to Judaism by circumcision. They had used the arts of flattery and fair speech (iv. 17), and had so 'bewitched' them (iii. 1) that some of them had actually begun to observe Jewish festivals (iv. 9 f.), and some wanted to be 'under the Law' altogether (iv. 21).

According to the theory of Lütgert,[1] however, which J. H. Ropes[2] accepted with some modifications, one must not assume that the hostile personal attacks on St. Paul came from the

---

[1] *Gesetz und Geist*, 1919.
[2] 'The Singular Problem of Galatians', *Harvard Texts and Studies*, xiv, 1928.

Judaizers. This would be to overlook the existence of a radical party in the Galatian churches opposed both to the Judaizers and to St. Paul. The latter was fighting on two different fronts. Ropes suggests that the Galatian churches included some ex-Gentiles who insisted that the Jewish law was necessary even for Gentiles who believed. They were confronted by a party of spiritual radicals or 'pneumatics' who rejected the rite of circumcision and claimed in reliance on the Spirit to be able to neglect moral discipline, in many ways resembling St. Paul's opponents in 2 Corinthians and anticipating the Marcionites. There may even have been a pro-Pauline party adopting the *via media* between the Judaizers and the 'pneumatics', cf. v. 9 f., vi. 6. Ropes claims that the arguments of Galatians are directed against both parties more or less alternately and that on this theory the Epistle can be dated comparatively late.

CONTENTS. St. Paul shapes his epistle to meet two lines of attack. (*a*) The attempt to undermine his authority he deals with in i–ii. 14, explaining that the original apostles were in no way superior to him in authority or spiritual knowledge, for he had received his Gospel direct from Christ Himself. The apostles did not teach it to him, and when they heard his account of what he preached they added nothing to it. To prove this he enumerates the occasions on which he was in contact with them up to the time when they formally recognized his apostleship to the Gentiles. And at the end of the epistle (vi. 11–17) he attacks the Judaistic opposition again. (*b*) He tries with all his might to draw back the readers from the peril into which they had allowed themselves to be led. This he does in three ways: (1) By controversial argument. He explains the nature of the Law as shown in the Law itself, and its purpose in the divine economy in relation to the promise made to Abraham (ii. 15–iv. 7). Again he explains its inferiority to the Christian dispensation as shown in a figure by a narrative in the Law itself—the story of Hagar the slave and Sarah the free woman and their sons (iv. 21–31). (2) By teaching as to the real meaning of life in the Spirit and of the freedom which it involves (v. 13–vi. 10). (3) These are interspersed by impassioned personal appeals (iv. 8–20; v. 1–12).

§ 6. ROMANS

CONTENTS. This epistle and Galatians are the chief sources of a peculiar and distinctive contribution made by St. Paul to Christian thought, in that they represent his fight with Judaism. Romans, no less than Galatians, is a general doctrinal treatise. Its first object was to frame 'a comprehensive *apologia* for the principle of a universal religion as set over against Jewish nationalism'. Since he is writing to a Church of which the members are not intimately known to him, the epistle does not vibrate with the passion of personal appeal which marks Galatians; but it is not the less alive. The argument is framed on the lines of a disputation with opponents, questions being rhetorically asked in order to be answered. It was impossible for St. Paul to put pen to paper on any subject without revealing *himself*. A Jew, and an ardent lover of his nation, he set himself the task of explaining why the Jewish religion was no longer *the* religion, but was superseded by one that was not national but universal. Two main problems presented themselves: 1. Seeing that Israel were the chosen race, and their religion was *the* religion, wherein did their failure consist? This forms the basis of i. 16–viii. 39. They failed because their system was essentially inadequate to the achievement of the end desired, i.e. the acquiring of 'righteousness'. Therefore God has now provided a new system which is completely successful in the case of all—Jew and Gentile alike—who adopt it and throw themselves into it. 2. The second problem is wrestled with in chs. ix–xi. Seeing that God chose Israel and made promises to them, how could He reject them without unfaithfulness and injustice? The following headings of this doctrinal portion of the epistle are taken from A. H. McNeile's manual *St. Paul*, pp. 191 f.:

A. i. 16–v. 21. Justification.[1]

    i. 16, 17. Thesis.

    i. 18–iii. 20. Universal failure of Gentile and Jew to attain to Righteousness.

---

[1] It is impossible to translate δικαίωσις and δικαιοῦν by one word in English (cf. O. C. Quick, *The Gospel of the New World*, 1944, pp. 54 f.). It means being reprieved, forgiven, and incorporated into Christ as part of His New Creation. The distinction from 'Sanctification' is not too hard and fast.

    (*a*) i. 18–ii. 29. Statement of their failure.
    (*b*) iii. 1–8. Three objections answered.
    (*c*) iii. 9–20. The failure proved from Scripture.
  iii. 21–31. The New System of attaining to Righteousness is explained.
  iv. 1–25. The New System corroborated by the case of Abraham.
  v. 1–21. The glorious effects of the New System.

    (*a*) *vv.* 1–4. The effects enumerated.
    (*b*) *vv.* 5–11. The consideration of God's love gives confidence of final salvation.
    (*c*) *vv.* 12–21. Adam and Christ. *vv.* 12–17. Their similarities and difference. *vv.* 18–21. Summary.

B. vi–viii. Sanctification.
  vi, vii. Four objections answered.

    (*a*) vi. 1–14. If more sin on man's part means more grace on God's, why not go on sinning?
    (*b*) vi. 15–vii. 6. If we are released from Law, are we not free to sin if we like?
    (*c*) vii. 7–12. If release from Law means release from sin, are not Law and sin identical?
    (*d*) vii. 13–25. Did the good Law, then, cause death?
  viii. The working out of the Christian's salvation by the indwelling of the Spirit.

C. ix–xi. The Rejection of Israel.
  ix. 1–5. Introduction.
  ix. 6–29. The Justice of the Rejection.

    (*a*) *vv.* 6–13. It is not inconsistent with God's promises.
    (*b*) *vv.* 14–29. It is not inconsistent with God's justice.

  ix. 30–x. 13. Causes of the Rejection.
  x. 14–21. The Jews had no excuse from want of warning.
  xi. Facts which lessen the difficulty.

    (*a*) *vv.* 1–10. The Rejection is not that of *all* Israel.
    (*b*) *vv.* 11–24. The Rejection is not final.
    (*c*) *vv.* 25–36. God's ultimate purpose is mercy to all.

After working out his thesis the apostle adds practical exhortations based upon it, i.e. the right attitude of Christians towards God (xii. 1, 2), towards the Body of which they are members (xii. 3–21), towards the civil rulers[1] (xiii. 1–7), and towards

    [1] O. Cullmann takes a rather unusual view when he says: 'The executive

men in general by love (xiii. 8–10), all this being enforced by a reminder of the nearness of the Last Day (xiii. 11–14). The exhortation ends with a warning against the misuse of the Christian 'liberty' which his universal Gospel involves (xiv. 1–xv. 7). Finally the duty of Jews and Gentiles to 'receive another', &c., both in the matter of foods and in other respects, is enforced by reminding the Gentiles on the one hand that their salvation was wrought to fulfil promises made to Israel, and the Jews on the other that the promises made to Israel did in fact include the saving of the Gentiles (xv. 8, 9a), four Old Testament passages being adduced as instances (xv. 9b–12). A closing prayer (xv. 13) forms a suitable ending to the main body of the letter. An epistolary conclusion follows in which St. Paul refers to his work in the past (xv. 14–21), and his proposed movements in the future (xv. 22–32), ending with a final prayer (xv. 33).

After this a new beginning in ch. xvi is unexpected (see below): Commendation of Phoebe (*vv.* 1, 2). Salutations to individuals and to groups of Christians (*vv.* 3–16). A doctrinal warning (*vv.* 17–20). Names of Corinthian Christians who send greetings (*vv.* 21–23). Doxology (*vv.* 25–27).

DESTINATION AND PLACE OF WRITING. The epistle as it stands indicates these clearly enough. The apostle greets 'all those who are in Rome beloved of God, called as saints' (i. 7); and he speaks of his eagerness 'to preach the Gospel to you also who are at Rome' (*v.* 15), which he had frequently purposed to visit, but had hitherto been prevented (*v.* 13). He had been prevented many times from coming to them, though he had longed for years to do so (xv. 22 f.). He wanted to stay with them for a passing visit on his way to Spain (*v.* 24). At the present moment he was about to start for Jerusalem, carrying the alms contributed by the churches in Macedonia and Achaia (*vv.* 25 f.), but as soon as he had accomplished that he would come to them *en route* for Spain (*v.* 29).

This fixes the place of writing of chs. i–xv as either Corinth

power of the state is the administrative organ for the "rulers of this world" (1 Cor. ii. 28). In the light of this fact we should also understand that the "authorities" of Rom. xiii. 1, in keeping with the meaning which this plural always has for Paul, are the powers that stand behind the actual executive power of the state.' (*Christ and Time*, Eng. trans., F. V. Filson, 1951, p. 37, n. 1.)

during the visit of Acts xx, just before he started for Jerusalem, or some point on the journey to Jerusalem. In ch. xvi, of those who send greetings Gaius (*v.* 23) was the name of one whom St. Paul had baptized at Corinth (1 Cor. i. 14), Erastus (*v.* 23) was that of one who 'stayed on at Corinth' (2 Tim. iv. 20), and Timothy and Sosipater (Sopater) (*v.* 21) were among the apostle's companions when he departed from Corinth (Acts xx. 4). Ch. xvi, therefore, was probably written from Corinth.

INTEGRITY. But the destination of the epistle involves the question of its integrity. There are indications which strongly suggest that ch. xvi was not originally part of the epistle, but was a separate letter, or portion of a letter. If so, it was probably a short personal communication, a brief ἐπιστολὴ συστα-τική, to commend Phoebe, but written to Ephesus, not to Rome. The reasons for this, the cumulative effect of which is strong,[1] are as follows:

(1) The numerous salutations suggest that St. Paul knew personally a large number of Christians in the place to which he wrote.[2] This is surprising at Rome which he had never visited before he wrote, but natural at Ephesus where he had worked for more than two years. And in the letters which he afterwards wrote from Rome not one of those who are saluted in ch. xvi are mentioned.

(2) A salutation is sent to Prisca and Aquila (*v.* 3). They had gone with the apostle from Corinth to Ephesus (Acts xviii. 18), where they had stayed (*v.* 19), not only till Apollos went thither (*v.* 26) but till St. Paul returned for his two-year visit, during which he wrote 1 Corinthians, in which he sent greeting from them 'with the Church that is in their house' (xvi. 19). But in Rom. xvi. 5 he greets them 'and the Church that is in

---

[1] Though Harnack, *Die Briefsammlung des Apostels Paulus*, pp. 13 f., thinks it a 'badly supported hypothesis'.

[2] Bp. Lightfoot's arguments that many names in ch. xvi are paralleled in Roman sepulchral inscriptions (*The Epistle to the Philippians*, 1903, pp. 171–8) have been met by K. Lake who has shown that the same names occur in inscriptions in the provinces (*The Earlier Epistles of Paul*, 1911, pp. 324–35). Lake answered de Rossi's argument that the Church of St. Prisca on the Aventine Hill was founded on the site of Prisca and Aquila's house by saying that evidence for this is lacking as is evidence for thinking that the church was called SS. Aquila and Prisca before the eighth century; cf. P. Styger, *Die Römischen Katakomben*, 1933, and Visscher, *Analecta Bollandiana*, lxix, 1951, pp. 39–54.

their house'. This points strongly to the same church and house at Ephesus, for it is very improbable that in the short interval between the writing of 1 Corinthians and Romans—within two years, possibly within one—they had returned to Rome and made their house a Christian centre.

(3) A salutation is sent to Epaenetus, 'the firstfruits of Asia unto Christ' (*v.* 5), i.e. the first convert in the province of Asia. This description of him would be suitable if he were then in Ephesus, but would have little point if he were in Rome.

(4) The commendation of Phoebe to a church whose members the apostle knew, and with whom his words would have their full weight, would be more natural than to a church which he had never visited.

(5) The antinomianism denounced in *vv.* 17, 18[1] seems to have been more hostile and pronounced than anything that is implied in the rest of the epistle, and would find congenial soil in the Asian capital.

(6) The words of xv. 33, 'Now the God of peace be with you all. Amen', have the appearance of being the conclusion of a letter.

It is quite likely that this commendatory letter has lost nothing but an epistolary formula at the opening and at the conclusion. But in its present form it ends with a rhetorical Doxology, which would be quite out of place in such a letter, and the style and language of which differ from those of the rest of Romans, approximating rather to those of Ephesians and the Pastoral Epistles. And the expression, 'the mystery which hath been kept *in silence* through times eternal, but now is manifested, &c.', is not in keeping with St. Paul's usual thought that the mystery was proclaimed in the Old Testament but not understood (cf. Col. i. 26) till it found its explanation in Christianity.[2]

---

[1] These verses bear a striking similarity to Phil. iii. 17–19, a passage occurring in a section which seems, like the present one, to be a fragment of another letter (see pp. 167 f.), perhaps addressed to a church in Asia.

[2] This argument of Corssen is dismissed as hypercritical by N. P. Williams. 'St. Paul was not a pedant, and it is unreasonable to expect minute and unvarying verbal consistency from him' (Gore, Goudge, and Guillaume, *A New Commentary*, iii, p. 448). Goguel (op. cit. iv. 2, pp. 250–3), however, argues tha the Doxology, though not the work of Marcion himself, since his text stopped at xiv. 23, came from a Marcionite milieu. J. Weiss (op. cit. ii. 284) suggests

If the Doxology was not from St. Paul's pen the question arises why it was added. Some have thought that it may have been the work of Marcion, or of a Marcionite after him. Lake holds that since Romans stands last of the epistles to churches (distinguished in the Muratorian Canon from epistles to persons) in the Bible of Tertullian as well as in the Muratorian Canon and in Origen's Bible, and since doxologies generally come at the end of books, and this Doxology belongs to the shorter recension of the epistle (see below), it is probable that it was added in some collection in which the epistle, in its short form, came last. The manuscript evidence with regard to the last two chapters is complicated. Some of the best manuscripts have the Doxology at the end of the epistle. In a few it stands there, and also at the end of ch. xiv; some have it only at the end of ch. xiv; the third-century Chester Beatty papyrus codex P[46] alone has the Doxology at the end of xv; others,[1] again, omit it altogether. Further, some Vulgate manuscripts seem to show clear traces of an Old Latin system of fifty-one *breves*, or chapter-divisions for the epistle, of which the fiftieth begins at xiv. 15, and the fifty-first corresponds with the Doxology. And Origen (according to the Latin translation by Rufinus) states that the heretic Marcion removed (*abstulit*) the Doxology, and *dissecuit* chs. xv, xvi; the latter may mean either the same as *abstulit*, or 'separated off', i.e. treated as not belonging to the epistle. It is not clear, therefore, whether Origen charges him with shortening the epistle or implies that he had received it in its already shortened form, and hence treated the last two chapters as unauthentic. It is noticeable also that Tertullian (*adv. Marc.* v. 14) makes no comment on Marcion's treatment of anything in the epistle after xiv. 10, and refers to that verse as occurring 'in clausula', i.e. at the close of the epistle. It is even more significant that Tertullian and also

that it was added by the collector of the Pauline corpus, perhaps the author of the Epistle to the Ephesians.

[1] G3 g leaves a space large enough for it at xiv. 23, showing that the scribe had reason to think that that was the place where it should occur, but it was lacking in his manuscript. Corssen (*Zeitschr. f. d. neutest. Wiss.* x, 1909, pp. 5 f.) thinks that the manuscript from which D was copied also lacked it, since the colometric arrangement in D suddenly ceases at xvi. 23, and the Doxology is written stichometrically, which points to the use of a different manuscript.

Irenaeus and Cyprian make no citations from chs. xv, xvi. Lastly, Origen,[1] 'Ambrosiaster', and G3 g omitted the words 'in Rome' in i. 7, and 'who are in Rome' in i. 15. Was the omission due to a Marcionite scribe's anti-Roman bias (Manson)?

There have been different explanations for this condition of things. The existence of a shortened form of the epistle at some stage of its history is certain. Lightfoot[2] thought that St. Paul shortened it himself, delocalizing it for general use; Moffatt,[3] that the Church shortened it for the same purpose; Sanday–Headlam[4] and Corssen,[5] that Marcion shortened it for doctrinal reasons. These views are summarized in A. H. McNeile's *St. Paul: his Life, Letters, and Christian Doctrine*, pp. 185–8. A different solution was suggested by K. Lake,[6] and accepted by Burkitt,[7] that the short form of the letter was the original, 'Written by St. Paul at the same time as Galatians, in connexion with the question of Jewish and Gentile Christians, for the general instruction of mixed churches which he had not visited.' 'Later on he sent a copy to Rome, with the addition of the other chapters to serve, as we should say, as a covering letter.' He explains xv. 1–13 as an addition 'continuing the thoughts of his original writing, probably because Aquila had told him that this would be desirable'. But no reason can be discerned why the general remarks of xv. 1–13 (especially of *vv.* 1–7) should have been desirable after the particular injunctions on the same subject in ch. xiv. F. C. Burkitt thought that the verses are a mere suture, leading on to the additional chapters that St. Paul was writing. But even so, the personal details in i. 8–15 need to be explained if they occurred in an epistle for general use. It is impossible that to each of the mixed churches that he had not visited, St. Paul wrote that he was always praying that he might do so, but had been prevented. The contents of those verses point to a particular church, and yet there is not the least evidence that they

---

[1] A codex (1739) at the Laura on Mt. Athos contains a text of the Epistle made from Origen's commentary.

[2] *Biblical Essays*, pp. 287 ff.   [3] *Introd. Lit. of N.T.*, p. 142.

[4] *Romans*, pp. xcvii f.   [5] Op. cit., pp. 1, 97.

[6] *The Earlier Epistles of St. Paul*, p. 362.

[7] *Christian Beginnings*, p. 126.

were absent when chs. xv, xvi were absent. If, on the other hand, St. Paul shortened the original epistle he would have omitted the personal matter that they contained together with those chapters. Any solution must take account of this personal matter. Dr. T. W. Manson[1] has put forward a theory covering most of the facts. He suggests that St. Paul wrote both chs. i–xv. 33, which he sent to Rome, and, later, i–xvi, which he sent to Ephesus. From the earlier letter Marcion took i–xiv and his short edition influenced the textual tradition in the West, as may be seen from D F G. From the longer edition to Ephesus is derived the Alexandrian tradition seen in B ℵ C. He suggests too that P[46] is derived from the earlier letter to Rome, with the (Marcionite) Doxology at the end of xv therefore. P[46] shows also the influence of Alexandrian texts in including xvi after the doxology. This theory also accounts for the high proportion of Western readings in chs. i–xv in P[46] but not in xvi. It is probable indeed that· non-Western readings have also infiltrated into chs. i–xv in this codex.[2]

C. THIRD GROUP OF EPISTLES

§ 7. COLOSSIANS[3]

PLACE OF WRITING. On the traditional view, the epistle was written from Rome, as is shown by its close connexion with Philemon (see pp. 180 ff. for the theory of the Ephesian origin of the imprisonment letters). In both epistles Timotheus joins in the opening salutation; Epaphras, Marcus, Aristarchus, Demas, and Luke are mentioned (iv. 7–14, Philem. 23, 24), and Archippus is greeted (iv. 17, Philem. 2); and Onesimus accompanies both (iv. 9, Philem. 10–12). Further, the words 'the mystery of the Gospel on account of which I have also been put in bonds' (iv. 3) and 'Remember my bonds' (iv. 18) show that St. Paul was writing in imprisonment, or in the custody that is related in Acts xxviii. There is no adequate reason for the conjecture accepted by several writers that he

---

[1] *Bulletin of the John Rylands Library*, xxxi, 1948, pp. 224–40.
[2] C. S. C. Williams, *Ex. T.*, lxi, 1950, pp. 125–7.
[3] The form 'Colassians' is the reading of B A P[46], 'Colossians' that of ℵ D F G.

wrote it at Caesarea. Still less for the curious *ab Epheso* in the Latin prologue to the epistle (see p. 148, n. 2).

CAUSE OF WRITING. It is probable that St. Paul had never been to Colossae (see ii. 1 with Lightfoot's note). He had reached Ephesus from the east on his third tour by 'the higher parts' (Acts xix. 1), and not by the main road through the valley of the Lycus, in which stood Colossae and Laodicea. He had sent others to preach to them, one of whom was a Gentile named Epaphras or Epaphroditus (not the Christian of that name who is mentioned in Phil. ii. 25, iv. 18). This seems to be indicated by the description of him in i. 7, 'a faithful minister of Christ on our behalf'.[1] But he thought of them as his own children in the faith, who needed a letter to guard them from a spiritual peril which threatened them. Epaphras had brought him a report of their condition. He had told him, on the one hand, as St. Paul says, of 'their faith in Christ Jesus, and the love which they had towards all the saints' (i. 4), and of 'their love in the Spirit' (*v.* 8). They were still true to the Christianity to which they were converted. But, on the other, he told him that they, and the Laodiceans for whom also the letter was intended, were in danger of being led into false ideas, which made it necessary to put before them, probably with much greater intellectual power than Epaphras or any other teacher had possessed, the central and fundamental fact of Christ. In writing to Churches in Asia Minor he uses language and methods of argument such as we find in no other epistles.

THE COLOSSIAN DANGER. The Colossian Christians were Gentiles, whom Jewish Christians were trying to seduce from pure Christianity. What they inculcated was not the plain Judaism which had been the chief trouble in Galatia a few years earlier. The danger now arose from a different quarter. Greek philosophical speculations were combining with a variety of oriental ideas to form a strange amalgam of mystical theosophy. Foreign religions, cults, and mysteries were being eagerly sought after by Western minds which had given up the ancient mythologies and longed for 'salvation' in some form or

---

[1] See Lightfoot, ad loc. ὑπὲρ ἡμῶν (B ℵ A P⁴⁶ D* G Lat.) is better attested than ὑπὲρ ὑμῶν.

other. Christianity in its own way offered salvation; but false teachers had tried to persuade the Colossian Christians 'not that Judaism with its circumcision and other ordinances was a necessary step towards Christianity, but that Christianity, as Epaphras had taught it when he evangelized Colossae, was only a preliminary step towards a deeper, vaster, and therefore humbler "philosophy"' (ii. 8).

Two chief aspects of their teaching are combated by St. Paul, arising from (1) astrology, and (2) philosophical dualism.

1. Oriental thought on the whole was tied and bound by a belief in the powers exercised by the cosmic forces of nature, and especially the stars, over the destinies of men. These forces were personified as supernatural or angelic, i.e. demonic, beings. The Colossians were in danger of being persuaded that merely to believe in Christ was an immature form of religion: they ought to go farther and be perfected (cf. i. 28, 'perfect in Christ') by initiation into something greater. Since man was brought into relationship with the Pleroma of the Godhead by angelic emanations or powers, the worship of Christ was not so 'perfect' as the worship of the angels with humility (ii. 18), which St. Paul characterizes as 'self-imposed worship (ἐθελο-θρησκεία) and humility' (v. 23).

2. But these theosophical ideas were bound up with the errors of dualism. God, it was thought, can have no contact with, nor can He be held responsible for, matter. To reach the Pleroma of the Godhead through the mediumship of the angels, man must free himself from the evil influences of matter. In particular he must purge himself from the malign effects of his material body. This involved a strict *asceticism*: 'handle not, taste not, touch not' (ii. 21); man must neglect his body (v. 23); to which St. Paul retorts that such neglect is of no value to remedy indulgence of the flesh.[1] While asceticism was one result of a dualistic philosophy, libertinism was another. If matter has no relation to God, the material body has no relation to religion; therefore man can indulge his body without

---

[1] See Lightfoot, ad loc. Over-ascetic rules 'have a rational or apparent justification in a voluntary form of worship, in "humility" and (om. P46 B al.) in bodily mortification but not in the honour, so to speak, which they pay to sensual gratifications; cf. H. S. Bettenson, *Theology*, xxvi, 1933, pp. 154–6.

restraint. But this deadly mistake is not referred to in the epistle (see p. 190 and n.). What St. Paul had to meet was the danger that his readers would submit themselves to Jewish rules of asceticism, man-made ordinances, injunctions, and teachings (ii. 21, 22), which included circumcision (*vv.* 11–13) restrictions as regards foods and drinks (*v.* 16), and—probably combined with astrological ideas—the observance of festivals, new moons, and Sabbaths (ibid.). This was a recrudescence of the old Judaistic mistake in a far more perilous form. It was a return to 'the tradition of men according to the elements (στοιχεῖα) of the world and not according to Christ' (*v.* 8). It was from these 'elements' that Christ died, and Christians with Him (*v.* 20).[1] At a later date these oriental ideas became greatly developed in contact with Christianity, and full-grown Gnosticism, claiming to be a higher, esoteric form of Christianity, became one of the most pressing dangers through which the Church ever passed. But there is little doubt that our epistle depicts it at an early stage in the form in which it was beginning to fascinate the Jewish mind in Asia.

To meet the danger St. Paul was not content with contradicting the false ideas. He held up before the Colossians in all its fullness the fact of Christ—i.e. of Him who was not one Emanation among many, but 'the Son of God's love' (i. 13); 'the Image of the invisible God, the First-begotten of every creature' (*v.* 15); in whom (so far from created matter being alien from God) all things were created, including 'the invisible things, whether thrones or lordships or principalities or authorities' (*v.* 16); the Agent and End of creation, prior to all things, and the centre of cohesion of all things (*v.* 17); the Head of the Body, the Church (cf. ii. 19), the Beginning,[2]

---

[1] The 'elements of the world' are probably not merely 'elementary ideas'—though that thought is not absent—but the elemental forces of nature which would be included in the angelic or demonic personifications which the Colossians were enticed to worship. Since angels, according to Jewish tradition, were instrumental in giving the Law at Sinai (cf. Gal. iii. 19), St. Paul thought of the Jews, in their obedience to Law, as 'enslaved under the elements of the world' (Gal. iv. 3). Christ, by being 'born under the Law' and dying and rising again, burst free from them and so conquered them. Cf. Col. ii. 15, referred to below, and 1 Cor. ii. 6, 8; cf. W. H. P. Hatch, *J.T.S.* xxviii, 1926–7, pp. 181–2.

[2] On the fullness of the meaning which St. Paul gives to ἀρχή see Burney, *J.T.S.* xxviii. 173–7; cf. A. E. J. Rawlinson, *The New Testament Doctrine of the*

First-begotten from the dead, in whom all the Pleroma dwells (cf. ii. 9) (*v.* 18), through whom all things are reconciled to God. He reconciled them in the body of His flesh through the Cross (*vv.* 20, 22). He is 'Christ in you, the hope of glory' (*v.* 27); the Mystery of God, even Christ, in whom are all the treasures of wisdom and knowledge hid' (ii. 3), and not in any pagan mysteries or esoteric theosophies; the Head of every [angelic] principality and authority (*v.* 10); who on the Cross 'stripped off' the domination of these principalities and authorities, and made a show of them openly, triumphing over them in it'—i.e. by virtue of His death on it (*v.* 15). Thus the fact of Christ is that He is the *centre* and the *whole* of the circle of all things that are.

CONTENTS. The epistle does not lend itself to exact analysis; but it falls roughly into four parts. After the opening salutation, and a thanksgiving and prayer for the readers (i. 1–14), the apostle plunges *in mediam rem.*

A. i. 15–20. Christ is the true Mystery. He is presented to the readers in His relation to God (*v.* 15a), to the Universe (*vv.* 15b–17), to the Church (*v.* 18), a threefold relationship which was necessary for the fulfilment of God's ultimate purpose of cosmic reconciliation to Him.

B. i. 21–ii. 3. The Colossians, as Gentile converts, had a share in this reconciliation, having been taught—owing to St. Paul's ministry and stewardship—the mystery of the indwelling Christ (i. 21–29). And he longs that they may be led to a full understanding of it (ii. 1–3).

C. ii. 4–iii. 4. Warnings against being led astray by the flattery and specious philosophy of false teachers.

D. iii. 5–iv. 6. Exhortations to live the moral life that is involved in the participation in the mystery. Some personal matter and salutations conclude the epistle.

GENUINENESS. There are critics who credit St. Paul with no ability to think on a plane other than that of 1, 2 Corinthians, Galatians, and Romans. This excludes his authorship of 1, 2 Thessalonians on the one hand, and Colossians and Ephesians on the other. But no genius can safely be judged in

Christ, 1926, pp. 163–5; W. D. Davies, *Paul and Rabbinic Judaism,* 1948, pp. 150–8.

so rigid a manner. In style and vocabulary a difference is indeed noticeable. The following Pauline words are absent from Colossians: ἀποκάλυψις, δικαιοσύνη, καυχᾶσθαι, νόμος, πιστεύειν, σωτηρία; also the following Pauline particles (cf. the list of particles absent from the Pastorals); ἄρα, διό, διότι, ἔτι, οὐδέ, οὔτε, οὐκέτι. But since the readers and the subjects of which he treats are of very different types, this is not unnatural. The style is smoother, less rapid, and more diffuse, grander and more rhetorical, as befits his theme. On the other hand he uses throughout characteristic words and expressions which are found in his earlier epistles, while those which do not occur elsewhere can be mostly accounted for by the needs of his subject. The stress which he lays on such words as 'wisdom', 'perfect', 'knowledge' (cf. 1 Cor. i. 24–27; xiii. 2, 8), 'Pleroma', 'mystery', is due to the language of the errorists themselves. The Christology, which is the main theme, is not essentially different from that in 1 Cor. i. viii. 6: 'one Lord Jesus Christ through whom are all things and we through Him'. And the doctrine that the death of Christ was a conquest over evil powers is found in 1 Cor. ii. 6, 8, where, however, it is only incidental, not, as here, central to his theme. There is nothing in the epistle which warrants any serious doubts as to the authorship. Theories of editorial interpolations or glosses, made in order to explain the combination of Pauline elements with those which are thought to be sub-Pauline, may be seen in Moffatt, *Intr. Lit. N.T.*, pp. 155–8; cf. M. Goguel, op. cit. iv. 1, pp. 29 f.; iv. 2, pp. 413 f.

C. Masson[1] has reached the same conclusions as did H. J. Holtzmann[2] (but by a different route) that Colossians 'in its actual form is a revision and development of the primitive Epistle of Paul to the Colossians by the author of the Epistle to the Ephesians, who, publishing both letters under Paul's name, has related them closely one to the other'. Moffatt's comment on Holtzmann's theory can be applied to Masson's too; 'such filagree-criticism has failed to win acceptance; the literary criteria are too subjective'. Many scholars, however,

---

[1] *L'Épître de St. Paul aux Colossiens*, p. 86.
[2] *Kritik der Epheser- und Kolosserbriefe*, 1872, refuted by H. von Soden, *Jahrbücher f. protestantische Theologie*, 1885, pp. 320–68, 497–542, 672–702.

including Masson,[1] treat i. 15–20 as a source which St. Paul used; its style is liturgical or it may be part of a Christological hymn. If so, the Christology of the community which produced it was more 'advanced' than most Form-critics have recognized hitherto. The same conclusion may follow if Phil. ii. 6–11 is also taken to be a hymn.[2]

The Pauline authorship of Colossians would, indeed, be impossible if the dangers against which the readers are warned were the fully developed Gnosticism of the second century. But evidence has been accumulating that the germs of that development, which came into being owing to the meeting of oriental and Jewish thought, were present in the area of the Dispersion some years before the time of St. Paul. It is idle to try to identify the errors attacked with any particular system—Ebionism, Mithraism, Gnostic Ebionism, and so on. Features of all of them were spreading gradually westward, and St. Paul wished to supply a universal antidote.

§ 8. PHILEMON

PURPOSE AND CONTENT. Philemon, to whom the letter was addressed, was a Christian living, probably, at Colossae. This is shown by the fact that in writing to the Colossians St. Paul describes Onesimus, as he does Epaphras, as 'one of you' (Col. iv. 9, 12), and states that he is sending him thither with Tychicus (vv. 7, 8). Onesimus, Philemon's slave, had run away from him, found his way to Rome, and been converted by St. Paul, who now sends him back with an affectionate recommendation to his master, who had also been converted by the apostle (Philem. 19), to receive him no longer as a mere slave but as a Christian slave, a beloved brother (v. 16). A runaway slave was usually treated with such harshness that it was a somewhat delicate thing to ask a master to receive him; and that is shown by the extremely tactful and tender way in which St. Paul pleads for him.

It is remarkable that in the collection of St. Paul's epistles

---

[1] Op. cit., pp. 104 f.
[2] E. Lohmeyer, *Der Brief an die Philipper*, 1928, pp. 90 ff., cf. his treatment of Eph. i. 3–14, *Theol. Blätter*, 1926, p. 120.

made by the early Church there should be included a short note to an individual[1] on a purely personal matter. But this brief note was rightly felt to be of lasting value, not only for the picture that it affords of the apostle himself—his warm-hearted love for his slave convert, and his delicacy of touch in advancing his cause—but for the principle which he lays down, which in the long run was to undermine the massive fabric of slavery. To have given any specific injunctions against the practice would have been futile. It was accepted by all ancient races as part of the natural order of things; and to incite a few slaves to break loose would do nothing but harm. In 1 Cor. vii. 20–24 his advice to Christian slaves is exactly the reverse. His principle was that Christianity places men in a status above the social distinctions of master and slave (*v.* 16; cf. 1 Cor. xii. 13; Gal. iii. 28; Eph. vi. 8, 9; Col. iii. 11). All alike were 'bought' by Christ for His service (1 Cor. vii. 22 f.). And there-fore, while he sends the slave back to his master, he does not suggest that Philemon should release him, but asks him to *love* him. In the early Church 'no effort was made to put a stop to the system of slavery, but its sting was drawn by the glad recognition of the fact that all were brothers in Christ'.[2]

TIME AND PLACE. The letter was written in captivity (*vv.* 9, 13), at the same time as Colossians (see p. 158), and prob-ably from Rome. It cannot have been the imprisonment at Caesarea (Acts xxiii. 33), because he tells Philemon to prepare him a lodging, since he hoped soon to be allowed to visit him (*v.* 22). At Caesarea, where he appealed to Caesar and was waiting to be sent to Rome, he could have had no such hopes. And a runaway slave would be much more likely to escape to Rome than to Caesarea (but see below, pp. 180 ff.).

§ 9. EPHESIANS

CONTENTS. As in Colossians, the rhetorical flow of lan-guage which is called forth by the sublimity of the theme makes exact analysis impossible. But the doctrinal portion (i. 3–iii. 13), concluding with a prayer and doxology (iii. 14–21), is distinct

---

[1] It was addressed, however, also, not only to two who were doubtless members of his family, but to 'the Church in thy house'.
[2] J. W. C. Wand, *A History of the Early Church*, 1937, p. 91.

from the hortatory portion (iv. 1–vi. 20), concluding with personal references to himself and Tychicus, greetings, and the Grace (vi. 21–24).

A. Doctrine. i. 3–14: The *purpose* of God is the holiness, the sonship, the redemption of Christians; and Christ is the *Medium* in whom this is being accomplished, the ultimate aim being the summing up of all things in Him. An assurance to the readers of the apostle's prayers for them that they may have wisdom to understand and know the great things of God (i. 15–19) introduces i. 20–23: The *method* of God. God (1) raised Christ from the dead, and (2) set Him at His right hand, gave Him victory over His enemies, and made Him Head over all things to the Church. ii. 1–10: The purpose of this was that in Christ God might also (1) raise Christians from the death of sin, and (2) set them with Him in the heavenlies. ii. 11–22: The *result* of this plan was the unity of Jews and Gentiles in Christ. iii. 1–13: And this great mystery was entrusted to St. Paul, the apostle of the Gentiles, to proclaim.

B. Exhortation. The moral exhortations are mainly concerned with the nature and the preservation of the unity which God intended. iv. 1–6: The readers are exhorted to live in unity. iv. 7–16: It is the unity of a living and growing Body, the members of which possess a wide diversity of gifts and functions, and which receives its vital force from Christ the Head. iv. 17–v. 21: As converted Gentiles they must put off all that constitutes the old Self, the 'old man', and put on all that constitutes the 'new man'. v. 22–vi. 9: Particular injunctions towards the preservation of unity are added for wives and husbands (v. 22–33), children and parents (vi. 1–4), slaves and masters (vi. 5–9). vi. 10–20: For such a life the whole armour of God is required (vi. 10–17), with prayer and intercession (vi. 18–20).

GENUINENESS. A glance at the epistle is enough to show the very close connexion between it and Colossians. Moffatt[1] prints the parallels in full, which amount to large portions of both the epistles; cf. M. Goguel, op. cit. iv. 2, pp. 458 ff., and E. J. Goodspeed, *The Meaning of Ephesians*, 1933, pp. 82–165, where Goodspeed prints parallels to Ephesians from all the

[1] *Introd. Lit. N.T.*, pp. 375–81.

authentic Pauline epistles. Moffatt says (p. 375) 'Those who hold that both were written by the same author either place them together in the second century or attribute them both to Paul. On the latter hypothesis he read over Colossians (or a copy of it) before writing Ephesians, or else composed the letter when his mind was still full of what he had just addressed to the Church of Colossê. The relationship in this event would resemble that of the Thessalonian letters, when 2 Thessalonians is accepted as genuine.' That the epistle was written (or is represented as having been written) at the same time as Colossians is indicated in vi. 21, 'Now that *you also* may know my affairs, &c.', an allusion to Col. iv. 7. But many who accept Colossians as the work of St. Paul doubt or deny the genuineness of Ephesians on account of its language and style, its affinities with other writings, and its doctrine.

(a) *Language.* This undoubtedly shows marked differences from that of the earlier epistles. But since the readers and subject-matter are different, this alone, some scholars maintain, would be no more evidence of spuriousness than it is in the case of Colossians. Where the subject-matter is closely allied to that of Colossians the similarity of its language is very close, though some differences are noticeable. Differences are sufficiently accounted for, on this view, by saying that St. Paul possessed enough literary power to express similar thoughts with a variety of expression. Moffatt[1] notes that it contains thirty-eight words which are not used elsewhere in the New Testament literature, and forty-four[2] which, while employed elsewhere in the New Testament, are never used by St. Paul. But figures like these can be balanced by others. The length of Colossians is to that of Ephesians about as eleven to sixteen. It contains thirty-eight words of the former type (a much larger proportion) and eighteen of the latter. To these must be added eleven which occur only in Colossians and Ephesians and would be *hapax legomena* in Colossians if they were not imitated in Ephesians: ἀνθρωπάρεσκος, ἀπαλλοτριοῦσθαι, ἀποκαταλλάσσειν, αὔξησις, ἀφή, ὀφθαλμοδουλεία, πλήρωμα (of God), ῥιζοῦσθαι,

---

[1] Ibid., pp. 385 f.

[2] Forty-three if ἅπαντες (Gal. iii. 28) is included, otherwise forty-two (Goguel, op. cit., p. 456).

συνεγείρειν, συνζωοποιεῖν, ὕμνος, and seven which are found elsewhere in the New Testament but not in St. Paul's epistles outside Colossians and Ephesians: δόγμα, θεμελιοῦσθαι, κατοικεῖν, κράτος, κυριότης, σύνδεσμος, ᾠδή. It is clear that *hapax legomena* and 'non-Pauline' words alone cannot settle the question. It is remarkable, further, how large a number of words in Ephesians or [and] Colossians have New Testament parallels only in 1 or 2 Corinthians. And there are at least twenty-five thoroughly Pauline words and expressions in Ephesians (found in Rom., 1, 2 Cor., Gal., Phil.) which do not occur in Colossians. Thus 'the linguistic data may be allowed to leave the problem of the authorship fairly open' (Moffatt, p. 387), unless we deduce with Goodspeed that the writer, *c*. 90–96, was familiar with a Pauline corpus.

(*b*) *Style.* This must be used with caution as a criterion, since much depends on the reader's individual feelings as to what is probable and improbable in a writer's change of style. The epistle is nearer to being a poem in prose than any other of St. Paul's writings. What was said above on the style of Colossians is true of that of Ephesians in an advanced degree. It is lyrical, diffuse, and elaborate. The train of thought is slow. The author is fond of synonyms and epexegetical genitives (Goguel). But while in Colossians he had definite enemies in view, here he has none. And the question, which does not admit of a confident answer, is whether one who could pass from the style of the four *Hauptbriefe* to that of Colossians could not pass farther to that of Ephesians, the change being accounted for by his freedom from the pressure of controversy, and by the sublimity and cosmic vastness of his subject.

The theory that a Paulinist wrote the epistle in his master's name cannot be ruled out as impossible. The bulk of the material in the Pastoral Epistles is probably to be explained in that way (see p. 194 and n.) ; and 2 Peter is certainly pseudonymous. But in the case of Ephesians the problem has a psychological aspect. It is not easy to decide whether a follower of St. Paul, writing in his name, with his mind steeped in the language and thoughts of Colossians, and greatly influenced also by the other Pauline epistles, could or could not have risen to the height, and reached the wide expanse, attained in this epistle. It is this which places the problem on a different plane from that of any other imitation, or use of sources, in the New Testament.

(*c*) *Literary affinities*. Affinities with other writers, in so far as they are not merely reflections of the common language of early Christianity, might arise from more than one cause. Either they are due to the direct influence of the epistle on the writers, or to the influence of the epistle on the *totum* of Christian thought which they inherited, or the author of the epistle, together with the other writers, shared in a development of Christian thought and language which grew up spontaneously in the Church after St. Paul's death. In other words, did the author of our epistle breathe with others an existing atmosphere, or did he help to create it? As far as language goes, the affinities which are pointed out do not, for the most part, amount to very much.

LUKE AND ACTS. Moffatt,[1] who notes some dozen words peculiar to Ephesians and St. Luke's vocabulary, also gives the following parallels: men are the objects of the divine εὐδοκία (Lk. ii. 14; Eph. i. 5), and the Ascension is emphasized (Lk. xxiv. 51; Eph. i. 20; iv. 8, 10); he compares Lk. xii. 47, 'that slave which knew his lord's will and prepared not nor did according to his will', with Eph. v. 17; vi. 6; Lk. xii. 35, 'Let your loins be girded', with Eph. vi. 14;[2] and gives two parallels (ii. 5; v. 18) with the parable of the Prodigal Son, from which he notes that Resch[3] draws a long series of parallels with Eph. ii. 1–19, a passage which may well be compared with the parable for purposes of devotional study, but which can hardly be imagined to have any literary connexion with it.

All the similarities to our epistle that he suggests in the Acts are in St. Paul's address at Miletus: the βουλή of God (i. 11), the commission of the apostle (iii. 2, 7; iv. 11), the purchasing of the Church (i. 14), the 'inheritance' of Christians (i. 14), and the 'shepherding' of the Church (iv. 11). But St. Paul's commission or διακονία was a fact on which he laid frequent

---

[1] *Intr. Lit. N.T.*, p. 384.
[2] But the thought is different. The former is a simile of household slaves, the latter of soldiers.
[3] *Paulinismus*, 1904, pp. 373 f.

and vehement stress in earlier epistles; the inheritance of Christians is the subject of Rom. iv. 14; viii. 17; Gal. iii. 18, 29; iv. 7; and the purchasing of the Church in Ephesians and Acts respectively is probably derived from two different passages of the Old Testament.[1] Other passages to which he attaches significance are Acts xx. 21 'faith in (εἰς) our Lord Jesus' and Eph. i. 15, 'your faith in (ἐν) the Lord Jesus'; xx. 19 and Eph. iv. 2, vi. 7, 'humility' and 'serving God'; xx. 32, 'to give *you* the inheritance *among* them that are sanctified', and Eph. i. 18, 'the wealth of the story of *His* inheritance *in* the saints'. The differences are at least as noticeable as the similarities. But parallels would be sufficiently accounted for if St. Paul wrote Ephesians, and if St. Luke obtained a more or less trustworthy summary of the contents of his address at Miletus. Alternatively, a Pauline disciple writing towards the end of the first century may have had access to a copy of Acts or to material used by Luke.

PASTORAL EPISTLES. There are several parallels of thought and language which place the Pastoral epistles somewhat nearer to Ephesians than to the earlier epistles of St. Paul. Moffatt, however, dismisses them with the remark, 'But beyond suggesting a sub-Pauline milieu of thought and language, these coincidences amount to very little'. The question, as said above, is whether the sub-Pauline author of Ephesians lived in the same milieu, or whether St. Paul himself by his epistle helped to create it.

I PETER. In this case a difference of opinion exists as to whether there are any significant parallels at all. There are not many verbal coincidences; the most striking are 'Blessed be the God and Father of our Lord Jesus Christ' (Eph. i. 3; I Pet. i. 3), πρὸ καταβολῆς κόσμου (Eph. i. 4; I Pet. i. 20), ἀκρογωνιαῖον (Eph. ii. 20; I Pet. ii. 6), περιποίησις (Eph. i. 14; I Pet. ii. 9), τοῖς ἰδίοις ἀνδράσιν (Eph. v. 22; I Pet. iii. 1), εὔσπλαγχνοι (Eph. iv. 32; I Pet. iii. 8). But there are distinct

---

[1] The former (περιποίησις) from Exod. xix. 5 (quoted in I Pet. ii. 9 with the same word, instead of the LXX περιούσιος); the latter (περιεποιήσατο) from either Is. xliii. 21 (LXX λαός μου ὃν περιεποιησάμην) or Ps. lxxiv [lxxiii]. 2 in some current translation of Old Testament *logia* (LXX τῆς συναγωγῆς σου ἧς ἐκτήσω). With 'He purchased through His blood' he also compares Eph. i. 7, 'the redemption through His blood'.

echoes of thought which cannot safely be explained as expressing, independently, current Christian ideas. Few, probably, would agree with H. A. A. Kennedy's[1] verdict: 'while there are a few vague parallels, it is hard to trace any close interrelation of ideas.' Hort,[2] on the other hand, holds that 'the connexion, though very close, does not lie on the surface. It is shown more by identities of thought and similarity in the structure of the two epistles as wholes than by identities of phrase.' If Ephesians is not the work of St. Paul, the writer may have borrowed from 1 Peter; but if it is, the probability is much greater that 1 Peter, which made large use of Romans, also used Ephesians.

JOHANNINE WRITINGS. There is an approach towards the doctrinal position of the Fourth Gospel and 1 John (see below). Moffatt and Lock[3] collect several similarities of thought, some of which, however, find parallels in St. Paul's earlier writings. But there is very little linguistic parallelism. Moffatt holds that 'the likelihood is that the unknown *auctor ad Ephesios* was a Paulinist who breathed the atmosphere in which the Johannine literature afterwards took shape'. Similarly of the parallels with Hebrews he says that they do not 'prove more than a common atmosphere of religious feeling and phraseology'. But if St. Paul wrote Ephesians it is more likely that he began to create the atmosphere which was afterwards charged more deeply with the particular significances represented by the Johannine writings and Hebrews respectively.

GALATIANS. C. F. D. Moule[4] has drawn attention to the reference in Eph. iii. 3 to the writer having already described in writing how the mystery of the inclusion of the Gentiles in the Church had been known to him by a revelation so that his readers could assure themselves of his understanding in these matters by reading what he has written. The passage in our Pauline corpus exactly fitting this reference is Gal. i. 10 ff., where Paul states that it was through a revelation that he was

---

[1] *Ex. T.* xxvii, p. 264.

[2] *The First Epistle of St. Peter, i. 1–ii. 17*, p. 5. M. Goguel discusses the parallels (op. cit. iv. 2, pp. 447–50) and concludes that Eph. and 1 Pet. are independent one of the other.

[3] Hastings's *D.B.* i. 716 f.   [4] *Ex. T.* lx, 1949, p. 225.

called to preach the good news among the Gentiles. 'On Good-speed's showing, the readers only had to look in the new Pauline corpus to which Eph. (by a disciple) formed an intro-duction, to find the reference in Gal.'

DOCTRINE. This is the criterion to which most importance can be attached, and upon it those who deny the genuineness of the epistle lay the chief weight. It must be remembered, however, that if Colossians is genuine, it is not enough to point to the undoubted fact that St. Paul's thoughts show an advance in several respects upon those in the epistles of the earlier groups. They must show an advance upon the doctrine of Colossians marked enough to render the unity of authorship improbable. This is not the case with several of the minor Johannine parallels which can be found. The doctrinal differ-ences between the two epistles can be explained, to a con-siderable extent, by the fact that Colossians is polemical and Ephesians is not. In the former, Christ is declared to be supreme and central in the *cosmos*; in the latter, the immanent Principle in the unity and spiritual growth of the *Church*. Thus the subject-matter of the two epistles is in some degree differ-ent, and it is impossible to maintain that while the former could be emphasized by St. Paul the latter could not, and must be sub-Pauline. This will account for some of the affinities with the Johannine writings noted by Moffatt (p. 385): 'The unity of the church, including Gentiles as well as Jews, is the divine object of Christ's death'; 'the church is the πλήρωμα of Christ and of God'; 'exceptional stress is laid on the functions of the Spirit, the word, and baptism, the unity of the church as the result of the divine unity between Christ and God and as the means of advancing the gospel'; 'the emphasis on ἁγιάζειν and cleansing' and 'on the duty of Christian love'. One of the notable similarities between the two epistles is the absence of Jewish eschatological ideas. A faint trace of the old language is seen in Col. iii. 4, 'When Christ shall be mani-fested—our Life—then shall ye also with Him be manifested in glory'. But the idea is not that of a Parousia, but of an inward and spiritual triumph. Similarly in Ephesians the writer looks forward to a great End, but it is spiritualized; it is a consummation to be reached in the far future by the spiritual

growth of the Church; it is the (final) redemption of the
purchased possession, of which the seal of the Spirit is the
present pledge (i. 14 f.); similarly iv. 30; hence 'this age' can
be contrasted with τῷ μέλλοντι (i. 21); the Body of Christ must
be built up 'till we all attain to the unity of faith in, and knowledge of, the Son of God, to a perfect Man' (iv. 13); the
inheritance in the Kingdom of Christ and of God is a present
one (v. 5; cf. Col. i. 13); so also is the coming of the wrath of
God upon the sons of disobedience (v. 6); and this leaves room
for 'ages to come' (ii. 7). This spiritualizing of the great End
was part of St. Paul's advance in thought,[1] which many[2] have
unaccountably refused to admit, and was due to the lapse of
time, in which his early expectations of the imminence of the
Parousia were unfulfilled.

The differences between Colossians and Ephesians are
mainly concerned with the meaning of Christ's Person and
Death. With this is connected the thought of the union of Jew
and Gentile, which in Ephesians plays an important part,
while in Colossians it appears only in iii. 11, 'where there cannot be Greek and Jew, &c.', a sentence directed against the
exclusive pride of Gnostic claims. In Colossians the Mystery
is 'Christ in you, the hope of glory' which is preached to the
Gentiles (i. 27); 'the Mystery of God, (even) Christ' (ii. 2);
'the Mystery of Christ', i.e. the Mystery which is Christ (iv.
3). These passages emphasize the indwelling of Christ in
Christians, which Gentile Christians were privileged to experience. But in Ephesians 'the Mystery of Christ' is the fact
that the Gentiles were allowed to be fellow-heirs (iii. 5 f.). It
is their *inclusion* that is the mystery.

In Col. μυστήριον is equated with Christ, the Word of God. . . .
Compared with Paul's earlier uses, it is a new and remarkable
development. Clearly Paul himself feels that this is so. For the time
being it is the dominant feature of his thinking. If Ephesians were
also from his hand, written at the same time as Colossians, we
should expect to find some echo of this significance when the word

[1] Cf. R. H. Charles, *Eschatology*, 1913, pp. 437 ff.; C. H. Dodd, *Bulletin of the John Rylands Library*, xvii, 1933, pp. 91–105, and xviii, 1934, pp. 68–110; W. L. Knox, *St. Paul and the Church of the Gentiles*, 1939, pp. 111 ff.

[2] J. Lowe, *J.T.S.* xlii, 1941, pp. 129–42 and (for a well-informed criticism) W. D. Davies, *Paul and Rabbinic Judaism*, 1948, pp. 285–320.

was used again. But we look in vain in the three contexts (i. 9, iii. 4, v. 32) for any trace of it. Here the meaning of the word is not only different (though partially related) but, as with πλήρωμα, lacking in precision and clarity.[1]

Correspondingly, the reconciliation effected through Christ's death is in Colossians (i. 20) that of 'all things', 'whether things on earth or things in heaven', the latter being the angelic powers; and with all these the Gentiles also are reconciled to God. In Ephesians, on the other hand, the cosmic significance of His death is not mentioned; His cosmic function of 'summing up all things' (i. 10) is not connected with His death; the reconciliation is that of Jew and Gentile in one Body (ii. 14–16). Further, in Ephesians Christ's death is the means of redemption (i. 7). In Colossians it is His Person (i. 14). But the former is the more usual Pauline thought.

In Colossians it is maintained that in Christ 'dwelleth all the Pleroma bodily', i.e. in concrete reality (ii. 9). This is in opposition to the Gnostic idea that Christ is only one among many emanations proceeding from the Pleroma. And He is the Head of every (angelic) principality and authority (ii. 10). In Ephesians He as the Pleroma of God is immanent in Christians, the full spiritual wholeness towards which they must strive (iii. 19, iv. 13). And He is the Head as the centre of coherence and unity of the Body, the true safeguard against false teaching and schism (iv. 15 f.). C. L. Mitton argues that apart from Colossians and Ephesians the use of πλήρωμα is without theological significance but that in Colossians it is used in a new and daring way to mean that the sum total of the divine character inhabited the human personality of Jesus but that in Ephesians it is used differently in a vague and obscure way, which would not be possible if Ephesians were Pauline and were written soon after Colossians (op. cit.).

There might seem to be an advance of thought in respect of the Agent of reconciliation. In Col. i. 20–22 (as in 2 Cor. v. 18) it is God who reconciles to Himself all things in heaven and earth, supernatural powers and sinners, 'through Christ',

---

[1] C. L. Mitton, Ex. T. lx, 1949, pp. 320 f. In Eph. v. 32 μυστήριον may be used in a sense derived from the theology of the 'mystery' cults, cf. W. L. Knox, St. Paul and the Church of the Gentiles, pp. 182 f. and 227 f.

'through the blood of His Cross', 'in the body of His flesh'. In Eph. ii. 16 it is Christ Himself[1] who reconciles Jew and Gentile in one Body to God through the Cross. But that can be balanced by a converse difference: in Eph. iv. 32 'God in Christ forgave you', while in Col. iii. 13 'the Lord (i.e. Christ, as another reading has it) forgave you'.

Apart from these fundamentals there are expressions which might suggest a date later than St. Paul. Perhaps the most striking are the use of 'the devil' (iv. 27, vi. 11), as in the Pastoral epistles, instead of 'Satan' as in 1, 2 Thess., 1, 2 Cor., Rom., the unique 'in the heavenlies' (i. 3, 20, ii. 6, iii. 10, vi. 12), the mention of 'His holy apostles and prophets' as having received the revelation of the mystery (iii. 5), and of 'the apostles and prophets' as a recognized body constituting the foundation of the Church (ii. 20).

These facts will appeal differently to different minds. To some they will seem to be real differences in points of view, which could have been reached only by a 'sub-Pauline' writer approximating to the Johannine position, a Paulinist with a style of his own and the beginnings of a later vocabulary. Any conclusion must be reached with hesitation. If Ephesians is not Pauline, there is much to be said for Goodspeed's view that it served as an introductory epistle by a disciple to a Pauline corpus of letters.

TIME AND PLACE OF WRITING. The indications suggest that the epistle was written at Rome, at the same time as Colossians. The writer was in captivity; see iii. 1, 'I, Paul, the prisoner of Christ Jesus on behalf of you Gentiles'; iv. 1, 'I the prisoner'; vi. 20, 'the mystery of the Gospel, on behalf of which I am an ambassador in a chain'. And, if Ephesians is St. Paul's, his conception of the Church as an organic unity, kept and controlled by Christ its Head, may well have owed something to the fact that he was in Rome, the capital of an empire which was highly organized and closely knit into a unity under Caesar its head. The similarities with Colossians place the epistles, if St. Paul was the author of both, in immediate juxtaposition. And Tychicus is spoken of (vi. 21 f.) as

---

[1] Similarly, as Moffatt points out, in 1 Cor. xii. 28 God is the giver of spiritual gifts; but in Eph. iv. 11 it is Christ.

bringing news of the writer, in words almost identical with Col. iv. 7 f.[1]

DESTINATION. This is an enigma. According to the Textus Receptus, followed in our A.V. and R.V., the opening words are 'Paul . . . to the saints which are at Ephesus (ἐν Ἐφέσῳ) and the faithful in Christ Jesus'. But the most important authorities[2] omit ἐν Ἐφέσῳ; Marcion (and, according to Tertullian,[3] other heretics) styled the epistle 'to the Laodiceans'. A place-name is required by the sense, τοῖς ἁγίοις and πιστοῖς, 'the saints' and 'faithful', being a double description of the same persons,[4] unless we take τοῖς οὖσιν to mean 'local', cf. the phrase in papyri τοῦ ὄντος μηνός 'the current month', ὁ ὤν meaning 'local' of place and 'current' of time, cf. Acts v. 17, 'The local school of the Sadducees'. Without it the words would mean 'to the saints who are also faithful', which is next to impossible. And yet, if the epistle was written to the Christians at Ephesus, it is surprising that it contains no greetings to individuals, and even more so if the theory is correct that Rom. xvi. 1–23, with its numerous salutations, was a letter to Ephesus (see pp. 154, 158 f.). This has led many to think that it was a circular letter intended for more than one Church, so that no salutations were possible, and that St. Paul's amanuensis left a blank to be filled in with the name of each Church to which Tychicus was to carry a copy. The further suggestion has been made, assuming that the theory of the circular letter is correct, that that letter is referred to in Col. iv. 16 in the injunction that the Colossians are to 'read the letter that is [i.e. that will be forwarded to them] from Laodicea'. It is thought that since the Colossians were receiving a letter of their own, St. Paul might think it unnecessary to send them also a copy of the circular letter. But this is unlikely, because if he wished them to read it as well as their own, it would be more natural that he should send them a copy. But the circular letter theory is not without its difficulties. If the amanuensis wrote out several

---

[1] See p. 166.
[2] B ℵ P⁴⁶, 1739, ancient codices known to St. Basil, Origen.
[3] *Adv. Marc.* v. 11.
[4] J. P. Wilson has suggested that ἐνί could easily have dropped out between οὖσιν and καί. If so, the original sense was 'to the saints who are one and faithful in Christ Jesus'. (*Ex. T.* lx, 1949, p. 225.)

copies, it was as easy for him to insert the place-name as for anyone else. And even if he left a blank, why should he omit the preposition ἐν? Did it drop out after ἐνί? Moreover, our earliest manuscripts, all of which omit ἐν and the place-name, must have been copied from earlier manuscripts, which finally go back to an archetype, which omitted them, for it is impossible to think that any scribes would omit them if they found them in the archetype. We are thus reduced to the improbable supposition that the archetype of our manuscripts was a spare copy which omitted them, and which was never delivered. If Ephesians was a circular letter, a solution which is just possible would be that the Laodiceans, being bidden to send it on to Colossae, and not wishing to part with their own letter, sent a copy which they made themselves, omitting ἐν Λαοδικίᾳ; that this was the copy used when the collection of Pauline epistles was made, and if, as is possible, that took place at Ephesus the words ἐν Ἐφέσῳ were inserted later. Yet another solution has been proposed—that the letter was written to a single Church, and originally ended with some salutations, but that when a desire was felt to use it for general purposes in the Church, editors omitted ἐν and the place-name together with the salutations. In this case, if Ephesus was not its original destination, Marcion and others may have been right after âll in styling it 'to the Laodiceans'. After the collection of letters was made, the presence of a place-name in the other letters made its absence in this one noticeable, and ἐν Ἐφέσῳ was inserted. Harnack suggests, rather fancifully, that the name Laodicea was omitted when it had become a name of ignominy in the Church (see Rev. iii. 14–16). But there are two objections to the theory. The writing is much more suitable as a general epistle than addressed to a particular Church. And the general salutations in the last two verses—'peace be to the brethren', 'grace be with all those who love', &c.— make it difficult to think that they were originally preceded by particular salutations. Perhaps the true solution has yet to be found, unless Goodspeed's theory is accepted, that Ephesians was written by a Pauline disciple as a preface to a corpus of Pauline letters.

§ 10. PHILIPPIANS

CONTENTS. Apart from iii. 2–iv. 1 (see below) this affectionate letter to St. Paul's best-loved converts is mainly concerned with personal matters. After the opening salutation, thanksgiving, and prayer (i. 1–11) he gives an account of himself—the spiritual result of his imprisonment (i. 12–18), and his hopes of 'salvation', i.e. probably his acquittal and release from bonds; for himself he would prefer death, but for their sakes he wants to live, and is confident of regaining his freedom and of seeing them again (i. 19–26). He will send Timothy, of whom he speaks in the highest praise, as soon as his own affairs are settled (ii. 19–24). Meantime he is sending Epaphroditus, who had brought a contribution from them. Epaphroditus had almost worked himself to death in supplying the apostle's needs, and was greatly troubled that the Philippians had heard of his consequent illness (ii. 25–30). He concludes the letter by expressing his thanks for their contribution, adding that he quite understood that their lack of opportunity had prevented them from helping him earlier. He had learnt, indeed, to be content in any circumstances, but their kindness was good, and they knew that he had accepted help, when he left Macedonia, from no other Church (iv. 10–18). And he ends with a closing prayer for them, salutations, and the Grace (iv. 19–23).

But with all these friendly messages he was obliged to speak of things which were not right with them. There were dissensions among them, so that he must appeal to them to show a united front (i. 27–30), and to live in unity and humility (ii. 1–4). This he enforces, in a sublime passage,[1] by pointing to the Self-emptying of Christ and of His glory which followed (ii. 5–11). They must therefore avoid murmurings and disputings, and set a shining example to the non-Christians round them (ii. 12–18). He begins to draw the letter to a close (iii. 1), but is constrained to renew his appeal—first, to two women, Euodia and Syntyche, who were probably the chief source of the dissensions (iv. 2, 3), and then to all, to let every-

---

[1] Derived from a Christian hymn perhaps, cf. E. Lohmeyer, *Der Brief an die Philipper*, 1928, pp. 90 ff.

one see their selfless yielding of their own rights and wishes, because Christ is coming soon who will put everything right, to pray and give thanks and be guarded in the peace of God (iv. 4–7). If their minds are set on the highest things, the God of Peace will be with them (iv. 8, 9).

The contents, as here sketched, form a complete and simple whole. The remaining passage, iii. 2–iv. 1, is quite foreign to it, and raises the question of the unity of the epistle.

UNITY. In the midst of grateful messages, and gentle and loving admonitions, this unexpected passage reveals the apostle in a wholly different mood. His pen suddenly becomes the rapier of the combatant, with which he attacks a twofold enemy. 1. He is on fire against Judaizers, as in Galatians. He hurls at them the epithet 'dogs', which they used of Gentiles, and scornfully speaks of circumcision as 'concision', mere mutilation (iii. 2). And, as in 2 Corinthians, he asserts with vehemence his own authority, high status, and aims as a Christian (*vv.* 4–14), calling upon the readers not to take a retrograde step (*vv.* 15 f.), but to imitate him (*v.* 17). 2. He laments that many do not. They are not only Judaizers, but, like the false teachers attacked in Rom. xvi. 17 f. (see p. 155), libertines, 'the enemies of the Cross of Christ, whose end is perdition, whose God is their belly and whose glory is in their shame, whose mind is centred upon earthly things'. The body of the true Christian, on the contrary, belongs already to the heavenly polity, whence Christ will appear, and is being prepared for the final transformation into the body of His glory (*vv.* 17–21).

It is scarcely possible to resist the conclusion that this is a fragment of another letter written by St. Paul to other readers. There is no evidence that the simple-minded Philippians were troubled either by Judaism or by libertinism. And Lightfoot's artificial explanation is unconvincing—that St. Paul was interrupted in his writing, and in the interval heard that these enemies were making trouble at Philippi, so that when he sat down to write again he plunged into violent controversy before resuming his affectionate appeal to the readers to be at unity. That fragments were incorporated in other letters has been shown to be probable in the case of 2 Cor. vi. 14–vii. 1 (pp. 139 f.), and possibly Rom. xvi. 1–23 (pp. 154 f.). Many would add 2 Cor. x–xiii (pp. 139 ff.). Opinions differ as to whether the words of iii. 1b, 'To write the same things unto you is not irksome to me but safe for you', belong to the fragment or not. 'To write the same things' may mean 'to bring up the subject of your dissensions again' (so Lightfoot; and the setting of the verse in Westcott and Hort's text implies the same). If this is right it is almost certain that iv. 2 ff., in which the subject is brought up again, must have followed immediately. Another explanation is that the half-verse belongs to the fragment, and 'to write the same things' means to bring up again the subject of the heresies, which we must suppose the apostle had already attacked in the earlier, lost portion of the letter to which the fragment belongs. But the former seems the more probable.

TIME AND PLACE. The theory has been so widely accepted that our epistle, together with the other three in this group, was written in captivity at Rome that it was thought best to study it at this point. The apostle was clearly a prisoner, for he speaks three times of his 'bonds' (i. 7, 13, 17). And this could not have been at Caesarea, just before starting for Rome, since he hoped soon to visit the Philippians (ii. 24), and speaks of his renewed presence with them (i. 26). But it is possible that he wrote the letter at Ephesus during his long stay there after leaving Antioch for the third time for missionary work. The arguments for Rome and Ephesus respectively are as follows:

1. *Rome.* (*a*) He says that 'his bonds have become manifest in Christ in the whole *praetorium*, and to all the rest' (i. 13). The last words make it probable that the *praetorium* is not the Emperor's 'palace' (A.V.), nor its barracks, nor the military camp outside the walls, but a body of persons. And these have been held to be either the 'praetorian guard' (R.V., following J. B. Lightfoot[1]) or the imperial court, 'the whole body of persons connected with the sitting in judgment' (Ramsay[2]). Lightfoot (p. 19) thinks of 'the praetorian soldiers, drafted off successively to guard him and constrained while on duty to

---

[1] *Philippians*, pp. 99–104.
[2] *St. Paul, the Traveller and the Roman Citizen*, p. 357.

bear him company'. But since they numbered some 9,000 men,
and he was guarded by one soldier at a time, the words must
be hyperbolical, not literal. If, however, the words were
written at Rome, this remains the best explanation. The
objection to Ramsay's meaning is that there is no evidence for
it. (b) Among the Christians who send greetings are 'especially
they of Caesar's household' (iv. 22). There were, no doubt,
Christians to be found in the enormous numbers of the
Emperor's slaves and courtiers. See Lightfoot, *Philemon*, p.
319, and Sanday and Headlam on the households of Aristo-
bulus and Narcissus, Rom. xvi. 10, 11. (c) Timothy joins in the
opening salutation as in Colossians and Philemon.

But among those who accept this evidence there is a difference of opinion as to whether the epistle was the earliest or the
latest of the Roman group.

(i) For the earlier date Lightfoot points to the very close
affinity in language and thought with Romans (see his parallels,
Philippians, pp. 43 f.), and the great difference from them of
the language and thought of Colossians and Ephesians. He
says, 'The heresies, which the apostle here combats (*sc.* in Col.
and Eph.), are no longer the crude, materialistic errors of the
early childhood of Christianity, but the more subtle speculations of its maturer age'. But these differences are, in fact, too
great to render the argument safe, since on the theory of Rome
as the place of writing all the development and growth to
maturity take place within the two years or so of his imprisonment there. It would be easier to recognize that the minds of
the Philippians were simpler and more elementary than those
of the Asiatic Christians, and therefore needed different
teaching.

(ii) For the later date it is argued: (a) That some time was
needed for the communications between St. Paul and the
Philippians—for them to send a contribution by Epaphroditus,
for him to fall ill by overwork on St. Paul's behalf, for the news
of it to reach them, and for St. Paul to hear that they had
received the news. Lightfoot contrives to explain it all by two
journeys; but in any case, if the journey between Rome and
Philippi occupied about a month, as he reckons, not more
than, say, five months are required. (b) St. Paul's 'defence

(*apologia*) of the Gospel' (i. 16) is explained by Ramsay as the defence of his own case in the Emperor's court; and his 'salvation' (*v*. 19) as the acquittal which he expected with some confidence, though he was prepared for the possibility of martyrdom (ii. 17). (*c*) If Ramsay's explanation of the word *praetorium* is correct, it is another indication that the trial was actually in process. The epistle would thus be placed close to the end of the captivity of Acts xxviii.

2. *Ephesus.*[1] The three arguments for Rome can be used with equal force for Ephesus. (*a*) An inscription[2] found there shows that praetorian soldiers were stationed in the city. And they would be much fewer in number than in Rome, so that St. Paul's words could be understood literally. (*b*) Another inscription[3] speaks of 'the slaves of our Lord Augustus', which shows that they and his freedmen were numerous enough to form burial clubs. (*c*) Timothy was with the apostle at Ephesus (Acts. xix. 22), but there is no certainty that he was at Rome. (If Heb. was addressed to Rome, Heb. xiii. 23 suggests that he was known there.) (*d*) Further, the similarities with Romans can be accounted for if the epistle was written at Ephesus just before St. Paul started to go via Macedonia to Corinth, where he wrote Romans. (*e*) And his expectation to visit the Philippians soon was natural, since he would certainly stop at Philippi on his way through Macedonia. (*f*) The Philippians had waited a long time to send him a contribution, because, as he says, they 'had lacked opportunity' (iv. 10). If he wrote from Ephesus this was really the case, because he had been far away in Palestine and Galatia since leaving Corinth (Acts xviii. 18–23, xix. 1). But if he wrote from Rome, it was after staying three months in Corinth (Acts xx. 3), when they could easily have sent him supplies as they had done during his previous Corinthian visit. Indeed they could actually have

---

[1] The arguments for the Ephesian theory are discussed by F. B. Clogg, *Introduction to the New Testament*, pp. 67–80, and C. H. Dodd, *Bulletin of the John Rylands Library*, xxiv, 1934, pp. 92 ff., cf. M. Goguel, op. cit. iv. 1, pp. 414 ff. The fullest defence of this theory is to be found in G. S. Duncan's *St. Paul's Ephesian Ministry*, 1929.

[2] J. T. Wood, *Discoveries at Ephesus*, 1877, App. 7, p. 4: 'T. Valerio T. F. Secundo Militis Cohortis VII Praetoriae Centuriae Severi.'

[3] Ibid., p. 18: 'Quorum [a monument and sarcophagus] Curam Agunt Collegia Libertorum Et Servorum Domini Nostri Augusti.'

given them to him in person when he was passing through Macedonia to Corinth. Written from Rome the words convey a rebuke, which, however gentle and tactful, is unexpected after their previous liberality on more than one occasion, which he gratefully records in iv. 15, 16. (g) The Parousia of Christ is still thought of as imminent; 'the Lord is at hand' (iv. 5) is similar to 'Maran-atha' (1 Cor. xvi. 22). It is difficult to place this in close conjunction with Colossians and Ephesians, in which, as has been said, the eschatology is largely spiritualized. The same must be said of the fragment iii. 2–iv. 1, in which 'heaven' is that 'from which we wait for a Saviour, the Lord Jesus Christ' (iii. 20); and the transformation of our bodies at the Parousia (v. 21) carries on the thought of 1 Cor. xv. 51–53.

No one would hesitate to regard this evidence as conclusive were it not that there is no mention in the Acts of an imprisonment at Ephesus. But neither is there any mention of the acute sufferings and perils of which the apostle himself speaks. His fighting 'with beasts at Ephesus' (1 Cor. xv. 32), whether this refers to men[1] or to actual wild animals, implies physical hardships which point to imprisonment. And the same is true of his affliction in Asia, an overpowering burden that made him despair of life (2 Cor. i. 8), and the anguish of mind and body depicted in 1 Cor. iv. 9–13 (written at Ephesus), and in 2 Cor. iv. 8–12 (written shortly afterwards, cf. Acts xx. 18 f. Moreover, the sufferings recounted in 2 Cor. vi. 4 f., xi. 23–27, including 'prisons' in the plural, the only imprisonment previously related in the Acts being that at Philippi (xvi. 24), show how little weight can be attached to St. Luke's silence about one at Ephesus.

That silence makes it impossible to place the writing of the epistle with complete certainty at Ephesus, but the theory has great probability. If it is accepted, Philippians must be placed in the second group, in close conjunction with 1 Corinthians

---

[1] With the metaphorical use cf. Ignatius, *Rom.* 5. But if 'beasts' is literal, the words must be rendered 'If after the manner of men I *had* fought with beasts at Ephesus, what advantage would it have been to me, &c.?', since a Roman citizen could not suffer the disgrace of the arena. If he was condemned *ad leones*, and escaped only because his Roman citizenship was discovered (cf. Acts xvi. 38 f., xxii. 26–29), he was almost certainly in prison for a short time.

and probably Galatians, and before 2 Corinthians and Romans. And the fragment iii. 2–iv. 1 was probably written at the same time, perhaps to some neighbouring Church in Asia.

Dr. T. W. Manson[1] would go farther, arguing that if the Roman origin of Philippians is abandoned, there is no need to suppose that when St. Paul wrote this letter he was in prison. The references to the 'bonds' in i. 7 can be taken to mean all the unpleasant experiences which he underwent from his first day at Philippi; ii. 17 can be taken to mean, 'We are in the same straits; let us show the same invincible joy in facing the odds together.' In iv. 14 θλῖψις need not mean 'the tribulation of imprisonment' but tribulation in the widest sense, such as lack of food, shelter, and friends. The reference to the Praetorium in i. 13 is taken to indicate a 'Government house' somewhere in the provinces. The suggestion is that St. Paul had been detained while awaiting trial but that now the trial is over; St. Paul has been acquitted and, being free, he can propose to visit Philippi. This letter may well be from Ephesus, says Dr. Manson, but not from prison.

Similarly, H. Wedell[2] has considered the Pauline words like (σύν)δοῦλος, δέσμιος, δεσμός, συναιχμάλωτος, ἄλυσις, and he finds that they are all used metaphorically to express 'spiritual imprisonment' or 'total apprehension in the service of Christ'. But this may well seem a *reductio ad absurdum* of this theory.

Most scholars, however, are prepared to admit that, despite the silence of Acts, St. Paul may have been imprisoned at Ephesus even if they treat as a different question whether St. Paul wrote any other letters, besides Philippians possibly, from Ephesus. Setting aside the late tradition of the lion to whom St. Paul was thrown at Ephesus licking his feet or of the building there known as his prison or of the Monarchian Prologue to Colossians, probably Marcionite in origin despite Lagrange, which speaks of St. Paul thus, 'Apostolus iam ligatus scribit eis ab Epheso', and which is as unreliable as the other Prologues ascribing Philemon and 'Laodiceans' to Paul at Rome, we have references in 2 Cor. i. 8–10; xi. 23; 1 Cor. xv. 30–32; Rom. xvi. 3, 7, which are best explained by the

---

[1] *Bulletin of the John Rylands Library,* xxiii, 1938, pp. 182 ff.
[2] *Theology,* l, 1947, pp. 366–72.

theory that St. Paul was imprisoned at Ephesus, though St. Luke did not think it necessary to include a reference to it in Acts. But whether Colossians, Philemon, and Ephesians (if Pauline) were written from Ephesus possibly during imprisonment is a different matter. When the two former letters were written, St. Luke was with St. Paul. We are told that he was with him in Rome, but we do not learn that they were together in Ephesus; as Acts xix is not part of the 'We-sections' the implication is that if Luke wrote Acts he was not with Paul at Ephesus. Against that, Timothy, another companion of the imprisonment letters, is known to have been with Paul at Ephesus but is not known for certain to have been with him at Rome. It is doubtful, it may be argued, whether Onesimus, the runaway slave, would have fled to Ephesus or to distan Rome, to escape detection. If Colossians, with which Philemon must go closely, was written from Ephesus, it was penned not long after 2 Cor. i–ix, which seems unlikely.[1] F. B. Clogg[2] has concluded, 'The cumulative evidence may seem to favour Ephesus as the place of writing of Philippians—but it does not amount to proof. On the other hand, the balance of evidence supports Rome, the traditional place of writing of the other three captivity epistles.'

BOOKS AND ARTICLES

E. H. Askwith, *The Epistle to the Galatians, its destination and date,* 1899.
B. W. Bacon, *Jesus and Paul,* 1921.
A. E. Barnett, *Paul becomes a literary influence,* 1941.
W. Bousset, *Kyrios Christos,* 2nd ed., 1921.
F. C. Burkitt, *Christian Beginnings,* 1924, pp. 116–34.
P. Carrington, *The Primitive Christian Catechism,* 1940.
S. Cave, *The Gospel of St. Paul,* 1928.
W. D. Davies, *Paul and Rabbinic Judaism, Some Rabbinic Elements in Pauline Theology,* 1948.
A. C. Deane, *St. Paul and his Letters,* 1944.
C. H. Dodd, *The Bulletin of the John Rylands Library,* xvii and xviii, 1933.
W. P. du Bose, *The Gospel according to St. Paul,* 1907.
E. J. Goodspeed, *The Meaning of Ephesians,* 1933.
—— *New Solutions of New Testament Problems,* 1927.
W. Goossens, *L'église, corps du Christ d'après St. Paul,* 1949.

[1] C. A. A. Scott, *J.T.S.* xxxi, 1929–30, pp. 197–9.
[2] Op. cit., p. 80.

Th. Haering, *Der Römerbrief des Apostels Paulus*, 1926.

F. J. A. Hort, *Prolegomena to the Epistles to the Romans and Ephesians*, 1895.

A. M. Hunter, *Paul and his Predecessors*, 1940.

H. A. A. Kennedy, *St. Paul and the Mystery Religions*, 1913.

—— *The Theology of the Epistles*, 1919.

J. H. Kennedy, *The Second and Third Epistles to the Corinthians*, 1900.

J. Klausner, *From Jesus to Paul*, Eng. trans. by W. F. Stinespring, 1942.

W. L. Knox, *St. Paul and the Church of the Gentiles*, 1939.

—— *St. Paul and the Church of Jerusalem*, 1925.

—— *Some Hellenistic Elements in Primitive Christianity*, 1944.

K. Lake, *Paul, his Heritage and Legacy*, 1934.

—— *The Earlier Epistles of St. Paul*, 2nd ed., 1919.

K. Lake and F. J. F. Jackson, *The Beginnings of Christianity*, vols. i–v, 1920–33.

C. L. Mitton, *The Epistle to the Ephesians*, 1951.

J. G. Machen, *The Origin of Paul's Religion*, 1921.

A. H. McNeile, *New Testament Teaching in the Light of St. Paul's*, 1923.

—— *St. Paul, his life, letters, and Christian doctrine*, 1920.

W. Morgan, *The Religion and Theology of Paul*, 1917.

A. D. Nock, *St. Paul*, 1938.

E. Percy, *Die Probleme der Kolosser- und Epheserbriefe*, 1946.

F. C. Porter, *The Mind of Christ in Paul*, 1930.

F. Prat, *The Theology of St. Paul*, 1926.

J. H. Ropes, 'The Singular Problem of the Epistle to the Galatians', *Harvard Theological Studies*, xiv, 1929.

A. von Schlatter, *Gottesgerechtigkeit*, 1935.

P. Schubert, 'Form and Function of the Pauline Thanksgivings', *Beihefte zur Zeitschrift f. d. N.T.-Wissen.* xx, 1939.

A. Schweitzer, *Paul and his Interpreters*, 1912.

—— *The Mysticism of Paul the Apostle*, Eng. trans. by W. Montgomery, 1931.

C. Anderson Scott, *Christianity according to St. Paul*, 1927.

H. St. J. Thackeray, *The Relation of St. Paul to contemporary Jewish thought*, 1900.

J. Weiss, *The History of Primitive Christianity* (completed by R. Knopf), Eng. trans., 1937.

N. P. Williams, *Essays Catholic and Critical*, ed. E. G. Selwyn, 1927, pp. 367–423.

—— *The Ideas of the Fall and of Original Sin*, 1927, pp. 93–163.

COMMENTARIES

Romans: K. Barth (1926, trans. by Sir E. C. Hoskyns, 1933), E. Brunner (1948), C. H. Dodd (1932), K. E. Kirk (1937), M. J. Lagrange (1931) H. Lietzmann (3rd ed., 1937), W. Sanday and W. Headlam (1900), E. F. Scott (1947).

1 Corinthians: E. B. Allo (1935), E. Evans (1930), H. L. Goudge (1903),

J. Héring (1948), H. Lietzmann (1949), N. Micklem (1920), J. Moffatt (1938), A. Robertson and A. Plummer (1911), J. Weiss (9th ed., 1910).

2 Corinthians: E. B. Allo (1937), A. Crosthwaite (1919), H. L. Goudge (1927), A. Menzies (1912), A. Plummer (1915), R. H. Strachan (1935), H. Windisch (1924).

Galatians: F. Amiot (1946), A. W. F. Blunt (1925), E. de W. Burton (1921), G. S. Duncan (1934), C. W. Emmet (1912), M. J. Lagrange (4th ed., 1942), H. Lietzmann (1932), J. B. Lightfoot (10th ed., 1890), Sir W. M. Ramsay (1899), H. Schlier (1949).

Ephesians: T. K. Abbott (1897), C. Gore (1898), W. Lock (1929), J. Armitage Robinson (1903), E. F. Scott (1923), B. F. Westcott (1906).

Thessalonians: E. J. Bicknell (1932), M. Dibelius (1937), J. E. Frame (1912), E. Lohmeyer (3rd ed., 1937), G. Milligan (1908), W. Neil (1948), A. Plummer (1918).

Philippians: P. Bonnard (1950), M. Dibelius (1937), M. Jones (1918), J. B. Lightfoot (2nd ed., 1869), E. Lohmeyer (1937), J. H. Michael (1928), A. Plummer (1919), E. F. Scott (1923), M. R. Vincent (1897).

Colossians: T. K. Abbot (1897), M. Dibelius (1927), J. B. Lightfoot (1875,) E. Lohmeyer (1930), C. Masson (1950), L. B. Radford (1931).

VII

1, 2 TIMOTHY, TITUS

THE title 'Pastoral Epistles', which is commonly used to designate this group of writings, does not describe their contents very accurately. It has some suitability in the case of 1 Timothy, less in that of Titus, and for 2 Timothy it is hardly suitable at all. Zahn[1] traces it to some lectures by Paul Anton in 1726–7, afterwards edited by Maier as *Exegetische Abhandlung der Pastoral-Briefe Pauli an Tim. u. Tit.*

CONTENTS. In none of these is a definite plan or course of thought to be traced. The object of the writer was to offer some sound advice to those who were in positions of responsibility in the Church. The chief trouble through which the Church was passing was the prevalence of false teaching of a Gnostic type allied with Jewish speculations. To this he constantly recurs, dwelling on the necessity of sound teaching in opposition to it. He also gives advice, chiefly in 1 Timothy but also in Titus, on Church organization, and the attitude that its leaders should adopt towards various individuals and classes in the Christian community. All this, however, is in view of the heretical teaching which is the burden that chiefly weighs on his mind; any advice that is given which is not concerned directly with heresy arises out of the danger or leads up to it. Apart from this there are personal details in 2 Tim. iv. 6–21 and Tit. iii. 12–14, which are of great importance in their bearing on the authorship of the epistles. They will be discussed below. The following analysis will show how the writer's thoughts oscillate between the condemnation of heresies and practical advice which the Church needed in view of them.

1 *Timothy.* i. 1, 2 : Salutation.

i. 3–11.   Timothy was left at Ephesus to oppose heresies into which some had fallen. *vv.* 12–17: The heresies are contrasted with the apostle's manner of life in the ministry which God's grace had entrusted to him after

[1] *Einleitung in d. N.T.*, i. 447 n.; Eng. *Introd. to the N.T.*, 1909, ii, p. 67 n.

his conversion. *vv.* 18–20: Timothy is exhorted to live the same life, in contrast with that of the errorists, of whom two are named.

ii. 1–8.　Prayer is to be offered for all men. *vv.* 9–15: The subordination of women in Church life. iii. 1–7: The qualifications of a bishop, and, *vv.* 8–13, of deacons, including (*v.* 11) their wives.

iii. 14–16.　The Church must be so ordered because it is the pillar and basis of Christian truth, of which a rhythmical formula is quoted. iv. 1–16: The teaching and manner of life, exemplified in those of Timothy, which are to be an antidote to the errors of those who oppose the truth.

v. 1, 2.　Timothy's manner of life in relation to individual Christians; *vv.* 3–16 to widows; *vv.* 17–25 to presbyters; vi. 1, 2 to slaves.

vi. 3–10.　Condemnation of false teachers.

vi. 11–16.　The right manner of life in contrast with theirs. *vv.* 17–19: Charge to rich Christians.

vi. 20, 21a.　Warning to preserve the deposit of faith in opposition to false 'knowledge'. vi. 21b: 'Grace be with you.'

2 *Timothy.* i. 1, 2: Salutation. *vv.* 3–5: Thanksgiving for Timothy's spiritual state.

i. 6–14.　Admonitions to follow the apostle's manner of life and to be true to his Gospel. *vv.* 15–18: Onesiphorus is given as an example. ii. 1, 2: Timothy is to entrust this Gospel to men who can teach others. *vv.* 3–13: And he must show endurance himself; for though adherence to Christian truth is a stern fight, yet the reward is sure.

ii. 14–23.　Empty and pernicious controversies must be avoided. *vv.* 24–26: The Lord's servant must not be contentious, but tactful, in order to win over opponents. iii. 1–10: A stern rebuke of the opponents.

iii. 11, 12.　Timothy must imitate the apostle's endurance in sufferings; all Christians must endure them.

iii. 13–17.　In the face of deceivers he must be true to the teaching of the Bible which he had known from childhood; and, iv. 1–5, be devoted in his work of teaching the truth.

iv. 6–8.　The writer is in momentary expectation of death.

iv. 9–21.   Personal details.
iv. 22.   'The Lord be with thy spirit; grace be with you.'

  Titus. i. 1–4: Salutations.

  i. 5, 6.   Titus was left at Crete to order the Church and ap-
               point fitting presbyters. *vv.* 7–9: Qualifications of a
               bishop.
  i. 10–16.   This is in view of antinomian heretics.
  ii. 1, 2.   Sound teaching must be given to older men; *vv.* 3–5
               to women; *vv.* 6–8 to younger men; *vv.* 9–10 to slaves.
               vv. 11–15: This is because of God's purposes for which
               men were redeemed by Christ. iii. 1–8: And the same
               purposes require Christians to preserve a blameless
               life in their dealings with all men.
  iii. 9–11.   The foolish teachings of heretics are to be shunned,
               and a heretic after admonition is to be personally
               avoided.
  iii. 12–14. Personal details.
  iii. 15.   Salutations. 'Grace be with you all.'

THE FALSE TEACHING. It will be seen how central a place
the false teaching occupies in the writer's thoughts; he is
unable to take his mind away from it for long, and comes back
to it again and again. The harm that it was doing to the Church
gives a ground and force to all his other exhortations. It is
possible that it was beginning to affect some who held office
in the Church, which would give additional point to his injunctions as to their character and behaviour, and the discrimina-
tion needed in ordaining them.

1. He speaks of some who are 'insubordinate, vain talkers,
and deceived in mind, especially they of the circumcision'
(Tit. i. 10), showing that some, but not all, were Jewish Christians. They claimed to be 'law teachers', though they were
incapable of understanding the true meaning and purpose of
the law (1 Tim. i. 7–10). But their error was quite different
from that of the 'slavery' to law of the earlier Judaism, against
which St. Paul fought in his second group of epistles. They
seem to have taught that Christians could be above law, that
a state of superior *gnosis* made them indifferent to God's moral
commands.[1] This leads the writer to declare that 'the law is

---

[1] The writers of the Apocalypse, Jude, 2 Peter, and 1 John were all faced with
the same dangerous tendency.

good if one treats it as law', i.e. as a prohibition of grievous
sins, and that every passage in the Old Testament (*sc.* including the law), given by inspiration of God, is intended to be
morally and spiritually profitable (2 Tim. iii. 16, 17). An
element of antinomianism was already to be felt when St. Paul
wrote to the Galatians (v. 13) and Romans (vi. 15). But that
was due, not to Gnostic esoteric teaching, but to an unintelli-
gent misuse of the 'freedom' from Judaic rules which St. Paul
claimed for Christians. A peculiarly bad feature is attacked in
1 Tim. vi. 5, the corruption and perversion of the minds of
men who could use their religiousness as a means of making
money.

  2. The alliance of Gnosticism with Judaism (such as was
seen, for example, in the Naassenes, an early form of the
Ophites) probably explains the references to 'myths and endless genealogies' (1 Tim. i. 4), 'old women's myths' (iv. 7),
'Jewish myths' (Tit. i. 14). Gnostics indulged in speculations
about aeons and emanations intervening between God and
created matter. But it is not necessary to bring the date of our
epistles down to the time when these speculations became fully
developed, or to restrict the term 'Gnostic' to the second-
century systems. The writer probably refers to myths and
legends in apocryphal Jewish works in which Gnostic and
other Oriental elements were mingled.

  3. The effect of Oriental thought upon some minds was to
lead them to the idea that matter was evil. The possessor of
true *gnosis* must suppress, and be superior to, the claims of the
body. They taught a rigid asceticism (1 Tim. iv. 8, E.V.
'bodily exercise') involving renunciation of marriage and of
the use of certain foods (*v.* 3). The writer controverts this mistaken dualism by the plain statement that all foods were
created by God, and that every creature of God is good and to
be received with thanksgiving offered to Him as a religious act
(*vv.* 3–5). It was possible to bid Timothy to keep himself pure,
and yet to drink a little wine for the sake of his health (v. 22,
23). The teaching that 'the resurrection is past already' (2 Tim.
ii. 18) is perhaps another aspect of the same depreciation of
matter unless it was due to a misunderstanding of 'realized
eschatology'; the true Gnostic was thought to be already in the

spiritual sphere and independent of the body. If so, it was a travesty of the language of true Christian mysticism: e.g. Rom. vi. 1–11; 2 Cor. v. 14 f.; Gal. ii. 20; Col. ii. 12 f., 20; iii. 1; Eph. ii. 5 f.; see also John v. 21, 24; 1 John iii. 14; writings in which true *gnosis* is taught in opposition to the spurious.

We are justified in using the word Gnosticism of these various types of error, since the false teachers themselves claimed a *gnosis* which the writer calls 'pseudonymous', 'falsely named' (1 Tim. vi. 20). Their pride ('puffed up', *v.* 4) in their esoteric teaching is probably to be seen in what he describes as *antitheses*, 'oppositions', which they drew between it and ordinary Christian doctrine, but which he couples with 'profane babblings' (*v.* 20). And he speaks of their discussions and disputes about words as nothing short of a disease (*v.* 4). Hort[1] tried to explain the *antitheses* as purely Rabbinic, 'the endless contrasts of decisions founded on endless distinctions which played so large a part in the casuistry of the scribes as interpreters of the law'. But this cannot be considered probable in face of the double product of dualism condemned in the epistles—asceticism and antinomianism. He admits the possibility, in St. Paul's lifetime, of influences at Ephesus and in Crete 'connected with a speculative form of Judaism out of which some forms of "Gnosticism" may later have been developed', but strangely holds 'that there is a total want of evidence for anything pointing to even rudimentary Gnosticism'. Still less is it necessary to take the *antitheses* to refer to Marcion's work as though this were an anti-Marcionite and late gloss. That the heresy attacked here and in Colossians is only Judaism with 'a quasi-Hellenic varnish' is a conclusion with which most modern writers do not agree.

AUTHORSHIP. The words 'Paul an apostle of Jesus Christ' form the opening of 1, 2 Timothy, and 'Paul a servant of God and an apostle of Jesus Christ' of Titus. Irenaeus, Tertullian, and Clement Alex. are known to have accepted them as the work of St. Paul. On the other hand, Tertullian (*adv. Marc.* v. 21) and Jerome (*Praef. in Tit.*) state that Marcion rejected them all; so also, according to Jerome, 'Basilides and all the

---

[1] *Judaistic Christianity*, 1894, pp. 130–46.

heretics'. He says further that Tatian accepted Titus as St.
Paul's, implying that he rejected 1, 2 Timothy. From Irenaeus
until modern times the Pauline authorship is assumed; and
some writers today defend it. In 2 Timothy and Titus occur
passages containing personal allusions which seem almost certainly to be the work of the apostle. The question is whether he
wrote the whole of the three epistles, or whether a devoted
disciple, being in possession of some genuine Pauline fragments,
built up the epistles out of them in order to give to the Church
a message which he felt sure that the apostle would have given
had he been alive, and quite naturally wrote them in the
apostle's name. That would not be the modern method of
treating precious fragments, but ancient methods were very
often not modern ones. The evidence in favour of the latter
theory is cumulative; although each point, taken by itself,
might with ingenuity be deprived of decisive weight, taken
together they appear irresistible.

1. The great stress laid, as shown above, on the danger of
Judaic Gnosticism or Gnostic Judaism suggests that it had
become more acute and more developed than in St. Paul's day.
And it is met, not, as in Colossians, by argument, but simply
by authoritative contradiction and denunciation. A lesser mind
can contradict and denounce, while it is not equal to the task
of refuting.

In the same spirit the writer exhibits a somewhat stereotyped *conception of orthodoxy*. St. Paul fought for what he believed to be true with the skill of a fencer, and with a creative
genius which helped him, as a master builder, to erect a firm
edifice of Christian doctrine. But here a later date is suggested
by the fact that the whole body of Christian doctrine is
assumed to be standing in its entirety. It is 'the Faith' (1 Tim.
i. 19; iii. 9; iv. 1, 6; v. 8; vi. 10, 21; 2 Tim. iii. 8; iv. 7; Tit. i.
13); 'the truth' (1 Tim. iii. 15; iv. 3; vi. 5; 2 Tim. ii. 15, 18;
iii. 8; iv. 4; Tit. i. 14); 'knowledge of truth' (1 Tim. ii. 4;
2 Tim. ii. 25; iii. 7; Tit. i. 1); 'the teaching' (1 Tim. iv. 13,
16; vi. 1; cf. iv. 6; vi. 3; 2 Tim. iii. 10; Tit. ii. 10); 'the commandment' (1 Tim. vi. 14); 'the charge' (1 Tim. i. 5); 'the
[my] deposit' (1 Tim. vi. 20; 2 Tim. i. 12, 14); 'the healthy
teaching' or 'words' (1 Tim. i. 10; vi. 3; 2 Tim. i. 13; iv. 3;

Tit. i. 9; ii. 1; cf. i. 13; ii. 2, 'healthy in faith'), 'safe-' or 'sane-mindedness' and the corresponding verb, adjective, and adverb (1 Tim. ii. 9, 15; iii. 2; 2 Tim. i. 7; Tit. i. 8; ii. 2, 4, 5, 6, 12). That is not the language of a pioneer, interpreting the fact of Christ, and putting in their true light the errors that endanger it. 'His was altogether a different kind of spirit from that which burns and throbs in every page of the genuine Paulines' (Harrison[1]).

2. Connected with this is the quality of the *style* which is 'correct and diffuse, somewhat lacking in warmth and colour'. 'The syntax is stiffer and more regular' (Lightfoot[2]). 'The comparative absence of rugged fervour, the smoother flow of words, and the heaping up of epithets, all point to another sign-manual than that of Paul' (Moffatt[3]). Even if St. Paul wrote the epistles in a period of release and a second Roman imprisonment, which is improbable (see below), it is difficult to believe that his mind could have lost so much of its fire and force in two or three years.

3. Not only in style but in *vocabulary*, e.g. Latinisms, new compounds, particles, favourite expressions, &c., the difference from the Pauline epistles is very great, in spite of several Pauline words and expressions which the writer adopts. And what is un-Pauline is scarcely more remarkable than the absence of words, particles, and constructions which are distinctive of St. Paul. The absence of the following Pauline particles and prepositions is very striking, as particles express the style and 'the style is the man': ἄρα, ἄρα οὖν, ἄρτι, διό, διότι, ἐπεί, ἐπειδή, ἔτι, ἴδε, ἰδού, νυνὶ δέ, ὅπως, οὐκέτι, οὔτε, πάλιν, ποῦ, ὥσπερ, ὥστε. The vocabulary stands on the whole nearer to that of the Christian writings of the second century than to the Pauline epistles. This is shown in the exhaustive study by Harrison, to which the reader is referred.[4]

4. The *ecclesiastical organization* includes directions regarding the bishop, presbyters, deacons and their wives, widows. None

---

[1] P. N. Harrison, *The Problem of the Pastoral Epistles*, 1921.
[2] *Biblical Essays*, p. 402.
[3] *Introd. Lit. N.T.*, p. 407.
[4] But it must be noted that Dr. Harrison's list of Pastoral *hapax legomena* gives not the earliest but the latest appearance of these words; cf. the valuable criticism by F. R. M. Hitchcock, *J.T.S.* xxx, 1928–9, pp. 272–9.

of these, indeed, imply a state of development impossible in St. Paul's lifetime. But when he deals with them it is mostly in answer to questions, and often on the basis of the highest moral principles and profound Christian doctrines. The writer of these epistles, on the other hand, is occupied with questions of ecclesiastical arrangement and *personnel* as such, in the hope that a well-ordered Church may stand as a bulwark against the flowing tide of heresy. And for this purpose he simply lays down a series of authoritative directions.

5. In *doctrine* the writer is a devoted Paulinist. He teaches 'life eternal, won by Christ's death, which has brought salvation to all mankind; and this life must show itself by a high Christian morality, and be ready to face the appearing of Jesus Christ' (Lock[1]). But the last sentence should be noted. In earlier days St. Paul, as a Jew, had placed eschatology in the forefront of his teaching. But a comparison of 1, 2 Thessalonians with Colossians and Ephesians (if Pauline) shows how his mind was changing its point of view; in Colossians and Ephesians the emphasis was on the 'Coming Age' as an eternally existent reality, not on it as a future event.

The emphasis which the writer lays on the nature of God by means of epithets,[2] μόνος ('only'), σωτήρ (Saviour), μακάριος ('blest'), ἄφθαρτος ('imperishable', 'immortal'), ἀόρατος ('invisible'; cf. 1 Tim. vi. 16), τοῦ ζωογονοῦντος τὰ πάντα ('who quickeneth, *or* endueth with life, all things'), μέγας ('great'), ζῶν ('living'), ἀψευδής ('without deceit', 'that lieth not'), was occasioned by the heresies which he was combatting. But St. Paul, in Colossians and Ephesians, though he is dealing with similar heresies at an earlier stage, gives little direct teaching on the nature of God. He mostly takes that for granted, as understood by his readers; and throughout his epistles his point of view is Christocentric.

An expression unique in the New Testament occurs in 1 Tim. ii. 5: 'There is one Mediator (μεσίτης) between God and men, [being Himself] Man, Christ Jesus.' This is connected with the preceding words 'our Saviour God who willeth all men to be saved, &c.', and with the following, 'who gave

---

[1] Hastings's *D.B.* iv. 773.
[2] See A. H. McNeile's *New Testament Teaching*, pp. 207–13.

Himself a Ransom on behalf of all as being their Equivalent' (ἀντίλυτρον ὑπὲρ πάντων). Being both God and Man, the Equivalent of our Saviour God and the Equivalent of man who is to be saved, He is able to ransom all. The meaning of the word 'mediator' should be compared with that in Gal. iii. 20, where St. Paul says that in the New Dispensation no mediator corresponding with Moses is needed, and in Heb. viii. 6; ix. 15; xii. 24, where Jesus is the 'Mediator of a new covenant' transcending Moses. Both St. Paul and the writer of Hebrews are concerned mainly with the death of Christ. For the former His birth into human life, 'born of a woman, born under the law', was only the necessary step for placing Himself under law and curse, and being 'made sin on our behalf', in order that by death He might burst free from them, and so conquer them. St. Paul never speaks of the Incarnation as having the significance in the plan of salvation that is accorded to it by the writer of 1 Timothy.

The conclusion, as has been said, is irresistible. The epistles, as they stand, cannot be from St. Paul's pen. The theory that the differences from his other epistles are due to the work of an amanuensis[1] is quite inadequate to account for the facts. Some have thought that 2 Timothy was written by the apostle, and not the other two. But all the three as wholes are too closely similar in style, language, and thought to be thus differentiated.[2] They must stand or fall together.

A more probable theory, as said above, is that they contain some original Pauline fragments incorporated by a disciple: these seem to form a larger portion of 2 Timothy than of the others, and to consist for the most part of personal allusions.[3]

PERSONAL ALLUSIONS. If St. Paul wrote the whole of the three epistles as they stand, these allusions are impossible to explain except on the assumption that he was released from the imprisonment with which the book of the Acts closes, and

---

[1] So, for example, Rackham, *The Acts of the Apostles* (1911), p. 19, who suggests St. Luke.

[2] Cf. Goguel, op. cit. iv. 2, pp. 500–4.

[3] W. Lock, *Pastoral Epistles* (Intern. Crit. Comm., 1924), thinks it possible that these fragments and the epistles are alike genuine, but originally unconnected. The fragments were bound up with the rest, as, for example, was Rom. xvi.

wrote them afterwards, 1 Timothy and Titus during the period of his freedom, and 2 Timothy in a second imprisonment. If the latter epistle was written in the imprisonment of Acts xxviii, great difficulties are raised, four of them by the single passage 2 Tim. iv. 9–21 :

(1) He writes to Timothy, 'Do thy diligence to come to me quickly' (*v.* 9); 'Do thy diligence to come before winter' (*v.* 21). This does not sound as if Timothy had been with him in the same imprisonment when he wrote Colossians (i. 1), Philemon (*v.* 1), and ?Philippians (i. 1).

(2) He says that Titus has gone to Dalmatia (*v.* 10). But this would mean that he had deserted his charge of the Church in Crete (Tit. i. 5), where he still was when St. Paul wrote his epistle to him, came to the apostle at Rome, and then left him, not to return to his work, but to go elsewhere.

(3) Because Titus, Demas, and Crescens had gone, only Luke was with him (*v.* 10). But he does not explain the absence of four other Christians who were with him just before in the same imprisonment, and sent greetings to the Colossians (Col. iv. 10–14) and (three of them[1]) to Philemon.

(4) He tells Timothy, 'Take Mark and bring him with thee, for he is useful to me for service' (*v.* 11). The words suggest that St. Paul was sending for him to come to be his personal attendant in Rome for the first time. And yet he was already with him when he wrote to the Colossians (iv. 10) and to Philemon (*v.* 24), and was about to pay Colossae a visit, which he would probably not do if St. Paul needed him for service.

No one disputes that the Pauline authorship of all these epistles requires a period of release and a second imprisonment. This is rendered still more certain if the apostle made a journey to Spain, as he hoped to (Rom. xv. 24, 28). But the evidence for this journey is very slender. Apart from the sentence in the Muratorian Canon, 'sed et profectionem Pauli ab urbe ad Spaniam proficiscentis', which need not be more than a deduction from Rom. loc. cit., there is only an obscure remark of Clement Rom. (*ad Cor.* v), that St. Paul 'having come to the limit of the West (ἐπὶ τὸ τέρμα τῆς δύσεως), and

---

[1] Perhaps all four. Jesus Justus can be included if 'Ιησοῦς is read for 'Ιησοῦ, or added after it.

having borne witness before the rulers, so was released from the world and went to the holy place'. When we find that Ignatius (*ad Rom.* ii) uses the same word δύσις, 'West', of Rome, it is unsafe to conclude that Clement means Spain.[1] Apart from this, the internal allusions in our three epistles are our only guides. But even the assumption of a second imprisonment is not free from difficulties. St. Paul might have wanted his cloak[2] in prison, and conceivably his books and parchments (2 Tim. iv. 13); but his request for the latter, and the injunction, 'Do thy diligence to come before winter' (*v.* 21), hardly sound as if he were on the point of martyrdom, as he declares in *v.* 6. If only Luke was with him (*v.* 11), how is it that he can send greetings from Eubulus, Pudens, Linus, Claudia, and all the brethren (*v.* 21)? And after the careful injunctions to Timothy as to his behaviour in the execution of his office at Ephesus (i. 6–iv. 5), it is strange that St. Paul should urge him to leave his post and rejoin him as speedily as possible (iv. 9, 21). If, on the grounds stated above, it is impossible to assign the three epistles as wholes to St. Paul, the genuine fragments which his disciple incorporated probably refer to events not later than, but within, the period of the Acts.

In this case the personal allusions afford no indication of the order in which the epistles were written. But since 1 Timothy is the richest in doctrinal and ecclesiastical matter, and 2 Timothy contains least of these but apparently most of St. Paul's own work, it is probable that the order of writing was 2 Timothy, Titus, 1 Timothy. The present order will, in that case, have been due to the editors of the Pauline *corpus*, who collected the epistles, probably at Ephesus. They placed first the two to Timothy, who was left at Ephesus, and the longer was prefixed to the shorter.

Several suggestions, some of them more plausible than others, for the identification of the fragments may be seen in Moffatt.[3] A more recent attempt is made by Harrison (op. cit.).

---

[1] See A. H. McNeile's *St. Paul*, pp. 256 f.

[2] If φελόνης means a cloak (= φαινόλης = *paenula*). But Chrysostom says that some understood it to mean τὸ γλωσσόκομον (the bag, cf. John xiii. 29) in which the books lay. So the Syriac. Or it may have been a travelling bag or case, not necessarily for the books.

[3] *Introd. Lit. N.T.*, pp. 403 f.

He finds five genuine notes: (1) Tit. iii. 12–15, written from western Macedonia several months after 2 Cor. x–xiii, and before 2 Cor. i–ix (see pp. 139–42 above), bidding Titus, who was at Corinth, join him in Epirus—which he did, bringing the good news of the submission of the Corinthians. (2) 2 Tim. iv. 13–15, 20, 21a, written from Macedonia after the visit to Troas mentioned in 2 Cor. ii. 12 f., bidding Timothy, who had returned to Ephesus, join him before winter. On leaving Ephesus St. Paul had gone first to Miletus, taking Trophimus the Ephesian with him, and had left him there sick. Meanwhile Timothy, since he was with St. Paul when 2 Cor. i–ix was written, must have returned to Ephesus, and there received a note, i.e. the present fragment, telling him to come. (3) 2 Tim. iv. 16–18a (? 18b), written from Caesarea soon after the soldiers had escorted him from Jerusalem (Acts xxiii. 31 ff.). His 'first defence' was the *apologia* of Acts xxii. 1, when none of the brethren supported him. (4) 2 Tim. iv. 9–12, 22b, written from Rome to recall Timothy, probably from Philippi (Phil. ii. 19, 23). All the friends who had been with the apostle at Rome were scattered, with the exception of Luke. Mark was at some place known to Timothy, probably Colossae (Col. iv. 10), who would pick him up *en route*. (5) Various fragments, 2 Tim. i. 16–18; iii. 10, 11; iv. 1, 2a, 5b, 6–8, 18b, 19, 21b, 22a, which Harrison thinks were the principal *Grundschrift* of the epistle, written from Rome as a farewell to Timothy when the apostle was hourly expecting martyrdom. It would reach him at Ephesus as he was hurrying Romewards in response to the preceding note (4).

Moffatt says that 'the net result of such investigations is negative'. But though certainty may never be reached as to the exact extent of Pauline material which the author incorporates, there is little doubt that parts of the epistles—or at least of 2 Timothy and Titus—are the work of St. Paul, and larger parts are not.

BOOKS

M. Goguel, *Introduction au Nouveau Testament*, iv. 2, 1926, pp. 476–561.

P. N. Harrison, *Problem of the Pastoral Epistles*, 1921.

A. H. McNeile, *St. Paul, His Life, Letters, and Christian Doctrine*, 1920, pp. 241–64.

J. Moffatt, *Introduction to the Literature of the N.T.*, pp. 395–420.
H. Windisch, *Zeitschrift f. d. neutest. Wissenschaft*, xxxiv, 1935, pp. 213–38.

COMMENTARIES

M. Dibelius (2nd ed., 1931), B. S. Easton (1948), Sir Robert Falconer
    (1937), W. Lock (1924), R. St. J. Parry (1920), E. F. Scott (1936),
    C. Spicq (1947).

VIII

GENERAL EPISTLES AND HOMILIES

THE remaining writings of the New Testament are not, and do not profess to be, the work of St. Paul. The epistles are of various dates, 1 Peter or Hebrews being possibly the earliest, and 2 Peter the latest. But they can best be studied according to the prevailing colour of their contents: James and 1 Peter may be described as ethical, Hebrews as Christological, Jude, 2 Peter, and the Apocalypse (which is clearly intended to be an epistle) as eschatological.

§ 1. JAMES

CONTENTS. The epistle consists, for the most part, of a series of little groups of maxims, and the only analysis that is possible is to distinguish the groups. Their order does not appear to be determined by any particular plan; a thought, or even a word, sometimes leads the writer on from one to another. But the main thread on which many of them are strung is the obvious but important truth that a man's faith, his attitude towards God, is unreal and worthless if it is not *effective*, if it does not *work* practically in life.

i. 1. Address. *vv.* 2–4. Trial is useful to test the worth of your faith, and endurance tends to perfectness and wholeness, so that you may be lacking in nothing. *vv.* 5–8. Any one who lacks divine wisdom can obtain it only by single-hearted effort in prayer. *vv.* 9–12. The poor brother can rejoice in the exaltation which divine wisdom gives, and the rich brother ought also to rejoice at the salutary trial of losing his wealth, because endurance of trial leads to moral and spiritual reward.

vv. 13–18. An examination of the true meaning and nature of trial: a man is tried not by God but from within. Evil desire which succeeds in seducing the soul gives birth to death. What comes from God is not trial but every good and perfect gift; of His own will He gave birth to us. *vv.* 19–21. Anger, filthiness, malice cannot work the righteousness of God, the salvation of the soul. That is gained by God's ἔμφυτος λόγος. *vv.* 22–25.

Moral results are not produced by hearing God's word without doing it. *vv.* 26, 27. Pure religion is not shown by an unbridled tongue, but by charity and chastity.

ii. 1–13. Religious faith is not sincere if it does not involve a right relationship to the poor, in accordance with the royal law 'Thou shalt love thy neighbour as thyself'. To transgress that command in any respect is to transgress the whole law. *vv.* 14–26. More generally, religious faith is worthless if it is not effective in 'works', the practical conduct of daily life. iii. 1–12. No one can be τέλειος, much less a teacher of others, if he cannot control his tongue. *vv.* 13–18; iv. 1–6. To claim heavenly wisdom is boastfulness and lying if you give way to bitter jealousy and factiousness; that is the very reverse of heavenly. The friendship of the world, which issues in these quarrels and jealousies, is the very reverse of the friendship of God. iv. 7–10. An appeal to submit to God in humble repentance. *vv.* 11, 12. To speak evil of others is opposed to the law of the divine Judge. *vv.* 13–17; v. 1–6. Two stern warnings against the proud self-sufficiency of wealthy traders, and against the wantonness of the rich and their exploiting of the poor.

v. 7–11. An exhortation to sufferers to exercise unmurmuring patience, both because the Lord is soon coming, and because all trial has a divine purpose (τέλος Κυρίου). v. 12. Swear not. *vv.* 13–18. The value of prayer, and in particular the healing value of the prayer of Church leaders with unction. *vv.* 19, 20. The spiritual reward of reclaiming a wanderer from his errors.

In ch. i there are some verbal links, and as far as iv. 6 the 'thread' spoken of above is more or less discernible; but after the appeal in iv. 7–10 the advice given is varied and quite miscellaneous. The epistle thus answers well to Ropes' description[1] of it as an imitation of the *diatribē*, a homiletic exhortation which passed into popular use from the Cynics.

A. Meyer takes James to be a unit composed of twelve short homilies upon the twelve patriarchs taken in turn (*Das Rätsel des Jacobusbriefes*, 1930, pp. 179–94). But according to W. L. Knox[2] the epistle contains three addresses in *diatribē* form, ii. 1–13 and 14–26 and iv. 1–10. To him the real problem lies in i. 2–27 and iii, underlying which he finds a basic document,

---

[1] *St. James* (I.C.C.), p. 3.   [2] *J.T.S.* xlvi, 1945, pp. 10–17.

i. 2–4, 9–12, 19–20, 26–27, and iii. 13, presenting a coherent line of thought based on the recognized standards of Jewish piety: but the rest of this section he takes to be the work of some Hellenistic commentator, concerned to give a running commentary on the basic document and introducing Hellenistic ideas which frequently are quite out of place and Greek words which are often forced into a doubtful or impossible sense. The remainder of the later chapters consist of a series of detached moral and religious maxims. Knox was inclined to suggest that the high authority which the basic text must have possessed may be due to its having been an utterance of James the Lord's brother while the 'commentator' may have been Ariston of Pella.

AUTHORSHIP. The writer names himself James, but we have no means whatever of identifying him. Tradition ascribes the epistle to the Lord's brother, who was leader of the Church in Jerusalem, whose martyrdom at the hands of the Jews is variously assigned to the reigns of Nero[1] and of Vespasian.[2] During the growth of the canon a book that was not thought to be 'apostolic' had little chance of universal reception. And the fact that James was the brother of Jude, to whom an epistle was ascribed, might contribute to the growth of the tradition. But it was, in fact, very slow in attaining to canonical authority. No writer is known to have attributed it to the Lord's brother before Origen,[3] and even he frequently quotes him quite loosely as 'the apostle James'. And Eusebius (loc. cit.) in the fourth century could still say only 'it is said to be by James the Lord's brother'. The tradition, therefore, rests on a somewhat slender foundation. And considerations can be urged against it:

(1) The lack of early evidence and the slowness with which the epistle was received as canonical are unfavourable to the idea that it was written by the head of the mother-Church of Christendom.

(2) It is difficult to think that a brother of the Lord, who had become a believer in Him, writing certainly before A.D. 69—some think at a much earlier date—could have written

---

[1] Joseph. *Ant.* xx. 9, followed by Jerome, *De vir. illustr.* 2.
[2] Heges. *ap.* Eus. *H.E.* ii. 23.   [3] *In Rom.* Lommatsch, vi. 286.

without speaking of His death or resurrection (unless a veiled reference to His death is to be seen in v. 6), and have contented himself with naming Him only twice (i. 1; ii. 1)—or only once, if, as is probable, the name in the latter passage is an interpolation. Although he refers to words of our Lord (see below), he shows little sign, such as we see in 1 Peter, of His 'personal spell'. And the moralizings and aphorisms which are the principal feature of the book, while they are natural from the pen of a Judaistic Christian, hardly seem to belong to the age of the Church's first life and inspiration, marked by enthusiasm and *charismata*. In particular the gift of healing, which St. Paul says that the Spirit distributed to Christians as He willed (1 Cor. xii. 9, 11, 28), has become, in this epistle, an official endowment of Church elders (v. 14 f.).

(3) The language and style of the whole epistle belong to a stage of literary ability and culture that could hardly be expected from a countryman of Galilee. The grandsons of Jude the brother of James, in the reign of Domitian, remained simple and hard-handed sons of the soil,[1] and it is difficult to think that the religious ascetic described by Hegesippus[2] had so far outstripped the rest of the family, long before, in learning and thought. The author writes not as a Palestinian but as a Jew of the Dispersion. He not only knows the LXX, and echoes the Wisdom literature of the Old Testament, but some of his thoughts and language are reminiscent of Alexandria,[3] and his $\tau\rho o\chi o\grave{s}$ $\tau\hat{\eta}s$ $\gamma\epsilon\nu\acute{\epsilon}\sigma\epsilon\omega s$ (iii. 6) is possibly an echo of an Orphic phrase, used as loosely as the word 'Evolution' is today. His language is idiomatic, and his style shows signs of literary, Hellenistic art. He even uses an hexameter line, $\pi\hat{a}\sigma a$ $\delta\acute{o}\sigma\iota s$ $\dot{a}\gamma a\theta\grave{\eta}$ $\kappa a\grave{\iota}$ $\pi\hat{a}\nu$ $\delta\acute{\omega}\rho\eta\mu a$ $\tau\acute{\epsilon}\lambda\epsilon\iota o\nu$ (i. 17), which is probably a quotation from a Hellenistic author known to his readers. The question is whether the thoughts may have come from James the ascetic of Jerusalem, while the Greek in which they are expressed is the work of another unless we accept Knox's theory. Wordsworth held that the epistle was a translation from the Aramaic; and Burkitt[4] revives the theory. The

---

[1] Heges. *ap.* Eus. *H.E.* iii. 20.   [2] Ibid. ii. 23.
[3] See *N.T. Teaching in the Light of St. Paul's*, p. 108.
[4] *Christian Beginnings*, pp. 69 f.

original, he thinks, was an exhortation to a particular congregation, and the translator has turned it into a general epistle to the twelve tribes of the Dispersion. He points out that Hegesippus, in relating the martyrdom of St. James, speaks of 'all the *tribes*' coming to the Feast of the Passover; and he holds that, if the translator was not Hegesippus himself, he was of the same community in Gentile Aelia Capitolina, and of the same tendencies. But it is easier to suppose that such a person was the author, not the translator, and that the epistle stood to St. James's teaching in somewhat the same relation that St. Mark's gospel stood to the Aramaic instructions of St. Peter. If he was the 'interpreter' of St. James it is easy to understand how the latter's name was adopted by the writer. The theory that it was pseudonymous was already known to Jerome.[1] Moffatt doubts whether it was the name of James the Lord's brother that the writer intended to assume, since 'many indeed are called James', as Jerome says in the same passage; he asks why a pseudonymous Judaistic writer did not 'make more of Paul's opponent'. But if he was not arguing with St. James's name as a handle, but simply expressing what he felt to be his mind, it was enough for his purpose to state his case in the plain, direct language of an authoritative teacher. Anyone who knew the early conditions knew that St. James could not have written the epistle in its Greek shape, and yet it gradually acquired 'apostolic' repute.

CHARACTER OF THE READERS. 'There were rich members as well as poor (i. 9–11; ii. 15). There was religiousness together with social snobbery (ii. 1–3); a desire to be thought religious, and to be teachers, together with an inability to control the tongue (i. 26; iii. 1–12; cf. iv. 11); and the ambition to be esteemed wise and understanding led to jealousy and a factious spirit (iii. 13–16; cf. v. 9); and there was not only jealousy but bitter fightings and even murder[2] (iv. 1, 2), together with worldliness and pride (*vv.* 4–6), filthiness and overflowing of wickedness (i. 21).'[3] If the Christian congregations in any part of the empire answered to the description, an

---

[1] *De vir. ill.* 2.
[2] Perhaps the word is used metaphorically.
[3] A. H. McNeile's *N.T. Teaching in the Light of St. Paul's*, p. 89.

early date for the epistle is scarcely possible. But how much of this denunciation was the stock-in-trade of a *diatribē* writer? Some have thought that it was a Jewish writing with Christian interpolations. But apart from i. 1; ii. 1,[1] the reminiscences of sayings of our Lord (see below) cannot be interpolations, and the Christianity of the writer gleams behind his words with a subdued light that no redaction could produce. A Christian interpolator would almost certainly have added more, and his additions would have been more easily separable from the original. J. H. Moulton[2] suggested that James of Jerusalem wrote it for Jews, but in that case it must have been written in Aramaic. It is difficult, indeed, to think that Christians are directly addressed in the two stern warnings, typical of a moralist, beginning ἄγε νῦν, to wealthy traders, and to the wanton rich who oppress the poor (iv. 13–17; v. 1–6). But the facts are probably best accounted for by supposing that a Hellenistic Christian wrote for *both Jews and Christians*. He wanted to describe for all alike the true principles of Christian morality, his writing being called forth partly by sins to which Jews were especially prone, and partly by the antinomian spirit in Christian circles which grew out of a misunderstanding or perversion of St. Paul's teaching on freedom. That is very different from the view that he was a Judaizer who deliberately attacked that teaching. But there was nothing in the epistle from which a good-minded Jew could not derive pleasure and profit. And several of his words and phrases— whether deliberately chosen for the purpose or not—are in fact capable of either a Jewish or a Christian interpretation; e.g. 'The twelve tribes that are in the Dispersion' (i. 1) would be understood literally by Jews, metaphorically by Christians. 'The Lord' could refer either to Yahweh or to Christ (i. 7; iv. 10, 15; v. 7, 8, 10, 11, 14, 15; in iii. 9; v. 4, it refers to Yahweh only). Our 'begetting' by God with the word of truth, that we might be, so to speak, a firstfruit of His creatures (i. 18) might be either the first creation (cf. the allusion in iii. 9 to Gen. i. 27) or the second, spiritual, Christian creation. 'The

---

[1] In the latter passage the words ἡμῶν 'Ιησοῦ Χριστοῦ are very likely a *scribal* addition which has made havoc of the syntax.

[2] *Expositor*, 7th series, iv. 44–55.

perfect law, the law of liberty' (i. 25; cf. Ps. cxix. 45), 'the royal law according to the scriptural passage, Thou shalt love thy neighbour as thyself' (ii. 8), is the moral law thought of either as contained in the Pentateuch or as fulfilled by Christ. 'The honourable Name which was called upon you' (ii. 7) is in keeping with the Hebrew thought that Yahweh's Name was 'called upon' the nation, and on those who spiritually attached themselves to it (Amos ix. 12;[1] Is. lxiii. 19, &c.), while Christians would think of the Name called upon them at their Baptism when they were incorporated in the New Israel. 'The elders of the *ecclesia*' (v. 14) may, perhaps, be intended to refer only to Christian elders; but that cannot be gathered from the expression itself. The word *ecclesia*, used in the LXX of the nation of Israel as a sacred assemblage, occurs in the same sense in Acts vii. 38, and it was not felt to be incongruous as placed in the mouth of our Lord (Matt. xviii. 17), a Jew speaking to Jews. συναγωγή (ii. 2) could naturally be read by Jews as meaning 'synagogue', if the word denotes a building; and it is found in early days used of a Christian church.[2] But it probably means simply 'assembly', 'congregation'. 'Brother' (i. 9; ii. 15; iv. 11) is frequent in Deuteronomy (xv. 3, 7, 9, &c.), and '[my] brethren' (i. 2 + 11 times) occurs in Gen. xxix. 4 and elsewhere.[3] 'The Parousia of the Lord' (v. 7 f.) and 'the Judge standeth before the doors' (*v.* 9) are expressions of Jewish no less than Christian eschatology. 'Ye murdered the righteous man' (v. 6) refers to the persecution of the poor and pious by the rich and worldly—a thought to which Jews had been accustomed for centuries, cf. Wisd. ii. Christians would naturally think of the supreme instance of it, the death of Jesus. Besides ambiguous language, the author uses the Old Testament, but never in Christian polemic, or as predicting anything fulfilled in the Messiah or in Christianity; the characters to whom he refers—Abraham and Rahab (ii. 21–25), the prophets and Job (v. 10, 11), Elijah (v. 17, 18)—and all the passages which he quotes or echoes, are only supports and illustrations of his moral teaching and appeal. 'He desires to

---

[1] Quoted in the speech of St. James as given in Acts xv. 17.
[2] *Encycl. Bibl.* 4833.
[3] 'My beloved brethren' (i. 16, 19; ii. 5) has a more Christian sound.

prove nothing doctrinal, and to "proselytize" no one, but to show that the highest standard of ethics for Jew and for Christian could be one and the same.' Luther could describe this as a 'right strawy epistle' but only in comparison with other New Testament writings. Luther's other remark is not so well known. 'It seems that [James] was some good man who obtained some of the words of the Apostles' disciples and put them on paper or perhaps someone else made notes on a sermon of his. Therefore I cannot put his among the chief books, but I will not ask anyone else not to, for [the epistle] contains many good sayings.'

Literary Connexions

(a) *Synoptic Gospels*. Parallels are found in utterances of our Lord; but the number of these has been greatly exaggerated. Plummer[1] gives a list of no less than nineteen in parallel columns, and six other references in Matt. i–iv. In most of them, while the moral teaching is akin, the language is quite different; in a few the thought is wholly different though the passages happen to contain some verbal similarities. The clearest parallel is in v. 12: 'But before all things, my brethren, swear not, neither by heaven (τὸν οὐρανόν) nor by earth nor by any other oath, but let your Yea be Yea, and your Nay Nay, that ye fall not under judgment.' Matt. v. 34–37: 'But I say unto you not to swear at all, neither by heaven (ἐν τῷ οὐρανῷ), because it is God's throne, nor by earth, because it is the city of the great King. . . . But let your speech (λόγος) be Yea, Yea, Nay, Nay; and what is superfluous beyond these is of the evil one.' The differences forbid a direct literary connexion with Matthew, but the author of our epistle evidently knew the *logion* in a form in which it was orally current. And if he knew one he probably knew others: e.g. the contrast of hearing and doing the word, illustrated by a simile (i. 22 f. = Matt. vii. 24, 26); the poor as heirs of the kingdom (ii. 5 = Lk. vi. 20); peacemakers (τοῖς ποιοῦσιν εἰρήνην iii. 18 = εἰρηνοποιοί Matt. v. 9). And his general attitude towards wealth is similar to that of several sayings recorded in Luke. 'It would look', says Streeter,[2]

---

[1] *Expositor's Bible*, St. *James*, 1891, pp. 310 ff.

[2] *The Primitive Church*, 1929, p. 193.

'as if the author of James had read Q in the recension known
to Luke.' But the only conclusion to be drawn from these, or
any other, parallels is that he was in contact with circles in
which sayings of the Lord were becoming common property,
and were moulding Christian language.

(b) *Acts xv. 14–21, 23–29.* Stress has sometimes been laid
on the parallels with the speech and letter ascribed to St.
James as a sign of identity of authorship. They are as follows:
'Men, brethren, hear me' (*v.* 14) = 'Hear, my beloved
brethren' (Jas. ii. 5). 'Greeting' (χαίρειν) *v.* 23 = Jas. i. 1.
And the words κρίνειν, ἐπισκέπτεσθαι, and ἐκλέγεσθαι occur in
both, but the force is different in each case. On the other hand,
in *v.* 19 ἐπιστρέφειν (act.) is intransitive while in James (v. 19,
20) it is transitive. χαίρειν is the ordinary Greek salutation at
the opening of a letter (cf. Acts xxiii. 26), and the other parallels
amount to nothing at all.

(c) *1 Cor., Gal., Rom.* In the first two of these epistles Moffatt
notes the following parallels: Jas. i. 26 'If anyone think himself to be religious = 1 Cor. iii. 18 'If anyone think himself to
be wise', Gal. vi. 3 ' . . . to be anything'. Jas. ii. 5 'Hath not
God chosen the poor in the world? = 1 Cor. i. 27 'God chose
the foolish things of the world'. Jas. iii. 15 'Wisdom that is not
from above, but is ψυχική = 1 Cor. ii. 14 'The ψυχικὸς ἄνθρω-
πος '. Jas. iv. 4 f. 'Friendship of the world is enmity against
God', 'The spirit . . . yearneth unto envy' = Gal. v. 17 'The
flesh lusteth against the spirit, and the spirit against the flesh'.
Jas. ii. 8–12, the thought of love to one's neighbour as the fulfilment of the law, is found in Gal. v. 14; Rom. xiii. 8 f. (But
see also Matt. xxii. 37–40.)

In Romans Moffatt's parallels are: Jas. i. 2–4 Rejoice in
trials because 'the δοκίμιον of your faith worketh endurance
(ὑπομονήν)' = Rom. v. 3–5 Let us boast in afflictions, because
'affliction worketh endurance, and endurance δοκιμήν, and
δοκιμή hope'. Jas. i. 6 'Let him ask in faith, nothing doubting
(διακρινόμενος)' = Rom. iv. 20 'He doubted not (οὐ διεκρίθη)
at the promise through unbelief'. Jas. i. 22 'Be ye doers of the
word, and not hearers only, deluding your own selves' =
Rom. ii. 13 'For not the hearers of law are righteous with God,
but the doers of law shall be justified'. Jas. ii. 11, the thought

that one commandment is as important to keep as another, appears quite differently expressed in Rom. ii. 22–25. Jas. ii. 21 'Was not Abraham our father justified by works?' = Rom. iv. 1. Jas. iv. 4, 7 'The friendship of the world is enmity against God'. 'Be subject therefore unto God' = Rom. viii. 7 'The mind of the flesh is enmity against God, for it is not subject to the law of God'. Jas. iv. 11, to judge one's neighbour is to judge law = Rom. ii. 1, to judge one's neighbour is to judge oneself.

Sanday and Headlam[1] omit two of these, Jas. ii. 11 and iv. 4, 7, but add Jas. i. 21 'Putting off all filthiness, &c.' = Rom. xiii. 12 'Let us therefore put off the works of darkness'. Jas. iv. 1 'your pleasures which war in your members' = Rom. vii. 23 'I see another law in my members warring against the law of my mind'. And further resemblances are collected by Mayor.[2] But direct literary indebtedness is hard to prove. Both writers probably refer to current Jewish discussions, and the author of James very likely found it necessary to utter a warning against an antinomian tendency fostered by a misunderstanding or misrepresentation of St. Paul's teaching on salvation 'apart from works of the law'. At most, therefore, it is possible to acquiesce in Moffatt's vague phrase that our author 'draws upon the conceptions which Paul had already minted for the primitive Church'.

(d) *1 Peter*. In this case the literary connexion is much clearer. Jas. i. 1, the address to those in the Diaspora = 1 Pet. i. 1; Jas. i. 2 f. τὸ δοκίμιον ὑμῶν τῆς πίστεως[3] in connexion with πειρασμοί = 1 Pet. i. 6 f.; Jas. iii. 17 ἀνυπόκριτος = 1 Pet. i. 22; Jas. i. 27 ἄσπιλος = 1 Pet. i. 19; Jas. i. 25 παρακύπτειν = 1 Pet. i. 12; Jas. v. 20, the quotation from Prov. x. 12 in a peculiar form = 1 Pet. iv. 8. And the following parallels in thought may be noted: Jas. i. 18 'He brought us to birth by the word of truth' = 1 Pet. i. 23 'begotten again (cf. *v.* 3) . . . of the word of the living and abiding God'; Jas. i. 21 'putting off all filthiness . . . receive the inborn word' = 1 Pet. ii. 1 f. 'putting off all wickedness . . . long for the λογικὸν ἄδολον γάλα ';

---

[1] *Romans*, p. lxxviii.   [2] *St. James*, p. xciii.

[3] i.e. 'what is genuine in your faith' (Hort, *1 Peter*, p. 42). For parallels from the papyri see Moulton and Milligan, *Vocabulary of the Gk. Test.*, s.v. δοκίμιος.

Jas. iv. 1 'your pleasures which war in your members' =
1 Pet. ii. 11 'your fleshly lusts which war against the soul';
Jas. iii. 13 'a good ἀναστροφή', 'meekness of wisdom' = 1 Pet.
iii. 2, 4 'your pure ἀναστροφή', 'a quiet and meek spirit';
Jas. i. 12 'he shall receive the crown of life' = 1 Pet. v. 4 'ye
shall be rewarded with the unfading crown of glory'; Jas. iv.
6 f., the quotation from Prov. iii. 34, followed by submission
to God and resistance to the devil = 1 Pet. v. 5f., 8; Jas. iv. 10
'Humble yourselves before the Lord and He will exalt you' =
1 Pet. v. 6 'Humble yourselves therefore under the mighty
hand of God that He may exalt you in due season'.

There is very little to indicate on which side the indebtedness lies; but perhaps the scale is turned by the first passage.
It is probable that the general expression 'the twelve tribes
that are in the Diaspora' (Jas. i. 1) is borrowed from the more
specific geographical description in 1 Pet. i. 1. 'If direct
dependence exists, then 1 Peter is much more likely to be
original than James: B. Weiss's arguments[1] seem to me far
more cogent than those of A. Meyer on the opposite side', says
E. G. Selwyn.[2]

DATE. On the assumption that the author was James the
Lord's brother[3] an early and a later date have been assigned
to the epistle. Mayor (op. cit.) and others would place it before
the Council of Jerusalem (Acts xv), 'as otherwise it must have
contained some reference to the question, which was then
agitating the Diaspora, as to the admission of Gentiles into the
Church', and because St. Paul's epistles are directed against
mistakes to which our epistle gave a handle. The latter is more
than doubtful (see above); and the former can be explained as
well by a late date as by an early one. The same reasoning
would place before the Council most of the books of the New
Testament! Hort,[4] Parry,[5] and others date it c. 62–65, allowing

[1] *Manual*, ii. 106 n. [2] *The First Epistle of St. Peter*, 1946, p. 463.
[3] On the different traditions about his date, A.D. 62 or c. 69, see Schürer, *The
Jewish People in the Time of Jesus Christ* (transl. of fifth edition, 1902), Div. I,
vol. ii, pp. 186 f.
[4] *Judaistic Christianity*, pp. 148 f. He accepts the genuineness of the reference
in Jos. *Ant.* xx. ix. 1 to the death of James, 'the brother of him who is called
Christ', and the date, A.D. 62, which it implies; and he thinks that the epistle
was written not long before, because of the references to persecution in i. 2;
v. 10. [5] *A Discussion of the General Epistle of James* (1903).

time for the author to have known some of St. Paul's epistles, and accounting for 'the development of the Christian conscience, social and individual' (Parry) which it shows.

If, on the other hand, the author is unknown and subapostolic, the *terminus ad quem* must be supplied by external evidence. Some have found echoes in Clement Rom.,[1] *ad Corinth.*, 'Because of faith and hospitality a son was given to him [Abraham] in his old age' (x. 7). 'Because of faith and hospitality Rahab the harlot was saved' (xii. 1). But these are not written in order to balance the teaching of St. Paul and St. James. Clement only gives a list of examples on which we should 'fix our eyes'. Enoch was 'found righteous in obedience'. 'Noah, being found faithful, by his ministration preached regeneration unto the world.' Abraham was 'found faithful in that he rendered obedience to the word of God'. 'Because of hospitality and godliness Lot was saved from Sodom.'

Similarly in ch. xxxi: 'Wherefore was our father Abraham blessed? Was it not because he wrought righteousness and truth through faith?' This is only noted as one among the records of the blessings received by the patriarchs, without the least indication of the influence of our epistle. The reference in xxiii. 3 and Jas. i. 8 is to a common source, *?Eldad and Modad*; that in xxx. 2 and Jas. iv. 6 (1 Pet. v. 5) to Prov. iii. 34; and that in xlix. 5 and Jas. v. 20 (1 Pet. iv. 8) to Prov. x. 12. Apart from these, the few verbal parallels which can be found are no evidence of literary connexion: they belong to the common language of hortatory moralizings. The editors of *The New Testament in the Apostolic Fathers* (1905) do not so much as mention a point of comparison between the two writings. The earliest author in whose work they find marked traces of our epistle is Hermas, *c.* A.D. 130. They cannot, indeed, place it higher than class C, indicating a low, but not the lowest, degree of probability of the use of the epistle, but they conclude, 'Although the passages which point to dependence on James fail to reach, when taken one by one, a high degree of probability, yet collectively they present a fairly strong case'

---

[1] F. W. Young inclines to the belief that James was indebted to 1 Clement, *J.B.L* lxvii, 1948, pp. 339–45.

(p. 113). E. J. Goodspeed,[1] however, concludes that the re-semblances between the two are so slight that they are prob-ably due to the common forms of popular preaching—the *paraenesis* of the day.

If, then, our epistle was influenced by 1 Peter, and if it influenced the *Shepherd* of Hermas, the limits of date are *c.* 67, at the earliest, and 130, and there is no external evidence to reduce the period. But since the tone of the writer and the character of the readers give the impression of a late rather than an early date, it is hardly safe to place it before the end of the first century.

BOOKS AND ARTICLES

A. T. Cadoux, *The Thought of St. James*, 1944.
G. Kittel, *Zeitschrift f. d. neutest. Wissenschaft*, xli, 1942, pp. 71–105.
W. L. Knox, *J.T.S.* xlvi, 1945, pp. 10–17.
A. Meyer, *Das Rätsel des Jacobusbriefes*, 1930.
R. St. J. Parry, *A discussion of the General Epistle of James*, 1903.
G. H. Rendall, *The Epistle of James and Judaic Christianity*, 1927.

COMMENTARIES

F. J. A. Hort (1909), J. B. Mayor (2nd ed., 1897), W. O. E. Oesterley (1910), J. H. Ropes (1916), H. Windisch (2nd ed., 1930).

§ 2. 1 PETER

CONTENTS. Two threads of thought are intertwined throughout the epistle. (1) Hopeful endurance under trial, because trial leads to glory and joy. 'The temper inculcated by Peter in view of suffering is not a grey, close-lipped stoi-cism, but a glow of exultation such as Jesus (Matt. v. 11 f.) and Paul (Rom. v. 3 f.) had already counselled. Christians can only be patient under their trials by being more than patient' (Moffatt[2]). (2) This 'more than patience' includes holiness and innocence of life. These two thoughts are combined with a free simplicity which forbids any formal analysis of the epistle. Further, the first portion i–ii. 10 is coloured throughout by the thought—not, as in St. Paul, that Christians have taken the

---

[1] *Introduction to the New Testament*, p. 293.
[2] *Introd. Lit. N.T.*, p. 319, note 2.

place of a rejected Israel, but—that Christians *are* Israel in the true form for which it was divinely destined. The following summary will show the alternation of the two thoughts of Christian endurance and Christian conduct.

i. 1, 2. Opening salutation to Christians in Asia Minor as the true Diaspora. 3–12. The glory which follows trial is the salvation of Christians as the New Israel, to which they have been begotten anew, and to which the Old Testament pointed. 13–21. Live, then, as the New Israel should, who have been redeemed by the blood of Christ the Lamb without blemish. 22–25. In particular, having been begotten anew, love one another. ii. 1–10. And being new born, desire the pure spiritual milk, and grow as a building into union with Christ the Foundation, who was foretold in the Old Testament, as also was your call to be His sacred people. ii. 11–iii. 7. An appeal to show a good manner of life before pagans (*vv.* 11, 12) is particularized in the duties of subjects (*vv.* 13–17), slaves enduring suffering with Christian patience (*vv.* 18–25), wives (iii. 1–6), husbands (*v.* 7). iii. 8–22. Christian social virtues (*v.* 8) are to be combined with endurance under suffering (*vv.* 9–17), because Christ gave us the example (*v.* 18), and in view of the crisis foreshadowed by the deluge (*vv.* 19–22). iv. 1–11. For these reasons pagan sins must be avoided (*vv.* 1–6), and Christians must show love and mutual helpfulness; first conclusion (*vv.* 7–11).

iv. 12–19. Suffer in fellowship with Christ with true Christian endurance, and not as a consequence of evil-doing. v. 1–5. Appeal to elders in the performance of their office; appeal to younger men and to all Christians to show humility. 6–11. Closing moral exhortations in the face of suffering. 12–14. Personal details, and conclusion.

DESTINATION AND READERS. The epistle is addressed to 'elect sojourners of the Dispersion in Pontus, Galatia, Cappadocia, Asia, and Bithynia' (i. 1), which means Christians who are the true Israel dispersed in the provinces mentioned. If it is to be understood from v. 13 that the writer was actually in Babylon, the geographical order of the names is more than surprising. See Hort, *1 St. Peter*, pp. 6, 167 f.[1] The whole of his

---

[1] See also Salmon, *Introd. N.T.*, pp. 440 f., and Lightfoot, *Clement*, ii. 491 f.

valuable chapter (pp. 157–84) on the provinces of Asia Minor
should be read. Following Ewald, he explains that if 'Babylon'
means Rome (which became a common precaution when persecution began), the writer could think of the bearer of the
epistle as landing at a port in Pontus, travelling through
[northern] Galatia, probably via Ancyra its capital, or perhaps
Tavium, into Cappadocia, no doubt to its capital Caesarea;
then westward along the great Ephesus road into Asia; and
finally northward through Bithynia, to take ship either at some
Bithynian port or where he had landed in Pontus.[1] 'In thus
following by natural and simple routes the order of provinces
which stands in the first sentence of the epistle, Silvanus would
be brought into contact with every considerable district north
of the Taurus in which there is reason to suppose that Christian
communities would be found.'

An alternative theory must not be ruled out as impossible—
that St. Peter avoided writing to districts in which St. Paul
had laboured. If the 'south Galatian' theory of St. Paul's
activities (see pp. 143–6) is accepted, and if we may suppose
Silvanus to have travelled not by the high road but by some
less frequented route from Cappadocia into the northern portion of the province of Asia, then the destination of the epistle
was a circuit of districts in the northern half of Asia Minor,
all St. Paul's fields of missionary work being omitted. St. Peter
himself had probably not preached in the districts to which he
writes; see i. 12. But in any case there had been plenty of time
since St. Paul's work in the south of the peninsula for Christianity to have spread to the north by the work of other missionaries, as that passage shows. And this in turn might account
for the absence of all reference to St. Paul—a salutation from
him if he was alive, or a mention of his martyrdom if he was
dead—which some have found surprising.

That the bulk of the readers were Gentiles is evident. Before
conversion they had lived in their 'former lusts in their ignorance' (i. 14). They had been called out of darkness into God's
light; they had once been 'not God's people' but were now
'God's people', once 'not pitied' but now 'pitied' (ii. 9, 10,

---

[1] This explanation is rejected by F. W. Beare, *The First Epistle of Peter*, 1947,
pp. 22 f.

adapted from Hos. i. 10; ii. 23; cf. Rom. ix. 25 f.). Their former manner of life handed down from their ancestors (i. 18) was the pagan manner of life. And this meant 'doing the will of the Gentiles, walking in lasciviousness, lusts, wine-bibbings, revellings, carousings, and abominable idolatries' (iv. 3, 4).

LITERARY CONNEXIONS. There is clear evidence for the author's dependence on Romans;[1] it is drawn out with the use of parallel columns by Sanday and Headlam, *Romans*, pp. lxxiv ff., to which the reader is referred. The connexion with Ephesians, which has been discussed on pp. 170 f., is less striking, but it is difficult to deny it, though Wand does so (ibid.). After examining the parallels between Colossians, Ephesians, and 1 Peter, C. L. Mitton[2] has shown that 'the author of 1 Peter was closely enough acquainted with Ephesians for its phrasing and thought to be from time to time reproduced in his own epistle'. Connexion with James is clearer; see pp. 210 f. But the relation which has been claimed to exist with 1, 2 Timothy, Titus is very hard to discover. The passage on the dress and behaviour of women in 1 Pet. iii. 1–6 may be compared with that in 1 Tim. ii. 9–11;[3] and the appeal to presbyters in 1 Pet. v. 1–4 with the description of a good ἐπίσκοπος to guide Titus in his choice of presbyters, Tit. i. 5–9. But these are not enough to prove literary dependence.[4]

Of uncanonical writers Polycarp certainly, and Clement Rom. possibly, knew our epistle.[5] The use of it by Polycarp is stated by Eusebius, *H.E.* iv. 14.

AUTHORSHIP AND DATE. The epistle was therefore written, *pace* Wand, after Romans and before *Ep. Polycarp*, i.e.

---

[1] J. W. C. Wand challenges this verdict, 'Out of eight passages from Romans in which Sanday and Headlam see a close parallelism with 1 Peter it is noteworthy that two are Old Testament prophecies . . ., two give lists of common Christian duties . . ., a fifth is semi-liturgical . . ., a sixth depends rather on thought than words . . ., while the remaining two are doubtful . . .' (*The General Epistles of St. Peter and St. Jude*, 1934, p. 19). On the other hand, it is doubtful whether C. Bigg is right in saying that 1 Pet. iv. 1 has no connexion with Rom. vi. 7.

[2] *J.T.S.*, N.S. i, 1950, pp. 67–73.

[3] Cf. Weidinger, *Die Haustafeln* and J. W. C. Wand, op. cit., pp. 3–9.

[4] On Hebrews see Moffatt, op. cit., p. 440, cf. E. J. Goodspeed, *New Solutions of New Testament Problems*, 1927, pp. 110 ff.

[5] See *The N.T. in the Apost. Fathers*, pp. 86–89 and 55–57.

between A.D. 56–57 and 115.[1] If it was written after *Ephesians*
and before Clement *ad Corinth.*, the period is narrowed to
A.D. 61–63 (or later if Eph. is post-Pauline) to 96. But within
these thirty-five years or so opinions differ among those who
accept the Petrine authorship. There is a general agreement
that the early tradition was correct that St. Peter and St. Paul
were martyred at Rome. But it is not certain that they met
their death at the same time. Harnack[2] believes it on the
strength of Clem. *Cor.* 6: 'To these men [St. Peter and St.
Paul] . . . was gathered a vast multitude of the elect, who
through many indignities and tortures . . . became a splendid
example among us.' But the words prove no more than that
the two apostles and the vast multitude suffered death in the
same persecution. Lightfoot[3] thinks that St. Peter died in the
year 64 at the outbreak of the Neronian persecution, St. Paul
in 67. It seems more probable that the dates should be exactly
reversed. Swete[4] places St. Paul's death as the earlier, and
St. Peter's in 70 or even later. He holds that St. Peter must
have written after St. Paul's death because some of the communities to whom he wrote 'were distinctly Pauline churches
and had received letters from St. Paul during his imprisonment', that Silvanus, who carried the epistle, was a well-known
colleague of St. Paul, and that it contained reminiscences
of Romans and Ephesians. But these considerations do not
of themselves require a date later than 67. To place it, as
he does, in the eighth decade, or (Ramsay[5]) in 80, is to aban-
don the theory that St. Peter suffered under Nero, and could
be justified only if it were certain that the descriptions of the
readers' sufferings implied a systematic persecution such as is
not known to have begun in Asia before 70.

The theory that St. Peter was not the author presents difficulties. (1) An examination of 2 Peter, which was certainly
pseudonymous (see p. 246), shows the methods which could be
adopted to give colour to the use of his name; 'the apostle is
made to speak prophetically of a future age, stress is laid on

---

[1] Or 135 if P. N. Harrison's date for *Pol.* i–xii, A.D. 135, is accepted (*Poly-carp's Two Epistles to the Philippians*, 1936).

[2] *Chronologie*, pp. 708 ff.   [3] *Clement*, ii. 497 f.

[4] *St. Mark*, pp. xvii f.

[5] *The Church in the Roman Empire*, pp. 279 ff.

his qualifications as an eye-witness of Jesus, and an irenical allusion to Paul occurs' (Moffatt[1]). In 1 Peter there is a marked absence of any such stress on the apostle's claims or qualifications. Moreover, pseudonymity is a device mostly adopted when a writer has a specific purpose for which he borrows the authority of a greater name; he denounces a heresy, or teaches a particular doctrine or belief, or lays down rules for Church life or organization. But there is no sign of that in this epistle of grace and hope. The Tübingen theory, that it represents an attempt to mediate irenically between the hostile Petrine and Pauline factions in the Church, has been almost universally abandoned. (2) The name Silvanus was known in Christian tradition only as that of a close companion of St. Paul. He is not, of course, necessarily the Silas of the Acts; but since it would be natural for the readers of the epistle to identify them, it is one of the last names that a pseudonymous writer would have selected to play the part of amanuensis to St. Peter (v. 12). (3) The order of the geographical names in i. 1, which can be explained, as shown above, if the bearer of the epistle was to carry it to definite districts on a circular route beginning and ending with Pontus, is almost inexplicable if the writing is an open letter to the Church at large.

It may be added that there are slight but important indications that the author was a disciple of the Lord. If there is a marked absence of any stress on the apostle's claims and qualifications, yet hints are not wanting.[2] In the same sentence in which he joins himself modestly with the elders as their 'fellow-elder', he claims to be a 'witness (μάρτυς) of the sufferings of Christ, and a partaker in the glory that is about to be revealed'. Christ's sufferings and resurrection and exaltation (cf. i. 11) formed the main substance of the early Christian message published on the authority of the apostolic witnesses. On the other hand, His earthly life and teaching did not at first occupy a large place in it, as the speeches in the Acts show; and the absence of detailed references to them is rather a sign of early

---

[1] *Intr. Lit. N.T.*, p. 335.

[2] Not much weight can be attached to the words 'whom not having seen *ye* love' (i. 8), as though they distinguish the readers from the writer who *had* seen Jesus Christ. With the exception of i. 3 (ἡμῶν, ἡμᾶς) and iv. 17 (ἀφ' ἡμῶν) the second person plural is used throughout the epistle.

date than the reverse. Some who place the epistle late, strangely understand the pseudonymous writer as referring to St. Peter as a 'martyr', who had already partaken in the consequent glory. But to write under the apostle's name, and yet to refer to his martyrdom, would be a self-contradiction and a blunder too great for any writer to commit.

The words 'gird yourselves ($\dot{\epsilon}\gamma\kappa o\mu\beta\omega\sigma a\sigma\theta\epsilon$)[1] with humility' (v. 5) may be an allusion—not, indeed, to the wording, but—to the event recorded in John xiii. 4 f. And the injunction to 'shepherd the flock of God' recalls the incident in John xxi. 15–17. The numerous echoes of our Lord's teaching which Bp. Chase[2] finds in the epistle are not so striking as those in James. There are a few which may be reminiscences. But a later writer who knew the synoptic Gospels would probably have represented St. Peter as using them to a greater extent than he has.

Again, there are many parallels between 1 Peter and the Petrine speeches in the early chapters of Acts, cf. Wand, op. cit., pp. 26–30. Were these due to St. Peter or to a late writer with a copy of Acts before him?

The objections to the Petrine authorship are mainly as follows: Harnack[3] rejects it partly on the ground that no writer before Irenaeus (c. 180) names St. Peter as the author. But feeling the difficulties of the pseudonymous theory he suggests that the body of the epistle (i. 3–v. 11) was written by some Christian teacher at Rome (McGiffert,[4] who agrees with him, suggests Barnabas), between 83 and 93, or possibly earlier; and, despite the absence of textual evidence for this view, the opening and closing sentences (i. 1, 2 and v. 12–14) were added later, between 150 and 175; so that we have no means of knowing whether the main portion was originally an epistle or

---

[1] Hesychius gives for this rare word the synonym $\sigma\tau o\lambda\dot{\iota}\sigma a\sigma\theta a\iota$, to put on (beautiful) apparel but Pollux (c. A.D. 180) suggests that the noun $\dot{\epsilon}\gamma\kappa\dot{o}\mu\beta\omega\mu a$ meant the slave's apron tied over his garment, cf. Apollodorus Carystius (iv–iii cent. B.C.) who is cited as using the verb meaning 'to gird oneself with'.

[2] Hastings's *D.B.* iii. 787 f.

[3] *Chronologie*, pp. 457 ff.

[4] *History of Christianity in the Apostolic Age*, p. 599. Bornemann (*Zeitschr. f. d. neutest. Wiss.* xix. 143–65) goes farther, and finds in i. 3–v. 11 a baptismal sermon delivered by Silvanus in Asia Minor, about 90, with close affinities with Psalm xxxiv.

not. Finding resemblances between these sentences and 2 Peter he thinks that the writer of the latter may have been the interpolator. The improbabilities of the theory are pointed out by Bp. Chase (op. cit., p. 786). Other theories of extensive interpolations in an originally non-Petrine homily to produce a Petrine epistle are less probable without the merit of ingenuity.

A more serious objection arises in connexion with the style and language of the writing. Bp. Chase (pp. 781 f.) notes that the author has an intimate knowledge of the Septuagint, that he uses a considerable number of words and expressions which do not occur elsewhere in the New Testament, and which may briefly be described as classical,[1] and a remarkable series of words for which there seems to be no earlier or contemporary authority;[2] also that within certain limits he had a very considerable appreciation of, and power over, the characteristic usages of Greek, which is confirmed 'when we note the delicacy and accuracy of his perception in regard to the rhythmical arrangement of words, the use of synonyms, and the arrangement of tenses, prepositions, &c.' The question arises whether a fisherman, brought up in bilingual Galilee, could or could not have gained, in the course of years, this command of the Greek language and knowledge of the Septuagint, although Aramaic was his native language (cf. Matt. xxvi. 73). The question does not admit of a confident answer. It has been suggested that we must either credit St. Peter with this literary ability, or put it down to the account of Silvanus. The latter seems to be the more likely. Silvanus may only have improved St. Peter's Greek, or he may have played the more important part of virtually writing the epistle himself when St. Peter had expressed his thoughts to him in outline.

The latter theory has been defended at length by E. G. Selwyn,[3] who compares this epistle with the two Thessalonian

---

[1] e.g. ἀναγκαστῶς, ἀνάχυσις, ἀπέχεσθαι ἐπιθυμιῶν ἀπογενέσθαι (metaph.), ἀπόθεσις, βιοῦν, ἐμπλοκή, οἰνοφλυγία, ὁμόφρων, ὁπλίζειν, πατροπαράδοτος, προθύμως.

[2] e.g. ἀλλοτρι(ο)επίσκοπος, cf. Epict. 3. 22. 97, ἀμάραντος and ἀμαράντινος, cf. Wisd. vi. 12, Apoc. Petri v. 15, ἀνεκλάλητος, ἀπροσωπολήμπτως (a Hebraism), ἀρτιγέννητος, περίθεσις. It should be noted that these words and those in the previous footnote are found in 'both parts' of the epistle if a break should be made after iv. 11.

[3] *The First Epistle of St. Peter*, 1946.

letters, where Silvanus is mentioned as if he might be joint author with Paul and Timothy. The many 'affinities of thought and phrase' between these three Epistles are taken to indicate a stock of common material already formed before 1 Peter was composed. Silvanus may have helped to shape this material or belonged to the circle of Christians who did so.

A third objection of a different kind is drawn from the words of iv. 16: 'but if (any one suffer) as a Christian let him not be ashamed, but let him glorify God in this name.' This is thought to mean that the readers in Asia Minor were suffering official persecution for *the name 'Christian'*, of which we do not possess actual evidence before the time of Trajan. His reply to Pliny's letter (A.D. 112) is the first imperial pronouncement known to us of Rome's attitude to Christianity; but it was clearly a pronouncement for the needs of the moment, and not an initiation of policy. Pliny, as his letter shows, had already tried repressive measures. And Christianity, as soon as it was seen to be distinct from Judaism, lost the advantage of being coupled with a *religio licita*, and was 'unincorporated', not illegal. This had come about, not by edict, but by the force of circumstances, the fall of Jerusalem and the hostility of Jews to Christians. The latter had been active from the first. The nickname 'Christian' was flung at them from an early date (Acts xi. 26). And whatever reason Nero might give for his persecution, it would be to the Christians themselves a suffering for Christ, or for the name of Christ.[1] Moreover, the epistle contains no indication that the readers were in a persecution which involved martyrdom. The state of things reflected in ii. 18–25; iii. 13–17 is comparable with the condition of the readers of Hebrews, who had not yet 'resisted unto blood'. They were suffering—and Christian slaves in particular—from hostility which might frequently be shown them by Jewish or pagan opponents (cf. Acts v. 41; ix. 16; xv. 26; xxi. 13; Phil. i. 29). If Tacitus says that Christians were convicted of *odium humani generis*, private malice and persecution must have been their lot long before, cf. Mk. xiii. 9–13. It is not easy to decide to what extent, if at all, official punitive measures

---

[1] See the discussion of the whole question by Merrill, *Essays in Early Christian History*, 1924, chs. 3, 4.

had begun to be taken in Asia Minor when the epistle was written. They had almost certainly begun at Rome, since the cryptic 'Babylon' had come into use (v. 13).[1] On the other hand, they do not appear to have been extended systematically over the empire, or the injunction in ii. 13–17, to honour governors as sent by the emperor for the punishment of evildoers and the praise of well-doers, could hardly have been written, unless with E. J. Goodspeed we take the view that 1 Peter was written after Rev. xviii and partly to counteract the latter's seditious tendencies by appealing to St. Paul's teaching, as in Rom. xiii, to support the civil powers.

Some scholars, like F. W. Beare, take the references to persecution, especially in iv. 12–19 and v. 8 f., to apply to that under Trajan (A.D. 98–117) long after Peter's death. As Wand admits, op. cit., p. 14, there are phrases in Pliny's correspondence with Trajan 'which might almost have been taken from 1 Peter', cf. Pliny, *Epp.* x. 96. But as Wand shows, the situation confronting Pliny was different from and no doubt later than that envisaged in this epistle. Pliny alludes to some Christians having given up the faith some three years before, and one as many as twenty years previously. Does this point to sporadic persecution in the region of Bithynia–Pontus as early as A.D. 93? If so, it would support the theory of other scholars who think that 1 Peter was written while Domitian was emperor (A.D. 81–96). The difficulty here is that despite ecclesiastical historians from Orosius to Fliche and Martin, the evidence that Domitian persecuted Christians as such is very slender. 'Domitian was quite ready to persecute anyone who stood in his way but there seems no reason to suppose that he selected the Christians as a class for harsh treatment, though individual Christians would not have been exempted from it.'[2] 'The date under Domitian seems to combine all the difficulties of the other views' says K. Lake.[3]

---

[1] Unless v. 12–14 is a later addition, despite the absence of textual support for omission. 'Babylon' is used for 'Rome' in Rev. xiv. 8 and xviii. 2 and *Sib. Oracles* v. 143, 159 and 2 Baruch xi: cf. Baruch vi. 1–4.

[2] R. L. P. Milburn, *Church Quarterly Review*, cxxxix, 1945, pp. 157 ff., cf. H. Last, 'The Study of the Persecutions', *Journal of Roman Studies*, xxvii, 1937, pp. 80–92.

[3] *Introduction to the New Testament*, pp. 166 f.

A fourth objection to the Petrine authorship of 1 Peter is based on the maturity of its doctrinal teaching, especially that on the Descent into Hades, which seems akin to that of the Old Roman Creed rather than to that of first-century Christians. The weight of this objection, however, has been removed by the study of the theology and ethics of this epistle and by the essay on 1 Pet. iii. 18–iv. 6 by E. G. Selwyn.[1]

A date about 67, just before St. Peter's death and after St. Paul's, seems to many to satisfy the requirements best, and is adopted by the majority of English scholars. Christians at the capital were still feeling the after-effects of Nero's mad outburst, but at the outskirts of the empire they were at peace so far as official persecution was concerned.

There are some, however, like B. H. Streeter,[2] who are impressed by the indications of a later date and by the change of tone in iv. 12–end. Streeter divided the work into two parts, (a) i. 3–iv. 11, a bishop's sermon to a group of newly baptized converts, and (b) iv. 12–v. 11, either the bishop's address to the general congregation including presbyters from neighbouring villages or the bishop's pastoral letter written some years later with reference to the 'fiery trial' of an unexpected character (iv. 12). Like Harnack, Streeter thought that i. 1–2 and v. 12–14 were later additions to give the work an epistolary form and Petrine character. He made the tentative suggestion that parts (a) and (b) were by Aristion.

E. J. Goodspeed,[3] again, would date 1 Peter with 1 Clement after the Epistle to the Hebrews, c. A.D. 95. The latter, he thinks, had issued a challenge to the Church in Rome to undertake the instruction and leadership of other churches, cf. Heb. v. 12. This letter and 1 Clement were the response, so that later Ignatius could say to the Church in Rome, 'You have taught others' (Rom. iii. 1). The book of Revelation had already adopted the apparently unchristian attitude of hatred against Babylon, and the author of 1 Peter was concerned with the real danger that Christianity might degenerate into a religion of hate and Christians into disloyal revolutionaries. The Church in Rome could already speak in

---

[1] Op. cit., pp. 64–115 and pp. 314–62.
[2] *The Primitive Church*, 1929, pp. 123 ff.   [3] Op. cit., p. 258.

St. Peter's name and while 1 Clement went to Macedonia and Greece 1 Peter went to the rest of the Christian Church, apart from Syria, and especially to the churches influenced by the Letters to the Seven Churches. Goodspeed thinks that 1 Peter was strongly influenced by the Pauline letters and that the mention of Silvanus is a mere epistolary touch; also that Heb. xiii. 22 points forward to 1 Pet. v. 12; Heb. xiii. 20 to 1 Pet. v. 4; and the doctrine of priesthood and sacrifice found everywhere in Heb. to 1 Pet. i. 19 and ii. 9.

COMMENTARIES

F. W. Beare (1947), C. Bigg (1901), F. J. A. Hort (i. 1–ii. 17, 1898),
    J. H. B. Masterman (1900), J. Moffatt (*The General Epistles*, 1928),
    E. G. Selwyn (1946), J. W. C. Wand (1934).

§ 3. HEBREWS

PURPOSE. The occasion of this writing, as of 1 Peter, was the readers' need of encouragement in the face of trouble. They were suffering tribulation for their faith, though it had not actually reached the point of martyrdom (xii. 4), and the author tries to rouse them to hold firmly to their Christian steadfastness. Their danger, however, was not merely despondency but religious apostasy; and he therefore supports his appeal by means of a carefully composed doctrinal argument, the various stages of which lead up successively to exhortations and warnings. In the sufferings which had come upon them, their dullness and denseness of faith and understanding were letting them drift towards the point of spiritual shipwreck, and he aimed at putting before them a presentation of Christ and Christianity such as would brace them to spiritual effort.

The doctrinal argument[1] is shaped under the influence of Alexandrian, and ultimately of Platonic, thought.[2] There is an antithesis between that which is Real, the heavenly Idea permanent and perfect, and the earthly 'copy' (ix. 23), 'shadow'

---

[1] See A. H. McNeile's *New Testament Teaching*, pp. 222–6.

[2] The Platonic influence on Heb. is sometimes exaggerated. As O. Cullmann has shown, our author remains true to the biblical conception of time (*Christ and Time*, Eng. trans., F. V. Filson, 1951, pp. 54 f.).

(x. 1), 'copy and shadow' (viii. 5), 'figure' (ix. 9), 'type' (ix. 24) which is imperfect, inadequate, transitory. The latter is seen in the sacrificial religion and priesthood of the Old Testament, and in the whole economy of God's people Israel; the former in Christianity. This does not mean, however, that the Real is merely substituted for the copy, but that the copy became obsolete when the heavenly Ideal was realized, actualized, in Christ and Christianity. The author says, in effect, 'That which is perfect is come, and if you fall away from it you lose everything. If it was perilous to disobey and disbelieve the divine message as imperfectly revealed in the Mosaic system, how much more perilous now that it is perfectly revealed in the ideal Christian system. On the other hand, if you hold firmly to your confidence and faith you enjoy all that is contained in the Ideal.'

CONTENTS. Many different analyses of the epistle have been offered by commentators, but they often fail to present it as a literary whole, and an organic unity. Some writers speak of 'digressions' and 'parentheses' as though the main outline would have been complete without them. This results from regarding the writing as primarily a doctrinal treatise, in the course of which the author takes the opportunity, at frequent intervals, of improving the occasion by homiletic exhortation. But even when it is recognized that the exhortations are as essential to the plan as the doctrinal portions, and that the former are throughout the ground and purpose of the latter,[1] another feature of the epistle is seldom explained, i.e. the *repetition* both of doctrinal statements and of exhortations. The best analysis known to the present writers is that of von Haering in the *Zeitschrift f. d. neutest. Wissenschaft*, xviii, 1918, pp. 145–63. He refers to von Soden's fourfold division of the epistle,[2] corresponding broadly to the fourfold division of a discourse which was conventional among ancient rhetoricians:[3]
1. προοίμιον πρὸς εὔνοιαν, leading up to the πρόθεσις. 2. διήγησις πρὸς πιθανότητα. 3. ἀπόδειξις πρὸς πειθώ. 4. ἐπίλογος. And while

---

[1] This is well shown by B. Weiss, *Texte u. Untersuchungen*, vol. xxxv, 1910.
[2] In the *Handkommentar zum n.T.* (Freiburg, 1890).
[3] The rhetorical care with which it was written is evident. Blass even prints it in στίχοι as rhythmical, a striking example of *Kunstprosa*.

the contents of the epistle are very different from those of a conventional discourse, he divides it as follows:

A. The *prooimion* (i. 1–iv. 13) leads up to the main thesis (iv. 14–16) which is expressed in a simple and undeveloped form.

B. The *diēgēsis* (v. 1–vi. 20) is a preliminary treatment of the doctrinal theme, followed by a preliminary exhortation.

C. The *apodeixis* (vii. 1–x. 18) is a fuller treatment of the doctrinal theme.

D. The *epilogos* (x. 19–xiii. 21) is a fuller exhortation.

A. The greatness of the final revelation which Christ brought, and of the salvation which He wrought, are due to His greatness as 'Apostle' and 'High Priest'. Correspondingly great is the responsibility of despising, disbelieving, falling away from, Him and His salvation (i. 1–iv. 13).

(*a*) The Son, Heir of all things, is the Bringer of the final revelation, and performs the High Priestly function of cleansing away sin (i. 1–3). The uniqueness of His office and Person measured by comparison with the angels, the bringers of the Old Testament revelation (cf. ii. 2), and the proof from Scripture (i. 4–14).

(*b*) Exhortation to take heed to this unique revelation (ii. 1–4).

(*c*) The temporary subordination to the angels, which seems to conflict with the superiority, was the very means of His exaltation, that by the subordination He might become the *archēgos* of our salvation, being identified with man. This is proved from Scripture (ii. 5–9). The reason why this was the means, befitting God (*v*. 10), to such an end—because to bring many sons to glory the Son must take blood and flesh to rescue them, and to have sympathy with men as a merciful and faithful High Priest (*vv*. 10–18). [Thus the consideration of the greatness of the Son as the Bringer of revelation leads dialectically to His worth as High Priest, and so the thesis of iv. 14–16 is prepared for.]

(*d*) Exhortation combining the thoughts of 'Apostle' and 'High Priest', all that has been said being completed by reference to Moses, the Old Testament Apostle and High Priest. Like him in faithfulness Christ is superior to him as the Preparer of the house is greater than the house, and the son than the servant. Therefore on our faithful holding to the hope depends our belonging to the house (iii. 1–6). [And so His faithfulness is the motive and force of ours.]

Exhortation which takes content and colour from the leading thought of the *prooimion* of the Son as Bringer of revelation. Refuse not the word which Christianity receives from Psalm xcv. 7 f. (iii. 7–iv. 13).

THESIS. The heavenly High Priesthood of the Son, whose greatness does not alienate us from Him, because He was tempted as we are, and can sympathize with us, is the ground of our free, bold access to the Throne of grace to obtain help (iv. 14–16).

B. Preliminary treatment of the thesis (v. 1–vi. 20).

(*a*) Preliminary treatment of the Son's High Priesthood, to which the Old Testament pointed (v. 1–10):

> His priestly *function* (v. 1). [In section *C* the functions are placed second (viii. 1–x. 18) and the qualifications first (vii). See v. 1 repeated in viii. 3.]
>
> His priestly *qualifications*, which are twofold:
>
> Sympathy with men because He shares human nature (v. 2 f., 7–9).
>
> Distinction from men because (like Aaron) He is called by God, His call being 'according to the order of Melchisedek' (*vv.* 4 f., 10).

(*b*) Preliminary exhortation (v. 11–vi. 20).

Rebuke of the undeveloped state of the readers towards the truth of Christ's High Priesthood (v. 11–14). Exhortation to develop (vi. 1–3). Warning that no second repentance is possible (*vv.* 4–8). [Parallel to x. 26–31.] Ground for hope: God will consider their behaviour in the past (vi. 9–12). [Parallel to x. 32–39.] The spurring thought of the certainty of God's sworn promise (vi. 13–20). [vi. 20 takes up the Melchisedek priesthood again.]

C. Fuller treatment of the thesis, showing the meaning of Christ's High Priesthood as the mediation of the New *Diathēkē* (vii. 1–x. 18).

(*a*) His priestly *qualifications* (vii. 1–28).

What the Melchisedek priesthood means: a priesthood *for ever* (*vv.* 1–3).

It is greater than the Levitical priesthood because (i) Abraham gave tithes to Melchisedek, (ii) Abraham was blessed by Melchisedek, (iii) Levitical priests are many in number because of death (*vv.* 4–10).

The superiority of the Melchisedek priesthood involves the changing of the old for the new, which means the change of the whole law and all that that includes (*vv.* 11, 12).

That takes place in Jesus, for He was Judaean not Levite; and His priesthood is of a wholly different kind, due not to an external command but to internal power of life, and that a life indissoluble because the oath was 'for ever' (*vv.* 13–17).

That means the annulling of the old, which could not accomplish what the bringing in of the better hope accomplished (*vv.* 18, 19).

The measure of the change is the superiority of the new priesthood (*vv.* 20–28):

in that it is (i) by oath (*vv.* 20–22), (ii) eternal (*vv.* 23–25), (iii) that of one who is ethically perfect (*v.* 26), (iv) eternally permanent in its operation, not constantly repeated (*vv.* 27, 28).

(*b*) His priestly *function* in the heavenly sanctuary is greater than the Levitical; hence the New *Diathēkē* mediated by it is greater than the old, as the old itself testifies (viii. 1–x. 18).

This chief thought (κεφάλαιον) stated summarily (viii. 1–13).

The function is executed in the True Tabernacle (*vv.* 1–5).

The correspondingly better *Diathēkē* foretold by Jeremiah (*vv.* 6–13).

The same thought worked out more fully (ix. 1–x. 18):

The Old Testament type: the place (ix. 1–5), the function (*vv.* 6, 7), the result (*vv.* 8–10).

The New Testament fulfilment (ix. 11–x. 18):

(i) Summary statement (ix. 11–15).

(ii) Why an offering, and that a better one? (ix. 16–28): Because every *diathēkē* is mediated with blood (*vv.* 16, 17); the old one (*vv.* 18–22); the new one (*vv.* 23–28).

(iii) Why is Christ's offering a better one? (x. 1–14): Because the old could make nothing perfect (*vv.* 1–3), being only that of animals (*v.* 4), while Christ's is one of obedience to God's will (*vv.* 5–9), and can sanctify

for ever (*v.* 10). And because the priests had to sacrifice often, and without result (*v.* 11), while Christ,
after one offering, sits throned with eternal success
(*vv.* 12–14).

(iv) Proof from Scripture that the New *Diathēkē* will be
successful in doing away with sins, and therefore need
never be repeated (x. 15–18).

D. Fuller warning and encouragement to hold fast (x. 19–
xiii. 21).

(*a*) Arising immediately out of the doctrinal teaching (x.
19–39):

Exhortation to hold fast to what Christ's High Priesthood
has done for us (*vv.* 19–25).

Warning that no second offering is possible for deliberate
sin (*vv.* 26–31).

Ground for hope: they can themselves consider their past
behaviour (*vv.* 32–39).

(*b*) The expectant faith demanded by the doctrinal teaching
(xi. 1–xii. 29):

Its essence (xi. 1), and past heroes of faith (*vv.* 2–40).

Motives for patient faith: The cloud of witnesses (xii. 1),
Jesus the great Example (*vv.* 2, 3).

Suffering is a Father's discipline (*vv.* 4–13):

A warning from Esau (*vv.* 14–17).

The greatness of the new Economy, the new *Diathēkē*,
Christ's saving work, and of the divine revelation,
makes disobedience more terrible than disobedience to
the Mosaic law (*vv.* 18–29). [A summing-up of the main
thoughts of the epistle.]

(*c*) Closing exhortation (xiii. 1–17).

Epistolary ending appended to the homily (*vv.* 18–25).

NATURE OF THE WRITING. The unusual fact has to be
accounted for that it has an epistolary ending but not an
epistolary opening. It has been suggested that the latter has
been accidentally lost; but the conjecture is without evidence
and is unnecessary. James has an opening address but no
epistolary ending; and the theory of accidental mutilation is
no more likely in the one writing than in the other. The problem is to determine the relation of the closing verses to the

main body of the writing. If it was originally a homily or treatise which someone wished to transform into a (?Pauline) epistle by means of an epistolary ending, he would certainly have provided it also with an opening address. Conversely, if it was originally an epistle which was altered into a treatise for general use by the omission of the opening address, the ending also would have been omitted.

It is not easy to determine how far the 'epistolary ending' extends. G. A. Simcox[1] thinks that the whole of ch. xiii consists of one, or perhaps two, commendatory letters, or parts of them, written by St. Paul or some other apostle, and attached to the writing, so that the whole acquired apostolic authority; and that 'I have written unto you briefly' (xiii. 22) refers not to chs. i–xii, but to ch. xiii only. Such expressions, however, were not uncommon in early Christian letter-writing. Moffatt refers to 1 Pet. v. 12 δι' ὀλίγων,[2] and Ep. Barn. i. 5 ἐσπούδασα κατὰ μικρὸν ὑμῖν πέμπειν (cf. i. 8 ὑποδείξω ὀλίγα), and to the writer's own words in v. 11; xi. 32. To these may be added Ignat. *Magn.* 14 συντόμως παρεκάλεσα ὑμᾶς, and *Polyc.* 7 δι' ὀλίγων ὑμᾶς γραμμάτων παρεκάλεσα. But ch. xiii, in fact, shows no trace of the commendation of anyone to any community. Perdelwitz[3] confines the epistolary ending to *vv.* 22–25. He thinks that the writing was a sermon actually preached, perhaps by a wandering prophet, to a congregation (probably) in Asia Minor, and that someone sent it in writing to Italy, probably Rome, with a brief covering letter, consisting of the last four verses. This would account for several of the phenomena, but the simplest solution is that it was a written, not a spoken, homily, which the author sent to a community whose members, and needs, he knew well. The advice to them becomes more personal at xiii. 1, but homiletic again in *vv.* 8–16, and he passes into an epistolary conclusion at *v.* 18, reverting, however, to solemn rhetoric in the prayer, *vv.* 20, 21. E. F. Scott[4] suggests that the author is a Roman writing to Rome; he sends a homily, with an epistolary ending, to an inner group

---

[1] *Ex. T.*, x. 430 ff.

[2] Goodspeed suggests that the words in 1 Pet. are based on those in Heb. xiii. 22, διὰ βραχέων.

[3] *Zeitschr. f. d. neutest. Wiss.*, 1910, pp. 59 ff., 105 ff.

[4] *Harvard Theol. Rev.* xiii, 1920, pp. 205–19.

of advanced converts as an example of Christian *gnosis* for the τέλειοι, the maturely developed, or those who ought to be τέλειοι.

READERS. Since the argument rests upon a comparison between the Hebrew and Christian economies, it has often been thought that the readers were Jewish Christians, and that their danger was a relapse into Judaism, or that they were tempted to apostatize in despair because of the terrible catastrophe of the fall of Jerusalem, either recent or imminent. But the author says nothing about Judaism; did he have Jewish Gnosticism in mind? 'It is difficult to believe that if the problem in question had been the connexion between the readers . . . and ordinary Judaism, it would have been referred to as "divers and strange teachings" '[1] (xiii. 9); he does not refer to Jewish ordinances as a rule of life, but, dialectically, to the Levitical system in the Pentateuch. He never mentions the Temple, either as standing or as destroyed, but uses the tabernacle as a 'shadow' of the perfected system of worship in the Christian dispensation. The Old Testament was read by all Christians, and any argument based upon it was as valid for Gentiles as for Jews. And he shows no sign of drawing the least distinction between them; St. Paul's battle was over and won. The writing has a universal appeal, leading the readers to rejoice in their possession of the Real which has rendered the Copy obsolete. If something in pagan life could have been taken as the Copy the argument would have been equally sound, but the Old Testament was the only basis from which he could appeal to all his readers alike.

No weight can be attached to the title prefixed to the epistle. In the A.V. this stands as 'The Epistle of Paul the Apostle to the Hebrews', and is unfortunately retained in the R.V. This was due to a gradual growth in some late manuscripts, and has no authority. In the earliest authorities that we possess[2] it is simply πρὸς Ἐβραίους, 'to Hebrews'. But this does not go back earlier than the third century, and cannot be original. The writing was sent to a definite group of persons, who would be

---

[1] F. D. V. Narborough, *The Epistle to the Hebrews*, 1930, p. 21.

[2] ℵ A B P⁴⁶, in the subscription of C (the opening is mutilated as far as ἁγίου in ii. 4), and in the Egyptian versions, bohairic and sahidic.

interested, for example, in the release of Timothy (xiii. 23), and to whom the author hoped soon to be restored (v. 19); they could not be vaguely described as 'Hebrews'. And, as has been shown, they were probably not Jewish Christians. The title 'was probably added to the epistle during the earlier part of the second century as a reflection of the impression made by its apparently Hebrew preoccupation upon the mind of a generation which had lost all direct knowledge of the writing's origin and standpoint' (Moffatt[1]). If so, our only guidance is the interpretation of the epistle as a whole, which points to a community of Gentile Christians, or, if Jewish, one whose 'training must have been that of Hellenistic Judaism such as Stephen was trained under—liberal, biblical, and to a certain extent syncretistic'.[2]

Some facts about them which we learn from the epistle (x. 32–34; xii. 4) are important in their bearing on its destination and date. They had undergone persecution in 'former days', when they had first become Christians ('illuminated'). This points to a definite period, after which persecution had ceased for a time and had now begun again. At that time they had associated themselves in sympathy with others who were similarly persecuted. These were fellow Christians in the same Church, or members of another Church or other Churches, according as the epistle was written to a single group or circle, or to a whole community. The sufferings which they endured had not yet reached the point of martyrdom. It is not, however, quite clear whether this was the case with the Christians, 'the prisoners', with whom they had sympathized in former days. There is possibly a hint of the martyrdom of their Church leaders who had spoken to them the word of God in the past (xiii. 7). 'The reference here seems to be to some scene of martyrdom in which the triumph of faith was plainly shown' (Westcott, ad loc.). This does not necessarily contradict xii. 4, which may refer only to the present persecution, not to the former one; or the epistle may have been written to a small circle, none of whose members had been martyred in either persecution. It is generally supposed from ii. 3 that disciples

---

[1] *Introd. Lit. N.T.*, p. 448.
[2] Ibid., p. 449.

of Jesus had personally evangelized them; but possibly 'us' means more generally the Christians of that generation.

DESTINATION. If the readers were Gentile Christians, or if they were Jewish Christians of a markedly Hellenistic type, the epistle can hardly have been written to any town in Palestine, least of all Jerusalem. The Alexandrian colour of the argument need not point to Alexandria, since that type of thought was widely diffused.[1] And there is not a semblance of evidence for deciding on any other of the numerous localities which have been proposed in Syria, Asia Minor, or Greece. But there are two indications in favour of Rome or some other town in Italy: 1. οἱ ἀπὸ τῆς 'Ιταλίας (xiii. 24), according to the most natural meaning, are Italians (a small, definite group) who are in company with the writer away from their own country, and send greetings to those at home. It can grammatically mean 'those in Italy'; but it is hardly possible that the author could have sent greetings from Italians generally. 2. The epistle was certainly known to Clement of Rome, who (in ch. xxxvi) closely follows the language and thought of Heb. i, but the Church in the west did not ascribe it to Paul at first; as Loisy says, 'One of the best reasons, perhaps the strongest, that one has for supposing that the Roman community was the destination of the letter, is that Rome originally knew that the document was not Paul's, and two generations were necessary for the community to forget its own tradition about the non-apostolicity of a writing which it knew, one can say, since it first saw the light'. (*Remarques sur la littérature épistolaire du Nouveau Testament*, 1929, p. 104).

DATE. Clement's epistle to Corinth is usually dated *c.* 96. Merrill,[2] indeed, maintains that it was not written by Clement, Bishop of Rome, and that no such person existed; he places it *c.* 140, shortly before the *Shepherd* of Hermas. But in either case it is the only safe *terminus ad quem* supplied by external evidence,

---

[1] Heb. came to have an honoured place among letters addressed by Paul to Churches in the Alexandrian uncials, B ℵ A C H I P. P⁴⁶, the third-century Chester Beatty papyrus codex, giving an Alexandrian text, is unique in placing Heb. directly after Rom. rather than after 2 Thess. D E K L place it at the end of the Pauline canon, after Philemon, cf. W. H. P. Hatch, *H.T.R.* xxix, 1936, pp. 133–51.

[2] *Essays in Early Christian History* (1924), ch. ix.

since the connexions which some have found with the epistles of Ignatius and Polycarp are doubtful. The *terminus a quo* is difficult to determine. The writer seems to have known some of St. Paul's epistles, especially Romans; there is a connexion also probably with 1 Peter,[1] though scholars differ on the question which is prior or whether both use common material. The connexion with the Lucan writings is very doubtful,[2] although Clement Alex.[3] conjectured that the epistle was written by St. Paul in 'the Hebrew tongue', and that St. Luke 'translated it for Greeks', so that it and the Acts are coloured by the same style. An early date for Hebrews is indicated, if Dr. T. W. Manson[4] is right in suggesting that St. Paul knew Heb. i–iv, when he penned Colossians, and that both writers had the same group of heretics in the Lycus valley in mind. This is supported if xiii. 23 is no mere literary touch but a reference to Timothy still being actively engaged in missionary work. Manson argues that in any case a date before 70 is extremely probable as Heb. v–x points to the Levitical priesthood with all its ritual being superseded by Christ's Melchisedekian High-Priesthood, while the author does not argue that God has destroyed the temple, which would have been 'the clinching argument' used if he wrote after A.D. 70.

As regards internal evidence, there is no indication of the existence of ἐπίσκοποι and διάκονοι, only the general word ἡγούμενοι being used (xiii. 7, 17). But πρεσβύτεροι, who existed from the first, are not mentioned either. The writer had no occasion to speak of them. The only indication is supplied by the references to persecution mentioned above. If the epistle was written to Rome, it was at a date when Christianity had flourished long enough in the capital for persecution to have been suffered some time previously, in 'former days'. This places it some years later than Nero's wild outburst against the Christians in the city (as scapegoats for the fire of which he was himself suspected of being guilty), since, according to Acts xxviii. 22, the Jews at Rome, some two years before, evidently knew nothing about the Christian sect, which was

---

[1] See Moffatt, *Introd. Lit. N.T.*, p. 440.
[2] Ibid., pp. 435 f.   [3] Eus. *H.E.* vi. 14.
[4] *Bulletin of the John Rylands Library*, 32, 1949, pp. 1–17.

impossible if it had already been persecuted there. If the persecution in 'former days' was not Nero's, and there were no
martyrdoms in it, it must have been trouble suffered at a later
time from the general malice of Jews and pagans. It is the *two*
persecutions at a considerable interval which require a date
some time after Nero, if the epistle was written to Rome. The
question remains whether the later one, from which the readers
were suffering when the epistle was written, could have taken
place in Rome, without martyrdoms, during the reign of
Domitian (81–96). Merrill[1] reduces the persecution under
Domitian to a minimum, arguing that the tradition of it,
which grew in explicitness in the Christian writers of the suc-
ceeding centuries, had no foundation in fact. Domitian began
to take more severe official cognizance of those who refused
the civic-religious duty of burning incense to the Emperor.
They were not charged with being Christians; but if any Christians were of the number, as is most probable, some of them no
doubt suffered death, as seems, from the Apocalypse, to have
been the case in other parts of the empire. Merrill makes light
of the burning language of the Apocalypse, but its references
to martyrs, and the horror and hatred of Rome shown by the
writer, cannot be summarily dismissed. If, then, Christians,
with Jews and other persons, were executed under Domitian
because they refused to worship the Emperor, the author of our
epistle would certainly have thought of it as martyrdom. Therefore the epistle must be placed, if written to Rome, as long as
possible after Nero, and before Christians came under Domitian's notice as guilty of treason, say *c*. 81–85. But there were
Christians in Italy outside Rome, as at Puteoli, Acts xxviii.
13 f., and perhaps at Pompeii, if the Sator[2] inscription there
was written before A.D. 79. Such Christians may not have suffered 'unto blood' under Nero.

Those who think that Hebrews is an encouragement to
Jewish Christians, in view of the imminent destruction of Jerusalem, place it shortly before that event, at dates varying from

---

[1] Op. cit., ch. vi, cf. R. L. P. Milburn, cited above (p. 222 n.).

[2] D. Atkinson, *Bulletin of the John Rylands Library*, 22, 1938, pp. 419 ff., and
Journal of Ecclesiastical History, ii, 1951, pp. 1 ff., cf. D. Daube, *Ex. T.* lxii, 1951,
p. 316; cf. *D.A.C.* vi, cols. 1482–4; cf. Dr. H. Last, *J.T.S.*, N.S. iii, 1952, pp. 92–97.

58 to 70. But it is recognized by most modern writers on the epistle that the references in the present tense to Old Testament worship (e.g. λαμβάνουσιν vii. 8, καθίσταται, ὄντων, λατρεύουσιν viii. 3–5, εἰσίασιν, προσφέρει, προσφέρονται, ἁγιάζει ix. 6 f., 9, 13, ἔχουσιν xiii. 10) afford no evidence that the Temple was still standing. See John v. 2 : 'There is in Jerusalem at the sheepgate a pool.' Clem. *ad Cor.* 41 : 'Not in every place, brethren, are the continual sacrifices offered . . . but in Jerusalem alone.' *Ep. Diogn.* 3 : 'The Jews, considering that they are presenting them [animal sacrifices] to God, as if He were in need of them, ought in all reason to count it folly. . . . Those who think to perform sacrifices to Him with blood and fat and whole burnt-offerings . . . seem to me in no way different from those who show the same respect towards deaf images.' It was a common literary method employed by writers long after the fall of Jerusalem, and affords no indication of date. Dr. Manson's arguments (above) for a date before 70 remain, independent of the references to the present tense.

AUTHOR. The title which stands in the A.V. and R.V., as has been said, is entirely without authority or value. The mind of St. Paul worked on a plane very different from that of the author of this epistle. They are at one in their exalted conception of the eternal existence and the Divinity of Christ. There are some parallelisms of language, which naturally occur in the work of one who knew some of the Pauline epistles. But on the score of language alone it would be equally possible to suppose St. Peter to have been the author. Origen (*ap.* Eus. *H.E.* vi. 25) suggested that while the thoughts were those of St. Paul, the style and composition were 'more Greek' than his, so that it might have been written by someone who preserved reminiscences of what the apostle said, and wrote them up at leisure. Clement Alex. (ibid. 14) even thought, as said above, that it was written by St. Paul 'in the Hebrew tongue' (i.e. Aramaic), and that *St. Luke* translated and edited it for Greeks, whence the similarity of 'colour' between it and the Acts. And he refers to 'the blessed presbyter'[1] as having previously (ἤδη) held St. Paul to have been the author, but to have suppressed his name through modesty, both for the sake

---

[1] Westcott (*Hebrews*, p. lxvii) suggests Pantaenus.

of the honour of the Lord, 'who being the Apostle of the Almighty was sent to Hebrews', 'and because it was a work of supererogation for him to write to Hebrews, since he was herald and apostle of Gentiles'. But the similarity, such as it is, is accounted for by the fact that both writers lived in much the same religious atmosphere, wrote at about the same time, and were in command of somewhat more literary Greek than other New Testament writers, and both were influenced by the LXX. Eusebius (iii. 37) accepted the tradition that it was written in 'Hebrew', but thought it more likely that Clement of Rome translated it, because of its similarity in style and thoughts to Clement's epistle. Tertullian (*De Pudic.* 20), who may be taken as representing the opinion both of Africa and Rome at his time, attributed it to *Barnabas*. This has had several modern supporters. As a Levite, and therefore officially connected with Jewish worship, and one able to give exhortation (υἱὸς παρακλήσεως Acts iv. 36), he might have written this 'word of exhortation' (Heb. xiii. 22). The 'Epistle of Barnabas' attributed to him is similarly based throughout on Old Testament material, and is deeply influenced by Alexandrian thought, though no one who reads the two epistles side by side could entertain for a moment the idea of a common authorship. It is less impossible to suppose him to have written Hebrews than the epistle which bears his name. But these facts are enough to account for the tradition. Barnabas, however, was one of the earliest 'apostles', and could hardly have written ii. 3 : 'so great a salvation, which, having its beginning in being spoken through the Lord was confirmed unto us by them that heard Him.' The supposed Pauline authorship of Hebrews was probably the chief reason for its reception as canonical, whereas, though Barnabas was an apostle, the Epistle of Barnabas was rejected. And if Barnabas was really the author of Hebrews, it is difficult to see how the Pauline tradition arose.

Without any early tradition modern guesses have been made, perhaps the most plausible of which, made by Luther, is Apollos, learned in the Old Testament, a thinker of an Alexandrian type, and connected with St. Paul and his friends. But if the epistle was written to Rome, the probability of his authorship is small in the absence of all evidence that he was in a position to write such an exhortation to the Christians at the capital. Dr. T. W. Manson (op. cit.) suggests that Apollos wrote it, sending it not to Rome but to the churches of the Lycus valley including Colossae. He takes Heb. i–x as a complete refutation of the Colossian heresy. On the other hand the work was known very early at Rome, and known not to be by Paul. If sent to the Lycus valley by Apollos, how did a copy reach Rome so that Hebrews was taken by Clement Rom. to be authoritative (but not Pauline) twenty or thirty years later? St. Peter has been suggested, on account of the similarities of language to be found in 1 Peter. But that the same mind could have produced the two epistles is practically impossible. The same must be said with regard to Silvanus (Silas), who may be supposed to have taken part in the composition of 1 Peter, and was connected with St. Paul and Timothy. Philip the Deacon, who no doubt conversed with St. Paul at Caesarea, is conjectured to have written the epistle to commend Paulinism to Jewish Christians at Jerusalem. Finally, Harnack proposes the name of Prisca (Priscilla); she collaborated with her husband Aquila, but wrote the epistle herself; hence the loss of the personal address at the opening of the epistle and the use of the masculine participle διηγούμενον in xi. 32, since no writing by a woman would have been admitted into the Canon. Aquila had already been suggested by Alford and others, and there is nothing in the epistle to suggest either the hand of a woman or the hands of two persons.[1]

None of these guesses has the least intrinsic merit, and we must be content, as Origen was, though loosely he called it Pauline, to leave the writing anonymous as we find it. If the epistle was written to Italy, the author was probably some Italian presbyter, highly esteemed in his own Church, who wrote it while he was away from home, perhaps in Asia, for it was in or for churches in Asia that all early Christian writings dealing with priesthood were composed.[1]

---

[1] C. Spicq, 'Aux sources de la tradition chrétienne' (*Goguel-Festschrift*, 1950, pp. 265 f.).

BOOKS

A. B. Bruce, *The Epistle to the Hebrews*, 1908.
W. P. Du Bose, *High Priesthood and Sacrifice*, 1908.
W. Manson, *The Epistle to the Hebrews*, 1950.
G. Milligan, *Theology of the Epistle to the Hebrews*, 1899.
J. A. Nairne, *The Epistle of Priesthood*, 2nd ed., 1915.
E. F. Scott, *The Epistle to the Hebrews*, 1923.
C. Spicq, 'Le Philonisme de l'Épître aux Hébreux', *Revue Biblique*, lvi, 1949, pp. 542 ff. and lvii, 1950, pp. 212 ff.

COMMENTARIES

J. Chaine (1927), O. Michel (1949), J. A. Nairne (1921), F. D. V. Narborough (1930), T. H. Robinson (1933), B. F. Westcott (2nd ed., 1892), E. C. Wickham (2nd ed., 1922), H. Windisch (1931), J. Moffatt (1924).

§ 4. JUDE

NATURE AND CONTENTS. This short writing is a tract or pamphlet rather than an epistle. It is addressed to no particular Church or locality, but quite generally to 'those who are beloved in God the Father and Jesus Christ, kept, called',[1] though perhaps it was primarily intended for the circle of Christians of which the writer was the pastor or a leading prophet. It presents a combination, which has not been without its modern imitators, of stern Jewish eschatology and zealous Christian orthodoxy, thus standing in line with the two writings next to be studied, 2 Peter and the Apocalypse. The writer begins with the tantalizing statement that he was about to write with diligent zeal 'concerning our common salvation' (an expression which suggests that he was a Jew writing for Gentiles), but thought it necessary instead to utter a warning to his readers 'to strive for the faith once for all delivered to the saints' in opposition to certain heresies that were creeping into the Church. We are thus left without the information, which would have been valuable to us, as to what 'the faith', 'your most holy faith' (*v.* 20), and the truth about 'our common salvation' meant to him. In what he does

---

[1] The punctuation is doubtful and the text probably corrupt, though the only omission, that of 'and kept for Jesus Christ' is not well attested (om. 630 and the Harklean Syriac).

give us, his Christian standpoint is seen in the fact that he speaks of 'God the Father' (*v.* 1), of Jesus Christ (whom he names six times) as 'our Master and Lord', and of himself as His 'slave' (*v.* 1); and it is seen especially in the closing doxology (*vv.* 24 f.), which has the sonorous effect of a liturgical form, an ascription to God of glory, majesty, power, and authority from everlasting and now and to everlasting through Jesus Christ, thereby implying the eternity of Jesus Christ.

No particular order can be seen in the contents. The denunciations of the heretics are enforced by examples of punishment drawn from the Old Testament and from Jewish tradition, and by eschatological warnings inspired by the Jewish apocalyptic of his age. The punishment awaiting the heretics is compared with that of the Israelites, who after being saved from Egypt believed not and were destroyed[1] (*v.* 5), and of the fallen angels who were 'kept with everlasting chains under darkness unto the judgment of the great day'[2] (*v.* 6; cf. *v.* 13b), and of Sodom and Gomorrah and the neighbouring cities steeped in immorality, whose burning was an example, i.e. a figure or symbol, of the eternal fire which awaits all sinners (*v.* 7). The behaviour of the heretics is contrasted with that of Michael the archangel: they speak evil of the 'glories' (i.e. probably the angelic powers) and of all the supernatural things which they cannot understand (*vv.* 8, 10), but Michael, meekly quoting Zech. iii. 2, did not dare to speak evil against the devil himself when disputing with him concerning the body of Moses[3] which Satan claimed as Lord of matter and because Moses, having slain the Egyptian, was a murderer and deserved no burial (*v.* 9). And their behaviour is likened to 'the way of Cain', 'the error of Balaam for a reward', and 'the

---

[1] The text is doubtful, since the *v.l.* ᾽Ιησοῦς for Κύριος, though intrinsically improbable, has some strong support. See Westcott and Hort, *The N.T. in Greek*, App., p. 106.

[2] Cf. Enoch x. 5 f., 12 f.

[3] This strange legend occurred, according to Clem. Al., Orig., and others, in a Jewish apocalypse of the first century A.D., probably entitled the *Testament of Moses*, itself perhaps the epilogue of the book of *Jubilees*. The extant Latin fragments, which bear the name *Assumption of Moses*, do not contain it, but some similarities of language with iv. 8; vii. 4, 9, 3; i. 10 are to be found in Jude *vv.* 3, 12, 16, 18, 24. See edition by R. H. Charles, pp. 105 ff., and Bp. Chase in Hastings's *D.B.* ii. 802.

gainsaying of Korah' (*v.* 11), and characterized by a series of rhetorical similes (*vv.* 12, 13). That the wicked shall receive punishment is stated not on the authority of the Old Testament, but of a work which the writer seems to have regarded as no less inspired, the book of Enoch, from which (En. i. 9) is quoted the prophecy of Enoch the seventh from Adam, 'Behold the Lord [i.e. God, Yahweh] came with His holy myriads'[1] (*vv.* 14, 15), and of the language of which Jude contains a few reminiscences. After denouncing the character of the heretics (*v.* 16) he adds Christian tradition to Jewish—the prediction of 'the apostles of our Lord Jesus Christ; for they said unto you, At the last time there shall be mockers, &c.' (*vv.* 17, 18). Over against their unchristian condition (*v.* 19) he enjoins faith, prayer, love of God, and the hope of eternal life (*vv.* 20, 21), the saving of doubters, and the pitying of those who dispute[2] (*v.* 22). Their 'fawning upon' others suggests a sense of inferiority producing the desire both to attack spiritual beings above them and to indulge in sexual depravity; by satisfying this desire a victim attains for a time a compensating sense of mastery and of power in fantasy which he does not possess in real life. The association here of being 'agin' the government' with moral laxity and day-dreaming seems true to life and not merely to be a pleasantry of theological vituperation.

Thus his eschatology is concerned wholly with punishment at the hands of God when He comes. The Parousia of Christ is not mentioned, but it is implied that He takes part in the judgement: those who are true to their Christianity 'look for the mercy of our Lord Jesus Christ unto eternal life'. The author of Jude is steeped in the Apocalyptic literature of the Pharisaic school, the *Assumption of Moses*, dated by R. H. Charles *c.* A.D. 7–30, the *Book of Enoch*, dated by Charles 200–64 B.C., and perhaps the *Testaments of the Twelve Patriarchs*, dated by Charles between 130 B.C. and A.D. 10. There is nothing here to preclude a first-century date for Jude.

DATE AND AUTHORSHIP. The writer describes himself as 'brother of James', i.e. probably of the Bishop of Jerusalem; he

---

[1] Westcott and Hort, who refer only to the Old Testament (Deut. xxxiii. 2, Zech. xiv. 5), print ἰδού as though it were not part of the quotation, but it occurs in Enoch.　　　　　　　　　　　　　　[2] The verse is corrupt.

and St. Jude were of the number of the Lord's brethren. It is not easy to determine whether the writing is pseudonymous or genuinely the work of St. Jude. The deeply Jewish colouring and the use of apocalyptic literature point to the author's having been, before his conversion, a member of the pious Jewish class to whom the apocalypses were dear. And to such the Lord's family belonged. But it is open to question whether St. Jude is likely to have lived, and to have been able to write with the nervous force of this fervid appeal, at a date as late as is implied by the development of heresy and of Christian thought which the writing presents.

Bp. Chase[1] gives some not very striking parallels of language and thought with St. Paul's epistles, and says further:

A Christian dialect has arisen. Certain words, e.g. κλητοί, σωτηρία, πίστις,[2] have attained, largely through the teaching and writings of St. Paul, a fixed and recognized meaning among Greek-speaking Christians.

The 'psychic' or natural is opposed to the 'spiritual' (v. 19), cf. 1 Cor. ii. 14, James iii. 15. This use of an accepted Pauline vocabulary would forbid a date before c. 65. But more significant is the affinity with 1, 2 Timothy and Titus.

The errorists whom both writers opposed were of a similar type, and both speak of them in the same severe tone of authoritative denunciation without argument, and with the contemptuous οὗτοι (vv. 8, 10, 12, 16, 19; cf. 2 Tim. iii. 8, where the reference to the apocryphal story of Jannes and Jambres is in the same vein as our author's references to apocalyptic literature). Both use the epithets μόνος, 'only', and σωτήρ, 'Saviour', of God (v. 25) to oppose the prevailing dualism, and the claim of the mysteries to lead to salvation. Both speak of 'the faith' as a recognized body of Christian belief (vv. 3, 20; cf. 1 Tim. i. 19; iii. 9; iv. 1, 6; v. 8; vi. 10, 21; 2 Tim. iii. 8; iv. 7). And both understand the appearance of the heretics to be a sign of the near approach of the End. The writer of the Pastorals, speaking in St. Paul's name, expresses this as his own prediction (1 Tim. iv. 1; 2 Tim. iii. 1; iv. 3); our author, who makes no claim to apostleship, gives it as a prediction of the apostles who had previously taught his readers (vv. 17 f.).[3]

---

[1] Op. cit., p. 802.
[2] But πίστις is not used with the distinctive meaning which St. Paul usually gives to it (see below).   [3] A. H. McNeile's N.T. Teaching, p. 202.

Reasons have been given on pp. 195–9 for thinking that 1, 2 Timothy, Titus were built from a Pauline nucleus by a later writer. They may have influenced our author, or vice versa; but it is quite possible that the writers were independent of each other, and that their similarities are due to their having written at about the same time, in similar surroundings, to meet similar dangers.

The only suggestion of date in the epistle itself is that in *vv.* 3, 17, where the writer looks back at the apostolic age as past.

In the light of these considerations the epistle can hardly be dated earlier than A.D. 70–80, and if the author was not St. Jude, it may be placed at any time within the generation of those who had heard the apostles (*v.* 17).

The date of St. Jude's death is not known, but an indication is perhaps afforded by the story of his grandsons related by Hegesippus,[1] though some have doubted its trustworthiness. Having been tried before Domitian and released, 'they were leaders of the Churches and lived till the reign of Trajan'. Their trial, therefore, appears to have taken place some time before the reign of Trajan, probably not very late in that of Domitian (81–96). At that time they were making their living by working a plot of land, and were therefore grown men. And they were 'those who survived of the Lord's family'; that is, their father and their relatives of his generation were already dead, and their grandfather presumably at a considerably earlier date. Nothing can be concluded with certainty, but under ordinary circumstances the story suggests that St. Jude had died long before the year 70. With this would agree the 'Epiphanian' view, accepted by Lightfoot,[2] that the brethren and sisters of our Lord were children of Joseph by a former wife.

B. H. Streeter[3] suggests that the author was not an apostle but could write authoritatively. He was therefore probably a bishop of some important see. Streeter points to the *Apostolic Constitutions*, vii. 46, which gives the name of the third Bishop of Jerusalem as 'Judas of James', who succeeded Symeon, the successor of James the Lord's brother. C. H. Turner's[4] comment on Epiphanius's list of bishops at Jerusalem, taken no

---

[1] *Ap.* Eus. *H.E.* iii. 20.
[2] *Galatians*, p. 272.
[3] *The Primitive Church*, p. 180.
[4] *J.T.S.* i, 1900, p. 540.

doubt from tradition there, was 'I imagine that the Jerusalem list may have run 'Ιουδαῖος 'Ιοῦστος or more probably 'Ιουδᾶς 'Ιοῦστος.' The third name occurs in later lists either as 'Judas' or 'Justus' or both. Streeter suggests that the original opening of Jude was 'Judas of James, a servant of Jesus Christ'. If so, the author was Bishop of Jerusalem early in Trajan's reign (98–117). Streeter, like Harnack before him, thinks that 'brother of (James)' was a late addition; the latter took the letter to be aimed at Syrian Gnostics *c.* 100–30. Other suggestions of a still later date are confronted with the difficulty that Jude is largely incorporated into 2 Peter, the date of which is probably A.D. 125–50 (see below).

COMMENTARIES

C. Bigg (1901), J. B. Mayor (1907), J. W. C. Wand (as on 1 Pet.).

§ 5. 2 PETER

NATURE AND CONTENTS. This is the latest writing in the New Testament, but it is studied here both because its main concern is eschatology, and because it is very closely connected with Jude. The same two characteristics are prominent— stern Jewish eschatology, and zealous Christian orthodoxy in opposition to heresy; and the denunciations of the heretics are enforced in an exactly similar manner by examples of punishment in the past and apocalyptic warnings of the future. Like Jude also the writing is a tract or pamphlet, addressed to no particular Church or locality, but to those whom the author, writing under the name of Simon Peter, describes as 'those who have obtained a like precious faith with us', as though he were a Jew writing for Gentiles.

In fulminating against heretics, or 'false teachers' (ii. 1), he writes a passage (ii. 1–17) which is closely parallel with Jude *vv.* 4–12. Apart from similarities of language he speaks, with the writer of Jude, of the fallen angels imprisoned in darkness and kept for judgement (*v.* 4), of Sodom and Gomorrah (*v.* 6), of defiance and evil-speaking of the 'glories', in contrast with 'angels greater in strength and power' who 'bring not against them a judgment of evil accusation before the Lord' (*vv.* 10 f.), and of 'the way of Balaam' (*v.* 15). Compare also *v.* 13 with Jude 12: σπίλοι—σπιλάδες, ἀπάταις[1] [?ἀγάπαις]—ἀγάπαις, and *v.* 17 with Jude 13 οἷς ὁ ζόφος τοῦ σκότους . . . τετήρηται. The relation of the two passages will be studied below.

On the other hand the rest of the epistle, except for certain words and expressions, stands apart from Jude. The writer's main object was not warning against heretics, but insistence on the coming of the End as a reason for living a good Christian life. In Jude the heretics are libertines first and last, whose future punishment is sure; in 2 Peter they are at the same time scoffers who deride the idea of the coming of the End; but that End, with its cosmic convulsions, is also sure, and therefore Christians must be zealous to be found spotless and blameless in peace.

The epistle falls into four parts:

A. i. 1–11. Be zealous in the Christian life, 'for so shall the entrance be richly supplied to you into the eternal kingdom of our Lord and Saviour Jesus Christ'.

B. i. 12–21. For this teaching the readers have two sources of authority. Firstly, the apostles: 'we made known unto you' (*v.* 16), i.e. including St. Peter (with whom the writer identifies himself) who was privileged to receive the personal prediction of his death from our Lord (*v.* 14), and to behold His glory in the Transfiguration (*vv.* 17 f.). Secondly, 'something even surer, the prophetic word' of inspired men of old (*vv.* 19–21).

C. ii. 1–22. With these inspired prophets must be contrasted the false prophets and teachers, who are denounced in the manner of Jude.

D. iii. 1–18. The Christian prophets and apostles foretold that scoffers would come, denying the Parousia of Christ (*vv.* 1–4). But the world will be destroyed by fire, as they wilfully forget that it was once destroyed by water (*vv.* 5–7); and though to men the End appears to tarry, it will come, and the heavens and the elements and the earth will be burnt up,

---

[1] The original text may have been ἀπάταις (C ℵ A* Syr.[hl] Cop.[bo] Arm) and ἀγάπαις may have been introduced from Jude into B A[cor.] Ephr. Lat.[m(vg.)] Syr.[ph. hl.mg.] If so, is this one of the several instances of a misunderstanding of Jude by the author of 2 Peter?

giving place to new heavens and a new earth in which righteousness dwelleth (*vv.* 8–13). Wherefore they must strive earnestly to be found spotless, remembering that St. Paul himself taught in his epistles that the delay was due to the Lord's long-suffering, that men might have a chance of salvation (*vv.* 14, 15). Some wrest his words to their own destruction, but the readers must guard themselves from error, and grow in grace and in the knowledge of Christ (*vv.* 17, 18).

AUTHORSHIP. It is as certain as any conclusion drawn from internal evidence can be that the author was not St. Peter. Bp. Chase[1] concludes a careful study of the style and language (to which the reader is referred for details) with the following cautious words:

We have no right to assume that an epistle of St. Peter would be written in good Greek, or even that it would be free from offences against literary propriety and good taste. But style is an index of character. The epistle does produce the impression of being a somewhat artificial piece of rhetoric. It shows throughout signs of self-conscious effort. The author appears to be ambitious of writing in a style which is beyond his literary power. We may hesitate to affirm that the literary style of the epistle in itself absolutely disproves the Petrine authorship. But it must be allowed that it is hard to reconcile the literary character of the epistle with the supposition that St. Peter wrote it.

The irresistible impression produced by the style and language is felt in its full force, as the Bishop points out, only when the epistle is read in Greek, not in the English of the A.V., the beauty of which tones down much of its ungainliness.

Whether St. Peter could have written in this style or not, it is inconceivable that he wrote both our epistle and 1 Peter. '2 Peter is more periodic and ambitious than 1 Peter, but its linguistic and stylistic efforts only reveal by their cumbrous obscurity a decided inferiority of conception, which marks it off from 1 Peter' (Moffatt[2]). Whatever part Silvanus may have played in the production of that epistle, he could not have improved it out of anything of the style of 2 Peter. Further, the epistle contains no allusion to the facts of the Gospel history, except two incidents relating to St. Peter (i. 14 and 16–18)

---

[1] Hastings's *D.B.* iii. 809.   [2] *Introd. Lit. N.T.*, p. 364.

introduced to support the adoption of his name, as is also the allusion to a First Epistle in iii. 1. It is wholly improbable that the apostle, if he were the author (or authority behind the writer) of 1 Peter, having in the First Epistle laid stress on our Lord's Passion, Resurrection, and Ascension, on the Christian Church as the true Israel, on Faith in the sense of hopeful trust, on Prayer, and on Baptism, wrote another which hinted at none of these things. Or that Knowledge should play no part in the First, but be represented as one of the principal aims of the Christian life in the Second (i. 2, 3, 6; ii. 20; iii. 18). And many other differences might be noted. It is impossible to avoid the conclusion that the two writings are expressions of two different minds.

DATE. To these arguments must be added the decisive indications that the epistle was written at a date in the second century, eighty years or more after St. Peter's death. It is uncertain whether Clement Alex., in his *Hypotyposes*, commented on it.[1] In no extant work does Clement cite it or name the author, though there are some possible echoes of its language and thought. If he knew it and commented on it, it must have been written by *c.* 175–80. There are a few doubtful echoes also in the Epistle of the Churches of Vienne and Lyons (177), and in Justin Martyr's *Dialogue* (*c.* 155).[2] If the last shows a knowledge of it, its date cannot be later than 150. But there is no evidence at all that it was known earlier than that. The same *terminus ad quem* is probably provided by its close connexion with the *Apocalypse of Peter*, dated *c.* A.D. 135–50, the parallels with which may be seen in Bp. Chase's article, cf. M. R. James, *The Apocryphal New Testament*, 1924, pp. 505–24. It has even been suggested by Sanday[3] and others that both writings were the work of the same author. At any rate it is probable that, if there is dependence of one writer upon the other, the apocalyptic work was dependent on the epistle, and not vice versa.[4] But they may have been composed by two different writers of the same school of thought, at about the same time. Still later 'Petrine' apocalyptic works are

---

[1] The conflicting evidence is given in Bp. Chase's article, op. cit., pp. 802 f.
[2] See Moffatt, op. cit., p. 372.   [3] *Inspiration*, 1893, p. 347.
[4] See Spitta, *Zeitschr. f. d. neutest. Wiss.* xii, 1911, p. 237.

Fragment ii of the *Gospel of Peter* (M. R. James, op. cit., p. 507), *The Preaching of Peter* (ibid., pp. 16–19), and the *Acts of Peter* (ibid., pp. 300–36), with which 2 Peter compares very favourably especially in its reference to the Transfiguration.

The latest certain *terminus a quo* is the date of Jude. Some have thought that the author was dependent upon the *Antiquities* of Josephus (A.D. 93); but this can hardly be considered proved, although 'a number of the coincidences of language and style occur not only in the compass of two short paragraphs of Josephus, but in a sequence and connexion which is not dissimilar' (Moffatt). But the connexion with Jude, as we have seen, is unmistakable. Attempts have been made, in the interest of the Petrine authorship, to prove that 2 Peter is the earlier; but the evidence to the contrary is too strong: (1) Passages in Jude which are simple and straightforward are elaborated in 2 Peter. (2) If the writer of Jude was the borrower, why did he make such full use of a single passage of 2 Peter, ignoring the Christian appeal in the rest of the epistle? That a single passage in 2 Peter bearing on the heretics should have been based on practically the whole of Jude is quite natural. (3) The sentence in Jude about Michael disputing with the devil (*v.* 9) appears in 2 Pet. ii. 11 in a vague form which requires the other passage to explain it. The author of 2 Peter may not have read Enoch and so he misunderstood Jude. In Jude *v.* 13 the blackness of darkness is reserved for the wandering stars, a natural and suitable conception; in 2 Pet. ii. 17 the picture is much less suitable, the blackness of darkness being reserved for the heretics who are likened to wells and mists. And if Jude *v.* 10 is compared with 2 Pet. ii. 12 it will be seen that 2 Peter has missed Jude's point. Jude referred to the order and harmony of the angelic hosts uncomprehended by false Christians with their lower appetites, what they understood naturally (φυσικῶς) being expressed and corrupted: 2 Peter expands the verse unintelligently, taking Jude's adverb as though it were a neuter plural, τὰ φυσικά, 'mere animals' who in seeking to satisfy their appetites are captured and destroyed. Bp. Chase[1] is justified in saying: 'All the expressions in Jude (except ὅσα . . . ἐπίστανται) have some-

---

[1] Op. cit. ii. 803.

thing corresponding to them in 2 Peter, and it is almost impossible to conceive that the ill-compacted and artificial sentence of the latter should have been the original of the terse,
orderly, and natural sentence of the former.'

Some have tried to explain 2 Peter as an original work by
the apostle with later interpolations;[1] but none is in the least
convincing. J. W. C. Wand has shown how weak are the
arguments brought by Spitta, Zahn, and Bigg in favour of the
priority of 2 Peter compared with Jude (op. cit., pp. 131–3).

There are other signs of a later date: (a) The reference in
iii. 16 to 'all the epistles of St. Paul', in such a way as to place
them on a par with 'the other Scriptures' (τὰς λοιπὰς γραφάς),
implies that the Pauline epistles were known in a collection,
and that they were canonical. (b) 'Your holy prophets and
apostles' (iii. 2) describes the sacred two-fold collection of the
Old and the New Testaments. (c) The Christians of the first
generation are called 'the fathers' (iii. 4), implying, with the
whole context, that they have long passed away.

We may see in the heretics denounced an early Gnostic sect
of the second century, c. A.D. 125–50. There is no sure evidence
for identifying the false teachers with the ascetic teachers denounced in the Pastorals for condemning meats and marriage,
or with the Carpocratians or any other similar sect like the
Ophites,[2] to whom in particular the Fathers gave the name
Gnostic.[3] They illustrate the tendency in all periods of Christian history for certain Christians to claim intellectual and
spiritual enlightenment, as though they were superior in
knowledge to their fellows, while in fact they deny by their
tacit assumptions and by their whole way of life the meaning
of the Incarnation and of the Sacraments of the Church and
the fact that the spiritual makes use of the material as its instrument and for its self-expression. In connexion with the denial
by these heretics of the Parousia, F. C. Burkitt's[4] words are
most valuable:

As I understand it, what is commonly known as 'Gnosticism' was

---

[1] See Moffatt, *Introd. Lit. N.T.*, pp. 369 f.
[2] J. B. Mayor (*Jude and 2 Peter*, 1907, pp. clxvii ff.).
[3] R. P. Casey, 'The Study of Gnosticism', *J.T.S.* xxxvi, 1935, pp. 45 ff.
[4] *Church and Gnosis*, 1932, pp. 146 ff.

a gallant effort to reformulate Christianity in terms of the current astronomy and philosophy of the day, with the Last Judgement and the Messianic Kingdom on earth left out. It failed. The Church decided still to wait, to let the old beliefs fade or survive, and meanwhile to organise itself for an extended career on this earth, and to put its trust less on constructive theories than on tradition, on the annals of what God had done in the past. . . . The science and sociology of the ancient world in the Roman Empire of the second century of our era was not sound . . . a too close alliance of Christianity with that science would have proved a burden and not a bulwark . . . when the Church of the second century rejected what seemed to be a scientific account of Religion and clung to an annalistic account it was taking a course that was appropriate to the time and therefore truly scientific.

Gnosticism was a Christian heresy, as Burkitt has shown; Gnostics were the 'modernists' of their day, trying to fit their religion into a structure based on an undeveloped science and philosophy, neither of which had sure answers to the deepest human problems.

COMMENTARIES

C. Bigg (1901), M. R. James (1912), J. B. Mayor (1907), J. W. C. Wand (1934), H. Windisch (1951).

§ 6. THE APOCALYPSE

PURPOSE. St. Peter exhorts Christians in northern Asia Minor to be joyful through hope and patient in tribulation because trial leads to glory. The writer of the Apocalypse exhorts Christians in western Asia Minor with the same message, but spends a wealth of imagination on descriptions of what the glory will be, and of the divine means to bring it about. All Jewish apocalyptic had the same object, to offer encouragement under trials which were so great that this life, the present order of things, could provide no adequate compensation. This bent of mind, which belonged exclusively to the Jewish race, is found with some frequency in the New Testament; but the writing now to be studied is the only Christian work admitted into the Canon which professes explicitly to be an apocalypse: 'The apocalypse of Jesus Christ which God gave Him to show to His servants the things which must come to pass shortly, and signified it by sending through His angel to His servant John' (i. 1).

In form the writing is an epistle to 'the seven Churches which are in Asia'. After an opening proemium it begins with an epistolary salutation (i. 4, 5). It addresses each of the Churches by name, with suitable commendations and rebukes (chs. ii, iii), and ends with the Grace (xxii. 21). The encouragement that the writer offers is on a plane different from that of any Jewish apocalypse. It is not only that the Messiah will come, but that the Messiah *has* come; that He has conquered death and redeemed men by His own death: that He is now reigning, however loudly the blatant power of scarlet Rome may appear to contradict it; and that therefore His servants are potentially kings. With a series of supernatural and destructive judgements Rome will be annihilated, Christ will come back to reign with the martyrs in a new and heavenly Jerusalem on earth for a thousand years, after which there will be a final conquest by Christ of all enemies, a final judgement by God, a final destruction of all evil men and evil powers, and the establishment of the kingdom of God and Christ in which the saints shall reign for ever.

METHODS OF INTERPRETATION. The book has at all times proved an enigma, and many writers, finding themselves unable to arrive at any satisfactory interpretation, have contented themselves with studying its language philologically. This must, of course, form part of its study, but by itself it is barren of results. Those who have tried to interpret it have followed in the main three methods:

1. *Allegorical.* This was the method adopted first by Alexandrian scholars. The spirit of Philo still lived in Clement and Origen, who went far to obscure the true meaning of the whole of Scripture by allegorizing everything that they could not understand, and a great deal that they could. The mature Christian was thought to have advanced beyond the literal interpretation to the spiritual, and the results differed *ad infinitum* with the imaginative vagaries of each writer. As regards everything chiliastic in particular the method was adopted even by such Latin scholars as Tyconius, Jerome, and

Augustine; and this threw back the true understanding of the book until the saner methods of earlier fathers were revived at the Reformation.

2. *Literary.* Along this path the modern study of the Bible has made some of its greatest strides. But the method, especially if pursued by itself, is always open to the danger of hyper-criticism, and to mistaken conclusions drawn from *a priori* assumptions of what a writer must have written, or could not have written. In the case of the Apocalypse it has taken three directions: (*a*) It is supposed that the original work was altered—and spoilt—by interpolations, rearrangements, and 'corrections', at the hands of a succession of editors or redactors. Probably no book in the Bible has entirely escaped such manipulation, certainly not the Apocalypse; but the method has been carried to extremes in the unsuccessful attempt to use it to explain all the difficulties of the book. (*b*) Attempts are made to find a variety of independent sources, Jewish and Jewish-Christian, strung together. Some of these are given by Swete,[1] others by Moffatt.[2] And the use of sources cannot be altogether denied. According to R. H. Charles,[3] they include vii. 1–8, xi. 1–13, xii–xiii, (xv. 5–8?), xvii–xviii. The book was written in the last years of the reign of Domitian, but it contains material which presupposes events under Nero and Vespasian. (*c*) The sympathetic student, however, is not satisfied with literary dissection. He realizes that it is not a case of the mere stringing of passages together. The writer has employed his sources with skill and deliberation to produce a unity which shall serve his purpose; so that the meaning of events and symbols in the sources is sometimes quite different from the meaning with which he uses them. Swete rightly says, 'The book has clearly passed through the hands of an individual who has left his mark on every part of it; if he has used old materials freely they have been worked up into a form which is permeated by his own personality'. But the recognition that he did use old materials is essential to the understanding of the book. And Gunkel[4] is probably right in

---

[1] *The Apocalypse of St. John*, p. xlvi (2nd ed., 1907).
[2] *Introd. Lit. N.T.*, pp. 489 f.   [3] *Commentary*, pp. lxii–lxv.
    Schöpfung und Chaos.

maintaining that his incorporation of sources was not merely a literary use of them; he was attempting reverently to determine the true and ultimate meaning of the expectations in traditional apocalyptic. Sometimes, indeed, it is possible that there are 'details which have no meaning at all for him, but which he retains as parts of the picture' (F. C. Porter[1]). He was trying to do for the material before him what numberless students have since tried to do for his writing. Gunkel goes very far in tracing the apocalyptic tradition to Babylonian mythology; but though many of his results—due to a 'pan-Babylonian' tendency in vogue at the time that he wrote—have not been accepted, his 'tradition-historical' theory accounts for many of the phenomena of the book.

3. *Literal*. But though these theories of literary compilation contain elements of truth, they fall far short of explaining the book. It is of the utmost importance to realize that, while the writer made use of imagery and metaphor, and worked upon earlier apocalyptic material, he was endeavouring himself to express something quite concrete and literal. 'No obscurity which confronts the modern reader was either intended by him or caused through any uncertainty in his purpose', writes M. Kiddle.[2] Modern psychological studies are rendering it increasingly probable that some of his material was shaped by visions or trances which he experienced in ecstasy; and the basis of those experiences was the actual happenings of his day. On the one hand he makes use of facts as they were during the period *c*. A.D. 64–94, the condition of Christians, as it appeared to him, under persecuting Rome with its power, luxury, and sins. On the other he had before his mind a more or less definite outline of the course of events immediately to come—the punishment of Rome, and the salvation of God's people; he expected literal plagues and destructions, and a literal millenium. That his ideas were largely alien to those of the modern mind constitutes our chief difficulty in understanding him. But historically and eschatologically he meant what he said. The strange notion is still, unfortunately, alive, and dies very hard, that he was predicting, not single events, but events which would take place successively in the world's

---

[1] Hastings's *D.B.* iv. 244.　　[2] *The Revelation of St. John*, 1940, p. 18.

history century after century in the future, so that each prediction would have countless different fulfilments. 'No one who
realizes that the prophecy is an answer to the crying needs of
the seven Churches will dream of treating it as a detailed
forecast of the course of medieval and modern history in
Western Europe' (Swete). The supernatural events that would
arise out of the contemporary conditions would occur 'shortly'
(i. 1; xxii. 6; cf. ii. 16; iii. 11; xxii. 7, 10, 12, 20), and he meant
'shortly'.

That does not mean that the book is not of permanent
spiritual value. It emphasizes the great truths that sin inevitably brings its awful results, that Christ the King of glory
is reigning now, that He has wrought salvation for His people,
and that the kingdoms of the world will one day become the
kingdoms of God and of His Anointed.

PLAN. After centuries of study there is still no approach
to a general consent as to the plan of the book. The most useful
analyses for English readers are those of Swete,[1] Moffatt,[2] and
Charles.[3] *Swete* divides the book into two parts, chs. i–xi, and
xii–xxii. 5. These form distinct prophecies. 'The theme of the
second prophecy is the same on the whole as that of the first,
but the subject is pursued into new regions of thought, and the
leading characters and symbolical figures are almost wholly
new. The Churches of Asia vanish, and their place is taken by
the Church considered as a unity, which is represented by the
Woman who is the Mother of the Saints.' He sums up the
scheme of the book in its briefest form as follows: Prologue
(i. 1–8). Part i. Vision of Christ in the midst of the Churches
(i. 9–iii. 22). Vision of Christ in Heaven (iv. 1–v. 14). Preparations for the End (vi. 1–xi. 19). Part ii. Vision of the Mother of
Christ and her enemies (xii. 1–xiii. 18). Preparations for the
End (xiv. 1–xx. 15). Vision of the Bride of Christ, arrayed for
her husband (xxi. 1–xxii. 5). Epilogue (xxii. 6–21). *Moffatt*
brings into prominence the arrangements of seven: seven
churches (ii. 1–iii. 22), plagues of seven seals (vi. 1–17; viii. 1),
of seven trumpets (viii. 6–ix. 21; xi. 15–19), of seven bowls

---

[1] *Apocalypse*, pp. xxxiii–xxxix, cf. R. H. Charles's Schweich Lectures on the
Apocalypse, 1919.
[2] *Introd. Lit. N.T.*, pp. 485–8.   [3] *Revelation*, vol. i, pp. xxv ff.

(xvi). These are followed by two sets of visions: (*a*) of doom on Rome the realm of the beast (xvii. 1–18), on the beast and his allies (xix. 11–21), on the dragon or Satan and his adherents (xx. 1–10); (*b*) of the great white throne (xx. 11–15), the new heaven and earth (xxi. 1–8), the new Jerusalem (xxi. 9–xxii. 5). The seals, trumpets, and bowls are introduced by visions of heaven (iv. 1–v. 14; viii. 2–5, and xv. 1–8). The seventh trumpet introduces threefold war: in heaven with the dragon or Satan (xii. 1–17), on earth with the beast from the sea, the dragon's vice-regent (xiii. 1–10), and with the beast from the land, the ally of the former beast (xiii. 11–18). And there are three 'intermezzos': (*a*) after the sixth seal: the sealing of the redeemed on earth (vii. 1–8), and the bliss of the redeemed in heaven (vii. 9–17); (*b*) after the sixth trumpet: episode of angels and a booklet (x. 1–11), and the apocalypse of the two witnesses (xi. 1–13); (*c*) bliss of the redeemed in heaven (xiv. 1–5), episode of angels and doom on earth (xiv. 6–20). Moffatt does not discuss the movement of the drama, but he holds that its action is not continuous; e.g. the white horse (vi. 2), the demonic cavalry (ix. 13–21), and the drying up of the Euphrates (xvi. 12–14) all refer to the Parthian invasion. The plagues and woes are described in recurring cycles each more terrible and ornate than the last. But while he sees a 'general unity of conceptions and aims', he recognizes that many of the strange features of the book require the theory that it is composite, and 'show that source-criticism of some kind is necessary in order to account for the literary and psychological data', while at the same time the general unity arises from the fact that the writer has incorporated sources and written them up himself; they were not strung together by an editor. *Charles* recognizes the general unity, together with the incorporation of sources. But he differs from the above writers and from most English commentators in rejecting any theory of 'recapitulation', maintaining that the action of the book is continuous. Not, however, of the book as it stands, since it has been seriously interfered with by disarrangement, alterations, and interpolations[1] at the hand of a redactor, whom he charges with

---

[1] Interpolations include i. 8, viii. 7–12, xiv. 3c and 4a, b, xiv. 15–17, xxii. 18b–19, according to R. H. Charles.

incompetence and dishonesty. When the necessary corrections are made his result is as follows: Prologue (i. 1–3). I. John writes to the Seven Churches to tell them that he has seen Christ and been bidden by Him to send them the visions written in this book (i. 4–20). II. Problem of the book set forth in the Letters to the Seven Churches, which reflect the seeming failure of the cause of both God and Christ on earth (ii, iii). III. Vision of God, to whom the world owes its origin, and of Christ, to whom it owes its redemption (iv, v). IV. Judgements. *First Series*: The first six seals (vi). *Second Series* (vii–xiii): Sealing of God's servants as a security against the Three Woes (vii. 1–8). [Proleptic vision of a vast multitude of the faithful in heaven, i.e. of those who had just been sealed and had died as martyrs—a vision subsequent in point of time to the visions in xiii.] The Seventh Seal, and silence in heaven during which the prayers of God's servants on earth for security against the Three Woes are presented in heaven (viii. 1, 3–5, 2, 6, 13). First and Second Woe (ix. 1–21; xi. 14a). [Proleptic digression on the Antichrist in Jerusalem—a vision contemporaneous in point of time with xiii (x–xi. 13).] Heralding of the Third Woe, and two songs of triumph (xi. 14b–19). Third Woe: the climax of Satan's power; all the faithful are martyred (xii, xiii). [Proleptic vision (*a*) of the Church triumphant *on earth* in the Millenial Kingdom and the conversion of the heathen—a vision contemporaneous with xx. 4–6 (xiv. 1–7); (*b*) of the judgement of Rome and of the heathen nations —a vision contemporaneous with and summarizing xviii; xix. 11–21; xx. 7–10 (xiv. 8–11, 14, 18–20).] Vision of the martyred host (xv. 2–4). *Third Series* (xv. 5–xx. 3): (*a*) Seven Bowls (xv. 5–xvi. 21). (*b*) Successive judgements affecting the several powers of evil: (α) Destruction of Rome (xvii, xviii); Thanksgivings of the angels and martyrs (xix. 1–4; xvi. 5b–7; xix. 5–9). (β) Destruction of the Parthian hosts (lost). (γ) Destruction of the hostile nations, the beast, and false prophet (xix. 11–21), and Satan chained (xx. 1–3). V. Millenial Kingdom: Jerusalem come down from heaven to be its capital; reign of the martyred saints for a thousand years (xxi. 9–xxii. 2, 14–15, 17; xx. 4–6). Final attack of the evil powers: destruction of them and Satan (xx. 7–10). VI. Heaven and earth having

vanished, the dead are judged before the great white throne
(xx. 11–15). VII. The Everlasting Kingdom (xxi. 5a, 4d,
5b, 1–4c; xxii. 3–5). Epilogue (xxi. 5c, 6b–8; xxii. 6–7, 18a,
16, 13, 12, 10, 8, 9, 20–21).

There is much that is illuminating in this. But it is doubtful
if the recapitulation theory has really been disposed of. Pro-
leptic visions contemporaneous with later material are not unlike recapitulation in an inverted form. And it is difficult to
avoid the conclusion that the Last Day is described in vi. 12–
17. The earthquake, the turning of the moon into blood, the
falling of the stars, the removal of the sky 'as a rolled-up book',
and of every mountain and island from their places, the panic
of the mighty and of slaves 'because the great day of their
wrath is come', are all signs of the End, and a long series of
subsequent woes is impossible, and Charles's explanations
hardly remove the difficulty. The theory also requires that all
the first four Trumpets (ch. viii) be assigned to the troublesome redactor. The most successful part of it is the rearrangement of the material in xx. 4–xxii. Some rearrangement is
clearly needed, and Charles makes it probable that the New
Jerusalem which comes down from heaven is not that in which
the saints live for ever, but the scene of the Messiah's temporary, millenial reign on earth with the martyrs only, during
which Satan is bound, and spiritual work is carried on for the
conversion of the heathen.

A theory of a different kind was proposed by *J. W. Oman*,[1]
i.e. that the present arrangement of the book was due to the
accidental transposition of sheets. He supposes 'a codex of
seven quires of double sheets, with the last page left blank as a
cover and protection of the writing, so that the last quire
consists of three and the others of four sections. In such a codex
one sheet was laid above another, then both were folded, then
all the quires were sewn together through the fold.' But an
editor found the sheets in confusion, and in transcribing them
made many additions, enough to fill between three and four
sheets, his work being frequently vitiated by his misunderstanding of the writer's meaning. The editorial additions being
omitted, the rearrangement of the book is as follows:

---

[1] *The Book of Revelation*, 1923.

Previous Order	*New Order*	
Sections 1–4	1–4	i. 9–iii. 22.
11–15	5–9	x. 1–xiv. 5, transposing xxii. 6–8a to follow x. 10, and omitting xi. 14–19.
18	10	xv. 5–xvi. 16, omitting xvi. 15.
23	11	xix. 11–21, transposing xiv. 19b, 20 to follow xix. 16.
7	12	vi. 2–17.
19–22	13–16	xvi. 17–xix. 9a.
26, 27	17, 18	xxi. 9–xxii. 17, omitting xxii. 6–9.
24	19	xvi. 15; xix. 9b, 10; xx. 1–10.
5, 6	20, 21	iv. 1–vi. 1.
8–10	22–24	vii. 1–ix. 21.
16	25	xi. 14–19; xiv. 6–11.
17	26	xiv. 12–xv. 4, omitting xiv. 19b, 20.
25	27	xx. 11 xxi. 8.

This order Oman arrived at by putting the sections of the Greek text on separate sheets, and arranging them simply in what appeared to be their natural sequence. But the remarkable result was reached that, when the editorial glosses were omitted, nearly every section[1] occupied, within a word or two, one sheet or more of thirty-three lines in Gebhardt's text.

The reader's first feeling is that the result is too good to be true. That, however, would be an unjust criticism if the result were substantiated. But there appear to be three objections to the theory: (1) Oman's sketch of the course of thought of his rearranged text is a more consistent and coherent whole than it actually yields. (2) Too much manipulation seems to be required. In some cases the editorial glosses appear to be due to the theory, and are not always self-evident. (3) It is psychologically improbable that a seer, writing in the heat of his spirit, fitted his sections so exactly (with two exceptions) to his sheets. And if he had really done so, would he have allowed himself the two exceptions?[2] The same objections can be urged against Oman's[3] revised theory, according to which 'glosses'

---

[1] 19 is one line, and 25 more than a line and a half, too long, 20 and 26 being short by the same amounts.

[2] See a criticism by A. E. Brooke, *J.T.S.* xxv, 1924, pp. 303–9.

[3] *The Text of Revelation. A Revised Theory*, 1928.

were all 'doublets', 'that is to say, repetitions by the original editor from his author'. Compared with the '*New Order*' above, §§ 1–4 remain the same; § 5, xxii. 10–12, x. 1–11; § 6, xi. 1–13; § 8, xii. 1–14; § 9, xii. 14–xiii. 11; § 10, xiii. 11–18, xiv. 6–12; § 11, xv. 5–6, xvi. 2–16, viii. 6–11 with passages from viii inserted; § 12, xix. 11–15, xiv. 19–20, xix. 16–21; § 13, xvi. 17–xvii. 9; § 14, xvii. 9–xviii. 6; § 15, xviii. 6–19; § 16, xviii. 19–xix. 9; § 17, i. 7, iv. 1–v. 2; § 18, v. 2–vi. 1; § 19, vi. 2–17; § 20, vii. 1–17; § 21, viii. 1–5, xvi. 4–7, viii. 6–13, ix. 1–7; § 22, ix. 7–21; § 23, xi. 14–19, xiv. 1–5, 13–14; § 24, xiv. 14–19, xv. 1, xv. 6–xvi. 1, xv. 2–4; § 25, xxi. 9–24; § 26, xxi. 24–xxii. 5, 6, 8, 9, xvi. 15, xxii. 14–17, 20, with passages from xix. 10; § 27, i. 3–6, xx. 1–10; § 28, xx. 11–xxi. 1, 3–8, xxii. 18, 19, 21; the rest being doublets. According to this theory the text runs more smoothly but the manipulations to achieve this result are even greater than before. § 7 is intentionally omitted by Oman (pp. 5, 34).

According to A. M. Farrer,[1] the structure of the Apocalypse, rightly understood, provides the key to its interpretation. At first the Ariadne thread seems based on the number seven, as seen in the letters to the seven Churches, the Sabbath, and the Christian week culminating in worship on Sunday. The thread changes and is drawn from Jewish liturgical custom, and from the feasts of Passover, Pentecost, New Year, Tabernacles, and Dedication. The thread again changes, being drawn from astrology, leading us through the maze of the signs of the zodiac,[2] the twelve tribes of Israel, the twelve stones of the High Priest's breastplate, and the twelve Apostles. But as Dr. T. W. Manson[3] has shown, 'the various schemes do not fit the facts without a considerable amount of adjustment, not to say forcing'. Where a scheme breaks down, an explanation is always forthcoming. Then with regard to the method by which correspondences in detail are established between St. John's text and the text of the Old Testament, 'time and time again one can hardly resist the conclusion', says Manson, 'that by

[1] *A Rebirth of Images*, 1949. See his chart facing p. 348.
[2] Cf. C. E. Douglas, 'The Twelve Houses of Israel', *J.T.S.* xxxvii, 1936, pp. 49–56.
[3] *J.T.S.* l, 1949, pp. 206–8.

using the methods of exegesis used in this study it would be possible to establish connexions between almost anything in the New Testament and almost anything in the Old. . . . The book is full of curious learning and ingenious conjecture . . . to one reader at least it is completely unconvincing.' But the book remains the most stimulating and original one on the Apocalypse that has been written in the last quarter of a century.

According to R. J. Loenertz,[1] the main part of the work relates two visions, i. 9–iii. 22 and iv. 1–xxii. 5, which together make up seven 'septenaries'. Each septenary has an opening introduction and in the second vision the seventh part of each septenary breaks out into the following septenary until the final one is reached, which has its seventh element complete. If seven is the number of completeness and perfection, Loenertz's book would suggest that the work was in a sense incomplete till the final septenary, xix. 6–10 to xxi. 1–xxii. 5, crowns the whole. If Loenertz is correct, the author, though a seer, worked according to a careful plan and his sources have been completely assimilated into the structure of his work.

On the other hand, M. E. Boismard,[2] impressed by the 'doublets' in this book, finds two parallel series of prophetic visions in it, though the same style now in both does not point to two different authors. One series[3] he dates in Nero's time, the other[4] after A.D. 70 under Vespasian or at the beginning of Domitian's reign, while the Letters to the Seven Churches are later still.

DATE. (a) *External evidence*. The incorporation in the book of sources belonging to different dates is probably one reason for the variations in the patristic tradition. (i) *Trajan*. This date is given by two late writers. See Swete, *Apocalypse*, p. xcvi, who suggests that this may have been due to the statement of Irenaeus (II. xxii. 5) that John 'remained with them till the

---

[1] *The Apocalypse of St. John*, trans. by Hilary J. Carpenter, 1947.

[2] *Revue Biblique*, 1949, pp. 507–39, especially p. 528.

[3] x. (1), 2a, 3–4, 8–11; xii–xvi; xvii. 10, 12–14; xviii. 4–8, 14, 22–23, 20; xix. 11–20; xx. 11–12; xxi. 1–4; xxii. 3–5, xxi. 5–8.

[4] iv–ix; x. 1, 2b, 5–7, xi. 14–18; xvii. 1–9, 15–18, xviii. 1–3; xviii. 9–13, 15–19, 21–24; xix. 1–10; xx. 1–6; xx. 7–10; xx. 13–15; xxi. 9–xxii. 2, 6–15. (Appendix: xi. 1–13, 19.)

time of Trajan'. Other traditions favour a date before Domitian. (ii) *Nero* (54–68). Jerome (*adv. Jovin*. i. 26) understands
some words of Tertullian to mean that the exile in Patmos was
in Nero's reign. The same is stated in the title prefixed to both
the Syriac versions of the Apocalypse. And Theophylact
(*Praef. in Joan.*) rather confusedly says that John wrote the
Gospel in the island of Patmos thirty-two years after Christ's
Ascension, i.e. *c.* 64. B. W. Henderson[1] accepts a date shortly
after Nero's death in 68, when the first pseudo-Nero threatened
Galba. (iii) *Claudius* (41–54). This is the date twice given by
Epiphanius (*Haer.* li. 12, 33). (iv) But the best evidence points
to the reign of *Domitian* (81–96). Iren. (v. xxx. 3, Eus. *H.E.* iii.
18; iv. 8): 'almost in our own generation, towards the end of
Domitian's reign.'[2] Victorinus (*in Apoc.* x. 11; xvii. 10). Eus.
(iii. 18) relates it as a tradition (κατέχει λόγος) that John
escaped from Patmos after the death of Domitian. Similarly
Jer. (*De vir. ill.* 9). See also Clem. Al. *Quis dives*, 42.

(*b*) *Internal evidence*. Some of the writer's sources seem to
belong to the reign of Nero, or at least to a date before the fall
of Jerusalem. In xi. 1, 8 it is assumed that the temple and city
are still standing, though the writer probably gave his own
spiritual interpretation to the words. xii. 14–16 seems to refer
to the escape of Christians from the city, and their safety
during the 'time, times, and half a time' of Antichrist's rule.
(This, however, might belong to Vespasian's reign.) In the
reign of Domitian, which our author regards as the time of
Antichrist, all escape would be impossible. The thought of the
approaching fall of Jerusalem as being the imminent coming
of the End, pictured by the author, led Lightfoot, Westcott,
and Hort to date the book before 70.

Vespasian is probably referred to in xvii. 10: the sixth
emperor who 'is' seems to be Vespasian, reckoning from
Augustus, and excluding Galba, Otho, and Vitellius who were
little more than insurrectionary leaders: unless with M. Kiddle[3]
we take 'seven' to have here only symbolical force, intended to

---

[1] *The Life and Principate of the Emperor Nero*, 1903, pp. 420, 443.
[2] But F. H. Chase argued that Irenaeus's evidence can be taken to point to
a date earlier than the close of Domitian's reign, *J.T.S.* viii. 1906/7, pp. 431–5.
[3] *The Revelation of St. John*, 1940, p. 350.

convey the *complete number* of the emperors. And some have
thought that xviii. 4 'Go forth, My people, out of her . . . that
ye receive not of her plagues' is an isolated fragment from the
time of Nero or Vespasian, because it is held that after ch. xiii
the plagues are poured upon a wholly pagan world, all Christians having been martyred.

But the book in its complete form is probably to be dated in
the reign of Domitian. The spiritual deterioration of Ephesus
(ii. 4–6), Sardis (iii. 1–3), and Laodicea (iii. 15–19), and the
development of the Nicolaitan party (ii. 6), suggest a date some
time after St. Paul's death. The Church of Smyrna, which did
not exist in St. Paul's day (Polyc. *Phil.* xi), had apparently
been developing for some years. The emperor-worship described in the terrible picture of the two beasts (ch. xiii), with
the persecution inflicted on those who refused, were features of
Domitian's reign, of which there is no evidence at an earlier
date. Above all there are clear references to the expectation
that Nero would reappear. This took two forms: at first the
belief was current that he was not dead, but had fled to Parthia
whence he would appear with the Parthian forces; and between
69 and 88 three pretenders appeared in the East. This belief
appears in the Sibyll. Or. v. 143–8 (A.D. 71–74), and the
Parthian invasion is probably spoken of in Rev. vi. 2; ix. 13–
21; xvi. 12–14, also, according to Charles, in the Jewish source
lying behind xvii. 12–17. Then the myth of *Nero redivivus*
became fused with the myth of Antichrist. He was expected
to appear not as a man but as the beast from the abyss. This
idea was impossible till after the last pretender appeared in 88,
and therefore the passages which reflect it in chs. xiii, xvii
must belong to the latter half of Domitian's reign. Charles is
probably right in holding that Domitian is not identified with
him; the part was to be played by a supernatural monster.
vi. 6 may well allude to Domitian's short-lived decree of
A.D. 92, as E. Huschke[1] suggested. Such a date is confirmed
by the use made of Matt., as well as of Lk., 1 Thess., 1 and 2
Cor., Col. and Eph. (Gal.?), 1 Pet., and James.[2]

---

[1] *Das Buch mit sieben Siegeln*, 1860.
[2] R. H. Charles, *Lectures on the Apocalypse*, p. 74, cf. his *Commentary*, pp.
xxxiii–lxxxvi.

AUTHORSHIP. The tradition of the apostolic authorship is met with from the middle of the second century. Justin speaks of the author as 'one of the apostles of Christ', *Dial.* 81 ; cf. Eus. (*H.E.* iv. 18). Tert. (*Adv. Marc.* iii. 14) 'The apostle John in the Apocalypse describes a sword proceeding from the mouth of God'. Hippol. (Lagarde, p. 17) 'Tell me, O blessed John, apostle and disciple of the Lord, what didst thou see and hear concerning Babylon?' Orig. (*in Ioan.*, tom. i. 14) 'John the son of Zebedee says in the Apocalypse'. Victorinus (*De fabric. mundi*)[1] 'The angels . . . who are called elders in the Apocalypse of John the apostle and evangelist'. To these must be added Irenaeus, who three times assigns the book to 'John the disciple of the Lord' (IV. xx. 11, xxx. 4; v. xxvi. 1). This does not call him an apostle, but throughout his pages he appears to know (apart from John the Baptist) of no other John than the son of Zebedee. He uses the same expression of the author of the Fourth Gospel (e.g. v. xviii. 2).

Further, i. 9 implies that the author belonged to Asia, to the Churches of which he was writing; and tradition tells of a John of Asia who was banished to Patmos and returned to Ephesus. Eus. (*H.E.* iii. 20) gives it as a traditional statement of 'the ancient men amongst us' that in Nerva's reign (i.e. *c.* 96) 'the apostle John after his flight to the island took up his residence at Ephesus', which is probably based, as Lawlor[2] shows, on the Memoirs of Hegesippus (*c.* 150–80). It is supported by Clem. Al. (*Quis dives* 42), and *Acta Ioh.* Orig. (*in Matt.* xvi. 6) says that the Roman emperor, 'as tradition teaches', condemned him to the island of Patmos; Tert. (*Praescr.* 36) that he was banished to the island after being plunged, at Rome, into boiling oil. And Victorinus (*in Apoc.* x. 11) says that 'when John saw the visions he was in the island of Patmos, having been condemned *in metallum* by Domitian Caesar'.

But there were many Johns in the early Church; and against the uncritical assumption (for it is probably no more) that an inspired writer named John must have been the apostle there are serious objections. As early as Dionysius Alex. (*c.* 240) criticisms were heard. He could not assign the book to the

---

[1] Routh, *Reliquiae Sacrae*², iii. 461.   [2] *Eusebiana*, pp. 51 ff.

apostle John who wrote the Fourth Gospel and 'the Catholic Epistle' (i.e. 1 John) for three reasons: (1) The writer's use of his own name, which the evangelist avoids; (2) the difference of ideas and thoughts, and the absence of some which are markedly characteristic of the Gospel; (3) the linguistic eccentricities, barbarisms, solecisms, provincialisms, which are completely lacking in the smooth and flowing Greek of the Gospel and Epistle (Eus. *H.E.* vii. 25). The last point is abundantly illustrated in Charles's study of the grammar.[1] Even if the book was written at the earliest date claimed for it, it is psychologically impossible for the same author afterwards to have written the Gospel. And this difficulty is greatly increased if it was written in the reign of Domitian, very shortly before the Gospel. Burney[2] suggests that while the Fourth Gospel was written in Aramaic, and translated by someone well acquainted with Greek, the Apocalypse, which also reflects an Aramaic mind, was written by the same author in such Greek as he could compass, after he had gone to live in Asia. To identify the author of the Apocalypse with that of the Gospel is not, indeed, the same as to assign it to the son of Zebedee. Apart from any other considerations, the latter is rendered practically impossible by the words of Rev. xxi. 14. Could the apostle John have written of the twelve foundations of the walls of the city, upon which were written 'the names of the twelve apostles of the Lamb'? But the book cannot, in fact, have been written by any immediate associate of Jesus, despite the evidence of Justin, which M. Kiddle[3] stresses. There is not a sign that the author had been His companion, or that he had a first-hand knowledge of His words. He does not reproduce a trace of His teaching on the Fatherhood of God, or His spiritual Kingdom. The whole idea of his ordered eschatological scheme is alien to the thought of Mk. xiii. 32: 'Of that day and hour knoweth no man' (cf. Acts i. 7). In xi. 1 the temple, as distinct from the court (*v.* 2), is measured for protection against destruction, in contrast with Mk. xiii. 1, 2. In iii. 21 Christ says, 'I will grant him to sit with Me on My throne', a prerogative which Jesus

---

[1] *Commentary*, vol. i, pp. cxvii–cxliv.
[2] *The Aramaic Origin of the Fourth Gospel*, p. 149.
[3] Op. cit., pp. xxxv f.

Himself disclaimed (Mk. x. 40). The improbability that the author was the son of Zebedee is extreme, apart from the tradition that the latter suffered martyrdom at a date long before the reign of Domitian (see pp. 287–90). Dionysius, dissenting from the idea that the author was John Mark, makes a vague suggestion that it was 'another of those who were at Ephesus, since people say that there are two tombs at Ephesus, and each is called John's'. And we must content ourselves with being similarly vague. The writer was a prophet, as he claims himself (i. 3; xxii. 9), and evidently a Palestinian who had lived in Asia, to which he could write with the spiritual authority which prophets could always exercise in the first century.

Many would therefore agree with E. F. Scott that the author of Revelation was an unknown Asian Christian, not the apostle nor the author of the Fourth Gospel nor of the three Johannine epistles. However, it must be added that whereas in 1897 Harnack was almost alone among Protestant scholars in holding the view that the author of Revelation was that of the Fourth Gospel, this view has gained currency, largely owing to E. Lohmeyer's commentary in which he supports the view that both works were written by the 'Elder'. It would not follow from this that one must accept the whole of H. Preisker's[1] argument that the Fourth Gospel was the 'first part of an Apocalyptic twin-work'.

BOOKS

H. E. Boismard, *Revue biblique*, 1949, pp. 507–39.

R. J. Brewer, 'The Influence of Greek Drama upon the Apocalypse', *Anglican Theological Review*, xviii, 1936, pp. 74–92.

J. E. Carpenter, *The Johannine writings*, 1927.

R. H. Charles, *Lectures on the Apocalypse*, 1919.

—— *Studies in the Apocalypse*, 1913.

A. M. Farrer, *Rebirth of Images*, 1949.

J. Freundorfer, *Die Apokalypse und die hellenistische Kosmologie und Astrologie*, 1929.

H. L. Goudge, *The Apocalypse and the Present Age*, 1935.

J. F. Gunkel, *Schöpfung und Chaos in Urzeit und Endzeit*, 1895.

R. J. Loenertz, *The Apocalypse of St. John*, trans. H. J. Carpenter, 1947.

J. W. Oman, *The Book of Revelation*, 1923.

—— *The Text of Revelation*, 1928.

[1] *Theologische Blätter*, 1936, pp. 185–92.

A. S. Peake, *The Revelation of John*, 1919.
F. C. Porter, *The Message of the Apocalyptic Writers*, 1905.
—— in Hastings's *D.B.*, iv. pp. 239–66.
Sir W. M. Ramsay, *Letters to the Seven Churches*, 1904.
J. Sickenberger, *Erklärung der Johannes-Apokalypse*, 1942.
E. Vischer, *Die Offenbarung Johannis* (2nd ed., 1895).
J. Weiss, *Die Offenbarung des Johannes*, 1904.

COMMENTARIES

E. B. Allo (1921), J. Behm (1935), R. H. Charles (1920), W. Hadorn (1928), M. Kiddle (1940), E. Lohmeyer (1926), E. F. Scott (2nd ed., 1940), H. B. Swete (1907), J. Weiss (1907).

IX

THE JOHANNINE GOSPEL AND EPISTLES

§ 1. THE FOURTH GOSPEL

THIS Gospel has long been one of the chief battlegrounds of New Testament criticism. To estimate the true inwardness of the Johannine problem it is essential to obtain a grasp of the contents of the Gospel as a whole. Many analyses have been made, but none of them has succeeded in exhausting 'the brooding fullness of thought and the inner unity of religious purpose which fill the book' (Moffatt). It is clear that the writer's purpose was religious rather than biographical; and it is from that point that we can go on to study the relation of the Gospel to the Synoptic three, its authorship, and the historical trustworthiness of its narrative.

Apart from ch. xxi, which has been added as an appendix (see pp. 277 f.), the book divides into two sections of unequal length, i–xii, and xiii–xx, which teach respectively that Christ brought Life into the world, and that the Life became fully available only through His self-sacrifice and death.

A. i–xii. *Christ brought Life into the world*

(1) i. 1–14. The fact is involved in the eternal Nature of the Logos, and in His Incarnation.
15–51. Witnesses to Him.

(2) ii. 1–iv. 42. The religion of the new Life is spiritual, superseding all others.

(*a*) ii. 1–22. Christ illustrated this by 'signs': *vv.* 1–11, Water turned to Wine, i.e. the New is better than the Old; *vv.* 12–22, Cleansing of the temple, i.e. the New purges out the Old; *vv.* 23–25, the signs produced apparent belief.

(*b*) iii. 1–iv. 42. The same is taught in three discourses: iii. 1–21, Christ teaches Nicodemus that Christianity is the religion of *spiritual* regeneration; *vv.* 22–36, the Baptist declares that Christ is superior to himself, for He is from above, and giveth the *Spirit* without measure; iv. 1–42,

Christ teaches the Samaritan woman that Christianity is a *spiritual* and therefore universal religion.

(3) iv. 43–vi. 59. The new Life is health and peace.

   (*a*) iv. 43–v. 18. Christ illustrated this by 'signs': iv. 46–54, The healing of the nobleman's son; v. 1–18, The healing of the man at the pool of Bethesda. (In the latter case the peace which he wins is not only health but freedom from the law of the Sabbath.)

   (*b*) v. 19–47. The same is taught in a discourse: v. 19–30, The Son can give the new Life because of His oneness with the Father in power and function; v. 31–47, Witness was borne to Him by John (in whom they delighted), Scripture (in which they thought to have eternal life), Moses (in whom they hoped), and, greater still, by the works which His Father had given Him to do, and by the Father Himself.

   (*c*) vi. 1–21. Two more signs: vi. 1–15, The Feeding of the Five Thousand, i.e. the preservation of life; vi. 16–21, The immediate arrival of the boat when He came to them on the water, i.e. the preservation of peace.

   (*d*) vi. 22–59. Discourse on the Bread of Life.

(4) vi. 60–viii. 59. The offer of the new Life sifts believers from unbelievers.

   (*a*) vi. 60–vii. 13. The Spirit that giveth Life, i.e. Christ's teaching (63), sifted those disciples who deserted Him from the others (66), and Judas Iscariot from the rest of the twelve (67–71); the Jews sought to kill Him (vii. 1); His brethren did not believe in Him (2–10); and the multitude were divided (11–13).

   (*b*) vii. 14–52;[1] viii. 12–59. Two discourses on His Nature, in conflict with His opponents.

(5) ix, x. The new Life gives the Light of truth in contrast with the darkness of error.

   (*a*) ix. 1–7. Christ illustrated this by a 'sign': the healing of the man born blind.

   (*b*) ix. 8–34. The discourse takes the form of the man's dialogue with the Jews, followed by
   ix. 35–41. The Lord's comment to the effect that He does not give light to those who think that they see.

   (*c*) x. 1–18. Discourse on the Good Shepherd, leading to
   x. 19–42. Renewed division and opposition.

---

[1] vii. 53–viii. 11, the story of the woman taken in adultery, is a later addition to the Gospel.

(6) xi, xii. The new Life is reached through Death.

    (*a*) xi. 1–44. Christ illustrated this by a 'sign': the raising of Lazarus.

    (*b*) xi. 45–57. The Sanhedrin plot to kill Him, i.e. they unwittingly acted so as to bring about life through death; and (50) Caiaphas unwittingly pronounced the truth.

    (*c*) xii. 1–11. The anointing at Bethany was an unwitting consecration to death.

    (*d*) xii. 12–19. The triumphal Entry was the crowd's unwitting pronouncement of the truth.

    (*e*) xii. 20–36a. The same is taught in a discourse.

    (xii. 36b–43. Epilogue.

    xii. 44–50. Summary of Christ's teaching.)

B. xiii–xx. *The Self-sacrifice and Death which issued in Life*

    (1) xiii. 1–30. In figure and prediction.

    (2) xiii. 31–xvii. 26. In discourse.

    (3) xviii–xx. In act.

No account is here taken of the transpositions which have been suggested (see pp. 274 ff.). If they are accepted the analysis will be slightly modified, but the writer's meaning and method as a whole are not affected. Action, 'sign', and discourse are carefully planned in such a way as to make the whole story of Christ's life and death a working out of a grand thesis.[1]

RELATION TO THE SYNOPTISTS. The Fourth Evangelist is so largely independent that some have doubted whether he even knew the other Gospels; e.g. Windisch,[2] because (1) the evangelist says so little in actual words to show that he was consciously correcting them; (2) the agreements are too few; (3) to make divergences so wide from writings recognized by the Church would be too bold. But it would be surprising that none of the Synoptic Gospels should have been known to a writer in Ephesus, or still more in Antioch, at a date at least twenty years after the publication of the earliest of them; and of course the earlier they are dated the more surprising it

---

[1] See H. Windisch, *Der Johanneische Erzählungsstil, Eucharisterion*, ii. 175–213, cf. W. F. Howard, *The Fourth Gospel in Recent Criticism and Interpretation*, 2nd ed., 1935, pp. 109–24.

[2] *Zeitschr. f. d. neutest. Wiss.*, 1911, p. 174: but later he held that 'John' intended, by his 'absolute Gospel', to displace the others.

becomes. In language, and in some ideas and narratives, there is more affinity with Mark and Luke than with Matthew.[1]

P. Gardner-Smith,[2] however, followed Windisch's earlier views, maintaining that the Fourth Evangelist neither knew nor used any of the Synoptic Gospels. Even the view that he was familiar with Mark and perhaps Luke is set aside on the ground of insufficient evidence. Divergences from the Synoptic Gospels far outweigh any similarities. Any striking agreements are due to common oral tradition. If the Fourth Evangelist wrote independently of the other three, then the *terminus a quo* hitherto set for the Fourth Gospel by the latest of the Synoptic Gospels, probably Matthew, is removed. The Fourth Gospel may have been written earlier than has been supposed and it may have incorporated traditions older than those found in the other three Gospels. T. Sigge's[3] arguments against Windisch remained, however, unanswered as did also C. H. Dodd's,[4] when he showed that Jn. vi. 1–vii. 10 is based on Mk. vi. 31–x. 1, the Fourth Evangelist knowing the 'doublet' of the journey in Mark and using the latter in written form, not departing from Mark's order of events. After a most careful examination of the evidence, Sir Edwyn C. Hoskyns and F. N. Davey[5] concluded that the original readers of the Fourth Gospel knew much about the life and death of Jesus 'and what they knew, they knew roughly at least in the form in which it lies before us in the Marcan Gospel'. They had some knowledge of Luke and even of Matthew. The Fourth Evangelist 'presumes this synoptic material to be less before the eyes of his readers than in their hearts'. If so, one may go farther than R. H. Strachan[6] when he finds in the Fourth Gospel sources 'parallel to and cognate with those employed by Mark and Luke'.

A few of the more important divergences of John from Mark and Luke may be noted. In Mk. i. 10 f. the vision of

---

[1] See Moffatt, *Introd. Lit. N.T.*, pp. 535 f.; Streeter, *The Four Gospels*, pp. 393–426; cf. Jn. i. 34 א Syr.[c] with Lk. ix. 35, xxiii. 35.

[2] *St. John and the Synoptic Gospels*, 1938.

[3] *Das Johannes-Evangelium und die Synoptiker*, 1935.

[4] *Expositor*, 1921, pp. 286 ff.

[5] *The Fourth Gospel* (one-vol. ed. 1947), pp. 67–85.

[6] *The Fourth Gospel*, 1941, p. 28.

the Dove, with the Voice at the Baptism, is experienced only by Jesus (εἶδεν); in Matthew and Luke it is not clear whether others saw it; but in Jn. i. 32 f. it was specially vouchsafed to the Baptist, and a prediction is recorded that he should see it. In Lk. iii. 23 Jesus was 'about thirty years' of age; but in Jn. viii. 57 'Thou art not yet fifty years old' seems to imply that He was a good deal more than thirty. The Synoptists place the cleansing of the Temple at the end, John at the beginning. In Matthew and Mark Jesus is not recorded to have visited Judaea between His departure to Galilee after the temptations and the triumphal entry into Jerusalem; Luke, however, has indications, and (according to the best reading in iv. 44) one explicit statement, that He was in Judaea during part of His ministry (see the writer's note on Matt. v. 1); in John He went four times to Jerusalem (ii. 13; v. 1; vii. 10; x. 23), and once to Bethany in Judaea (xi. 7), before the later visit to Bethany and the entry, and the greater part of the Gospel is concerned with His work at the capital. According to Jn. iii. 22–24 Jesus began His ministry and was baptizing in Judaea while 'John was not yet cast into prison'; but it is as clearly stated in Matt. iv. 12; Mk. i. 14, and implied in Lk. iii. 18–20, that His ministry began *after* John's imprisonment. As against the Synoptic records of teaching in Galilee the only piece of Galilean teaching in John is in vi. 26–59, part of which (?*vv.* 41–59) is placed in the synagogue at Capharnaum, where, however, a controversy with 'Jews' (*vv.* 41, 52) is unexpected. In Matthew and Mark, if not in Luke, the Last Supper is the Passover; in John it is held on the day before. In Matthew and Mark there are Resurrection appearances in Galilee; in John, as in Luke, they are confined to Jerusalem and the neighbourhood. These instances will illustrate the way in which the writer dealt with the Synoptic traditions. On some points he probably had the more trustworthy information; in other cases alterations and rearrangements were the result of his use of the events as falling into line with the spiritual scheme of thought which the Gospel presents.

More important than discrepancies in historical details are the differences in the potraiture of our Lord. In his attractive work *According to St. John* (1926), ch. ix, Lord Charnwood is compelled to show 'the ways in which this falls short, or seems to do so, of presenting to us our Lord as we can believe Him to have been'. He thinks, indeed, that chs. xii–xvii set before us, for the most part, a figure of our Lord which is very vivid, and, so far, true to the impressions which we get from the other Gospels, adding to its consistency, its compactness, and its force. On the other hand there are elements in the portraiture, chiefly in chs. i–xi, which are felt to be discordant with that in the Synoptists. There is an absence of practical counsel on the details of daily moral life; and an absence of the human compassion of the Man who went about doing good; both of which impress us deeply in the other Gospels. By the time of the evangelist it had become necessary to guard the Christian community from being merged in surrounding masses, and its belief from fading out amid a chaos of loose, fantastic ideas; and, therefore, with the sharp line which he felt obliged to draw between the brotherhood and the world, between the believer and the unbeliever, 'it is not surprising that we miss certain notes which sound loudly elsewhere in the New Testament; only in missing them we miss what we believe to have been the accents of our Lord'. Another note that we miss is the 'elasticity' with which our Lord discouraged the idea of a saved and exclusive community; the writer, as a divine rather than a missionary, shows no positive sign of such vitality of human sympathy. Again, 'The Jesus of the other Gospels is meek, and above all forgiving. Is He so here, and, if at all, has the Evangelist himself acquired His temper? . . . Strange that no echo of this wonderful note which sounds throughout the story is heard when we read the Fourth Gospel. The very design of the book is fraught with the writer's anger.' Above all, in this Gospel our Lord from the very first publishes His own personal claim, and confronts the Jewish people with challenging statements of it. But 'no sort of gainsaying of Christ's personal attributes could, according to the other Gospels, be His ground of quarrel with any man. . . . The business in hand is the kingdom, not Himself. There is here the whole difference which again and again in history has distinguished the man who leads and governs from the man interested in obtaining due acknowledgement of his right to govern.' The evangelist enters into the cloud, and sees a transfigured Christ, so that in attempting to convey his impression of the 'glory' of the Incarnate Logos he departs from the threefold portrait of the Jesus that we know.

COMPOSITION. A broad distinction between the Synoptic Gospels and the Fourth is that while the former are compilations the latter is a composition. Nothing satisfactory has yet been written, though many have taken in hand to draw up schemes, to show that an originally apostolic writing has been incorporated by an editor or editors with expansions and additions. Ch. xxi, indeed, is an addition to the Gospel as originally written, and the writer who was responsible for that may perhaps have touched up chs. i–xx in respect of some details. But the general unity of plan and spirit forbids the idea either of partition into sources or of extensive revision. Instances of attempts of this kind may be seen in Moffatt (op. cit., pp. 558–61). And see Cheetham, *Church Quart. Review*, April 1924, pp. 14–35. The author had, indeed (as Moffatt says), 'access to some reliable historical traditions for his work', and among them 'a certain oral tradition (Johannine or not) upon the life of Jesus, which had hitherto flowed apart from the ordinary channels of evangelic composition'. But that is something quite different from the editorial working up of written sources.

Despite the failure of previous attempts, R. Bultmann[1] has tried to rearrange the text of this Gospel, which he believes reached the editor in complete chaos, though the latter has reduced it partly to order. At the same time Bultmann thinks that sources can be discerned, the most important of which are the *Offenbarungsreden* or *Redenquelle*, which were derived from a pre-Christian or Gnostic author, imbued with an early form of eastern Gnosticism, but saved from a thoroughgoing dualism by the influence of the Old Testament. These sayings came to the editor in Aramaic or Syriac, cast into the form of Semitic poetry, except for Jn. x which is in prose. Next in importance comes the *Semeia-quelle* or Miracle-story source with

---

[1] *Das Evangelium des Johannes*, 1941. As this work consists simply of commentary, without introduction or summary of results, the review by B. S. Easton (*J.B.L.* lxv, 1946, pp. 73 ff.) and his article (ibid., pp. 143–56) are indispensable for the study of it. The influences of Form-criticism and of Barthian theology are apparent throughout the commentary.

its rough style and odd Greek phrases. Bultmann discerns ten or more other smaller sources, some of which may belong to either of the two mentioned above, and some of them akin to synoptic or to oral tradition. Ch. xxi he takes to be the work of an editor weaving together an account of a Resurrection appearance with that of the commission to Peter. The Prologue, however, is part of the Gnostic *Redenquelle*, which speaks of a real incarnation of the Revealer (i. 14) and later of his real atoning death, x. 11. Bultmann does not know where to place vi. 28–29 and he suspects viii. 26–27 of being corrupt. He ignores vii. 53–viii. 11 but the rest of the Gospel he has, in effect, rearranged in what he thinks was the original order because it seems to him to be the logical one. (Any value which this rearrangement has is due to its presentation of themes handled in the Fourth Gospel.) On this view the body of the work falls into two parts: (*A*) The Revelation to the World, ii–xii, and (*B*) The Revelation to the Church, xiii–xx. The themes under (*A*) include 'Encounter with the Revealer, 'Revelation as Judgment', 'Encounter with the World', and 'The secret Victory', and those under (*B*) 'The Farewell' and 'Passion and Easter'. As Easton says, the rearrangements are too drastic. 'How did the text ever arrive at the utter confusion that Bultmann postulates?' If the four winds scattered the leaves of the original roll or codex, it seems strange that none of the breaks occur in the middle of a word or sentence. Perhaps, as Easton suggests, the theory is that the evangelist originally wrote sentences on separate slips of papyrus and his not too competent editor did his best to put them into an order now achieved by Bultmann.

While, however, if we reject such views the general unity of the book is recognized, it cannot be denied that it contains difficulties which suggest the possibility of dislocations, some, perhaps, scribal and accidental, others, apparently, editorial and deliberate. Bacon[1] points out the anticipation by Tatian of some of the modern proposals of transposition. The instances given here are not all equally striking, but they will show the sort of difficulties that present themselves.[2]

---

[1] *The Fourth Gospel in Research and Debate*, ch. xix.
[2] Cf. W. F. Howard, op. cit., pp. 125–41, cf. *App. D.*, p. 264.

John's witness of himself in i. 15 is an awkward parenthesis referring by anticipation to his words in *v.* 30; it may originally have stood elsewhere, or was possibly a marginal note, perhaps on *v.* 8. In iii. 22 the statement that Jesus came into the land of Judaea is a little strange, because, according to the present order of the text, He went thither from Jerusalem; and some would transpose iii. 22–30 to follow ii. 12, so that He would go from Capharnaum into the land of Judaea, where He stayed and baptized, and then to Jerusalem. In iv. 43 f. we are told that, after spending two days in the Samaritan district, the Lord departed thence into Galilee, 'for Jesus Himself witnessed that a prophet in his own country (πατρίς) hath no honour'. Since Samaria was not His own country, the words, as they stand, seem to refer to Judaea which He had just left (iv. 3); but the evangelist knew that though Bethlehem was the village in which He was actually born, Galilee and not Judaea was His πατρίς (vii. 41 f.). If the words are in their right place we must adopt some such explanation as that of Brooke:[1] 'Jesus in spite of His success stays only two days. His true work is in Galilee, His own country, where He is not likely to receive honours which at present would be dangerous.' But this is difficult, and the words may belong to another context. Some writers wish to transpose chs. v, vi, because the words 'Jesus went away across the sea of Galilee' imply that He had been in Galilee and not in Jerusalem (as in ch. v). He will then have crossed after being in Cana (iv. 46), and fed the Five Thousand before going to Jerusalem at the unnamed feast (v. 1), which in that case would be Pentecost. During that visit the Jews persecuted Him (*v.* 16), and sought to kill Him (*v.* 18); and vii. 1, in which this is given as His reason for going to Galilee, naturally follows at once the account of the danger. Further, besides the transposition of chs. v, vi, there is something to be said for transposing vii. 15–24 to follow ch. v. The question 'Is not this He whom they wish to kill?' (vii. 25) is strange immediately after Jesus had spoken with the Jews about it (*vv.* 19, 20), but not unnatural if He had been away in Galilee, and had just come up secretly to the feast, and taught in the temple (*v.* 14). In the latter case 'Behold He speaketh openly' (*v.* 26)

[1] Peake's *Commentary*, ad loc.

follows well upon *v.* 14; also 'How knoweth this man writings', &c. (*v.* 15) suitably echoes 'If ye believe not his writings', &c. (v. 47). In x. 1 the metaphor of the sheepfold is introduced so abruptly that some would place *vv.* 1–18 after *v.* 29, following sayings about sheep. And this brings into closer conjunction the second σχίσμα (x. 19) with the first (ix. 16).¹ In xii. 44 'Jesus cried and said', &c. is unexpected after *v.* 36b 'Jesus departed and was hidden from them'. The whole statement of His rejection by the Jews (*vv.* 36b–43) is a natural conclusion of the narrative before the final events, and it seems probable that *vv.* 44–50 should be transposed to follow *v.* 36a. In xiv. 31 the words 'Arise, let us go hence' scarcely seem to leave enough time for the further long discourse in chs. xv, xvi. The sequence of thought is as good, if not better, if these chapters are placed before ch. xiv, bringing 'I am the Vine' into conjunction with the Last Supper, and the words about unfruitful branches into conjunction with the departure of Judas. Writers disagree as to the exact point to which they belong; either before 'Now is the Son of Man glorified' (xiii. 31b) or after xiii. 38 would be suitable. xviii. 13–24 has very likely suffered dislocation. In *v.* 13 Caiaphas is stated to be high priest; and in *v.* 19 'the high priest' questions Jesus; but not till *v.* 24 is it related that Annas sent Him to Caiaphas. Again, it is hardly probable that the story of Peter's denial was originally broken into two pieces, *vv.* 15–18 and 25–27, the last words of *v.* 18 being repeated almost verbally at the beginning of *v.* 25. For a rearrangement in this case we are able to point to some textual support: Syr.[sin] places *v.* 24 between *vv.* 13 and 14, and *vv.* 16–18 between *vv.* 23 and 25, which is not the arrangement of the Diatessaron in any form known to us. The latter transposition may also have stood in the Old Latin codex *e*, in which case the evidence is greatly strengthened.²
On the other hand, it may be best to compare the Fourth Gospel with an opera. The Prologue corresponds to the 'overture' in which the dominant themes of the work are antici-

---

¹ It may be noted that the only textual support for *any* dislocation according to the papyri is found in P[44] where ix. 3–5 follows x. 10.

² See C. H. Turner, *J.T.S.* i, 1900, pp. 141 f.; C. F. Burkitt, *Evang. da-Mepharreshe*, ii. 316.

pated, after which the themes are presented, variations are introduced, new themes appear, and old themes are then taken up in a new guise, while the unity of the work as a whole is apparent.

Further, although F. R. Hoare,[1] who has presented the most thorough exposition of the theory of textual dislocation in the Fourth Gospel, has taken into account that every section transferred to its 'original order' must be a multiple of the same spatial unit and also that 'every interval between these breaks in the text throughout the book must be the equivalent of one or more physical units', even he has not faced all the difficulties confronting any theory of dislocation at all. As W. G. Wilson[2] has shown, critics have assumed that the original text was written on sheets of papyrus which were accidentally disarranged before being pasted together to form a roll or that the pages in an original codex became displaced. Against the former view he cites Sir Frederic Kenyon's statement that 'the scribe did not write his text on separate sheets and then unite them to form a roll, for the writing frequently runs over the junction of the sheets'; and against the latter view, Wilson argues that if leaves in a codex became displaced the length of each passage so dislocated, and the space between its 'original' and its present position would in every case be equivalent to a multiple of two pages (i.e. sufficient to cover one or more complete leaves of two pages each). Wilson takes seven widely favoured dislocations and finds that in no case is his two-page test satisfied.

Two passages, the story of the woman taken in adultery (vii. 53–viii. 11) and the last chapter (xxi), were not originally parts of the Gospel. In the former case the manuscript evidence[3] as well as the style and vocabulary are decisive, though there can be little doubt that it is a genuine incident. The latter is obviously an Appendix added after the conclusion of

---

[1] *The Original Order and Chapters of St. John's Gospel*, 1944.

[2] *J.T.S.* l, 1949, pp. 59 f.; cf. F. G. Kenyon, *Books and Readers in Ancient Greece and Rome*, 1932, p. 53.

[3] It is omitted in B ℵ (C) 33 L Ψ 0124 W Θ 157 1080 a f q Syr.[vet.] p. Cop. Arm. Geo., and it is found after Lk. xxi. 38 in the Caesarean fam.[13] but at the end of Jn. in other Caesarean manuscripts, fam.[1] 1076 1582 and some Armenian codices.

the Gospel (xx. 30 f.). Moffatt[1] thinks that it was not the work of the evangelist, and notes some linguistic features and peculiarities in which it differs from the Gospel. Are they striking enough to make the difference of authorship certain? M. E. Boismard[2] shows that while xxi contains characteristic phrases found in i–xx, it also has 'figures of grammar and style' which cannot reasonably be attributed to the evangelist. He notes the points of contact with Luke and suggests that xxi was written by 'a disciple of John' familiar with Luke's Jerusalem sources.

AUTHORSHIP. The results here arrived at on this disputed subject are as follows: (1) The Fourth Gospel was not written by John the son of Zebedee, but by a person known as John the Elder, who exercised authority in the Church at Ephesus towards the end of the first century. (It must be stressed that this statement is keenly debated and it must be treated as a 'working hypothesis'.) (2) He was accustomed to think in the Aramaic language, and had been in Jerusalem, where he obtained some of his material from local tradition. (3) He had been an eyewitness of the Crucifixion, which must have been in his boyhood; and had known something of John the son of Zebedee, whom he deeply revered, and thought of as the ideal disciple of Jesus, him whom He loved;[3] and from him he gained some more material.

The internal evidence, apart from a single verse, is all against the apostolic authorship: (a) The author nowhere claims to be an apostle; the writing is anonymous. (b) It is in the last degree improbable that he should have spoken of himself as 'the disciple whom Jesus loved'. (c) It is very unlikely that the son of Zebedee, one of the innermost and most intimate circle of the twelve, should have made use of the work of St. Mark and St. Luke (if he did so, *pace* Windisch and Gardner-Smith), who were not apostles. (d) It is very unlikely that the son of Zebedee would have reached the type of thought that is sketched in the following words of Streeter (pp. 424 f.):

The Gospels of Mark, Luke and John form, it would seem, a

---

[1] *Introd. Lit. N.T.*, p. 572.

[2] *Revue Biblique*, liv, 1947, pp. 473–501, cf. M. Goguel, *Introd. au N.T.* ii, 1924, pp. 285–91.

[3] The identity of the Beloved Disciple with the son of Zebedee is proved by J. H. Bernard, *Commentary*, vol. i, pp. xxxiv ff.

series—Luke being dependent on Mark, and John on both the others. This conclusion of documentary analysis is confirmed by its correspondence with a parallel evolution in the doctrinal emphasis in the several Gospels. Here also Mark, Luke and John form a progressive series the characteristic direction of which is a tendency to make more and more of the idea of Christianity as the universal religion, free from the limitations of its Jewish origin, and, along with this, to lay less and less stress on the original Apocalyptic expectation of an immediate visible return of the Master. The Fourth Gospel is thus the climax reached in the development of theology in the New Testament towards the naturalisation of Christianity in the Hellenic world.

One verse in the Appendix (xxi. 24),[1] written in the first person plural, declares that the writer of the Gospel was the beloved disciple with whom the foregoing incident is concerned: 'This is the disciple who witnesses concerning these things and who wrote these things, and *we* know that his witness is true.' The words would not have been written if the fact had not been disputed; and the leaders at some Church centre found it necessary to write them. But could the authorship of such a book, if it was really written by one of the Twelve, have been for one moment disputed anywhere? In the fight against Gnosticism it became necessary to urge the continuity of tradition from the apostles; and the result was that in some cases writings which formed a very early factor in that tradition were believed to be not only 'apostolic', but actually written by the pen of apostles. Matthew and Hebrews are instances in point.

John xxi. 24 is probably the earliest evidence of that belief in the case of the Fourth Gospel. But the same necessity for defending the apostolic authorship was felt in the West till the end of the second century. Irenaeus (c. 190) is at pains to emphasize the fact that there can be, from the nature of things, neither more nor less than four Gospels, in opposition to some who accepted more and some less. Hippolytus, at the close of

---

[1] There is no textual doubt about this verse, as there is often alleged to be about the last verse, xxi. 25; but H. J. Milne and T. C. Skeat have shown with the help of ultra-violet photography that in ℵ *v.* 24 was followed by a regular *coronis* and subscription but that these were washed out and verse 25 was superimposed, with a new *coronis* and title to follow, *by the original scribe.* The evidence of the inclusion of 25 is as old as that of its omission! If ℵ* omitted, it was unique. (*Scribes and Correctors of Codex Sinaiticus*, 1938.)

the century, in Rome, wrote a work, not now extant, 'In
defence of the Gospel and Apocalypse of John'; and, as
Streeter says, 'no one defends what nobody attacks'. The
attacks do not appear to have come from heretics; most of the
Gnostics accepted the Fourth Gospel; Basilides knew it, c. A.D.
117–38, and c. 170–80 Ptolemaeus and Heracleon also, the
latter being author of a commentary on it:[1] and the Montanists valued it highly for its teaching on the Spirit, the
Paraclete. But some persons whom Epiphanius nicknames
Alogi, i.e. ἄλογοι, which 'may be translated equally well by
"Anti-Logosites" or "Irrationalists"' (Streeter), ascribed both
the Gospel and the Apocalypse to the heretic Cerinthus, and,
among other criticisms, laid stress on the differences of order
between it and the Synoptic Gospels. And Gaius of Rome,
whether he was one of their number or not, ascribed the
Apocalypse to the same heretic, he himself being quite an
orthodox person in his opposition to the Montanists. Once
more, the writer of the Muratorian fragment, expressing, perhaps, the official view of the Roman Church (see p. 360),
reveals the same need for the defence of the apostolic authorship, stating that the Gospel was written by the apostle John,
with the endorsement of all the apostles; and therefore that
the divergences in the Gospels do not affect the faith of
believers. And in speaking of 1 John he says of the writer, 'For
so he declares himself not an eye-witness and a hearer only,
but a witness of all the marvels of the Lord in order', which
looks like an answer to the criticisms of the Alogi.

The Logos doctrine was at first alien to Western Christian
thought (though it was derived from Jewish thought, the
Word, identified with the Torah, being the mediating principle in creation and revelation while at the same time it was
connected with the Logos of Hellenistic speculations[2]), and
might be considered to have a Gnostic tendency. So that for

[1] Cf. J. N. Sanders, *The Fourth Gospel in the Early Church*, 1943, pp. 37–55. He
suggests that Irenaeus was the first Catholic writer to overcome the prejudice
which appears to have been felt against the Fourth Gospel, at least in Rome,
c. 180 (p. 66), but Streeter, op. cit., p. 441, suggested that Justin, quoting from
the Fourth Gospel as from the 'Memoirs of the Apostles' had already introduced it to the West (c. 145), as authoritative; contrast Sanders, op. cit., p. 32.

[2] P. H. Menoud, *L'évangile de Jean d'après les recherches récentes*, 2nd ed., 1947,
pp. 50–53.

something like a century after the Gospel was written, Rome does not seem to have felt itself bound by any ancient and authoritative tradition of the apostolic authorship.

Further, we should expect that many in earlier days who did believe the Fourth Gospel to be the work of an apostle would say so, or indicate in some way their belief in its apostolic authorship. And yet the study of its canonical recognition (see pp. 314–25) shows that there is 'a steady decrease in the employment and recognition of the Fourth Gospel by those who might reasonably be supposed to know it, as we approach the date and region where its currency and authority should be at a maximum' (Bacon[1]). A striking instance is seen in Ignatius. If the apostle John died in Ephesus within twenty years before the letters of Ignatius, it is strange that the latter should write to the Ephesians, 'Ye are associates in the mysteries of Paul', and say not a word about the authority of John, which would to them be supreme, and that although it is pretty clear that he knew the Fourth Gospel. The 'silence of Ignatius', in spite of all attempts to explain it, remains difficult.[2] And not less so is the silence of Polycarp, if (as Irenaeus said) he was a companion of John.

The uncertainty in the patristic traditions has been caused by a complex of facts: (1) A John was known at a late date at Ephesus. (2) The name John is claimed by the author of the Apocalypse, who wrote to the Churches of Asia. (3) Papias speaks of a John whom he calls the Elder. (4) The author of 2, 3 John styles himself the Elder. (5) Dionysius of Alexandria had heard of two Johns buried at Ephesus. (6) The Apostolic Constitutions, usually dated c. A.D. 370 but preserving older material, had access to an authentic list of the bishops of Smyrna while for the bishops of Ephesus it gives 'Timothy ordained by Paul; and John ordained by (the Apostle) John'.[3] (7) A. Mingana[4] quotes a Syriac manuscript dated 1749 but

---

[1] *The Fourth Gospel in Research and Debate*, 2nd ed., 1918, p. 334.

[2] J. N. Sanders does not think that it is certain that Ignatius knew or used the Fourth Gospel (op. cit., pp. 12–14), though according to *The New Testament in the Apostolic Fathers*, 1905, p. 83, 'Ignatius's use of the Fourth Gospel is highly probable, but falls some way short of certainty' (W. R. Inge).

[3] B. H. Streeter, *The Primitive Church*, 1929, pp. 96 f.

[4] *Bulletin of the John Rylands Library*, xiv, 1930, pp. 333 ff.

probably copied from an eighth-century manuscript. Before the gospel it has 'The holy Gospel of our Lord Jesus Christ (according to) the preaching of John the Younger' and after it, 'Here ends the writing of the holy Gospel (according to) the preaching of John who spoke in Greek in Bithynia'.

Irenaeus writes: 'All the elders, who consorted in Asia with John the disciple of the Lord, witness that John delivered [the Apocalypse]; for he abode with them till the times of Trajan' (II. xxii. 5, Eus. *H.E.* iii. 23). 'And there are those who heard him [*sc.* Polycarp], and that John the disciple of the Lord went, &c.' (III. iii. 4, Eus. *H.E.* iv. 14). 'The Church that is in Ephesus was founded by Paul, but John, who abode with them till the time of Trajan, is a true witness of the tradition of the apostles' (ibid., Eus. *H.E.* iii. 23). He speaks of Polycarp, whom he had seen in lower Asia when he was himself a boy, and 'his companionship with John, as he declared, and with the rest of those who had seen the Lord' (*Epist. to Florinus*, Eus. *H.E.* v. 20). Polycrates, Bishop of Ephesus, wrote to Victor of Rome on the Paschal question, A.D. 195. In his letter he says: 'And further, John also, who lay on the Lord's bosom, who became a priest wearing the priestly plate (τὸ πέταλον), and a martyr and teacher, he sleeps at Ephesus' (Eus. *H.E.* iii. 31; v. 24). And Eusebius states (*H.E.* v. 18) that Apollonius (*c.* 186) 'used passages from John's Apocalypse, and relates that a dead man, through the power of God, was raised to life by John at Ephesus'.

For all the Aramaic colouring of its language the Gospel was suited to readers surrounded with Hellenistic perils, which supports the tradition of its Asiatic origin. And the knowledge of its characteristic teaching and vocabulary shown in the *Odes of Solomon*, and by Ignatius and Polycarp whether they knew the actual Gospel or not, tends to confirm this.

Irenaeus nowhere speaks of 'John the Apostle', but, as has been said, it is improbable that (apart from the Baptist) he ever meant any other John. In I. ix. 2 the name John and the title Apostle are applied to him in successive clauses; and the collocation of John with 'the rest of those who had seen the Lord' (*Ep. to Florinus*) should be compared with words in III. iii. 4 (Eus. *H.E.* iv. 14): 'Polycarp was not only taught by apostles, and companioned with many who had seen the Lord, but was appointed bishop by apostles', &c. If, then, his recollections of Polycarp's words are correct, and if Polycarp meant the apostle, it follows that the latter did, in fact, visit Asia. But we must not underrate the facility with which writers in an uncritical age could confuse the early Christian traditions. Thus James the son of Zebedee was not infrequently confused with James the head of the Church in Jerusalem. Irenaeus himself appears to do this in III. xii. 14. And he actually refers to the account of St. Peter in Acts v. 15 as if the words applied to Jesus.[1] He argues on the basis of doctrine and Scripture, but also states on the authority of 'the Gospel and all the elders in Asia who associated with John' that John had taught that our Lord's life was extended to fifty years, so that His ministry was some twenty years in length (II. xxv. 5). And he states that Papias, a companion of Polycarp, was a hearer of John, a mistake pointed out by Eusebius (*H.E.* iii. 39). Another signal instance is that of Polycrates who confuses Philip the deacon with Philip the apostle (Eus. *H.E.* iii. 39), and Eusebius apparently accepts the confusion without demur. See Salmon,[2] who concludes: 'We can believe, then, that in process of time the veneration given Philip as a member of the Apostolic company caused him to be known as the Apostle . . . and eventually to be popularly identified with his namesake of the Twelve.' If a mistake of that magnitude could be made about Philip and James it could be made about John. It cannot, then, be pronounced impossible that Irenaeus was mistaken in the recollections from boyhood which he claimed to have of Polycarp's teaching. He stood, according to his own statement (IV. xxvii. 1), in the third generation after the apostles, and it is quite possible that the John with whom Polycarp had been associated was another than the apostle. It is true that other contemporaries of Polycarp were alive; but if he could make other obvious slips without correction he could make this one; and the more easily because those who could have corrected him

---

[1] In his work *Eἰς ἐπίδειξιν τῶν ἀποστόλων κηρύγματος*, ch. 71. *Texte u. Untersuch.* xxxi. 1, p. 40; cf. J. A. Robinson, *St. Irenaeus, The Demonstration of the Apostolic Preaching*, 1920, p. 132.

[2] *Introd. N.T.*, pp. 313 f.

were in Asia, and he was in Gaul where there was probably no one who could.

That the person with whom he confused the apostle was John the Elder is suggested by a passage of Papias, to which Eusebius refers to show that Irenaeus was mistaken (*H.E.* iii. 39) :

And I shall not hesitate to put down, together with my own interpretations, all that I carefully learnt at any time from the elders and carefully remembered, guaranteeing their truth. For I did not take pleasure, as the many do, in those that say a great deal, but in those who teach what is true, nor in those who remember foreign commandments, but in those who remember the commandments given from the Lord to faith, and coming to us from the Truth itself. If, further, anyone came who had actually been a follower of the Elders, I used to enquire as to the words of the Elders, (about) what Andrew or Peter said, or Philip, or Thomas or James, or John or Matthew or any other of the Lord's disciples ; also as to what Aristion and the Elder John, the Lord's disciples, say. For I supposed that things out of books were less useful to me than what could be learnt from a living and abiding voice (i.e. of one who is still alive).

It is possible that 'as to what Aristion, &c.' should be 'about what Aristion, &c.' The former makes ἅ τε Ἀριστ. depend upon 'inquire' (ἀνέκρινον), the latter upon the λόγους of the Elders. But the former is the more probable, because Papias's dependence on the Elders was for information as to the apostles, not as to Aristion and John who were alive in his day. The contrast between 'said' and 'say' must be allowed its full force. The word 'about' has been inserted in the translation to make clear the probable meaning, i.e. that the Elders were not Andrew and the other members of the Twelve, but that the words of the Elders were the source of information about what Andrew, &c. said.[1]

It may be noted in passing that it is difficult to reconcile the late date of the apostle's death with the evidence of Papias. Many who had been in personal contact with St. John would still be alive in or near Hierapolis, and yet Papias was obliged to depend upon *third*-hand information about him, according to the above translation.[1] Moreover, he would have had an

[1] Contrast, however, H. J. Lawlor and J. E. L. Oulton, *Eusebius, Ecclesiastical History*, 1928, ii. 112 f.

importance for him so great that it is scarcely possible that he could mention him only sixth in a list of seven apostles, even though, as Lightfoot pointed out, the order and selection of names is that of the Fourth Gospel itself.

So far nothing[1] has been written which proves that Eusebius, in insisting on the two Johns, misunderstood Papias, though he may wrongly represent him as claiming to have been an actual hearer of Aristion and the Elder John. This Elder John need not be considered more shadowy than Aristion. Probably he was the 'Elder' of 2, 3 John, and if so, of the Fourth Gospel and the First Epistle. In that case he cannot have been the author of the Apocalypse (see p. 264), as Eusebius suggests when referring to the tradition of Dionysius that there were two tombs of Johns at Ephesus.

Behind the 'Anti-Marcionite' Prologue to John[2] may lie the germ of truth that John the Apostle was the authority behind but not the actual author of the Fourth Gospel. For while at the end of the Lucan Prologue there is a reference to Luke writing Acts after the third Gospel, followed by the words, 'Afterwards John the Apostle' (the Greek has 'of the Twelve' as well) 'wrote the Apocalypse in the island of Patmos and after this the Gospel' (the Latin adds 'in Asia'), the writer of the Johannine Prologue, which is extant only in Latin, has:

Evangelium Iohannis manifestatum et datum est ecclesiis ab Iohanne adhuc in corpore constituto sicut Papias nomine Hierapolitanus, discipulus Iohannis carus, in exotericis (id est in extremis) quinque libris retulit, descripsit vero evangelium dictante Iohanne recte; verum Marcion hereticus, cum ab eo fuisset improbatus eo quod contraria sentiebat, abiectus est ab Iohanne. Is vero scripta vel epistulas ad eum pertulerat a fratribus qui in Ponto fuerunt.

The Prologue-writer was unfamiliar with Papias's five *Exegetical Books* and the words in brackets *id . . . extremis* are an obvious gloss on the impossible *exotericis*. The Prologue also calls Papias 'the beloved disciple of John' and attributes to Papias,

---

[1] Not even by G. Salmon, *Dictionary of Christian Biography*, iii. 398–401.

[2] de Bruyne, *Revue Bénédictine*, 1928, pp. 193; A. von Harnack, *Sitzungsberichte der preussischen Akademie, Phil.-hist. Kl.*, 1928, pp. 322 ff.; A. Huck and H. Lietzmann, *A Synopsis of the First Three Gospels* (Eng. ed. by F. L. Cross, 1935), p. viii.

the Chiliast, the penning of the Fourth Gospel which stresses 'realized eschatology' almost but not quite to the exclusion of futurist eschatological views. It also assumes that John the Apostle was alive in A.D. 120 and capable of dictating accurately to Papias, who flourished then. The usual interpretation of the Latin is as follows:[1]

> The Gospel of John was published and given to the churches by John still present in the body, as Papias, entitled Hierapolitanus, the beloved disciple of John, related in the five *Exegetical Books*; indeed, he, Papias, took down the Gospel, John dictating accurately. But the heretic Marcion, when he had been condemned by him, Papias, because he held opposed views, was expelled by John. Marcion indeed had brought documents or letters to him, Papias, from the brethren who were in Pontus.

But as B. W. Bacon[2] has suggested, the Prologue-writer was probably dependent on Tertullian's work 'against Marcion' (IV. vi): 'He (Marcion) has erased everything that was contrary to his own opinion' and the Prologue-writer has misunderstood Tertullian, *On the Flesh of Christ*, iii, 'If you had not purposely rejected in some instances, and corrupted in others, the Scriptures which are opposed to your opinion, you would have been confuted in this matter by the Gospel of John . . .'. The interpretation of the second part of the Prologue therefore should be: 'But the heretic Marcion was expelled by John, when he had been condemned by him (John). Marcion indeed had brought documents or letters to John . . . .' The Prologue-writer was guilty of the anachronism of making the son of Zebedee a contemporary of Marcion (*fl.* 140) and has missed Tertullian's point that the Johannine writings condemned Marcionite doctrine long before Marcion appeared. Finally, *manifestatum* would seem more applicable to Revelation than to the Gospel. If Papias had indeed written anything resembling the above Prologue in the five *Exegetical Books*, why did not Eusebius, who used Papias as a source concerning Gospel origins, quote this passage? Would it have escaped the eyes of other Patristic searchers too engaged on a similar quest? It would seem that this and the other Anti-Marcionite Prologues

---

[1] T. W. Manson, *Bulletin of the John Rylands Library*, xxx, 1946–7, pp. 312 ff.
[2] *J.T.S.* xxiii, 1921–2, pp. 134–60 and *Journal of Bibl. Lit.* xlix, 1930, pp. 43–54.

must sacrifice their pride of place in the last edition of Huck's synopsis where they stand before Irenaeus as though they were prior to and independent of him and of Tertullian.

In addition to these problems, there is some evidence, which is valued differently by different minds that the apostle did not live to an advanced age and die a peaceful death, but suffered martyrdom. Both sides of the problem must be considered:

(1) In Mk. x. 39 Jesus said to the two sons of Zebedee 'the cup which I drink of ye shall drink, and with the baptism wherewith I am baptized ye shall be baptized'. The obvious conclusion some would say, which only the strongest evidence could prove mistaken, is that the evangelist who preserved that saying must have known that John, as well as his brother James, suffered martyrdom. And the confused traditions of an aged John at Ephesus, in which the apostle and the writer of the Apocalypse came to be identified, can hardly be called strong enough to empty our Lord's plain and explicit statement of half its meaning. Those who accepted the Apocalypse as the apostle's work were able to persuade themselves that the words were fulfilled by his banishment to Patmos.[1] And yet, later, Eusebius gives a tradition, not of banishment but of *flight* to the island (see p. 263); whoever John was, he fled from persecution in Asia, which is far from being a fulfilment of our Lord's words to the sons of Zebedee.[2] Attempts to get nearer to a fulfilment are probably to be seen in the stories that he was compelled by Domitian to drink poison, which did not hurt him,[3] or that he was plunged into boiling oil, and suffered nothing,[4] and in each case banished afterwards. Perhaps also in the modified form in which the words appear in Syr.[sin]: 'Ye are able that ye should drink . . . ye are able that ye should be baptized'; similarly Syr.[cur] (in Matt.): 'Ye are able that ye should drink.' But those who cannot accept any of these

---

[1] Orig. *in Matt.*, tom. xvi. 6, Eus. *H.E.* iii. 18; and especially Jer. on Matt. xx. 23.

[2] In Rev. i. 9 the writer does not speak of banishment. He had been a sharer with his readers in their affliction, and his words are quite consistent with flight, at the same time very likely expressing his purpose of Christian teaching in the island (διὰ τὸν λόγον κτλ.).

[3] James, *The Apocryphal N.T.*, p. 228; cf. Mk. xvi. 18.

[4] Tert. *De Praescr.* 36, Jer. *in Matt.*

expedients feel irresistibly the force of Christ's words as evidence of St. John's martyrdom, or at least of the evangelist's belief in it. To sit on Christ's right and left hand would be thought of as an equal reward for equal suffering, while mere endurance of persecution, and faithfulness during a long life, would not be thought of as suffering equal to martyrdom. The force of the words is enough to carry conviction to some, even if the subsequent references to St. John's martyrdom could be proved to be only deductions from them.

The first of these is a quotation from Papias, who has shown us that John the presbyter was distinct from John the apostle. In the Coislin MS. (ninth century) of Georgius Hamartolus we read: 'Papias in the second *logos* of the *Dominican Logia* states that he [John] was killed (ἀνῃρέθη[1]) by Jews.' Georgius adds, 'thus plainly fulfilling together with his brother the prediction of Jesus about them, and their own confession and agreement concerning them', and then quotes Mk. x. 39.

This is supported in an extract printed by C. De Boor[2] from an Oxford manuscript of 7th or 8th (M. R. James, 14th) century, an epitome probably based on the Chronicle of Philip of Side (fifth century): 'Papias in his second *logos* says that John the θεολόγος[3] and James his brother were killed by Jews.' As Swete says, 'With this testimony before us it is not easy to doubt that Papias made some such statement. . . . But if Papias made it, the question remains whether he made it under some misapprehension, or merely by way of expressing his conviction that the prophecy of Mk. x. 39 had found a literal fulfilment. Neither explanation is very probable in view of the early date of Papias.'[4]

A Syriac calendar early in the fifth century commemorates on 27 December John and James together as martyrs, with which the Armenian and the Gothico-Gallic agree. And a calendar of Carthage (early in the sixth century) on the same day places together John the Baptist and James the Apostle; but since the former is commemorated on 24 June, John the

---

[1] The word which is used in Acts xii. 2 of the death of James his brother.

[2] *Texte u. Untersuch.* v. 2, 1888, p. 170.

[3] This word 'theologian' or 'divine', as Sanday suggests, was probably added by the writer of the fragment.

[4] *Apocalypse*, p. clxxv.

Apostle is evidently meant. All the existing Western calendars are based on the Hieronymian martyrology, which commemorates on 27 December the 'Assumption' of St. John the Evangelist and the consecration to the episcopate of St. James, the Lord's brother. This, perhaps, detracts from their value, but it does not affect the Syriac martyrology; nor does Gregory of Nyssa[1], who shows that he accepted the Ephesian tradition, and the attempt to harmonize it with our Lord's words by the story of the boiling oil, and by John's continual willingness to die for the name of Christ.

Aphrahat (Aphraates)[2] in his *De Persecutione* (A.D. 344) writes, 'After Him [*sc.* Christ] was the faithful martyr Stephen whom the Jews stoned. Simon also and Paul were perfect martyrs. And James and John walked in the footsteps of their Master Christ.' He does not speak of James and John as martyrs, but he knew that the former certainly was, and clearly implies that what was true of one was true of the other. And in the anti-Cyprianic North African treatise *De Rebaptismate* (*c.* A.D. 260) occur the words, 'He said to the sons of Zebedee, Are ye able? For He knew that the men had to be baptized not only in water but in their own blood.' Some have found other possible, but uncertain, traces of the tradition.

(2) On the other hand it can be shown that the Epitomizer of Philip of Side was dependent on Eusebius for any knowledge of Papias. The Epitomizer or his source was a bungler and he used of the martyrdom of James the Great a phrase which really belonged to the martyrdom of James the Just according to the Chronicle of Eusebius.[3] 'All that can be said with confidence is that the sentence as found in the *Epitome* is corrupt, and that no historical inference can be drawn from a corrupt sentence in a late epitome of the work of a careless and blundering historian' (Bernard). Neither Eusebius nor Irenaeus, who both knew what Papias wrote, hints at such a

---

[1] *De Persecutione*, xxiii (cf. *Nicene and Post-Nicene Fathers*, xiii. 401).

[2] Aphraat was not a scholarly but a simple, pastorally minded monk, capable of misquoting Matt. xxviii. 19, cf. C. S. C. Williams, *Church Quarterly Review*, cxlv, 1947, pp. 48–58 and *Alterations to the text of the Synoptic Gospels and Acts*, pp. 33–36.

[3] J. H. Bernard, *Studia sacra*, 1917, pp. 271 f. and *Commentary on John*, vol. i, 1928, pp. xxxviii–xlii.

statement as the one alleged by the late Epitomizer and still later George the Sinner. Secondly, the early church-calendars commemorated the great 'leaders of the apostolic chorus' after Christmas, irrespective of their witness being by death or by life.[1] Thirdly, 'it is more likely that Mark x. 35 gave rise to the idea that the two brothers must have suffered martyrdom than that not a trace of such an event should have survived in early Christian literature'.[2] The words of Mk. x. 39 f. were misinterpreted to convey the idea of a 'baptism of blood', whereas 'to drink the cup' and 'to be baptized with' were Old Testament metaphors meaning 'to undergo tribulation' or 'to be overwhelmed with calamity', but not necessarily 'to die'.[3]

Another reference to John as a 'witness', $\mu\acute{a}\rho\tau\upsilon s$, rather than as a 'martyr' was made by Polycrates, Bishop of Ephesus, who wrote to Victor, Bishop of Rome, in A.D. 190 on the question of the date of the observance of Easter, defending the Quartodeciman custom of Asia Minor of keeping Easter on Nisan 14. He mentions the 'great, principle men' among his fore-runners in the Church there who followed this custom. After mentioning Philip the Apostle and his daughters, he cites John, Polycarp, and four others in an order due no doubt to that of their appearance as $\mu\epsilon\gamma\acute{a}\lambda a$ $\sigma\tauο\iota\chi\epsilon\hat{\iota}a$ of his church (Eus. H.E. v. 24, 2–7). He describes John as 'he who "leant back" on the Lord's "breast", who was a priest wearing the sacerdotal plate, both witness and teacher. He has fallen asleep at Ephesus.' It is clear that Polycrates intended to refer to John the Beloved Disciple and not to the Elder. It cannot be supposed[4] that the son of Zebedee was ever high priest among the Jews and mention of the 'petalon' or sacerdotal plate is probably due to the (uncertain) identification of the Beloved Disciple with 'the other disciple[5] who was known to the high priest', Jn. xviii. 16. $\gamma\nu\omega\sigma\tauό s$ could mean 'acquainted

---

[1] Bernard, Commentary, vol. i, pp. xlii–xliv.
[2] W. F. Howard, The Fourth Gospel in Recent Criticism and Interpretation, p. 250, cf. Menoud, op. cit., p. 9.
[3] Bernard, Commentary, vol. i, p. xlv.
[4] Contrast Bernard on xviii. 15 f., Commentary, ii. 594 ff.
[5] R. H. Strachan suggests that the 'other disciple' was the evangelist himself as opposed to the son of Zebedee, the Beloved Disciple, and that the former was a converted Sadducee, The Fourth Gospel, pp. 85 f.

with' or 'kinsman of' and tradition probably turned the 'other disciple' not only into the beloved one but also into a member of the High Priest's family and one who had been High Priest himself. If Polycrates confused Philip the Evangelist with Philip the Apostle, he may well have given credence to such a tradition.

PLACE OF ORIGIN. During his boyhood Irenaeus, who came originally from Ephesus, had known Polycarp, who in turn had known at least *a* John there, probably about A.D. 90.[1] Irenaeus[2] himself says, 'John, the disciple of the Lord, who leaned back on His breast, himself too set forth the Gospel while dwelling in Ephesus, the city of Asia'. But Irenaeus, who may have confused the two Johns, may also have been mistaken on this point too. For the two tombs at Ephesus to which Dionysius of Alexandria[3] drew attention in distinguishing the author of the Gospel from that of Revelation need not have been those of the Apostle and the Elder, despite Eusebius. Yet the tradition that the Fourth Gospel originated in 'Asia' and particularly in Ephesus has some support in (*a*) Papias being the first external witness, unless Clement of Rome[4] was even earlier in quoting the Fourth Gospel, (*b*) the rejection of this Gospel by the Alogi and its popularity among the Montanists, and (*c*) the connexion between this Gospel and the Apocalypse and the Johannine Epistles, the last especially being closely connected with 'Asia'. But if the evangelist wrote in Ephesus, how can one explain the silence of Ignatius even in his letter to the Ephesians or of Polycrates in his letter to Victor of Rome?

According to manuscripts of the Armenian version of Ephraem's commentary on the Diatessaron cited by F. C. Conybeare,[5] 'John wrote in Antioch, where he lived till Trajan's time'. It is possible that a first draft of the Gospel was made in Antioch before it was taken to Ephesus, as Goguel[6] suggests.

---

[1] Eusebius, *H.E.* v. 20.
[2] *Adv. Haereses*, III. i. 1.
[3] *H.E.* vii. 25, 16.
[4] C. C. Tarelli, *J.T.S.* xlviii, 1947, pp. 208 ff.
[5] *Zeitschr. f. d. neutest. Wiss.* iii, 1902, pp. 193 ff.
[6] Op. cit. ii. 550, cf. T. W. Manson, *Bulletin of the John Rylands Library*, xxx, 1946–7, pp. 325–8.

Goguel discussed the hypothesis of an Egyptian origin, saying that it could be envisaged but that one could scarcely invoke in its favour only the affinity of Johannine thought with Judaeo-Alexandrian speculation and perhaps certain other forms of Egyptian thought. The arguments of this kind are far from decisive, he said, for an age when the exchange of ideas was active in the Mediterranean basin. J. N. Sanders has advanced other arguments in favour of Alexandria as the place of origin besides the Logos doctrine used by Philo (op. cit., p. 40). He has suggested affinities between this Gospel and the *Epistle of Barnabas* and both parts of the *Epistle of Diognetus*, for all of which an Alexandrian origin has been suggested. He has pointed to the use of the Gospel by Egyptian Gnostics; certainly their welcome of it might explain to some extent the reluctance of the Church in the West to receive it at first. In fact he thinks that the early Church in Alexandria was not orthodox (p. 41). He points also to the existence of papyri of an early date (see below, p. 294) found in Egypt showing a knowledge of John there. But little is known of the early Church in Alexandria. As Sir Idris Bell[1] has said, 'There is no satisfactory evidence in our documents for the existence of a Christian community at Alexandria in the first century of our era; but that does not justify the inference that no such community existed. The probabilities are all the other way.' Sanders, however, concludes tentatively, 'There is some evidence to point to Alexandria as the place of origin but this suggestion is not advanced as more than a possibility where certainty is not to be expected' (p. 66). The possibility had already been mentioned by Lake[2] and has been discussed independently by A. M. Perry.[3]

DATE. That the writer does not refer to the fall of Jerusalem is no evidence that he wrote before 70. Nor is the present tense in v. 2 ('There *is* in Jerusalem at the sheep gate a pool') an indication that the city had not yet been destroyed. The past tense is used in iv. 6; xi. 18; xviii. 1. As said above (p. 236), it was a common literary usage. The past tense is actually substituted in the Syriac, Egyptian, and Armenian versions.

---

[1] *Harvard Theol. Rev.*, xxxvii, 1944, p. 190.   [2] *Introd. to N.T.*, p. 53.
[3] *Journal of Biblical Lit.* lxiii, 1944, pp. 99–106.

The limits within which the book must lie are fixed by the use of Luke by the author if he used it, and the use of John or of Johannine thought by Ignatius, i.e. between 85 and 115. On the one hand, there had been time for the Third Gospel to come from Rome to Ephesus or Antioch or Alexandria, and for the Elder to have meditated upon it and absorbed its material into his thoughts. On the other, there had been time for those thoughts to have influenced the outlook and theology of Ignatius at Antioch. This probably reduces the limits to 90 and 100. But the Elder could speak (if 1 John is his) of what he had heard and seen (i. 1), unless he speaks there not in his own name but in that of the community, and could claim to have been an eyewitness of the Crucifixion (John xix. 35). And this must bring the date nearer to the earlier than to the later limit. It is sometimes said that Johannine language, found in patristic writers who make no distinct quotations, may have been due not to the Gospel but to the teaching of the Ephesian school, 'a compact body of teaching like that which we find in the Fourth Gospel' (Sanday). But at least the evangelist must have created and inspired the school, if there was one, and not vice versa.

On the other hand, if the evangelist used no Synoptic Gospel but only sources akin to them, the *terminus a quo* may be earlier than 90[1]; in the mind of a religious genius the development of the Logos Christology might have occurred at any time after the Epistle to the Colossians.

But confirmation of the *terminus ad quem* being *c.* 100 has come from one if not two papyrological discoveries. In 1935 Sir H. Idris Bell and T. C. Skeat[2] published a papyrus from the Nile valley dated within the first half of the second century containing what may be a 'mosaic'[3] of Synoptic and Johannine phrases. But did the author use our Fourth Gospel? It is possible to conclude with G. Mayeda[4] that this *Papyrus Egerton 2*

---

[1] Cf. E. R. Goodenough, 'John a Primitive Gospel', ibid. lxiv, 1945, pp. 145–82; contrast R. P. Casey, ibid., pp. 535–42.

[2] *Fragments of an Unknown Gospel*, 1935.

[3] The description used by M. J. Lagrange, *Critique textuelle, ii, La critique rationelle*, 1935, pp. 633–49.

[4] *Das Leben-Jesu-Fragment Papyrus Egerton 2 und seine Stellung in der urchristlichen Literaturgeschichte*, 1946; cf. Sir Idris Bell's favourable review, *Harvard*

represents a type of popular Christian literature, not a canonical Gospel, but dating from the time before the Canon was formed, and independent, at least to some extent, of the Gospels and perhaps as early as they are.

But also in 1935 C. H. Roberts[1] published a fragment of a papyrus codex of John containing xviii. 31–34 (recto) and 37–38 (verso), also from Egypt, and also dated on palaeographical grounds within the first half of the second century. This papyrus, now styled P^{52}, proves conclusively that those critics were wrong who used to date the Fourth Gospel c. 130 or later. But it must be added that if Sanders's suggestion is right and the Gospel was written in Alexandria, less time presumably would be needed for its dissemination and copying than if the Gospel had been penned in distant Ephesus or Antioch. Bultmann,[2] however, is satisfied that this P^{52} shows that the Fourth Gospel must have been known in Egypt c. A.D. 100, when taken in conjunction with Papyrus Egerton 2.

ORIGINAL LANGUAGE. It is remarkable that while the contents of the book are obviously suited to minds which needed an antidote to docetic Gnosticism, the language and literary style are markedly Aramaic. The simplest explanation is that it was written by a Jew[3] whose native tongue was Aramaic, and who thought in that language, but who went to live in Asia, and found that the Christians there were sorely in need of such a book as he could write. If he wrote it in Greek which he had acquired, and with which he was not perfectly familiar, it would naturally be coloured more or less strongly with Aramaisms, and in this respect be comparable with Mark (see p. 42). But a theory, suggested as early as 1645 by Salmasius, that it is a Greek translation of an Aramaic original, has been revived by C. F. Burney,[4] who adduces not only a large

---

Theol. Rev., xlii, 1942, pp. 53–63. In the Revue des sciences religieuses, xvii, 1937, pp. 54 ff., L. Vaganay discusses the affinity of this papyrus with Tatian's text.

[1] An unpublished fragment of the Fourth Gospel in the John Rylands Library (1935), cf. the Bulletin of the John Rylands Library, xx, 1936, pp. 45–55 and Catalogue of the Greek and Latin Papyri in the John Rylands Library, iii, 1938, pp. 1–3, cf. H. Lietzmann, Zeitschr. f. d. neutest. Wiss. xxxiv, 1935, p. 285, and Sir H. I. Bell, Journal of Egyptian Archaeology, xxi, 1935, pp. 266 f.

[2] Das Evangelium des Johannes, p. 203.

[3] Cf. Bernard's discussion of the evangelist as a Jew, Commentary, i, pp. lxxviii–lxxxiii.   [4] The Aramaic Origin of the Fourth Gospel (Oxford, 1922).

number of Aramaisms in the grammar and syntax, but several passages in the Greek which he thinks point clearly to mistranslation. They can only be enumerated here, and must be studied in his book. דְּ with a relative sense mistranslated by ἵνα = 'who', 'which' (i. 8; v. 7; vi. 30, 50; ix. 36; xiv. 16); by ὅτι = 'who' (viii. 45; ix. 17; less certainly i. 16); by ἵνα = 'when', properly 'which . . . in it' (xii. 23; xiii. 1; xvi. 2, 32). דְּ = 'because' mistranslated as a relative (i. 3, 13). דְּ a relative, lacking gender and number, has led to misunderstanding: in x. 29 the true reading ὅ is a mistranslation, the variant ὅς, found in most manuscripts, being a correction which gives the right sense. Similarly xvii. 11, 12 ᾧ, and xvii. 24 ὅ are rightly corrected in some manuscripts to οὕς. vi. 37; xvii. 2 πᾶν ὅ (with no variant) meant 'all who' (masc.) in the original Aramaic. i. 5; xii. 35 καταλαμβάνειν = קַבֵּיל 'take', 'receive' is a misunderstanding of אַקְבֵּיל 'darken'. i. 9 ἦν = הֲוָא is a misreading of הוּא 'he'. i. 15 γέγονε = הֲוֵי is a misreading of the participle הֲוֵי 'is going to be'; and πρῶτός μου = קָדְמַי of קַדְמַי 'because He was First (of all)'. i. 29 ἀμνός 'lamb' = טַלְיָא which means also παῖς 'boy', 'servant'. There is a play on the word, the reference being to the suffering Servant of Is. liii, who was meek as a lamb when brought to the slaughter. ii. 22 ἔλεγεν 'He was saying' = אֲמַר הֲוָא is a misreading of אֲמַר הֲוָא 'He had said'. vi. 63 (perhaps 68) ῥήματα should mean 'things', a sense which the Aram. מִלָּה can bear. vii. 37, 38 κοιλίας 'belly' = מְעִין is a misreading of מַעְיָן 'fountains'; changing the punctuation Burney renders, 'He that thirsteth let him come unto Me; and let him drink that believeth in Me. As the Scripture hath said, Rivers shall flow forth from the fountain of living waters.' viii. 56 ἠγαλλιάσατο 'exulted'; Western Aramaic probably had a word like the Syriac ܣܘܚ which in Peal and Pael means both 'exulted' and 'longed', the latter being the required meaning. ix. 25 ἕν = חֲדָא is a misreading of הָדָא 'this', which is the reading of the 'Palestinian' Syriac. xx. 2 οὐκ οἴδαμεν 'we know not' = לָא יְדַעְנָא is a misreading of לָא יָדְעָנָא 'I am not knowing'. xx. 18 ἑώρακα 'I have seen' = חֲמֵית is a misreading of חֲמָיַת 'she had seen'.

Burney studies also the twenty quotations in the Gospel from the Old Testament. Six of these (i. 23, 51; vi. 45; xii. 39 f.;

xiii. 18; xix. 37) presuppose direct use of the Hebrew, containing points for the explanation of which the Hebrew is vital. But some of the remainder conform to the LXX.[1] The writer, says Burney, cannot have quoted some from the one and some from the other. The assimilations to the LXX might be due to an editor or redactor, but are probably the work of the translator.

Torrey[2] accepts Burney's theory, but rejects some of his instances of retranslation, while advancing some further ones of his own. This raises suspicion against the theory, which ultimately rests on the mistranslations; and it has not found universal acceptance.

T. W. Manson[3] has suggested that as the Aramaisms to which Burney drew attention are not evenly distributed throughout the Gospel it is possible to separate certain blocks (A), in which they are found, from other blocks (B), in which they are not. (A) would include i. 1–34, ii. 13–22, iii. 1–6, iv. 1–26, 31–38, v. 1–47, vi. 22–71, vii. 14–24, 32–52, viii. 12–59, ix. 8–41, x. 1–18, 22–39, xi. 1–44, 47–53, xii. 20–50, xiii. 1–30, xiv. 1–4, 8–21, 25–31, xv. 1–27, xvi. 1–15, 25–33, xvii. 1–26, xviii. 1–11, 19–24, 28–37, xix. 1–16, 31–37. (B) would include the rest with the exception of the Pericope Adulterae. But Torrey finds two Aramaisms in i. 51, five in ii. 23–25, one in vi. 21, two in vii. 3–8, two in xii. 6–11, one in xiv. 7, also in xiv. 22, xvi. 18, but he has retracted his earlier suggestion that there are traces of Aramaisms in xxi. Similarly J. de Zwaan,[4] who on the whole supports Torrey, finds some in xii. 7, 11, xvi. 16. Matthew Black,[5] who suggested translating Jn. i. 16 'even grace instead of disgrace' because the Heb. חֶסֶד, Aram. חִסְדָּא means both, in his more recent work[6] has treated the whole subject with caution. Out of five instances of Burney for Jn. i alone, Black rejects three while he approves of two.

[1] A. Faure, Zeitschr. f. d. neutest. Wiss. xxi, 1922, pp. 99–121.

[2] Harvard Theol. Rev., 1923, pp. 305–44; The Four Gospels, a new translation, 1923; Our Translated Gospels; cf. E. Littmann, Zeitschr. f. d. neutest. Wiss. xxxiv, 1935, pp. 20–34.

[3] Bulletin of the John Rylands Library, xxx, 1946–7, pp. 322 f.

[4] 'John wrote in Aramaic', Journ. of Bib. Lit. lvii, 1938, pp. 155–71; cf. J. A. Montgomery, ibid. liii, 1934, pp. 79–99.

[5] J.T.S. xlii, 1941, pp. 69 f.

[6] An Aramaic Approach to the Gospels and Acts, 1946.

His conclusion (p. 207) is that the evidence of mistranslation is not unimpressive, especially of d^e, but he doubts whether written documents covered the whole of the Fourth Gospel; there may have been an Aramaic sayings-tradition probably in an early Greek translation. This verdict is not unlike G. R. Driver's[1] that John was mentally translating, as he wrote, logia, handed down by tradition and current in Christian circles in Aramaic, from that language into the Greek in which he was actually composing the Gospel. A view still more strongly opposed to Burney's and Torrey's is that of E. C. Colwell.[2] He makes the most of the disagreements between Aramaic scholars on this subject and then he examines the papyri and the works of Epictetus for similar phenomena to those alleged. But while his denial that the Greek of the Fourth Gospel is a translation from a written Aramaic document may be correct, he goes too far in suggesting that no Aramaic influence in thought and diction can be seen. In conclusion it may be said that the theory of an Aramaic written document underlying this Gospel still remains to be proved but even if parts of the Gospel were shown to be derived from Aramaic written sources, such as collections of sayings rather than narratives, the most probable hypothesis would be that the translator was the evangelist who imposed his own style on to his material, making the style of the whole book essentially one just as he made the Fourth Gospel a unity.[3]

THE HISTORICAL ELEMENT. 'One result of our studies throughout this book', writes W. F. Howard,[4] 'is the discovery how inadequate any interpretation of this Gospel is which ignores the Evangelist's interest in the actual events of the past.' H. Scott Holland[5] and J. A. Robinson[6] cannot be dismissed as conservative scholars pleading a case. Nor can

[1] *The Jewish Guardian*, 5 and 12 Jan. 1923.

[2] *The Greek of the Fourth Gospel*, 1931, cf. W. F. Howard's *Appendix to Moulton's Grammar of N.T. Greek*, ii, 1929.

[3] Cf. E. Schweizer, *Ego Eimi*, 1939, the importance of whose criterion of the 'Johannine characteristics' has been stressed by P. H. Menoud, op. cit., pp. 14–16.

[4] *The Fourth Gospel in Recent Criticism and Interpretation*, p. 236.

[5] *The Fourth Gospel*, 1923.

[6] *The Historical Character of the Fourth Gospel*, 2nd ed., 1929. Cf. his article on 'Jesus Christ', *Enc. Brit.*, 11th ed., xv, pp. 348–58.

Goguel,[1] who has made a real attempt to combine genuine historical details given in this Gospel with those in the Synoptic narratives. While he recognizes that the evangelist is actuated by doctrinal and religious motives in such a way that he has made not 'plain biography' but a selection of profound meditations on the deeds and sayings of Jesus, to bring out their spiritual meaning, yet in so doing John has adopted early traditions in the Church, which can be picked out and reconstructed despite the accretions that have grown about them. Though the warp and woof of the 'seamless robe' of the Fourth Gospel are history and interpretation, many of its historical threads can be selected, tested, and found strong. One of Goguel's criteria is provided by 1 Cor. xv. 3 f. A deed or saying implying ideas foreign to those that St. Paul had received must go back to such very early tradition that it may be accepted as genuine. Another criterion is provided by contradictions and anomalies within a section of this Gospel, revealing traits which do not fit John's scheme nor support his doctrinal motives. A third criterion, for sayings, is that if they have been handed on in a pure or highly original Hebraic form, they are older than the transposition of the material from the Jewish-Christian to the Hellenistic milieu. Goguel concludes that after being a follower of John Baptist for many months, Jesus conducted a ministry lasting more than a year. Contradictions in iii. 22–iv. 3 reveal that Jesus disagreed with John over Baptism and left him no longer to preach only Baptism and Repentance but also the imminence of the Kingdom, the coming of which would be due to no meritorious act of man but to the forgiving, compassionate God. The Law was but a means to an end. After leaving John Baptist, He ministered in Galilee. His teaching on submission to authority led to Pharisaic hostility; He incurred Herod's suspicion and then enmity, which led to His becoming a wanderer and a fugitive from him. Yet the Feeding of the Multitude revealed that He was undismayed, being dispenser of the Messianic Banquet. It is historically true that the people on this occasion sought to make Him king—a fact omitted by Mark from fear of political repercussions—from which time onwards His claim to be

---

[1] *The Life of Jesus*, Eng. trans. O. Wyon, 1933.

Messiah was foremost. Since Jesus recognized evil to lie not in men's circumstances but in their hearts, His consciousness of His own sinless purity is especially important 'when we remember that the moral consciousness of Jesus was extremely fine and sensitive' (p. 389). This sense helped Him to believe in His unique vocation, leading Him to see that He was God's Son and Messenger as others are not. This was the root of His consciousness as suffering Messiah. It was at the feast of Tabernacles that He arrived in Jerusalem, where He remained till the feast of Dedication, retiring to Peraea before returning again to Jerusalem six days before the Passover. A willing sacrifice, He faced death deliberately, as His words over the broken bread show. The evidence for the date of the death of Jesus in relation to the Last Supper is self-consistent in the Fourth as opposed to the Synoptic Gospels. Jesus' arrest by the Roman governor at the instigation of the Jews on the charge of being an agitator was followed by His appearance before the Sanhedrin on a religious charge; yet the Sanhedrin did not judge Him officially for He was Pilate's prisoner, Pilate insisting that the Jews should be fully implicated and be unable to trap himself by inciting the people to rise after the death sentence was passed or by an accusation to Rome that an innocent man had been killed. The trial contained two historical elements: it began with Pilate's question about His claim to be King and it closed with the sentence of death preceded by scourging. 'In asking Jesus, "Art thou the King of the Jews?", Pilate was perhaps less formulating a question than indicating the motive for the sentence which he intended to pronounce . . .' (p. 521). Jesus died in A.D. 28.[1]

At the same time historical events are seen *sub specie aeternitatis* by a mystic. As von Hügel[2] has said,

The book's character results from the continuous operation of four great tendencies. There is everywhere a readiness to handle traditional, largely historical, materials with a sovereign freedom, controlled and limited by doctrinal convictions and devotional experiences alone. There is everywhere the mystic's deep love for

---

[1] J. K. Fotheringham gives the more usual conclusion on the date. 'If we hold with St. John that the Crucifixion was on Friday, Nisan 14, we have a choice between A.D. 30 and A.D. 33.' He inclined to the date 3 April 33. *J.T.S.* xxxv, 1934, pp. 146–62. [2] *Encycl. Brit.*, 11th ed., xv, p. 454.

double, even treble meanings. . . . There is everywhere the influence of certain central ideas, partly identical with, but largely
developments of, those less reflectively operative in the Synoptists.
. . . There is everywhere a striving to contemplate history *sub specie
aeternitatis* and to englobe the successiveness of man in the simul-
taneity of God.

It may be impossible ever to arrive at a definite conclusion
about the historicity of a particular 'event' recorded only
in the Fourth Gospel. Is the raising of Lazarus, for instance,
to be taken as historical or mystically allegorical? von Hügel[1]
would seem to incline to the latter alternative. On the whole
it would appear, however, that the Fourth Evangelist began
with what he took to be historical and by profound contempla-
tion of it he uncovered deeper and deeper meanings, often
allowing the characters or events 'on the surface' to fade away
into the backcloth of his scene or the conversation to run 'into
the sand'.

§ 2. THE FIRST EPISTLE

PLAN AND PURPOSE. The word 'Epistle' does not accurately describe the writing. It has neither address nor salutations, and there is not a word to indicate the circumstances of
the author. The readers are appealed to in the second person,
as in a homily; and it must be regarded as a tract in homily
form, issued for the help and warning of Christians in some
district in which they were assailed by doctrinal and moral
perils. The nature of these perils suggests that it was Asia
Minor.

It is even less possible than in the Fourth Gospel to trace any
definite plan or arrangement.[2] The writer wishes to enforce
two main ideas, and in doing so passes, with no set plan or
order, from the one to the other.

1. His doctrine starts with the assumption, found also in the
Fourth Gospel, that all men belong to one or other of two
categories: life and death, love and hate, light and darkness,
truth and untruth, in other words God and the world. And on

---

[1] *Encycl. Brit.*, 11th ed., xv, p. 455. It is the weak point of Hoskyns and
Davey's *Commentary* that the issue is raised but not faced.

[2] See C. H. Dodd's *Commentary*, 1945, pp. xxi–xxvi.

the intellectual and the moral plane alike there is an acid test, an infallible criterion, as to which of the two categories each man belongs. On the intellectual plane this test consists of a great spiritual fact which is either recognized or repudiated. The presentation of Christianity as a *gnosis*, the knowledge of a fact, is the weapon with which the writer attacks the false *gnosis* of those who were led astray by the rising Gnosticism of the time. The theosophical speculations that were gradually permeating Asia Minor and Europe from the East are met by insistence on the supreme fact of the Incarnation: 'Jesus is the Christ' (ii. 22; v. 1), 'Jesus Christ is come in the flesh' (iv. 2), 'Jesus (Christ) is the Son of God' (iv. 15; v. 5); and every man is in the higher or the lower category according as he recognizes or repudiates that. As John of Asia had personally to stand up against Cerinthus (Polycr. *ap.* Eus. *H.E.* iii. 28; iv. 14), so this writing stands up against the tendencies of which Cerinthus was a representative. It opposes the docetism which had its roots in oriental dualism. The emphasis with which it is stated that 'God is light, and in Him is no darkness at all' (i. 5) suggests that there were some against whom it was necessary to maintain God's moral purity.

Cleansing from sin (i. 7; ii. 2) is due to Christ's blood and propitiation alone, not to a knowledge of, and participation in, the mysteries. The divine anointing gives to all Christians alike the knowledge of the truth (ii. 27); 'ye all know' (ii. 20); so that they must not be deceived by those who claimed that the knowledge was confined to those who were initiates in esoteric theosophy. The latter despised and 'hated' the rank and file of believers, and the writer protests that that kind of illumination is not light but darkness (ii. 9).

2. But Gnosticism tended to produce antinomianism. The superior persons, the initiates, felt themselves to be above good and evil. 'We have no sin' (i. 8); 'we have not sinned' (*v.* 10). Bodily vices could be indulged in because their higher state of *gnosis* rendered these things of no importance, and made Christ's death for human sin of no meaning to them. Little wonder that when they speak 'of the world the world heareth them' (iv. 5); the attraction of a *gnosis* which was compatible with fleshly vices was naturally great.

Hence to the former test on the intellectual plane there is a parallel test on the moral plane. The category to which a man belongs is determined by his obedience or disobedience to the divine commandments, which are centred in love to God and man. Sin, therefore, is ἀνομία (iii. 4).

The two tests thus form the *foci* of the epistle, which is excellently shown in von Haering's arrangement,[1] on which Brooke's analysis[2] is based. Haering also[3] suggested an alteration in his plan, adopting which we may divide the epistle as follows:

i. 1–4. Christological.

ii. 18–27. Christological.

iv. 1–6. Christological. Instead of the corresponding ethical passage, in iv. 7–v. 12 the Christological and ethical are inextricably combined.

v. 13–21. Conclusion.

i. 5–ii. 17. Mainly ethical.

ii. 28–iii. 24. Mainly ethical, but in iii. 22–24 emphasis is laid on their connexion.

RELATIONSHIP TO THE FOURTH GOSPEL. The similarity of style and language between the two writings is undoubted. Moffatt[4] mentions 'the same combination of negative and positive statements, the use of contrast, the aphoristic tone, the playing on ideas, &c.' See the parallels drawn out by Brooke.[5] Moffatt notes, on the other hand, differences in vocabulary and grammar, and Charles[6] thinks that linguistically 2, 3 John stand nearer to the Gospel than 1 John. The similarities, side by side with the differences, make it improbable that the writer of the epistle imitated the Gospel. If there was a movement of thought at Ephesus conditioned by the intellectual environment, and quickened by the need of opposing certain errors, Christian writings within the movement would tend to be similiar in style and language as well as in thought. The Deuteronomic movement affords a parallel; products of it

---

[1] *Theolog. Abhandlungen* dedicated to C. v. Weizsäcker, 1892 (Mohr).
[2] *Epistles of St. John*, pp. xxxiv ff.
[3] *Zeitschr. f. d. neutest. Wiss.*, 1918, pp. 163 f.
[4] *Introd. Lit. N.T.*, p. 589.   [5] Op. cit.
[6] *Revelation*, vol. i, p. xlii, though he assigns all the four to the same author.

are seen in Deuteronomy, in Jeremiah, in the Deuteronomic elements in other parts of the Hexateuch, and in 1, 2 Kings, and no one thinks of them all as the work of one pen.[1]

More noteworthy, however, are differences in ideas and points of view, which may possibly be due to different authors. These are indicated in A. H. McNeile's *New Testament teaching in the light of St. Paul's*, pp. 303–9, and may here be summarized. In the epistle there are no quotations from the Old Testament or even clear allusions to it except the mention of Cain (iii. 12). No hostility is shown to Jews as such, and there is no reference to popular Messianic ideas. Eschatology plays a larger part, and allusions are made to the current Jewish expectations of Antichrist (ii. 18; iv. 3). The conception of God is shaped by ethical rather than metaphysical considerations; He is 'Light' (i. 5) and 'Love' (iv. 8, 16) rather than 'Spirit' (John iv. 24). Correspondingly, it is on what Christ means for men rather than on His eternal relation with the Father that stress is laid; the word 'Glory', frequent in the Gospel to describe the attributes or characteristics of Deity, does not occur. 'The Gospel teaches what Christ is, and consequently what He does to unite men with God. The epistle dwells rather on what God is, and consequently what He does to unite men with Himself through Christ.' Salvation, as in the Gospel, consists of passing from the lower to the higher category, but the epistle is more definitely concerned with the way in which it is done; the saving work of Christ occupies a larger place; His destroying of the works of the devil (iii. 8), His 'propitiation for our sins' (ii. 2; iv. 10), our cleansing by His blood (i. 7), His advocacy with the Father (ii. 1) are momentous ideas, all of them absent from the Gospel, the first reminiscent of St. Paul, and the others of Hebrews. In the last there is a marked difference from the Gospel as regards both the meaning and the Person of the Paraclete (cf. John xiv. 26; xv. 26; xvi. 7).

The writer does not speak of these in such a way as to suggest that he wished to supplement or correct the Gospel. Does he make any reference to it? The threefold ἔγραψα (ii. 13b, 14) has been so explained.[2] But the words 'because ye have known

---

[1] Cf. A. Lods, *Histoire de la littérature hébraïque et juive*, 1950, pp. 376–97.
[2] Wendt, who thinks (*Das Johannesevangelium*, 1900, pp. 158 ff., and *Zeitschr.*

. . . because ye have known . . . because ye are strong', &c.
read very unnaturally as a reason why the Gospel was written.
If they are not a reference to 2 John or to a lost epistle, they
may be only a rhetorical repetition of the preceding γράφω
clauses,[1] all referring to the present epistle. The reason for
writing is that the readers have been privileged to share in the
blessings of Christianity. The author recalls to them their
privileges, while he warns them not to allow errorists to rob
them of what they have gained. And the same purpose under-
lies i. 1–3. If the opening words had run 'He who was from the
beginning, whom we have seen . . . that is, the Word of Life', it
would have been natural to see in them a reference to the subject of the Prologue of the Gospel, the eternal Logos who has
life in Himself and who became Flesh. But the remarkable use
of the neuter, 'That which was, &c.', and the expression 'concerning the Word of Life' probably yield a different thought,
i.e. that the divine 'Message the acceptance of which gives
Life' was that of the indwelling, Incarnate Christ in humanity,
which the Church had mystically experienced. 'From the
beginning' no doubt means 'from all eternity', as in ii. 13,
since the indwelling, which formed the subject of the message,
was in the eternal counsel of God. There is no reason to suppose that it means, as some have thought, 'from the beginning
of Christianity'. In any case the thought of the writer seems to
be, 'We, the Christians of an older generation, have had immediate personal experience[2] of the indwelling Christ, which
is the burden of the life-giving message of Christianity; and
we [i.e. I, as representing this older generation] write to you
that ye also may have your full share in our privileges'. If the
ἔγραψα clauses do not refer to the Gospel, the passage has no
bearing on the priority of either writing.

Examination, however, of 1 Jn. ii. 7–8 and iii. 8–15 in com-

---

f. d. neutest. Wiss., 1911, pp. 53 ff.) that the Discourses and the Prologue belong
to a different stratum of the Gospel from the narratives, finds a connexion of
1 John with the former but not with the latter. But he holds (op. cit., 1922,
pp. 140–6) that ἔγραψα refers not to either of these but to 2 John, which he
dates before the First Epistle.

[1] If the passage meant that he was as confident of his readers now as when
he wrote before, the ἔγραψα clauses would more naturally have come first, with
aorists and imperfects instead of ἐγνώκατε, νενικήκατε, and ἐστε, μένει.

[2] Cf. the use of ψηλαφήσειαν in Acts xvii. 27.

parison with Jn. xiii. 34 and viii. 44–47 respectively leads to the conclusion that the First Epistle was written after the Fourth Gospel and with a knowledge of it, as C. H. Dodd has said.[1] The latter has given the fullest presentation of the case against the unity of authorship of the First Epistle and the Fourth Gospel, his work superseding that of H. J. Holtzmann, E. von Dobschütz, H. Windisch, and A. H. McNeile[2] in this field. He adduces linguistic, stylistic, and doctrinal arguments the author of the First Epistle having a far less flexible and a more monotonous vocabulary. 1 John contains no Semitisms, as one would expect of the author of the Fourth Gospel. Yet he writes as though he had picked up some of the evangelist's phrases, such as (πᾶς) ὁ with the participle or certain forms of the conditional sentence, and as though he were running these mannerisms to death. Doctrinally he is closer, Dodd alleges, to the thought of the primitive Christian community than the evangelist, especially in his eschatology and his doctrines of the Atonement and of the Holy Spirit. At the same time, Dodd argues, he is much nearer to Gnostic thought than the evangelist had been. These arguments have been subjected to very searching criticism especially by W. F. Howard[3] and independently by W. G. Wilson,[4] with the result that one may conclude that the verdict reached after careful linguistic analysis by R. H. Charles[5] and A. E. Brooke[6] that the Fourth Gospel and all three Johannine epistles were penned by the same person has not been overthrown.[7]

§ 3. 2, 3 JOHN

THE ELDER. Papias, the *fons et origo* of many problems, appears to use the word πρεσβύτερος, not in the ecclesiastical sense of one who held an official position in the leadership of a local Church, but in the sense of one who belonged to an older

---

[1] *Bulletin of the John Rylands Library*, xxi, 1937, pp. 129–56.
[2] McNeile inclined to this view in the first edition of this book.
[3] *J.T.S.* xlviii, 1947, pp. 12–25.
[4] *J.T.S.* xlix, 1948, pp. 147–56.
[5] *Revelation*, i, pp. xxxiv ff.   [6] *Johannine Epistles*, pp. lxxiii ff.
[7] This conclusion detracts in no way from the excellence of the recent commentary on the Johannine epistles by Dr. Dodd.

generation of Christians, a 'senior', an 'ancient worthy'. See the passage (*ap.* Eus. *H.E.* iii. 39) quoted on p. 284, where the conclusion is reached that when he speaks of the Elder John he appeals to the authority of one who was still alive, but old enough to relate things that had been said by apostles. In the same chapter Eusebius quotes him as saying, with reference to the work of St. Mark, 'This also the Elder used to say'. And this usage was taken over by Irenaeus. Since, then, the writer of 2, 3 John calls himself 'the Elder', the tradition, voiced by Jerome,[1] may very well have been correct that he was the Elder John of whom Papias wrote. In the former passage Jerome shows that tradition expressly distinguished between the writer of 1 John and that of 2, 3 John, the former being the work of the evangelist, the latter of the Elder, 'to the memory of whom another sepulchre is shown to this day'. Dionysius of Alexandria also, though he rejects the view that the *Apocalypse* was written by the apostle, mentions the tradition of two tombs of Johns at Ephesus. Eusebius (loc. cit.), on the other hand, thought it probable that the *Apocalypse* was written by John the Elder, 'unless anyone should prefer' to ascribe it to the apostle. Many modern writers, with Jerome, assign 2, 3 John to the Elder, and 1 John to another writer. Some go farther and assign to the Elder the Apocalypse also. But it is no easier to account for the differences in style and grammar between the epistles and the Apocalypse than between the Gospel and the Apocalypse (see Charles, *Revelation*, i, pp. xxxiv ff.). There is no insuperable difficulty, in spite of some differences of language, in supposing that the author of the First Epistle wrote also the other two, especially if there was some interval of time between them, according to the suggestion made above. And if that is correct, he can have been the writer of the Gospel also.

2 JOHN. For the understanding of the two epistles it is important to notice that in 2 John the 2nd person plural is employed from *v.* 6 onwards, and in 3 John the 2nd person singular throughout. This suggests that the former was written to a Church, while the latter was clearly addressed to an individual named Gaius. Moreover, he appears to have been a

---

[1] *De vir. illustr.* 9. 18.

member of the same Church, 'I have written somewhat to the Church' (3 John 9) being best explained as referring to the other letter. The expression 'to the elect lady (ἐκλεκτῇ κυρίᾳ) and her children' has in it a touch of official formality as well as of pastoral affection, a community being addressed to which the presbyter feels that he has the right to speak with authority. Some who think that the 'lady' is an individual suggest that she is either 'the lady Eklekta' or 'the elect Kyria'; the latter, but not the former, is known to have been a proper name. The former is rendered very improbable by the greeting (v. 13) from 'the children of thine elect sister', evidently another Church in which the writer holds a position of authority. And the use of the feminine singular for a Church is supported by 1 Pet. v. 13: 'the fellow-elect [lady] in Babylon greeteth you', which our writer has perhaps imitated. In any case the contents are not suitable to an individual lady and her children. She is loved by 'all who know the truth, because of the truth which abideth in us [*sc.* in the community and in the presbyter who represents it]' (*vv.* 1 f.). '[The command] which we had from the beginning' (v. 5), 'as ye heard from the beginning' (v. 6) looks back to the Christian tradition of the Church from the earliest days.[1] 'I found *some* of thy children walking in the truth' (v. 4) points to a community, not to a family; some of its members were in danger, and needed the warning in v. 8. And *vv.* 10, 11 would have very little point if it were merely advice to a certain lady not to receive heretics into her house. It is an injunction to the whole community to use the disciplinary measure of excommunication. The heretics are of the same Gnostic type (*vv.* 7, 9) as those attacked in 1 John.

3 JOHN. This letter teaches us more about the writer. While writing authoritatively to one Church, of which Gaius was a leading representative, he is also, as we have seen, in authority in the Church from which he writes. He had recently sent certain Christians who were unknown to Gaius (v. 5) with a recommendation to receive them and to forward them on their journey. The system of letters of commendation (cf. Rom. xvi. 1, 2; 2 Cor. iii. 1) was common, and under ordinary circumstances he would probably not have written a special

[1] Cf. 1 Jn. i. 1, ii. 13.

word of praise to Gaius and to another member of the Church, Demetrius (*v.* 12), for acting according to instructions. But a certain Diotrephes had risen in rebellion against his authority; he had tried to usurp the leadership of the Church, and, not content with reviling the presbyter, had refused to receive the visitors whom he had recommended, and had excommunicated any who did so (*vv.* 9, 10). Gaius and Demetrius are therefore warmly thanked for defying him, as the visitors, on their return, had reported (*v.* 6), and an exhortation is given to continue to do so (*v.* 11), which suggests that the bearers of the letter were visitors of the same kind. The presbyter says that he will deal with the offender when he comes (*v.* 10). The visitors 'had gone forth on behalf of the Name, receiving nothing from the Gentiles', i.e. they were probably itinerating prophets who went from church to church preaching, and depending for their maintenance on the charity and goodwill of the Christians. If a conjecture is allowable, Diotrephes may have had Gnostic tendencies which easily fostered spiritual pride. If so, this letter and the warning in 2 John 10, 11 reflect the two sides of the conflict.

BOOKS

For a full bibliography, as well as an excellent introduction, see P. H. Menoud, *L'évangile de Jean d'après les recherches récentes*, 1947, esp. pp. 78–88.

E. A. Abbott, *Johannine Grammar*, 1905.
—— *Johannine Vocabulary and Grammar*, 1906.
B. W. Bacon, *The Fourth Gospel in Research and Debate*, 2nd ed., 1911.
—— *The Gospel of the Hellenists*, 1933.
R. Bultmann, *Johanneische Schriften und Gnosis*, 1940.
C. F. Burney, *The Aramaic Origin of the Fourth Gospel*, 1922.
Lord Charnwood, *According to St. John*, 1925.
E. C. Colwell, *The Greek of the Fourth Gospel*, 1931.
C. H. Dodd, *Bulletin of the John Rylands Library*, xix, 1935, pp. 329–43, and xxi, 1937, pp. 129–56.
P. Gardner, *The Ephesian Gospel*, 1915.
P. Gardner-Smith, *St. John and the Synoptic Gospels*, 1938.
A. E. Garvie, *The Beloved Disciple*, 1922.
W. F. Howard, *The Fourth Gospel in recent Criticism and Interpretation*, 1931.
—— *Christianity according to St. John*, 1943.
H. Latimer Jackson, *The Problem of the Fourth Gospel*, 1918.
M. Lidzbarski, *Das Johannesbuch der Mandäer*, 1905–15.

T. W. Manson, *Bulletin of the John Rylands Library*, xxx, 1946–7, pp. 312–29.

C. Masson, *Revue de théologie et de philosophie*, 1940, pp. 297–311, and 1944, pp. 92–96.

H. Odeberg, *The Fourth Gospel* . . ., 1929.

E. B. Redlich, *An Introduction to the Fourth Gospel*, 1940.

A. Schlatter, *Der Evangelist Johannes*, 1930.

E. Schweizer, *EGO EIMI* . . ., 1939.

V. H. Stanton, *The Gospels as Historical Documents*, iii, 1920.

B. H. Streeter, *The Four Gospels*, 1924, pp. 363–481.

COMMENTARIES

On the Fourth Gospel: W. Bauer (2nd ed., 1935), J. H. Bernard (1929), F. Blass (1902), R. Bultmann (1941), W. Heitmüller (4th ed., 1918), Sir E. C. Hoskyns and F. N. Davey (2nd ed., 1947), M. J. Lagrange (3rd ed., 1928), A. Loisy (2nd ed., 1921), G. H. C. Macgregor (1928), A. Plummer (1893), A. Schlatter (4th ed., 1928), J. Wellhausen (1908), B. F. Westcott (1908), T. Zahn (6th ed., 1921).

On the Johannine epistles: A. E. Brooke (1912), F. Büchsel (1933), J. Chaine (1939), C. H. Dodd (1945), A. Plummer (1886), B. F. Westcott (1883), H. Windisch (1930).

X

THE GROWTH OF THE NEW TESTAMENT CANON

§ 1. THE WORD CANON

THE word κανών denotes a straight rod or bar, especially as used to keep something straight, such as a rule or line employed by masons. Cf. Eurip. *Tro.* 6 πύργους . . . ὀρθοῖσιν ἔθεμεν κανόσιν.[1] Hence metaphorically it means a 'rule', 'norm', 'standard'. Aristotle, *Eth. Nic.* iii. 4 f., calls the good man the κανών and μέτρον of the truth. The statue of a spearman by Polykleitos was considered a κανών or standard of physical beauty (Müller, *Archäol. d. Kunst*, § 120. 4). To the Alexandrian grammarians the old Greek classics were 'canons', models of excellence. In the early Church only the metaphorical force is found. See 2 Cor. x. 13, 15, 16; Gal. vi. 16, the only passages in which the word occurs in the New Testament. Clement Rom. *ad Cor.* i. 3: women are under 'the canon of obedience'; xli. 1: 'The canon of his service.' Hegesippus (*ap.* Eus. *H.E.* iii. 32) speaks of 'the sound canon of the saving preaching'; Clement Alex. (*Strom.* vi. 15) of the harmony between the Old and the New Testaments as the 'ecclesiastical canon', and (vii. 16) of heretics as those who 'steal the canon of the Church'. Gradually the meaning became more concrete. The canon of the Church, or the ecclesiastical canon, was the rule of doctrine or practice. Cornelius told Fabian (*ap.* Eus. *H.E.* vi. 43) that Novatus, who was baptized when he was ill, after recovery did not receive what was necessary 'according to the canon of the Church' including the sealing by the bishop. A synod at Antioch in A.D. 266 declared a doctrine of Paul of Samosata to be 'foreign to the ecclesiastical canon'.[2] And the council of Nicaea in 325 frequently refers to the general orthodox doctrine simply as 'the canon'. A further step was taken

---

[1] It is connected with κάννα 'cane', 'reed'; but that word was generally used for something made of reeds.

[2] See A. Hahn, *Bibliothek der Symbole*, 1877, p. 98.

towards the middle of the fourth century when the decisions or rules of councils, called *dogmata* in earlier times, came to be called also 'canons' in the plural.

But if 'the canon' was the general rule of doctrine or practice, the Scriptures that were generally recognized by the Church could be described as 'canonical' or 'canonized'. The 59th canon of Laodicea (see p. 369) laid down that 'Psalms privately composed are not to be read in the churches, nor uncanonized (ἀκανόνιστα) books, but only the canonical [books] of the New and the Old Testaments'.[1] Origen (Latin trans.) speaks of 'canonized Scriptures',[2] and Athanasius of 'books which have been canonized'.[3] In these cases the word appears to be used as though well understood, and the origin of this usage most probably dated in the middle of the fourth century.

Finally, the recognized custom of the Church with regard to a group of books would naturally cause the books which conformed to it to be written in a list. And thus the Canon of Scripture became equivalent to the contents of Scripture contained in an authoritative list.

§ 2. THE FORMATION OF A CANON OF THE NEW TESTAMENT

The Bible of the first Christians was the Old Testament, whether confined as in Palestine to that which we usually call the Old Testament, or extended to include several apocryphal writings which were held in high honour among Hellenistic Jews, many of which are included in the Septuagint. The Old Testament was not discarded, as it might have been, when Christianity emancipated itself from Judaism; it was recognized as containing the Christian economy in symbol and prediction and type. And part of the duty and delight of the early preachers was to show how these found their fulfilment in the narratives of the Lord's life, especially those of the Passion. But first came the oral tradition of the Lord's words, which were as authoritative as the Old Testament; and side by side with them the apostolic interpretation of them, and the

[1] See Westcott, *The Canon of the New Test.*, p. 540.
[2] *Comm. in Matt.*, § 28.
[3] *Epist. Fest.* xxxix; see Westcott, op. cit., pp. 554 f.

teaching of what He was and meant to men. This apostolic doctrine consisted partly, as has been said, of the Messianic application of Old Testament passages, and partly of dogma such as was afterwards enshrined in Creeds. Thus the Lord's words and the teaching of the apostles formed a parallel to the Law and the Prophets.

Soon came the time when they began to be written down. The Lord's words were put together in collections (such as Q), the contents of which would be somewhat different in the different local centres, and the words would be accompanied by brief narratives of the circumstances under which they were spoken. These, together with accounts of events in which was seen the fulfilment of the Old Testament, began to form the nucleus of the Gospels. Such collections as each Church possessed would be read at the services on the First day of the week, and the copying of them would go on apace, so that each Church would obtain a larger and larger store of evangelic material. But as long as it was available the living voice of the apostles and those who consorted with them would be preferred to the writings. See the words of Papias quoted on p. 284. St. Paul does not refer to any Gospel written-material, but to oral tradition—'that which I also received' (1 Cor. xv. 3). And he speaks of the Romans as having been 'delivered into' a form of tradition, as though put into a mould (Rom. vi. 17). The apostolic *kerygma* was such a mould or pattern (cf. Ch. II above).

With St. Paul also we reach the stage when the apostolic doctrinal interpretation of facts began to find expression in writing. In his widening activities he began to send letters to his converts in various Churches, containing dogmatic teaching and pastoral advice and injunctions. Such letters were read, as St. Paul expressly intended them to be read, in church on Sunday, because in that way, though absent in body, he could be present in spirit, and teach the whole community. Other teachers afterwards imitated this practice of pastoral letter-writing, but for some time the letters of St. Paul stood far the highest in the Church's estimation. The sayings and doings of the Lord in the Gospels, and the apostolic teaching in St. Paul's epistles formed the indispensable groundwork of the New Testament.

Somewhere between 65 and 70 St. Mark wrote his Gospel, in all probability in Rome. It would help to inspire with faith and courage the stricken Christians who had survived the persecution under Nero.[1] Copies of it found their way in a very short time to different parts of the empire. It was far the best account of the Lord's life that had yet appeared, supplementing on the narrative side the existing collections of His words. It was known to be the work of one who had been in close connexion with St. Peter, despite the Form-critics; and its production at Rome gave it additional prestige. It was therefore treated as of high value by the authors of Matthew and Luke, the former probably in Antioch and the latter in Greece. A few years later, at the end of the century, came the Fourth Gospel, probably from Ephesus. But in the early centuries the favourite and most highly valued Gospel was Matthew, and this in spite of three considerations: Matthew was the most Judaic of all the Gospels; and to anything which savoured of Judaism the spirit of second-century Christianity was in strong opposition. St. Mark and St. Luke were the immediate followers of the two greatest apostles, St. Peter and St. Paul. And they produced their Gospels at the two most influential Churches, Rome and Ephesus. The reason was that the First Gospel was universally believed to be the actual work of an apostle. But though highly valued, as being from the pen of one who had stood in the closest intimacy with the Lord, there was no inclination at first to treat the *book* as divinely inspired, on a level with the Old Testament, though the inspiration and authority of the Lord's words contained in each of the Gospels was supreme. Oral tradition, for something like half a century, was felt to be better than any writing. There is not a passage in the New Testament which is certainly quoted from words of our Lord. In Acts xx. 35 occurs the only sentence which is avowedly a quotation of them, and that is one which is not contained in any of the Gospels. But it is possible that the author of the Apocalypse knew Matthew.[2]

The evidence that some of St. Paul's epistles (all of which

---

[1] See A. E. J. Rawlinson, *St. Mark*, pp. xvi f.

[2] See Charles, *Revelation*, vol. i, pp. lxxxiv ff., where, however, the extent of his dependence on books of the New Testament is greatly exaggerated.

were earlier than any of our written Gospels) were known to other New Testament writers is unmistakable, though the extent of their indebtedness is probably less than has often been supposed. It is not clear that any of them—except, perhaps, the writer of 2 Peter—knew 'all' his epistles; some seem to have known only one or two.

We take our stand, then, at the beginning of the second century, and during, roughly, the first three-quarters of it we find the conception of a canon being formed, i.e. the separation of a group of apostolic writings from all other Christian writings to be reverenced on a level with the Old Testament. The Christian writings were of four main kinds: Gospels, Acts, Epistles, and Apocalypses; in the case of all four classes some being rejected, most of them decisively from the first, but some after hesitation and sporadic use as Scripture. Conversely, of our canonical epistles some were accepted slowly and late, while our canonical Apocalypse had a unique history, being accepted with practical unanimity in early times, but rejected in the third and fourth centuries with equal unanimity in the East.

In order, therefore, to gain a clear idea of the development, we must keep these four classes distinct. But we must also keep distinct the four chief geographical areas in the Church, the ganglions of its system—Rome and the West, Carthage, Alexandria, and what may be broadly called the East, i.e. Asia Minor, Syria, and Palestine.

§ 3. THE SUB-APOSTOLIC AGE

(a) The Gospels

Rome gives us the first Christian writer outside the New Testament. CLEMENT OF ROME wrote in the name of his Church to the Corinthians a letter usually cited as *1 Clement* (because a writing commonly known as *2 Clement*, and indeed a large literature, afterwards appeared to which his name was attached). He frequently quotes the Old Testament with such expressions as 'it is written', 'that which is written', 'the (holy) writing', 'the Holy Spirit saith'; and he uses the LXX with considerable accuracy. But his allusions to passages in the New Testament are loose and inexact,[1] which seems to imply that some of them were known and valued at Rome when he wrote (c. A.D. 96), but that none of them was yet sacred, as Scripture was sacred. He must have known Luke, and also the Acts, and it is possible that he knew Matthew. But he seems to have possessed a collection of sayings of the Lord which had reached him in forms partly like, and partly unlike, sayings in those Gospels. He writes, for example, 'Especially remembering the words of the Lord Jesus which He spake, teaching forbearance and long-suffering; for He said: Shew mercy that ye may receive mercy; forgive that it may be forgiven unto you. As ye judge so shall ye be judged; as ye are kind so shall kindness be done to you. With what measure ye mete, in it shall it be measured to you' (xiii. 1 f.). 'Remember the words of Jesus our Lord, for He said: Woe to that man, for it were good for him that he had not been born; it were better for him for a millstone to be hung round him ($\pi\epsilon\rho\iota\tau\epsilon\theta\hat{\eta}\nu\alpha\iota$), and that he should be drowned in the sea, than that he should pervert one of my elect' (xlvi. 8).

For forty years or more no Roman writing is forthcoming. But by the time that Jerusalem had finally passed away, and been replaced by Aelia Capitolina, and we reach the period 135–50, we find that a great advance has been made. The so-called *2 Clement* is not an epistle, but a homily by an unknown writer which was wrongly ascribed to Clement.[2] The writer sometimes uses formulas of quotation which imply that the Lord's words now stand permanently in writing. We read, for instance, side by side with 'the Lord said' (as in Clement), 'the Lord *saith*' ($\lambda\epsilon\gamma\epsilon\iota$ or $\phi\eta\sigma\iota$). His quotations, indeed, are often loose, but not looser in the New Testament than in the Old. In xi. 2–4 a passage is quoted from a lost apocryphal work (?*Eldad and Modad*) with the formula 'For the prophetic discourse ($\lambda\acute{o}\gamma os$) also saith'; so that it is not surprising to find passages apparently from an apocryphal Gospel or Gospels: 'The Lord said, If ye are with Me united in My bosom and do not My commandments, I will cast you away, and say unto you, Depart from Me, I know not whence ye are, workers of

---

[1] Cf. W. K. L. Clarke, *First Epistle of Clement*, 1937, pp. 32 f.
[2] Eusebius (*H.E.* iii. 16) knew of only one epistle of Clement.

iniquity' (iv. 5). 'For the Lord saith, Ye shall be as lambs in the midst of wolves. And Peter answering saith unto Him, What then if the wolves tear the lambs? Jesus saith unto Peter, Let not the lambs after they are dead fear the wolves. And you, fear ye not them which kill you and can do nothing to you, but fear Him who, after ye are dead, hath authority over soul and body to cast into the Gehenna of fire' (v. 2–4). 'For the Lord Himself, when asked by someone when His kingdom should come, saith, When the two shall be one, and the outside as the inside, and the male with the female, neither male nor female' (xii. 2). 'For the Lord said, I come to gather all nations, tribes, and tongues' (xvii. 4). (It has been conjectured that all these are from the *Gospel according to the Egyptians*.) In viii. 5 words identical with part of Lk. xvi. 10 are combined with extraneous matter under one formula: 'For the Lord saith in the Gospel, If ye have not kept that which is little, who will give you that which is great? For I say unto you that he which is faithful in that which is least is faithful also in much.' And after quoting and commenting on Is. liv. 1, the author writes, 'And another Scripture saith, I came not to call the righteous but sinners' (ii. 4). And there are other passages which appear to be quotations from, or allusions to, the Gospels, but with great differences in wording. Some have thought that he may have used an early harmony of various evangelic material, which contained much that stands in our Gospels but also much besides. However that may be, his attitude seems to be that the words of the Lord are authoritative, and the writings in which he found them are 'Scripture', but the wording, as such, of our Gospels is still short of being regarded as sacred. It was that kind of attitude which admitted most of the important corruptions of the original text which lie behind all our manuscripts. Finally, there is the interesting expression, 'The Books and the Apostles say that the Church existeth not now [for the first time] but from the beginning' (xiv. 2). 'The Apostles' seems to mean all that the apostles have bequeathed, both in the epistles that he knew (especially those from which he derived the idea in question) and the Gospels. His New Testament formed a parallel with the Old, though it had not yet become clearly enough defined as a *corpus* to be described as 'the

Books'. It should be noted that Lightfoot assigned 2 *Clement* to Corinth, dating it 120–40 and Harnack to Rome, *c.* 130–60, but Streeter to Alexandria before 140.[1]

The DIDACHE is of uncertain date. J. Armitage Robinson[2] contended that the author borrows from both 'Barnabas' and Hermas. He holds that 'Barnabas' was probably the author of the piece of writing known as 'The Two Ways', which, therefore, had no Jewish original such as was conjectured by C. Taylor[3] and accepted by Harnack; and that it was echoed by Hermas and by the writer of the Didache. The language of Did. i. 5 seems clearly borrowed from Hermas, Mand. ii. 4b–7.[4]

This strange writing may be tentatively dated 145–50. It is of little help towards the history of the Gospels. The writer shows no knowledge of Mark or John; but the nature of his work would give no occasion for quoting the latter. In the first part, The Two Ways (chs. i–vi), an apocryphal sentence, 'Let thine alms sweat into thine hands until thou knowest to whom thou givest', is introduced with 'it has been said'. In the ecclesiastical portion (chs. vii–xv) we read, 'The Lord said, Give not that which is holy to the dogs' (ix. 5), which occurs in Matt. vii. 6. (Similarly, in reference to the Old Testament in xiv. 3, 'This was what was spoken by the Lord' introduces a free reproduction of Mal. i. 14 and 11.) And in vii. 2 'As the Lord commanded in His Gospel, Thus pray ye' is followed by the Lord's Prayer, very nearly, but not quite, identical with that in Matthew, together with a doxology in the form, 'Thine is the power and the glory for ever'. This is apparently not quoted from Matthew but from current liturgical usage. Also, 'But concerning Baptism thus baptize ye: having recited all things, baptize into the name of the Father and of the Son and

---

[1] *The Primitive Church*, 1929, pp. 233 ff.
[2] *Barnabas, Hermas, and the Didache*, 1920.
[3] *The Shepherd of Hermas*, 1903–6.
[4] Many have thought that i. 3b–ii. 1 is a later interpolation; but the evidence for this has been weakened. See Dom Connolly, O.S.B., *J.T.S.*, xxiv, 1923, pp. 147–57, and xxv, 1924, pp. 151–3; cf. J. M. Creed, *J.T.S.* xxxix, 1938, pp. 370–87 who concluded that it has yet to be shown that the Didache will fit easily into the conditions of any period considerably later than the first three decades of the second century. F. E. Vokes (*The Riddle of the Didache*, 1938) has not convinced everyone that the Didache was written after the Montanist heresy arose and as Montanist propaganda.

of the Holy Spirit, in running water' (vii. 1). In the closing, apocalyptic chapter (xvi) Zech. xiv. 5 is loosely quoted with 'as it was said'. Besides these 'the Gospel' is mentioned three times: 'But concerning the apostles and prophets [i.e. their reception when they visited a Church] according to the ordinance (δόγμα) of the Gospel so do ye' (xi. 3). 'Reprove one another not in wrath but in peace, as ye have in the Gospel' (xv. 3). 'Your prayers and alms and all your deeds so do as ye have in the Gospel of our Lord' (xv. 4). The first and third may be allusions to Matt. x. 40 f. and vi. 1–18; the second is apocryphal. There are numerous other echoes, mostly loose and inexact, of the language of Matthew and Luke, especially the former, without formula of quotation; but also, no less loose and inexact, of the Old Testament. It and the First and Third Gospels and apocryphal sayings are all treated as if they were on a par.

But when the second half of the century begins we have clear evidence from Rome as to the position of the four Gospels in JUSTIN, often called Justin Martyr. He was a Greek Samaritan who was converted to Christianity at Ephesus, and came to Rome where he taught as a Christian philosopher and died for his faith c. 165. Between 151 and 163 he wrote two *Apologies* for Christians to the Roman government (or rather one, since the second is little more than a postscript or appendix to the first), and then a *Dialogue* with Trypho, a Jew who knew the Gospel tradition. At Ephesus he would have read Matthew and John, and at Rome Mark and Luke. He quoted a great deal from the first and last, and a little from the other two; but he quoted very loosely, sometimes combining separate passages; sometimes even quoting them more than once with differences. There was, naturally, not much peculiar to Mark which he could use; but it is noteworthy that he did not quote much from John, though his apologetic system was profoundly influenced by its Logos doctrine. This is probably to be explained by the fact that the Roman Christians had not yet been persuaded that it was written by an apostle, and a Gospel coming from Ephesus without apostolic authority was not valued very highly.

He mentions the Gospels under the name of the *Memoirs*

(ἀπομνημονεύματα) *of the Apostles,* or simply the *Memoirs,* prob-
ably in imitation of Xenophon's *Memoirs of Socrates.* In the
Apology there are only three references to them, but in the
Dialogue there are thirteen. A few of them are important:

1. The account of the Last Supper is given with the words,
'For the apostles, in the Memoirs made by them, which are
called "Gospels", handed down, &c.' (*Apol.* lxvi). This is
probably the earliest known writing in which the plural appears. In *Dial.* x he still uses the singular—'the commands in
that which is called the Gospel'—as was done by many writers
after him; and in *Apol.* xcviii he uses the plural in referring to
a passage in a single Gospel. That is to say he used the word
with exactly the same varieties as it might be used today.

2. The fact is stated that the memoirs of the apostles were
still read, together with the writings of the prophets, in the
weekly services (*Apol.* lxvii).

3. 'It is written in his [Peter's] Memoirs as having taken
place' (*Dial.* cvi). This can refer only to Mark. It was thought
to have St. Peter's apostolic sanction, as Luke was to have
St. Paul's. The apocryphal *Gospel of Peter* even if it was written
by that time,[1] had a Docetic colour, and could not have been
in general use.

4. 'Memoirs . . . which I say were composed by His apostles
and those who followed them' (*Dial.* ciii). This is usually taken
to mean that the First and Fourth Gospels were attributed to
apostles, and the others to those who were not apostles but
their followers. It is quite as likely that the First and Second
were thought of as the work of apostles (the Second being
derived immediately from St. Peter), and the Third and
Fourth by their followers (the writer of the Fourth being not
yet raised to the rank of 'apostle' at Rome).

With all his use, however, of the written Gospels, Justin did
not, in fact, speak of them quite in the same way as of the Old
Testament. He frequently refers to the former with 'it is

---

[1] M. R. James (*The Apocryphal N.T.*, p. 90) thinks that it is not safe to date
it much earlier than A.D. 150. Its Doceticism was recognized by Serapion,
Bishop of Antioch, *c.* 190 (Eus. *H.E.* vi. 12). But see Gardner-Smith, *J.T.S.*
xxvii, 1926, 255–71, 401–7, who dates it 80–100. The evidence is set out in
L. Vaganay's edition, 1930, pp. 147 ff.

written' (γέγραπται), but never, as in the case of the latter, as 'Scripture' (γραφή).

He has a few uncanonical details, but he does not refer any of them to the Memoirs. He may have derived them from written sources, but they can probably be accounted for as reminiscences of floating tradition.

It will be seen that Justin is a landmark. It was probably owing to his teaching, and perhaps still more to his martyr death, that the Fourth Gospel was accepted at Rome before the last quarter of the second century. In all likelihood it was accepted still earlier in the East, but now the weight of Rome was added to the general consensus.

The date at which Carthage was first evangelized is unknown to us, and it supplies no writing in our period. Alexandria must have received Christianity at an early date, but for some time it lay outside the main current of Church life. The so-called EPISTLE OF BARNABAS may not have been written there, but it is marked by a characteristic Alexandrian colouring, and an allegorical use of the Old Testament. Some would date it 70–79, others 100–30. The answer to this debatable problem depends on the answer to three others: Did Hermas quote from it? (see p. 317). Did Hermas write as early as 100? Did the author of *Barnabas* know Hebrews? (see p. 334). Whatever his date his evidence with regard to our written Gospels is indecisive. 'His handling of the Passion in terms of Old Testament types, especially from the Psalms, seems parallel to, rather than dependent on, Matthew's narrative' (Bartlet[1]); e.g. 'Having been crucified He was given to drink vinegar and gall' (viii. 3); cf. Ps. lxix [lxviii]. 22; but in Matthew the gall is given before the Crucifixion, the vinegar after. 'When they shall smite their Shepherd, then the sheep of the flock shall perish' (v. 12) is an allusion to Zech. xiii. 7, with no hint of the context in which the similar allusion stands in Matthew, Mark. 'For my garment they cast a lot' (vi. 6), from Ps. xxii [xxi]. 19, is combined with other passages from the same Psalm and from cxviii [cxvii]. 12, to which no reference is made in the Gospels. Traditions of the trial and mocking by the Sanhedrin and by the soldiers (cf. Matt., Mk.) are combined in vii. 9

[1] J. V. Bartlet in *The N.T. in the Apostolic Fathers*, 1905, p. 18.

with verbal touches reminiscent of Luke. If the earlier date is assigned to the writing, any use of Matthew or Luke is impossible; the writer must have been dependent on earlier written material, or oral tradition, or both. With the later date he may have combined other material with a free use of Matthew and Luke. One passage requires special notice: 'Let us take heed lest, as it is written, we may be found many called but few chosen.'[1] This has the appearance of being an explicit quotation from a written Gospel to which authoritative value is attached. This might be possible at the later date,[2] and would stand as the earliest known instance of the quotation of a Gospel with such a formula, which would be of importance for the history of the Canon. But the writer may be quoting from a Jewish apocryphal work containing a contrast between 'many' and 'few' such as is found in 4 Esdr. viii. 3; x. 57.[3] Or he is referring to our Lord's words, but 'he had forgotten the reference, and consequently has employed the formula "as it is written" by inadvertence for the more appropriate "as the Lord said to His disciples", or something of that kind'.[4]

If Africa and Egypt do not yet help us much, we get plenty of light from the East. The probability that Matthew was written at Antioch is supported by the fact that it is IGNATIUS, Bishop of Antioch, who gives us the first clear evidence of it. He wrote the seven letters that we possess on his way to martyrdom at Rome, c. 115. He speaks (*Trall.* xi. 1; *Philad.* iii. 1) of errorists who are 'not the Father's plant' (cf. Matt. xv. 13); and says that Jesus Christ was 'truly born of a virgin, and baptized by John that all righteousness might be fulfilled by Him' (*Smyrn.* i. 1), the latter clause of which, as Sanday said, it is unreasonable to refer to any other than Matthew. 'He that receiveth let him receive it' (*Smyrn.* vi. 1), and 'Be thou

---

[1] This saying, popularized in the East by Tatian, is added to Matt. xx. 16 in some manuscripts and versions, of which Syr.sin. pesh agree with *Barnabas* in omitting γάρ.

[2] H. Windisch 'Der Barnabasbrief' in *Handbuch z. N.T.*, 1920) holds the writing to be a compilation; behind it lie a collection of *testimonia* and a work on 'The Two Ways', and the book underwent a revision. He places it between 100 and 135, though he thinks that the first edition could have been earlier.

[3] The formula of citation does not forbid this, since he uses 'it is written' and 'the Scripture saith' when citing Enoch (iv. 3, xvi. 5).

[4] Burkitt, *The Gospel History and its Transmission*, p. 320.

wise as the serpent in all things and harmless always as the dove', are echoes of Matt. xix. 12 and x. 16. The only possible reference to Luke is the statement that Jesus Christ was cruci-fied 'under Pontius Pilate and Herod the tetrarch' (*Smyrn.* i. 1). Oral tradition might have supplied the last words. But the tone of his letter to Rome is perhaps the result of his having read Clement's letter to Corinth; and if that could reach him from Rome or Corinth, Luke could reach him. He would not, however, treat it with anything like the same deference as his own local Gospel written by an apostle. The often-quoted passage, 'Take, touch Me, and see that I am not a bodiless demon' (*Smyrn.* iii. 2), is like Lk. xxiv. 39, and yet so unlike that a use of the written words is improbable.[1] Eusebius (*H.E.* iii. 36) confesses ignorance of its source; Jerome (*De vir. illustr.* 2) and Origen (*De Princ.*, praef. 8) refer it respectively to the *Gospel acc. to the Heb.* and the *Doctrine of Peter.*

A knowledge of John by Ignatius, if it cannot be proved with certainty, is highly probable despite J. N. Sanders. Their theology is akin, and there are echoes of wording, the clearest being the sentence about the Spirit (*Philad.* 7): 'for It knoweth whence It cometh and whither It goeth' (cf. John iii. 8).

Two interesting passages show how the Old Testament was valued chiefly as pointing to Christ and Christianity. 'That I may attain unto the inheritance wherein I have obtained mercy, fleeing for refuge to the Gospel as the Flesh of Jesus, and to the Apostles as the Presbytery of the Church. Yea and we love the prophets also, because they too pointed to the Gospel in their message, and hoped in Him, and awaited Him' (*Philad.* v. 1). The 'Gospel' here means not the written Gospels but the whole Christian tradition, oral and written, in many forms and fragments, about the life and teaching of Christ. The 'Apostles' means the whole apostolic teaching, as it had been preached and written in letters. And the prophets are the Old Testament prophets. Ignatius, therefore, probably does not refer, as Westcott suggested, to a definite collection of

---

[1] Was Ignatius quoting a Syriac phrase originally? *Shi'da'* could be trans-lated into Greek by either δαιμόνιον or φάντασμα, the word used in D in Lk. xxiv. 37, cf. F. H. Chase, *The Syro-Latin Text of the Gospels*, 1895, pp. 72 f.

books as on a par with the written prophecies, but to Christian truth as that to which Old Testament hopes pointed. Similarly in *Philad.* viii f. :

I heard certain persons saying, If I find it not in the charters (τοῖς ἀρχείοις) I believe it not in the Gospel. And when I said to them, It is written, they answered me, That is the question. But as for me, my charter is Jesus Christ, the inviolable charter His Cross and Death and Resurrection, and faith which is through Him. . . . But a singular value hath the Gospel, [namely] the Advent of the Saviour, our Lord Jesus Christ, His Passion, His Resurrection. For the beloved prophets pointed to Him in their message, but the Gospel is the perfect provision of immortality.

That is to say, the charter of Christians consisted, not in writings corresponding to those of the prophets, but in the facts which the evangelic message proclaimed. And some people had questioned whether certain passages in the Old Testament contained predictions which Ignatius insisted in finding in them.

POLYCARP, Bishop of Smyrna. Though important in the history of the Christian tradition, he does not supply much evidence as to the canonicity of the Gospels. He lived till 155/6, but his only letter that we possess was written to the Philippians soon after the martyrdom of Ignatius, forty years earlier[1] —so soon after that he asks them to send him such news as they can obtain of Ignatius and his companions. His references to the Old Testament are so allusive and inexact that we cannot expect great precision in his quotations from Christian books. He appears to have known the Acts (see below), and, if so, he must have known Luke; and if Luke, then Mark may also have reached him from Rome. And Matthew would probably have come to Smyrna from Antioch by 115, but we cannot be sure. He gives some sayings of our Lord similar to those in

[1] According to P. N. Harrison, chs. i–xii were written *c.* A.D. 135 (*Polycarp's Two Epistles to the Philippians*, 1936) but if his theory of two letters of Polycarp is accepted there is no necessity to date these chapters so long after the remainder, chs. xiii–xiv. He finds (pp. 328–35) numerous references and possible allusions in i–xii to Matt. and to Lk. (over twenty times each), a dozen to Acts and half a dozen to Mk., but none to the Fourth Gospel, the expression in v. 2 'According as he promised to raise us from the dead' being referred to 2 Cor. iv. 14, Rom. viii. 11 and not to Jn. v. 21, as in *The New Testament in the Apostolic Fathers*, 1905, p. 103.

St. Luke's Sermon on the Plain, and one clause in a Matthaean form: 'Remembering what the Lord said teaching, Judge not that ye be not judged; forgive and it shall be forgiven unto you; shew mercy that ye may receive mercy; with what measure ye mete it shall be measured to you again. And, Blessed are the poor, and *they that are persecuted for righteousness' sake*, for theirs is the Kingdom of God' (ii. 3). But his form of quotation, and his catena of sayings, are similar to those in Clement (see above), which he apparently knew, and the sayings as they appeared in Matthew and Luke were not more sacred to him than as they appeared in the collection known to Clement. 'According as the Lord said, The spirit indeed is willing but the flesh is weak' is verbally identical with Matthew–Luke. 'According to the truth of the Lord who became Servant of all', διάκονος πάντων (*v.* 2), preserves the thought of Matt. xx. 28, while πάντων διάκονος occurs in a different context in Mark ix. 35.

Irenaeus, who had seen Polycarp, tells us that he was a companion of John (see p. 282). And if the Fourth Gospel was written in Ephesus, the Bishop of Smyrna would certainly know it twenty years later. But if it was not the work of an apostle, and if Polycarp knew it was not, he would have little inducement to quote it, differing widely as it did from the apostolic Matthew. Only one sentence, 'According as He promised to raise us from the dead' (*v.* 2), might seem to point to John v. 21 ; vi. 44, the Synoptic Gospels containing no such promise.

PAPIAS, Bishop of Hierapolis, has been variously dated, but most of the suggestions border round 140. His importance for the history of the Canon lies not in any quotations from the Gospels but in the fact that, in the fragments that we possess, he voices an earlier tradition with regard to Matthew and Mark. The passages are quoted on pp. 4–6. The latter is the first explicit evidence in patristic writings that we possess of the existence of the Second Gospel, but it shows that it was well known to the Elder whom he quotes, and recognized as carrying apostolic sanction, since St. Mark, as St. Peter's interpreter, did his best in putting down what he remembered of the apostle's teaching of Christ's deeds and words. The theory of

an Ur-Marcus, to which some have thought that he was referring, is discussed on pp. 65–67, and shown to be improbable.
The First Gospel was believed by the Elder to be the work of
an apostle, no less than the Second; it was one of the translations made by various persons, as best they could, of St.
Matthew's work. It had been enlarged, as we know, far beyond
the limits of his original collection of the *logia*, and was current
among Eastern Christians with all the apostolic authority of
St. Matthew's own Gospel.

As regards John Papias is important in relation to the
authorship; and as Bishop of Hierapolis he must have known it.
But we have no words of his which afford any help with regard
to its canonicity, unless he understood the Elder's remark
about Matthew as (according to Streeter) a disparaging contrast with the Fourth Gospel. Possibly the quotation by Irenaeus (v. xxxvi) from 'the Elders', which contains the words of
John xiv. 2, is from the comments of Papias. But the statement of the latter himself shows that, though he knew written
records, 'what could be learnt from a living and abiding voice'
(see p. 284), i.e. oral tradition, was still of the first importance
to him. And the title of the work attributed to him by Eusebius,
An exposition of Oracles of the Lord, does not conflict with this. A
passage is sometimes quoted from Irenaeus (IV. xxxii. 1) as
referring to him: 'In the same manner also the Elder, a disciple of the apostles, used to discuss concerning the two *testa-
menta*, showing that both were from one and the same God.'
If 'a disciple of the apostles' is correct, this cannot have been
Papias. But whoever it was, 'de duobus testamentis' must be
a translation of περὶ τῶν δύο διαθηκῶν, an echo of Gal. iv. 24,
where the word means 'dispensations', not the Jewish and
Christian Canons (see p. 2).

By about 160, then, the Gospels had emerged into prominence in the East and in the West. They were perhaps not yet
explicitly defined everywhere as a *corpus* of Four, though with
Justin at Rome they were near to it. But by their intrinsic
superiority they had risen into unique recognition. 'As soon as
the feeling of the need of authoritative writings grew up,
Christian sentiment took to the Four as instinctively as a child

to its mother's milk.'[1] And if the interpolations in the Western text go back to a single interpolated copy (see p. 438), the Four were a unity at about the middle of the century. The esteem in which they were held is only emphasized by the fact that there were other Gospels in existence, and in sporadic use, before the middle of the century: the *Gospel according to the Hebrews*; the *Gospel of the Nazarenes*[2] (see pp. 16, 44); the *Gospel according to Peter*[3]—used, apparently, by Justin, and still read at the close of the century at Rhossus, but condemned as docetic by Serapion, Bishop of Antioch (*c.* 190); the *Protevangelion of James*—known to Origen, and possibly to Justin; the *Gospel according to the Egyptians*—coloured with Encratite views, known to the author of *2 Clement*, to some Gnostic writers, and later to Clement of Alexandria; and the Gospel as edited by Marcion (140–50), i.e. an arbitrary recension of the Third Gospel with its contents manipulated in accordance with his views. His text (as restored) will be found in Zahn, *Geschichte d. nt.lichen Kanons*, ii. 455 ff., and Harnack, *Marcion* (*Texte u. Untersuch.* xlv, 1921). None of these was ever a serious rival to the Four. Either on account of date or authority or character they were recognized as inferior to them.

(b) The Acts

There is very little sign that anyone in this period possessed or knew the Acts. It must, of course, have been known in Rome when it first appeared. In writing for Theophilus St. Luke no doubt wrote for a wider public, and his accounts of the life of the Lord and of the life of the Church were two volumes of the same work. But the separation between them, as regards general use, would soon take place. Few among the rank and file of the Church would at first be interested in the deeds of the apostles, while every Christian was eager to know the deeds and words of Christ. So that the former would supply little material as compared with the latter for catechetical in-

---

[1] C. H. Turner, *J.T.S.* x, 1908–9, p. 166.

[2] At the very beginning of the century there are Talmudic allusions, in a play on the word εὐαγγέλιον, to the 'Gospel' in *Greek* as used by Minim, i.e. Palestinian Christians (see Burkitt, *Christian Beginnings*, pp. 47 f.).

[3] In its story of the Passion strands from all our four Gospels can perhaps be traced, woven together.

struction or for mission preaching. Thus the Gospels would be copied and read widely, but not the Acts. And all that we can find are a few echoes, more or less doubtful. CLEMENT OF ROME, who must have known a work composed at the capital as a kind of public *apologia* only five or six years possibly before he wrote, combines (in xviii. 1) words from Ps. lxxxviii [lxxxix]. 21 with words from 1 Sam. xiii. 14, and reads ἄνδρα (Ps. δοῦλον, 1 Sam. ἄνθρωπον) as in Acts xiii. 22. But the clause 'a man after My own heart' is transposed; and while Acts ends with 'who shall do all My will', Clement ends with 'in eternal mercy (ἐλέει[1]) have I anointed Him'. It might almost seem as if Clement was influenced by a collection of *testimonia* as well as by the Acts. 'Ye were all humble . . . with more pleasure giving than receiving' looks like an allusion to Acts xx. 35, though he may have known the Lord's words independently from oral tradition. The author of the *EPISTLE TO DIOG-NETUS*, an *apologia* to a pagan, has a clear allusion (ch. iii) to the *apologia* to pagans in Acts xvii. 24 f.: 'For He that made heaven and earth and all things that are in them, and supplies us with all that we need, Himself would need none of those things which He affords to them that think they give [to Him].' To these may be added one doubtful parallel in HERMAS (*Vis.* iv. ii. 4): 'Having believed that by nothing canst thou be saved but by the great and glorious name' (cf. Acts iv. 12); and one in the DIDACHE (iv. 8): 'Thou shalt share all things with thy brother, and not say that they are thine own' (ἴδια εἶναι, cf. Acts iv. 32).

In the East there is similar fragmentary evidence. IGNA-TIUS says[2] that 'each man will go [*sc.* after death, μέλλει χωρεῖν] to his own place', which reads like an allusion to Acts i. 25, although the latter has πορευθῆναι. And 'After His Resurrection He ate and drank with them' (*Smyrn.* iii. 3) recalls the general statement in Acts i. 4 (συναλιζόμενος) rather than the particular story in Lk. xxiv. 41–43. POLYCARP has a striking coincidence with Acts ii. 24: 'Whom God raised up (ἤγειρεν, Acts ἀνέστησεν), having loosed the pangs of

---

[1] The Psalm has, according to one reading, 'in holy mercy', ἐλέει for ἐλέῳ (= ἐλαίῳ).

[2] *Magn.* v. 1.

Hades' (Acts 'Death'[1]). Both have the same structure of the sentence, and both have 'pangs' (ὠδῖνας), a mistranslation of חֶבְלֵי which also means 'cords'. In Ps. xvii [xviii]. 5, 6 (LXX) occur both 'pangs of death' and 'pangs of Hades', and the former in Ps. cxiv [cxvi]. 3. If Polycarp's expression is not due to a collection of *testimonia*, it is a pretty clear instance of quotation from the Acts. He has a few other uncertain echoes of language.[2]

Reference has already been made (p. 122) to W. L. Knox's argument (*The Acts of the Apostles*, 1948, pp. 40 f.) that the Pastoral writer knew and used Acts especially in 2 Timothy and that Ignatius knew and used the Pastorals as authoritative writings.

(c) The Pauline Epistles

Behind our Gospels there was oral tradition, and there were early attempts at the writing of Gospel material, both of which might be the source of some of the patristic language. But in the case of the epistles there is no such uncertainty. If a writer clearly echoes or paraphrases a passage it proves his knowledge of the epistle containing it. St. Paul's writings would be eagerly copied, mostly, of course, in full, but sometimes probably with the omission of what had purely local and immediate reference. If one Church made a copy for another, some salutations or personal details, possibly also some rebukes to individuals, might be excised; it might even happen that there would be sent, or a visitor might copy, only a fragment which it was thought would be of general Church interest. It is possible, as we have seen (pp. 157 f.), that Romans was an instance of such editing if we reject T. W. Manson's theory that St. Paul wrote two recensions of Romans, the later including xvi and being sent to Ephesus. And the Pauline *corpus* finally contained, in all probability, some fragments of epistles that found their way into the Canon attached to other epistles, e.g. 2 Cor. vi. 14–vii. 1; Phil. iii. 1–iv. 1; (Rom. xvi. 1–23). Only deliberate editing of all the available material will account for this. When this was accomplished is unknown. It has

---

[1] θανάτου ℵ A B C &c.; but ᾅδου D e vg. pesh. cop.
[2] See P. V. M. Benecke, in *The N.T. in the Apostolic Fathers*, pp. 98 f.

been thought that it was Marcion who first formed the *corpus*.[1] Christians in general possessed a Bible in the Old Testament; but Marcion, rejecting that, was without a Bible at all. And he therefore made his own Bible; he defined for the first time (some hold), quite clearly, a New Testament Canon, which consisted of his recension of Luke and of the Pauline epistles, i.e. his 'Gospel' and 'Apostolicon', in which he 'erased' (as Tertullian says) by his 'heretical industry' what did not suit him. But there is no evidence that he formed the *corpus*. If he did, not only was this heretic's collection accepted in all parts of the Church less than half a century later, but within that time it was contrived to reintroduce into it both whole epistles (1, 2 Tim. and Tit.) which he had omitted, and all the sections, sentences, and words which he had 'erased'; e.g. in Galatians and Romans appeared the ideas of the righteousness of Abraham, and of the pedagogic function of the Jewish Law, which fundamentally altered St. Paul's presentation of Christianity. It is easier to suppose that Marcion issued his revised edition of an already existing *corpus*, as he did of an already existing Gospel of St. Luke. There is not much weight in the fact that St. Paul is comparatively little quoted by the Fathers in the second and third centuries. The literature is largely apologetic and controversial, directed against pagans and Gnostics. And for this purpose the apostle's language in argument against Judaizers did not supply much material.

There is evidence that a quarter of a century before Marcion some, at least, of the Pauline epistles were beginning to be collected in the East. A treasuring-up of his letters is antecedently probable; and it may very likely have been owing to the fact that the apostle's letters were beginning to be collected that the Philippians wanted to do the same with those of Ignatius. They asked Polycarp to send them a copy of the letter that Ignatius had written to him, with any others that he had. At least, as Turner says, this action would give an impetus to the collection of the Pauline letters. Polycarp himself, as his letter in reply to them shows, knew at least Rom., 1, 2 Cor., Gal., Eph., Phil., and 1, 2 Tim., so that some of them had been collected at Smyrna. And before that, again, Ignatius, in writing

[1] Cf. J. Knox, *Marcion and the New Testament*, 1943.

to the Philippians, says to them that St. Paul makes mention of them 'in every letter', which implies a collection of at any rate some of them. And when we remember that every one of his letters, except that to the Romans, was written to a Church either in Asia Minor, or in Macedonia or Achaia on the other side of the water, it is natural to suppose that it was in those regions that the first collections were made. And they must have been made independently, which explains why, in collections known to us a little later, they are arranged in different orders. Textually this is an advantage to us, because it gives us independent evidence of text from different local centres.

In accordance with the probability that it was in the East that the *corpus* began to be formed, CLEMENT OF ROME shows a knowledge of very few epistles. Since he wrote from Rome to Corinth it is not surprising that the only two epistles with which he shows undoubted acquaintance are Romans and 1 Corinthians.[1] In xlvii. 1 he writes, 'Take up the epistle of the blessed Paul the apostle. What did he first and foremost write to you in the beginning of the Gospel [i.e. soon after your conversion]? Of a truth he spiritually enjoined you concerning himself and Cephas and Apollos.' 'The epistle' need not necessarily mean that Clement did not know the Second Epistle to Corinth. (Lightfoot ad loc. shows that similar expressions were used by several later writers about the First Epistle, and also by Origen and Chrysostom about 1 Thess. and 2 Thess. respectively.) But in fact he shows no sign that he knew it. Romans he would of course know, though only in one passage does he quite clearly echo it. In xxxv. 5, 6 he gives a list of thirteen sins, eight of which occur, in the same order, in Rom. i. 29–32; and he adds a remark similar to St. Paul's: 'For they who do such things are haters of God, and not only they who do them but also they who take pleasure in them [*sc.* that do them].'

But Rome must rapidly have received other letters of St. Paul. MARCION, as has been said, issued his own edition of them, consisting of ten epistles in the following order (accord-

---

[1] 1 Clem. xlvi. 6 may echo Eph. iv. 4–6, and the phrase 'ready unto every good work', 1 Clem. ii. 7, cf. xxxiv. 4, may echo Tit. iii. 1; cf. also 1 Clem. xxix. 1 'lifting up holy and undefiled hands' with 1 Tim. ii. 8 'lifting up holy hands'.

ing to Tert. *Adv. Marc.* v.) : Gal., 1, 2 Cor., Rom., 1, 2 Thess., Laodiceans (=Eph.), Col., Phil., Philem.[1] In some Vulgate manuscripts, including cod. Amiatinus, are preserved prologues to these epistles, which many authorities[2] hold to be the work of Marcion. 1, 2 Timothy and Titus are not of such a character that he would reject them *in toto* for subjective reasons. He probably did not know them, and it is questionable if they were known at all in Rome at his date.[3] Hebrews he would certainly reject if he knew it; but it was not accepted at Rome as the work of St. Paul till late in the fourth century.

This very able and wrong-headed New Testament critic was opposed by JUSTIN,[4] who must, therefore, have known at least the ten epistles in his Apostolicon. His thoughts and language are not infrequently moulded by the epistles, especially Rom., 1 Cor., and 2 Thess. This is most noteworthy in the case of his Old Testament citations. In *Dial.* xxvii, for instance, he quotes part of the catena of passages in Rom. iii. 10–18. In *Dial.* xxxix the words of Elijah, and the answer made to him, are given in a form very similar to that in Rom. xi. 3, 4, but widely different from the LXX of 1 Kings xix. 10, 14, 18. See others in Westcott, *Canon of the N.T.*, p. 171 note. The EPISTLE TO DIOGNETUS may be mentioned here, if Lightfoot is right in dating it *c.* 150, but B. Altaner,[5] who cites Dom Connolly's suggestion that the author was Hippolytus, dates it at the beginning of the third century. The genuine chapters, i–x, have very few verbal parallels with the New Testament, but the writer is one who may be called a Pauline Christian. In ch. ix the whole section shows the influence of Rom. iii.

---

[1] The theory that Marcion's order of the Pauline Epistles gives us a clue to the original order in the Church's canon has been seriously challenged by C. H. Buck, *Journal of Biblical Literature*, lxviii, 1949, pp. 351–7.

[2] Besides De Bruyne and Corssen, who first maintained this, Harnack (*Zeitschr. f. d. neutest. Wiss.*, 1925, p. 205) names Rendel Harris, Lietzmann, Armitage Robinson, Souter, Wordsworth–White, Zahn, and himself, as supporting it.

[3] Later Marcionites added prologues on these epistles, and also on Eph. when the spurious *Epistle to the Laodiceans* had become known. 'Ambrosiaster' afterwards made use of the prologues, unaware, as were the scribes of the Vulgate, of their heretical origin.

[4] Iren. iv. vi. 2, Eus. *H.E.* iv. 18.

[5] *Précis de patrologie*, 1941, p. 106.

21–26, and ch. v that of Phil. iii. 18 ff. There are echoes of
1, 2 Corinthians and several Pauline words and phrases.[1]

The EPISTLE OF BARNABAS, as has been said, savours of
Alexandria. It contains little that is decisive. Echoes, more or
less clear, can be heard of 1, 2 Corinthians and Ephesians. But
the only thing that is really striking is in xiii. 7: 'What, then,
saith He to Abraham, when he alone believed and was appointed for righteousness? Behold, I have appointed thee,
Abraham, a father of nations that believe in God (v.l. the
Lord) in uncircumcision' (δι' ἀκροβυστίας).' Here the writer,
as often, blends two Old Testament passages (Gen. xv. 6; xvii.
4 f.), but he also blends with them reminiscences of Rom. iv. 3,
10 f. (cf. vv. 17 f., where St. Paul also quotes Gen. xvii. 5),
showing that he felt little or no difference between the authority of Genesis and of the words of St. Paul.

In the East many of the Pauline epistles were well known
fifty years after the apostle's death. IGNATIUS certainly knew
1 Cor., and scarcely less certainly Rom. and Eph.; very possibly Gal., Phil., and Col., and perhaps 2 Cor. and 1, 2 Tim.
POLYCARP perhaps knew more. Turner speaks of his epistle
as 'crowded with indubitable echoes of at least eight'. Besides
using Rom., 1 Cor., and Eph., he combines words from 2 Cor.
and 2 Thess. when he writes to the Philippians as those 'among
whom the blessed Apostle Paul laboured, who were his epistles
in the beginning. For he boasteth of you in all the Churches
which alone at that time knew God.' And he speaks of the
letter which St. Paul wrote to them. He shows a knowledge of
1, 2 Timothy when he says of St. Paul and others that 'they
loved not this present world' (ix. 2); and when he combines
and transposes 1 Tim. vi. 7, 10, prefixing 'knowing that'
(εἰδότες ὅτι) as a sort of quotation-formula to the words 'We
brought nothing into this world, &c.' The same formula in
v. 1 introduces 'God is not mocked' from Gal. vi. 7, and in i. 3
words similar to Eph. ii. 8. The most interesting passage is in
xii. 1, which unfortunately has come down to us only in a
Latin translation: 'For I am persuaded that you are well
practised in the sacred writings (sacris literis). . . . As it is said
in these scriptures (scripturis, i.e. passages of Scripture), Be ye

---

[1] Westcott, op. cit., p. 91 note.

angry and sin not; and, Let not the sun go down upon your wrath.' The two halves of Eph. iv. 26, only the former of which occurs in Ps. iv. 4, are quoted as passages from the sacred writings. This, and the passage quoted above from the *Epistle of Barnabas*, speaks volumes for the reverence in which the apostle was held. Similarly the author of 2 PETER (who probably wrote somewhere in the East) in iii. 16 seems to rank St. Paul's writings ('all his epistles') on a level with the Old Testament ('the other Scriptures').

(d) The Epistle to the Hebrews

This epistle must be treated by itself. In later times it was gradually accepted as the work of St. Paul, and on that account canonical. But in this period very few writers show any knowledge of it, and there is not a sign that anyone thought it was St. Paul's. It is open to question, indeed, whether it was known outside Rome. The fact that CLEMENT shows a clear knowledge of it is one of the reasons for thinking that the epistle was addressed to Rome (see p. 233). Among other echoes of language, those in xxxvi. 1–5 are decisive:

This is the road, beloved, on which we found our salvation, Jesus Christ the High Priest of our offerings, the Assister and Helper of our weakness (cf. Heb. ii. 18; iii. 1). Through Him let us gaze at the heights of the heavens; through Him we see mirrored His faultless and most excellent visage. . . . Who being the effulgence (ἀπαύγασμα) of His majesty is so much greater than the angels as He hath by inheritance obtained a more excellent name. For it is written thus: Who maketh His angels spirits and His ministers a flame of fire. But of His Son thus said the Master, Thou art My Son, I this day have begotten Thee. Ask of Me, and I will give Thee nations as Thine inheritance, and as Thy possession the ends of the earth. And again He saith to Him, Sit Thou on My right hand till I make Thine enemies a footstool of Thy feet.

This is clearly an abbreviation of Heb. i. 1–13 with some alterations, preserving the πυρὸς φλόγα of Hebrews instead of πῦρ φλέγον[1] of the LXX of Ps. civ. 4. HERMAS uses the words 'to depart from the living God'; 'those who finally depart from the living God' (*Vis.* II. iii. 2; III. vii. 2); cf. Heb. iii. 12. And

---

[1] Aᵃ πυρὸς φλέγα.

he says 'For your city is far from this city . . . he, then, that prepareth for this city does not look to return (ἐπανακάμψαι) to his own city' (*Sim.* I. i. 2); cf. Heb. xi. 15 f. But he seems to have heard the language of the epistle in sermons or instructions rather than read it, for in denying the possibility of repentance after post-baptismal sin (*Mand.* IV. iii), as in Heb. vi. 4–8 (cf. x. 26–31), he says that he had 'heard it from certain teachers'. JUSTIN twice (*Apol.* xii, lxiii) speaks of Jesus as 'Apostle', a designation of Him confined in the New Testament to Heb. iii. 1. But in the latter of the two passages it is 'Angel and Apostle', and reference is made to the Lord's words, 'he that heareth Me heareth Him that sent (ἀποστεί-λαντα) Me'; so that the thought of the divine Messenger sent by God may not be due to Hebrews at all.

Passing from Rome it is doubtful if we find any trace of the epistle in this period. The relation to it of the EPISTLE OF BARNABAS is of interest. On the surface it seems to be connected at various points, but their spirit and purpose are widely different. In Hebrews the Jewish economy of priesthood, sacrifices, tabernacle, covenant, and law are the copy, shadow, figure, type of which the Christian economy is the perfect Ideal made real. In *Barnabas*, on the other hand, the Jewish economy was one huge mistake, and Christianity as the Truth has taken its place. In the one the Perfect was evolved out of the Imperfect (Heb. i. 1); in the other, the Perfect was present all the time, but wholly misunderstood and misinterpreted by the Hebrew race. So the question to be decided is whether the two teachers of an Alexandrian type independently made the Jewish system the basis of their presentation, or whether the author of *Barnabas* knew Hebrews and deliberately rejected its line of argument in favour of another. The former alternative is kinder to him, and also more probable. But if the latter is the true one, he treats Hebrews as anything but sacred and authoritative.

In Asia there is no evidence at all. IGNATIUS (*Philad.* ix) says, 'The priests also (were) good, but better (is) the High Priest who hath been entrusted with the Holy of Holies, who only hath been entrusted with the deep things of God. And POLYCARP (xii. 2) says, 'May the God and Father of our

Lord Jesus Christ, and the eternal High Priest Himself, the Son of God, Jesus Christ, build you up'. But the comparison in the former case with the priests of Israel is different in kind from that in Hebrews, and it is impossible to suppose that the idea of Christ as the High Priest, and of His eternity, could not have occurred to anyone without dependence on that epistle.

Hebrews, then, existed in Rome, but was not thought of as apostolic, and elsewhere was virtually, if not entirely, neglected.

(e) The Catholic Epistles

The position held by the acknowledged Pauline epistles during this early period may be gathered from some indications a little later, in the last quarter of the century. In the Passion of the Scillitan martyrs (A.D. 180) we read, 'Saturninus the Proconsul said, "What are the things in your satchel?" Speratus said, "The books [sc. presumably the Gospels] and the letters of one Paul, a righteous man".' The New Testament rolls which they considered worthy to be kept in one satchel, their sacred collection, were the Gospels and the Pauline epistles; no others were thought of as canonical. That was in Africa. But in the East we find the same thing. The *Doctrine of Addai* says, 'The Law and the Prophets and the Gospel . . . and the Epistles of Paul . . . and the Acts of the twelve apostles . . . these books read ye in the Church of God, and with these read not others'. This was in the Syriac Church of Edessa, and belongs to the latter half of the fourth century when the Catholic epistles were still not included in the Canon. And therefore, once more, when we read in Tertullian (*De Praescr.* xxxvi), 'She [the Church at Rome] combines the Law and the Prophets with the Evangelic and the Apostolic writings', we understand that 'Apostolic' means 'written by *the* Apostle', St. Paul. Throughout the whole Church, so far as we can see, no other epistles were canonical.

The only ones of which there is any trace are 1 Peter, 1 John, and perhaps James. It is possible, of course, that St. Peter's letter (if Petrine) to the churches in Asia Minor was known by CLEMENT in Rome thirty years or so later. But the signs that he knew it are far from decisive. Prov. iii. 34 is quoted in xxx. 2, and in 1 Peter, but also in James. The quotation of Prov. x. 12 (in xlix. 5) is more noticeable; 'a multitude of sins', found also in 1 Peter, differs from the Heb., which has 'all sins', and is quite different from the LXX. Various explanations of this, however, are possible; e.g. a variant reading in the LXX, not preserved in our manuscripts. The only other coincidences which have been found are the words ἀγαθοποιΐα (ii. 2) and ἀδελφότης[1] (ii. 4), which are peculiar to 1 Peter in the New Testament. But we do not possess enough early Christian literature to determine whether two isolated words must have been borrowed by Clement. Goodspeed's theory has already been mentioned, that Hebrews challenged the Church in Rome to produce leaders in thought and deed and that 1 Peter and *1 Clement* were the result; written about the same time in the same community.

There are signs at Rome of a knowledge of 1 John. In the *EPISTLE TO DIOGNETUS* we read, 'For God loved men . . . to whom He sent His only-begotten Son'; cf. 1 John iv. 9. And 'How shalt thou love Him who so loved thee before?' cf. *v.* 19. (Behind both passages John iii. 16 can also be felt.) And JUSTIN writes (*Dial.* 123): 'We Christians are called the true children of God, *and we are*, who keep Christ's commandments'; cf. 1 John iii. 1. Again, it is possible that HERMAS knew James. 'Although the passages which point to James fail to reach, when taken one by one, a high degree of probability, yet collectively they present a fairly strong case'.[2]

The writer of *EP. BARNABAS* perhaps knew 1 Peter. In vi. 2–4 he quotes Is. xxviii. 16 and Ps. cxviii. 22 as in 1 Pet. ii. 6–8 with textual variations. But this may have been due, in both writings, to a collection of *testimonia*. And in v. 6 it is said that 'the prophets having their grace from Him [Christ] prophesied of Him'. But the thought that Christ inspired the Old Testament prophets, though it is not found elsewhere in the New Testament, may easily be supposed to have been current in the circles in which *testimonia* were current.

But in the East a knowledge of 1 Peter and 1 John is fairly

---

[1] The former is unique in biblical literature, the latter occurs in the sense of 'brotherly affection' in 1, 4 Macc.

[2] J. Drummond in *The N.T. in the Apostolic Fathers*, p. 113.

clear. The former seems to be echoed by IGNATIUS (*Rom.* ix)
in his collocation of God as the 'Shepherd' of the Church in
Syria and Jesus Christ as its 'Episcopos'; cf. 1 Pet. ii. 25 (cf.
v. 2). POLYCARP is strongly influenced by it. Several close
parallels may be seen in *The N.T. in the Apost. Fathers*, pp. 86 ff.
(Benecke). And he seems certainly to use 1 John. 'For everyone who does not confess that Jesus Christ has come in the
flesh, is anti-Christ. And whosoever does not confess the witness of the Cross, is of the devil' (vii. 1; cf. 1 John iv. 2; iii. 8).
If he did not use the epistle he may, at any rate, have known
the author.[1] PAPIAS is stated by Eusebius (*H.E.* iii. 39) to have
made use of 'the former Epistle of John, and that of Peter
likewise'. Finally, 2 PETER explicitly refers (iii. 1) to the First
Epistle, and shows the high regard in which he held its value
and apostolic authority.

(*f*) The Apocalypse of John

It is pointed out by C. H. Turner[2] that much might be said
for admitting apocalyptic works into the Canon. They corre-
sponded to, and carried on, Old Testament prophecy; and if in
successive periods of persecution these comforting 'revelations'
were produced, inspired messages of consolation to the
Church, must not all these be as authoritative as the inspired
messages of the Old Testament prophets? The Canon would
thus be susceptible of infinite expansion. But in fact only two
of these, which were finally rejected from the Canon, enjoyed
sufficient recognition at first to be able to hover on the borders
of it—the *Apocalypse of Peter* and the *Shepherd of Hermas*.
M. R. James dates the former early in the second century, and
says,[3] 'The second book of the *Sibylline Oracles* contains (in
Greek hexameters) a paraphrase of a great part of the Apocalypse: and its influence can be traced in many early writings—
the *Acts of Thomas* (chs. 55–57), the *Martyrdom of Perpetua*, the
so-called *Second Epistle of Clement*, and, as I think, the *Shepherd* of
Hermas.' Both it and the *Shepherd*[4] are included in the canonical

---

[1] See further, Stanton, *The Gospels as Historical Documents*, i. 20, notes 3, 4.
[2] *J.T.S.* x, 1908–9, p. 366.   [3] *The Apocryphal N.T.*, p. 505.
[4] Some people, as we learn from Tert. (*De Orat.* xvi), treated its words with
such reverence that because Hermas said (*Vis.* v. 1) 'when I had prayed in my
house and sat down on my bed' they sat down after concluding prayer.

list appended to cod. Claromontanus (D₂); a passage from the *Shepherd* is quoted as ἡ γραφή in Iren. IV. xx. 2; Clem. Alex. uses it; in Pseudo-Cypr. *Adv. Aleatores* it is 'Scriptura divina'; and Orig. (*in Ep. Rom.*, Lommatzsch, vii. 437) says of it (according to the Lat. translation), 'scriptura valde mihi utilis videtur, et ut puto divinitus inspirata'; and owing doubtless to Origen's authority it was included in cod. Sinaiticus (ℵ). Turner,[1] from the numerations of the gatherings of the manuscript conjectured that the *Shepherd* originally stood at the end of the Old Testament as part of the prophetic Canon; but Mercati (op. cit. xv. 452) argues that this is impossible, and that it stood in its present position at the end of the New Testament.

But for different reasons both works soon failed to obtain canonical recognition. The *Apoc. Pet.* was seen to be tainted with the Docetic heresy, and the *Shepherd* was not apostolic. Origen, indeed, claimed that it was, and identified Hermas with his namesake mentioned in Rom. xvi. 14; but the writer of the Muratorian fragment (see below) rejected it because it was so recent; and Tertullian, as a Montanist, because he was shocked at any idea of reconciliation after post-baptismal mortal sin. And he claims that it is not worthy to be included in the 'divine Instrument' because it was judged 'by every council even of your own Churches to be among the apocryphal and false writings' (*De Pudic.* 10). Generally speaking, it was opposition to the Montanists which prevented late apocalypses from being added to the Canon; nothing in the ecstatic vagaries of Montanus and his prophetesses could contribute anything new to the divine Revelation, which was given in its final and complete form by the apostles.

The *Apocalypse of St. John* had a unique history, in that it was the only book of the New Testament which, after being accepted in the East at an early date, was later rejected there, though it at last came fitfully into its own. That will be shown later. In this period there are already signs of its use both in the East and West. The date of its composition was practically contemporary with that of the letter of CLEMENT OF ROME, and therefore a knowledge of it by Clement is not to be expected

---

[1] *J.T.S.* xiv, 1912–13, pp. 404–7.

of him. But HERMAS seems to be familiar with its imagery: the Church as a woman (*Vis.* ii. 4); the enemy of the Church as a beast (iv. 1, 2), from whose mouth fiery locusts come forth (iv. 1); the apostles and teachers are stones in the heavenly tower (iii. 3); the faithful receive crowns and white robes (*Sim.* viii. 2). And JUSTIN definitely refers to it by name: 'Moreover also among us a man named John, one of the apostles of Christ, prophesied in a revelation made to him that those who have believed on our Christ shall spend a thousand years in Jerusalem' (*Dial.* lxxxi). And he says (*Apol.* i. 28), 'The leader of the evil demons is called Serpent, and Satan, and Devil'; cf. Rev. xx. 2. Where the book was thus received as the work of 'one of the apostles of Christ' its authority was assured, and its acceptance in the West remained uninterrupted.

In the East we learn that Papias, among others, was a witness to its credibility (τὸ ἀξιόπιστον), as stated by Andreas in the prologue to his commentary on the book. And a quotation of Papias from Rev. xii. 9 is given in Cramer's Catena, viii, p. 360. Irenaeus (v. xxxiii. 3, 4) says that certain elders 'who had seen John the disciple of the Lord' (of whom 'Papias the hearer of John' is just afterwards expressly mentioned) remembered that they had heard from him—and then follows, in the form of teaching ascribed to our Lord, words expressing a materialistic chiliasm, condemned by Eusebius (*H.E.* iii. 39), in the development of which the Apocalypse probably played a part.

Note on some early Heretics

Some of those who differed from the Catholic Fathers in doctrinal matters are important in the Church's history because they felt it necessary to appeal to apostolic authority for the support of their views. Some of them claimed a secret tradition from the apostles. And when the Church met this by pointing to the open and public tradition of its writings, they made use of the same writings, or such of them as suited them. But they also published other works for the dissemination of their heretical ideas, in some cases gaining currency for them by attaching to them apostolic names. This led the Church-writers to define more clearly those which early tradition had handed down as truly apostolic. Heretics thus gave an impetus to the crystallizing of the Canon, which persecution helped to complete.

SIMON MAGUS (see Acts viii. 18–24), a Samaritan Gnostic, exercised an influence which can be traced in the second century. Of the views attributed to him we have some account in a work called *Philosophumena*, written, in all probability, by Hippolytus, to whom a summary of them was available in a Simonian work named the *Great Pronouncement* (ἀπόφασις). In the notices of it by Hippolytus there are two echoes of the language of Matthew and Luke, and one of John. And the value put upon apostolic writings is shown by the fact that the Simonians 'wrote books in the name of Christ and His disciples, and gave them currency' to deceive believers (*Apost. Const.* VI. 16. 1). CERINTHUS, an Egyptian Jew, was thought of in tradition as the special opponent of St. John. This probably reflects the fact that the Cerinthians were strongly Judaistic. Epiphanius (*Haer.* xxviii. 5) says that 'they make use of the Gospel according to Matthew on account of the human genealogy, but part of the Gospel, not the whole'; and that they opposed the genealogy to the Johannine prologue. But since he confused both the *Gospel according to the Hebrews* and the *Gospel of the Ebionites* with Matthew, we cannot be sure of the facts. (On the strange ascription of the Fourth Gospel and the Apocalypse to Cerinthus see p. 280). BASILIDES (*c.* 120–30) is more useful to us, if the accounts of him are to be trusted. In a *Disputation between Archelaus and Manes* (3rd cent.), originally a Syriac work, it is stated that he lived 'not long after the times of our apostles'; and Clement Alex., who knew his writings, and Jerome place him in the reign of Hadrian. Origen, followed by Ambrose and Jerome, speaks of his 'Gospel', which is probably to be understood in the same sense in which St. Paul wrote 'my Gospel' (Rom. ii. 16; cf. xvi. 25), viz. his presentment of Christian truth. He wrote ἐξηγητικά or Expository Comments, and, according to Hippolytus, referred to words in Matt. ii. 1 and to some Pauline epistles with the formula 'it is written', to Lk. i. 35 with 'that which is written', and to John i. 9; ii. 4 with 'that which is said in the Gospels', while a passage in

1 Corinthians is cited as ἡ γραφή. If these are genuinely the language of Basilides, the use of such formulas by an Alexandrian heretic at so early a date is remarkable. A further fact about him is noteworthy. According to Clem. Alex. (*Strom.* vii. 17) he appealed to the authority of Glaucias, whom he claimed to be an 'interpreter of Peter', as Papias his contemporary claimed for St. Mark. Whether he knew the work of Papias, and tried to imitate it by a rival claim, we cannot say; but it is a further indication that for sufficient proof of Christian doctrine heretics and orthodox alike appealed to the sanction of an apostle. Similarly, VALENTINUS (c. 140), who propounded his views at Rome, thought it necessary to link himself with an apostle, and claimed to have listened to Theodas, who was acquainted with St. Paul (ibid.). But Tertullian supplies us with an important piece of evidence. He says (*De Praescr. Haer.* 38) that 'Even if Valentinus appears to have used the *whole Instrument*', and did not, like Marcion, mutilate Scripture, he perverted the text by verbal additions and alterations with even greater impunity; 'alius manu scripturas, alius sensus expositione intervertit.' 'The whole Instrument' need not imply that Valentinus quoted from every book of the Canon as known to Tertullian, but it does imply that the latter thought of a definite Canon as being then recognized by the general agreement of Christians. He could not accuse him of rejecting whole books as Marcion did. HERACLEON, a contemporary and follower of Valentinus, has an importance of his own, in being the earliest known New Testament commentator. Origen refers repeatedly to his comments on the Fourth Gospel,[1] which, no doubt, modified his Valentinianism. The extent of these suggests that he treated of the whole of John; if so, he may perhaps have written on the other Gospels in the same way, but we have a comment on only one passage in Lk. xii quoted by Clem. Alex. (*Strom.* iv. 9). His work shows that he regarded the language of the Fourth Gospel as the language of the Old Testament was regarded; the smallest verbal detail was significant, and capable of yielding hidden truth. PTOLEMAEUS, another contemporary and follower of Valentinus, in a letter to an 'honourable sister Flora' (quoted by Epiph. *Haer.*

---

[1] See E. A. Brooke, 'The Fragments of Heracleon', *Texts and Studies*, i. 4.

xxxiii. 3 ff.) uses sayings of our Lord which occur in Matthew and words from the prologue of John. MARCION,[1] son of a bishop of Sinope, came to Rome *c.* 140, where he soon afterwards left the Church, and expounded his heretical ideas with great ability and stormy force. C. R. Gregory describes him as 'the most active and influential man, bearing the name of Christian, between Paul and Origen'. He did not aim at adding to or extending Christian truth, but of purifying it from the false ideas with which it had been overlaid, i.e. that the God and Messiah of the Old Testament were the God and Christ of the New. The God who made the world, the Demiurge, was just but not good—hard-hearted, cruel, and bloodthirsty; and all Jewish, Old Testament notions of Him must be purged out of Christianity. The Third Gospel and ten of St. Paul's epistles (1, 2 Tim. and Tit. being omitted) alone supplied him with the required material, which he revised and expurgated (see p. 329). TATIAN, an Assyrian who came to Rome, was converted to Christianity by Justin, after whose death he developed Gnostic views. The tendency of the Gnostic ideas on the inherent evil of matter, which was created by the Demiurge, was either towards antinomianism, or, as in Tatian's case, towards a rigid asceticism. He returned to the East, where he became head (Eus. ἀρχηγός, Jer. *patriarches*) of the Encratites. On the speculative side he was allied to Valentinus, on the ascetic to Marcion. But this did not lead him to Marcion's conclusions on the Christian writings. His chief importance consists in the fact that he arranged a harmony of the Four Gospels (probably composed at Rome in Greek unless Baumstark and Plooij are right in their theory of a Syriac original or Burkitt in that of a Latin one), known by the Greek title *Diatessaron*,[2] which was naturalized in Syriac, and also the (to us) less known Syriac title *Evangelion da-Mehalleṭē*, 'Evangel of the Mixed ones'. This supports the evidence from other quarters that the Four were

---

[1] See Harnack's 'Marcion', *Texte und Untersuchungen*, xlv, 1924; E. C. Blackman, *Marcion and his Influence*, 1948, and C. S. C. Williams, *Alterations to the Text of the Synoptic Gospels and Acts*, pp. 10 ff.

[2] Cf. ibid., pp. 19 ff., A. J. F. Klijn, *A Survey of the Researches into the Western Text of the Gospels and Acts*, 1949, pp. 87–110, and M. M. Parvis and A. P. Wikgren, *New Testament Manuscript Studies*, 1950, pp. 28 f. (by B. M. Metzger).

by this time a recognized group. The combination into one rendered it easier and less noticeable to excise those passages which did not suit his views. Theodoret says that he 'removed the genealogies, and all the other passages which show that the Lord was born of David according to the flesh. And not only did the members of his party use this, but also those who followed the apostolic doctrines, not realizing the evil design of the composition, but quite simply using the book as being concise.' This was probably the earliest form in which the Gospel reached the district of which Edessa was the literary centre. A Greek fragment of the *Diatessaron* discovered at Dura in 1933 was published by C. H. Kraeling. A translation of the separate Gospels (*Evangelion da-Mepharreshē*), which we call the 'Old Syriac', was made (about A.D. 200), but it does not seem to have had much vogue, and remains to us only in two somewhat different manuscripts (see pp. 386 f.). The *Diatessaron* was completely put aside, first by Rabbula (411–35), who, though he continued quoting sometimes from older manuscripts, substituted in Edessa his own revision known as the *Peshitta*, containing the separate Gospels, and a rather larger Canon than had been recognized by the Syriac-speaking peoples; and secondly, by Theodoret of Cyrrhus (423–57), who 'swept up more than two hundred copies of it in the churches of his diocese, and introduced the four Gospels in their place'.[1] It would be wrong, however, to infer that the *Peshitta* completely displaced the *Diatessaron*, which was known in Armenia in the fifth century, or the older translation(s) of the separate Gospels.

Besides the Gospels he recognized some of St. Paul's epistles. Jerome (*Praef. in Tit.*) says that he rejected some, but disagreed with Marcion and others in accepting Titus.

§ 4. A.D. 170–300

In this period the intercommunication between the Churches increased, one result being the growth of a closer agreement, as regards the canonicity of some books and the rejection of others. This process was helped by the mere lapse of time. The 'ancients' became regarded as more honourable the farther

[1] Wright, *Syriac Literature*, p. 9.

they receded into the past. No new letter or book had now the slightest chance of being treated as sacred, though it might still be read in Church as an important and interesting communication. Both facts are well illustrated in the letter of Dionysius of Corinth (*c.* 167–70) to the Romans under their bishop Soter, parts of which are quoted by Eusebius (*H.E.* iv. 23) : 'Today, then, we passed the Lord's Day, a holy day, in which we read your epistle, which we shall ever hold by, reading it for admonition, as also the one written to us formerly by Clement.' 'When the brethren asked me to write letters [*or* a letter] I wrote. And these the apostles of the devil have mingled with tares, taking some things out and adding some things; for whom the Woe is appointed. It is not be wondered at, then, if some have put their hand to deal deceitfully with the Dominical writings (τῶν κυριακῶν γραφῶν), when they have taken counsel against those that are not such.' The position as regards the Canon is summed up by Turner :[1]

As a bulb germinates beneath the ground, striking root slowly and deeply into the earth, and only then emerges above the surface to shoot up suddenly into foliage and flower, so the real and effectual canonization of the Apostolic writings had been silently wrought in the inner chambers of the life of the Christian society before history can lay her finger upon any open proofs. But when once the evidence comes, it comes, in the last quarter of the second century, abundantly and with a rush.

(a) The Gospels

It is unnecessary to adduce further quotations from the Gospels. They were not only known, but by the end of the century had received the titles which they hold today: 'The Gospel—according to Matthew', &c., i.e. the one Gospel of Jesus Christ in so far as it is related by Matthew, &c. Thus the Muratorian fragment (see below) speaks of 'the third book of the Gospel—according to Luke', and, with a conjecturally emended text, 'the fourth book of the Gospel—according to John'. All four, together with their discrepancies, were needed to present the Gospel. But there were some besides heretics who chiefly valued one or another. John had held the first place,

[1] *J.T.S.* x, 1908–9, p. 25.

as was natural, in Asia Minor, where Papias, perhaps, implied its superiority to Matt. and Mk. (see p. 79), Matt. in Antioch, Mk. in Rome, and Lk., perhaps, in Greece. But there may have been, as Harnack[1] thinks, a compromise between the preferences arrived at, not by a harmony, but by including all four as authoritative. It might be thought that this fourfold arrangement would not be likely to continue, because, if the history was to be authoritative, differences between the accounts would detract from its value. The differences were too obvious to escape notice, and called for harmonizing expedients. Matthew and Luke had each been a harmonizing compilation, as we now know, made out of Mark, Q, and other sources; why should not the four Gospels be similarly harmonized? All difficulty would thus be removed by the production of one work. And attempts were, in fact, made in this direction. Some have thought that Justin shows indications of having used a harmony. This is uncertain; but Jerome (*Ep. ad Algasiam*) uses language which may imply that Theophilus, Bishop of Antioch (*c.* 180), compiled one and commented on it, and refers to a commentary 'on the Gospel' which went under his name (*De vir. ill.* 25). And some ten years earlier appeared the famous *Diatessaron* of Tatian, which, in its Syriac form (it is almost certain that Syriac was not its original language), he introduced into Mesopotamia. The four separate Gospels were afterwards translated into Syriac; but this harmony was probably the first Gospel writing that was there known. And yet no harmony permanently succeeded. In spite of the difficulties involved in divergences the Four retained their supremacy, partly because they had already been established as 'classics' each in its own region or district, and partly because the authors were understood to be 'apostolic' men, and apostolic authority was the surest shield against heresy. The secret traditions claimed by the Gnostics were opposed by the open and public traditions claimed by the Church. To combine the Four, therefore, into one was to lose the guarantee of authenticity. That which preserved the Four was the same principle that underlay the preservation and selection of the epistles. But it was not brought about by the

---

[1] *The Origin of the N.T.* (trans. Wilkinson), p. 73.

authoritative action or definite decision of any one Church or locality, because in that case we should not find the Four arranged, as we do, in different orders; e.g. the order commonly found in the West was Matt., Jn., Lk., Mk.; but that in the Curetonian Syriac is, curiously, Matt., Mk., Jn., Lk., while our present order is found in the Sinaitic. The Gospels were four and canonical according to the oldest witnesses that we possess of the Old Syriac and the Old Latin, to Clement in Alexandria, and to Irenaeus representing Rome and Gaul. For the latter (III. xi. 8) the number Four lay in the divinely ordered nature of things, as the four regions of the earth, the four winds, and the four faces of the Cherubim with which he fancifully illustrates the characteristics of each Gospel.

(b) The Acts

It might seem surprising that the epistles, with their widely different styles and subjects, and spiritual and moral values, should ever have come to be placed on a par with the words and deeds of our Lord, so that their inspiration and authority were thought of as on the same plane as those of the Gospels. But this was due to the conception of the Church which was afterwards represented in the Nicene Creed by the term 'Apostolic', and which finds expression as early as Clement of Rome (ch. xlii): 'The Apostles received the Gospel for us from the Lord Jesus Christ; Jesus the Christ was sent forth from God. The Christ, then, [is] from God, and the Apostles from Christ.' In other words the Apostles *are* Christ as manifested in the succession from Him; the Church is the extension of the Incarnation, and the Apostles are the first stage in the extension. It was a working-out of the thought in such a passage as Matt. x. 40, 'He that receiveth you receiveth Me'. The foundation-stones of the new Jerusalem are the twelve apostles of the Lamb (Rev. xxi. 14), although 'other foundation can no man lay than that which hath been laid, which is Jesus Christ' (1 Cor. iii. 11). The epistles of *the* apostle, St. Paul, had already established themselves, and others were beginning to emerge into recognition. But there was one writing, hitherto almost unnoticed, though written by an 'apostolic' man, which related the first stages of the Church's growth, the first manifestation of Christ in the apostolic body. Though it relates little of anyone except St. Peter and St. Paul, yet it is πράξεις τῶν ἀποστόλων, or 'the Acts of all the Apostles' as the Murat. fragment has it. It thus legitimized the placing of epistles on the same canonical level as the Gospels, a place already won by St. Paul's epistles because of the weight of their own intrinsic authority; and at the same time it constituted an independent authority for placing St. Paul and the other apostles on an equal footing. So that when once the idea of a sacred Canon began to include the Pauline *corpus*, the book of the Acts, which helped to justify this, leapt suddenly into prominence, and was placed in such a position that it formed an introduction to the apostolic part of the Canon. The arrangement was not, indeed, universal or immovably fixed. Two centuries later, when the need for any justification was no longer felt, we meet with some lists in which the Acts holds a less central position. But, so far as the evidence goes, it was very widely adopted. The importance now accorded to the book is illustrated by the extent to which Irenaeus quotes it (in Bk. III); and he says, 'Thus Paul's *annuntiatio* is consonant with, and so to speak the same as, what Luke testifies of all the apostles' (III. xiii. 3). And it stands in the Murat. Canon after the Gospels; and the writer states that Luke related to Theophilus things which took place when he was himself present. In Africa Tertullian vigorously defended its canonicity against Marcion (*Adv. Marc.* v. 1, 2; and cf. *De Praescr.* xxii. 1). In Alexandria Clement not infrequently cites 'The Acts of the Apostles' by name, sometimes quoting extended passages. And in the East an Old Syriac translation, argued by Bishop Chase,[1] was further deduced by J. Rendel Harris[2] from the quotations of Ephraem Syrus from the Acts in his Commentary on the Pauline epistles, preserved in an Armenian translation, which was made generally accessible by the Mechitarists in Latin, Venice, 1893. A translation of the Armenian (into Latin) and of the sections drawn from it in an ancient Armenian catena (into English) by F. C. Conybeare appears on pp. 373–453 of

---

[1] *The Old Syriac Element in Codex Bezae*, 1893; *The Syro-Latin Text of the Gospels*, 1895.
[2] *Four Lectures on the Western Text*, 1894.

the *Beginnings of Christianity*, Part I, *The Acts of the Apostles*, iii, 1926.

(c) The Pauline Epistles

It is as unnecessary as in the case of the Gospels to quote instances of the use of passages. Irenaeus quotes from every one of the thirteen epistles except Philemon, which, however, had already been accepted by Marcion, saved, according to Tertullian, by its brevity. And the language of Tertullian himself, and of Clement of Alexandria, is similarly steeped in them.[1]

The collection of the Pauline *corpus*, as has been said, had probably been going on independently in various places during the sub-apostolic period, since the epistles now appear in different orders. Marcion's order, according to Tert., was Gal., 1, 2 Cor., Rom., 1, 2 Thess., Laodiceans (=Eph.), Col., Phil., Philem. Epiph. gives the same, except that he transposes the last two. But the Murat. fragment has 1, 2 Cor., Gal., Phil., Col., 1, 2 Thess., Eph., Rom. And Tert. (*De Resurr. Carn.* 33 ff.) and Cyp., (*Testim.*, esp. iii. 11) agree with it in placing Corinthians first and Romans last. 'Ambrosiaster', in the fourth century, and Pelagius, early in the fifth, have the order Rom., 1, 2 Cor., Gal., Eph., Phil., 1, 2 Thess., Col., Tit., 1, 2 Tim., Philem. At the end of the century, then, the Gospels, Acts, and Pauline epistles were universally established as the Church's Canon, while other books were beginning to make their way towards being included in it.

(d) The Epistle to the Hebrews

During the last decades of the second century this epistle made no advance towards canonicity, since it was not ascribed to St. Paul. The MURAT. FRAGMENT states that he wrote to 'seven Churches', 'following the plan (*ordinem*) of his predecessor John', and hence Hebrews is omitted; and the rejection of its Pauline authorship remained the continuous tradition of the Roman Church till the fourth century. 'The custom of the Latins received it not' (Jerome). IRENAEUS, in one of his

---

[1] Melito of Sardis, according to the recently discovered *Homily on the Passion*, seems to have known Gal., Col., and 1 Cor. at least, despite C. Bonner's cautious verdict. (*Texts and Studies*, xii, 1940, pp. 41 f.)

works known to Eusebius (*H.E.* v. 26), is said to have quoted from it, and from 'the so-called Wisdom of Solomon'. And (in II. xxx. 9) he uses the phrase 'by the word of His power' (Heb. i. 3), referring, however, not to Christ but to God the Father. But though Irenaeus knew the epistle, Stephen Gobar, a sixth-century writer, states, according to Photius, that Irenaeus and HIPPOLYTUS (215–35) rejected the Pauline authorship. The latter, indeed, is held by some to have been the writer of the Murat. fragment (see below).

The attitude of Carthage, which learnt its Christianity from Rome, as Tert. says, was the same as that of Rome. TERTUL-LIAN was a lawyer of Carthage, who, after wielding his mordant pen in behalf of the Church, went over to the sect of the Montanists less than twenty years after he became a Christian. Converted *c*. 195 at the age of thirty-five, and living to extreme old age, he represents the opinion on the Canon of African Christianity during the first half of the third century. It is still disputed whether his Scriptural quotations were taken by him from the Greek, and turned into his own Latin, or whether he used a Latin translation already existent.[1] He may, of course, have done both at different times. But that there was a Latin translation of at least the Gospels and the Pauline epistles seems clear from the account of the Scillitan martyrs, in 180 (see p. 335). But while the Acts and the Pauline epistles were for him the *Instrumentum Apostolicum*, Hebrews was not. After speaking of 'the discipline of the apostles' he adds, *ex abundantia*, a quotation from 'a certain companion of the apostles', i.e. Hebrews, which he assigns to Barnabas, 'a person of sufficient authority, as being one whom Paul placed with himself in the matter of continence: and certainly the *Epistle of Barnabas* is more widely received by the Churches than that apocryphal *Shepherd* of the adulterers'. Written by a companion of the apostles it had some authority, but not that of the apostles themselves, and therefore was not strictly canonical. This comparatively favourable verdict does not seem to have influenced CYPRIAN, a younger contemporary (baptized 246, martyred 258), who revered Tertullian as 'the Master'. He makes no

---

[1] Cf. M. J. Lagrange, *Critique textuelle, II. La Critique rationelle*, 1935, pp. 259–62.

allusion to the epistle, and does not consider it St. Paul's, since he states, as the Murat. fragment had done, that the apostle 'writes to seven Churches', the symbolism of the mystical number being repeated in the epistles to the seven Churches in the Apocalypse.

The Church of Alexandria has not hitherto been mentioned, except in connexion with the *Ep. Barnabas*, in which the allegorical treatment of the Old Testament was in the Alexandrian style. Its spiritual and intellectual development went on quietly and apart from the Church as a whole. But a product of it was the Catechetical School which became famous under such leaders as Pantaenus, Clement, Origen, and Dionysius. We know of no written work of the first of these, but Clement, who succeeded him, and deeply revered him, sometimes quotes sayings of his. CLEMENT OF ALEXANDRIA, probably born at Athens, having journeyed widely in south Italy, Syria, and Palestine, joined the School at Alexandria, and became head of it just before 200. He frequently quotes Hebrews, and speaks of the writer as 'the Apostle' (*Strom.* vii. 1). According to Eusebius (*H.E.* vi. 14) he explicitly assigns it to St. Paul, but says that he wrote it to 'the Hebrews in the Hebrew language', and that St. Luke translated it for Greeks, which accounts for the similarity of 'colour' between it and the Acts. He refers to 'the blessed presbyter' (probably Pantaenus) as teaching to the effect that St. Paul, being the apostle of the Gentiles—the Lord having been sent to the Hebrews as the Apostle of the Almighty—in modesty, and doing honour to the Lord, would not describe himself as the 'apostle' of the Hebrews, since he need not have written to them at all. This is the first appearance of the acceptance of the epistle as the work of St. Paul, and therefore in the fullest sense canonical. ORIGEN, a pupil of Clement, who followed him as head of the School in 203, and died, after living for some time at Caesarea, as a confessor in the Decian persecution in 254/5, accepted the books recognized by his teacher. He did not, however, follow him in attributing Hebrews to St. Paul. His opinion has been given on p. 236. After stating it he adds, 'if any Church, then, holds this epistle as St. Paul's it may be approved for doing so; for it was not without reason that the men of old time have handed it down as Paul's. But who it was that wrote the epistle God knoweth the truth.' But he had heard both Clement of Rome and St. Luke spoken of as the author. On the other hand DIONYSIUS, a pupil of Origen, who succeeded Heraclas as head of the School c. 231, and then as Bishop of Alexandria c. 247, agreed with Clement that the epistle was the work of St. Paul, referring to x. 34, 'They received with joy, like those to whom Paul bore witness, the spoiling of their goods'. The third-century Chester Beatty papyrus codex of St. Paul's Epistles, P⁴⁶, places Hebrews directly after Romans, whereas Athanasius and most Alexandrian uncial manuscripts put it after the other epistles addressed to Churches, i.e. after 2 Thessalonians, and not, like D, E, K, L, and Erasmus, after Philemon at the end of the Pauline Canon. It is probable that Hieracas, the heretical ascetic of Egypt, followed the same order as P⁴⁶ about A.D. 300.[1]

In Asia Minor GREGORY, Bishop of Neo-Caesarea in Pontus, was a convert of Origen, and was probably taught by him which books were to be held sacred, and Origen in a letter to him uses the words of Heb. iii. 14. And METHODIUS, bishop of an obscure place called Olympus in Lycia (Socr. *H.E.* vi. 13), who opposed the doctrine of Origen, frequently used the epistle, though he nowhere ascribed it to St. Paul. In Caesarea PAMPHILUS, one of Origen's most devoted disciples, must have accepted the epistle either as St. Paul's or, as Origen thought, Pauline though written by someone else. There is evidence of this, if a colophon is to be trusted which is attached to the Pauline epistles in cod. H (Paul), where Hebrews is placed before the Pastoral epistles, stating that the manuscript (i.e., no doubt, an ancestor of the manuscript) was 'collated with the copy in the library of St. Pamphilus at Caesarea, written with his own hand'.

Farther east, in the Syriac-speaking Church, it was accepted as the work of St. Paul. Ephraem the Syrian (died 373) included it in his commentary on the Pauline epistles. His younger contemporary, Aphraat, frequently quotes Hebrews in his *Demonstrations*, calling the author 'the Apostle'.

---

[1] H. F. D. Sparks, *J.T.S.* xlii, 1941, pp. 180 f.

(e) The Catholic Epistles

Rome was very slow in accepting these. The MURAT. FRAGMENT includes only two Epistles of John, and the Epistle of Jude; and even these are mentioned rather as an afterthought, as though the writer admitted them chiefly because other churches had already done so. This can be seen from the context. After enumerating the epistles of St. Paul, he writes: 'There is current also an epistle to the Laodiceans, and another to the Alexandrians, forged under the name of Paul for the heresy of Marcion, and many others which cannot be received into the Catholic Church, for gall does not suit to be mixed with honey. The epistle, indeed (*sane*), of Jude, and two superscribed as John's are held in the Catholic [?Church], and Wisdom written by the friends of Solomon in his honour.' Possibly 'in Catholica' in the last sentence should be emended to 'in Catholicis', i.e. among the Catholic epistles; but since the writer recognizes no others in the group known as the Catholic epistles, he can mean no more than the epistles received in the Catholic Church. 'The two superscribed as John's' is the rendering of an emended text, that of the fragment being corrupt; but it is clear that the two epistles are ascribed to John. The First Epistle is mentioned also earlier. After relating the legend of the origin of the Fourth Gospel the writer says, 'What wonder is it, then, that John brings forward each detail with so much emphasis even in his epistle(s), saying of himself, What we have seen with our eyes, and heard with our ears, and our hands have handled, these things we have written.' By the 'two' epistles he must have meant the First and Second, not the Second and the Third, for the only place elsewhere in which a vestige of knowledge of the Third is shown is Alexandria, where there was always an inclination towards a wider and looser Canon than in Rome, which generally tended to be strict. IRENAEUS quotes from both the First and the Second (see I. xvi. 3, III. xvi. 7), naming the writer. A knowledge of I Peter seems to have reached Gaul from the East before there is any sign of it at Rome. The letter from Vienne and Lyons alludes to v. 6: 'They humbled themselves under the mighty hand by which they are now greatly exalted' (Eus.

H.E. v. 2); and possibly *v.* 8: 'The devil thinking that he had already devoured (καταπεπωκέναι) Biblias' (ibid. 1). Irenaeus quotes 1 Pet. i. 8 with the words 'And Peter says in his epistle' (IV. ix. 2); and Eus. (*H.E.* v. 8) says that he quoted many passages from 'the former epistle of Peter'. But with the possible exception of Clement (see above) there is no sign that 1 Peter was known at Rome till the fourth century. Hippolytus twice has words from it, but in one case it is from the heretical work *The Great Announcement*, and in the other probably from Irenaeus.

Of James, 2 Peter, and 3 John there is no trace in Rome in this period. After Hippolytus no great writer appears there till Jerome, towards the end of the fourth century. The Roman Church was mainly occupied in matters of discipline, and her biblical knowledge was taught her by teachers in other lands.

In Carthage 1 Peter was known, and soon accepted as canonical. Tertullian uses it sparingly. C. H. Turner[1] shows that the internal evidence of the Latin version suggests a different translator, and a later incorporation into the Canon. Tertullian may have known only the Greek of the epistle. Cyprian speaks of 'Peter in his epistle' (*Ad Martyres* ix), and evidently accepts it as canonical. 1 John was assigned by Tertullian to the same author as the Apocalypse, i.e. 'John the Apostle', these two, with the Fourth Gospel, comprising the 'Instrumentum Johannis'. They were thus included in his Canon, while 2, 3 John were definitely excluded. He included also Jude, as being written by 'Jude the Apostle', and cites it in order to prove the authority of Enoch which is quoted in it. Cyprian does not refer to it, but it is quoted in the contemporary tract (pseudo-Cypr.) *Ad Novatianum* (Hartel, Cypr. iii. 67). He speaks of 'John in his epistle', as though he did not recognize any other epistle as his. This, however, does not necessarily follow, since at a Council of Carthage (256) at which he was present, one bishop having quoted 1 John as 'the epistle of John', another quoted 2 John (*vv.* 10 f.) as 'by John the Apostle in his epistle'[2] (cf. Origen and Dionysius Alex. below). In Carthage, then, 1 John and Jude were established,

---

[1] *Ch. Quart.*, Apr. 1890, p. 157, and *J.T.S.* x, 1908–9, p. 356.
[2] Cypr. *Sent. Episc.* lxxxi.

and 1 Peter and 2 John soon came to be established, as canonical. As in Rome, James, 2 Peter, and 3 John are at present outside the sacred pale.

In Alexandria, as would be expected, there was greater freedom in accepting books. CLEMENT, who accepted Hebrews as St. Paul's, is stated by Eusebius (*H.E.* vi. 14) to have made comments in his *Hypotyposes* (*Outlines*) on 'every canonical writing, not omitting the disputed ones, I mean Jude and the rest of the Catholic Epistles, also the Epistle of Barnabas and the Apocalypse that is called Peter's'. Cassiodorus (sixth century) mentions comments only on 1 Peter, 2 John, and James (a mistake for Jude). But Photius (ninth century) described the *Outlines* as consisting of 'interpretations of Genesis, Exodus, the Psalms, the Epistles of St. Paul, the Catholic Epistles, and Ecclesiasticus'.[1]

But while James, 2 Peter, and 3 John were not in Clement's Canon, other books besides *Ep. Barnabas* and *Apoc. Peter* still hung on the borders of the Alexandrian Bible, viz. the *Epistle of Clement* and the *Shepherd* of Hermas. He calls the former 'the Apostle' (*Strom.* iv. 17), identifying him, as has been said, with his namesake of Phil. iv. 3; and the latter also 'the Apostle' (ii. 6), and 'the apostolic Barnabas, who was of the Seventy and a fellow-worker of Paul' (ii. 20). These identifications gave to these writings in Alexandria an apostolic prestige without which it had become impossible for any books in this period to be considered sacred.

ORIGEN shows an advance in that James, 2 Peter, and 3 John definitely come into sight. He once uses language (*in Matt.*, tom. xvii. 30) which seems to imply that Jude had only a secondary authority, but he quotes it frequently and ascribes it to the Lord's brother (ibid. x. 17). In the same passage he says much of St. James, but does not say that he wrote an epistle; elsewhere, however (*in Joan.*, tom. xix. 6), he quotes Jas. ii. 20 with the words, 'as we read in the epistle current as James's', which hardly suggests that it had a high value for him. In the portions extant only in Latin he quotes it, speaking of the author as 'the Apostle', and once as 'the Lord's brother'

---

[1] Cf. the curious mention in the Murat. fragment of *Wisdom* between the Epistles of John and the Apocalypses of John and Peter.

(*in Rom.*, tom. iv. 8), but that may be due to the translator. He mentions 'the Catholic Epistle by Peter' (*Selecta in Ps.*, Lomm., xi. 420) and 'the Epistle by John' (*in Matt.*, tom. xv. 31), as though he recognized no others ascribed to them. (See, however, the same usage in Cyprian and Dionysius.) But he knew them, for he says, 'Peter has left behind one epistle generally acknowledged; perhaps also a second, for it is a disputed question' (*ap.* Eus. *H.E.* vi. 25). In the Latin version, again, 2 Peter is quoted more than once with the formula 'Peter said' (e.g. *in Lev.* iv. 4), and 'As Scripture says in a certain place' (*in Num.* xiii. 8). And after speaking of St. John as the author of the Gospel and Apocalypse he writes, 'He has left also one Epistle of very few lines; it may be also a second and a third, for all do not hold these to be genuine; but both together do not extend to more than a hundred lines' (*ap.* Eus. *H.E.* vi. 25). Origen, therefore, was inclined to extend his Canon to all our present books, but with doubts about James, 2 Peter, and 2, 3 John.

Too little of DIONYSIUS has reached us to give clear evidence as to the Alexandrian Canon. Beside 1 John, which he quotes, he appears to have accepted 2, 3 John as the work of the apostle, the author of the Fourth Gospel and the First Epistle. He points out, in contrast with the Apocalypse, that in neither of the latter, 'nor in the current Second and Third of John, although short epistles, does John appear by name, but "the Presbyter" is written anonymously' (*ap.* Eus. *H.E.* vii. 25). In the same context, indeed, he speaks of the First Epistle more than once as 'the Epistle', 'the Catholic Epistle', as though there were only one by that author. But that usage has already been noted in Origen and Cyprian. He makes one quotation from James, but does not mention 1, 2 Peter or Jude in the fragments that we possess.

From the East there is practically no direct evidence. THEOPHILUS OF ANTIOCH perhaps echoes 1 Pet. i. 18 and iv. 3 in using the expressions πλάνη πατροπαράδοτης and ἀθέμιτος εἰδωλολατρία (*Ad Autol.* ii. 34); and possibly 2 Pet. i. 21, when he speaks of 'the men of God being πνευματόφοροι of the Holy Spirit, and Prophets' (ibid. ii. 9). ii. 13 is also cited: 'His word, appearing like a lamp in a confined place'; but this is not very similar either to 2 Pet. i. 19 or to 4 Esdr. xii. 42, from which the latter is borrowed. In Asia Minor APOLLONIUS accuses a Montanist named Themison of venturing 'in imitation of the Apostle to compose a Catholic Epistle' (*ap*. Eus. *H.E.* v. 18), a reference apparently to 1 John. GREGORY THAUMATURGUS, Bishop of Neo-Caesarea in Pontus, was a convert of Origen, and had probably, therefore, been instructed by him as to the books to be held sacred. Origen, in writing to him, quotes from Heb. iii. 14, and he himself, according to a catena,[1] is credited with words which recall Jas. i. 17: 'For it is clear that every perfect good comes from God.' And PAMPHILUS of Caesarea, an ardent admirer of Origen, must have known, and probably accepted, his Canon. Two cursive manuscripts of the Acts and Catholic epistles (see p. 396) have a colophon stating in each case that it was collated (which means that an ancestor was collated) with the copies of Pamphilus at Caesarea, which implies that, if Pamphilus did not copy them himself, he at least knew the Catholic epistles as a definite collection. On the other hand, in the Syriac-speaking district of which Edessa was the centre, the Catholic epistles were not for a long time included in the Canon (see the *Doctrine of Addai*, quoted on p. 335).

(*f*) *The Apocalypse of John*

We have seen that as early as Justin this book was established at Rome as the work of an apostle. And this opinion of it did not vary in the West. The letter from VIENNE and LYONS quotes it three times, once with the formula 'that the Scripture might be fulfilled'. IRENAEUS uses it frequently as the work of John who was 'a disciple of the Lord', and whom he identifies with the disciple whom Jesus loved. He refers to its date 'not long ago, but almost in our own time, at the end of Domitian's reign' (v. xxx. 3, Eus. *H.E.* iii. 18). Possibly he owed this and other traditions to Papias. In the MURAT. FRAGMENT it is said, 'The apocalypses of John and Peter alone we receive, which latter some of our number will not have read in the Church' (see p. 347). And HIPPOLYTUS is said to have

---

[1] *Ap*. Ghisler, *Comm. in Jerem*. i. 181. This reference is taken from Westcott.

written a commentary on it which he ascribed to the apostle John.

In Carthage TERTULLIAN recognized it as the work of 'John the apostle', and, as has been said, the Fourth Gospel and 1 John, with the Apocalypse, comprised for him the *Instrumentum Johannis*. CYPRIAN constantly used it as Scripture, though he nowhere ascribes it to the apostle John. And LACTANTIUS, at the end of the century, refers to it by name.

In Alexandria it was no less strongly established as canonical. CLEMENT frequently quotes it, assigning it to the apostle John. ORIGEN states (*ap*. Eus. *H.E.* vi. 25) that John, who lay on the breast of Jesus, and who left a Gospel, 'wrote also the Apocalypse, having been commanded to keep silence and not to write the voices of the seven thunders'.

But criticism began to make itself heard. DIONYSIUS broke away from the opinion of Clement and Origen, though his view found no endorsement, so far as we know, from subsequent Alexandrian writers. Portions of his words, as given by Eusebius (*H.E.* vii. 25) are here translated. Their significance for our present purpose lies not so much in the nature of the criticisms as in the fact that a learned teacher of the third century was open-minded enough to accept the book as canonical, as Origen had accepted Hebrews, while denying its apostolic authorship. John of Ephesus, who was not the son of Zebedee, was for Dionysius only one who had lived in touch with the apostolic age. He points out that neither in the Gospel nor in any of the three epistles is John named, while the writer of the Apocalypse names himself four times. On the other hand, he never says of himself, as is frequently said in the Gospel, 'the disciple loved by the Lord', nor 'he thât lay on his breast', nor 'the brother of James', nor that he was an eye-witness and hearer of the Lord. There were many Christians called after the apostle (as there were after Paul and Peter)— John Mark, for instance. He thinks, however, that the author was some other John in Asia, and mentions the report that there were two tombs of Johns at Ephesus. This is followed by a discussion first of the subject-matter, and then of the style and vocabulary:

And from the thoughts, too, and from the words and their

arrangement, this writer may reasonably be supposed to be different from the other. For the Gospel and Epistle agree with one another, and begin in a similar manner. The one says, 'In the beginning was the Word', the other 'That which was from the beginning'. The one says, 'And the Word became Flesh . . . &c.', the other the same a little varied, 'That which we have heard . . . &c.' These things he puts as a preface, in strenuous opposition (as he shows in what follows) to those who say that the Lord has not come in the flesh; wherefore also he carefully adds, 'And that which we have seen we witness, and declare unto you the eternal Life, &c.' He is consistent with himself, and does not depart from his purposes, but goes through everything with the same headings and names, some of which we will mention briefly.

After enumerating them, Dionysius proceeds:

In short, when we note all their characteristics it is obvious that the complexion of the Gospel and Epistle is the same. But the Apocalypse is quite different from these, neither touching nor bordering on any of them, scarcely having even a syllable, so to speak, in common with them. Nay more, neither has the Epistle (for I let alone the Gospel) any remembrance or thought of the Apocalypse, nor the Apocalypse of the Epistle, while Paul by his Epistles gave some hint of his revelations which he did not severally insert. Further, by the diction one can judge the difference of the Gospel and the Epistle from the Apocalypse. For the former are written not only correctly as regards the Greek, but very elegantly in their wording, their reasonings, and the arrangements of their explanations; one is far from finding in them a barbarous word or solecism, or any vulgarism at all. For he had, it seems [the power of delivering] the message in either form, the Lord having given him both—that of knowledge and that of expression. That the other saw a revelation, and received knowledge and prophecy, I will not gainsay. I see, however, that his dialect and language are not accurately Greek, but that he uses barbarous vulgarisms, and in some places actual solecisms. It is not necessary to pick these out now, for it is not in mockery that I have made these remarks—let none think it—but only to draw out the dissimilarity of the writings.

Scholarship and tradition are here complementary influences; the latter made him think of the author as 'a holy and inspired man', but it was not the apostle.

In the East there is not much evidence in this period. In Syria, THEOPHILUS of Antioch quoted it (Eus. *H.E.* iv. 24), and PAMPHILUS of Caesarea, if his Apology for Origen is to be trusted, referred to it as the work of St. John. This, however, may be due to Eusebius, who was responsible for the completion of the work. In Asia Minor APOLLONIUS (according to Eus. *H.E.* v. 18) 'used passages from the Apocalypse of John'. It was natural that he should oppose the claims of the Montanists, against whom he wrote, by the 'apostolic' book of revelation. And METHODIUS, Bishop of Olympus in Lycia at the end of the century, quoted from it, naming the author 'the blessed John'; and Andreas mentions him, with Papias, Irenaeus, and Hippolytus, as a witness to its divine inspiration. But a reaction was beginning in the East. 'The rise of Greek scholarship during the "long peace" after Severus (A.D. 211–49) made men more conscious of the critical difficulties of common authorship of Apocalypse and Gospel. The slackening of persecution set free the natural recoil of the Hellenic spirit against the apparent materialism with which the rewards of the blessed and the glories of the heavenly Jerusalem are portrayed.'[1] The effects of this reaction are seen in the next period.

Note on the Muratorian Fragment on the Canon[2]

The Latin fragment first published by Muratori in 1740 is an important piece of evidence with regard to the Western Canon. It seems to be part of a longer treatise which contained more than the writer's judgement on the Canon, since he says that he must deal separately with the epistles to the Corinthians, Galatians, and Romans, i.e. no doubt in the portion lost to us. It was probably written at Rome, and many think that it was originally written in Greek. Whether Latin-speaking Christians at Rome were numerous enough at that time to need a Latin translation, or whether it was translated for, or in, some other place, is not known. The manuscript in which it has been preserved, together with several other pieces of patristic writing, was written by a careless and illiterate scribe of the seventh or eighth century, and some of its sentences,

---

[1] Turner, op. cit. x. 372.
[2] Cf. M. J. Lagrange, *Introduction à l'étude du Nouveau Testament*, I, 1933, pp. 78–84.

which are corrupt, have received a variety of interpretations. The writer evidently made some statement about Matthew and Mark, the fragment beginning with six words which presumably refer to the latter. He goes on to speak about Luke as the third book of the Gospel, and then relates a story about how St. John came to write his Gospel. His views on the other books of his Canon have already been noted. On the *Shepherd*, he writes, 'Hermas wrote the Shepherd quite recently in our own times, while Bishop Pius his brother occupied the Chair of the Church of the city of Rome'; and, therefore, he is of opinion that, while it ought to be read, it ought not to be published, either among the prophets or the apostles for ever (which seems to mean either among the Apocalypses, two of which he has just named, or among the apostolic epistles). In the concluding clauses of the fragment, which are corrupt, he repudiates certain Gnostic writings.

Harnack[1] holds that the tone of the writing is that of an authoritative utterance, independent of the views of others, delivered by one who felt himself in a position to state the use of his own Church (or the majority of its members) as a norm for other Churches: There are two forged letters of Paul, 'and many others *which cannot be received into the Catholic Church*', 'The Apocalypses of John and Peter only *we receive*'. (But if we accept Zahn's emendation and suppose that a line has dropped out, the reference will be not to the Apocalypse but to the Epistle 'of Peter [one Epistle which] alone we receive'.) The work of Hermas '*ought* to be read, but *cannot* be published'. The writings of the Gnostics, Arsinous, &c., '*we do not receive at all*'. 'We' and 'the Church' and 'the Catholic Church' are treated as synonymous, implying that 'the whole Catholic Church ought to follow our example'.

Salmon[2] and Lightfoot[3] argue for Hippolytus as the author. Harnack suggests Victor (Bishop of Rome 189–99), or less probably Zephyrinus (199–217), or someone under his authorization. If it was the work of a bishop of Rome, it must have had a

---

[1] *The Origin of the N.T.* (trans. Wilkinson), pp. 106–8. In the *Zeitschr. f. d. neutest. Wiss.*, he gives the reasons offered by Lightfoot and others for a Greek original, and controverts them.

[2] *Introd. to the N.T.*, p. 122.

[3] *Clement*, ii. 411 ff., cf. Lagrange, op. cit.

wide effect in the West. And the principle on which it is constructed is evidently that of confining the Canon to books
which could claim 'apostolic' authority. But it was not by
any means a final judgement on the Canon.

§ 5. THE FOURTH CENTURY

The Gospels had long formed, in every part of the Church,
an immutable quartet, and St. Paul's epistles were a definite
corpus, consisting of either thirteen or fourteen according as
Hebrews was excluded or not.

At the opening of the fourth century a new impetus was
given to the demarcation of sacred books by the persecution of
Diocletian. These books were now so closely bound up with the
life of the Church that he hoped to ruin her by destroying
them. His first edict was to the effect that the churches should
be razed to the ground and the writings destroyed by fire
(Eus. *H.E.* viii. 2). The phrase officially used to describe the
latter seems to have been 'the Writings of the Law' (*scripturae
legis*), which implies a fairly definite collection. But the fact
that some writings which were read here and there in Church
did not occupy the same status as the bulk of the collection
made it possible for some Christians to surrender certain books
to the Roman officials which satisfied their demands. Others,
however, viewed this as a traitorous subterfuge, and the violent opposition of the strict party to those whom they considered 'traditores' developed into the long-drawn-out Donatist
controversy. An effect of the persecution is seen in the fact that
we now begin to meet more frequently with lists of sacred
books. Marcion, indeed, had made his own list, by which he
expressed his conception of the impassable chasm between
Christianity and Judaism. The author of the Muratorian list
had delivered the judgement of his Church. But the judgement
of particular Churches can now be seen with increasing clearness.

For any development of the Roman Canon we have no
evidence for three-quarters of a century, but no doubt the
ecclesia principalis continued to learn from her visitors, as she
had in earlier years. In 382 a Council was held at Rome, which

issued a list of canonical books.[1] It was held under the presidency of Damasus the bishop, and Jerome, to whom the compilation of the list was probably due, attended it, having just come to Rome. In the light, however, of the work of von Dobschütz (*Texte und Untersuchungen*, xxxviii, 4, 1–362 (1913)), which proved the decrees of the 'Damasine Council' to be of the sixth century, this evidence and the date 382 must be set aside.

This list expressed the mind of the great scholar who revised the Latin New Testament. Sophronius Eusebius Hieronymus (JEROME), a native of Stridon on the border between Dalmatia and Pannonia, had travelled far and read widely. While accepting all the books of our English Bible, he knew of others which were to be 'placed among the apocryphal writings', which included the *Shepherd* with Wisdom, *Sirach*, Judith, Tobit, and 1, 2 Maccabees, and was well acquainted with the doubts entertained in regard to Hebrews, the Catholic epistles, and the Apocalypse.

On these he writes as follows:

On Hebrews and the Apocalypse. 'Paul the apostle writes to seven Churches, for an eighth to the Hebrews is put by many outside the number' (*Ep. ad Paulinum*). This shows a leaning against the Pauline authorship. But twenty years later, in *Ep. ad Dardanum* (No. 129) he speaks of it as 'received not only by the Churches of the East, but by all Church writers of the Greek language in previous times as [the work] of Paul the Apostle, though many judge it to be [the work] of Barnabas or Clement. And it does not matter whose it is since it is [the work] of a Churchman, and is daily employed in the reading of the Churches.' He recognizes that 'the custom of the Latins received it not', but neither for that matter (as he points out) do the Greek Churches receive the Apocalypse. 'Nevertheless we receive both, by no means following a custom of the present time only, but the authority of ancient writers, who for the most part quote passages from each of them, not as they are accustomed to do sometimes from the apocryphal writings, and even very occasionally use passages from pagan literature, but as canonical and churchly.'

---

[1] The text is given by C. H. Turner, *J.T.S.* i, 1900, pp. 554 ff.

On James. 'James who is called the Lord's brother . . . wrote only one Epistle . . . which is asserted to have been published by someone else under his name, though it gradually in process of time acquired authority' (*De vir. ill.* 2).

On 2 Peter. '[Peter] wrote two Epistles, which are named Catholic, the second of which is denied by many to be his because of its difference from the former in style' (ibid. 1). He himself explains the difference by supposing that St. Peter had two interpreters (*Ep. ad Hedibiam*; No. 120).

On Epp. John. '[John] wrote one Epistle . . . which is approved by all Churchmen and learned men; the other two are asserted to be [the work] of John the presbyter' (*De vir. ill.* 9).

On Jude. 'Jude the brother of James left a small Epistle which is one of the seven Catholic Epistles. And because he inserts in it a passage from the book of Enoch, which is apocryphal, it is rejected by many. Yet by age and use it has now deserved authority, and is reckoned among the sacred Scriptures' (ibid. 4).

These passages excellently illustrate the method by which the disputed books found their way into the Canon. No authority of a General Council ever pronounced them Scripture; but they were written by Churchmen, and used by Churchmen, and gradually acquired, and deserved, authority, whoever their authors may have been.

Jerome's Latin Bible, the 'Vulgate', played a large part in moulding the Canon in the West; and it is due to him that our New Testament contains what it does. As regards the New Testament he was supported by Augustine,[1] who contributed still further to the establishment of our Canon.

In Africa there are signs which appear to indicate a conflict of opinion, some moving towards a wider Canon than in the last century, while more conservative minds refused. A Latin manuscript which goes by the name of Mommsen, who found

---

[1] In the Old Testament Augustine included without reservation Tobit, Judith, Esth. (including the Greek additions), 1, 2 Macc., Wisd., Ecclus. Jerome, on the other hand, followed Hebrew tradition, excluding from the Canon the Greek works which we know as the Apocrypha. He has been followed by the Anglican and the Free Churches, while the Roman and Eastern Churches retain the Canon of Augustine, following the early Christian tradition.

it, or of the 'Cheltenham list', contains a list of the books of the Old and New Testaments dated about A.D. 360.[1] In the latter the following words occur:

> eplae Johannis III ūr CCCL
> una sola
> eplae Petri II ūer CCC
> una sola

> i.e. 'Three epistles of John [containing] 350 verses
> one only
> Two epistles of Peter [containing] 300 verses
> one only'.

The writer appears to have been of reactionary opinions, for he omits Hebrews and Jude as well as James. As to 2, 3 John and 2 Peter the explanation is probably this: he copied the first and third lines from some earlier list, and in doing so could not separate 2, 3 John from 1 John, and 2 Peter from 1 Peter, because they were bound to them by the enumeration of verses; but he expressed his own opinion that they were un-canonical by adding, with unshaken conviction, that there was 'one only' by John and Peter. Harnack's suggestion is very improbable—that the second line refers to James, and the fourth to Jude. The word 'sola' would be quite superfluous, and the names could not have been omitted.

But the reactionary spirit could not win the day against the general trend of opinion. Jerome, by influencing Augustine, influenced the African Church. In 397 was held the third COUNCIL OF CARTHAGE, at which Augustine was present. The 39th canon names the books of Scripture, stating that 'It was resolved that beyond the canonical Scriptures nothing be read in the Church under the name of Divine Scriptures', an exception, however, being made for the reading of the Passions of the Martyrs on their anniversaries. The New Testament Canon is the same as our own, the order being: Gospels, Acts, thirteen epistles of St. Paul, 'one to the Hebrews by the same name', 1, 2 Peter, 1, 2, 3 John, James, Jude, Apocalypse. A note was added later, probably when the canons of the several Carthaginian councils were codified: 'Let this also be notified

---

[1] Cf. A. Souter, *Text and Canon of the New Testament*, 1912, p. 212.

to our brother and fellow priest Boniface [Bishop of Rome, 418], or to other Bishops of those parts, for the confirming of this Canon, because we have received from the Fathers that these are to be read in the Church.'

AUGUSTINE, Bishop of Hippo in Africa (395–430), supported Jerome, as has been said, in respect of the New Testament. He gives our present list of books (*De Doctr. Christ.* ii. 12) in the order: Gospels, fourteen epistles of St. Paul (Hebrews last), 1, 2 Peter, 1, 2, 3 John, Jude, James, Acts, Apocalypse. But though he includes Hebrews among St. Paul's epistles, he elsewhere pointedly refrains from quoting it as his. And he exercises a critical judgement, recognizing that some books are received on weightier authority than others:

Among the canonical Scriptures let him [the Christian reader] follow the authority of the majority of Catholic Churches, among which, of course, are those which have been worthy of having apostolic sees and receiving Epistles. He will hold, therefore, this measure in the canonical Scriptures, that he will prefer those which have been received by all Catholic Churches to those which some of them do not receive; and among those, moreover, which are not received by all, that he prefer those which the more numerous and the weightier Churches receive to those which the fewer and less authoritative hold. But if he find some held by the more numerous, and some held by the more weighty, though he will not find this easily, I think that they ought to be held of equal authority.

In Alexandria, fifteen years before the Council at Rome under Damasus, the great Bishop ATHANASIUS shows us that the Canon in Egypt had arrived at the same condition of completeness as at Rome. He returned to his see after his fifth banishment, and in the next year (367) wrote as usual a Festal Epistle, his 39th, of which fragments remain. In it he gives a list of canonical books, identical with our New Testament, but in the following order: Gospels, Acts, seven Catholic epistles (of James, Peter, John, Jude), fourteen Epistles of St. Paul, and the Apocalypse. This follows a list of the Hebrew Old Testament Canon, with the addition of 1 Esdras, Baruch, and the *Epistle of Jeremiah*, and the omission of Esther. These are 'fountains of salvation'. No one must add to them or take away from them. Other books, which he appends merely 'for the sake of greater accuracy', he rates lower than Eusebius was prepared to do (see below). One class contains the Wisdom of Solomon, *Wisdom of Sirach*, Esther, Judith, and Tobit, and among Christian writings the *Teaching of the Apostles* and the *Shepherd*. These are 'not canonized, but authorized by the Fathers as of a kind fit to be read to catechumens'. Another class consists of 'apocryphal books', which he leaves unnamed, written by heretics and falsely represented as ancient to deceive the simple. He gives no hint of any official action of synods. The Canon of the New Testament had made itself, and for Athanasius was complete and sharply defined; and this in spite of the greater latitude characteristic of Alexandria in earlier days.

His opinion, however, did not prevent DIDYMUS, the blind head of the catechetical School, who died some twenty years later than Athanasius, from expressing the doubts that were still felt about 2 Peter. He wrote, indeed, a commentary on the seven Catholic epistles, but said (according to the Latin translation), 'It should be known, therefore, that this Epistle *esse falsatam*, which, though publicly read, is not in the Canon'. The Latin words probably represent νοθεύεται (as Eusebius said of James), i.e. 'held by some to be spurious'.

In the East the progress of the Canon went on more slowly in some parts than in others. Palestine and Asia Minor were in advance of Antioch and the Syriac-speaking Edessa. The fullest and most interesting treatment of the books is that by EUSEBIUS, Bishop of Caesarea (*c.* 313–30), who, with Pamphilus, was an ardent admirer of Origen, and shows the influence of his open-mindedness. The following passages should be studied: (*a*) *H.E.* ii. 23 (martyrdom of James, *ad. fin.*); (*b*) iii. 3 (concerning the epistles of the apostles); (*c*) iii. 24 (concerning the order of the Gospels); (*d*) iii. 25 (concerning the acknowledged Divine Scriptures and those that are not such). It is unnecessary to give them here in full. They will be found translated in Lawlor and Oulton's edition of the *H.E.*[1] (*a*) The first passage speaks of 'the seven Epistles called Catholic', implying that they were widely recognized as forming a dis-

---

[1] And see Westcott, *The Canon of the N.T.*, pp. 415–20, or Gregory, *The Canon and Text of the N.T.*, pp. 257–62.

tinct group; but some, it is said, regard James as spurious (νοθεύεται); neither it nor Jude was often mentioned by the ancients, but both are publicly read with the others in many Churches. (*b*) In iii. 3 it is said, 'Of Paul the fourteen Epistles are clear and manifest', though some rejected Hebrews because the Roman Church counted it disputed. This gives another definite group. Eusebius says that the *Acts of Paul* had not reached him in the Christian tradition as indisputable. Of the numerous Petrine writings he speaks of 1 Peter only with a certain voice; it was frequently used by the presbyters (or ancients) of old as indisputable. 2 Peter ('that which was current as his second') had not reached him as part of the Testament (ἐνδιάθηκον, canonical), but many found it useful and read it diligently with the other Scriptures. On the other hand, neither in his own time nor earlier had Church writers made use of passages from the work entitled *Acts of Peter*, the *Gospel* named after him, that which is called his *Preaching* (κήρυγμα), and his so-called *Apocalypse*; they had not been handed down in the collection of Catholic books. (*c*) In iii. 24 he deals at some length with the four Gospels. Of writings other than the Fourth Gospel, 1 John had been acknowledged, in his own time and in the past, as indisputable, but 2, 3 John were disputed, and regarding the Apocalypse opinions still differed. (*d*) In iii. 25 is his actual catalogue in which he proceeds 'to sum up the writings of the New Testament already mentioned'. These he distinguishes, as he says, into (1) the writings which, according to ecclesiastical tradition, are true and genuine and thoroughly acknowledged: the Four Gospels, Acts, Epistles of Paul, 1 John, 1 Peter, and ('if it should possibly appear right') the Apocalypse; and (2) others which are 'not part of the Testament but disputed, but nevertheless acknowledged by most of the Church writers'. This second division is subdivided. In his words just given the whole division consists of 'disputed' books, but in the actual sub-divisions they are (i) disputed, (ii) spurious (νόθοι). The former are James ('current under the name of James'), Jude, 2 Peter, and those named 2, 3 John ('whether belonging to the Evangelist or perhaps to another of the same name'). The latter are the *Acts of Paul* (which he distinguishes from other Acts of the several apostles by naming it and leaving the others unmentioned till the end), the book named the *Shepherd*, and the *Apocalypse of Peter*; further, the epistle current as that of *Barnabas*, and the *Teaching of the Apostles*. 'And, moreover, as I said, the Apocalypse of John, if that appears right, which some, as I said, reject; while others reckon it among the acknowledged books.' Finally, some include among 'these' (i.e. probably the spurious books) the Gospel according to the Hebrews.

Thus he shows that he had himself no doubt about Hebrews. It was in the fullest sense canonical because its author was St. Paul; its value was belittled by those who denied that. But as to the authorship, and therefore the value, of the Apocalypse he was far from certain. *If* it was by the evangelist St. John (εἴ γε φανείη), it must stand in the first class; if not (to which, influenced by the Eastern opinion of his day, he seems slightly to incline—εἰ φανείη), it must take a low place. To these two classes he appends a third, i.e. heretical, pseudonymous works which no one in the succession of Church writers has ever deigned to quote, at variance with the apostolic *ethos*, unorthodox, and forgeries, not to be classed even as spurious, but avoided as monstrous and impious. These are the writings purporting to contain a Gospel of Peter, Thomas, or Matthew, and also the Acts of Andrew, John, and the other apostles.

Eusebius thus recognized, as many scholars have done since, different degrees of canonicity:

> Class I. Gospels, Acts, epistles of St. Paul (including Hebrews), 1 Peter, 1 John, ?Apocalypse.
>
> Class II. (*a*) James, Jude, 2 Peter, 2, 3 John.
> (*b*) *Acts of Paul, Shepherd, Apocalypse of Peter, Barnabas*, the *Teaching*, ? Apocalypse.

Near Caesarea was Jerusalem, of which CYRIL was bishop. Soon after his consecration, just before 350, he delivered catechetical lectures, in one of which he gave a list of the canonical books of the Old and New Testaments. He excluded the Apocalypse, but otherwise his list is identical with ours (with the addition of Baruch and *Ep. Jeremiah*). After mentioning the Four Gospels he says, 'but the rest are pseudepigrapha and harmful'; the Manichaeans also wrote a Gospel 'according to

[margin handwritten note:] Eusebius

Thomas'. At the end of the list he writes, 'And let all the rest lie (outside) in the second rank'. But Epiphanius, Bishop of Constantia (Salamis) in Cyprus, a countryman of Cyril, received at the end of the century the whole of our Canon including the Apocalypse.

In Asia Minor exactly the same New Testament Canon as Cyril's is found in some metrical lines of GREGORY, Bishop of NAZIANZUS in Cappadocia (372–89), ending with the words, 'Thou hast all. If any is outside these, it is not among the genuine ones.' The Apocalypse, therefore, was uncanonical; but this did not prevent him from alluding to it with the remark 'as John teaches me by the Apocalypse'. On the other hand BASIL, Bishop of CAESAREA in Cappadocia, his contemporary, and GREGORY, Bishop of NYSSA, Basil's brother, both refer to the Apocalypse as the work of the evangelist St. John, but the use of it by all three is very sparing. Another contemporary, AMPHILOCHIUS, Bishop of ICONIUM, wrote iambic lines, *Iambi ad Seleucum*, warning the reader against spurious books and giving a list of the 'inspired books' of the Old and New Testaments. After enumerating the Four Gospels, Acts, and fourteen epistles of St. Paul he writes:

Some say that that to the Hebrews is spurious, not speaking well, for its grace is genuine. Let be. What remains? Of the Catholic Epistles some say that seven, others that only three, ought to be received, one of James, one of Peter, and one of John. And some receive the three [of John] and the two of Peter besides them, and that of Jude the seventh. And the Apocalypse of John, again, some include, but still the majority say that it is spurious.

Here is our full Canon, but with the recognition that there is difference of opinion on all the disputed books, especially the Apocalypse. At about the same time all our books except the Apocalypse are named by an unknown writer or scribe, as an addition to the last canon of the Council of Laodicea, a small gathering of clergy from parts of Lydia and Phrygia, held in 363.[1] It was not till the close of the next century that the Apocalypse was fully recognized in Asia Minor. ANDREAS, Bishop of Basil's see of Caesarea in Cappadocia, wrote a commentary

---

[1] See Westcott, *The Canon of the N.T.*, pp. 432–9.

on it, and even he felt obliged to adduce previous testimonies to its inspiration, those of Papias, Irenaeus, Methodius, and Gregory of Nazianzus. And ARETHAS after him also wrote a commentary on it, with a similar defence.

Further East, however, the history of the Canon was very different. In the Syriac-speaking churches, till early in the fifth century, no advance was made on the primitive Canon— Gospels, Acts, and Pauline epistles (see *Doctrine of Addai*, quoted on p. 335). But the Syriac version known as the PESHITTA omitted from our New Testament books only 2 Peter, 2, 3 John, Jude, and the Apocalypse. This was the work of Rabbula, who was Bishop of Edessa from 411 till his death in 435 and organized and regulated the Syriac-speaking churches. The great probability of this origin of the Peshitta, as against the much earlier date which used to be assigned to it, is demonstrated by Burkitt,[1] who shows that before Rabbula there is no trace of the Peshitta in Syriac writings, and hardly a trace of any other writings after him.[2] His Canon was that of Antioch at that date, as his text reflected the current text of Antioch–Constantinople. The Canon of Antioch is indicated by the writings of CHRYSOSTOM, its bishop at the close of the fourth century, and THEODORET, Bishop of Cyrrhus in Syria (423–57), who nowhere quote the books which the Peshitta omitted. And Constantinople inherited the same tradition, the *Synopsis scripturae sacrae*, found among the works of Chrysostom, omitting the same books. They were still omitted from the catalogue of EBED-JESU, a Nestorian bishop at the beginning of the fourteenth century; and to this day they have formed no part of the Peshitta, which has always been the 'Authorized Version' or 'Vulgate' of Syriac Christians. In the sixth century JUNILIUS, an African bishop, learnt from a Persian the views on the Canon which were taught in Nisibis. These were that the primitive Canon described in the *Doctrine of Addai*, with the addition of 1 Peter, 1 John, contained the New Testament books which were of 'perfect authority', while

---

[1] *Evangelion da-Mepharreshe*, vol. ii, ch. 3.

[2] This verdict should be questioned in view of the researches of Vööbus (*Contributions of the Baltic University*, lix, 1947) and M. Black (*Bulletin of the John Rylands Library*, xxxiii, 1950/1, pp. 203–10). Rabbula used an old Syriac text sometimes.

all the four minor Catholic epistles and also James were of 'secondary (*mediae*) authority'. But Junilius is very vague about the Apocalypse; *apud Orientales admodum dubitatur*. The Nestorians have always held to the Canon of the Peshitta; but among the Jacobites (i.e. the Monophysite Syrians) two subsequent attempts were made to translate the full Greek Canon. In 508 a revision of the Peshitta was made for Philoxenus, Bishop of Mabbōg (hence called the PHILOXENIAN SYRIAC), the four Catholic epistles and the Apocalypse, which were lacking to it, being added. The text of the former is probably that which is usually bound up with modern editions of the Peshitta. In 616 another bishop of Mabbōg, Thomas of Heraclea (Ḥarḳel), made at Alexandria an elaborate revision[1] of the Philoxenian, the Apocalypse of which is probably that commonly printed with the Peshitta. This revision is called the HARKLEAN SYRIAC.

At the beginning of the fifth, or the end of the fourth, century, Syria made an advance upon the Canon of Chrysostom and Theodoret. In the writing known as the *Apostolic Constitutions*,[2] traditionally ascribed to Clement of Rome, the concluding section is known as the APOSTOLIC CANONS, the last of which consists of the Canon of the Old and New Testaments. The latter includes all our books except the Apocalypse, with the addition of *1, 2 Clement*, and was afterwards ratified by the Quinisextine Council at Constantinople in 692. For this reason JOHN OF DAMASCUS, in the eighth century, recognized all our present books, but included also the *Apostolic Canons* in his New Testament.

Constantinople and the Greek Church generally continued to waver with regard to the Apocalypse. LEONTIUS, early in the seventh century, admitted it, but NICEPHORUS and PHOTIUS in the ninth did not. In the Orthodox Church it has

---

[1] This view, adopted by G. Zuntz ('The Ancestry of the Harklean New Testament', *The British Academy Supplemental Papers*, vii. 76) and others, is opposed to that of W. D. McHardy (*J.T.S.* xliii, 1942, p. 168) and others, that Thomas did no more than add marginal notes from a few Greek manuscripts to a copy of the Philoxenian text. See also Zuntz, *Revue Biblique*, lvii, 1950, pp. 550–82.

[2] A composite work, probably by the author of the pseudo-Ignatian epistles, based upon the *Didascalia*, the *Didache*, and other material.

never, in fact, attained to the secure position, canonical and authoritative, that it holds in the West.

With Eusebius, Augustine, and many later writers the modern student feels compelled to prefer some books to others, realizing that some books stand on a higher level than others. Gradations of value, which are subjectively determined, are not, indeed, identical with gradations of canonicity but, in fact, they correspond fairly well. The books made their own place by a process which can be called, on the whole, the survival of the fittest, so that they were gradually set apart from all others as containing the sacred message of God.

BOOKS

F. C. Burkitt, *Evangelion da-Mepharreshe*, 1904, vol. ii, ch. 3.

E. J. Goodspeed, *The Formation of the New Testament*, 1926.

A. von Harnack, *The Origin of the New Testament* (tr. J. R. Wilkinson, 1925).

E. Jacquier, *Le Nouveau Testament dans l'église chrétienne*, i, 1911.

M. J. Lagrange, *Introduction à l'étude du Nouveau Testament*, i, 1933.

J. Leipoldt, *Geschichte des neutestamentlichen Kanons*, 1908.

A. Souter, *The Text and Canon of the New Testament*, 1912.

B. F. Westcott, *A General Survey of the History of the Canon of the New Testament*, 7th ed., 1896.

T. Zahn, *Geschichte des neutestamentlichen Kanons*, 1888–92.

The New Testament in the Apostolic Fathers (Oxford Society of Historical Theology, 1905).

XI

TEXTUAL CRITICISM

§ I. THE NEED

THERE are still readers of the Bible whose thoughts have never been carried to any stage in its history behind the Authorized Version. They know that the Greek Testament has come down to us; but how, they have never thought of inquiring. Printing having begun in the age of Caxton, the books must have been preserved in nothing but handwriting during the centuries before that. And the study of the manuscripts themselves (apart from their contents), which is called palaeography, is a fascinating study, possible only to a few experts, but the results of which are indispensable for the scientific examination of the text of the New Testament. The material of which they are composed, the arrangement of sheets, columns, and so on, the style of handwriting, scholia or notes by the scribes, even the ink employed, can all help in the determination of their date, and sometimes of their place of origin.

But more important than all palaeographical details is the 'text' found in them. If the reader were to examine twenty manuscripts of, say, the First Gospel, he would find, in all probability, that no two of them were verbally identical throughout a single chapter. That is to say, their text would not be identical. Not one of them would contain a text exactly the same as what the evangelist wrote, but the object of textual criticism is to discover that as nearly as possible. If it were found that the manuscripts divided themselves into four groups, those in each group containing a text very similar to each other's, but with a good many marked differences from the text in the other groups, we should say that they presented four types of text. And if, on studying the history of the manuscripts, we found reason to believe that the four types of text represented more or less the forms in which the Gospel was read in four well-defined areas or districts, we should speak of them as 'local texts'. And that is, in fact, what we do find, as we shall see later on.

A printer can make a thousand copies of a book absolutely identical because each sheet is an impression of the same type. But when scribes copied manuscripts they were always subject to limitations of eye and hand. Add to that the fact that in the early days of writing there were numerous abbreviations, no spaces between the words, no small as distinct from capital letters, and practically no stops, and it will be seen that the opportunity for slips was very large. If we imagine the opening of this chapter to run:

THEREARESTILLREADERSOF T̄
BIB̄WHOSETHOUGHTSHAVENEV̄
B̄NCARRIĒTOANYSTAGEINITS

we get some idea of how a careless or sleepy scribe could go wrong. Jerome himself speaks of *librariis dormientibus* (Pref. to Vulg. Gospels). The following are among the commonest of purely clerical errors: Confusion between letters, e.g. *O* and *Θ*. Omission of a final word or letter before a clause or word beginning with the same word or letter, and conversely of an initial word or letter after a clause or word ending with the same word or letter ('Homoeoteleuton') i.e. the passing of the scribe's eye from words or letters in one sentence to the same words or letters in a subsequent sentence, omitting everything between. (The name implies that the words or letters stand at the end of a clause, but the same slip is often made in respect of words or letters which stand in any position.) 'Dittography', i.e. the accidental repetition of one or more letters. Transposition. The misunderstanding of an abbreviation; e.g. in Acts xiii. 23 cᴧᴛнⲣα ιнⲥοᴧνn was apparently abbreviated cᴧᴛнⲣαῑν or ⲥⲣ̄αῑν which a scribe read as cᴧᴛнⲣιαν or ⲥⲣ̄ιαν These have operated at all times, and the most conscientious and highly trained scribes never wholly escaped them.

But the great majority of corruptions had found their way into the text before the end of the third century, in a period during which a much more disturbing element was at work. The history of the Canon makes it clear that it was some time before the books of the New Testament came to be invested with a sacredness equal to that of the Old. If a scribe repro-

duced what he felt to be the exact sense that the writer intended, 'the reverence', as Hort says, 'paid to the apostolic
writings, even to the most highly and widely venerated among
them, was not of the kind that exacted a scrupulous jealousy
as to their text as distinguished from their substance'. So that
it was 'quite possible to intend nothing but faithful transcription, and yet to introduce changes due to interpretation of
sense'. Sometimes this took the form of a scarcely conscious
alteration, which was, from the scribe's point of view, an
emendation in order to preserve what he felt sure the writer
meant, but it did, in fact, depart from the writer's wording,
and often from his meaning. Often, though not as often as
von Soden imagined, a scribe familiar with a harmony like
Tatian's would be influenced by it. Let us picture an earnest-
minded Christian, say from Rome, visiting Antioch. He has
known the Third Gospel for the last year or two; he has heard
it read on Sundays, and loved and valued it, and knows parts
of it by heart. And he now, for the first time, hears the First
Gospel read, and obtains permission to make a copy of it.
When Matthew and Luke are very similar, he is in constant
danger of putting down the words from Luke that he knows by
heart, instead of looking word by word at the manuscript
before him, to be sure of preserving all the little differences, in
which he would not be greatly interested. Thus he carries
home a 'text' of Matthew which has been corrupted by
assimilation with Luke, and all the manuscripts which are
copied from his, and all which are in turn copied from them,
will carry on the corrupt text. Conversely, a Christian from
Antioch comes to Rome, and in copying Luke corrupts his
manuscript by assimilation in other passages, and those corruptions are handed on by other copyists. This kind of thing
happened with practically every copy made. Sometimes, too,
intentional alterations were made to 'improve' the narrative
even doctrinally.[1]

Assimilation, though the commonest, was not the only
source of corruption. The author might quote an Old Testament passage in a translation known to him, or might possibly translate it himself from the Hebrew, while the scribe

[1] Cf. C. S. C. Williams, *Alterations to the Text of the Synoptic Gospels and Acts.*

inadvertently put down the wording of the better-known LXX. Or the manuscript that was being copied contained an Old Testament sentence, and the scribe carelessly continued it to the extent of a few words because he knew the LXX passage by heart. Or he had heard some preacher tell a story about Jesus Christ, and when he found the same story in the manuscript that he was copying, he deliberately enriched it by some details or words from his own knowledge. The critical sense had not yet been born which would make people anxious to compare copies with the original to be sure of their accuracy. And when copies had begun to be made, perhaps on better papyrus, or more durable vellum, it was not thought worth while to preserve the original, which was very likely beginning to be faded or frayed, though to us it would be worth many times its weight in gold. Lastly, if a scribe had before him two manuscripts of the same writing, each with its different heritage of corruption, he would be convinced that they were both too valuable to disregard, and he would copy details from both, some right and some wrong, thus making a 'mixed' text which other copyists would perpetuate after him.

So the history of every book and chapter, almost of every verse, was a history of corruption. And the task of textual criticism is to discover these corruptions and by the scientific means known to modern scholars to try to arrive at a text as close as possible to that which the author wrote. It is obvious that the need for it is great. Very small, it is true, for that kind of reading of the New Testament which is by far the most important. We steep ourselves in it in order to know the great facts and doctrines of our religion, to obtain the spiritual food that comes from a devotional study of the words and deeds and character of our Lord, and of those who knew Him best. For that greatest of all purposes any text, or, for that matter, any translation, will suffice. But for an intellectual grasp even of these great things it is important, and for scientific, literary study it is essential, to search for the text of every verse and clause which is as far as possible free from corruptions. How much needs to be done can be realized from the fact that, apart from the more ancient papyri, the oldest Greek manuscripts that have come down to us are not earlier than the fourth century, and only two are earlier than the fifth. When the books had become canonical, accepted as sacred and inspired Scripture, they were copied with far greater care by expert scribes; but in the second and third centuries the care taken over them was nothing like so scrupulous, and most Christians were confined to the humbler classes and largely devoid of literary or clerical skill. Quotations by Christian writers, and translations of the books made before the fourth century, are often a help in determining the text of a given passage at that time and place, before later corruptions sprang up. But the copyists of these translations, and of the works of the Fathers, made mistakes in them of exactly the same kinds –clerical slips, errors of assimilation, and so on—requiring textual criticism of the versions and Fathers if they are to be of use in the textual criticism of the Greek manuscripts of the New Testament.

§ 2. THE MATERIAL

Before studying the methods which have been employed it is necessary to have some idea of the material at our disposal. In extent and variety it is many times as great as that for any other literature in the world.[1] That might seem to be favourable to an accurate knowledge of the original wording. And broadly speaking it is. For the great purposes of the Christian religion we may be confident that we possess a very close approximation to what was originally written, and that no future discoveries have the least chance of altering our New Testament in any essential. But in details of scientific study the multiplicity of the material offers complex problems which only a long succession of scholars can expect to solve.

The manuscripts here given are not in their alphabetical or numerical order, which has no relation to their value or date. They comprise only the more important ones, and are arranged in groups, the meaning of which will be explained later. The capital letters denote manuscripts written, as all Greek manuscripts of the New Testament were in the early centuries, in

[1] An introduction to one of the modern editions of the Greek text, such as A. Merk's or J. M. Bover's or A. Souter's (2nd ed., 1947), indicates the wealth of material and the *sigla* employed.

large letters like capitals, called Uncials; the numerals those written in the ordinary, small running hand, called Cursives or Minuscules; while small italic letters stand for the manuscripts of the Old Latin version. The cursives were mostly later in time than the Uncials, and date from the ninth century; but some of them are of greater value than some of the Uncials, having been copied from good early manuscripts. The grouping here indicated represents the general position which these manuscripts may be said to occupy in the distribution of texts. But it must be remembered that every one of them contains a larger or smaller proportion of readings which belong to other groups, some deeply affected by the Byzantine revision. The mention of some of them—only a few of the more important—implies only that readings characteristic of the group can be found in them in sufficient quantities to warrant their being placed as members of the group.

Gospels

(a) *Alexandrian*: B ℵ C L Δ (in Mk.) 33 Ψ T Z Ξ 579 (except Matt.) 892 1241 157 X and the following papyri, P¹ P³ P⁴ P⁵ P¹⁹ P²² P²⁸ P³⁵ P³⁹ P⁵⁵, and the Coptic versions, the Sahidic and Bohairic.

(b) *Eastern*: 1. '*Antiochene*': the old Syriac, extant in the Sinaitic and Curetonian MSS.
    2. '*Caesarean*': (i) P⁴⁵ W (in part) fam.¹ 28 fam.¹³ and (ii) Θ 565 700 P⁶(?) P³⁷.

(c) *Western*: 1. *African*: W (for Mk. i. 1–v. 30) *k* (Mk. Matt.) *e* and *c* (Mk. Lk.) [*m*].
    2. *European*: D *b a ff²h* (Matt.) *i r c* (Matt. Jn.) *nff g g² l q*.

Acts

(a) *Alexandrian*: B ℵ A C Ψ 33 81 P⁴⁵.

(b) *Eastern*(?): 181 307 88 1739 P⁸(?) P⁴¹(?).

(c) *Western*: (i) *African*: *h*(?) *p m* and citations in Cyprian and Augustine. (ii) *European*: D E₂ P²⁹ P³⁸ P⁴⁸ *gig g² s m t d* and the Harklean Syriac margin.

Pauline epistles

(a) *Alexandrian*: B ℵ A C I M P Ψ 17 1739 P¹⁰ P¹¹ P¹³ P¹⁴ P¹⁵ P¹⁶ P¹⁷ P²⁶ P²⁷ P³⁰ P³¹ P³² P³⁴ P⁴⁰ P⁴⁶ P⁴⁹ P⁵¹ P⁶¹.

(b) *Eastern*: H_3.
(c) *Western*: (i) *African*: No true representative. [m]. (ii) *European*: $D_2 F_2 G_3$.

Catholic epistles

(a) *Alexandrian*: B ℵ A C Ψ P_2 33 81 P^{20} P^{23} P^{54}.
(b) *Western*: h m ff s q and citations in Tertullian.

Apocalypse

A ℵ C P_2 (025) B_2 (046) 44 (051) 183 (052) 38 (2020) 95 (2040) P^{18} P^{24} P^{43} P^{47}.
African: h [m]. *European*: g.

Byzantine ('*Syrian*' or '*Antiochian*') representing on the whole the later, standardized or Antioch–Constantinople text: For the Gospels: A E S V; for Acts and the Epistles: $H_2 L_2 P_2$ (in Acts and 1 Pet.) and (except Acts) K_2. These may be mentioned as typical, but the revised text is to be found in several other uncials, and in the mass of cursives.

The *Versions*, other than those named above, will be described on pp. 408–13.

GOSPELS

(a) Alexandrian

Codex VATICANUS (B). This famous codex is in the Vatican library at Rome, and was already there when the first catalogue was made in 1475, the library having been founded by Pope Nicholas in 1448. It originally contained the whole Bible, but parts of both Testaments are now lost. From the New Testament are lacking part of Hebrews (from the middle of the word καθαριεῖ in ix. 14), 1, 2 Tim., Tit., Philem., Apoc. According to one series of its chapter divisions the Pauline epistles are treated as if they were one continuous book, and the figures show that in some earlier manuscript from which they were taken Hebrews stood after Galatians. Hort[1] says, 'The scribe reached by no means a high standard of accuracy, and on the other hand his slips are not proportionately numerous or bad'; and he goes on to describe them. Although it is not the age of a manuscript that is important but its text, it is

[1] Introd., p. 233.

of interest that B is the oldest known vellum codex of the New Testament, having been written in the fourth century. (A papyrus fragment of the first half of the second century has been found, P⁵².)

Its chapter divisions require a separate note. Eusebius divided each of the Gospels into little sections. These he numbered, and arranged tables consisting of parallel columns in which were placed the numbers of those sections in each Gospel dealing with the same event. This was equivalent to making a harmony of the Gospels without writing out all the sections at length. This division was based on a harmony, which is lost to us, made by Ammonius of Alexandria on the basis of Matthew. It has been noticed that the chapter divisions in cod. B ℵ (partly) Ξ 579 seem to be the remains of a scheme which appears to have belonged originally to such a harmony; and A. Schmidtke in his edition of codex 579 (Leipzig, 1903) suggests that it was that of Ammonius. And accepting the view that B represents the Hesychian revision (see p. 434), he thinks that Hesychius may have extended the system of Ammonius. The latter, in basing his harmony on Matthew, omitted a good deal of material in the other Gospels, and Hesychius preserved his divisions but went on, with less care and minuteness, to divide the passages which Ammonius had not used. But when the separate Gospels were written in full, the apparatus for the harmony was of no further use, and, when considered apart from the original scheme, the length of the several divisions was very different. Eusebius, therefore, made a new division into chapters and subdivisions to combine the usefulness of the Ammonian harmony with the presentation of the separate Gospels. Lake[1] thinks that though this is not proved, it is very likely true. At any rate a harmony lies behind B ℵ, their relationship to which is somewhat analogous to that of the sin. and cur. Syriac MSS. to the Diatessaron.

Codex SINAITICUS (ℵ). Discovered by Tischendorf in the monastery of St. Catherine on Mt. Sinai in separate pieces in 1844 and 1859, finally published by him and presented by the monks of Sinai to the Czar of Russia in 1862. It was bought in 1933 from the Soviet Government for the British Museum for

---

[1] *J.T.S.* vii, 1905–6, pp. 292 ff.

£100,000. It contained the whole Bible, with the addition of *Ep. Barnabas* and a mutilated fragment of the *Shepherd* of Hermas, written in four columns to a page. It suffered from the hands of a succession of correctors, and illustrates the process of conforming manuscripts to the Byzantine standard (see pp. 430 f.). Of the seven detected by Tischendorf the third (ℵ^c or ℵ$^{c.a.}$) has an importance of his own, since he has written a colophon at the end of Esther stating that the manuscript had been collated with a copy which had itself been corrected by the hand of the holy martyr Pamphilus. His corrections thus have a connexion with the Eastern text. The codex belongs to the fourth, or perhaps the fifth, century.

Codex EPHRAEMI rescriptus (C). In the National Library at Paris. This is a palimpsest, as the Latin participle in the title indicates, i.e. a manuscript from which the original writing was almost erased by a later scribe who used it as material for another writing. A twelfth-century scribe wrote over it a Greek translation of thirty-eight tractates of Ephraem the Syrian. Before it was mutilated it contained the whole Greek Bible. It now contains portions of the Old Testament, and considerable fragments of every book of the New except 2 Thessalonians and 2 John. It is written in one column to a page, which became the usual practice. As in the case of ℵ, correctors endeavoured to bring it into conformity with the Byzantine standard. Tischendorf speaks of two, whose work, however, affected Matthew and Luke more than Mark and John. Codex C, with L and the Boh., shows the most characteristic forms of grammatical and stylistic correction which Hort classed as Alexandrian and thought might be the work of the reviser Hesychius (see p. 431). At the same time C has a good deal of mixture with the Western text. It belongs to the early fifth century.

Codex REGIUS (L). In the National Library at Paris. Two columns to a page. Contains the Four Gospels, with small lacunae in each of them except the Third. It is badly written by a scribe who was perhaps ignorant of Greek, a feature which, as Streeter[1] points out, is noticeable in other important manuscripts which have a large non-Byzantine element, e.g.

---

[1] *The Four Gospels*, p. 2.

D Δ 28, and still more conspicuously Θ; he thinks that they must have been written in out-of-the-way places, where the Byzantine revision had not yet, or had only recently, penetrated. Next to B ℵ it is the most important witness to the Alexandrian text of the Gospels, the Byzantine infusion being found chiefly in Matt. i–xviii; Mk. i, ii. It belongs to the eighth century.

Codex SANGALLENSIS (Δ). In the monastery of St. Gall, where it was probably written; but it was perhaps brought thither by an Irish scribe of the ninth century. One column to a page. Contains the Four Gospels, with a short lacuna in John xix. It is a Graeco-Latin manuscript, the Latin being written between the lines of the Greek. The Latin is of little value, except for the occasional Old Latin readings which it preserves; it is mainly Vulgate with some assimilations to the Greek. And the Greek is of interest only in Mark, especially chs. iii–xii, where the text is closely allied with that of the C L 33 group; in the other Gospels it is mostly Byzantine with a few earlier readings. It belongs to the ninth century or possibly later.

CODEX 33 (= Acts 13, Paul. 17). In the National Library at Paris. One column to a page. Contains the New Testament except the Apocalypse. This manuscript, which Eichhorn called 'the Queen of Cursives', is a great deal more valuable than many of the Uncials, because in spite of many Byzantine, and some 'Western', readings it sides, on the whole, with the foregoing manuscripts, and is thus the best cursive that we possess containing an Alexandrian type of Gospel text. It belongs to the ninth century.

Codex LAURENSIS (Ψ). In the Laura on Mt. Athos. One column to a page. It originally contained the New Testament except the Apocalypse, but has lost Matthew and Mark i–ix. 5 (to σοὶ μίαν), and one page of Hebrews. The Catholic epistles are in the curious order Pet., Jas., Jn., Jude. The whole of it except Mark has been more or less corrected into conformity with the Byzantine text. In Mark, on the other hand, the fundamental text is later Alexandrian of the C L 33 type, with a few Byzantine readings, but also[1] some Western readings of

[1] Lake, *J.T.S.* i, 1900, pp. 290 ff.

an early, pre-Origenistic type, which hold somewhat the same textual position as the Western elements in Clem. Alex. In the other Gospels there is a rather larger proportion of Alexandrian readings than in Δ. It probably belongs to the eighth century.

Codex BORGIANUS (T). In Rome at the College De Propaganda Fide. Two columns to a page. It is a remarkable manuscript in more ways than one. It is Graeco-Sahidic, containing fragments of Lk. xxii, xxiii; Jn. vi–viii, of which the Greek has preserved a little more than the Sahidic. The text is Alexandrian, and the presence of the Sahidic is one of the proofs that this type of text belongs to Egypt. It is valuable in that it stands even nearer to B than to א, so that if we possessed more of it than these fragments, it would probably rank next to B as a primary authority for the early Alexandrian text. It belongs to the fifth century.

Codex DUBLINENSIS (Z). In the library of Trinity College, Dublin. One column to a page. It is a palimpsest containing fragments of Matthew amounting to about one-third of the Gospel, the upper writing being various patristic passages. The text is valuable, having a close affinity with that of א. It belongs to the sixth, or possibly the fifth, century.

Codex ZACYNTHIUS (Ξ). In London, the property of the British and Foreign Bible Society; obtained from the island of Zacynthus, and presented to the Society in 1820. It possesses chapter-divisions found in B and 579. It belongs to the eighth century.

CODEX 579. In the National Library at Paris. One column to a page. Contains the Four Gospels, but lacking Jn. xx. 15–xxi. 25. In Matthew it has an ordinary Byzantine text; but in the other Gospels it affords a good instance of the possibility of a late cursive having a high value. It belongs to the thirteenth century, but is probably copied directly from a sixth-century Uncial[1] which was thoroughly Alexandrian, without being more markedly akin to one manuscript than to another in the main group. Its non-Byzantine readings, therefore, which are most numerous in Luke, have all the value of the

---

[1] So A. Schmidtke, *Die Evangelien eines alten Uncialcodex*, 1903; cited by Streeter.

text of its Uncial parent. 'The value of a MS. of this kind', as Streeter says, 'appears where it supports a reading of B, ℵ, or L, which is otherwise unsupported.'

CODEX 892. In the British Museum. One column to a page. Contains the Four Gospels, but lacking John x. 6–12, 18; xiv. 24–xxi. 25. Like the foregoing it has suffered a large amount of Byzantine admixture, but the basis of its text is Alexandrian, which, as frequently, is best preserved in Mark. It belongs to the ninth or tenth century.

CODEX 1241 (= Acts 290, Paul. 338). In the monastery at Mt. Sinai. Contains the whole New Testament, with a text somewhat similar to that of the foregoing. It belongs to the twelfth, thirteenth, or fourteenth century.

CODEX 157. In the Vatican Library at Rome. One column to a page. Contains the Four Gospels. It is to be noted that although it was made for the Emperor its text is not simply the standard Byzantine, but is Alexandrian to much the same extent as the three preceding manuscripts. At the same time points of contact have been found between it and the Palestinian Syriac (Syr.[hier]) on the one hand and the text of Marcion on the other. It contains a colophon at the end of each of the Gospels stating that it was 'copied and corrected from the ancient exemplars from Jerusalem preserved on the Holy Mountain', i.e. probably Sinai. This is found in the compound half-Uncial, half-Cursive MS. Λ–566, and in several cursives of little value. It was made for John II Comnenus in the twelfth century.

Codex MONACENSIS (X). In the University Library at Munich. Two columns to a page. Contains two fragments of the Four Gospels, in the order Jn., Lk., Mk., Matt., with patristic comments on each of them except Mark, which illustrates the noticeable fact of the small attention paid to Mark as compared with the others. A few notable readings are to be found in it of the later Alexandrian type. It belongs to the end of the tenth century.

P[1] is a third- or fourth-century papyrus codex, Oxyrhynchus Pap. 2. It gives a fragment of the text of Matt. i. P[3] is a fifth- or sixth-century lectionary codex[1] giving fragments of Lk. vii

---

[1] C. Wessely, *Wiener Studien*, iv. 198 ff.

and x. P⁴ is a fourth-century lectionary codex[1] giving parts of Lk. i–vi. P⁵ is a third-century (lectionary?) papyrus, Ox. Papyri 208 and 1781, giving fragments of Jn. i, xvi, and xx.[2] P¹⁹ is a fifth-century codex, Ox. Pap. 1170, giving parts of Matt. x. 32–xi. 5. P²² is a late third-century roll, Ox. Pap. 1228, having fragments of Jn. xv. 25–xvi. 32. P²⁸ is a fourth-century codex, Ox. Pap. 1596, with fragments of Jn. vi. P³⁵ is a seventh-century codex, having fragments of Matt. xxv.[3] P³⁹ is a fourth-century codex, Ox. Pap. 1780, having part of Jn. viii. 14–22.[4] P⁵⁵ is a sixth-century codex, *Pap. Gr. Vindob.* 26214, having fragments of Jn. i.[5]

The Coptic version in the SAHIDIC and BOHAIRIC dialects (called by Hort Thebaic and Memphitic respectively) of southern and northern Egypt. The former contains fragments of all the books of the New Testament, except Titus and Philemon; the latter contains the whole New Testament, in the order Gospels, Pauline epp., Catholic epp., Acts, Apocalypse. But in both forms of the version the last book is treated as occupying an inferior position, which may perhaps have been due to the criticisms passed on it by Dionysius of Alexandria. Since St. Antony is said to have heard the Gospels read in church in the vernacular when he was a boy, Egypt (if the tradition is correct) must have had a version of them at least by the middle of the third century, if not by the end of the second. And Hort claimed this date for the versions that have come down to us, supporting thereby the high antiquity of the B text. Many scholars were doubtful whether the Bohairic version was older than the seventh or eighth century, however, though some of them have revised their opinion since Sir Herbert Thompson[6] published a fifth-century manuscript of John written in sub-Akhmimic. The Sahidic version, according

---

[1] V. Scheil, *Revue Biblique*, i, 1892, pp. 198–214 and J. Merell, ibid. xlvii, 1938, pp. 1–22, cf. M. J. Lagrange, *Critique textuelle*, pp. 118–24.

[2] Cf. C. Wessely, *Patrologia Orientalis*, iv. 142–4.

[3] *Papiri Greci e Latini*, i. 1, ed. G. Vitelli, 1912.

[4] Cf. Lagrange, *Revue Biblique*, xxxv, 1926, p. 90.

[5] P. Sanz, *Griechische literarische Papyri christlichen Inhaltes*, i (1946), pp. 58 f.. For fuller information about the papyri see G. Maldfeld and B. M. Metzger, *Journal of Biblical Literature*, lxviii, 1949, pp. 359–70.

[6] *The Gospel of John according to the earliest Coptic Manuscript*, 1924, cf. his *The Coptic Version of the Acts and the Pauline Epistles in the Sahidic Dialect*, 1932.

to most modern scholars, dates from the third to the fourth centuries, though Thompson and Horner urge a second-century date. The latter[1] published anonymously both versions, with an apparatus which still remains an indispensable supplement to Tischendorf's *octava maior*, for its evidence not only of the Coptic manuscripts but also of the Syriac, Armenian, and Ethiopic versions. The comparative purity of the Coptic text is explained by Tischendorf as due, first, to the schism between the Jacobites and the Melchites, then to the Arab pressure, a century and a half later, which began to thrust out the Coptic language, and lastly to the critical care of scholars in Egypt in the twelfth century.

Besides these there are fragments of Middle-Egyptian versions, Fayyumic, Memphitic, and Akhmimic manuscripts having been found.[2]

(b) Eastern

(1) 'Antiochene'

The most important witness to the Eastern[3] text is not a Greek manuscript but the Old Syriac version, which has reached us in two manuscripts.

SINAITIC SYRIAC. This is a manuscript of what was called the *Evangelion da-Mepharreshe*, 'The Evangel of the Separated ones', i.e. the Four Gospels as separate writings, not combined into a harmony such as the *Diatessaron* of Tatian. It is a palimpsest, the upper writing consisting of lives of saints written in 778, discovered by Mrs. Lewis[4] and Mrs. Gibson of Cambridge in the convent of St. Catherine on Mt. Sinai in 1892, from which year till 1897 successive transcriptions and photographs were taken. It appears to have been written at some place near Antioch, possibly Edessa, though it is uncertain whether the translation itself belonged to Antioch or Palestine

[handwritten margin note: Sinaitic Syriac seems to be earlier than the 5th c.]

---

[1] *The Coptic versions of the New Testament*, 1898–1924.

[2] Cf. M. M. Parvis and A. P. Wikgren, *New Testament Manuscript Studies*, 1950, pp. 35–38.

[3] The term 'Eastern' is misleading if it implies that the Old Syriac version is not closely related to the 'Western' text, which it is, though it does not contain the more obvious 'Western' vagaries. Syr.cur is inferior to Syr.sin as a witness to this type of text in the East.

[4] *The Old Syriac Gospels*, 1910; cf. F. C. Burkitt, *Evangelion da-Mepharreshe*, 1904.

(see pp. 436 f.). It contains some Georgian signatures, and formed part of a collection of manuscripts which found its way to Mt. Sinai. Two columns to a page. Contains the Four Gospels in the usual order. It seems to be earlier than the fifth century.

CURETONIAN SYRIAC. So called because it was first edited by Dr. Cureton in 1858. There are 82½ leaves in the British Museum and 3 at Berlin. It came from the library of the Convent of St. Mary Deipara in the Natron valley, west of Cairo, to which it was presented by the monk Habibai.

Eighty of the surviving leaves reached England in 1842 as part of a volume of the Gospels made up in the year A.D. 1222 from various MSS. of the same size; the other leaves of the volume were taken from copies of the Peshitta, and the binder hardly seems to have been aware that the text of *C* was different from the rest. The remaining leaves came to Europe as fly-leaves to strengthen the bindings of other books. . . . Two more detached leaves reached the British Museum in 1847.[1]

Two columns to a page. Contains fragments of the Four Gospels in the unusual order Matt., Mk., Jn., Lk., the only fragment of Mark (xvi. 17b–20) being followed immediately by John on the same page. It cannot be later than the early part of the fifth century.

The date of the Old Syriac version and its precise relation to Tatian's *Diatessaron* are still matters of dispute.[2]

(2) *'Caesarean'*

It is to B. H. Streeter more than anyone that credit is due for the emergence of a theory that a textual family existed other than the Alexandrian and Western, though related somehow to both, and other than the Byzantine, however much he was indebted to the work of others like Ferrar and Lake before him for the isolation and grouping of certain minuscules like the fam.[13] and the fam.[1] groups (see below) respectively. He thought that the Koridethi MS. Θ (see below) stood at the head of this family and that 28, 565, and 700 with fam.[1] and fam.[13] and W for Mark (after v. 30) provided secondary

[1] Ibid., p. 7.
[2] Cf. Parvis and Wikgren, op. cit., pp. 27 ff. See also A. Vööbus, *Theologische Zeitschrift*, vii, 1951, pp. 30–38.

support, believing most emphatically that von Soden had erred greatly in putting D in close conjunction with Θ. He examined Origen's citations in his commentary on John, the first five books of which were written in Alexandria, but the rest in Caesarea where he made his home after A.D. 231. Streeter thought that in its first ten books this commentary has an Alexandrian text for Mark, while Origen's later works, such as the Exhortation to Martyrdom and the commentary on Matthew, give a text resembling that of Θ. This he took to be proof that Origen had used an Alexandrian text in Alexandria and for a short time at Caesarea, and a 'Caesarean' or Θ text at Caesarea. His *Four Gospels* appeared in 1924; and when the Chester Beatty papyrus of the Gospels (P⁴⁵) was discovered in 1930 and published[1] in 1933, and when its readings of Mark were seen to support many of the manuscripts of this family, if one disregarded their variants which appeared to be Byzantine intrusions, it seemed as though Streeter's hypothesis had been brilliantly vindicated.

But in the meantime a most thorough examination[2] of all the relevant evidence had been conducted by K. Lake, R. P. Blake, and S. New (Mrs. Lake), whose work indicated that while the manuscripts concerned are related, they are far from being homogeneous, and that the patristic evidence in fact leads to the conclusion that Origen used a 'Caesarean' text at Alexandria, later also an Alexandrian text at Caesarea, and then a Caesarean text there. When it is remembered that papyri of a 'Western' as well as of a 'Caesarean' character have been found in Egypt, at least for Acts, it will be seen that Streeter's 'local texts' have lost their clear-cut divisions. Further, when it was observed that P⁴⁵ sometimes supports 'Byzantine' readings almost alone, though it was written, of course, long before the Byzantine revision was made, doubt was thrown on the whole method of excising 'Byzantine' readings from manuscripts of this group and of concentrating solely on the remainder.

---

[1] *The Chester Beatty Biblical Papyri*, Fasc. ii, 1933, ed. Sir F. G. Kenyon.

[2] 'The Caesarean Text of the Gospel of Mark', *Harvard Theol. Rev.*, xxi, 1928, pp. 207–404; cf. B. M. Metzger, *Journal of Biblical Literature*, lxiv, 1945, pp. 457–89; T. Ayuso, *Biblica*, xvi, 1935, pp. 369–415.

Caesarean (handwritten marginal note)

For the present it may be well to regard the members of this group as those of a clan rather than of a family and to suppose that they came up out of Egypt into Palestine, where they had a local influence at first, which spread later, perhaps, owing to Origen himself and the scribes in the library of Pamphilus at Caesarea as far as to Armenia and to Georgia. There is as yet no certain proof that a 'Caesarean' text of any part of the New Testament ever existed beyond the Gospels, and even for the Gospels themselves it may be that the origin of this clan did not lie in one particular manuscript but in several attempts made by a few Egyptian scribes to compromise between Alexandrian and the 'Western' texts known to them. Any hopes based upon Streeter's work[1] that here we should find a pre-Byzantine textual type independent of and as valuable as the 'Western' and the Alexandrian seem now very remote.

Following the suggestion of T. Ayuso,[2] some of the 'Caesarean' clan may be regarded as pre-Caesarean and the rest 'Caesarean' proper. To the former would belong P[45] W (partly) fam.[1] 28 and fam.[13] P[45] is a third-century codex, containing parts of Matt. xx, xxi, xxv–xxvi, Mk. iv–xii, Lk. vi–xiv and Jn. x–xi.[3]

The FREER codex (W), in Washington, was probably written in Egypt; it was bought from an Arab dealer in 1906. It has one column to a page. It contains the Gospels in the order Matt., Jn., Lk., Mk., which is characteristic of Western manuscripts till Jerome. It lacks Jn. xiv. 26–xvi. 7 and Mk. xv. 12–38. The text differs so widely in different parts that Lagrange calls it Protean. Its editor, H. A. Sanders,[4] suggested that its ancestor was a composite book made up of several rolls of the Gospels which were saved in the time of Diocletian's persecution, when the emperor tried to suppress Christianity by destroying its sacred books. He also suggested that it represents the Greek column of a trilingual, originally Greek–Latin–Syriac, the Syriac being replaced later by a Cop.[sah] version. It seems probable that there are traces of Syriac influence upon

---

[1] *The Four Gospels*, p. 84.

[2] Loc. cit.

[3] With Kenyon's edition compare M. J. Lagrange, *Revue Biblique*, xliii, 1934, pp. 1–41.

[4] *Facsimile of the Washington Manuscript . . .*, 1912.

the text.[1] While in Mk. i. 1–v. 30 its text is strikingly Western, affording the only Greek evidence of a text akin to that of African Latin manuscripts, in Mk. v. 31–end, according to Streeter, it is Caesarean. (Lagrange's figures[2] suggest, however, that here W was akin to a Western text.) In Mk. xvi it has after verse 14 the 'Freer Logion' inserted into the Longer Ending and hitherto known, only in part, from a citation by Jerome.[3] Lk. i–viii. 12 is mainly Alexandrian. Jn. i–v. 11 does not appear to have belonged to the original manuscript; it is written on different parchment by a different hand. For the textual affinities of the various parts of W the reader should consult Lagrange's *Critique textuelle*. W is probably a fifth-century manuscript.

The group of cursives or minuscules 1–118–131–209 was shown by K. Lake[4] to be derived, in the Gospels, from a common ancestor; other cursives have been found akin to these: 22, 1582, 872 (in Mk.), 1278, and 2193.

28, of the eleventh century, contains the Gospels with lacunae in all but Mk., where its readings are chiefly valuable.

FAM.[13] denotes another group of cursives, 13–69–124–346, which W. H. Ferrar and T. K. Abbott collated. Apart from 124, they were brought to Calabria. They possess a stichometric reckoning of ῥήματα, which occurs in a series of Syriac manuscripts, the earliest of which is of the ninth century. The most important manuscripts of this group are 69[5] and 124: E. A. Hutton[6] showed that anything of value in the readings of this 'family' is to be found in either the one or the other. Other cursives have been added to the group since the first four were edited: 230–543–788–826[7]–828–983–1689–1709.

The Koridethi codex (Θ) was discovered by Bartholoméen the church of St. Kerykos and Julitta at Koridethi, which

---

[1] Cf. C. S. C. Williams, *J.T.S.* xlii, 1941, pp. 177 f.

[2] *Critique textuelle*, p. 147.

[3] C. S. C. Williams, *Alterations to the Text of the Synoptic Gospels and Acts*, pp. 42 f.

[4] 'Codex 1 of the Gospels and its Allies', *Texts and Studies*, vii, 1902.

[5] See T. K. Abbott, *The Origin of the Leicester Codex . . .*, 1887. Manuscripts of the same scribe are known, Emmanuel of Constantinople, which is a link with the East (*J.T.S.* v, 1904, pp. 445 ff.).   [6] *J.T.S.* xii, 1910–11, p. 621.

[7] On 826–828 see K. Lake, *J.T.S.* i, 1900, pp. 117 ff.; for fam.[13] as a whole see K. and S. Lake, *Studies and Documents*, xi, 1941.

lies in a high valley in the district of the Swaneten in the west of Caucasia. It is now at Tiflis. It was written probably by a Syrian scribe who knew little Greek, in two columns to a page. It has the four Gospels in the usual order but lacks Matt. i. 1–9, 21–25; ii–iv. 4; iv. 17–v. 4. It was edited by G. Beermann and C. R. Gregory in 1913 with a study of the history of the manuscript as gleaned from numerous marginal notes in different dates in Greek and Gruse, which fix its date between the seventh and ninth centuries.

For 565 and 700 see Streeter, op. cit., p. 574.

Two papyri may belong to the Caesarean group, P⁶ and P³⁷: P⁶ is a fragment of Jn. x and xi on a fifth- or sixth-century codex.[1] P³⁷ is a third-century codex having part of Matt. xxvi. 19–52.[2]

(c) Western

(1) African

The Freer codex (W), which for Mk. i. 1–v. 30 has a Western text has been described above.

Codex BOB(B)IENSIS (k) is at Turin; it is extant only for Mk. viii–xvi, Matt. i–xv. It is by far the most important Old Latin manuscript, containing a text closely akin to that of Cyprian's citations, whence the name 'African' given to this type of text. It belongs to the fourth or fifth century. Mme A. Bakker has published a study (1933) and a collation (1938) of it.[3] F. C. Burkitt valued very highly those readings of k which it shares with Syr.ˢⁱⁿ, as a reaction from Westcott and Hort's reliance on the B ℵ text.

Codex PALATINUS (e) of which parts are in Trent, Dub- lin, and London, contains portions of the Four Gospels in a text which is somewhat later African Latin than k, with a slight European admixture. It belongs to the fifth century. The best edition is that of H. J. Vogels, 1926.[4]

Codex COLBERTINUS (c). In Paris. Contains the Four

---

[1] F. Rönsch, *Bruchstücke des 1 Clemensbriefes* . . ., 1910, pp. 144–6.

[2] H. A. Sanders, *Harvard Theol. Rev.* xix, 1926, pp. 215–26; cf. M. J. Lagrange, *Critique textuelle, I*, pp. 157 f. and *Revue Biblique*, xxxii, 1929, pp. 161–77. The latter is more definitely 'Caesarean'.

[3] Cf. J. Wordsworth, *Old Latin Biblical Texts*, ii, 1886, cf. *J.T.S.* v, 1903, p. 88, and xxvii, 1925–6, pp. 91 ff.

[4] Cf. A. Souter, *J.T.S.* xxiii, 1922, pp. 284–6.

Gospels. Its text in Mark and Luke is about half Old Latin and half Vulgate, the former approximating to an African type.[1] It belongs to the twelfth century.

The SPECULUM (*m*). At Rome. This is not a New Testament manuscript, but a collection of passages from the whole New Testament which used to be ascribed to Augustine. Its text has some affinity with that of Priscillian, and it may be of Spanish origin. It belongs to the eighth or ninth century.

(ii) *European*

Codex BEZAE (D). At Cambridge. A Graeco-Latin manuscript containing the Four Gospels in the order Matt., Jn., Lk., Mk. (with lacunae), and the Acts, but at one time it contained also the Catholic epistles. These stood, curiously, before the Acts; the Latin has preserved the last five verses of 3 John with the subscription 'epistulae Johannis III explicit incipit Actus apostolorum'. Jude, therefore, either was absent or stood in an earlier place. The Greek is on the left-, the Latin on the right-hand page, the former being the place of honour. It contains one column to a page, and the lines consist of *cola*, or short clauses according to the sense, so that the corresponding words in the Greek and the Latin could more easily be kept parallel. And a curious feature of the script is that the Greek letters are formed in such a way that they somewhat resemble the Latin. Providing the only complete Greek 'Western' text of the Gospels, it has given rise to a whole literature on this text.[2]

It was given to the University of Cambridge by the reformer Beza in 1581, who succeeded Calvin as head of the Church at Geneva. When he gave it he said that it had been found in 1562 in the monastery of Irenaeus at Lyons. But some years later he wrote in his notes on the New Testament that it was found in the monastery at Clermont, at no great distance, and he named it Codex Claromontanus, which is the title given to the MS. D$_2$ of the Pauline epistles, which also belonged to him. The similarity of its text to that of Irenaeus (noted by Sanday and Turner, *Novum Testamentum S. Iren.*, 1923) is in favour of

---

[1] Cf. F. C. Burkitt, *J.T.S.* ix, 1908, pp. 307 ff.

[2] Cf. A. F. J. Klijn, *A Survey of the Researches into the Western Text of the Gospels and Acts*, 1949.

the south of France as its original home. But it contains certain lection marks which Brightman[1] holds to be Byzantine, and to point to south Italy where the Byzantine use was followed. Kenyon,[2] however, says

the chief objection to this theory is that Greek was so well known in that region that we should have expected the Greek part of the MS. to be better than it is. In point of fact, the Greek has the appearance of having been written by a scribe whose native language was Latin; and some of the mistakes which he makes (e.g. writing *l* for *λ* or *c* for *κ*) point in the same direction. We want a locality where Latin was the prevalent tongue, but Greek was still sufficiently known to make it desirable to have copies of the Scriptures in their original language as well as in a translation.

Two or three localities would suit the requirements better than south Italy, but certainty is at present impossible. A. C. Clark favoured an Egyptian origin or a Palestinian.[3] E. A. Lowe[4] gives reasons for thinking that it was already in Lyons in the ninth century. It belongs to the fifth century.

Codex VERONENSIS (*b*). At Verona. Contains the Gospels (with lacunae) in the Western order, as in D.[5] H. J. White says, '*b*, indeed, seems to be almost a typically European manuscript; as the other manuscripts of European and of Italian origin, such as *a f h i q r*, all resemble *b* more closely than they resemble each other'.[6] It belongs to the fifth century.

Codex VERCELLENSIS (*a*). Among the relics at the cathedral of Vercelli, and traditionally said to have been written by Eusebius of Vercelli. Contains the Gospels (with lacunae) in the Western order, as in D. Its text stands between those of *b* and *k*, containing many African readings, and is farthest from *b* in Mark, where it may be said to contain a text which is neither the typical European of *b* nor African. Souter

---

[1] *J.T.S.* i, 1900, pp. 446 ff.
[2] *Handbook to the Textual Criticism of the N.T.*, p. 75.
[3] *The Acts of the Apostles*, 1933, pp. lxii f.
[4] *J.T.S.* xxv, 1924, pp. 270 ff.
[5] This order is found also in W (see above) and several O.L. manuscripts. It is stated in the 'Monarchian Prologues' to the Gospels to be the order in the official Canon.
[6] *O.L. Bibl. Texts*, vol. iii, 1888, p. xxii.

holds that (at least in Lk.) it was the type of text used by Jerome for his revision.[1] It belongs to the fourth century.

Codex CORBEIENSIS (ff^2). At Paris. Contains the Gospels (with lacunae in all but Mk.) in our usual order. Its text is nearest to that of b. Belongs to the fifth or sixth century.

Codex CLAROMONTANUS (h). In the Vatican. Contains the Gospels; Matthew mutilated. In Matthew alone it has an O.L. text; in the other Gospels it is Vulgate. It belongs to the sixth century.

Codex VINDOBONENSIS (i). At Vienna, formerly at Naples. A purple vellum manuscript containing only parts of Luke and Mark (in that order). It belongs to the fifth or sixth century.

Codex USSERIANUS (r). At Trinity College, Dublin. Contains the Gospels in the Western order, as in D. It belongs to the sixth century.

Codex COLBERTINUS (c). See above. Its text is of a European type in Matthew and John.

Codex SANGALLENSIS (n) and (two leaves) CURIENSIS (formerly called a^2). At St. Gall and Chur respectively. The former[2] contains parts of Matt., Jn., Mk., the latter of Lk., all fragments of the same manuscript, whose text stands closest to that of a. It belongs to the fifth century.

Codex CORBEIENSIS (ff). At Leningrad. Contains Matthew only. Its text is mostly Vulgate, and more so after ch. ix. It may be a manuscript fundamentally Vulgate into which O.L. readings found their way (Hort), or it may exhibit a transmission from a 'Gallican' to a Vulgate text (Gregory). It belongs to the tenth century.

Codex SANGERMANENSIS (g). At Paris. Contains the Gospels. Only in Matthew is it O.L., the rest being mostly Vulgate. Hort thought the whole to be of the same character as the last, but Wordsworth regarded the text of Matthew as mixed O.L., in many respects peculiar, but occasionally corrected to the Vulgate. It belongs to the eighth century.

Codex SANGERMANENSIS (g^2). At Paris. Contains the Gospels, written, apparently, by an Irish hand. There is a

---

[1] *J.T.S.* xii, 1910–11, pp. 583–97.
[2] See Burkitt, *J.T.S.* v, 1904, p. 106.

similar difference of opinion regarding the whole manuscript
between Hort and Wordsworth. It belongs to the tenth
century.

Codex REHDIGERANUS (*l*). At Breslau, in the church of
St. Elizabeth. Contains the Gospels, but lacking Jn. xvi.
13–xxi. 25. Hort, as in the case of the three foregoing
manuscripts, thought it was a Vulgate MS. into which O.L.
readings had intruded. Its value is almost confined to Luke
and John. It belongs to the early eighth century.

Codex MONACENSIS (*q*). At Munich. Contains the Gospels
(with lacunae) in the Western order, as in D. Its text is
similar to that of *f*, but with some approximation to the true
European type of *b*. It belongs to the sixth century. On *f* see
pp. 442 f.

There are other fragments, some of them extending to only
a few verses; but the above form the main part of the O.L.
material.[1]

ACTS

(*a*) *Alexandrian*

B אּ *and C* have been described above. J. H. Ropes printed
the text of B opposite that of D in his edition, *Beginnings of
Christianity*, Pt. I, vol. iii, 1926.

A, Codex ALEXANDRINUS: see below under 'Byzantine'
cf. Ropes, op. cit., pp. li–lv.

Ψ, Codex LAURENSIS, in the monastery of the Laura on
Mount Athos, belongs to the eighth or ninth century, cf.
K. Lake, *J.T.S.* i, 1899–1900, pp. 290–2 (see above).

81, in the British Museum, written in A.D. 1044, has parts
of Acts i–iv, vii–xvii, and xxiii, cf. Scrivener, *Codex Augiensis*,
1859, pp. 415–53.

33, of the ninth or tenth century; see above.

P[45], see above, belongs to the Alexandrian family for Acts,
cf. Sir F. G. Kenyon, *The Chester Beatty Biblical Papyri*, Fasc. ii,
1933, p. xviii; cf. M. J. Lagrange, *Revue Biblique*, xliii, 1934,
pp. 164–71. It contains parts of Acts iv–xvii. Its most striking

---

[1] For further information about editions of the above manuscripts see M. J.
Lagrange, *Critique textuelle*, pp. 240 ff., cf. C. S. C. Williams, *Alterations to the
Text of the Gospels and Acts*, pp. ix ff.

variant[1] is the omission of καὶ τῆς πορνείας but not of πνικτοῦ in xv. 20.

Jerome may also witness to an Alexandrian text.[2]

(b) Eastern

181, an eleventh-century codex at the Vatican, contains the Acts and Epistles, with the Apocalypse as a later addition. A 'Euthalian' manuscript (see below), it was used by Zacagni as the basis of his edition of the Euthalian Acts and Epistles.

307, a codex of the tenth or eleventh century at Paris, has some connexion with the ancient text of the East, for both it and the next manuscript contain a colophon stating that it (i.e. an ancestor) was compared (or collated) with a codex of Pamphilus at Caesarea.

88, a tenth-century codex at Naples, cf. cod. 307.

1739, a tenth-century codex on Mt. Athos, was written by a scribe, Ephraim, who may have had access to a critical edition of the New Testament made at Caesarea according to manuscripts and Fathers preserved in the library of Pamphilus at Caesarea, cf. E. von der Goltz, *Texte und Untersuchungen*, xvii, 1899; also K. Lake, J. de Zwaan, and M. S. Enslin, *Six Collations of New Testament Manuscripts*, 1932.

P[8], a fourth-century papyrus fragment of a roll possibly rather than a codex, is usually regarded as supporting the Alexandrian text (e.g. M. J. Lagrange, *Critique textuelle*, p. 416). But the variant readings oscillate between B and D in such a way that the question has been asked[3] whether this papyrus is not rather a 'Caesarean' one, if a 'Caesarean' text of Acts ever existed as it did in a sense for the Gospels.

The same question might be asked of P[41], which is 'probably a twelfth- to thirteenth-century papyrus' (J. H. Ropes), printed by C. Wessely (*Studien zur Paläographie und Papyruskunde*, xv, 1914, pp. 107–18). Though it agrees with B in xix. 14, 15, and 16, xx. 12, 38, yet it agrees with the 'Western' text, xix. 3, xx. 15, 24, xxi. 1 (Myra).

The relationship for Acts between 181 307 88 917 1874

---

[1] Cf. C. S. C. Williams, op. cit., pp. 72–75.

[2] J. H. Ropes, op. cit., pp. cxxvii ff., thinks that Jerome's Latin Vulgate text of Acts was derived largely from a manuscript akin to B ℵ A C 81.

[3] Cf. C. S. C. Williams, op. cit., pp. 87 f.

1898 1829 431 307 36 610 453 and 1739 and the papyri P⁸ and P⁴¹ needs fuller investigation; with them the Armenian text of Acts should be compared.

(c) *Western*

(i) *African*

Codex FLORIACENSIS (*h*) was at Fleury but is now at Paris. It contains fragments of Apoc., Acts, 1, 2 Pet., 1 Jn. in that order. Its text is similar to that of Cyprian in his *Testimonia* where he quotes iii. 6 and iv. 8–12. For this reason it is usual to call *h* 'African' (cf. H. von Soden, *Das lateinische Neue Testament in Africa zur Zeit Cyprians*, 1909, pp. 551–67). But its editor, E. S. Buchanan,[1] says also that it is similar to that of the Latin of Irenaeus, which represents rather a European type, and A. C. Clark,[2] after a careful examination of some of the variants, concludes that it would be a mistake to think of the Greek text represented by *h* as limited to Africa. 'What is clear is that the Greek text on which *h* is based was widely circulated in the East at an early date. This is shown by the numerous agreements between *h* and the quotations of Ephraem, the *Peshitta* and the Sahidic version . . . .' It is a palimpsest of the sixth century, the *De Mundo* of Isidore of Seville being written on top.

PERPIGNAN codex (*p*). At Paris. It contains the New Testament, but only Acts i–xiii. 6, xxviii. 16–30, and the Catholic epistles are Old Latin, perhaps copied from a mutilated O.L. manuscript of the fourth or fifth century; the rest is Vulgate, except where, like *m*, it agrees with Augustine. The text is of a different strain from that of *h*, apparently Spanish, and in some ways unique.[3] It belongs to the thirteenth century, illustrating the fact that a manuscript of late date can preserve an early text.

SPECULUM (*m*). See under Gospels, above.

Augustine, *Acta de Felice Manichaeo*, i, chs. 3, 4 contains a quotation from Acts i–ii. 11 in a very pure African text.

---

[1] *Old Latin Biblical Texts*, vol. v, 1907.
[2] *The Acts of the Apostles*, 1933, pp. 247–55; contrast J. H. Ropes, op. cit., pp. cvi f.
[3] E. S. Buchanan, *J.T.S.* xii, 1910–11, pp. 497 ff.

Cyprian earlier had quoted from a Western, presumably African, text, cf. A. C. Clark, op. cit., pp. xli, 247, 249, 254, 259, 340, 360 f.

(ii) *European*

Codex BEZAE (D). See under Gospels, above. Cf. J. H. Ropes, op. cit., iii.

Codex LAUDIANUS (E_2). At Oxford; formerly in Sardinia, where it may have been written; brought to England, very likely by Theodore of Tarsus in the seventh century. It was one of the manuscripts used by Bede; and was finally presented to the Bodleian by Archbp. Laud (whence its name). Two colums to a page. A Graeco-Latin manuscript, with the Latin occupying the place of honour on the left. Contains the Acts only, and lacking xxvi. 29–xxviii. 26. At one time it was held that the Latin has been assimilated to the Greek; later, the opposite was held to have occurred. A. C. Clark concluded after discussion of the readings (op. cit., pp. 234–46) that there can be no doubt that the basis of the Greek side was a non-Western manuscript, which was collated with a version presumably Latin which had the extra material of the Western text and which resembled *h*. These additions were translated into Greek different from Codex Bezae's. Later the enlarged Greek text was used as the Greek side of a bilingual manuscript and it was given a Latin translation which, though full of Graecisms, resembles *g* and the Vulgate. As in D, the text is arranged in *cola*, sometimes very short. It belongs to the sixth century.

To list three papyri found in Egypt under the heading of 'Western' European may seem strange till it is realized how widely diffused this type of text was early in the second century. Any implication that it arose in the West and spread to the East rather than vice versa is not intended. P^{29} is a third- or fourth-century codex, *Oxyrhynchus Pap.* 1597, containing parts of Acts xxvi. 7 f. and 20. Cf. J. H. Ropes, *Beginnings of Christianity*, iii. 235–7 and A. C. Clark, op. cit., pp. 382 f. P^{38} is a fourth-century codex, though its editor, H. A. Sanders, dates it *c.* A.D. 200–50 (*Harvard Theol. Rev.* xx, 1927, pp. 1–20). It contains parts of Acts xviii and xix.

P⁴⁸ is a third-century papyrus from Oxyrhynchus (*Pubbli-cazioni della società italiana*, x, 1932, pp. 112–18) containing parts of Acts xxiii, for which D is lacking. See Lagrange, *Critique textuelle*, pp. 407–9.

Codex GIGAS (*gig*), so named from its great size, is at Stockholm. It contains the whole Bible, but only Acts and Apocalypse are Old Latin, their text being closely akin to that of Lucifer of Cagliari in Sardinia. It belongs, like *p*, to the thirteenth century but preserves an early textual type.

Codex MEDIOLANENSIS (*g²*) at Milan is a lectionary frag-ment, containing some verses of Acts vi–viii. Its text re-sembles that of *g*. It belongs to the tenth or eleventh century.

Codex VINDOBONENSIS or BOBIENSIS (*s*) is a sixth-century palimpsest which contains parts of Acts xxiii–xxviii. Its text is similar to that of *g*. Formerly at Vienna, it is now at Bobbio.

For *m* see p. 392.

LIBER COMICUS (*t*) is a lectionary of the eleventh century, the name of which is a corruption of *Liber Comitis* or *Comes*. Parts of it give an Old Latin text, parts a Vulgate. It has some affinity with *g*, though if Clark is correct (op. cit., p. 267) in thinking it to be closer to *p* and to *h* than to *g*, it should be listed with the Western African authorities.

d is the Latin text of Codex Bezae (see above).

For the Harklean Syriac Marginal readings, see below.

PAULINE EPISTLES

(a) Alexandrian

For *B* ℵ *A C Ψ 17* see above, 17 being 33 of the Gospels.

I, the WASHINGTON manuscript of the Epistles of Paul, edited by H. A. Sanders, 1918, is a sixth-century codex, containing fragments of all the epistles, including Hebrews after 2 Thessalonians, and the Pastorals.

M, Codex RUBER, is written in red ink: two leaves are in the British Museum, two in the public library at Hamburg, the former containing fragments of 1, 2 Corinthians, the latter of Hebrews. It belongs to the ninth century. See Tischendorf, *Anecdota sacra et profana*, 1861, pp. 177–205.

P, Codex PORPHYRIANUS, is at Leningrad. It contains

fragments of all the epistles. It belongs to the ninth century. See Tischendorf, *Monumenta sacra inedita*, v, 1846.

1739 (see above) has a text of the Pauline epistles, especially of Romans,[1] closely akin to that of Origen, but though it is almost certainly descended from a manuscript written at Caesarea it supports, in the epistles, the Alexandrian text on the whole.

P[10] is a fourth-century fragment of an amulet or possibly a schoolboy's exercise, containing the text of Rom. i. 1–7. It is *Oxyrhynchus Pap.* 209.

P[11] is a fifth-century fragment, possibly of a roll, containing the text of 1 Cor. i. and vi (fragments). At Leningrad.[2]

P[13] is a fourth-century roll, *Oxyrhynchus Pap.* 657, containing large parts of Heb. ii–v and x–xii.

P[14] is a fifth-century codex containing part of the text of 1 Cor. i–iii. See J. R. Harris, *Biblical Fragments from Mount Sinai*, 1896, pp. 54–56.

P[15] is a fourth-century codex, *Oxyrhynchus Pap.* 1008, containing part of 1 Cor. vii–viii.

P[16] (which may be part of the same codex as P[15]), *Oxyrhynchus Pap.* 1009, contains part of Phil. iii and iv.

P[17] is a fourth-century codex, *Oxyrhynchus Pap.* 1078, containing fragments of Heb. ix.

P[26] is a sixth- or seventh-century fragment, possibly of a roll, *Oxyrhynchus Pap.* 1354, giving a text of Rom. i. 1–10, which its editors declare to be 'only of slight interest'.

P[27] is a third-century codex, *Oxyrhynchus Pap.* 1355, giving the text of parts of Rom. viii and ix.

P[30] is a third- or fourth-century codex, *Oxyrhynchus Pap.* 1598, containing fragments of 1 Thess. iv and v and 2 Thess. i. 1.

P[31] is part of a lectionary(?) codex, containing part of Rom. xii. It is *Rylands Pap.* 4 (see the *Catalogue of the Greek Papyri in the John Rylands Library*, i. 9). It is of the sixth or seventh century.

P[32] is a third-century codex, *Rylands Pap.* 5, containing fragments of Titus i, ii, in a text like that of א.

---

[1] Cf. O. Bauernfeind, *Der Römerbrieftext des Origenes . . .*, 1923.
[2] Cf. C. R. Gregory, *Textkritik*, p. 119.

P[34] is a sixth- or seventh-century codex (C. Wessely, *Studien zur Paläographie und Papyruskunde*, xii, 1912, 191, p. 246) containing fragments of 1 Cor. xvi, 2 Cor. v and xi.

P[40] is a fifth- or sixth-century codex (F. Bilabel, *Griech. Pap.*, Heidelberg, 1924, lvii, pp. 28–31) containing parts of Rom. i–iv but with many omissions due to homoeoteleuton.

P[46] is the famous third-century Chester Beatty papyrus text of Paul, containing originally all the Pauline epistles except probably the Pastorals, for which there seems to have been no room. (Lagrange,[1] however, argues that the scribe intended to include them and that he wrote his lines closer together towards the end of the codex to do so and that if it was necessary a few extra pages could have been folded and added as leaves at the beginning and at the end, which have now been lost.) The order in which the epistles occur is remarkable: Rom., Heb., 1 and 2 Cor., Eph., Gal., Phil., Col., 1 and 2 Thess.

Apart from one or two lines at the foot of each page and comparatively small lacunae, the text is fairly complete, and though it is a century older than our oldest Uncials it vindicates in general the soundness of their text, as anyone will agree who has worked through the variants given by Sir F. G. Kenyon comparing with the the apparatus of Tischendorf, Horner (Sahidic version), A. Merk, A. Souter, and J. M. Bover.

P[49] is an unpublished third-century codex containing parts of Eph. iv–v.

P[51], *Oxyrhynchus Pap.* 2157, is a fourth-century codex, containing part of Gal. i.

P[61] is an unpublished seventh-century codex containing parts of Rom. xvi, 1 Cor. i, v, Phil. iii, Col. i, iv, 1 Thess. i, Tit. iii, and Phil.

(b) Eastern

Codex COISLINIANUS (H$_3$). Formerly in the monastery of the Laura on Mt. Athos, where it was used as binding material for several books which were afterwards scattered in various parts of Europe. There are known at present eight leaves on

---

[1] *Critique textuelle*, pp. 473, 652.

Mt. Athos, twenty-two at Paris, three at Leningrad, three at Moscow, three at Kiev, and two at Turin. They contain parts of the Pauline epistles, except Rom., Phil., Eph., 2 Thess., Philem. It probably belongs to the sixth century. Its importance lies in the fact that it is the earliest known respresentative of the Euthalian edition of the Acts and epistles. At the end of Titus are words which were probably copied as they stood from an earlier manuscript: 'I, Evagrius, wrote this volume of Paul the Apostle to the best of my power stichometrically. . . . And the book was compared with [i.e. collated from] the exemplar in Caesarea belonging to the library of the holy Pamphilus, written by his hand.' That is to say, Euthalius's own manuscript of his edition, made two centuries earlier on the basis of a Caesarean text, seems to have been the ancestor of our fragments.

Note on Euthalius

Someone who was traditionally known as Euthalius issued an edition of the Pauline epistles, and then of the Acts and Catholic epistles, in which the text was arranged in *cola* as an aid to intelligent reading. J. Armitage Robinson[1] showed it to be probable that, while Euthalius supplies prologues, full tables of Old Testament quotations in the books, and chapter summaries, other material which found its way into some manuscripts was added later. The work of Euthalius is dated between 323 and 396. Later material included, for example, the *Martyrium Pauli*, expanded out of the prologue to the Pauline epistles; and stichometrical calculations were written down. Also a colophon was added to the Pauline epistles such as stands in the codex Coislinianus (H_3) and Ac. 83. The latter, however, contains further the *Navigatio Pauli*, which is frequent in manuscripts furnished with the 'Euthalian' apparatus. It begins with Εὐάγριος ἔγραψα, and the name Evagrius has been deciphered in the colophon of H_3 (see above). Research has not shaken the probability of Robinson's theory that the material reached its expanded form by additions which Evagrius made to the original work of Euthalius. The fact that

[1] *Euthaliana*, Texts and Studies, iii. 3, 1895; cf. A. Vardanian, *Euthalius Werke*, 1930; cf. H. Omont, *Notice sur un très ancien manuscrit . . . de S. Paul*, 1890.

an apparatus was attributed to Euthalius by the Armenians disposes of von Soden's identification of him with a seventh-century namesake, a bishop of Sulca, clearly a Westerner, who wrote a *Confession concerning the Orthodox Faith*. C. H. Turner[1] accepting, at that time, the identification, was obliged to suppose that this later Euthalius added to the work of Evagrius, and not vice versa. F. C. Conybeare and Zahn think that the work was originally anonymous, and that the title 'Bishop of Sulca', which is given in more than one manuscript, was attributed to the Euthalian editor only after the seventh century, when his namesake had become prominent.

(c) Western

(i) African

No manuscript of Cyprianic Latin is known, 'though some of its peculiar renderings reappear in the not inconsiderable quotations of Tyconius (flor. 380)' (Burkitt). A late form of it is seen in the *Speculum* (*m*, see above), with which the quotations of Priscillian, which are most frequent in the Pauline epistles, mostly agree.

(ii) European

Codex CLAROMONTANUS (D₂). Now at Paris, but formerly in the monastery at Clermont, where it was acquired by Beza. A Graeco-Latin manuscript like its namesake of the Gospels, the Greek being on the left. One column to a page, with very short *cola*, so that the Greek and Latin closely correspond. At the same time the scribe has been very faithful to his exemplar in both, so that the two texts are practically independent, and the Latin (*d₂*) has the value of an Old Latin manuscript; and it exhibits the same text as that of the quotations of Lucifer of Cagliari, which points to Sardinia as the place of origin. In the longer epistles, however, the text has been affected by the Vulgate. Contains the Pauline epistles with small lacunae, Phil. following Col., and Heb. Philem. Before Hebrews (which was not accepted into the O.L. Canon, and forms a sort of appendix at the end of the manuscript) is

---

[1] Hastings's *D.B.*, extra vol., p. 525.

written a more ancient list of the number of *stichoi* in each book of the New Testament, in which Hebrews and Philemon are omitted, and the books are named in very unusual order: Matt., Jn.,Mk., Lk., Rom., 1, 2 Cor., Gal., Eph., 1, 2 Tim., Tit., Col., Philem., 1, 2 Pet., Jas., 1, 2, 3 Jn., Jude, *Ep. Barnabas*, Apoc., Acts, *Shepherd, Acts of Paul, Apoc. of Pet.* It belongs to the sixth century. It was corrected by several hands; and after the fifth corrector a transcript of it was made which survives under the name codex Sangermanensis (E_3).

Codex AUGIENSIS (F_2). At Trinity College, Cambridge, formerly in the monastery of Reichenau (Augia Dives) on an island in Lake Constance. A Graeco-Latin manuscript, with the Latin always on the outside. Two columns to a page. Contains the Pauline epistles with lacunae, Hebrews being entirely lacking in the Greek. It belongs to the end of the ninth century.

Codex BOERNERIANUS (G_3). At Dresden. Named after C. F. Boerner, who bought it in 1705. Part of the same manuscript as codex Sangallensis (Δ) of the Gospels, and copied from the same exemplar as the slightly earlier F_2, while the corrector of F_2 seems to have had G_3 before him. Contains, with lacunae, the Pauline epistles except Hebrews. There is an interlinear Latin translation, but the Latin is so largely assimilated to the Greek that it is of no value. It belongs to the end of the ninth century.

CATHOLIC EPISTLES

(a) *Alexandrian*

For $B \aleph A C \Psi P_2$ *33* and *81* see above.

P[20] is a late third-century codex containing fragments of Jas. ii. 19–iii. 9 (*Oxyrhynchus Pap.* 1171). See Lagrange, *Critique textuelle*, pp. 533 f.

P[23] is a fourth-century codex, containing fragments of Jas. i. 10–12 and 15–18 (*Oxyrhynchus Pap.* 1229). See Lagrange, op. cit., p. 534.

P[54] is a fifth- or sixth-century papyrus containing fragments of Jas. ii and iii (*Papyri in the Princeton University Collections*, E. H. Kase, 1936: Princeton, xv. 1–3).

(b) Western

h, FLORIACENSIS, of the fifth century, contains parts of 1 and 2 Peter and 1 John. See E. S. Buchanan, *Old Latin Biblical Texts*, vol. v, 1907.

m, see above.

ff, CORBEIENSIS, of the tenth century, contains James: see J. Wordsworth, *Studia Biblica*, i, 1885, p. 113 and W. Sanday, ibid., pp. 233–63.

s, FRAGMENTA VINDOBONENSIA, now at Naples, contains fragments of James and of 1 Peter. Of the fifth or sixth century. See H. J. White, *Old Latin Biblical Texts*, iv, 1897.

q, FREISING, of the seventh century, contains parts of 1 Peter and 1 John; see D. de Bruyne, *Les fragments de Freising*, 1921.

For the citations in Tertullian, see Lagrange, op. cit., pp. 540 ff.

APOCALYPSE

Dr. Charles[1] has attempted to work out the relative value of the uncials containing the Apocalypse, i.e. the first six of the following manuscripts, which are placed in the order of value as estimated by him.

A (see below) ℵ *C P*$_2$ (see above).

Codex VATICANUS 2066 (B$_2$, Gregory 046). In the Vatican. Contains the Apocalypse, in company with some small writings of Basil, Greg. Nyss., and other Fathers. According to Charles it represents what he calls the cursive, as against the uncial, type of text; but it compares favourably with ℵ, considering its late date. It belongs to the eighth century.

Codex ATHOUS, PANTOKRATOR 44 (Swete 186, Gregory 051). On Mt. Athos. Contains Rev. xi. 15–xiii. 1; xiii. 3–xxii. 7; xxii. 15–21 in uncial script, each few verses being followed by the comments of Andreas in cursive (see Swete, *Apocalypse*, p. cxcv). It belongs to the tenth century.

Codex ATHOUS, PANTELEEMON 183 (Gregory 052). At Thessalonica. Contains Rev. vii. 16–viii. 14, with Andreas's comments. It belongs to the tenth century.

---

[1] *Revelation*, vol. i, pp. clx–clxxxiii: H. C. Hoskier's two volumes, *Concerning the Text of the Apocalypse*, 1929, contain a mass of essential data, though some of his conclusions are bizarre.

CODEX 38 (Gregory 2020). At the Vatican. Its text stands close to that of P_2. It belongs to the fifteenth century.

CODEX 95 (Gregory 2040). At Parham, formerly on Mt. Athos. Charles says that its text is better after xi. 8 than before. It belongs to the eleventh or twelfth century.

P^{18}, a third- or fourth-century roll, *Oxyrhynchus Pap.* 1079, contains Rev. i. 4–7, on the verso of the text of Exodus. It agrees mainly with A.

P^{24}, a fourth-century codex, *Oxyrhynchus Pap.* 1230, contains fragments of Rev. v and vi. Its text agrees with that of ℵ and A.

P^{43}, a (lectionary?) roll, probably of the seventh century, contains parts of Rev. ii, xv, and xvi. See W. E. Crum and Sir H. I. Bell, *Wadi Sarga*, 1922, pp. 43 ff.

P^{47}, the Chester Beatty papyrus of Rev., contains parts of ix. 10–xvii. 2. In an important article, R. V. G. Tasker[1] has argued that P^{47} 'reflects an early revision of the original text of the Apocalypse, similar to that reflected in the text used by Origen, and less thorough than that which eventually became standardised and resulted finally in the textus receptus'.

An Old Latin text almost in Cyprianic form is found in *h*, as in the Acts; and it is found in the very full quotations of Primasius in the sixth century. A late form is seen in *m*; see under 'Gospels'. A late European text is extant in *g*. Unlike the epistles, Acts and Apocalypse in their Latin texts did not suffer from the fourth-century revision.

BYZANTINE

Codex ALEXANDRINUS (A). At the British Museum. Given to the English king Charles I in 1621 by Cyril Lucar, patriarch of Constantinople, formerly of Alexandria. He had taken the manuscript with him on his translation, and it has therefore been assumed until recently that its original home and place of writing was Alexandria; hence its name. But it is now thought, with much more likelihood, to have come from the East—either from Constantinople, whence it found its way to Mt. Athos, and thence to Alexandria,[2] or, as

---

[1] *J.T.S.*, l, 1949, pp. 50–68; cf. Lagrange, *Critique textuelle*, pp. 586–91.
[2] Burkitt, *J.T.S.* xii, 1910–11, pp. 603 ff.

Streeter suggests,[1] from some place like Caesarea or Berytus (Beyrout), half-way between Antioch and Alexandria. Two columns to a page. Contains the Old and New Testaments, but in the latter has lost Matt. i–xxv. 6; Jn. vi. 50–viii. 52; 2 Cor. iv. 13–xii. 7. It contains also *1, 2 Clement,* and originally included the *Psalms of Solomon,* which is now lost, together with the last two sheets of *2 Clement.* It is the earliest manuscript which contains a text in the Gospels which approximates to the text of 'Lucian's' revision. In the rest of the New Testament it has an Alexandrian element. It belongs to the fifth century.

Codex BASILIENSIS (E). At Basle. One column to a page. Contains the Gospels. The text is Byzantine, but von Soden claims for it a slight 'Ferrar' admixture. It belongs to the eighth century.

Codex VATICANUS 354 (S). At the Vatican. Contains the Gospels. It is one of the earliest dated manuscripts, having a note stating that it was written by a monk named Michael in 949.

Codex MOSCUENSIS (V). At Moscow, to which it was taken from the Vatopedi monastery on Mt. Athos. Contains the Gospels. It belongs to the ninth century. S and V are the two manuscripts which probably contain the purest Byzantine text.

Codex MUTINENSIS (H₂). At Modena, in the grand ducal library. Contains the Acts with lacunae. (The Cath. and Paul. epp. were supplied by a cursive hand of the fifteenth or sixteenth century.) It belongs to the ninth century.

Codex ANGELICUS ROMANUS (L₂). At Rome, in the library of the Augustinian monastery. Contains Acts (from viii. 10), Cath. epp., and Paul. epp. (to Heb. xiii. 10). It belongs to the ninth century.

Codex PORPHYRIANUS CHIOVENSIS (P₂). See under Pauline epistles.

Codex MOSQUENSIS (K₂). At Moscow, formerly on Mt. Athos. Contains the Catholic and Pauline epistles. It belongs to the ninth century.

---

[1] *The Four Gospels,* p. 120.

VERSIONS

The material for the three primary versions has been described above—the Coptic, Old Syriac, and Old Latin, representing the Alexandrian, Eastern, and Western types of text respectively. The versions now to be mentioned are less important for critical purposes. They were revisions or translations reflecting (except the Vulgate) late forms of the Greek text, when the Antioch–Constantinople or Byzantine type was dominant.

LATIN VULGATE. This stands by itself, being based on the Old Latin, but revised according to good Alexandrian manuscripts. It was Jerome's revision of the many and various Old Latin texts which existed before his day, made (383–400) at the request of Pope Damasus. The fullest account of its history and manuscripts can be seen in the article 'Vulgate' in Hastings's *Dict. of the Bible*, by H. J. White, cf. B. M. Metzger[1] in M. M. Parvis and A. P. Wikgren's *New Testament Manuscript Studies*, 1950, pp. 55–61. The whole number of its manuscripts cannot be less than 8,000. But it is only in the Gospels that the text can really be called Vulgate, as Jerome's revision of the other books was very slight and cursory. Dr. White selects 181 which he groups and describes; and of these, 40 are contained in the list in the edition of the Vulgate N.T. by Wordsworth and White.

The best group is the Northumbrian, traceable to the schools of Wearmouth and Jarrow, founded in the seventh century by Benedict Biscop, and furthered by Ceolfrid, who was Abbot of both.

Codex AMIATINUS. This contains the purest known text of the Vulgate. It was written by Ceolfrid's orders for a gift to the pope, i.e. the see of Rome. Prefixed to it are some metrical dedicatory lines which have been found also in an anonymous life of Ceolfrid used by Bede. But afterwards, in

---

[1] As Metzger shows, questions about the Vulgate still hotly debated include: What was the nature of the Old Latin texts used by Jerome? *f* (Wordsworth and White) or *a* (Souter) or *e*, *ff*², *b*, *i*, and *q* (Vogels)? On the basis of what sort of Greek manuscripts did Jerome revise? B ℵ L (Wordsworth and White), B A (Burkitt), or B and A but mainly ℵ (Lagrange)? Did Jerome revise the epistles? Is the Vulgate text of the Pauline epistles that of Pelagius (de Bruyne)? Did Jerome revise the Apocalypse on the basis of ℵ (Vogels)?

the manuscript, the names Ceolfrid and the see of Rome were erased, and those of Peter Lombard and Monte Amiata were substituted regardless of the metre. Now in the Laurentian library at Florence. Two columns to a page. Contains the whole Bible. In the Gospels are numbered the Ammonian sections, and in the Acts the second numeration found in ℵ and B (see p. 380). It belongs to the early eighth century.

Codex LINDISFARNENSIS, known as the Lindisfarne Gospels. In the British Museum. It was written in honour of St. Cuthbert, who died in 687, and was preserved with his body. It therefore belongs to the late seventh or early eighth century.

Codex DUNELMENSIS. In the Cathedral library at Durham. Contains the Gospels, but is valuable only in John. It belongs to the seventh or eighth century.

Codex STONYHURSTENSIS. At Stonyhurst College, formerly at Durham. Contains John only. It belongs to the seventh century.

Codex FULDENSIS. At Fulda, in Germany. Contains the whole New Testament. The text is closely allied to that of the above group, though the manuscript itself is not Northumbrian. Apart from its text it has a value of its own, since it contains not the separate Gospels but the arrangement of them in Tatian's *Diatessaron*, the translation of the passages being taken from the Vulgate. It was written at the order of Victor, Bishop of Capua, in 541–6.

Another group with a fairly good text of a different type is represented by:

Codex HARLEIANUS. In the British Museum. Contains the Gospels. It belongs to the sixth or seventh century. A similar type of text is seen in the 'Canterbury MSS.', one in the Bodleian Library at Oxford, and one at Corpus Christi College, Cambridge.

Codex SANGALLENSIS belongs to the same class as Harleianus, and if C. H. Turner[1] was right, it approximates more to Jerome's text than does Wordsworth and White's reconstructed text. At St. Gall. It contains nearly half the text of

---

[1] *The Oldest Manuscript of the Vulgate Gospels*, 1931.

the Gospels on leaves used for binding. It belongs to the sixth century.

A third group is Irish, and includes:

Codex DUBLINENSIS, known as the BOOK OF ARMAGH. Contains the New Testament, and also the apocryphal Epistle to the Laodiceans. It belongs to the eighth or ninth century.

Codex KENANSIS, known as the BOOK OF KELLS (Kells is another name of Kennana in Co. Meath), and famous for its extraordinarily elaborate and beautiful Celtic illuminations, and for being written in the most perfect existing Irish script. It belongs to the seventh or eighth century.

There is also a Spanish group, and others with various degrees of mixture.

PESHITTA SYRIAC. This version, of which numerous manuscripts remain, a few as early as the fifth century, was a revision of the Evangelion da-Mepharreshe made by Rabbula, Bishop of Edessa 411–35, soon after he became bishop, in order to conform its text more closely with the Antioch–Constantinople text that was then current, though it retains some Old Syriac readings.[1] The name Peshitta means 'the Simple', and 'was in use as early as the ninth or tenth century; it has been conjectured that it originally served to distinguish the Syriac Vulgate of the Old and New Testaments from the Hexaplaric versions of the O.T. and the Harklean [see below] of the N.T., editions which were furnished with marginal variants and other critical apparatus'.[2] It is sometimes known as the Syriac Vulgate, because it was generally accepted by Syriac-speaking Christians.

PHILOXENIAN SYRIAC. A revision of the *Peshitta*, including the books which were absent from the latter, and based on the later current Greek text. It was made by a chorepiscopos named Polycarp in 508 for Philoxenus, the Jacobite, or Monophysite, Bishop of Mabbog or Hierapolis in eastern Syria, and used by the Monophysites. Philoxenian readings are probably to be found in manuscripts of the

---

[1] See M. Black, 'Rabbula of Edessa and the Peshitta', *Bulletin of the John Rylands Library*, xxxiii, 1951, pp. 203–10, and A. Vööbus, *Contributions of the Baltic University*, lix, 1947, cf. ibid. lxiv and lxv, 1948.

[2] Burkitt, *Encycl. Bibl.* 4999.

subsequent revision that was made (see below), but the only texts of the original version that are known are that of the four shorter Catholic epistles (2 Pet., 2, 3 Jn., Jude) now usually printed with the *Peshitta*, and that of the Apocalypse brought to light by J. Gwynn, of Dublin, in 1897.[1]

HARKLEAN SYRIAC. This may have been a revision of the Philoxenian made in 616 in Alexandria by another Monophysite bishop of Mabbog named Thomas of Heraclea (Ḥarḳel) but the problem of the relation of the Harklean to the Philoxenian version is extremely complicated (cf. Metzger in Parvis and Wikgren, op. cit., pp. 32 f.). Thomas adopted the method of extreme literalness, forcing the Syriac into accordance with the Greek. It is remarkable also for notes in the margin giving variant readings from two or three Greek manuscripts collated by Thomas at Alexandria. In the Acts these are sometimes of considerable importance, the readings being taken from a manuscript with a text akin to that of D. But the text itself is Byzantine practically throughout. Nearly forty manuscripts of this version are known, and the Apocalypse belongs to it which was published by De Dieu in 1627 and is usually printed with the *Peshitta*.

PALESTINIAN (or 'JERUSALEM') SYRIAC. This has nothing to do with Jerusalem, nor is it, properly speaking, Syriac. It is a variety of the Western Aramaic almost identical with that of the Galilean Jews. The better name for it, therefore, would be 'Jewish Aramaic'. Three complete Gospel lectionaries of the eleventh to twelfth centuries in this dialect are known, and fragments of at least two others, and of four continuous Gospel codices. There are also small fragments of Acts and Galatians, and much later ones of lections from all parts of the Bible, except the Gospels. Burkitt[2] has shown that it may originate from Antioch, and may have been a product of the time when Justinian, in the sixth century, was trying to abolish the religion of the Samaritans, and Heraclius, early in the seventh, was harassing the Jews. M. J. Lagrange rejected this date, preferring one in the second half of the fifth century (*Critique textuelle*, pp. 233–9). The

[1] *The Apocalypse of St. John in a Syriac Version.*
[2] *J.T.S.* ii, 1901, pp. 174–83.

text is mixed, being often influenced by the Peshitta, but in the main following the Greek.

ARMENIAN. There were Armenian Christians in the middle of the third century, for Dionysius of Alexandria wrote to them, and their bishop was Meruzanes (Eus. *H.E.* vi. 46). But their ecclesiastical language was Syriac, and an Armenian version of the Gospels did not appear till much later. Tradition ascribed it to Isaac and Mesrop (*fl.* 400). Whenever it was made, it may have been translated from Syriac manuscripts, as J. Armitage Robinson tried to show,[1] though this has been disputed.[2] Those opposed to this view think that an original Greek text was akin to the 'Caesarean' and that 'Syriacisms' are relics of an early translation or of the *Diatessaron.*

Though most Armenian manuscripts of the Gospels are no older than the ninth or tenth century, the text is a remarkably 'pure' one, revealing great scribal fidelity, and the language has sufficient flexibility to reproduce that of the Greek and to earn the title 'Queen of the versions'. The text of Acts and the Pauline epistles, to judge from the printed text of Zohrab, seems to compromise between Alexandrian and Western readings in much the same way as Caesarean manuscripts of the Gospels do. In the Catholic epistles, however, the affinity is rather with the Alexandrian. The Apocalypse was not accepted as canonical till the fifth century; though the text seems to have been dependent on the Greek, it was also influenced apparently by an Old Latin version.[3] It was revised by scholars working on Greek manuscripts, but despite its history this text is often of value in deciding doubtful readings.

No modern critical edition of the Armenian New Testament is yet available; until it appears and manuscripts can be collated with it, the exact amount of 'Caesarean' support that the Armenian version gives is difficult to assess.

---

[1] *Euthaliana*, Texts and Studies, iii. 3, 1895, pp. 72–91.

[2] By F. Macler, *Le texte arménien de l'évangile*, 1919, S. Lyonnet, in Lagrange's *Critique textuelle*, pp. 342–75, E. C. Colwell, *Anglican Theological Review*, xvi, 1934, pp. 113–32, and C. S. C. Williams, *J.T.S.* xliii, 1942, pp. 161–7, cf. xlviii, 1947, pp. 196–200.

[3] F. C. Conybeare, *The Armenian Version of Revelation*, 1907.

GEORGIAN. This version is that of the Iberian Church in the Caucasus and various scholars have supposed it to have been derived from the Syriac and from the Armenian rather than from the Greek directly. R. P. Blake[1] has produced the Georgian text of Mark and of Matthew from the Adysh MS., dated A.D. 897, compared with the Opiza (A.D. 913) and the Tbet' (A.D. 995) MSS. He has also produced the Georgian text of John.[2] Anyone working through the variants at least of this text will be convinced that the relationship of the Georgian to that of the Armenian versions is so close as probably to be that of child to parent. Sometimes the Georgian witnesses to an Armenian mistranslation, or sometimes to an Armenian variant that has been 'revised away' from the Armenian text now extant. A critical edition of the Georgian New Testament, like the Armenian, is still awaited. It too will probably reveal 'Caesarean' support,[3] with perhaps the influence of an Armenian Diatessaron probably based on Tatian's.

For the less important versions, *Ethiopic, Arabic, Sogdian*, and *Nubian*, see B. M. Metzger in Parvis and Wikgren, op. cit., pp. 45–51. The *Gothic* version deserves more than mention. Ulphilas was Bishop of the Goths 348–c. 380. He invented an alphabet for them, and then translated both the Old and New Testaments from the Greek. But the version was influenced from Latin sources, and the manuscripts that we possess contain a text which dates from the fifth century or later, when the Goths were in Italy and Spain, and appear to belong to north Italy. Of the New Testament the Gospels and the Pauline epistles (except Hebrews), with many gaps, remain. The Gospels are in the Western order, and the manuscripts contain both Western and Alexandrian readings, but the text is mainly Byzantine. Their text was edited by G. W. S. Friedrichsen, 1926, who also edited the Gothic version of the epistles in 1939.

Patristic writings

The writers whose text is known with sufficient accuracy for

---

[1] *Patrologia Orientalis*, xx. 3, 1929, pp. 435–574, xxiv. 1, 1933, pp. 1–168.
[2] R. P. Blake and M. Brière, ibid. xxvi. 4, 1950.
[3] Cf. S. Lyonnet in Lagrange's *Critique textuelle*, pp. 375–86 and 460–3, cf. p. 625.

critical purposes are comparatively few, but the great majority of the earlier Fathers support some form of Western text.

Alexandrian. Origen (partly), Athanasius, Cyril.

Eastern. Aphraates, Ephraem (where their readings are not influenced by Tatian's *Diatessaron*), Origen (partly).

Western. Justin, Tatian, Marcion, Irenaeus, Clement of Alexandria (predominantly; but his text contains different elements whose sources have not yet been traced), Tertullian, Cyprian, Hilary, Lucifer, Ambrose, Augustine (where he was not using the Vulgate), Tyconius, Priscillian, Primasius (on the Apocalypse).

BOOKS

The following bibliography, which is not complete, may indicate the importance of the text of various Fathers, notably of the text of Tatian's *Diatessaron*.

Origen: E. Hautsch, *Die Evangelienzitate des Origenes*, 1909; K. Lake, R. P. Blake, and S. New, *Harvard Theol. Rev.*, xxi, 1928, pp. 259–77; R. V. G. Tasker, *J.T.S.* xxxviii, 1937.

Eusebius of Caesarea: C. Peters, *Oriens Christianus*, xi. 1, 1936, pp. 1–25; R. V. G. Tasker, *Harvard Theol. Rev.*, xxviii, 1935, pp. 61–67; D. S. Wallace-Hadrill, *J.T.S.*, N.S., i, 1950, pp. 168–75, cf. Lake, Blake, and New, op. cit., pp. 277–85.

Aphraat(es): F. C. Burkitt, *Evangelion da-Mepharreshe*, ii, 1904, pp. 180–6.

Ephraem: F. C. Burkitt, *Texts and Studies*, vii. 2, 1901.

Justin: W. Bousset, *Die Evangeliencitate Justins des Märtyres*, 1891; M. J. Lagrange, *Critique textuelle*, pp. 169–74; E. Lippelt, *Quae fuerint Justini Martyri ΑΠΟΜΝΗΜΟΝΕΥΜΑΤΑ*, 1901.

Tatian: A. Baumstark, *Oriens Christianus*, 3. 5. 2, 1930, pp. 165–74 and ibid. 1, pp. 1–14; *Biblica*, xvi, 1935, pp. 257–99; *Oriens Christianus*, 3. 10. 2, 1935, pp. 244–52 and 3. 14. 1, 1939, pp. 19–37; F. C. Burkitt, *J.T.S.* xxv, 1924, pp. 113–30 and xxxvi, 1935, pp. 255–9; P. Essabalian, *Le Diatessaron de Tatien et la première traduction des évangiles arméniennes*, 1937; J. R. Harris, *The Diatessaron of Tatian*, 1890, and *Harvard Theol. Rev.* xviii, 1925, pp. 103–9, and *Bulletin of the Bezan Club*, ix, 1931, pp. 8–10; J. H. Hill, *The Earliest Life of Jesus ever compiled*, 1894; H. W. Hogg, *The Diatessaron of Tatian*, 1897; A. Jülicher, *Journal of Biblical Lit.* xliii, 1924, pp. 132–71; C. H. Kraeling, 'A Greek Fragment of Tatian's Diatessaron from Dura', *Studies and Docs.* iii, 1935; S. Lyonnet, *Biblica*, xix, 1938, pp. 121–50; A. S. Marmadji, *Diatessaron de Tatien*, 1935 (but see D. S. Margoliouth's review, *J.T.S.* xxxviii, 1937, pp. 76–78); A. Merk, *Biblica*, xvii, 1936, pp. 234–41; C. Peters, 'Der Diatessaron Tatians', *Orientalia Christiana Analecta*, 123, 1939; C. A. Phillips, *Bulletin of the Bezan Club*, ix, 1931, pp. 6–8; D. Plooij, *A primitive Text of the Diatessaron*, the Liège MS., 1923, cf.

Z.N.T.W. xxii, 1923, pp. 1–16, and (with C. A. Phillips) *The Liége Diatessaron*, 1929–38; O. Stegmüller, *Z.N.T.W.* xxxvii, 1938, pp. 223–9; H. J. Vogels, *Neutestamentliche Abhandlungen*, viii, 1919; C. S. C. Williams, *J.T.S.* xliii, 1942, pp. 37–42; T. Zahn, *Forschungen zur Geschichte des neutestamentlichen Kanons*, i, 1881.

Marcion: A. von Harnack, *Texte und Untersuchungen*, 1921 (2nd ed., 1924), and *Neue Studien zu Marcion*, 1923; A. J. B. Higgins, *Vigiliae Christianae*, 1951, v. 1, pp. 1–42; M. J. Lagrange, *Revue Biblique*, xxx, 1921, pp. 602–11; A. Pott, *Zeitschrift für Kirchengeschichte*, xlii. v, 1923, pp. 202–23; H. von Soden, *Festschrift für A. Jülicher*, 1927, pp. 229–81; C. S. C. Williams, *Alterations to the Text of the Synoptic Gospels and Acts*, 1951, pp. 10–18.

Irenaeus: B. Kraft, *Die Evangelienzitate des heiligen Irenäus, Biblische Studien*, xxi. 4, 1924; M. J. Lagrange, *Critique textuelle*, pp. 174–7; W. Lüdtke and H. Jordan, *Irenaeusfragmente (armenische), Texte und Untersuchungen*, xxxvi, 1913; W. Sanday, C. H. Turner, and A. Souter, *N.T. Sancti Irenaei Episcopi Lugdunensis*, O.L. Bibl. Texts, vii, 1923; H. J. Vogels, *Revue Bénédictine*, xxxvi, 1924, pp. 21–33.

Clement of Alexandria: P. M. Barnard, *Texts and Studies*, v. 5, 1899; M. J. Lagrange, *Critique textuelle*, pp. 177–81; H. von Soden, *Die Schriften des N.T.* i, 1902, pp. 1596–604.

Tertullian: G. J. D. Aalders, *Tertullianus' Citaten*, 1932; H. Rönsch, *Das N.T. Tertullians*, 1871; H. von Soden, see on Marcion above; M. C. Tenney, *Harvard Studies in Classical Philology*, lvi–lvii, 1947, pp. 257–60.

Cyprian: J. Heidenreich, *Der N.T. Text bei Cyprian*, 1900; H. von Soden, *Texte und Untersuchungen*, 1909.

Lucifer of Cagliari: A. M. Coleman, *The Biblical Text of Lucifer of Cagliari*, 1927 (Acts), 1946 (Pastorals), 1947 (Pauline Epistles and Hebrews); H. J. Vogels, *Theologische Quartalschrift*, 103, 1922, pp. 23–27, 183–200.

St. Augustine: F. C. Burkitt, *Texts and Studies*, iv, 1896, and *J.T.S.* xi, 1910, pp. 258–68; H. J. Vogels, *Biblische Zeitschrift*, iv, 1906, pp. 267–95.

Tyconius: H. J. Vogels, *Untersuchungen zur Geschichte der lateinischen Apocalypseübersetzung*, 1920; F. C. Burkitt, *Texts and Studies*, iii. 1, 1894; T. Hahn, *Tyconius-Studien*, 1900; A. Souter, *J.T.S.* xiv, 1912–13, pp. 338–58.

Priscillian: G. Schapss, *C.S.E.L.* xviii, 1899.

Primasius: J. Haussleiter, *Forschungen zur Geschichte des N.T.-Kanons*, 1891.

§ 3. THE HISTORY OF CRITICISM

Since the earliest days that differences between N.T. manuscripts began to be observed, critics of the text have been divisible into two main classes according to the aim which they set before themselves in dealing with it. The one class is concerned to produce unity. An eclectic method is employed in order to preserve all that is felt to be best in the multiplicity of texts. The other class aims at discovering, at all costs, the text which is the nearest possible to the original. 'The almost universal tendency of transcribers to make their text as full as possible, and to eschew omissions' (Hort), is reflected in some early editors, but not in all. The two methods are distinguished in an instructive passage of Eusebius, *On the Discrepance of the Gospels*, quoted by Hort:[1]

For at this point [i.e. at xvi. 8, ἐφοβοῦντο γάρ] the end of the Gospel according to Mark is determined in nearly all the copies of the Gospel according to Mark; whereas what follows, being but scantily current, in some but not in all copies, will be redundant [i.e. as such should be discarded], and especially if it should contain a contradiction to the testimony of the other evangelists. . . . [That is the view of one class of critic.] While another, not daring to reject anything whatever that is in any way current in the Scripture of the Gospels, will say that the reading is double, as in many other cases, and that each [reading] must be received, on the ground that this finds no more acceptance than that, nor that than this, with faithful and discreet persons.

The inclusive tendency, which is on a par with the harmonizing of commentators, is here sharply contrasted with what we think of as the critical method, the latter of which was chiefly characteristic of Alexandria, though there are manuscripts outside Alexandria which express a spirit of keen criticism. What were considered to be interpolations were carefully noted (both in pagan and Christian writings), and often obelized, or bracketed and dotted for deletion. The only course, however, open to an editor or commentator who desired as pure a text as possible was to employ the earliest manuscripts he could find. This was doubtless what was done by the scholars Origen and Jerome, who fill so important a place in the history of the text. The latter claims to have used ancient Greek codices rather than the emended ones containing the revisions attributed to Hesychius and Lucian.[2] This, however, was not the bent of mind of the Christian world in general. The opposite tendency, which Eusebius evidently preferred, was followed

---

[1] *The New Testament in Greek*, 1896, Appendix, p. 31.

[2] Whether these attributions are correct, which Jerome makes in his *Epistula ad Damasum*, is very doubtful; cf. Sir F. G. Kenyon, *The Text of the Greek Bible*, pp. 183, 209.

by Lucian, who deliberately enriched his text with material drawn from manuscripts of the main types which existed in his day. His revision was the earliest form of what became the standard text represented by the mass of manuscripts that have come down to us, and in conformity with which nearly all Greek manuscripts have, to a greater or less extent, been corrected. It was a text 'smooth and readable in structure, and competently exact for all practical purposes' (Warfield). And it continued to be the text of Christendom, untouched by critical hands, till the Renaissance.

PRINTED EDITIONS. In 1514 was undertaken the first printed edition of the New Testament, that of Stunica in Cardinal Ximenes's Complutensian (Alcala) Polyglot. But it was eight years before it saw the light. In the meantime Erasmus, at Basle, prepared an edition in great haste to outstrip the other, and published it in 1516. The humanist worked *ad maiorem Erasmi gloriam.* He admitted himself that it was *precipitatum verius quam editum.* He used late medieval manuscripts of the Byzantine text, its rival—when it appeared seven or eight years later—being based on earlier manuscripts of the same text. Other editions followed, which were little more than reprints of these, especially of the Erasmian. In 1550 appeared the magnificent edition of Stephanus, printed in Paris, which was almost entirely Erasmian. And an unsatisfactory revision of this, in five successive editions, by the reformer Beza was printed in the beautiful Elzevir 24mo editions issued at Leyden in 1624, 1633, &c. In that of 1633 it was stated that it contained 'the text now received by all'; and so the Stephanus–Elzevir text came to be known as the Textus Receptus, the Received Text, and is cited by the Greek symbol ς (= st for Stephanus). And reprints of the Stephanus or the Elzevir are the traditional text of the New Testament. No Greek text intended to reproduce exactly that which underlay our A.V. has ever been printed. Beza's fifth and last text, of 1598, was more likely than any other to be in the translators' hands, but they sometimes departed from it in retaining language inherited from Tyndale and his successors, which had been founded on the text of other Greek editions. They also adopted some readings which Beza had mentioned in his notes, and others, perhaps, on independent grounds. (The R.V. in 1881 was translated from a text produced by a compromise between 'the text presumed to underlie the Authorized Version' and the text of Westcott and Hort.)

An impetus seems to have been given to the critical study of the text by the presentation to King Charles I of the codex Alexandrinus (A) in 1628. Nevertheless for two centuries no attempt was made to produce an edition independent of the Textus Receptus, and based upon the best manuscripts, because the material for it was as yet almost non-existent. One edition after another appeared in which the editors tried to revise the T.R. with the help of the manuscripts that were coming to light. This stage of textual criticism lasted from 1657 to 1831, the chief editions being those of Walton's Polyglot (1657), Fell (1695), Mill (1707), Wells (1709–19), all English scholars; and then a succession of German ones: Bengel (1734), Wetstein (1751, 1752), Griesbach (1775–1827), Matthaei (1782–8), and Scholtz (1830–6). The most important of these were those of Bengel and Griesbach, the latter being helped by suggestions of Semler, and by the need of reinforcing his position in 1811 against theories of Hug.

But in 1831 Lachmann began to work upon scientific principles laid down more than a century before by the genius of Bentley, whose intention of producing an edition had not found fulfilment. He constructed a text directly from ancient documents without regard to printed editions, and issued better editions in 1842–50. He was immediately followed by Tischendorf (1840–72), whose eighth edition, published in parts in 1864 and 1872, is still the chief storehouse of variant readings, with which G. W. Horner's *apparatus criticus* to his Coptic editions may be compared. The last important edition before that of Westcott and Hort was that of Tregelles, in parts from 1857 to 1879.

The advance in the science of criticism was made possible by the continuous discovery of fresh material, which led to the recognition that manuscripts were to be classified according to the type of text which they contained. Bentley saw that they could be divided broadly into an earlier and a later class, viz., as we can now call them, pre-Byzantine and Byzantine. Bengel accepted this division, calling them African and Asiatic. But he went farther and perceived that the earlier was not homogeneous, and he divided it into two families represented by codex A and the Old Latin. He recognized also that his 'African' on the whole was of more value than his 'Asiatic'. Griesbach anticipated modern results with great acuteness by naming the latter class Constantinopolitan, and the two families of the former Alexandrian and Western. Not only so, but he was the first to perceive with any clearness that different families were, in some cases, represented in different parts of the same manuscript; and he even dimly detected the hardest part of the problem—the mixture of texts of different types in the texts of manuscripts. The Alexandrian and Western he held to have been types at least as early as the third century, and the Constantinopolitan not earlier than the fourth or fifth. From the work of Hug it became clearer that the Western text had a wide and early currency; and he thought that it was a corrupt text universally current in the second century, of which the existing manuscripts (except D) represented three revisions. Tregelles helped to substantiate scientifically the fact that Griesbach's Alexandrian and Western texts were earlier than, and superior to, the Constantinopolitan. Thus the increase of material, and a growing insight into true methods, prepared the way for the work of Westcott and Hort, which must be studied next.

§ 4. WESTCOTT AND HORT

The principles on which their edition is constructed are set forth by Hort in an *Introduction* and *Appendix*, which form the second volume of their *The New Testament in the Original Greek* (Cambridge and London, 1882); and those principles were summarized at the end of both the larger and smaller editions of their text. A second and corrected impression of the former appeared in December 1881, and the latter (a reprint of the former) in 1887.

The principles are of permanent validity; and scholarship owes a heavy debt to the two great Cambridge men for their clear grasp and formulation of them. But since science never stands still, their application of them has undergone some modification in the last forty years by further study and the discovery of fresh material.

The first thing to be done is to recognize the different kinds of evidence available for determining a given reading.

INTERNAL EVIDENCE OF READINGS. The most rudimentary form of criticism, when variant readings present themselves, is to adopt the one which seems to be the most probable. But even this cannot be done without weighing two kinds of probability—intrinsic and transcriptional.

(a) *Intrinsic Probability*. The reader may consider the context, the grammar, the style of the author and his manner in other passages; and may decide, with regard to a given reading, either by itself or in comparison with other readings, what he thinks that the author meant to say. The trained reader will be more likely to arrive at the truth than the untrained. But an author does not always express himself in the best way possible; and what the reader imagines he must have said may sometimes be an improvement, but textually a corruption, of his actual words. And it may all too frequently happen that a reader does not fully understand the mind or the circumstances or the purposes of the author, so that he may corrupt without improving his words.

(b) *Transcriptional Probability*. This is a safer, because a less subjective, basis of criticism. There are certain causes of corruption, mentioned on p. 374, which seem generally to operate in manual transcription of any kind. What Hort calls 'observed proclivities of average copyists' allow of generalizations on which transcriptional probability can be based. And the greater the experience of the trained reader in these sources of corruption, the more safely will he deal with this class of probability. But proclivities are awkward things to judge. It is extremely difficult for the most highly trained reader to determine which of various impulses may have acted upon a scribe. That which actually did may not have been the one which the reader might think the strongest. On the other hand, the reading which appeals to him as intrinsically the best may be only that which the scribe felt to be an improvement, and was therefore, in fact, a corruption. But in practice the two kinds of probability are not often in antagonism, because an ancient scribe was seldom able to make an 'improvement' which to the literary and historical sense of the trained student in modern times appears really better than the original. Transcriptional probability is chiefly of value when the trained student can feel the superiority of a given reading, and yet has reasons for thinking that an ancient scribe would probably prefer a variant. In such cases, which are of frequent occurrence, the mutual aid of the two kinds of probability can be of the utmost help in connexion with other methods of criticism. But when they coincide, and no likely cause can be assigned for the existence of a variant, then other methods must be sought to arrive at a decision.

INTERNAL EVIDENCE OF DOCUMENTS. An important part of the weighing of evidence is to consider whether a witness is normally credible and trustworthy; and the inquiry into the character and antecedents of a document offers a safer criterion than the mere balancing of probabilities, because it deals more with objective fact, and less with personal surmise. One fact about a manuscript which can be determined with approximate accuracy is its date. Sometimes a scribe actually dated it; sometimes the date is fixed within more or less narrow limits by external facts or records; more often the century, at least, to which it belongs is learned from the palaeographical details of the manuscript itself. It is far from being a final criterion, because a late manuscript may have been copied immediately from an early one; but broadly speaking, the later a manuscript the greater the number of corruptions it is likely to have inherited. The date, however, can be only a general guide, and by itself is useless in determining which is the better of two variants.

Here begins the first serious labour of the textual critic. He must not be content with deciding upon reading after reading, as they occur, on the lines of Probability. He must do so for the entire document in such a way that he becomes acquainted with its character as a whole, intimately enough to be able to gauge its relative value as compared with that of other documents which he has similarly studied. There is only a certain proportion of its variants on which he can, at first reading, decide from Internal Evidence. There will be many others which have left him in doubt; but on studying them again, he finds that his valuation of the manuscript as a whole helps to turn the scale in several places. If he has come to feel that the manuscript as a whole is good, he will be predisposed to prefer its readings in many instances where the Internal Evidence was not clear enough for a decision. That is an important factor in Westcott and Hort's system.

And yet no single document is free from errors. The student may feel certain that Internal Evidence sometimes condemns a reading in a 'good' document; but where his two lines of evidence are in conflict, nothing but personal caprice can lead him to follow either, if he does not possess a further criterion. Documents are never good or bad absolutely, but only comparatively, each having its obvious slips of scribes or translators. A good text was sometimes very badly transcribed, and vice versa.

But there are further difficulties. A document containing more books than one may have been copied from more exemplars than one, which may have been of various degrees of excellence. Or—the most perplexing of all—a document may contain a mixed text, i.e. its text may be the result of an irregular combination of two or more texts belonging to different lines of transmission. So that the words 'good' and 'bad' cannot be applied to the document as a whole, but only to this or that element which has come to it from entire lines of textual ancestry.

Lastly, the Internal Evidence of Documents decreases in utility when, with the increase of the number of documents, several of them appear on general grounds to be 'good', and yet are in disagreement with each other, in which case the student is again reduced to the uncertainties of personal judgement.

INTERNAL EVIDENCE OF GROUPS. Hort places this last, after the next type of evidence, because it would naturally ocme last in the order of discovery. But logically it must be placed at this point in the evolving of safe critical method. If the general value of one document can be gauged in relation to others by an examination of all its readings in the light of probability, it must be possible similarly to gauge the general value of a given *group* of documents in relation to other groups.

This has two advantages over the internal evidence of a single document: (1) If a document has a mixed text, i.e. contains elements derived from different ancestries, it can be ascertained which elements have descended to every member of the group that is being studied, and which have not. And thus the various mixed elements in a document can be studied separately as though a different document were being studied in each case, because every reading (accident apart) goes back to a previous document from which it is derived. (2) A very small group can be found 'good', while a very large one may be 'bad'. The counting of documents can play no part at all in textual criticism. All documents which contain a reading have inherited *that reading* from a common ancestor. 'Community of reading', as Hort says, 'implies community of origin.' But it should be observed that community in a true reading may imply only the common descent from the autograph. 'The only kind of consent between documents that shows community of origin [*sc.* short of the autograph] is community in error' (Burkitt). And so we are led to the best and surest kind of evidence that critics have learnt to use.

GENEALOGICAL EVIDENCE. To gauge rightly the value of a group in relation to other groups, it is necessary to know the genealogical relationship of all documents to each other. If of ten documents containing the same work nine coincide in a reading, while the tenth has a variant, the subjective weighing of probability between group and group is far from adequate. For the nine might all have been copies of the same document, in which case the choice would not be between nine and one, but between two single documents. Or the nine might all have been copied from the tenth, and their variations be nothing but corruptions, and as far as those ten are concerned the reading of the tenth is to be preferred. But the former case affords the better opportunity for the critic, because the two single documents point back to a common source, i.e. a point nearer to the autograph. Or, once more, the nine might be found to fall into two sets, five descended from one lost ancestor and four from another; and in that case the five and the four and the one resolve themselves into three single documents, and the process of tracing back would continue.

Let us suppose that there are three groups α, β, and γ; and that, in a large number of cases in which we are confronted by triple variants, the documents in the three groups are found normally or frequently arrayed together in support of them respectively. This teaches us that for a large proportion of their text the documents in each group have a common ancestor. Or it may happen that in a large number of other cases one of these groups is divided against itself, and each division of it must have had its own ancestor. Where there has been no mixture the ancestor from which the whole group has inherited a reading stands nearer to the autograph than the ancestor from which a division has inherited its reading. Again, let us suppose that x^1 and x^2 are copies of x, and that y^1 and y^2 are copies of y. Where there has been no mixture, the x's can side against the y's; x^1 or x^2 can go over to the y's; and y^1 or y^2 can go over to the x's; but neither x^1y^1 nor x^2y^2 can side together against the other two: these are cross-combinations due to mixture.

MIXTURE. This greatly increases the complexity of the task. From a variety of causes readings were introduced into manuscripts not from their proper line of descent but from one or more other lines. In this case there is no homogeneous text which can be traced back to an ancestor but, as has been said, to different elements in a document, each element representing, as it were, a separate document whose ancestor must be traced. One result is that the ancestor of the larger or more complex group cannot necessarily be assumed to stand nearer to the autograph than the ancestor of the smaller, because readings which had previously only a narrow distribution may have been given, in comparatively late times, a wide extension by favourable circumstances. The first step, then, is obviously to recognize mixture when we meet it. This is done most easily in the case of 'conflate' readings, i.e. where two variants are combined into one whole, forming a third reading. It is far more likely that the third is a combination of the other two than that the other two are independent simplifications of the third. If, then, we note a considerable number of conflate readings, and find practically the same groups of documents supporting the two shorter readings and the conflate reading respectively, we learn that the third group is certainly tainted with mixture, while the other two contain at least portions of two ancient texts which were eventually mixed together. The groups are seldom quite constant, though there is generally a nucleus of documents within them which is. But we feel certain that the documents, say in a group a which habitually supports conflates, witness to a later and less pure text than those from which they are habitually absent, say β and γ. But mixture does not always reveal itself in conflation. Two variants might frequently occur which could not possibly be combined into one. One of the two, say the reading of group β, is simply taken over into the documents which habitually favour conflates (group a). But since these are known, the real evidence for the two readings in the case of mixture remains as before. On the other hand, in so far as its readings are not due to mixture, the ancestor of group a was a manuscript in the same line of transmission as the ancestor of group β, and becomes an additional witness for the β reading.

TRUE AND FALSE READINGS. We now know the way in which the existing documents reveal their ancestry. But it remains to be seen how far this enables us to distinguish true from false readings. First, it is obvious that if a manuscript A is extant we can disregard all its descendants. Apart from mixture, all readings in which they differ from A are wrong, except in the rare cases where a scribe may have hit upon the true reading by pure accident when A is wrong. If a manuscript B with a different text has no descendants, and A has a dozen, a reading in the latter must not be reckoned as having a probability of 13 to 1: it is simply A against B. If A is lost, its descendants still have only the weight of one document against B; but we must use their evidence in such a way that we can detect the errors which have been introduced into them since A, before we compare them with B—that is to say, we must reconstruct A from them. In practice, however, we do not start from classified manuscripts; we have to discover which belong to the same families by an examination of their common readings, and thus reconstruct the ancestors of the various groups which may disclose themselves. The following genealogical tree is given by Hort as an illustration (*Introd.*, p. 54):

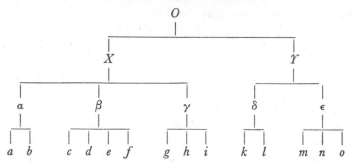

O is a manuscript descended from the autograph; and the use of this tree, therefore, will take us no nearer to the autograph than O. If, from another set of manuscripts, we could reconstruct another ancestor P, then O and P would point back to *their* common ancestor Q, nearer to the autograph. But when we have worked back with all the available evidence to the earliest ancestors we can, and have not yet reached the autograph, it is clear that genealogical evidence can help us no farther. And yet the period between the autograph and the earliest traceable ancestor was that in which it was most easy for corruptions to appear, because the books had not begun to be considered sacred. That is the position in which we are left with regard to every book of the New Testament. The number and complexity of the Gospel codices take us farther back than those of any other book; but in the last resort we are obliged to be content with subjective considerations, and fall back on the internal evidence of documents and groups.

But it is important to understand why complexity can be a help and not a hindrance. In Hort's imaginary tree, in all cases in which (say) the γ group agrees with that of the δε groups against the αβ groups, the αβ readings can be rejected (except in the cases of mixture or accidental coincidence), because, while a corruption can have occurred in an intermediate ancestor of αβ, it is possible for γ and δε to coincide only by having received the reading through X and Υ from O. And there is nothing (except mixture or accident) to make αβ agree with the autograph against O. The same is true when any one of α, β, γ, δ, ε stands against the others, or when (by mutual mixture among descendants of X antecedent to α, β, γ) any two of α, β, γ stand against the others. The consent of Υ with any part of the descendants of X leads back through O to the autograph. The same must be true, therefore, in the last generation, when any one of the five lesser sets is divided against itself.

But lastly, if mixture comes in from another line of descent than that of O, quite different conclusions may be reached. If, say, γ sides with δε against αβ, it may be that γ and Υ have both been affected by mixture, so that the reading of αβ may be that of X and of O. Or αβ may have received a mixture from a text independent of O, and this rival to O may have preserved the true reading of the autograph. But these suppositions need be entertained only when the reading in question is actually found in fairly numerous manuscripts, or when there is other good ground for supposing that mixture from without exists.

Such are the principles underlying the work of Westcott and Hort. Their *Introduction* elaborates them, but this may serve as a summary of their main argument. Their application of them to the then known documents must now be sketched.

Application of Principles

The 'Syrian' [i.e. 'Byzantine'] Text.[1] An overwhelming proportion of the readings common to the great mass of Greek manuscripts—cursives and late uncials—is identical with those of Chrysostom's quotations, of his fellow pupil Theodorus, and their teacher Diodorus. The first named spent the last ten years of his life first at Constantinople as bishop and then wandering as an exile; the second was at Mopsuestia; and the third at Tarsus; but all three belonged to, and worked at, Antioch. Thus the fundamental text of late Greek manuscripts generally is that which was dominant in the second half of the fourth century, which Hort calls 'Antiochian or Graeco-Syrian'. The varying degrees of corruption of our better manuscripts cannot be understood unless it is realized that this 'Syrian' text was either contemporary with, or earlier than, the oldest manuscripts that have come down to us, and that every one of them, with the exception of B and early papyri, has been to some extent affected by it. All the non-Syrian texts

---

[1] Cf. E. C. Colwell, *J.B.L.* liv, 1935, pp. 211–21.

to be found in our manuscripts are older than the Syrian. To prove this Hort examined: (1) eight conflate readings; (2) ante-Nicene patristic quotations; (3) the internal evidence of Syrian readings. (1) In each case two short readings are found in two different groups of documents, and they are conflated in a third. And in each case the ancestors from which the two former groups were descended were older than that of the third group. He names them 'Neutral and Alexandrian', 'Western', and 'Syrian' respectively. (2) On patristic writings he sums up by saying, 'Before the middle of the third century, at the very earliest, we have no historical signs of the existence of readings, conflate or other, that are marked as distinctively Syrian by the want of attestation from groups which have preserved the other ancient forms of text'. (3) The authors of the Syrian text selected or combined, with many alterations of their own, the readings of at least three earlier forms of text, an Alexandrian, a Western, and a third.

The net result is that a reading which is distinctively Syrian is worthless. And in the case of any other reading the ancestor of the Syrian text has the value of only one manuscript siding with the group which contains that reading.

The Western Text. Hort wrote before enough material was available for a just appreciation of the nature of the text to which was given this name, which came down from Griesbach. He holds it in lower esteem than that which it has gained in recent times. He admits that 'it is not uncommon to find one, two, or three of the most independent and most authentically Western documents' attesting 'a state of the Western text when some of its characteristic corruptions had not yet arisen, and others had'. But this means that in some cases they must attest the earliest known readings, and probably more often than he was willing to admit. Of characteristic corruptions he names three: (*a*) Readings due to a love of paraphrase. (*b*) Non-biblical alterations and additions. (*c*) Assimilations, e.g. between parallel passages of the Old Testament, of Ephesians and Colossians, of Jude and 2 Peter, and above all of the first three Gospels. So he concludes that, 'whatever be the merits of individual Western readings, the Western texts generally are due to a corruption of the apostolic texts'. He recognizes their merit, however, in a small number of passages, all (except Matt. xxvii. 49) in the last three chapters of Luke, where he believes interpolation to have taken place in all non-Western texts, but not in the Western. He names these 'Western non-interpolations', though modern scholars would say that this class is not homogeneous and that a simpler term would be 'Western omissions'. The trend of modern criticism is to recognize a larger number of passages in which the Western text has escaped interpolation where all other texts have suffered and at the same time to recognize, more than Hort did, the possibility of doctrinal modifications upon the text especially by 'Western' scribes.

The Alexandrian Text. It is not unnatural that a purer text should have been preserved at Alexandria with its exact grammatical School. Readings which are pre-Syrian and non-Western find the great bulk of their support in writers connected with Egypt, especially Alexandria and neighbouring places in north Egypt. But not there only; early non-Western readings were preserved in various degrees of purity in regions remote from Alexandria. Hort held, therefore, that it was misleading to use the term 'Alexandrian' for all such readings. It must be applied to those which are normally supported by distinctively Alexandrian authorities. 'The more startling characteristics of Western corruption are almost wholly absent from the Alexandrian readings. . . . The changes made have usually more to do with language than matter, and are marked by an effort after correctness of phrase. They are evidently the work of careful and leisurely hands, and not seldom display a delicate philological tact which unavoidably lends them at first sight a deceptive appearance of originality.' Thus the Alexandrian text, from Hort's point of view, was mostly the result of Alexandrian corrections.

The 'Neutral' Text. There are, then, readings which are pre-Syrian, but neither Western nor Alexandrian. They may be seen, for example, when documents normally Western attest non-Western readings in opposition to other Western manuscripts, in cases where mixture seems to be improbable. Such documents attest a state of the text when it had been only partially Westernized, and presuppose an earlier text which was not Western at all. And they can be seen most instructively when both the Western and Alexandrian texts err, 'especially when they severally exhibit independent modes of easing an apparent difficulty in the text antecedent to both'. No manuscript, version, or patristic writer preserves this text in its original purity; it can be arrived at only by a delicate comparison of pre-Syrian groups. But the nearest approach to it is to be found in B (except in the Pauline epistles and Apoc.), and next to it, but a long way after, comes ℵ. Of other manuscripts, which again come a long way after ℵ, it may be said in general that those which have most Alexandrian readings usually have also most neutral readings.

Modern criticism has only confirmed the fact that B contains a purer text than any other known manuscript, and that Westcott and Hort's edition contained a purer text than any that preceded it. But their argument with regard to a neutral text has been called in question, and it is usual now to put B and ℵ at the head of the Alexandrian text, not apart as 'neutral'. More recent editors have, indeed, reached not dissimilar results by other methods. And these methods must now be studied.

§ 5. FURTHER ADVANCE

Like all scientific results, those reached by Westcott and Hort were a stepping-stone to more. Their solid contribution was the safe foundation which they laid in the principle that manuscripts are to be judged not by their age, nor the numbers in which they support a given reading, but by the type of text which they exhibit, which enables them to be grouped genealogically. Salmon,[1] though he criticized their work, said that it could be called epoch-making quite as correctly as that of Darwin. And to a large extent the grouping which they mapped out holds good today. But since their time several discoveries have been made, and experts have been continuously at work, with the result that their conclusions are undergoing certain modifications.

Their first chief conclusion, which may be said to be permanently established, was that the text, generally speaking,

[1] *Some Thoughts on the Textual Criticism of the N.T.*, 1897, p. 5.

of later manuscripts, which superseded all earlier texts, was the result of a revision which was officially, and became universally, approved. No manuscript containing the actual text of the revision survives (unless it is Π, as Mrs. Lake's work[1] suggests), but in a slightly modified form it became authoritative throughout the Byzantine Empire from the ninth century. Hence the name 'Byzantine', akin to Griesbach's, is preferable to the name 'Syrian', which Hort uses (which might be thought to have something to do with 'Syriac'), or 'Antiochian' as it is sometimes called. But it no doubt emanated from Antioch, since it was used, as has been said, by Chrysostom, who worked there for nearly twenty years, and by no writer before his date. In 398 he became Patriarch of Constantinople, where the text was speedily adopted. The revision was possibly made about 300 by Lucian of Antioch, who was martyred there in 312. His authorship is supported by two statements of Jerome: 1. In his preface to his Vulgate Chronicles: 'Alexandria and Egypt in their Septuagint extol the authority of Hesychius; Constantinople to Antioch approves the manuscripts containing the text of Lucian the martyr; between these, the provinces of Palestine read the codices edited by Origen, which Eusebius and Pamphilus published. The whole world is thus divided between a threefold variety.' 2. In his preface to his Vulgate Gospels he speaks of the multitude of differences in Latin manuscripts, which must be corrected from the fountainhead of the Greek; but he will have nothing to do with the versions attributed to Lucian and Hesychius, of which he speaks very slightingly. But it must be noted that he may be referring only to the Greek Old and not to the New Testament at all. From the modern point of view the revision had deplorable results. Once an approved text had been issued, corrections were gradually made in earlier manuscripts to bring them into conformity with it; and of their descendants, the Greek manuscripts that we possess, not one (except probably B) escaped the infection, except the earlier papyri.

The revision was felt to be necessary because two centuries of corruption had produced a bewildering variety of texts. But

---

[1] *Family Π and the Codex Alexandrinus*, 1936; cf. B. H. Streeter, *J.T.S.* xxxviii, 1937, pp. 225–9.

when the unrevised elements in our manuscripts are examined, the texts are found to belong severally to certain areas. In the two centuries during which the books were only gradually becoming recognized as inspired, the manuscripts were subject to all the ordinary mistakes and corruptions of scribes, most of whom were not trained copyists but poor and often ignorant amateurs.

As soon as there were numerous copies of a book in circulation in the same area, one copy would constantly be corrected by another, and thus within that area a general standard of text would be preserved. But what we have to consider is that it is unlikely that the errors in the first copy of the Gospel of John, for example, which reached Rome would be the same as those in the first copy which came to Alexandria; and as each of these would become the parent of most other copies used in those respective cities, there would, from the very beginning, be some difference between the local texts of Rome and Alexandria. . . . In this way local texts would inevitably develop, not only in the greater, but also in the smaller centres of Christianity. But along with a growing veneration for the text as that of inspired Scripture, there would come a tendency, whenever a new copy of the Gospels for official use in the public services was wanted, to lay more and more stress on the importance of having an accurate text. This would naturally result in the smaller churches obtaining new copies from the greater metropolitan sees, since these would be thought likely to possess a pure text. From these any copies in private hands in the smaller churches would be corrected. Thus the local texts of smaller churches would tend to become assimilated to those of the greater centres in their immediate neighbourhood [Streeter[1]].

When we look for local texts we find three, at any rate, represented in the Coptic, Syriac, and Latin versions, which would be needed for missionary work in the areas where those languages were respectively spoken, i.e. in Egypt, in Mesopotamia, and in Italy, Gaul, and Africa. And they would be translated, for the most part, from Greek manuscripts which had developed each its different type of text in its own area. The descendants of those manuscripts may have suffered, in different ways and degrees, mixture and assimilation to the Byzantine standard; but we may antecedently expect to find,

---

[1] *The Four Gospels*, 1926, pp. 35 f.

by genealogical methods, types of text which may be called Alexandrian, Eastern, and Western.

(a) Alexandrian

The earliest Father whose writings afford any evidence of the text current in Alexandria is Clement. The text of his quotations is rather a puzzle when compared with that of Alexandrian manuscripts. P. M. Barnard[1] shows that it is strongly coloured by 'Western' elements. But he had travelled in south Italy, as well as in Syria and Palestine, before he went to Alexandria. And Streeter (op. cit., pp. 57 f.) suggests that he took with him thither a Western text, and that becoming familiar with an Alexandrian text which he heard read in church, he used Alexandrian readings when he quoted from his memory of what he heard, but Western readings when he used his own manuscripts brought from Italy. Further, that his pupils may have noted some of his Western readings, which thus became perpetuated in the Alexandrian text. But this does not explain all the phenomena. There are also readings which he may have brought from the East, and which point to pre-Origenian types of which little is known.

Origen is the first biblical scholar who is known to have interested himself in textual matters. But while his work on the LXX is well known, there is no clear evidence that he revised the text of the New Testament. And yet he was not a man who would be likely to accept the popular text without critical caution. The oldest papyri suggest that the B type of text was known in Egypt before his day[2] and he cannot be considered the source of it. But if he used there (and at Caesarea) a type of text which compromised between the short, austere B-text and the more popular and 'gossipy' D type of text, his choice no doubt influenced many scribes who resorted later to the library of Pamphilus.[3] However much older than Origen the B-א type is, there is an increasing agreement among scholars that it cannot be placed on quite so high a pedestal as Westcott

[1] *Texts and Studies*, v. 5, Cambridge, 1899.

[2] But L. Cerfaux would challenge this. He thinks that there is no trace of the B-א type of text in Alexandria to be found in second-century papyri or Gnostic authors (*Ephemerides Theologicae Lovanienses*, xv, 1938, pp. 674–82).

[3] Cf. Lagrange, *Revue Biblique*, iv, 1895, pp. 501–24.

and Hort placed their 'Neutral' text, a transcendent text raised above local corruptions whether Western or Alexandrian. Salmon[1] complained that the name is 'question-begging'; founded on the quality of the text, it presupposes the final establishment of their theory. The strongest evidence for it comes, on their own showing, from Alexandria. But our conceptions of what they called Western have been altered by the discovery of the Sinaitic Syriac, and by the higher value which modern study places on the ancient versions, of which the Old Syriac and the Old Latin are older than our oldest manuscripts. Alexandrian scholars were on a higher level of education and training than any others, but might be 'for that reason the more exposed to the danger of treating the text of the Gospels by the same *a priori* methods as their heathen teachers and contemporaries treated the text of Homer'.[2] When readings which can reasonably be regarded as 'Western' corruptions in all parts of the world have been discarded, there remain readings in the local texts of Europe and Africa on the one hand, and the East on the other, including those of early Egyptian papyri, which may, more frequently than Westcott and Hort imagined, be truer to the original than the Alexandrian.

Hort thought it possible that the 'Hesychian' revision was represented by the group which he called distinctively 'Alexandrian'. Bousset, on the other hand,[3] suggested that it was represented by B, the writing of which can have been only a few years after the revision. But the occasional Western, as against distinctively Alexandrian, readings in B render this doubtful. Whether it was the work of Hesychius or not, the text is on the lines of Origen's, but with a more ruthless pruning away of every trace of 'Western corruption'. That is to say, it is the early text of Alexandria refined in the crucible of Alexandrian scholarship, but not infected with the 'Alexandrianisms' found in the later local text.

The manuscripts of this later text suffered not only from the

---

[1] *Some Thoughts on the Textual Criticism of the N.T.*, p. 49.

[2] C. H. Turner, *Theology*, ix, 1924, p. 222 and *J.T.S.* xxviii, 1926–7, pp. 145–58.

[3] *Texte u. Untersuch.* xi, 1894, 4. 92.

infiltration of 'Western', i.e. unrevised, elements, but from grammatical and stylistic 'improvements', such as would be natural in the home of classical scholarship. Even ℵ is not quite exempt, but they are more frequent in C 33 Ξ Δ (Mk.) Ψ (Mk.), and most frequently of all in L; they are found also in the quotations of Alexandrian writers, especially Cyril, and in the bohairic version. It was to a text of this type that Hort confined the name 'Alexandrian', a 'partially degenerate form of the B text', as though the degeneracy in this direction constituted the Alexandrianism. It is truer to say that the later Alexandrian text is a degenerate form of the earlier. It is throughout a local text, as Salmon long ago insisted.

Finally, while 'Lucian's' recension, at the end of the third century, adhered more closely to the Alexandrian than to the Western text, the manuscripts of the later Alexandrian text suffered, on the whole, more than the Western from 'corrections' to bring them into conformity with the Byzantine standard.

In view, however, of the occasional support for readings hitherto considered 'Byzantine' given by P[46], dogmatism on this point would be out of place.

(b) Eastern

The stream of 'unrevised' readings which inundated Europe and Carthage flowed also eastward into the districts of Mesopotamia, Syria, and Palestine, of which Edessa, Antioch, and Caesarea were the chief centres. It is antecedently probable that in those areas a type of local text would grow up. In Hort's day, as has been said, there were known the Curetonian Syriac, some members of the Ferrar group, and some other cursives of a similar character to the latter. These contained some non-Byzantine readings which he had not evidence enough to place as a distinct type. The only course open to him, therefore, was to group all these with D (which was thought to be the most typical Western manuscript) and the Old Latin under the name Western. But since then there was discovered in 1892 the Sinaitic Syriac, which began to lead scholars to question the grouping, because, in re-enforcing the non-Alexandrian non-Western elements in the Curetonian, it made it clear that the Old Syriac, though on the whole it was nearer to D and the Old Latin than to the Alexandrian text, was distinct enough from them to be reckoned as a third type of text earlier than the Byzantine revision.

Evangelion da-Mepharreshe. In the first half of the third century the separate Gospels were translated from Greek manuscripts into Syriac. The translation received a considerable Western element from the *Diatessaron* (see pp. 444–7), but the importance of Syr.[sin] consists mainly in the fact that it contains a large number of readings which are neither Western nor Alexandrian, but belong to an independent Eastern text. The version as it left the translator's hands, we may assume, was a fairly faithful representation of the text used at Antioch about A.D. 200 though both manuscripts were written probably *c.* A.D. 400–50. The colophon of Syr.[sin] definitely states it to be a copy of the *Evangelion da-Mepharreshe.* It is true that there were something like two centuries between the original translation and our manuscript, during which time it was possible for corrections to be made to conform it to Greek manuscripts; but there are, in fact, very few cases in which this seems to have been done. It almost always represents the text either of the original translator or of the *Diatessaron.* The Curetonian MS., which is shown by the palaeographical details to be only a little later than the Sin., is less trustworthy[1] as evidence for the Eastern text, because it not only contains *Diatessaron* readings, but also shows signs of revision from a Greek manuscript,[2] which contained some, at least, of the more common additions to the Western text. The translation contained in Syr.[sin] 'bears all the marks of freedom and idiomatic vernacular rendering which everywhere (and nowhere more clearly than in Syriac) distinguish earlier translations from later'.[3] And the *Acts of Judas Thomas* (which Burkitt showed to have been written in Syriac), which cannot be dated later than the end of the third century, uses not the *Diatessaron* or the *Peshitta,* but the gospel text found in Syr.[sin] and Syr.[cur] If, then, the translation was made in the third

---

[1] Contrast M. J. Lagrange, *Critique textuelle,* pp. 213–18.
[2] Burkitt, *Evang. da-Meph.* ii. 215–19.
[3] Turner, *J.T.S.* xi, 1909–10, p. 202.

century from Greek manuscripts, it must probably have been made in Edessa. Now the Christianity of Edessa previously to this was probably open to the suspicion of being unorthodox, the only two Edessene teachers known to us in that period, Tatian and Bardesanes, having been—at least in Greek or Latin estimation—unorthodox. And in the seventh century the orthodox in Edessa were known as Palutians, which implies that those who were not Palutians were not considered orthodox. Moreover, Palut of Edessa, according to the *Doctrine of Addai*, went to receive consecration within Roman territory from Serapion, Bishop of Antioch. It may be concluded, therefore, that Palut introduced orthodox Christianity into Edessa. From that Burkitt (op. cit.) goes on to conjecture that he superseded the gospel of Tatian's *Diatessaron* by the four separate Gospels obtained at Antioch. But Turner notes indications which point to Palestine rather than to Antioch. On the one hand the Greek forms of Jewish proper names and place-names are given their correct Aramaic spelling; and on the other 'in at least two places, "Bethabara" for "Bethany" beyond Jordan in Jn. i. 28, and "Girgashites" for "Gerasenes" in Mk. v. 1, the Old Syriac agrees with Origen in readings which are the direct reflexion, through pious researches or local patriotism, of the growing cult for the holy places of Palestine' (Turner). The former alone might have been the work of an Edessene scholar; the latter alone might show that the Old Syriac was later than Origen. But the combination of the two strongly suggests that the translator was a Palestinian, or at least lived in Syria.

But there were variations in the Eastern type of text no less than in the Western. The evidence for the existence of a 'Caesarean' clan has already been discussed, though it now seems that this clan had its origins in Egypt, while it may have been popularized later at Caesarea.[1]

(c) Western

In Europe west of the Adriatic, and in Africa, there is little evidence of the critical spirit which seeks to preserve the purity,

[1] Cf. A. F. J. Klijn, *A Survey of the Researches into the Western Text of the Gospels and Acts*, 1950, pp. 110–46.

or improve the style, of the text. Consequently the popular
corruptions—paraphrase, interpolation, and assimilation—
are seen in their most pronounced form. The interpolations
are often striking, sometimes long, and occasionally inserted
awkwardly in positions which would not appear to be the most
natural. But manuscripts of different kinds, and belonging to
different localities, agree in their positions, and very largely in
their wording. Burkitt, accordingly, concludes[1] that they go
back to a single interpolated codex. The latest suggestion is
that of J. H. Ropes, *The Beginnings of Christianity*, vol. iii, 'The
Text of the Acts'. In his Preface he gives the upshot of it as
follows: 'the preparation of the "Western" text, which took
place early in the second century, perhaps at Antioch, was
incidental to the work of forming the collection of Christian
writings for general Church use which ultimately, somewhat
enlarged, became the New Testament; in a word, that the
"Western" text was the text of the primitive "canon" (if the
word may be pardoned in referring to so early a date), and was
expressly created for that purpose.' The suggestion, as he says,
is one worthy of further discussion. The possibility must also
be borne in mind that the 'Western' text arose at the time
when Christians started the habit (before pagans[2]) of using
codices rather than rolls for their books. The codex-form
made for ease of reference and for assimilation. In fact,
the 'primitive canon' may well have appeared in an early
codex capable of holding Gospels and Acts (at least) in one
portable object.

The Western text has been regarded successively from different points of view. In 1891 Rendel Harris[3] held that in the
Acts, where the text is most striking and characteristic, there
had been a reaction in the Greek text from the primitive Latin
translations, and occasionally from the Syriac. The Greek,
therefore, was not a true standard of the Western text; and
many of its glosses were due to Montanist and Marcionite
influence. Although the theory of Latin reaction suggested in
this pioneer work has failed to establish itself, except in the

[1] *Two Lectures on the Gospels*, 1901, pp. 23 f.
[2] C. H. Roberts, *J.T.S.* xl, 1939, p. 256.
[3] *A Study of Codex Bezae*, Camb. Text and Studies, ii. 1.

case of a very few readings, the work succeeded in putting the text of the codex in a truer light than when it was considered the standard for the Western text. In 1893 and 1895 F. H. Chase maintained a parallel view[1] that the phenomena of the Greek might be explained by Syriac rather than by Latin influence. But this has not obtained more acceptance than the other or, except in the *Bulletins of the Bezan Club*, received the attention that it deserved, owing perhaps to the dearth of Syriac scholars among New Testament critics. For the handling of his subject Dr. Chase chose the text of the Acts, because the peculiarities of the Western text are more strongly marked there than elsewhere. The Acts became the special study of Professor Ramsay, who pointed out the archaeological accuracy of some of the glosses in D, and suggested that they were the work of an early redactor who lived in Asia Minor. In 1894 they were credited with being the work of St. Luke himself, the theory being revived by Fr. Blass that St. Luke published two editions of the Acts. He extended this theory later to the Third Gospel.[2] He thought that St. Luke wrote (1) the 'Neutral' text of the Gospel for Theophilus; (2) the edition of the Acts containing the longer, 'Western', text, which was written and circulated at Rome; (3) the shorter, 'Neutral', text of the Acts, which he sent to Theophilus; (4) for the Roman Church the whole work by sending them the 'Western' text of the Gospel. The theory was favourably received by such scholars as Salmon, Nestle, and (for the Acts) Zahn. And it has the merit of having instilled the idea that some of the Western variants and 'interpolations' may be original. But it does not adequately explain many of the variants in the Third Gospel and Acts, and it leaves the Western text in other than Lucan writings with no explanation at all; furthermore, on close examination, it is clear that the same writer could not have written both recensions, even of Acts.[3]

Roman Christians, who were, in the first two centuries, mostly non-Latin in origin, spoke Greek. (This must not preclude the question whether there were Latin-speaking

---

[1] *The Old Syriac Element in the Text of Codex Bezae*, 1893, and *The Syro-Latin Text of the Gospels*, 1895.   [2] *The Philology of the Gospels*, London, 1898.

[3] C. S. C. Williams, *Alterations to the text of the Synoptic Gospels and Acts*, p. 54.

Christians in Italy, e.g. at Pompeii.) Marcion, Justin, Irenaeus, Hippolytus all wrote in Greek. On the other hand the Christians of Carthage spoke Latin from the time that they received Christianity. At the beginning of the third century Tertullian was already writing there in the vernacular; and how long before that time Latin was needed for missionary purposes we do not know. At Rome Latin began to be used for theological purposes during the third century, though there was no writer of note till Novatian, who was contemporary with Cyprian. It is natural, therefore, that with the dying-out of Greek as the spoken language the Western type of text should not be preserved in many Greek manuscripts. We possess only two that are of any value for the Gospels, the Freer MS. (W) and codex Bezae (D), the remaining authorities being manuscripts of the Old Latin version, and the quotations of Latin Fathers. The evidence of W is important—a manuscript unknown to Hort—because it shows that the African text (that of Cyprian's quotations, with which *k* is very closely similar) had a Greek origin, and that many of its idiosyncrasies were not merely corruptions current in Latin, or paraphrases of a better Greek text. C. H. Turner[1] holds that the primitive Latin version seems to have been made in a place where the spelling of Semitic names was familiar (though if Jewish Christians worked on the translation, they might have done so in the West as well as the East); and that even the Latin of Cyprian shows secondary elements, an earlier stage being probably traceable in Nemesianus of Thubunae.

When Latin began to be used by Christian writers in Rome, and, generally, west of the Adriatic, the African text gradually underwent textual and linguistic alterations, so that a type emerged which is known as 'European'. For this *b* is the norm, the nearest to which is *ff*[2]. The others cited on p. 378 show different degrees of fidelity to the type, but all of them are nearer to *b* than they are to each other. In the middle of the group stands the Greek MS. D, the text of which is closely related to that used by Irenaeus,[2] and, on the whole, nearer to the European than to the African. The oldest, but not the

---

[1] *J.T.S.* ii, 1901, 600–10.
[2] Sanday and Turner, *Nov. Test. S. Irenaei*, Oxford, 1923.

most typical, member of the European group is *a*, which possibly represents a transitional stage in its formation, since its text is intermediate between *k* and *b*; in Mark, which is the best testing-ground of texts, it is farthest removed from *b*.

While the word 'Western' is rightly geographical as regards the extant authorities, the place of origin of the European text may, after all, be Asia Minor. The evidence which Streeter adduces for this is as follows: The *Epistula Apostolorum* is thought by its editor, Carl Schmidt (*Texte u. Untersuch.* 1919), to be of Ephesian origin; and it has some points of agreement with the Western text, the most striking of which is that in ch. 2 the name Judas Zelotes is given in the list of apostles in Matt. x. 3, a curious combination which occurs, instead of Thaddaeus = Lebbaeus, in *a b h q*, &c. In ch. 3 the wording seems to imply the reading in Jn. i. 13 which asserts the Virgin Birth of Jesus Christ, ὅς . . . ἐγεννήθη for οἵ . . . ἐγεννήθησαν, which occurs in *b*, three quotations of Irenaeus, two of Tertullian, and was known to Ambrose, Augustine, and probably Justin. Possibly the text of the *Epistula* also included the longer conclusion of Mark, which is found in D and in all O.L. manuscripts except the African *k*, and in the text used by Irenaeus and Tatian. To these agreements between a (probably) Ephesian document and the European O.L. must be added the personal links between Asia Minor and the West. Tatian was Justin's pupil, and Justin was converted in Ephesus. And not only was Irenaeus in Smyrna as a boy, but the connexion maintained between Asia Minor and Gaul, which is shown in the *Letter* of the Churches of Vienne and Lyons to the Churches of Asia, was probably due to the intercourse, no doubt for trading purposes, between the cities of Ionia and the Greek-speaking communities of the Rhone valley, who had originally been colonists from Ionia. That would bring the Ephesian text to the Rhone valley. And the relation of Irenaeus to D and the O.L. 'suggests the possibility that the earliest Latin translation used in Gaul was derived, not from the Greek text used in Rome, but from that used in the Rhone valley. This translation might have spread thence into Gallia Cisalpina, the consanguineous district of N. Italy.'[1]

[1] Streeter, op. cit., pp. 70 ff.

Yet a third type of Old Latin was distinguished by Hort and by most scholars after him for a time. Augustine, who speaks of 'codices Afros' (*Retr.* i. 21. 3), says also, 'In ipsis autem interpretationibus Itala ceteris praeferatur; nam est verborum tenacior cum perspicuitate sententiae.'[1] This was understood to mean that he praised an Italian type as superior to all others. And it was thought that a revision of the European O.L. must have been made in northern Italy early in the fourth century. But Bentley had previously disbelieved in the existence of an Italian revision, and Burkitt laid the ghost. In 'The Old Latin and the Itala'[2] he maintained that Augustine's *Itala interpretatio* was simply the Vulgate. Augustine deprecated Jerome's great changes in the Old Testament, but he was warm in his praise of his translation of the Gospels. All his life, when he depended on his memory, he reverted to the Old Latin; but when he quoted with care from a written text of the Gospels it was from the Vulgate, as, for example, in the *De Consensu Evangelistarum* (*c.* A.D. 400); and in the *Acta de Felice* (404), a report of a trial for heresy, he quoted a long passage from the Gospels, and another from the Acts, the latter in pure Old Latin, the former in pure Vulgate.

Some scholars[3] have tried to emend Augustine's words, putting *Aquila* or *illa* for *Itala*. On the former view Aquila's version of the Old Testament was in mind.

The great scholar Jerome (Sophronius Eusebius Hieronymus) was commissioned by Pope Damasus in 381 to produce a revision, in view of the manifold corruptions of the Latin text. He took the Gospels in hand first, and published them, with an open letter to Damasus, in 383; and then followed a very cursory revision of the New Testament. The Gospels were critically edited by Wordsworth and White in 1889–95, and their text was printed in a pocket edition in 1911. They considered that the type of O.L. which Jerome used as his basis was such as was found in cod. Brixianus (*f*), representing the 'Italian' revision of the European Latin, in which the manuscript had been largely corrected in conformity with Greek manuscripts

---

[1] *De Doctr. Christ.* ii. 22.
[2] *Texts and Studies*, iv. 3, 1896; contrast Lagrange, *Critique textuelle*, pp. 257 f.
[3] See B. M. Metzger in Parvis and Wikgren, op. cit., p. 53.

of a Byzantine type. But it is probable that *f* should not be reckoned as an O.L. manuscript at all. Burkitt thinks that it received its text from a manuscript containing both Vulgate and Byzantine elements, and conjectures a Gothic-Latin manuscript of which the Latin side was largely Vulgate and the Gothic largely Byzantine[1]—a view which has gained further support from the phenomena of a more recently discovered Gothic-Latin manuscript, which the same writer describes.[2] He suggests, in the former article, that Jerome's manuscript was more like *b*. Souter, on the other hand, showed[3] that, for Luke at least, his Latin text was more akin to that of *a*, and thought it possible that his manuscript may have been made up of assorted texts, differing in different Gospels.

But whatever may have been the Latin text which he revised, the Greek text in accordance with which he revised it was more important. In the last eight chapters of Luke, a large part of John, and the Catholic epistles, his text is almost entirely Byzantine, while in the remainder of the Gospels there is rather more Alexandrian mixture. The large Byzantine element may have been due to the fact that he had just returned from Constantinople, where he had sat at the feet of Gregory of Nazianzus. But on the death of Damasus, at the end of 384, he went to Palestine, where Pamphilus, in the manuscripts of his library at Caesarea, kept alive, as has been said, the tradition of Origen, for whom Jerome, at this time, had a great admiration. This perhaps accounts for the fact that, in his revision of the Acts and in his commentary on Matthew, his text makes a much nearer approach to that of ℵ. The remainder of the New Testament he revised with much less thoroughness, so that the text of the epistles might almost rather be called Old Latin than Vulgate.

No sooner had he done his work, and copies began to multiply, than the old story of corruption was repeated; Old Latin manuscripts were 'corrected' from the Vulgate, and Vulgate manuscripts were 'corrupted' by the introduction of

---

[1] *J.T.S.* i, 1900, p. 129, cf. K. Lake, *The Text of the New Testament*, 6th ed., 1928, pp. 29 ff., according to whom *f* and *q*, sometimes wrongly called 'Italic', represent probably not a separate version but a modification of the general European type, probably due to the influence of the Vulgate and (for *f*) of the Gothic version.　　[2] *J.T.S.* xi, 1909–10, pp. 611 ff.　　[3] Op. cit. xii, pp. 583 ff.

Old Latin readings. No manuscript with a perfectly pure Hieronymian text survives, but by a critical use of a large number of them Wordsworth and White arrive at a close approximation to it. Its text is of comparatively little use as evidence for ancient readings, but for practical purposes it is a very much 'better' text than the O.L. in so far as it was purged of a great number of the paraphrases, glosses, and interpolations of the Western text.

The Diatessaron. For a knowledge of the Greek text of the Gospels lying behind the O.L. there is at present very little material. From a critical study of Marcion (as quoted by his opponents) and Justin it has been thought that their text was akin to the African. But what would really determine the Roman texts of the Gospels in the latter half of the second century would be the original text of Tatian's *Diatessaron*. Tatian was the first successful missionary in Mesopotamia, in the district of which Edessa was the literary centre. He went there about A.D. 172 after working at Rome. He seems to have died in the East a few years later, so that his work must have been published by 180. He combined the Four Gospels into a harmony, which implies not only the existence of the separate Four, but their canonical distinction from all others. It seems strange that such Christians of Mesopotamia as there were before Tatian's arrival should have had no New Testament at all till he came; but so it was. And they naturally became deeply attached to that form of the Gospel which had helped to build up their faith; so that it remained in popular use, and was read in churches (as is implied in the *Doctrine of Addai*, 36) until about 430, when it was superseded by the separate Peshitta Gospels. The text of the harmony would naturally be that which Tatian knew at Rome, and thus for two and a half centuries a Western type of text was current in the East. The influence of the *Diatessaron* has been exaggerated by some writers, especially von Soden and Vogels, but there is no doubt that it explains a great number of Western readings in the Eastern text.

The sources of our present knowledge of the *Diatessaron*—apart from the Greek fragment found at Dura[1] and the Gospel

---

[1] C. H. Kraeling, *Studies and Documents*, iii, 1935

quotations in Aphraates (Aphrahat), Ephraem in his genuine works, Marutha, and other Syriac writers—are: 1. Ephraem's Commentary on the *Diatessaron*, which is not extant in Syriac, but survives in an Armenian translation.[1] The Armenian work was rendered into Latin by Moesinger (1876), and Ephraem's quotations in it into English by J. Armitage Robinson (see below). 2. An Arabic translation of the *Diatessaron* from the Syriac made in the first half of the eleventh century, edited and rendered into Latin by Ciasca (1888) and into English by Dr. Hamlyn Hill in his *Earliest Life of Christ* (1894). (The latter contains as Append. X the rendering of Ephraem's quotations by J. Armitage Robinson.) It was rendered into French by A. S. Marmadji in 1935 with some refreshing but misplaced attempts at humour. Unfortunately the Syriac from which the Arabic was translated had been revised throughout in conformity with the *Peshitta*, and so, while giving us the Syriac mosaic, is of very little help for determining the original text.[2] 3. A Latin translation found in codex Fuldensis of the Vulgate.[3] It was prepared for, and corrected by, Victor of Capua in 546, whose annotations and signature (with the blot he made in signing his name) are still to be seen in the manuscript. For the purpose of determining the text of the *Diatessaron* this is of no more use than the Arabic, since the Latin employed is pure Vulgate, the purest, in fact, known, next to that of codex Amiatinus. 4. Medieval Dutch translations of the Latin, especially the Liège MS. (*c.* 1300).[4] There is another translation in a manuscript at Stuttgart which adheres more closely to the Vulgate than the former. 5. Late Armenian Fathers, and English, Italian, and Persian Harmonies and the Manichean writings extant in Coptic.[5]

---

[1] The translator, according to F. C. Conybeare (*J.T.S.* xxv, 1924, pp. 232–45), did not give Ephraem's quotations in an immediate rendering of his Syriac, but used another, lost, Armenian version of the Gospels (whether a Harmony or the separate Four is uncertain), the text of which was made from the 'Syriac base' of the Armenian Vulgate. The existence of this 'Syriac base' is now denied by many Armenian scholars.

[2] Cf. A. J. B. Higgins, *J.T.S.* xlv, 1944, pp. 187–99.

[3] Edited by E. Ranke, 1868.

[4] Edited by D. Plooij, C. A. Phillips, and others, 1929–38.

[5] Cf. P. Essabalian, *Le Diatessaron de Tatien*, 1937; V. Todesco, A. Vaccari, and M. Vattasso, *Studi e Testi*, lxxxi, 1937; M. Goates, *The Pepysian Gospel*

These five sources fall into two parts, the Arabic mostly following the order of the mosaic in Ephraem, and the Liège that of Fuld., but the Western part exhibits marked differences from the Eastern. The arrangement in F and L is rougher and cruder, and suggests that the smoother and more natural order of the Eastern part may have been the result of revision and correction. This leads Burkitt to conjecture that 'the agreement of F and L bears witness to a pre-Syriac form of the Harmony, something that Tatian left behind him before he returned to his native Mesopotamia;[1] that this was a Latin, not a Greek, harmony; and that when Tatian prepared a Syriac edition of it, he revised and rearranged it from his Greek manuscripts of the separate Gospels. If this is right there never was a Greek *Diatessaron*. By an examination of the few passages of Fuld. which are not Vulgate, Burkitt concludes that the ancestor of Fuld. (i.e. the manuscript which Victor found) was a Latin Harmony with a 'European' text like that of *b* and *ff*[2]. If so, it might, being Old Latin, be as early as 400 or 300, i.e. its history can be pushed back to an age comparable with that of Ephraem and the rest of the Syriac evidence. And this Latin Harmony may not have been the work of Tatian at all. Eusebius (*H.E.* iv. 29) speaks of Tatian as the leader of an heretical sect who 'put together somehow or other a sort of composition and collection of the Gospels'; 'this he named the Dia-tessaron, which is current among some even till now'. Eusebius does not appear to have seen the work, or known much about it, but was no doubt referring to the popular Syriac work current in the East. (The Syriac translator of Eusebius shortly afterwards showed that he knew it well.) But part of Burkitt's conjecture is that originally it was not intended to be a substitute for the separate Gospels, but was made at the time when Greek was beginning to give way to Latin as the spoken language of Christians in the West; it was 'a Latin epitome for Latin Christians who as yet had nothing but the Greek original' of the Gospels. Its usefulness must have

---

Harmony, 1922; G. Messina, *Biblica*, xxiii, 1942, pp. 268–305, and *Diatessaron persiano*, 1951; H. J. Polotsky, *Manichäische Handschriften*, 1934; and C. R. C. Allberry, *A Manichean Psalm-Book, Pt. ii*, 1938.

[1] *J.T.S.* xxv, 1923–4, p. 116.

been short, because within thirty years, or perhaps less, all four Gospels were available in Latin. This theory would explain the absence of any references to the work in the literature of the Christian West, and the rarity of surviving copies. The Latin *Diatessaron* may have influenced the text of the Gospels in the earliest days of the European Latin, 'when the Latin Gospels current in Roman Africa were being accepted and adapted for Roman and Italian use'; but it did not do so to anything like the extent that the Syriac *Diatessaron* influenced the Old Syriac Gospels.

To the ordinary methods of textual criticism one further consideration may be added, which is coming increasingly into recognition, where it is available, particularly in the Gospels, as a valuable ally. One of the commonest forms of corruption, as has been said, is assimilation, due mainly to the tendency of scribes to write in one Gospel what they remembered in another; but occasionally it seems to have been deliberate, from a wish to smooth down differences. And the advancing study of the Synoptic Problem has provided a criterion other than that of the manuscripts, and yet not subjective.

The new method, starting from the results of Synoptic criticism —not necessarily final or infallible results, but, nevertheless, results reached from the examination of a totally different set of phenomena and of *prima facie* validity in their own sphere—gives us a sort of objective test which reduces the danger of the individual's subjective preferences to a minimum. One accepts, that is to say, a reading, not because it is the reading of B or of D, but because it conforms, say, to Marcan usage, or because it removes a difficulty in the way of the conclusion (reached on an independent line of argument) that Matthew and Luke tapped their Marcan source without collusion with one another. In particular, the appeal to the *vera causa* of contamination of the text of one Gospel by the intrusion of matter from a parallel text in another (and especially a more familiar) Gospel, will often suggest the *prima facie* rejection of the reading of one group of authorities in favour of that of another group, without any absolute regard to their constituent members.[1]

It remains to summarize some of the more important work

[1] C. H. Turner, op. cit., p. 224. See his articles on Marcan usage, *J. T.S.* xxv, xxvi, xxvii, xxviii, xxix, 1924–8.

done in this field since Westcott and Hort. Without discussing the new and confusing nomenclature for all manuscripts adopted by H. von Soden,[1] one may point to his three divisions of textual types: (1) 'H', Hesychian (roughly speaking, 'Alexandrian'): B ℵ Ath. Did. Cyr. and Coptic versions; W (in part) C Ψ Z L Δ 33 892 579 1241. (2) 'I' (Jerusalem, i.e. roughly Western and Caesarean): D Θ 565 28 fam.¹ fam.¹³ Lat. Syr. (3) 'K' (Koine or Byzantine): W (in part) S V 461 655 661 476 E F G H Syr.ᵖᵉˢʰ and the mass of late manuscripts.

H. von Soden was criticized for assuming that he could recover the 'H–I–K' type of text older than our recensions; for his over-estimate of the influence of Tatian upon harmonizing scribes of the separate Gospels; and for associating D in close conjunction with manuscripts of the Θ type.

B. H. Streeter[2] saw that the most pressing problem was to split up the 'Western' text scientifically. In his theory of local texts, he advocated five divisions, not counting the 'Byzantine', under the headings Alexandria, Antioch, Caesarea, Italy and Gaul, Carthage for Gospel manuscripts. This theory may serve as a 'working hypothesis' provided that it is not allowed to obscure certain points. His table of local texts has, under the category of primary authority, manuscripts of very different values. The text of the Koridethi MS., Θ, is not of the same value as Vaticanus, B, though the former is put as a primary authority for Caesarea (Streeter wrote before P⁴⁵ was discovered) while the latter is the primary authority for Alexandria. If all five local texts were quite independent one of another, a majority of the primary authorities in favour of a particular reading would carry weight against the minority whenever internal evidence left one in doubt. But it is a questionable assumption to suppose that any 'primary' authorities arose independently: for example, five independent copies of Mark did not float down from the clouds to the five localities mentioned to serve as archetypes of the 'families'. Again, since Streeter wrote it has become clearer that the 'Caesarean' family or clan arose in Egypt (and was carried to Caesarea)

---

[1] *Die Schriften des Neuen Testaments in ihrer ältesten erreichbaren Textgestalt . . .*, 1902–13.

[2] *The Four Gospels*, 1924; see his chart, p. 108.

probably as a compromise or series of compromises between a text resembling the Alexandrian and one resembling the Western; also that Western manuscripts existed in Egypt, to judge from the papyri. It is also clear that early papyri make us revise our opinion of what we once dismissed as 'late Byzantine' readings. Again, with Streeter's chart in mind it is fatally easy to oversimplify the problem and to suppose that a scribe invariably adopted the same procedure with all parts of the text that he was copying; to suppose, for instance, that the scribe of the Chester Beatty papyri invariably took an Alexandrian text and based his compromise on it, inserting the less extravagant Western readings of other manuscripts known to him into it. Such may have been his (or his textual ancestor's) procedure when he copied the Epistle to the Hebrews, because it was accepted in Alexandria (and Syria) long before it was accepted in the West. But when he copied the Epistle to the Romans he may well have taken as his base for Rom. v. 17–xv. 33 (i. 1–v. 16 being lost) a Western text, perhaps of a pre-Marcionite character, if Dr. T. W. Manson[1] is correct; this was akin not only to D F G but also to the Marcionite text which was derived from it. Whereas the Marcionite text omitted xv, P^{46} naturally placed the doxology at the end of xv, where the Western text ended. But the scribe of P^{46} allowed a few non-Western readings into these chapters and drew on an Alexandrian manuscript for xvi, which he added after the doxology. In fact a textual critic has to take into account not only the intrinsic merit of a manuscript or of a group of manuscripts but also the history, so far as it is known, of the canon of Scripture and of the inclusion in that canon of any part of the New Testament with which he is concerned. He may have to allow for the possibility that the difference between the Alexandrian and Western readings is due to two copies of the original having been made and sent to different Churches by the author; for instance, Paul may have sent Rom. i–xv to Rome and then sent a copy, including Rom. xvi, to Asia, as Manson has suggested. The failure of Blass to establish his theory of two recensions of Luke and of Acts going back to

[1] *Bulletin of the John Rylands Library*, xxxi, 1948, pp. 224–40 and C. S. C. Williams, *Ex. T.* lxi, 1950, pp. 125 f.

St. Luke should not deter one from applying a similar hypothesis to other New Testament evidence.

F. C. Burkitt's distrust of the evidence for the 'Caesarean' text appeared in his review[1] of Streeter's *The Four Gospels*. He preferred to group under an 'Eastern' family Θ 565 fam.[1] fam.[13] and the Old Syriac, as opposed to the Alexandrian, Western, and Byzantine families. Burkitt had become known early in the century[2] when he showed that Syr.[sin] and Syr.[cur] represent the Old Syriac 'separated Gospels' and that Syr.[pesh] was no longer to be considered the ancient Syriac text as Cureton had thought but that it was due to Rabbula, Bishop of Edessa, A.D. 411–35, who used it, he said, to displace the *Diatessaron*. Burkitt favoured those readings which are supported by Syr.[sin] and by *k* rather than those of the Alexandrian text, his advice being, 'Let us come up out of the land of Egypt'. Recently Burkitt's views have been challenged by A. Vööbus[3] and M. Black.[4] Just as the *Diatessaron* was not altogether displaced by the *Peshitta*, so the *Peshitta* had not altogether displaced old Syriac versions used even by Rabbula himself.

M. J. Lagrange crowned many years' work on textual criticism for the *Revue Biblique* with his *Critique textuelle*,[5] in which the following divisions are implied:

1. For the Gospels
   - (*a*) B-recension. B $\aleph$ W[Lk. i-viii. 30] C Ψ L Δ 33 892 579 1241 Cop. P[1] P[5] P[22] P[4] 0161 0109.
   - (*b*) D-recension. D 0171 (Lat.[vet] Syr.[vet]).
   - (*c*) C-type (Caesarean) which Lagrange recognized as having been born in Egypt. W Θ 565 fam.[1] fam.[13] 700 28 P[37] P[45].
   - (*d*) A-type (Byzantine) A Ω K Π E F G H.

2. For Acts
   - (*a*) B-type. B $\aleph$ C A Ψ 81 33 G I[5] 1175 104 459 326 1261 P[45] P[8] 0165.
   - (*b*) D-type. D E P[38] P[48] P[29].
   - (*c*) A-type. 093 S P L H, &c.

---

[1] *J.T.S.* xxvi, 1924–5, pp. 285.   [2] *Evangelion da-Mepharreshe*, ii, 1904.
[3] *Contributions of the Baltic University*, lix, 1947 and lxiv, 1948.
[4] *Bulletin of the John Rylands Library*, xxxiii, 1950–1, pp. 203–10.
[5] *Critique textuelle, II. La Critique rationelle*, 1935.

Lagrange considered also the textual evidence for the rest of the New Testament.

J. H. Ropes[1] printed the text of codex Vaticanus side by side with that of codex Bezae or other Western evidence. In his introduction and notes he favoured the Alexandrian text but allowed that the Western text sometimes preserves the original.

A. C. Clark[2] favoured Western readings which he culled from all possible sources. The Alexandrian text was accounted for as being shorter owing to the omission of stichoi from the Western. (Contrast Dom C. Butler, *Downside Review*, 1933, and Sir F. G. Kenyon, *The Western Text in the Gospels and Acts*, pp. 17 ff.)

The modern study of textual criticism enables us to realize more clearly than was possible for Hort the width of the gulf fixed between the autograph and the three earliest types of text that we can trace. When research has brought us back to the Alexandrian, Eastern, and Western texts in the purest forms obtainable, we cannot, by genealogical methods, go behind them. There does not survive any manuscript which contains a 'neutral' text, independent of, and superior to, the three, though the earliest Alexandrian, as has been said, is probably the purest of them. But the agreement, say, of the Old Syriac with the Old Latin of *k*, in a case in which neither has been affected by the Western influence of the *Diatessaron*, points back to a common origin for the reading which must be far older than the oldest Alexandrian evidence of any kind that we possess. No early intercourse is known between Africa and Mesopotamia, so that a common origin is, in all probability, the autograph. Or if there were an agreement between Aphraates and the Sahidic which was known not to be due to Western mixture through the *Diatessaron* or other cause, it would have a strong claim to consideration, even if it were supported by no known manuscript. The giving to versions and Fathers a more rightful weight in the scale is one of the chief lines along which modern study has moved from Westcott and Hort's position. In the great bulk of the readings in which the three local texts agree, it is reasonable to be pretty confident

---

[1] *The Beginnings of Christianity*, iii, ed. F. J. F. Jackson and K. Lake, 1926.
[2] *The Acts of the Apostles*, 1933.

that they represent the autograph. When their reading, in spite of their agreement, appears to be intrinsically impossible or extremely improbable—in other words, when internal evidence of readings is in ultimate conflict with genealogical evidence—the former holds its own against the latter, and it is concluded that a corruption has occurred earlier than all our extant witnesses, a 'primitive corruption' as Hort called it; and room is then left for conjectural emendation. There are such cases, but they are very few. When the readings of all the three local texts in their earliest and purest forms differ, we are obliged (except in the special cases of assimilation mentioned by Turner, above), to fall back on subjective considerations. Internal evidence must be the last court of appeal. Textual criticism has done its utmost when it has eliminated the whole of the vast mass of errors which can be detected by means which are not subjective. And, finally, there must always remain some instances in which external data cannot help, and subjective criticism is at fault; there is no apparent reason for preferring any one of the two or three variants which present themselves.

The principles sketched in this chapter take us, in theory, less far towards the original than Hort's. But modern students, by methods in some respects differing from his, have recognized the great value of the early Alexandrian text represented by B. By pinning his faith to it as almost wholly 'neutral', he obtained an exceedingly good text, but discovery and scientific study are improving it, and will continue to improve it for a long time to come.

BOOKS

J. M. Bover, *Novi Testamenti Biblia Graeca et Latina*, 1943, *Prolegomena*.
F. C. Burkitt, *Texts and Studies*, iv. 3, 1896.
—— art. 'Text and Versions', *Encylopaedia Biblica*, iv, 1907.
—— *Evangelion da-Mepharreshe*, ii, 1904.
A. C. Clark, *The Primitive Text of the Gospels and Acts*, 1914.
—— *The Acts of the Apostles*, 1933.
C. R. Gregory, *Tischendorf's Novum Testamentum Graece*, 8th ed., iii, *Prolegomena*, 1884; or *Textkritik des Neuen Testaments*, 1900–2.
P. E. Kahle, *The Cairo Geniza*, Schweich Lectures, 1941, pp. 117–228.
Sir F. G. Kenyon, *Handbook to the Textual Criticism of the New Testament*, 2nd ed., 1926.

—— *Recent Developments in the Textual Criticism of the Greek Bible*, Schweich Lectures, 1933.

—— *The Text of the Greek Bible*, 1937.

—— *Our Bible and the Ancient Manuscripts*, 4th ed., 1933.

A. F. J. Klijn, *A Survey of the Researches into the Western Text of the Gospels and Acts*, 1949.

M. J. Lagrange, *Introduction à l'étude du Nouveau Testament: deuxième partie: critique textuelle, II. La Critique rationelle*, 1935.

K. Lake, *Texts and Studies*, vii. 3, 1902.

—— *The Text of the New Testament*, 6th ed., 1928.

K. Lake, R. P. Blake, and S. New, *Harvard Theological Review*, xxi. 4, 1928, pp. 208–404.

K. Lake and S. New, *Six Collations of New Testament Manuscripts*, 1932.

A. Merk, *Novum Testamentum Graece et Latine*, 1935, *Prolegomena*.

B. M. Metzger, *Journal of Biblical Literature*, lxiv, 1945, pp. 457–89.[1]

—— *Ex. T.* lxiii, 1952, pp. 309–11.

M. M. Parvis and A. P. Wikgren, *New Testament Manuscript Studies*, 1950.

A. T. Robertson, *Textual Criticism of the New Testament*, 1925.

J. H. Ropes, *The Text of the Acts of the Apostles* (F. J. F. Jackson and K. Lake, *Beginnings of Christianity, III, The Text*, 1926).

A. Souter, *The Text and Canon of the New Testament*, 1930.

B. H. Streeter, *The Four Gospels*, 1924.

A. Vaganay, *An Introduction to the Textual Criticism of the New Testament*, trans. B. V. Miller, 1937.

B. F. Westcott and F. J. A. Hort, *The New Testament in Greek, II, Introduction*, 1896.

H. Wheeler Robinson (editor), *Ancient and English Versions of the Bible*, 1940.

[1] See especially pp. 483–9 for 'future tasks and problems'; cf. Ropes, op. cit., pp. ccciii–cccvi.

XII

INSPIRATION AND VALUE

THERE are few more fruitful sources of error in religious thought than the use of metaphors. In every metaphor there is apt to lie, open or concealed, an 'argument from analogy'. An idea is never true or 'proved' because an analogy to it can be found in another department of life. A signal instance is seen in the word Inspiration. The word 'inspire' means 'breathe into'; and it is quite commonly supposed that its meaning is self-evident when it is used metaphorically to describe the part played by the Spirit of God in the production of the books of the Bible. To the primitive Hebrew it was no metaphor; the Divine Spirit was the Breath of God breathed as though physically into men. But we cannot use it to define or explain the action of God, but only to express in picturesque or illustrative form what we find His action to be. Some of the ideas which have been held on the inspiration of the New Testament correspond exactly with those on the Old Testament held by some early Christian writers. 'For the study of the attitude of the early Church towards the Old Testament, a starting-point is afforded by three passages in the New Testament. Rom. xv. 4: "All things that were written before were written for the purpose of instructing us, in order that by endurance and by the encouragement of the Scriptures we might have hope." St. Paul declares that the Old Testament is of abiding value for us Christians, in that it encourages us to keep fast to the Christian virtue of hope. Similarly, but more specifically, in 2 Tim. iii. 15, it is stated, not *how* Scripture was inspired, but for what purposes it is profitable. It is said to be profitable not for the study of science, history, philosophy, poetry, and so forth, but simply for spiritual improvement. The "sacred writings are able to make thee wise unto salvation, through faith which is in Christ Jesus. Every divinely inspired writing is also profitable for instruction, for conviction, for correction, for discipline which is in righteousness, that the man of God may be equipped, thoroughly equipped, for every good work." And in 2 Pet. i. 21 the writer says that "holy men spake from God, being carried along by [the influence of the] Holy Spirit". This states the divine source of the inspiration, but provides no definition of its nature and purpose. "Carried along by the Holy Spirit." Carried for what purpose? To what end? In what sense? It will be noticed that the last two passages occur in what are probably two of the latest epistles in the New Testament. Christians were just beginning to reflect upon the inspiration of the Old Testament, but there is not one syllable in the whole of Scripture which ties us down to any particular theory or definition. . . . The apostolic fathers are not more definite. They quoted the Old Testament as a divine book, but did not examine the nature of its inspiration.

'The first Church writer who gives a more explicit statement is Justin Martyr.

It was not possible [he says] for men to know things so great and divine by the light of nature, or by human intuition, but by the gift which came down at that time upon the holy men. They did not need the art of words, nor to speak in the spirit of rivalry or competition; all they needed was to offer themselves in purity to the activity of the Divine Spirit, in order that, as a plectron makes use of the harp or lyre as an instrument, so the divine influence, making use of righteous men, might reveal to us the knowledge of divine and heavenly things.

'Now it is not right to say that this is a purely mechanical theory of inspiration, because a stringed instrument, when it is played on, will give a sound the nature of which is determined by the structure of the instrument itself. It is not certain whether Justin had this in mind, but at any rate his words do not exclude the thought that the personal differences of the prophets might produce different results when the Divine Spirit played upon them. And it must be noted further that Justin reaches a conclusion which does not differ from that which we have seen in the New Testament, that Scripture was inspired in order to give the knowledge that is necessary for salvation. . . . And in the Odes of Solomon we read: "As the hand plays upon the harp, and the strings sound, so speaks the Spirit of the Lord in my members." Hippolytus uses the same metaphor of the plectron, but adds the important thought that the musical instrument must be tuned to give forth the harmony rightly. And Theophilus teaches the same without metaphor. Though he marks a new departure in definitely ascribing to divine inspiration the correctness, e.g., of the chronology in the writings of Moses and other similar subjects, yet he says that the prophets were men of God who were "deemed worthy" to be his instruments: they had to display a personal and moral fitness for their work.

'On the other hand, Athenagoras holds the extreme mechanical theory characteristic of the Montanists. He says that the reasoning powers of the writers were thrown by the Divine Spirit into a state of ecstasy, and they uttered that which was enacted in them, the Spirit using them as His instruments, like a flute-player playing on a flute. Here is sheer mechanism. That which a flute-player blows into a flute is his own breath, and that breath comes out again unchanged, but uses the instrument in its passage. Irenaeus is no less strict. "The Scriptures", he says, "are perfect, since they were spoken by the word of God and His Spirit. . . ." This idea of inspiration is a relic from very primitive thought. In the early days of Israel the prophets were men of the Dervish type, who threw themselves into ecstatic frenzy by music and dancing. And when Israel, at a later time, came into contact with Greek thought, this popular and inadequate notion of prophecy found its counterpart in the art of divination, as it was seen, for example, in the oracle priestess of Pytho or Delphi. Philo the Jew was the first who explicitly transferred this to afford an explanation of the written prophecies of the Old Testament.[1] But the idea found its way into Christian writings, especially into those of the Montanists, who attached supreme importance to the utterance of their own prophets and prophetesses when they spoke in a state of ecstatic unconsciousness. It is noteworthy that the word *Inspiratio*—a breathing into—seems to have been intro-

---

[1] There has been a growing recognition since 1900 that the prophets often conceived in mystic trance the messages which they delivered. See Hölscher, *Die Profeten*, 1914, followed by T. H. Robinson, *Prophecy and the Prophets*, 2nd ed., 1944; J. Hänel, *Das Erkennen Gottes bei den Schriftpropheten*, 1923, but contrast H. H. Rowley, *Harvard Theol. Rev.*, xxxviii, 1945, pp. 1–38; cf. his edition of *The Old Testament and Modern Study*, 1951, pp. 141–5, by O. Eissfeldt.

duced into theological language by Tertullian, who became a Montanist.

'Another fact which strengthened the idea of the divine inspiration of the Old Testament was the gradual acceptance of the inspiration of the New. The Old and the New became inseparably connected, and both were needed to make up the Word of God. Irenaeus says: "God did not teach that the one Testament offered old truths and the other new truths, but He taught that they were one and the same." Their contents are different—one is a law for slaves, the other precepts for free men—but both are given by the same Father of the family. Tertullian says: "The same Divine Power was preached in the Gospels which had been known in the Law, though the teaching was not the same." And he declares that the Church should drink in the faith made as a potion by mixing the Law and the Prophets with the evangelical and apostolic writings. And, lastly, Origen: "The sacred volumes breathe the fullness of the Spirit, and there is nothing in the Law, in Gospel, or in Apostle which does not descend from the fullness of the divine majesty."'[1]

Since, then, the idea of 'verbal inspiration' among Christians was a gradual growth, and the word 'Inspiration' is not defined in the Bible, we can discover what is the right application to give to the metaphor only by examining the books of the New Testament themselves, and discovering what they reveal to us of their nature and value. And the study of them establishes as an underlying principle that God inspires not books but men. If He had inspired the books in the sense of dictating the words to the writers' minds, they would all have reached the same uniform level of perfection. There could have been no disagreement in detail, and therefore no divergences from perfect accuracy; and there could have been no growth or development in the Christological or any other elements in Christian doctrine. But generations of study have made increasingly clear both the divergences and the development. Those who still cling to the idea of verbal inspiration do so because they are honestly convinced that to hold any other idea of the meaning of inspiration is disloyalty to God. It would be

[1] This sketch of early Christian ideas on inspiration is quoted from A. H. McNeile's *The Old Testament in the Christian Church*, 1913.

if God had ever made it clear by even a single statement that that was the true meaning. But since He has not done so, they are in danger, by their very loyalty, of shutting their eyes to His guidance. If He inspired not the books but the men, the way is left open for manifold differences in the temperament, environment, capacity of grasping truth and of appreciating facts, spiritual development, and so on, of the several writers.

1. *Gospels.* The inspiration of the Gospels is inseparably bound up with their historical value. On the Incarnation, Death, and Resurrection of Jesus Christ as historical events rests the Christianity of the Catholic Church; but it rests on them as they are interpreted by the Catholic Church. And therefore the spiritual value of the Gospels, in other words their inspiration, is to be measured, not by the 'photographic' accuracy of their details, but by the extent to which they embody and express that which is the life of Christianity. All history is a record of human life at earlier stages, a record which accounts for, and helps to the understanding of, human life in the present; it is a record of experience, and also a guide to behaviour. To gain a bare acquaintance with past events merely as events, to accumulate knowledge of what was, with no relation to what is, or what ought to be, is barren and useless. If we are to use history rightly, the modern mind feels it to be important, of course, that a narrative of the events should be as far as possible accurate. But absolute accuracy is impossible. Even an eyewitness of an event which occurred yesterday is psychologically incapable of recalling details literally as they were. His report of them is something which has passed through himself, with his limitations and presumptions, before it reaches his hearers. And when we read history we can gain no more than approximate knowledge, and that only of such few facts, among millions of others, as the narrator was led to select as being from his point of view salient and important. History is never an automatic or mechanical recital of events; it is the attempt of the narrator to present them as he understood them. Furthermore, in a record of which a single human being is the main subject the difficulty of accurate knowledge is heightened, because it is not only a report of facts but also, and primarily, a portraiture of personality. No

one can 'accurately' apprehend the personality of another; and still less can he accurately convey his impressions of it to others. He can only try, with the crude and inadequate instrument of language, to make others feel the effects which his apprehension of it has produced upon himself. There could be no guide to action more valuable than a real and full knowledge of a personality with all the conditions which developed it; but that we can never get, human nature being what it is.

It is of the utmost importance to apply these considerations to the Synoptic Gospels if we are to understand them aright. (1) They are three records containing a very small selection of events, actions, and words in the life of Jesus. Not one of the three writers was an eyewitness or an αὐτήκοος of all that he reports. And each account has passed not only through the writer himself but also through many before him, all of them with limitations and presuppositions. If the inspiration of the evangelists was such as to be independent of all that we know of human nature and psychology, and of a kind which forced them passively to produce 'accurate' reports of what they had received, we must postulate the same kind of inspiration for every Christian who had contributed to the oral tradition, and to the primitive Aramaic written sources, and to the primitive Greek reproductions of them. But an inspiration of that sort would not have resulted in three accounts widely differing from, and in a multitude of details disagreeing with, one another. However much we may regret it, an 'accurate' knowledge of details of the Lord's life is impossible. (2) We are concerned with the Personality which transcends all others as the central mystery of mankind. Eyewitnesses could record only the effects which their limited apprehension of it produced upon them. And many Christians tried to hand on by oral tradition and writings those features and aspects in the Portrait which formed themselves in their minds from hearing the record, until finally the evangelists put down on paper, each in his own way, the portraiture as they had received it, according to the different effects which it had produced upon *them*. And no two readers from then till now can have apprehended these portraits with identical results, because no two minds are identical.

It is well to begin our study of the problem by realizing how far we necessarily are from possessing an 'accurate' knowledge of facts of the life of Jesus, or of His Personality, which it is beyond the power of man fully to apprehend and therefore to delineate. 'Men were trying to apprehend that character; they had a glimpse here and a glimpse there; but they cannot have had more than a dim and vague surmise as to what it was as a whole' (Sanday[1]).

This has led some into almost complete scepticism about the historical value of the Gospels, though the extreme position represented by Drews[2] that Jesus was a purely mythical figure, created in the imagination of Christians under the influence of pagan thought, has been completely discredited by some of the keenest critics of the New Testament.[3] Still, it is asked, if the Gospels represent only the gradually evolved ideas of a generalization of Christians, are they not practically worthless as real accounts of the Lord? This seems to the present writer to be quite unwarranted for several reasons:

1. The general course of His ministry, as they relate it, appeals to us as psychologically natural and probable. He emerged from obscurity, carried to His work by the driving force of prophetic inspiration. For a short time He enjoyed a growing success; but soon His revolutionary handling of traditional ideas and customs raised official opposition. He retired for a time with a small group of His followers, but was at last done to death. If this main outline is true to fact, excessive scepticism as to further details is unnecessary, though each must, of course, be judged on its merits. K. L. Schmidt,[4] like other Form-critics (see Ch. III above), reduces the trustworthiness of the 'framework' of the Gospels to a minimum. 'The oldest tradition of Jesus is the tradition of pericopes, a tradition of individual scenes and utterances, handed down in the Church, and for the most part lacking any definite indication

---

[1] Hastings's *D.B.* ii. 626 b, and *Outlines of the Life of Christ*, p. 110 (ed. 2, 1906).

[2] *The Christ Myth*, trans. Burns, 1910.

[3] See, for example, F. C. Conybeare, *The Historical Christ*, 1914, and contrast M. Goguel, *Jesus of Nazareth, Myth or History* (trans. Stephens, 1926) and *The Life of Jesus* (trans. O. Wyon, 1933), pp. 61–69.

[4] *Der Rahmen der Geschichte Jesu*, 1919.

of time and place.' But if, as is probable, the general course of the history as we have it was due mainly to the preaching and teaching of the first disciples, although individual stories and sayings were undoubtedly handed down orally as isolated units, for which the evangelists found places in such a way as to suit their several purposes, yet the main outline must go back to the reminiscences of eyewitnesses.

2. Among His words certain sayings are attributed to Him which it is extremely difficult to imagine tradition placing in His mouth if they were not substantially genuine: e.g. 'Why callest thou Me good? None is good but One—[that is] God' (Mk. x. 18). 'Of that day or that hour none knoweth, not even the angels in heaven, nor the Son, but the Father [only]' (xiii. 32). 'My God, My God, why hast Thou forsaken Me?' (xv. 34). Similarly, statements are made about Him which no Christian would have invented or imagined: 'His relations (?) (οἱ παρ᾽ αὐτοῦ) came out to lay hold on Him, for they said, He is beside Himself' (iii. 21). 'He could not there do any mighty work, save that He laid His hands on a few sick folk and healed them; and He marvelled at their unbelief' (vi. 5–6). These are among the nine passages which P. W. Schmiedel[1] describes as 'absolutely credible', and 'the foundation-pillars for a truly scientific life of Jesus'. But the presence of such passages inspires confidence in St. Mark's source or sources, which must have contained many other perfectly genuine traditions about our Lord and His words. The writer who was faithful in a few matters may be trusted to have been faithful also in many.

3. The actions and words of Jesus, as the Gospels relate them, are to a very considerable extent entirely in keeping with His time, country, and race. As Sanday says, 'There was a certain circle of ideas which Jesus accepted in becoming Man in the same way in which He accepted a particular language with its grammar and vocabulary'.[2] This conviction has been deepened for modern students by the growing knowledge of Jewish life and literature in recent years.

4. And yet, conversely, His actions and words came like an exhilarating breeze, a grateful shower of rain upon a sultry and

---

[1] *Encycl. Bibl.* ii, 1891, 1881 f.
[2] Hastings's *D.B.* ii. 624 b, and *Outlines* . . ., p. 103.

thirsty land. The surprise and delight of the poor and ignorant, the scorned and neglected masses, is evident throughout the record of the ministry. And even if it were true that His character and life were gradually idealized in the course of oral and written tradition, owing to a gradual development and heightening of Christological beliefs, it would remain very difficult to credit first-century writers with the literary skill which could convey a general impression of exhilaration and spiritual uplift if His contemporaries had not, in fact, experienced it.

5. Above all, the portraiture of His Personality, i.e., as has been said, of the effects which were produced on the minds of the narrators by the traditions which they received, is altogether outside the region of mere idealization. Its combination of humility with majestic claims, of denunciation of sin with tenderness towards sinners, of flaming hatred of hypocrisy with that which in any other would be hypocrisy or worse—a complete absence of any consciousness of sin in Himself—is a paradox which no Christological idealization could produce. It is sometimes said that the enthusiasm of the first Christians, due to their belief that certain of them had seen the risen Lord, that He was exalted to the right hand of God as the Messiah, and that He was still present with them by His Spirit, which was the Spirit of God, was the result of 'mystical' experiences, generated by auto-suggestion, in the minds of those who claimed to have seen Him. But the more the argument is pressed, the greater becomes the need of postulating a depth and strength and mystery in the Character and Personality of the Man with whom they had a few days before walked and talked sufficient to account for the universal and immovable conviction. And the measure of the historical value of the Gospels is primarily and ultimately the extraordinary success with which they portray such a Character and Personality.

That there are limitations to the historical value we have already recognized; it is only equivalent to saying that the writers were human. In no single sentence can we be entirely certain that we possess the *ipsissima verba* of Jesus, even if it could be assumed that the Greek translations which have come down to us were always adequate. The variations in the reports of the same sayings in the different Gospels would alone be enough to render that certain. And yet we may feel confident that we possess to a considerable extent the real substance of them, because the substance of His words forms a large and indispensable factor in the production of the total Portrait which is required to account for the coming into existence of Christianity.

And the same must be said of His deeds. It was doubtless easier for first-century writers to heighten the wonder of deeds than of words. And the possibility must remain open that some of His miracles—e.g. the withering of the fig-tree (cf. Mk. xi. 12 ff., 20–25 with Lk. xiii. 6–9)—were originally parables or other utterances translated into actions in the course of tradition. But it is gratuitous to claim that all His recorded miracles must be so explained, simply because they are miracles. His Character and Personality were miraculous, and it is in the last degree improbable that none of the wonderful deeds were actually performed which contributed an integral element in the impression of Him that was handed on in tradition. The miracles of healing are mostly accepted today because some light is being thrown upon them by modern researches into the relation between the psychical and physical in man.[1] And we cannot say that future research will throw no light on other miracles concerning which we are at present in the dark. We have moved away from the materialism of the earlier part of the nineteenth century, and it is becoming scientific to think of Spirit as lying in and behind the energy displayed in the constitution of the atom. And if Science has only just begun to discover Spirit, we cannot place any limit on the extent to which it may reach a conception of the modes and possibilities of free and purposive action of the Spirit upon matter. In the days of our Lord such action was simply taken for granted, with no reasoned conception at all of modes and possibilities; the miracles of Jesus were one and all equally miraculous.

The truth is that the historian who tries to construct a reasoned picture of the Life of Christ finds that he cannot dispense with miracles. He is confronted with the fact that no sooner had the Life of Jesus ended in apparent failure and shame than the great body

---

[1] Cf. P. Dearmer, *Body and Soul*, 1909; P. Janet, *Psychological Healing*, 1925.

of Christians—not an individual here and there, but the mass of the Church—passed over at once to the fixed belief that He was God. By what conceivable process could the men of that day have arrived at such a conclusion, if there had been really nothing in His life to distinguish it from that of ordinary men? We have seen that He did not work the kind of miracles which they expected. The miracles in themselves in any case came short of their expectations. But this makes it all the more necessary that there must have been something about the Life, a broad and substantial element in it, which *they could recognize as* supernatural and divine—not that we can recognize, but which they could recognize with the ideas of the time. Eliminate miracles from the career of Jesus, and the belief of Christians, from the first moment that we have undoubted contemporary evidence of it (say A.D. 50), becomes an insoluble enigma.[1]

And if we cannot claim exact knowledge of His words and deeds, still less can we accept as certain the order of events or the positions in which the evangelists place His utterances. The order and position often differ widely in the different Gospels. The general course of the Ministry, as said above, is natural and probable. But many of the events and utterances current in Q, and many others which must have reached the evangelists from oral or written sources as separate and unrelated items, not infrequently reaching them in two or more forms, were an almost haphazard bundle of treasures, which they grouped and disposed each in his own way for his own reasons.

Another limitation must also be recognized. The reports of our Lord's words and of statements about Him may here and there reflect Christological and ecclesiastical conceptions arrived at in later years. But the extent to which this has occurred has been greatly exaggerated by some writers; and the tendency has been to attribute this for the most part to the influence of St. Paul. There will always, probably, be differences of opinion as to the amount which Pauline and other later ideas have contributed to the Gospels. Every alleged instance needs examination. They cannot be altogether denied; but most of them stand out pretty clearly, and the wonderful Portrait is seen to be independent of them.

[1] Sanday, in Hastings's *D.B.* ii. 627 a.

The records of the Virgin Birth are approached from different directions by different minds. Some will ask, Is not the historical value of the Gospels so high that this miraculous event must be accepted because it is recorded in them? Others will put their question more cautiously: Is the event so intrinsically congruous with the miraculous Character and Personality of Jesus that it may be accepted in spite of any literary difficulties which may be found in the records? Our study of the formation and transmission of the Gospels forbids us to speak of their 'inerrancy' in matters of fact, but allows us to feel confident that they are substantially trustworthy in their portraiture of the miraculous Person whom Christians learnt to worship as God. The second question, therefore, represents much better than the first the line of approach that is open to us. The Virgin Birth, if it is an historical event, must have become known from statements made either by the Lord's mother, or St. Joseph, or both. And it has often been thought that the former may have given rise to the account in Luke and the latter to that in Matthew. Whether this was so we have, of course, no means of knowing. The two Gospels contain wholly different accounts, coinciding only in the central fact; but both are purely Jewish, and emanate from Palestinian circles in which not only Aramaic but Hebrew appears to have been understood. This intensely Jewish character of the narratives makes it very improbable that they took their rise under the influence of pagan myths of heroes and virgin goddesses.[1] And it is doubtful if there is anything in the Old Testament which would suggest that the Messiah would be born of a Virgin; if there is, it is in the LXX, not in the Hebrew of Is. vii. 14 which the writer of Matthew quotes (i. 23). The narratives in Matthew which form the framework of the central fact contain much which must probably be regarded as *midrash* rather than history;[2] but that does not necessarily make the central fact less credible. Some have thought that St. Luke's source did not relate that the Birth was from a

---

[1] So Schmiedel, art. 'Mary', *Encycl. Bibl.*; Usener, art. 'Nativity', ibid.; W. Soltau, *The Birth of Jesus Christ* (trans. M. A. Canney, 1903), and others.
[2] See Box, *The Virgin Birth of Christ*, pp. 19 ff., and A. H. McNeile's *St. Matthew*, p. 23.

Virgin, and that the indications of it in i. 34–35 are due to the evangelist. (If so, *v.* 36 must be included, which relates of Elizabeth that 'she also' was giving birth to a son not in the ordinary course of nature.) But even if this were the case it is not impossible for the source to have been written by one who did not know of the Virgin Birth and for St. Luke to have added to it the fact which he had learnt by tradition. This would explain the parenthetical ὡς ἐνομίζετο in iii. 23. The narratives which surround the mysterious and unique event contain difficulties from the point of view of their historical accuracy. But some of them arise from its very uniqueness and mystery, and none of them are such as to supply positive evidence against it. In the last resort the evidence for it is not only literary but also doctrinal.[1]

The reports of the Resurrection stand on a different footing from those of the earthly Life. The traditions of the Lord's deeds and words arose out of the statements of those who saw and heard them. The traditions of His Resurrection arose out of a deduction. Strictly speaking there is no record of the Resurrection; there could not be, since no one saw Him rise. Those who saw Him alive after His death and burial inferred that He must have risen. And since the earliest appearances were on the third day they drew the further inference that He must have risen on the third day. All the accounts, differing widely in detail, so that the actual facts cannot be determined with certainty, are accounts not of the Resurrection but of the appearances, some of them emanating from Galilee and some from Jerusalem. The disagreements and obscurities in the narratives render them insecure as chronicles of detailed happenings, but they leave us as certain as we can be of anything in history that the stories arose from appearances of the Lord in which His spiritual body produced sense impressions which were real experiences of certain persons. The inference which they drew from them formed the immediate basis of the Church's belief that He had risen. But the credibility of the Resurrection does not rest only on the appearances or on the inference. It rests also on doctrinal grounds and considerations

---

[1] See F. H. Chase, *The Gospels in the light of Historical Criticism*, pp. 72 f. (reprinted from *Cambridge Theological Essays*, ed. Swete, pp. 414 f.).

of probability. Could physical death have been the end of One whose miraculous Character and Personality were such as the evangelists portray? Could Christianity and the Church be such as they have been, and are, if physical death had been the end?—and so on. The *mode* of the Resurrection, the empty tomb, and the third day, are matters on which opinions differ. The historical value of the Resurrection narratives, simply as narratives, lies in the unmistakable witness which they bear to the central fact which the apostles proclaimed: 'This Jesus hath God raised up, whereof we all are witnesses.'

And with regard to the work of the evangelists as a whole Sanday's words[1] remain as true (despite the Form-critics) as when he wrote them in 1899: 'The tendency of the researches in recent years has been to enhance and not to diminish the estimate of the historical character of the Gospels.' To which may be added Harnack's testimony: 'Sixty years ago[2] David Friedrich Strauss thought that he had almost entirely destroyed the historical credibility not only of the fourth but also of the first three Gospels as well. The historical criticism of two generations has succeeded in restoring that credibility in its main outlines.'[3]

The Fourth Gospel was planned with a definitely religious purpose. The writer lived at a time when Christians had learnt, by the experiences of Easter and Pentecost, that Christ was to be adored and worshipped as divine. At first the experiences were enough; but the need was soon felt of explaining *how* He who had lived a human life on earth could be identified with the eternal and universal Object of Christian devotion. In the New Testament writings the problem is approached, broadly speaking, from four different directions: (*a*) St. Paul shared the general view that Christ was the Messiah, but he was more influenced by his own mystical experience of His indwelling and oneness with the Christian Body. Such universality of Being is in its nature eternal, and has a cosmological significance which he finally worked out in Colossians (and Ephesians?). (*b*) The writers of the Synoptic Gospels and the

---

[1] Hastings's *D.B.* ii. 625 b, and *Outlines of the Life of Christ*, p. 106.
[2] The words were written in 1900.
[3] *What is Christianity?* p. 21 (trans. Saunders, 3rd ed., 1904).

Acts were not appreciably affected by St. Paul's distinctive doctrines. They contented themselves with showing that Christ was the destined Messiah, the Son of God, but in a higher and better sense than any Jewish speculations had reached. (*c*) In Hebrews also the mystical idea is absent; the thought of Christ is on the lines of a Priesthood; He is the Ideal which annuls the old earthly copy, but He was fitted for this function by being completely representative of man in virtue of His true Humanity perfected through suffering. (*d*) The Fourth Evangelist, while he shares St. Paul's mysticism, makes a different use of the truth. The cosmological idea scarcely appears, though it is seen in his Prologue, where Jewish Wisdom speculations are transferred to Jesus Christ: 'All things were made through Him, and apart from Him was not anything made that was made' (i. 3). His main object was to picture as a Man Him who was eternally the Logos. His thought starts with the universal, divine Christ as the accepted and recognized Object of worship, and he aims at showing that, by becoming Man and living a human life, He brought eternal life into mankind. For this purpose an epistle would not serve; he must write a Gospel which should portray the eternal Son of God in human features. Any accurate knowledge that he possessed of the details of that life he would naturally use. The extent to which he possessed accurate details, and the circumstances which contributed to his knowledge of them, are matters of dispute. It would certainly seem as if he was well informed, perhaps in some cases better informed than the synoptists, on matters of topography, and personal names, and dates. It is quite gratuitous to suppose that he introduced these artificially to lend verisimilitude to his narrative. As regards correctness each detail, of course, must be judged on its merits, and the decision must not be influenced by any preconceived idea of authorship. But the whole Gospel was planned, not for biography or history such as the modern scientific mind desires, but to draw a portrait, to convey by means of narrative the profound mystery of the Logos on earth, and what that means for mankind. He makes a larger use—very likely he possessed more knowledge —of our Lord's words and deeds in Jerusalem than in the North; he would certainly find more material for his picture in the controversies with scholarly and intellectual Jews at the capital than in the simpler teaching given to Galileans. That the discourses are His *ipsissima verba* is impossible, but there is no good reason for doubting that they were based on traditions of real utterances; and the work of Rabbinic scholars in recent years has tended to increase this probability. But his object must be kept steadily in view. 'These things', he says himself, 'have been written that ye may believe that Jesus is the Christ, the Son of God; and that believing ye may have life in His name' (xx. 31). When a writer avows his object, by that object alone ought he to be judged. And his inspiration, and the value of his work, can be estimated by the success with which, during the long lapse of the Christian centuries, he has accomplished his purpose.

2. *Acts.* The historical value of the Acts, in the sense of its trustworthiness as a record of events, has been discussed on pp. 103–23. It is a precipitate of early traditions and personal experiences in which a picture of the Church as it was accounts, and at the same time supplies a norm, for the Church as it is. St. Luke was inspired, not for the purpose of writing an accurate chronicle, however great the extent of the accuracy may be which modern research may find in it, but to portray the early life of the new people of God in such a way that it has provided the Church ever since with an inspiration and an ideal. In the first volume of his work he related what Jesus began to do and to teach until the day when He was taken up. In the second he related what He went on to do and to teach afterwards by the energy of His Spirit, i.e. by the Spirit of God Himself. The author's inspiration was such that he was able with wonderful success to describe on paper, and to make his readers feel, the ferment, the effervescence, of the young life of the Spirit-filled community, insurgent and expanding. It is not a peculiarity of style, it is of the essence of his work that 'Spirit' is spoken of more than sixty times in his twenty-eight chapters. The facts which he relates illustrated for all time the truth that a Christian community which is to reach the freedom wherewith Christ has made it free cannot keep its Christianity confined within the shell of Judaism. The apostles at Jerusalem were convinced by the pressure of events that they

must recognize the working of the Spirit of God in the Gentile mission, and that circumcision must not be forced upon its converts. This mission had started some time before St. Paul's conversion; it was, in fact, the direct continuation of our Lord's ministry in Galilee and Samaria, Tyre and Sidon, and the semi-Gentile cities of the Decapolis. But by the whirlwind activity of the Apostle of the Gentiles the sparks were fanned into a flame which swept from Palestine through Syria and Greece to the capital of the Empire. Granting all the compilation that literary and historical criticism demand, it is the pen of the inspired writer himself which has made the history a spiritual thing, and a record of the divine and irresistible growth of the Spirit-filled Church.

3. *Epistles.* But if the members of a community have life in them, there is internal as well as outward expansion. A growing love to God results in an intensifying of the moral life of obedience to Him, and a deepening intellectual understanding of His nature and purposes. This healthy internal life is guided and sustained by the teaching of the epistles. The best proof of their worth is the history of the formation of the Canon. In the large intercommunication between the Churches the numerous letters of bishops and other leaders were as a rule read to the congregations. Many—such, for example, as commendatory letters for Christians who were travelling, or brief notes on small matters of the moment—might not be read a second time. But if they were felt to be helpful for the spiritual or practical needs of the Church, they were read again and again at the will of the presbyters, and no doubt often at the request of members of the congregation. The proof of inspiration was the permanence of the books.

After the first generation of Christians had passed away, another factor, it is true, contributed to their permanence— the prestige of an 'apostolic' name. A good name is as ointment poured forth. Because a writing was believed to be the work of an 'apostolic' man, it was felt that he was in a peculiar sense inspired. Nevertheless, many pseudonymous works bearing apostolic names, though they were read sporadically, and survived for a time, fell out for various reasons. In the last resort it was the felt reality of the writers' inspiration, generally speaking, that caused books to be treasured by the verdict of the collective consciousness of the Catholic Church.

But the inspiration of the writers was such as to fit them for a particular work, not the dictation by God of infallible words which they were to put on paper. All the writings are not on the same level. 2 Peter, for example, stands a long way below Ephesians. And that is true even of different parts of the same book. When St. Paul teaches the Corinthians that the troubles which will accompany the End of the present world-order will be so severe, and are so immediately imminent that it is wiser for married people to live as though they were unmarried, and for everyone to hold himself detached from things of this life (1 Cor. vii. 29–31),[1] he is obviously not writing in the same intensity of inspiration as when he pours out his paean of Love in ch. xiii. 'It is as sunlight through a painted window. The light must come to us coloured by the medium. We cannot get it in any other way. In some parts the medium is denser and more imperfect; in others the golden glory comes dazzlingly through.'[2] The various media hold back some of the rays in varying degrees, but the New Testament, as a kaleidoscopic whole, reveals to us the 'many-coloured (πολυποίκιλος) wisdom of God' (Eph. iii. 10).

The epistles with the Apocalypse, which is one of them, may be said broadly to deal with four main subjects:

1. *Eschatology.* St. Paul began in 1, 2 Thessalonians by treating it as a matter of profound importance; it may be said, despite J. Lowe, that he ended in Colossians (and Ephesians?) by reducing it almost to the vanishing point. If, then, we are to choose between his earlier and his riper thoughts, the decision is not doubtful. The expectation of the imminent Advent of Christ, which pervaded the Church of the first century, was a heritage from their Jewish ancestry which no writer was so nearly able to transcend as St. Paul. In the Apocalypse the calamities which usher it in, and the terrors of judgement upon the sinful Roman empire, are pictured for the comfort

---

[1] Dr. K. E. Kirk thinks that St. Paul advances other reasons for preferring celibacy which do not depend for their validity on the imminence of the Lord's coming. Marriage brings troubles and distractions (*The Vision of God*, 1928, pp. 75 ff.).

[2] J. Paterson Smyth, *How God inspired the Bible*, p. 131.

and encouragement of the Christians who 'conquer' in stead-fast loyalty to Christ. Their bliss and glory in the new heavens and the new earth are portrayed in word-painting, the thrill and beauty of which have been the support of suffering and tempted Christians ever since. Thus the moral and spiritual value of the book is enormous. It is the classical expression of Christian optimism in its unconquerable certainty of the final victory of God's cause. So long as sin, oppression, and the pride of power and wealth remain will the humble and meek give full value to the work of the inspired genius who laid him-self out to fulfil the command, 'Comfort ye, comfort ye My people'. The enduring value of all apocalyptic is beautifully expressed by F. C. Burkitt in his essay, 'The eschatological Idea in the Gospels', in *Cambridge Biblical Essays*, pp. 195–213, cf. H. H. Rowley, *The Relevance of Apocalyptic*, 1944. But the spiritual value of the Apocalypse does not lie in the details of the programme of events which it lays down, or of its descrip-tions of punishment and bliss. The Jewish limitations of the writer show themselves in the fact that for him Rome is the one and only enemy, in whom the supernatural powers of evil find their embodiment; in the expectation of a millennial reign of Christ on earth; and in the greater part of his imagery, which can today be taken only as the outward vehicle—determined by his age and environment—which the writer employed to convey his spiritual consolation, warnings, and hopes. The same consolation, warnings, and hopes are expressed in simpler language by the other New Testament writers. The warnings in Jude and 2 Peter take a particular form: the destruction of libertine heretics; and of these heretics the writer of 2 Peter has especially in view those who denied the immediacy and cer-tainty of the coming of the Day of Wrath—characteristics, again, which were determined by the age and environment of the authors. Their inspiration is felt in the spiritual truths which their writings enshrine, not in the distinctively Jewish dress in which they clothe them.

Further, the epistles at least echo the faith of the apostolic *kerygma*. In a deep and true sense the Messianic Kingdom of Jewish expectation has arrived and the King has come. In so far as Christians have thrown themselves 'into Christ' by

Baptism and all that that implies, they are in Him by mystical union, members of a new world and a new creation, making up together His Body, the Church; already they taste the powers of the Age to Come (Heb. vi. 5); they are bound to their King by the Spirit, who is given to them as a pledge or first instalment of full redemption.[1]

2. *Ethics*. In the Hebrew religion, as represented by its highest and best minds, the expectations for the future were the immediate product of the morality to which the Israelite nation gave a higher value than any other nation on earth. Insight to the Jew is foresight. The inseparable oneness of a perfectly moral God with His people involved the conception that, ideally, His people also were perfectly moral. And God, at His Advent, would punish the wicked and avenge the righteous. In the period in which our Lord was born there was a humble class of Jews, the 'quiet in the land', in whom Hebrew morality was exhibited in its best and most beautiful form. The family of Jesus belonged to it; and through Him Hebrew morality was, from the first, a primary element in the essence of Christianity. He put into it new content and depth; He 'fulfilled' what the Law and the Prophets had taught. And the epistle-writers do not decline from the high level which the first Christian missionaries had reached under His influence, reinforced by the mighty experience of Pentecost. The moral ideal for the Church filled with His Spirit is nothing short of divine perfection; and the degree of beauty with which weak and limited men were enabled to portray it is a measure of their inspiration for this purpose. The spur of His example, the motive—'for His sake'—and the method—'by His Spirit'— are the *momenta* in the New Testament moral appeal which places the writings beyond all price.

3. *Christology*. In the late pre-Christian centuries there was a growing tendency to avoid the use of language which implied God's close, personal contact with men, and His personal activity in the world. His will, the will of a loving but majestic King, was performed by angels and other mediators.

[1] Cf. C. H. Dodd, *The Apostolic Preaching and its Developments*, 1936; O. C. Quick, *The Gospel of the New World*; O. Cullmann, *Christ and Time* (trans. F. V. Filson, 1951).

In line with this tendency was the growing definiteness and precision in the ideas about the heavenly Messiah. All that was expected of God in the great day of His coming would be performed through the agency of the Messiah. This conception passed over into the Christian Church, but it underwent a final transformation in the certainty that this Messiah was, in fact, the Man Jesus. Before His death many thought that He might be the political Messiah of popular expectation, though He did His best to show that He was not. But after His death and resurrection the belief in the latter led Christians along a gradually rising scale of their comprehension of what He was. His exaltation taught the first disciples that He had entered upon His heavenly office of Messiahship, and all Christian hearts speedily enthroned Him as 'Lord'. Up to that point His glorified human personality comprised all that they knew of Him. But the mystical experience of St. Paul led him to ascribe to Him a spiritual universality in which the human individual was understood to be endowed with all that is divine. And this led men to think back into the past, and to meditate upon the mystery of His nature from the first. It was endorsed by the Transfiguration, by His own vision at the Baptism, then by the Virgin Birth, and lastly the fullness of the Divine Nature 'in the beginning' was realized. That the doctrine of the three Persons in the Godhead had begun to shape itself before the end of the first century is shown by the baptismal formula in Matt. xxviii. 19,[1] cf. 2 Cor. xiii. 13, Rom. viii. 14–17, 26–29, but nowhere in the New Testament is there definite teaching of the metaphysical threeness in oneness at which the Church arrived later in conflict with heresy. But the Christological value of the writings lies in their gradual approach to the truth, itself inexplicable, which explains the universe.

4. *Soteriology.* To the Jew salvation was always in the future. The judgement on sinners and the salvation of God's faithful people were the obverse and reverse of the eschatological hopes. It was salvation from sinners rather than from sin. The present salvation from sin was not thought of under that term. Atone-

---

[1] For the genuineness of the text of Matt. xxviii. 19 cf. C. S. C. Williams, *Alterations to the Text of the Synoptic Gospels and Acts*, pp. 33–36.

ment for unwitting transgressions of the ritual law was provided for by means of the sin-offering. But for transgressions of
the moral law God's forgiveness could be gained by contrition,
and salvation from sin meant simply keeping free from it by
obedience to God's moral commands.

The writer of James, in his Jewish Christianity, adheres
honestly and wholeheartedly to this position, but the specifically Christian belief from the first was that 'there is no other
name under heaven given among men whereby we must be
saved but only the name of the Lord Jesus'. In the spiritual
value of the New Testament, which is the measure of the
inspiration of the writers, the soteriology and the Christology
hold an equal place, and are inseparably connected. It was
firmly believed that Jesus Christ came to save His people—
not from their earthly enemies; that would take place at His
second coming, but—from their sins. How, was not at first
clearly formulated; but in very early days the sufferings of
Christ began to gain significance in the light of Isa. liii, which
spoke of the vicarious value of the sufferings of the 'Servant of
Yahweh', words which Jesus may have applied to Himself.[1]
St. Paul received this interpretation in the Christian tradition
of his day, but his own distinctive contribution to the doctrine
of the Atonement was of a different kind. He was possessed by
the thought that Christ, by His birth into the world, put
Himself into union with man; put Himself under the Law,
under the Curse which the Law involved (owing to the fact
that no man could obey it perfectly), under the malign domination of the tyrant Sin (which used the Law as its instrument),

---

[1] One cannot be so dogmatic as was J. Moffatt, 'The suffering Servant conception was organic to the consciousness of Jesus and . . . He often regarded His
vocation in the light of this supremely suggestive prophecy' (*The Theology of the
Gospels*, 1912, p. 149) for apart from Mk. ix. 12b, which R. Otto stresses (*The
Kingdom of God and the Son of Man*, 1938, pp. 244 ff.) we have only allusions in
Mk. such as i. 11, x. 45, and xiv. 24, which despite H. Rashdall are no doubt
authentic sayings of Jesus. For a full expression of the identification of Jesus with
the Suffering Servant we turn to later strata than Mk.; Lk. xxii. 37 (L),
Matt. viii. 17 and xii. 18 (M), Acts iii. 4 and esp. viii; Rev. v. 6, 12; Jn. i. 29
(despite C. H. Dodd); 1 Pet. ii; *1 Clem.* xvi. But see Vincent Taylor, *Jesus and
His Sacrifice*, 1937. Further, there is some evidence that even in pre-Christian
Judaism the doctrine of a suffering Messiah was not unknown to the Jews, cf.
W. D. Davies, *Paul and Rabbinic Judaism*, 1948, pp. 276–84; Wm. Manson,
Jesus the Messiah, 1943, pp. 171–4.

and under the evil, supernatural, angelic Powers by which this age was governed. And then by death He burst free from them all, 'stripped them off', and left them behind nailed to His Cross. Every Christian who threw himself into union with Christ by 'faith', and was 'baptized into Christ', becoming a member of the Body of Christ and therefore a sharer in His Spirit by which that Body lived, was thenceforth 'in Christ', and all that had happened to Christ happened mystically to him. In Him he burst free from Sin, Law, and Curse, and the evil Powers, to live in the divine atmosphere of the Spirit (as a butterfly bursts free from his chrysalis fetters to revel in the free air of heaven), and thereby necessarily shared in His righteousness as his own. There is much more in St. Paul's teaching which is connected with this, but that is the kernel of his thought.

He was an inspired man, but not in such a way that he could set forth 'infallibly' the doctrine of the Atonement in its complexity. The sacrificial aspects of Christ's death, which played a very small part in his teaching, are seen in 1 Peter, 1 John, the Apocalypse, and above all Hebrews, the typology of which formed the chief basis of the conceptions which Christians have formed about Christ as Victim and Priest.

Since 1925 scholars have placed increasing emphasis upon the idea of revelation and on the essential unity, not only of the New Testament but of the Bible as a whole, interpreting the Bible by the Bible, the focal point of which is Christ, who is the perfect divine self-disclosure.

Authority

This study of the nature of the inspiration of the New Testament helps to point to an answer to the difficult question of the nature of its authority. The word covers two quite different conceptions. On the one hand there is the authority of the expert. When a great physicist makes a statement about radio-activity, or a physiologist about muscular activity, it is not difficult for the layman, who knows nothing about it, to accept his judgement in faith and trust. On the other hand there is the authority of an official—a king, a magistrate, a schoolmaster. The one can be represented by *auctoritas*, the other by *potestas*. Both come into consideration in connexion with the authority of the Bible. The Jewish Church gave a gradual, diffusive consent to the marking off of certain books as sacred; and Jews submitted to their Church's authority, the *potestas* thus exercised. Christians accepted the same Old Testament canon from them. A similar diffusive consent of the Christian Church gradually marked off the New Testament canon, which comes to us by the *potestas* of the Church of the first two and a half centuries. We must never forget that the Church was there first. It made the New Testament by gradually differentiating certain books from all others.

One aspect, then, of the authority of the Bible is the authority of the Church. But the question must, of course, be asked, What was it that led the Church gradually to rule in those particular books into the Canon and to rule out all others? Why was St. Matthew's Gospel felt to be sacred and not the *Gospel according to the Hebrews*? Why was the Epistle of Jude admitted and not the *Epistle of Barnabas*? The Apocalypse of St. John and not the *Apocalypse of St. Peter*—and so on? That brings us to the other aspect of authority, the *auctoritas* of the Bible, the inherent right of the authors to offer us their teaching and impart their ideas because they were experts. And the real centre of the problem is—experts in what? A thinking man will not bow to the authority of a mathematician when he happens to talk about botany or medicine. And we cannot be expected to bow to the authority of a biblical writer on whatever subject he may happen to write: on history, for example; the expert writing of history is quite a modern science; no one in the first century approached the standard of accuracy now required. Or natural science; how can any of them speak to us with infallible authority on natural science when they all, without exception, believed that the earth was the centre of the universe? Or psychology; what deference should we pay, on the subject of psychology, to any one in the twentieth century who held that the bowels were the organs of grief and compassion and other emotions? When we go to an expert we want him on his subject. It is quite certain that the Church of the second century did not reverence the books of the New Testament because of their science or psychology. They reverenced them for one reason only, and that was that the writers had lived so near to God, so intimate with Jesus Christ, or with those who had been intimate with Him, so deeply influenced by His Spirit, that they could write authoritatively on the things of God, on things spiritual and moral, on the great, main facts of history on which the Christian religion depended. Not absolutely free from errors even on their own subject. The greatest musician in the world does not always write perfect music. But when we want our soul to be filled with the spirit of music, we turn to Beethoven, Bach, Schubert, Chopin, and so on. Each of them does it differently for us, but on his subject each of them is a supreme expert. And every book of the Bible gives us something different. Some of the writers are more spiritual, more profoundly inspired, than others, and in parts of the books more than in other parts. But their authority on the things of God, which the test of centuries has only enhanced, ranks higher for us than that of any other writers in the world. The New Testament is a collection of masterpieces of spiritual music. Its authority is that of spiritual experts, and we treat it as we should treat the authority of any supreme expert *on his subject*.

BOOKS

C. H. Dodd, *The Bible To-day*, 1946.
A. E. J. Rawlinson, 'Authority as a Ground of Belief', in *Essays Catholic and Critical*, ed. E. G. Selwyn, 1926.
A. Richardson and W. Schweitzer, *Biblical Authority for To-day*, 1951, especially pp. 112–26, 129–54, 181–97, 219–39.
H. H. Rowley, *The Relevance of the Bible*, 1941.
W. Sanday, *Inspiration*, 1893.
T. B. Strong, *Authority in the Church*, 1903.
L. S. Thornton, *Revelation and the Modern World*, 1951.
—— *The Common Life in the Body of Christ*, 1941.

I. INDEX OF SUBJECTS

II. INDEX OF ANCIENT PERSONS AND WRITINGS

PRINTED IN GREAT BRITAIN
AT THE UNIVERSITY PRESS, OXFORD
BY VIVIAN RIDLER
PRINTER TO THE UNIVERSITY